IFIP Advances in Information and Communication Technology   507

Editor-in-Chief

Kai Rannenberg, Goethe University Frankfurt, Germany

Editorial Board

IFIP – The International Federation for Information Processing

IFIP was founded in 1960 under the auspices of UNESCO, following the first World Computer Congress held in Paris the previous year. A federation for societies working in information processing, IFIP's aim is two-fold: to support information processing in the countries of its members and to encourage technology transfer to developing nations. As its mission statement clearly states:

> IFIP is the global non-profit federation of societies of ICT professionals that aims at achieving a worldwide professional and socially responsible development and application of information and communication technologies.

IFIP is a non-profit-making organization, run almost solely by 2500 volunteers. It operates through a number of technical committees and working groups, which organize events and publications. IFIP's events range from large international open conferences to working conferences and local seminars.

The flagship event is the IFIP World Computer Congress, at which both invited and contributed papers are presented. Contributed papers are rigorously refereed and the rejection rate is high.

As with the Congress, participation in the open conferences is open to all and papers may be invited or submitted. Again, submitted papers are stringently refereed.

The working conferences are structured differently. They are usually run by a working group and attendance is generally smaller and occasionally by invitation only. Their purpose is to create an atmosphere conducive to innovation and development. Refereeing is also rigorous and papers are subjected to extensive group discussion.

Publications arising from IFIP events vary. The papers presented at the IFIP World Computer Congress and at open conferences are published as conference proceedings, while the results of the working conferences are often published as collections of selected and edited papers.

IFIP distinguishes three types of institutional membership: Country Representative Members, Members at Large, and Associate Members. The type of organization that can apply for membership is a wide variety and includes national or international societies of individual computer scientists/ICT professionals, associations or federations of such societies, government institutions/government related organizations, national or international research institutes or consortia, universities, academies of sciences, companies, national or international associations or federations of companies.

More information about this series at http://www.springer.com/series/6102

Jiří Hřebíček · Ralf Denzer
Gerald Schimak · Tomáš Pitner (Eds.)

Environmental Software Systems

Computer Science for Environmental Protection

12th IFIP WG 5.11 International Symposium, ISESS 2017
Zadar, Croatia, May 10–12, 2017
Proceedings

 Springer

Editors
Jiří Hřebíček
Masaryk University
Brno
Czech Republic

Gerald Schimak
Austrian Institute of Technology GmbH
Seibersdorf
Austria

Ralf Denzer
Environmental Informatics Group
Saarbrücken
Germany

Tomáš Pitner
Masaryk University
Brno
Czech Republic

ISSN 1868-4238   ISSN 1868-422X   (electronic)
IFIP Advances in Information and Communication Technology
ISBN 978-3-030-07897-3   ISBN 978-3-319-89935-0   (eBook)
https://doi.org/10.1007/978-3-319-89935-0

Jiří Hřebíček (1947–2017)

In Memory of Jiří Hřebíček

by Tomáš Pitner

Our dear colleague and friend, IFIP 5.11 member, co-author, and co-editor of ISESS proceedings, Prof. Dr. Jiří Hřebíček, PhD, passed away in autumn 2017. The following words and the 2017 proceedings of ISESS are dedicated to this exceptional colleague.

Jiří Hřebíček was a senior researcher and director at the Institute of Biostatistics and Analyses of Masaryk University. He was a professor at the Faculty of Science and Faculty of Informatics. He held an MSc in mathematics and informatics (1970) and a PhD in applied and numerical mathematics (1982). Since 1990, he had been working in the research of environmental informatics and modelling, computational science, and waste management.

In the mid-1990s, he became involved in the building of the newly established Faculty of Informatics under the leadership of Dean Zlatuška. He started to educate a new generation of experts in environmental informatics here. He established the Summer School of applied informatics, lasting two decades, which became an excellent working platform for joint meetings with colleagues from Masaryk and Mendel universities, Brno University of Technology, Ostrava University of Technology, and in recent years also numerous foreign guests.

His later career was tightly connected with the Institute of Biostatistics and Analyses and the Center for Research on Toxic Substances in the Environment, where he focused on eEnvironment services. He participated in numerous international projects, such as the FP6 Network of Excellence DEMO-net, eParticipation project FEED and FP7 projects ICT-ENSURE and TaToo. He had been the national representative of the Czech Republic at EIONET since 1996. The highlight of his career was the recurring appointment to the Scientific Advisory Board of the European Environmental Agency in Copenhagen in 2013.

Prof. Hrebicek authored more than 350 scientific publications. He wrote 17 books and one of them was translated into Portuguese, Chinese, and Russian.

He was an active member of the International Federation of Information Processing (IFIP) and secretary of WG 5.11 "Computer for Environment" of IFIP, member of the International Environmental Modelling and Software Society (iEMSS) and iEMSS board, the International Envirometrics Society (TIES), member of the Association and Mathematics of America, chairman of international conferences EnviroInfo 2005, ISESS 2007, 2011, vice-chairman of ISESS 2013, and held the Czech Presidency for the European conference Towards eEnvironment in 2009.

We miss him dearly.

Preface

The International Symposium on Environmental Software Systems (ISESS) is one of several overlapping forums discussing issues of environmental information and decision support systems.

ISESS was founded by Ralf Denzer and Gerald Schimak in 1995, with support from the German Informatics Society Working Group 4.6 "Computer Science for Environmental Protection," the International Federation for Information Processing (IFIP) Working Group 5.11 "Computers and Environment," and our friend David Russell at the Pennsylvania State University (PSU) campus in Malvern, PA. The first symposium received great support from PSU and turned out to be one of many success stories.

Since then, the symposium has been held in the following countries: the USA, Canada, Austria, New Zealand, Switzerland, Portugal, the Czech Republic, Italy, and Australia; over several years, joint sessions were held in conjunction with the biennial meeting of iEMSs (International Environmental Modelling and Software Society). ISESS has been an IFIP event since 1995 and is organized by WG 5.11.

Since its establishment, WG 5.11 has been led by Giorgio Guariso (1991–1999), Ralf Denzer (1999–2005), Dave Swayne (2005–2011), and Gerald Schimak (2011–2017). Since this conference was initiated, it has been in the hands of Ioannis Athanasiadis. Several individuals have served as vice-chairs and secretaries and many members of the WG have been active supporters for a long time without holding an official position.

For more than two decades, ISESS has brought together researchers dealing with environmental information challenges trying to provide solutions using forward-looking and leading-edge IT technology.

The 30-year anniversary of the EnviroInfo conference series (also called "Computer Science for Environmental Protection" at the beginning) was in 2017. To mark this occasion, we chose the subtitle "Computer Science for Environmental Protection."

During the past 20 years we have seen the publisher of IFIP change several times and electronic publishing has become the most important medium for scientific publications. ISESS has followed this transition and therefore there is *no single place* where all ISESS proceedings can be accessed.

The first and second proceedings (ISESS 1995, ISESS 1997) were published by IFIP publisher Chapman & Hall:

- R. Denzer, D. Russell, G. Schimak (eds.), Environmental Software Systems, Chapman & Hall, 1996, ISBN 0 412 73730 2 (print)
- R. Denzer, D. A. Swayne, G. Schimak (eds.), Environmental Software Systems Vol. 2, Chapman & Hall, 1998, ISBN 0 412 81740 3 (print)

Then IFIP changed publisher and the third proceedings (ISESS 1999) were published by IFIP publisher Kluwer Academic Press:

- R. Denzer, D. A. Swayne, M. Purvis, G. Schimak (eds.), Environmental Software Systems Vol. 3 — Environmental Information and Environmental Decision Support, Kluwer Academic Publishers, 2000, ISBN 0 7923 7832 6 (print)

As print publications were becoming increasingly difficult (particularly their cost for smaller conferences), the fourth and fifth proceedings (ISESS 2001, ISESS 2003) were published by the organizers of the symposium under IFIP ISBN:

- D. A. Swayne, R. Denzer, G. Schimak (eds.), Environmental Software Systems Vol. 4 — Environmental Information and Indicators, International Federation for Information Processing, 2001, ISBN 3 901882 14 6 (print)
- G. Schimak, D. A. Swayne, N.T. Quinn, R. Denzer (eds.), Environmental Software Systems Vol. 5 — Environmental Knowledge and Information Systems, International Federation for Information Processing, 2003, ISBN 3 901882 16 2 (print)

The sixth and seventh proceedings (ISESS 2005, ISESS 2007) were published, but this time as electronic versions, under IFIP ISBN:

- D. A. Swayne, T. Jakeman (eds.), Environmental Software Systems, Vol. 6 — Environmental Risk Assessment Systems, International Federation for Information Processing, 2005, ISBN 3-901882-21-9 (CDROM)
- D. A. Swayne, J. Hřebíček (eds.), Environmental Software Systems, Vol. 7 — Dimensions of Environmental Informatics, International Federation for Information Processing, 2007, ISBN 978-3-901882-22-7 (USB)

The eighth proceedings (ISESS 2009) were again published electronically, but not under IFIP ISBN:

- D. A. Swayne, R. Soncini-Sessa (eds.), Environmental Software Systems, Vol. 8, 2009, University of Guelph, ISBN 978-3-901882-364 (USB)

Today, Springer is the official IFIP publisher and ISESS is published by Springer in the IFIP *Advances in Information and Communication Technology* (AICT) series[1]. Proceedings number nine and ten were published as follows:

- J. Hřebíček, G. Schimak, R. Denzer (eds.), Environmental Software Systems, Vol. 9 — Frameworks of eEnvrionment, IFIP AICT 359, 2011; ISBN 978-3-642-22285-6 (eBook), ISBN 978-3-642-22284-9 (hard cover), ISBN 978-3-642-26878-6 (soft cover)
- J. Hřebíček, G. Schimak, M. Kubásek, A.E. Rizzoli (eds.), Environmental Software Systems, Vol. 10 — Fostering Information Sharing, IFIP AICT 413, 2013; ISBN 978-3-642-41151-9 (eBook); ISBN 978-3-642-41150-2 (hard cover)
- Denzer, R., Argent, R.M., Schimak, G., Hřebíček, J. (Eds.), Environmental Software Systems. Infrastructures, Services and Applications, IFIP AICT 448, ISBN 978-3-319-15994-2 (eBook), ISBN 978-3-319-15994-2 (hard cover)

---

[1] http://www.springer.com/series/6102.

Today Springer also has the rights of the early Kluwer and Chapman & Hall books (ISESS 1995, ISESS 1997, ISESS 1999), as Kluwer merged with Springer in 2004 and Chapman & Hall had been bought by Kluwer in 1997. Therefore, all proceedings that were published by a publishing house are in one place today and can be accessed through Springer. They are available as hard cover and/or soft cover, as eBooks and (most of them) as individual articles.

The proceedings which were self-published under the copyright of IFIP have been made available since 2015 at www.enviromatics.org by Ralf Denzer. Particular ISESS sessions at IEMSS are available through the IEMSS website[2]. The 2015 proceedings contain an overview article that gives a complete history of what ISESS has contributed to the research community in the past 22 years[3].

The ISESS conferences have always had a high standard of peer reviewing. For ISESS 2017, we summarize the reviewing process here:

As in 2015, we used extended abstracts of 3 to 4 pages, a strategy which we had applied in many early conferences but not in recent years. This year we only received 46 abstracts but they were, compared with 2015, of much higher initial quality. Logically, most of these abstracts made it into final papers, and therefore the rejection rate was only around 10%. Each extended abstract was assigned for review by three independent reviewers in the first stage. For stage 2, the review of the full papers, two independent reviewers were assigned to each full paper, and in many cases at least one individual was a different person than the reviewers in the first stage, which means that many papers had a total of at least three reviewers.

January 2018

Ralf Denzer
Gerald Schimak
Tomáš Pitner

---

[2] www.iemss.org.
[3] See: Ralf Denzer, Topics in Environmental Software Systems, ISESS 2015.

Organization

Conference Chairs

Gerald Schimak	Austrian Institute of Technology Austria
Jiří Hřebíček	Mazaryk University, Czech Republic

Program Chair

Ralf Denzer	Environmental Informatics Group, Germany

Organizing Committee

Jiri Hrebicek	Masaryk University, Czech Republic
Gerald Schimak	Austrian Institute of Technology, Austria
Ralf Denzer	Environmental Informatics Group, Germany

Program Committee

Gab Abramowitz	University of New South Wales, Australia
Ioannis Athanasiadis	Democritus University of Thrace, Greece
Allesandro Annoni	Joint Research Center, Italy
Dan Ames	Brigham Young University, USA
Robert Argent	Bureau of Meteorology, Australia
Lars Bernard	Technical University Dresden, Germany
Arne Berre	SINTEF, Norway
Lindsay Botten	National Computational Infrastructure, Australia
Ralf Denzer	Environmental Informatics Group, Germany
Albert van Dijk	Australian National University, Australia
Peter Fischer-Stabel	Hochschule Trier, Germany
Peter Fitch	CSIRO, Australia
Steven Frysinger	James Madison University, USA
Omar el Gayar	Dakota State University, USA
Lars Gidhagen	SMHI, Sweden
Reiner Güttler	Environmental Informatics Group, Germany
Denis Havlik	Austrian Institute of Technology, Austria
Daryl Hepting	University of Regina, Canada
Jiri Hrebicek	Masaryk University, Czech Republic
Tony Jakeman	Australian National University, Australia
Stefan Jensen	European Environment Agency, Denmark
Ari Jolma	AALTO, Finland
Kostas Karatzas	Aristotle University of Thessaloniki, Greece
Milan Konecny	Masaryk University, Czech Republic

Jose Lorenzo	ATOS Origin, Spain
Tim Pugh	Bureau of Meteorology, Australia
Werner Pillmann	ISEP, Austria
Nigel Quinn	Lawrence Berkeley Laboratory, USA
Iva Ritschelova	Czech Statistical Office, Czech Republic
Andrea Rizzoli	IDSIA, Switzerland
Francois Robida	BRGM, France
Mauno Rönkkö	University of Eastern Finland, Finland
Zohair Sabeur	IT Innovation, UK
Gerald Schimak	Austrian Institute of Technology, Austria
Katharina Schleidt	Environment Agency Austria, Austria
Sascha Schlobinski	Cismet GmbH, Germany
Kerry Taylor	CSIRO, Australia
Thomas Usländer	Fraunhofer IOSB, Germany
Alexey Voinov	University of Twente, The Netherlands
Bartel Van de Walle	Tilburg University, The Netherlands

Contents

Health and Biosphere

Risk and Disaster Management

Information Systems

Modelling, Visualization and Decision Support

Keynote Lectures

Real-Time Web-Based Decision Support for Stakeholder Implementation of Basin-Scale Salinity Management

Nigel W. T. Quinn[1(✉)], Brian Hughes[1], Amye Osti[1], Joel Herr[2],
Elwood Raley[3], and Jun Wang[3]

[1] Lawrence Berkeley National Laboratory,
1 Cyclotron Road, MS64-209, Berkeley, CA 94720, USA
nwquinn@lbl.gov
[2] Systech Water Resources, 1200 Mount Diablo Blvd., Walnut Creek, CA 94596, USA
joel@systechwater.com
[3] US Bureau of Reclamation, MP-740, 2800 Cottage Way, Sacramento, CA 95825, USA
{eraley,junwang}@usbr.gov

Abstract. Real-time salinity management increases annual average salt export from the agriculture-dominated and salt-impacted San Joaquin Basin. This strategy also reduces the likelihood of potential fines associated with exceedences of monthly and annual salt load allocations which could exceed $1 million per year based on average year hydrology and State-mandated, TMDL-based salt load export limits. The essential components of this program include the establishment of telemetered sensor networks, a web-based information system for sharing data, a basin-scale salt load assimilative capacity forecasting model and institutional entities tasked with performing weekly forecasts of River salt assimilative capacity and coordinating west-side drainage return flows. San Joaquin River (SJRRTM) Online (SJRO) is a new web portal that combines WARMF-Online a dedicated web portal for sharing model input data and salt assimilative capacity forecasts with an informational website for increasing stakeholder awareness of the unique characteristics and opportunities for enhanced water and water quality resource management in the River Basin.

Keywords: Salinity · TMDL · Decision support · Forecasting · Web-portal

1 Introduction

In the USA, the Total Mass Daily Load (TMDL) is a policy instrument, developed by the US Environmental Protection Agency (EPA) for attaining compliance with water quality objectives for pollutants of concern for receiving waters (CEPA 2002; CRWQCB 2004). A unique provision in the published salinity TMDL for the San Joaquin River Basin (SJRB) was the admission of a "real-time" management salt load control strategy which substituted the attainment of a 30-day running average pollutant (salt) concentration for the typical load-based salt load allocations developed for watershed sub-basins upstream

© IFIP International Federation for Information Processing 2017
Published by Springer International Publishing AG 2017. All Rights Reserved
J. Hřebíček et al. (Eds.): ISESS 2017, IFIP AICT 507, pp. 3–18, 2017.
https://doi.org/10.1007/978-3-319-89935-0_1

of the compliance monitoring point on the San Joaquin River (SJR). This strategy increases potential management flexibility for agricultural, wetland and municipal dischargers to the River and provides an opportunity to maximize salt load export from the Basin without exceeding environmental objectives – however it assumes a level of coordination and cooperation amongst stakeholders that does not currently exist. The core requirements of this program include: the development of a basin-scale, sensor network to collect real-time monitoring of flow and salinity data; an information dissemination system for effective sharing of data among basin stakeholders; a calibrated simulation model of hydrology and salinity in the SJR and its contributing watersheds to allow forecasting and daily assessment of River assimilative capacity (Fig. 1); the development of a stakeholder-based institutional entity responsible for coordinating salinity management actions and ensuring compliance with State salinity objectives; and finally the sanction of the Central Valley Regional Water Quality Control Board (CRWQCB). Not only could successful matching of salt load export with River salt load assimilative capacity permit greater export of salt load from the watershed during normal and wet years (Quinn and Karkoski 1998; Quinn and Hanna 2003; Quinn et al. 2005; Quinn 2009; Quinn et al. 2011) it would also help to overcome salt accumulation in the shallow groundwater system which would ultimately degrade the groundwater resource within the Basin. The combination of real-time monitoring, simulation modeling and forecasting of SJR assimilative capacity has the potential to optimize use of available River salt assimilative capacity, generated by releases of high quality Sierran water, which provides dilution to saline west-side agricultural and managed wetland return flows. However there needs to be coordination and sufficient lead time to allow entities being asked to charge drainage practices or alter reservoir release patterns to be able to respond. Agricultural return flows and salt loads are highest during the summer irrigation season whereas return flows and salt loads from seasonally managed wetlands are highest during the spring months of March and April, when most seasonal wetland ponds are drained to promote establishment of moist soil plants and habitat for waterfowl. These anticipated hydrologic patterns help to screen the array of practices on both the east and west sides of the Basin that will be most effective at managing salinity.

Given the uncertainty associated with estimates of salt assimilative capacity, the need for adequate lead time for stakeholders to adjust tributary inflow and drainage return flow schedules and the fact that most weather forecasts provided by news organizations rarely extend beyond two weeks – a two week forecast period and one week hindcast period was chosen for the real-time salinity management program (RTSMP). The one week hindcast refers to the technique of beginning the simulation one week in arrears so that the first week of the forecast can be compared to observed flow and electrical conductivity (EC) data. Model parameters affecting River and tributary inflow and water quality such as the partitioning coefficients that allocate watershed runoff and deep percolation to groundwater can be adjusted to recalibrate the model during periods when model output and River observations diverge. Stakeholders have embraced the suggested two-week forecast and one-week hindcast periods.

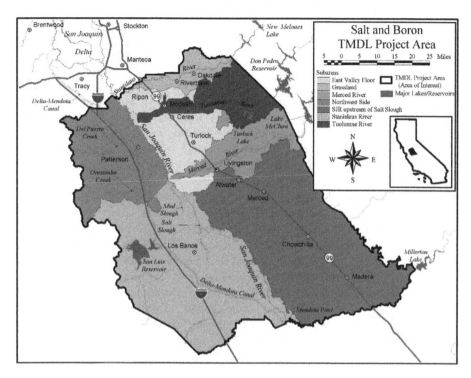

Fig. 1. Subareas within the San Joaquin River Basin draining to the San Joaquin River defined in the salinity TMDL (CEPA 2002).

2 Real-Time Salinity Management

2.1 Monitoring Networks – Data Measurement and Telemetry

The monitoring of flow and electrical conductivity (EC) at seven purpose-built monitoring stations along the SJR and from its major east-side and west-side tributaries is undertaken mostly by water agencies such as the California Department of Water Resources (CDWR) and the US Geological Survey (USGS). These stations include the current salinity compliance station at Vernalis on the San Joaquin River, the current upstream boundary monitoring station at Lander Avenue, two major salt load conveyances from the west-side that account for up to 65% of the annual salt load to the River and three major east-side tributaries – the Stanislaus, Tuolumne and Merced River's that receive releases of most Sierra water from eastside reservoirs. Most of these stations have more than 20 years of flow and EC monitoring records and are maintained monthly. The complementary San Joaquin River Restoration Program (SJRRP) is a comprehensive long-term effort to restore a self-sustaining Chinook salmon fishery in the San Joaquin River from Friant Dam to the confluence of Merced River, Full restoration flows began on January 1, 2014 and the previously dry sections of the River are now permanently re-wetted. Full merger of the current RTSMP with the SJRRP will add five or more River monitoring stations to the current sensor network and will enhance the reliability of model simulation of upper boundary inflow. Water districts and local agencies are responsible for flow and salinity monitoring within the watersheds, some of which directly discharges to the San Joaquin River. Critical data on SJR diversions is currently only collected for the major westside SJR diverters – however this data is not reported on a real-time basis. Recent California legislation requires estimation and reporting of SJR diversions by all riparians with an established right to SJR water supply. This new policy directive has provided an opportunity to coordinate and improve the reporting of stakeholder diversion data using a common reporting protocol. For the three largest diverters on the westside of the SJR this will require creating external ftp-accessible directories, firewalled from each water districts main server, that can be polled and the data contents uploaded to a single dataserver supporting the forecasting model.

A variety of telemetry technologies are used to transmit data from monitoring stations to the end user including CDMA cellular phone, GOES satellite and RF radio. State and federal agencies such as the CDWR and the USGS report real-time data to publicly available sites such as the California Data Exchange (CDEC) and the National Water Information system (NWIS) respectively – whereas most irrigation districts utilize SCADA-based monitoring networks which are private and require username and password access. One of the challenges of developing a basin wide real-time salinity management system is accessing and operationalizing these data in a timely manner that supports daily decision making while maintaining database autonomy and data security.

2.2   Data Quality Control and Assurance

Although data quality assurance protocols for discrete environmental sampling are well established and data quality control plans are necessary functions of all hydrologic and water quality monitoring projects - there has been incentive to integrate these activities to promote uniformity and coherence. For continuously recorded and reported data, the protocols for monitoring site visitation, rating procedures, data management, data processing and error correction are often inconsistent leading to a reluctance for stakeholders to share or rely on each other's data. Established software tools used by local water districts (WISKI) the CDWR (HYDSTRA) and the USGS (AQUARIUS) facilitate and guide these tasks that use QA data to error-correct and apply averaging techniques to continuous records. However the response time is currently insufficient to support daily forecast model runs with QA-censored data. In the case of CDWR a separate division is tasked with developing the agency-published time series data which occurs 6–12 months after data acquisition by CDEC. The USGS has a similar turnaround time for published data on their agency NWIS website. All data prior to being published is labelled "Preliminary". In the project we strive to produce a reliable data record that can be publicly shared and readily utilized in the salt assimilative capacity forecasting model. For forecasting purposes we seek daily mean data for flow, electrical conductivity (EC) and temperature (used to make corrections to EC which is temperature dependent) that has undergone at least a preliminary level of data quality assurance. Inaccurate or absurd data posted to a project website can cause irreparable harm by producing erroneous model simulations and forecasts that can quickly lead to a loss of confidence within the stakeholder community. Since four stakeholder entities have already adopted the (Kisters Inc. 2013) WISKI hydrological data management toolbox and the CDWR uses its sister product HYDSTRA we resolved to encourage more widespread use of this common IT platform as a means of fostering the collaboration and data sharing activities required under the RTMP. The WISKI platform is capable of a large number of data quality assurance operations – the most important for our purposes are the screening and removal of values that exceed normal upper and lower threshold values or that exhibit a rate of change between readings that cause the readings to be flagged (in the watershed abrupt changes in flow and EC are not typically observed and are considered aberrant). The software is able to interpolate missing values using a variety of linear and non-linear algorithms including cubic splines which pass through control points. A similar technique is also deployed to perform data shifts that allow real-time data to be fitted to flow and EC sensor quality assurance data, performed monthly in the case of the water agencies and weekly by water districts such as Grassland Water District.

3 Flow/Water Quality Modeling, Simulation and Forecasting

The Watershed Management Framework (WARMF) model (Herr et al. 2001; Chen et al. 2001; Herr and Chen 2006) is comprehensive decision support tool specifically designed to facilitate TMDL development at the watershed-level. The WARMF-SJR application simulates the hydrology of entire San Joaquin River Basin which is drained by the SJR – the model performs mass balances for a broad suite of potential contaminants including total dissolved solids (Chen et al. 1996). The model, whose simulation domain is shown in Fig. 2, simulates tributary inflows from the major east-side rivers, agricultural and wetland drainage return flows, accretions from shallow groundwater, riparian and appropriative diversions and uses hydrologic routing to calculate flow and water quality at approximately 1.6 km intervals along the main stem of the SJR. Wetland drainage from the Grassland Ecological Area is partitioned into component State, Federal and private wetland subarea watershed contributors to SJR salt load.

A GIS-based model graphical user interface (GUI) facilitates the visualization of model input flow and water quality data. Although data templates are built-in to expedite automated data retrieval from State and Federal agency hydrology and water quality databases to facilitate the automated updating of model input files we opted to utilize the OpenNRM engine (described later) to facilitate this retrieval for both the model and the SJRO web portal to avoid potential inconsistencies. Water managers can enter daily schedules of diversions and discharges using a customized spreadsheet-like data interface that is also operationalized through OpenNRM. Standardized model output graphics aid the dissemination of flow and water quality forecasts exported to the dedicated WARMF-Online web portal are now part of the combined SJRO web portal. What makes the new SJRO web portal unique is the integration of real-time watershed data and model-generated flow, salinity and salt load assimilative capacity forecasts.

The RTSMP serves a diverse stakeholder community consisting of agricultural, wetland and municipal entities. The agricultural community comprises more than 40

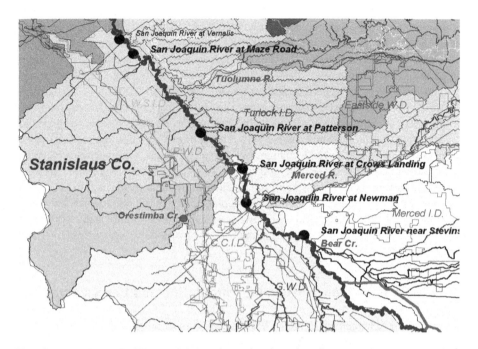

Fig. 2. The WARMF-SJR model interface showing the disaggregation of watersheds contributing flow and salt load to the San Joaquin River into component drainages. The hydrology of the San Joaquin Basin is such that the political boundaries of individual agricultural water districts are the most appropriate primary unit (sub-watershed) for monitoring, management and control of salt loading to the San Joaquin River from the west-side. Sub-watersheds on the east-side of the San Joaquin River are determined by the irrigation supply and surface drainage network.

individual water districts which exhibit their own distinct diversity among the 7 geographic subareas previously identified (Fig. 1) that also generally define: (a) native soil salinity; (b) irrigation supply water quality; (c) drainage relief with respect to proximity to the San Joaquin River; and institutional support within stakeholder-led coalitions. The eastside water districts are larger, wealthier with greater resources all of which serve both agricultural and municipal customers. Since the source of their water supply is the Sierra-Nevada mountains water quantity and electrical power rather than water quality have been the major focus of District activities. Because do not divert water from the SJR they are less impacted by salinity and have been more challenging to "bring-to-the-table" for real-time data coordination activities in support of the WARMF-SJR salt assimilative capacity forecast modeling. The westside divided into Grasslands and Northwest side subareas are distinguished from each other primarily by the higher concentration of native salts and the diminished reliance on SJR diversions as a source of irrigation water supply in the Grasslands subarea.

Outreach to westside agricultural stakeholders has concentrated on familiarizing farmers and water district managers with the concept of salt load assimilative capacity and how it varies with season and by water year type. These stakeholders have a well-evolved skepticism of models and model-based analyses and an important aspect of outreach has been the simultaneous display of model flow, EC and salt load assimilative capacity forecasts and real-time observations, as shown in an example (Fig. 3), to incrementally build trust in the ability of the model to simulate ambient conditions. Discussion in open forums of WARMF-SJR based salt assimilative capacity forecasts are also

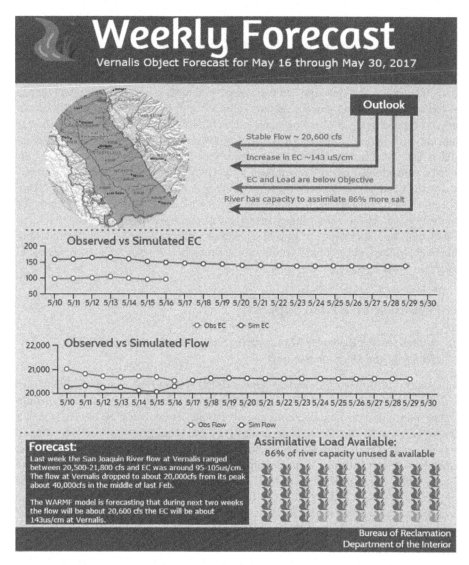

Fig. 3. Prototype WARMF-SJR model-based forecast graphic being used to encourage stakeholder interest and engagement in RTSMP activities. Given the newness of the concept of RTSM - stakeholders do not necessarily know a-priori their preferences for data visualization and quantitative representation of the concept of salt load assimilative capacity. The WARMF-Online web portal is being developed through feedback at scheduled stakeholder meetings.

used as a vehicle to encourage greater stakeholder engagement including sharing of real-time drainage discharge and River diversion information. We have demonstrated, during stakeholder presentations, the significance of errors that can occur, especially during dry and critically dry years, when default model diversion data (nine year averaged daily mean) are used in-lieu of actual data from westside riparian diverters. The threat of having inaccurate data associated with two of the three major westside riparian diverters has been effective in catalyzing initial data transfer of historic daily diversion data from these water districts.

The wetland entities that form the 140,000 acre (64,000 ha) Grassland Ecological Area (GEA) similarly exhibit their own unique diversity largely on account of their institutional status as State and Federal wildlife refuges on one hand and privately owned duck clubs (some that combine cattle grazing) on the other. Habitat objectives dictate the fall wetland flood-up schedule and more importantly the spring wetland drawdown period. Discharges of salt load between late February and the end of April each year coincide with agricultural pre-irrigation – problematic for those agricultural stake-holders that divert the majority of their water supply from the San Joaquin River. Coordination of salt load discharge schedules for the GEA is being undertaken by the Grassland Water District that has been the first to embrace the concept of RTSM – largely on account of being able to use the same sensor network of 50 flow and EC stations for both water conservation and salinity management purposes. We have found that technology transfer and embrace of web-based sensor technologies occurs faster and more effectively between stakeholders facing similar problems than from vendors of technical experts in water agencies.

4   Web-Based Decision Support

4.1   Collaborative Resource Management System for Data Visualization, Analysis and Decision Support

Collaborative, real-time salinity management (RTSM) is best facilitated when all stake-holders have a forum and toolset for aggregating and accessing the data and information used to inform management decisions and operations. The SJR RTMP has developed a comprehensive resource (San Joaquin River Real Time Management – (SJRRTM) Online (abbreviated to San Joaquin River Online-SJRO) that combines WARMF-Online - the dedicated web portal for sharing model input data and salt assimilative capacity forecasts (Figs. 4 and 5) - with an informational website for increasing stakeholder awareness of the unique characteristics and opportunities for enhanced water and water quality resource management in the River Basin. SJRO supports collaborative efforts to improve salinity management in the San Joaquin River and gives stakeholders access to resources (reports, GIS, datasets), reporting dashboards for viewing WARMF model output and supplemental data as well as a collaborative workspace for evaluating and discussing system conditions. SJRO aims to provide stakeholders with timely information and a transparent process for coordinating system-wide salt loading schedules with reservoir releases of high quality flows from the East-side of the Basin. The web based data management platform

OpenNRM, is a Collaborative Natural Resource Management software tool developed by 34-North Inc. in concert with the project team.

Fig. 4. San Joaquin River (SJRRTM) Online (SJRO) web portal using the OpenNRM visualization toolbox. The web portal provides data access to visualizations of WARMF-SJR model output. The model provides forecasts for weekly salt assimilative capacity and GIS-based data analysis.

OpenNRM allows users to create, modify and manage data and content collectively and provides filtering capability to parse information based on regions, areas of responsibility, hot spots, presets and more using mapping and data dashboard interfaces. Geocoded information is enabled for all data types extending the map and dashboards to include document libraries, projects databases, datasets, visualizations, wiki knowledge bases, publications and miscellaneous file types related to specific locations. The framework supports simple and robust construction of dashboards, common operating pictures, adaptive management scenarios, regional management cyberinfrastructure, workspaces and project collaboration tools.

OpenNRM is currently implemented as five hosted open data management platforms throughout the State of California. This open data federation approach provides instant access to State and Nationwide datasets and services including the California Irrigation

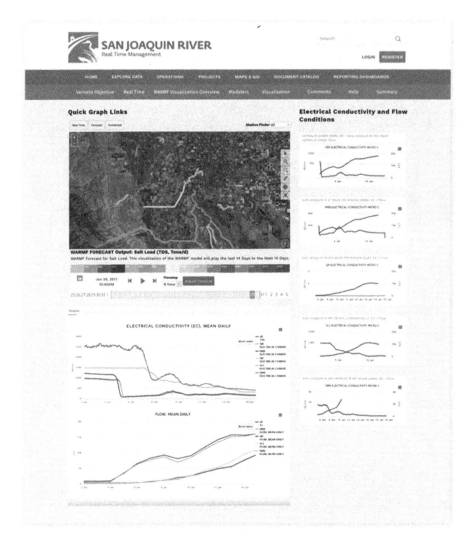

Fig. 5. Visualization of WARMF-SJR model results in SJRO - published daily for collaborative viewing of forecasted conditions of the River and its tributaries in the Basin. Visualizations are supported with additional analytics for comparing observed and forecasted data. The web portal provides data access to more than 365 monitoring sites throughout the basin. Reporting dashboards are in real time and can be compared with modeled data.

Management System (CIMIS), California Data Exchange (CDEC), National Water Information System (NWIS), National Oceanic Atmospheric, Administration (NOAA), water quality databases including STREAMWATCH, CEDEN, STORET and hundreds of GIS Layers. CIMIS, CDEC, NWIS and NOAA provide real-time data used in the development of San Joaquin River salt assimilative capacity forecasts using the WARMF-SJR model. The OpenNRM platform has been customized to provide stakeholders with the following decision support resources and tools:

1. Data tools to visualize and analyze current watershed conditions. Baseline data and baseline conditions.
2. Data and information needed to assess future environmental conditions and support management actions using the WARMF-SJR model and real time analytics.
3. Data aggregation and formatting tools to efficiently run the WARMF-SJR model and system wide assessments. Support resources to better understand how the San Joaquin Basin functions including research catalogs, regulatory resources, interactive maps, real time data visualizations, charts and graphs.
4. OpenNRM also addresses the need for a collaborative workspace for supporting, organizing, managing, analyzing, visualizing, archiving and reporting project and operations information.
5. The creation of SJRO facilitates analysis, synthesis, assessment and communication to develop a credible process in which stakeholders can participate in order to ensure that data are appropriately assessed, interpreted, and reported.

4.2 Customized SJRO Features for Real Time Salinity Management

The data aggregation toolset in SJRO prepares data packages from a variety of agencies and data sources that include approximately 356 monitoring sites (meteorological hydrologic, and water quality data) using preset and user defined time extents. The assembled data is formatted and converted to make the data compatible for import into the WARMF-SJR forecasting model as well as the online reporting dashboards and assessments. This tool also generates base line data for modelers and stakeholders running independent analytics. A second key feature is the simplification of data management and access by centralizing key datasets and management tools. To better understand the characteristic behavior of the SJRB sensor data is spatially organized using interactive maps and data dashboards allowing stakeholders to track flow, salinity, salt load export and irrigation diversions from the upper reaches of the SJR through to the Sacramento - San Joaquin Bay Delta. The data are collected from a wide range of sources and made comparable using map based data visualizations alongside interactive charts and graphs. Users can compare Electrical Conductivity (EC), River Discharge, and Salt Load from both the forecasted model output and real time observations.

Customized post-processed visual outputs such as the GOWDY Output (Fig. 6) allow the user to directly access WARMF-SJR model simulation results and toggle between views of flow, EC and salt load for the entire San Joaquin River between Lander Avenue and Vernalis (a 96 km reach) for a single day in the year. On the left panel flows into the River show as green horizontal columns superimposed over the input source whereas diversions from the River show up as red horizontal columns to the left of zero. In the top and bottom panels to the right of the screen are shown travel time showing an initial value of 1.8 days diminishing to zero days at the Vernalis compliance monitoring station. Flow is shown increasing from left to right as the east-side tributaries discharge into the River. The lower right-hand panel shows the same cumulative flow relative to cumulative River diversions. Powerful visualization aids such as the Gowdy Output provide the user with a comprehensive daily window into the complex characteristics of flow and water quality in the San Joaquin Basin.

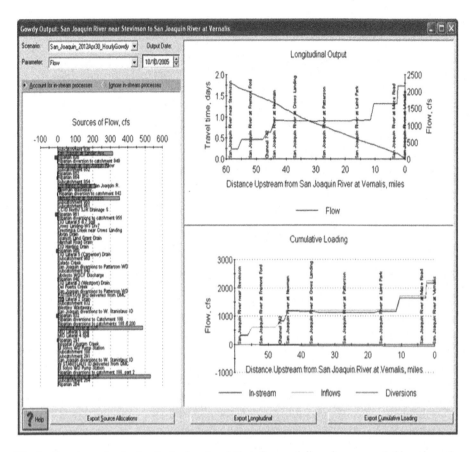

Fig. 6. Gowdy customized outputs showing daily inflow and diversions every 1.6 km along the mainstem of the San Joaquin River for a chosen annual time series output from the WARMF-SJR simulation and forecasting model. (Color figure online)

Although Basin stakeholders have endorsed the concept of RTSM the novelty of decision support implications of RTSM implementation are unclear to the majority of these stakeholders. Hence the primary initial goal of SJRO has been to educate stakeholders on the characteristics of the Basin, the various means of generating salt assimilative capacity within the Basin and the potential performance of various salinity management strategies (that include both incidental measures such as river diversions and drainage water reuse and deliberate strategies such as short-term ponding of drainage in small reservoirs). Other short-term goals are specific to water managers within each of the major contributing subareas to the SJR. For example west-side agricultural water districts that divert directly from the SJR for a portion of their agricultural water supply will be interested in assessing compliance with the newly promulgated upstream salinity objectives at the upstream Crows Landing monitoring station – which directly impacts the salinity of their River diversions. The wetland entities which include private duck clubs, State and Federal wildlife refuges will be concerned with scheduling of their annual wetland drawdown during the months of March and April so as not to exceed available River salt assimilative capacity. East-side water districts that control reservoir releases along tributaries to the SJR that generate much of the River's salt assimilative capacity will want to develop a better understanding of how to optimize the timing of these events with west-side salt loads and their own salt loading to the River and how to improve communication of these opportunities.

Data and model forecast visualization is a key component of SJRO. Model-based forecasts and simulations runs are shared and can be viewed as a recording or in video format. The OpenNRM application allows certain model outputs such as EC, flow and salt load to be interactive and viewed spatially on a map. Attribute tables determine how the values from surrounding monitoring stations are assigned to each watershed polygons and color coded using the OpenNRM display tools. Data is delivered using the OpenNRM content management system that ingests a binary and proprietary RIV file. The result allows the end user to see the salinity conditions over a user-specified time window – typically two weeks for the salt assimilative capacity forecast.

The SJRO visualization tools are designed so that model simulations and forecast runs can be repurposed and enhanced for additional studies or analysis. When fully implemented SJRO will supply real-time flow and salinity data from public water agency websites, cooperating water districts and other stakeholders to enable reliable daily simulations and forecasts of River assimilative capacity to the San Joaquin River. Future forecasts will utilize a single web-based version of the model application. This web based model will be continuously calibrated and upgraded with new algorithms and bug fixes. Future WARMF-SJR model forecast runs will be made by a small core group of stakeholder and/or agency personnel with write access privileges to the model. Model outputs and post-processed visualizations will continue to be made available to the public through SJRO web portal.

4.3 Coordinated Stakeholder Decision Support for Salinity Management

In early 2016 the San Joaquin Valley Drainage Authority (SJVDA) initiated informa-tional quarterly stakeholder meetings on behalf of the Westside San Joaquin River Watershed Coalition (WSJRWC) on the topic of data management, data coordination and mechanisms for data sharing - a core requirement for RTSM. The WSJRWC (www.sjvdc.org) currently: (a) represents water districts and other agricultural and wetland stakeholders located within the Grassland and North-West side subregions; (b) manages data collection at a large number monitoring sites and; (c) submits reports on these data to the CVRWQCB. Similarly on the east-side of the Basin the East San Joaquin Water Quality Coalition (ESJWQC) (www.esjcoalition.org) files required monitoring reports with the CVRWQCB on behalf of its 1000 + farmers and stakeholder entities, provides conditional waiver coverage for members of the coalition, develops and is responsible for implementation of the real-time water quality monitoring program. The ESJWQC communicates and advises landowners when water quality monitoring indicates the occurrence of a problem exist and helps with the timely development of equitable solutions. Ultimately the WSJRWC and the ESJWQC will need to develop a Memorandum of Understanding for joint implementation of the real-time management program recognizing the use of the WARMF-SJR model as a decision-making tool to forecast availability of River assimilative capacity. Realization of the potential of RTSM may require the formation of a basin-scale salinity management entity built upon the WSJRWC and the ESJWQC with the authority to encourage compliance with sub-basin salt load targets through incentives or penalties set at mutually agreed-upon salinity compliance monitoring locations.

In Fig. 7 a simplified workflow, feedback and control schema is shown that provides an overview of the current institutional decision support framework. Weekly salt load forecasts will be made for each of the seven subareas and compared to salt load allocations for these same subareas determined using the procedures published in the Water Quality Basin Plan for the San Joaquin Basin.

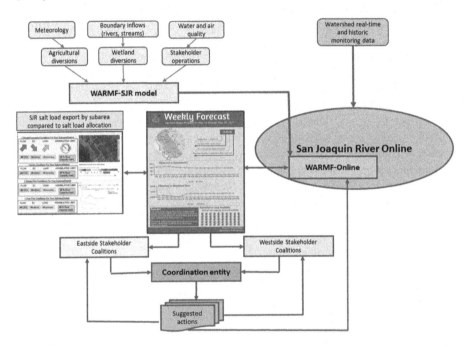

Fig. 7. Process workflow showing the main steps in developing weekly salt load assimilative capacity forecasts and the role of the coordination entity in allocating resources to improve San Joaquin River salinity during periods of exceedence.

The salt load allocation procedures are based on current flow conditions and subtract background salt loading, groundwater accretions and point source load allocations from River assimilative capacity (estimated by multiplying the same flow condition by the salinity compliance objective at the Vernalis monitoring station). It is assumed that only 85% of the available assimilative capacity is available – hence a factor of safety of 15% is applied to each salt load allocation for each of the seven contributing subareas. While salinity objectives are being met at Vernalis no action is required to control and make scheduling adjustments to salt export to the River. However at times, such as during dry or critically dry years, when the objective might be violated – those subareas not in compliance would be obligated to reduce salt export or enter a salt load trading arrangement with compliant subareas to bring the entire system into compliance.

Following the schema in Fig. 7 – real-time watershed data used by the WARMF-SJR model to develop weekly forecasts are compared with subarea salt load allocations using the same flow and EC predictions provide by the model and reviewed by the separate eastside and westside stakeholder coalitions. The (as yet un-named) coordination entity would be responsible for managing salt export in those subareas in instances where the model-based forecasts suggested a potential future violation. During the past decade there have been less than five violations of the Vernalis objective that would have required action by stakeholders that might invite complacency. However the Regional Water Quality Control Board requirements for real-time salinity management require that a response program be ready and implementable if stakeholders are to continue to enjoy the economic and environmental benefits of being part of the Program. The Board can impose a fine of up to $5,000 per day to any Subarea within the basin that is found in violation of Subarea salt load limits during any period of violation of the Vernalis salinity objective.

5 Summary and Conclusions

Technical advances in data acquisition and information dissemination technologies have made possible the initial stages of implementation of a real-time salinity management program in California's SJRB. Experience to date with respect to implementation of RTSM in the San Joaquin Basin suggests the following principles moving forward, that have been discussed in the paper: (a) necessary stakeholder participation in the design and operation of existing and planned flow and water quality monitoring stations and web-based IT solutions that provide easy access to the real-time data being collected; (b) decision support system enhancement that utilizes technical expertise within the WSJRWC and ESJWQC and works toward implementation of a common system; (c) WARMF-SJR simulation model enhancements with full GIS capabilities and made more robust in its ability retrieve real-time data through the current WARMF-Online and SJRO web browsing tools. A state-of-the-art visualization engine with imaginative graphics to enhance stakeholder understanding of the current system and how their actions can impact salt load export; (d) more widespread support for data quality assurance technologies such as WISKI and HYDSTRA to improve accuracy of the real-time data being utilized by the WARMF-SJR forecasting model and reduce the fear of posting erroneous data; (e) greater automation of the process of providing salt assimilative capacity forecasts and an eventual transition from weekly to daily forecasts which allow feedbacks between stakeholder actions that update the state of the system; (f) institutional arrangements that formalize and streamline salt loading trading between subareas within the eastside and westside stakeholder coalitions that minimize institutional oversight and remedy potential salinity compliance violations before they occur.

The process of implementing RTSM in the SJRB will further encourage innovation – successful implementation will have significant transfer value to other highly regulated river basins where water quality is a concern.

Acknowledgements. The authors acknowledge support from the US Bureau of Reclamation that has financed development of the essential tools for RTSM implementation and Dr Jobaid Kabir, Chief of the Decision Analysis Branch overseeing this work. Also to 34-North Inc. for their contributions to the WARMF-Online web portal.

References

California Environmental Protection Agency: Total Maximum Daily Load for Salinity and Boron in the Lower San Joaquin River. Staff report by the Regional Water Quality Control Board, Central Valley Region (2002)

California Regional Water Quality Control Board: Amendments to the Water Quality Control Plan for the Sacramento River and San Joaquin River Basin. Draft Final Staff Report and Technical TMDL Report, Sacramento, CA (2004)

Central Valley Regional Water Quality Control Board: Technical TMDL Report for Salt and Boron in the Lower San Joaquin River Appendix 1. July 2004 Draft Final Report (2004b)

Chen, C.W., Herr, J., Weintraub, L.H.Z.: Watershed Analysis Risk Management Framework: Update One: A Decision Support System for Watershed Analysis and Total Maximum Daily Load Calculation, Allocation, and Implementation. EPRI, Palo Alto, CA. Topical report 1005181 (2001)

Chen, C.W., Herr, J., Gomez, L.E., Quinn, N.W.T., Kipps, J., Landis, P.J., Cummings, E.W.: Design and Development of a Graphic User Interface for Real-Time Water Quality Management of the San Joaquin River. Prepared for California Department of Water Resources, San Joaquin District, California (1996)

Herr, J., Weintraub, L.H.Z., Chen, C.W.: User's Guide to WARMF: Documentation of Graphical User Interface. EPRI, Palo Alto, CA. Topical report (2001)

Herr, J., Chen, C.W.: San Joaquin River Model: Calibration Report. CALFED Project ERP-02D-P63 Monitoring and Investigations for the San Joaquin River and Tributaries Related to Dissolved Oxygen. Systech Water Resources Inc. San Ramon, CA (2006)

KISTERS Inc.: WISKI hydrological data management software. Citrus Heights, CA 95610-5800. kna@kisters.net (2013)

Quinn, N.W.T., Hanna, W.M.: A decision support system for adaptive real-time management of seasonal wetlands in California. Environ. Model. Softw. **18**(6), 503–511 (2003)

Quinn, N.W.T., Karkoski, J.: Real-time management of water quality in the San Joaquin River Basin. California. Am. Water Resour. Assoc. **34**(6), 1473–1486 (1998)

Quinn, N.W.T., Hanlon, J.S., Burns, J.R., Taylor, C.M., Lundquist, T., Stringfellow, W.T.: Real-Time Water Quality Monitoring and Habitat Assessment in the San Luis National Wildlife Refuge. Lawrence Berkeley National Laboratory Topical report # 58813, Berkeley, CA (2005)

Quinn, N.W.T., Ortega, R., Holm, L.: Environmental sensor networks and continuous data quality assurance to manage salinity within a highly regulated river basin. Decision Support Systems in Agriculture, Food and the Environment: Trends, Applications and Advances (2011)

Quinn, N.W.T.: Environmental decision support system development for seasonal wetland salt management in a river basin subjected to water quality regulation. Agric. Water Manag. **96**(2), 247–254 (2009)

Trends in Policy Relevant European Environmental Information Systems

Stefan Jensen[✉]

European Environment Agency, Copenhagen, Denmark
stefan.jensen@eea.europa.eu

Abstract. The paper presents the evolution of European environmental reporting and how it has transformed information systems. It connects systemic changes in policy assessments whilst acknowledging that information systems themselves have evolved both from a knowledge and a technology perspective. It starts out by setting the policy context where a review of the current legislation related to environmental monitoring and reporting goes hand in hand with initiatives to promote open and distributed data access. The knowledge management model of EEA has been developed over almost two decades and is the background against which an evolution related to the way environmental data is been reported and generated and indicators are been developed has to be seen. This evolution is triggered by a growing need to support systemic thinking and integrative projects involving a growing set of stakeholders. To support these new demands our ways to manage environmental data needs to change. We receive more volumes of often less homogeneous data in more frequent intervals. We need to combine data from very different sources – environmental data based on legislation; data from research and big earth observation programs; data from citizens and industry. This data is structured or unstructured. While we continue investing in streamlining the data management aspects of reporting, we have to step-wise engage in new approaches like big data analytics. With these newly emerging data flows we also need to revise our information technology infrastructure by introducing more modularity and new tools.

Keywords: Environmental policy · Environmental knowledge
Environmental information system · Knowledge management · Big data

1 Background

The first pieces of environmental legislation in the European Union (EU) entered into force more than four decades ago. Since then EU Member States have been regularly collecting and reporting comparable data on a wide range of environmental issues ranging from hourly pollutant concentrations in cities to seasonal measurements of bathing water quality. They also keep track of greenhouse gas emissions, energy consumption, pollutants released from industrial facilities, the size and location of protected areas, etc. These data streams are essential for monitoring progress and ensuring an effective implementation of environmental legislation.

© IFIP International Federation for Information Processing 2017
Published by Springer International Publishing AG 2017. All Rights Reserved
J. Hřebíček et al. (Eds.): ISESS 2017, IFIP AICT 507, pp. 19–27, 2017.
https://doi.org/10.1007/978-3-319-89935-0_2

In 2016, the relationship between legislation and environmental monitoring underwent a review. This has also been referred to as a "fitness check" on environmental monitoring and reporting [1]. This fitness check triggered a refocusing on key environmental data and created a legal basis for the coming years to better incorporate new trends and areas for environmental data collection. Meanwhile, the Shared Environmental information system (SEIS) [2] concept, itself a decade old, has been reinforced through ideas such as "active dissemination" and data harvesting. The data harvesting principle is already part of the SEIS principles (manage data as close as possible to the source; avoid duplication). The *active dissemination* concept is fairly new and has currently only been assessed by a set of pilot studies. The idea reflects the growth of environmental data and information which is too large to be reported in its entirety. The data should therefore be made available at the local or national level. Interested users in the EU Member States and the European Commission (as the owner of the data flows) would harvest national services on demand. This would occur in particular when the state of the specific environmental theme is not developing according to target. National data reporting would then be limited to a sub-set of data only. The EU's INSPIRE directive [3] follows a similar principle building on a common spatial data infrastructure (SDI) to which data can be flexibly connected or, when legislation demands, a thematic subset can be reported.

The 2016 EU Communication on data, information and knowledge management [4] supports the aforementioned trend. It encourages increased information sharing and collaboration between EU institutions such as through the establishment of knowledge and competence centres. It also calls for capacity to handle "big data" and machine-readable open formats as well as stronger use of particular data and metadata standards.

The paper presents the evolution of European environmental reporting and how it has been used. It connects systemic changes in policy assessments whilst acknowledging that information systems themselves have evolved both from knowledge and technology perspectives.

2   EEA's Knowledge Management Model

The European Environment Agency (EEA) has, since its establishment in 1993, provided a regular analysis of the state of environment using various methodologies. This analysis has been published in various forms such as reports, factsheets etc. The methodology underpinning this has always been based on the MDIAK concept (monitoring, data, indicators, assessment and knowledge) combined with the DPSIR (driving forces, pressures, state, impact and response) model.

While the five areas in the MDIAK model have not changed, the way they have been used has evolved over time. The technology used in collecting, reporting and analysing environmental data has developed remarkably in this period. We can now collect, store and process larger amounts of data. We can also interlink different data streams to draw increasingly more accurate analyses on what is happening and why it is happening.

Monitoring is coming from more sources and data of different kinds is emerging in high volumes. Our indicator and modelling activities are getting more substantial based on efforts to increase data and indicator quality. Assessments become more cross-cutting and systemic in order to target a user community which constantly grows in numbers and diversity.

A more in-depth look into these five areas (see Fig. 1) will be provided in the next two chapters.

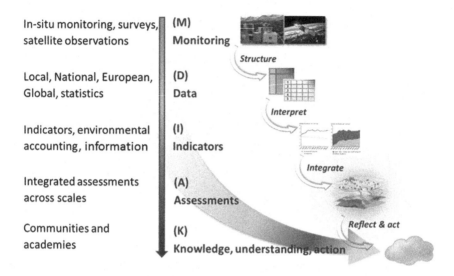

Fig. 1. EEA's knowledge management based on the MDIAK model

The EEA recognises that common EU rules ensure data compatibility and facilitate data and information exchanges across Europe. Yet to be able to fully understand environmental trends, it is essential to cooperate not only within the EU but also at the wider European and international level. The founding EEA legislation [5] established the Environmental Information and Observation Network (Eionet) as the instrument to link with the EEA Member Countries after 1993 and together with it, and a growing set of European and international partners, the EEA is in a unique position to process environmental information and foresee future knowledge needs.

3   Evolution of Environmental Monitoring, Data and Indicators

To underpin EEA analyses and reports with evidence, we needed to establish a solid data and information base. Since the start of EEA's mandate, this was carried out in agreement with the management board and with the support of Eionet. The EEA subsequently established data flows based on voluntary arrangements with Member Countries and increasingly serviced data reporting on behalf of DG Environment. Those data flows were established under the environmental *aquis* - the set of legislation related to environment available at the European level. Data flows have been growing substantially in number and volume over the past years as displayed in Fig. 2. This led to the need to modernize our data handling system Reportnet which was introduced in 2002.

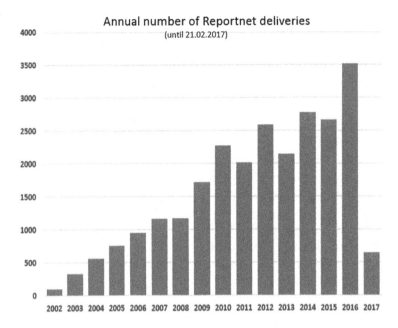

Fig. 2. Growth in reporting environmental data

Environmental indicators are another part of the way the EEA gathers and uses data thereby contributing to its "knowledge system". Indicators serve many purposes such as allowing data to be combined through the use of different models to represent complex relationships. Indicators are also widely regarded as communication tools to simplify environmental messages. The EEA has consolidated its indicators during the past year into a focused number of high quality core set indicators (Fig. 3). Data collaboration has also taken place with the European Statistical System (ESS). To highlight their policy relevance, EEA indicators have been submitted as part of the European contribution to the Sustainable Development Goals' (SDGs) indicators. This international policy

Focus / Type	Driving forces	Pressure	State	Impact	Response	Total
A – Descriptive indicators	17	22	19	34	7	99
B – Performance indicators	1	5	3	0	3	12
C – Efficiency indicators	2	5	0	0	3	10
D – Policy effectiveness ind.	1	2	1	0	4	8
E = Total welfare indicators	0	0	0	0	0	0
Total	21	34	23	34	17	129

Fig. 3. EEA's core set of indicators

process is a key driver for agreeing on environmental and other sustainable development related content for the years to come.

Such development highlights the evident growth in environmental data and information. This has been complemented by an increased collection of data by citizens and private companies. Therefore the EEA has been required to build new data partnerships between public and private, local and global data owners and collectors. A related area connects human well-being with data from classical environmental sources. This human biomonitoring increases in relevance and puts the human exposure to harmful substances and the causes and consequences of this into focus.

A further area of growing importance is the increased availability of remotely sensed data. Copernicus, the EU's earth observation programme, has been particularly responsible for driving growth through data from satellite observations which can be combined with data reported by monitoring equipment on land and at sea.

European environmental assessments are finally taking more advantage of research data as the open availability of this data is increasing. EU funded projects are increasingly obliged to make resulting data publically available. The open data movement in general and infrastructure initiatives like INSPIRE and the Copernicus program are further instruments through which free data availability is promoted.

In addition to particular data ownership and management issues, discussed later in this paper, large amounts of data present another challenge: how to distil relevant policy relevant knowledge out of large data flows. What do we need to know to improve the environment further? Such reflections may well lead to identifying new areas to monitor, others to discontinue or monitor less frequently. It might also require building new connections between data sets. Moreover, the knowledge needs of an urban planner may be very different from those of a European policy maker. How can environmental knowledge contribute to the management of complex systems like cities?

4   Systemic Assessment and an Extended Knowledge Approach

Despite some gaps, current knowledge on the environment is impressive and our understanding of specific issues has expanded over time. However, this enhanced understanding has also highlighted the need to look at the "bigger picture"—the need for more systemic analyses, looking at entire systems, such as on mobility and food. For example monitoring air pollutant concentrations can only take us to a certain point. The EEA cannot analyse and tackle air pollution without looking at other areas such as transport, the dieselisation of the vehicle fleet, agriculture, urban sprawl, and consumption patterns. The environment is complex and our knowledge base needs to factor in this complexity. It has become clear that we will increasingly need more systemic and cross-cutting knowledge in the future. In close collaboration with partners, and in support of the European Commission's 7th Environmental Action Program (7th EAP) [6], the EEA is contributing to Europe's environmental knowledge base with systems-based thematic assessments. The EEA does not only focus on past trends and the current state of play, but also on emerging issues and future knowledge needs. Further details on this approach and related work can be found in the most recent EEA Multiannual work programme (MAWP) [7].

Systemic analysis constitutes the core of the EEA's latest European environment—state and outlook report released in 2015. One section within this report has tried to assess the influence of global trends on Europe's environment and vice versa. Thematic EEA reports also address the issue at hand within a wider systemic analysis.

This very much pushes the need to adapt our data management to the new knowledge management approach. With input sources multiplying and data volumes growing we will have to adapt our information systems. This relates to many aspects: the governance structure around them – so who guides which process, the content they represent and the IT system which is used to process the data and disseminate the results.

While we used to work with a governance building on environmental datacentres (EDCs) we move to a wider governance steered by a European environmental knowledge community (EKC). A knowledge approach is widening scope and analytical opportunities. The demand for policy relevant knowledge is seen as coming from the interaction between many institutional players and those relationships develop subsequently. Due to the diversity of them, data variety is growing. Activities move from project type to more integrated program type (Fig. 4).

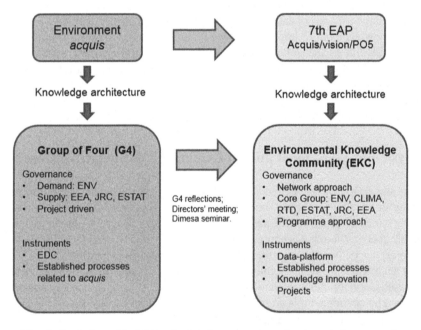

Fig. 4. Evolution of the EU institutional structure towards a knowledge approach

5   Data Management, "Big Data" and the Impact on the Information System

Several aspects have already been highlighted which are driving the future development of both data management and the information system as such. To acknowledge this, the EEA established a data and information management framework in 2015 [8]. Data management is far more complex as the input sources are much more diverse. Figure 5 shows the main areas from which data has been collected. Challenges lie, in particular, in the different quality standards, assurance and control which needs be addressed where data are jointly been processed into European data sets. The EEA runs a common work-space for processing the national reporting data which then needs to be complemented by data sets from other input streams.

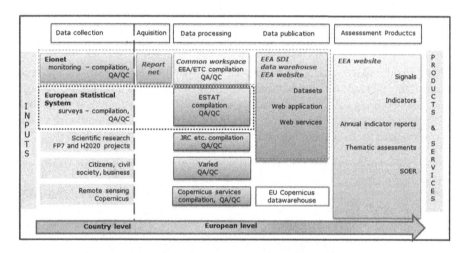

Fig. 5. Highlighted components for management of EEA multi-source data flows

This is especially the case when producing environmental indicators with sources which need to be integrated. It is here where we start meeting the issues which are addressed as part of the big data discussion. Out of the five big data characteristics (volume, variety, velocity, variability, veracity) the increase in *volume* is obvious in the area of national reporting data and the huge data stream generated by Copernicus. *Variety* is growing particularly when looking at research data and the new data emerging from citizen science (e.g. on species distribution) or data from the telecommunications industry. Here, spatial patterns derived from mobile phone data can be related to human movements and used to produce new population density or transportation flow related data sets. *Velocity*, the concept which addresses the speed in which data is generated and processed, is gaining a bigger share in the monitoring data. Here the near real time air quality monitoring is becoming more operational. Data *variability* grows the more the questions put forward become systemic, and finally data *veracity* – the differences in data quality – continues to place limits on producing integrated datasets of good overall quality.

Data publication, independent from its explicit usage in assessments, is one area which is seeing growth within the EEA. The demand to download datasets in flexible ways is increasing as is the need to create regular and interactive visualisations. The provision of map viewers, where user statistics have been monitored since 2007, has been growing steadily since 2009 and a larger variety of web services have been established and are increasing in popularity in part because they are integrated by stakeholders into their websites and information systems.

The typology of assessment products has also been changing. The number and volume of reports have been decreasing. Some elements of those reports are provided through the EEA website whilst others are more targeted, and offered in a briefing format alongside smaller information products. In general such products are not offered in hard copy format however users can often customize them to their needs and print them as PDF directly from the website.

6   Information Technology and Tool Related Challenges

As has been discussed, new data processing steps require new workflows and more integrated tools. Figure 6 explains the key components and tools used for the management of the reporting data. It incorporates the update of Reportnet and shows the tools used for data processing in the common workspace. On the dissemination side, a variety of tools has been used – depending on the type of data and the target audience.

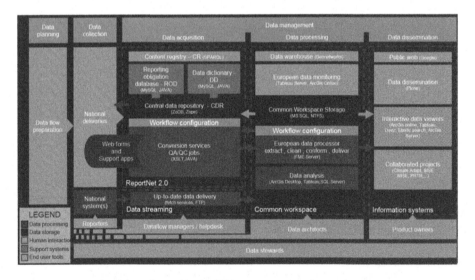

Fig. 6.   Tools used in the EEA management of reporting data

For a number of years, the EEA has been using cloud technology to host services and distribute data. We can be considered as a ground-breaker amongst the EU institutions. The use of cloud services has allowed EEA to better address the challenges posed by big data. Demands on our services tend to peak towards the end of a particular quarter when major *aquis* reporting is due or alongside the publication of popular reports such as the one on European bathing water due in June. Access to web map services can be exceptionally high.

There is one area which is not specific to the environment yet creates the need to take serious and partially costly measures. Information and communication technology (ICT) security needs to be tackled more intensely. This calls to enhance several functions in the information system: back-up solutions for data need to improve; security needs to be enhanced, that is why data access is been categorized into different security levels. Based on this, authentication levels for several of our services should be enhanced beyond the standard "public" and "restricted" designations, alongside other security measures.

References

1. European Commission: Fitness Check of reporting and monitoring of EU environment policy. Commission Staff Working Document SWD(2017)230 and Report on "Actions to Streamline Environmental Reporting" COM(2017)312
2. European Commission: Towards a Shared Environmental Information System (SEIS). Eur-lex. COM(2008) 46 final. http://eur-lex.europa.eu/legal-content/EN/TXT/PDF/?uri=CELEX: 52008DC0046&from=EN. Accessed 1 Feb 2008
3. European Parliament, Council of the European Union: Directive 2007/2/EC establishing an Infrastructure for Spatial Information in the European Community (INSPIRE) and related Implementing Rules. Eur-lex. http://inspire.ec.europa.eu/. Accessed 14 Mar 2007
4. European Commission: Data, Information and knowledge management at the European Commission. Communication to the Commission. C(2016)6626. https://ec.europa.eu/ transparency/regdoc/rep/3/2016/EN/C-2016-6626-F1-EN-MAIN.PDF
5. European Parliament, Council of the European Union: Regulation 401/2009 on the European Environment Agency and the European Environment Information and Observation Network. Eur-lex. http://eur-lex.europa.eu/legal-content/EN/ALL/?uri=CELEX:32009R0401. Accessed 23 Mar 2009
6. European Commission: Environment Action Programme to 2020 'Living well, within the limits of our planet'. Europa. http://eur-lex.europa.eu/legal-content/EN/TXT/?uri=CELEX: 32013D1386. 20 Nov 2013
7. European Environment Agency: Multiannual Work Programme 2014–2018: expanding the knowledge base for policy implementation and long-term transitions. http://www.eea.europa. eu/publications/multiannual-work-programme-2014-2018. Accessed 21 Jan 2014. ISBN 978-92-9213-418-1
8. European Environment Agency: EEA Data and Information management framework, 18 December 2015. Unpublished EEA internal

Big Data Storage and Management: Challenges and Opportunities

Jaroslav Pokorný[(✉)]

MFF UK, Malostranské nám. 25, 118 00 Praha, Czech Republic
pokorny@ksi.mff.cuni.cz

Abstract. The paper is focused on today's very popular theme – Big Data. We describe and discuss its characteristics by eleven V's (Volume, Velocity, Variety, Veracity, etc.) and Big Data quality. These characteristics represent both data and process challenges. Then we continue with problems of Big Data storage and management. Principles of NoSQL databases are explained including their categorization. We also shortly describe Hadoop and MapReduce technologies as well as their inefficiency for some interactive queries and applications within the domain of large-scale graph processing and streaming data. NoSQL databases and Hadoop M/R are designed to take advantage of cloud computing architectures and allow massive computations to be run inexpensively and efficiently. The term of Big Data 1.0 was introduced for these technologies. We continue with some new approaches called currently Big Data 2.0 processing systems. Particularly their four categories are introduced and discussed: General purpose Big Data Processing Systems, Big SQL Processing Systems, Big Graph Processing Systems, and Big Stream Processing Systems. Then, an attention is devoted to Big Analytics – the main application area for Big Data storage and processing. We argue that enterprises with complex, heterogeneous environments no longer want to adopt a BI access point just for one data source (Hadoop). More heterogeneous software platforms are needed. Even Hadoop has become a multipurpose engine for ad hoc analysis. Finally, we mention some problems with Big Data. We also remind that Big Data creates a new type of digital divide. Having access and knowledge of Big Data technologies gives companies and people a competitive edge in today's data driven world.

Keywords: Big Data · NoSQL databases · MapReduce · Hadoop · Big Data 2.0
Big Analytics

1 Introduction

One rather subjective definition by Kushal Agraval[1] says that Big Data can be as data that exceeds the processing capacity of conventional database systems. Consequently, its storage and processing require

---

[1] https://kushalagrawal.com/blog/big-data/.

© IFIP International Federation for Information Processing 2017
Published by Springer International Publishing AG 2017. All Rights Reserved
J. Hřebíček et al. (Eds.): ISESS 2017, IFIP AICT 507, pp. 28–38, 2017.
https://doi.org/10.1007/978-3-319-89935-0_3

- new data architectures, analytic environments,
- new analytical methods,
- new tools.

In the business sphere, Big Data is data whose scale, distribution, diversity, and/or timelines require the use these new technologies to enable insights to new sources of business value.

Usually some examples from the commercial world are presented for documenting the size of Big Data. The most known example concerning the Google's database mentions gross total estimate of all data Google saved by 2016 as approximately 10EBytes[2]. A. Orlova stated in 2015[3] that Facebook generates about 10 TBytes every day, Twitter generates about 7 TBytes and some enterprises generate TBytes every single hour. In general, the digital universe is doubling in size every two years, and by 2020 – the data we create and copy annually – will reach 44 ZBytes or 44 trillion GBytes[4]. In the near future, the "Big Data" problem will begin to emerge in every enterprise.

We will consider Big Data for both *data-at-rest* as well as *data-in-motion*. For Big Data at rest we describe two kinds of systems: (1) NoSQL systems for interactive data processing; (2) systems for large scale analytics, e.g. decision support, based on MapReduce paradigm, represented by tools such as Hadoop. Hadoop-based systems enable to run long running decision support and analytical queries consuming and possible producing bulk data. Data-in-motion is the process of analyzing data on the fly without storing it. We utilize real-time processing methods in this case.

Today, users have a number of options associated with the above mentioned issues [9]. For storing and processing large datasets they can use:

- traditional parallel database systems (shared nothing architectures),
- distributed file systems and Hadoop technologies,
- key-value datastores (so-called NoSQL databases),
- new database architectures (e.g., NewSQL databases).

The Big Data landscape is dominated by two classes of technologies: systems that provide operational capabilities, i.e. *operation systems* for real-time, interactive workloads where data is primarily captured and stored; and *analytical systems* that provide analytical capabilities for retrospective, complex analysis that may use most of all the data. Usually we talk about *Big Data analytics* (shortly *Big Analytics*). These classes of Big Data technology are complementary and frequently deployed together.

Big Data storage and processing are appropriate for cloud services. This approach reinforces requirements on the availability and scalability of computational resources offered by cloud services. Authors of [5] highlight this role of cloud computing. Cloud has given enterprises the opportunity to fundamentally shift the way data is created, processed and shared.

---

[2] https://www.quora.com/How-big-is-Googles-database/.

[3] http://blog.azoft.com/telcos-gain-valuable-insight-with-big-data/.

[4] https://www.emc.com/leadership/digital-universe/2014iview/executive-summary.htm.

The rest of the paper is organized as follows. Section 2 introduces traditionally some V's characterizing Big Data and some immediate challenges arising from them. Section 3 provides basic characteristics of NoSQL databases. Section 4 shortly introduces principles of MapReduce and Hadoop technology (Big Data 1.0). Big Data 2.0 processing systems are discussed in Sect. 5. Section 6 is devoted to the most important part of Big Data application domain - Big Analytics. Some problems with the Big Data are presented in Sect. 7. Section 8 gives the conclusion.

2   Big Data Characteristics

Big Data is most often characterized by several V's. In [11] we discussed eight such characteristics:

- *Volume*: Volume refers to the quantity of data generated and stored from various sources. Data scale in the range of TBytes to PBytes and even more. The big volume is not only a storage issue but also influences Big Analytics. Not only data samples, but often all data is captured for analysis.
- *Velocity*: Both how quickly data is being produced and how quickly the data must be processed to meet demand (e.g. streaming data). For many applications, the speed of data creation is more important than the volume. For example, a well-known source of high-velocity data is social media. Twitter users are estimated to generate nearly 100,000 tweets every 60 s.
- *Variety*: Data is of many format types – structured (e.g., call detail records in a telecom company), unstructured (product reviews on twitter), semi-structured (e.g., graph data), media, etc. Data does not come only from business transactions, but also from machines, sensors, GPS signals from cell phones, and other sources, making it much more complex to manage. There is a need to integrate this data together. From the analytics perspective, variety of data is the biggest challenge to effectively use it. It is becoming the single biggest driver of Big Data investments. Technically, some connectors are becoming crucial in integration of different data.
- *Veracity*: Managing the reliability and predictability of inherently imprecise data, e.g. to test many different hypotheses, vast training samples, etc. It means data needs to be cleaned before it can be integrated.
- *Value*: Indicates if the data is worthwhile and has value for business. Data value vision includes creating social and economic added value based on the intelligent use, management and re-uses of data sources with a view to increase business intelligence (BI). Also, an attention must be paid to the investment of storage for data. For example, storage may be cost effective and relatively cheaper at the time of purchase but it can be unreliable. Saving money can cause a risk in this case.
- *Visualization:* Concerns visual representations and insights for decision making. For example, SAS offers five Big Data challenges related to visualization and Big Data[5]:
  - meeting the need for speed,
  - understanding the data,

---

[5] https://www.sas.com/resources/asset/five-big-data-challenges-article.pdf.

- addressing data quality,
- displaying meaningful results, and
- dealing with outliers.

• *Variability*: The different meanings/contexts associated with a given piece of data is considered. Variability even refers to data whose meaning is constantly changing. Thus, variability is different from variety.

• *Volatility*: How long the data is valid and how long should be stored, i.e. at what point is data no longer relevant to the current analysis. For example, an online e-commerce company may not want to keep a one year customer purchase history.

The first three V's have been introduced by Gartner in [6], the V associated with Veracity has been added by Snow in his blog [13]. The fifth V was introduced by Gamble and Goble in [4].

Borne adds three other V's in [2]:

• *Venue:* Considers distributed, heterogeneous data from multiple platforms, from different owners' systems, with different access and formatting requirements, private vs. public cloud.

• *Vocabulary*: Includes schema, data models, semantics, ontologies, taxonomies, and other content- and context-based metadata that describe the data's structure, syntax, content, and provenance.

• *Vagueness*: Concerns a confusion over the meaning of Big Data. Is it Hadoop? Is it something that we've always had? What's new about it? What are the tools? Which tools should I use? etc.

Not only V's characterize Big Data. Often a quality is accentuated [8].

• *Quality*: Quality characteristic measures how the data is reliable to be used for making decisions. Saying that the quality of data is high or low is basically dependent on four parameters: (a) Complete: all relevant data is available, for example all details of vendors like name, address, bank account, etc., exist (b) Accurate: data is free of misspelling, typos, wrong terms and abbreviations (c) Available: data is available when requested and easy to find (d) Timely: data is up to date and ready to support decision.

These characteristics are not independent. For example, veracity (confidence or trust in the data) drops when volume, velocity, variety and variability increase. Sometimes, a *validity* (additional V) is considered. Similar to veracity, validity refers to how accurate and correct the data is for its intended use.

The characteristics represent challenges related to data itself, i.e. *data challenges* [8]. The tasks like data acquisition, cleaning, curation, integration, storage, processing, indexing, search, sharing, transfer, mining, analysis, and visualization are called *process challenges* in [8].

We can find a lot of other characteristics of Big Data. For example, Tyrone Systems[6] company distinguishes 10 Big Data challenges in two categories: cultural and

---

[6] http://blog.tyronesystems.com/the-top-10-big-data-challenges/.

technological. The former tackles the legal and ethical issues related to accessing data, e.g. privacy, security, and governance. In [8] they are called *management challenges*. The latter includes, in addition to the continued development of effective dealing with Big Data, putting results of Big Data Analysis in a presentable form for making decisions, i.e. it emphasizes a visualization and visual models.

3   NoSQL Databases

Considering Big Data we do not suppose an architecture with a database stored on the large disk. We refer to a much wider technology environment, which is coined under the term of *Big Data Ecosystem* (BDE) and relates to all interconnected parts, ranging from required infrastructure to data itself. A part of the BDE is represented by the NoSQL distributed databases. They include four main categories: key-value, column-oriented, document stores, and graph databases (see, e.g., [10]). Their data models are different and they can hardly be categorized in a precise way. Some typical user characteristics of these categories can be described as follows:

- *Key-value*. A user can store and retrieve data using keys in schema-less way. A key is a unique identifier for some data item. The data items, so-called values, are stored against these keys. They may be, e.g., a scalar (string), a hash, a list, a set, a sorted set, etc. Technically, a key-value store is just a distributed persistent associative array (map). It is suitable for rapid access to unstructured data, but it is inefficient when querying or updating part of a value is necessary. Examples of these databases are Redis[7] and Memcached[8].
- *Column-oriented*. A column is a key-value pair, where the key is a qualifier and the value is related to the qualifier. A data row has a sortable row key and an arbitrary number of columns. Columns are often grouped into columns families. These databases are suitable for very rapid access to structured or semi-structured data. Their examples include well-known systems Cassandra[9] and HBase[10].
- *Document datastores*. Data is stored as documents. Documents are data structures composed of key-value pairs. Documents can contain many different key-value pairs, or key-array pairs, or even hierarchically nested document parts (usually in JSON-style). Sometimes, a document database can contain a number of document collections. Examples of document databases include MongoDB[11] and Amazon Dynamo-moDB[12].
- *Graph databases*. Graph databases allow to store information about entities and relationships between these entities. In graph-oriented terms these databases use edges and nodes to represent and store data. These nodes are organized by some

---

[7] https://redis.io/.

[8] http://memcached.org/.

[9] http://cassandra.apache.org/.

[10] http://hbase.apache.org/.

[11] https://www.mongodb.com/.

[12] https://aws.amazon.com/dynamodb/.

relationships with one another, which is represented by edges between the nodes. Both the nodes and the relationships have some defined properties. The most known graph database available is Neo4j[13] and OrientDB[14].

There is DB-Engines initiative[15] to collect and present information on DBMSs. It provides a DB-engines ranking service which ranks DBMSs according to their popularity. The ranking is updated monthly. The examples of DBMSs presented above come from the first two places of ranking lists for particular categories.

4 MapReduce and Hadoop

Google introduced the MapReduce (M/R) [3] framework in 2004 for processing massive amounts of data over highly distributed clusters of nodes. M/R represents a generic framework to write massive scale data applications. It involves writing two user defined generic functions: *map* and *reduce*. In the map step, a *master node* takes the input data and the processing problem, divides it into smaller data chunks and sub-problems and distributes them to *worker nodes*. A worker node processes one or more chunks using the sub-problem assigned to it. Specifically, each map process takes a set of {key, value} pairs as input and generates one or more intermediate {key, value} pairs for each input key. In the reduce step, intermediate {key, value} pairs are processed to produce the output of the input problem. Each reduce instance takes a key and a set of values as input and produces output after processing a smaller set of values:

$$\text{Map}(k_1, v_1) \rightarrow \text{list}(k_2, v_2)$$
$$\text{Reduce}(k_2, \text{list}(v_2)) \rightarrow \text{list}(k_3, v_3)$$

Consequently, one of the main advantages of this approach is that it isolates the application from the details of running a distributed program, such as issues on data distribution, scheduling and fault tolerance.

Many NoSQL databases are based on Apache™ *Hadoop Distributed File System*[16] (HDFS), which is a part so-called *Hadoop software stack*. HDFS is a massively distributed file system designed to run on cheap commodity hardware. Open-source software Hadoop[17] is based on the M/R implementation along with HDFS.

The stack enables to access data by three different sets of tools in particular layers which distinguishes it from the universal DBMS architecture with only SQL API in the outermost layer. The NoSQL HBase is available as a column-oriented key-value layer with Get/Put operations as input. Hadoop M/R system server in the middle layer enables to create M/R jobs, i.e., programs in a programming language. It is often emphasised that writing custom M/R jobs is difficult and time-consuming.

---

[13] https://neo4j.com/.
[14] http://www.orientechnologies.com/.
[15] http://db-engines.com/en/.
[16] http://hadoop.apache.org/docs/r0.18.0/hdfs_design.pdf.
[17] http://hadoop.apache.org/.

Consequently, high-level languages HiveQL, PigLatin, and Jaql are at disposal for some users at the outermost layer. HiveQL is an SQL-like language representing a subset of SQL92, and therefore can be simply understood by SQL users. Jaql is a declarative scripting language for analysing large semi-structured datasets. Pig Latin is not declarative. Whose programs are series of assignments similar to an execution plan for relational operations in a relational DBMS.

NoSQL databases and Hadoop M/R are designed to take advantage of cloud computing architectures and allow massive computations to be run inexpensively and efficiently. This makes operational Big Data workloads much easier to manage, and cheaper and faster to implement. Some NoSQL systems provide native M/R functionality that allows for analytics to be performed on operational data in place. The term of *Big Data 1.0* was introduced for these technologies. Hadoop is its main representative.

5 Big Data 2.0 Processing Systems

For at least 10 years the M/R framework has represented the de facto standard for Big Data processing. Its fundamental principle is to move analysis to the data, i.e. to program applications in a data-centric fashion and not moving the data to an analytical system.

On the other, the research and development in the last years recognized some limitations of this approach. It is extremely complex to integrate, deploy, operate, and manage massive Hadoop environments. Hadoop cluster thinking requires special programmer skills to deploy the system and process data. Also, in processing large-scale structured data, several studies reported on the significant inefficiency of the Hadoop framework. The reason is that Hadoop is a file system built on batch processing. The Hadoop framework has also been shown to be inefficient within the domain of large-scale graph processing and streaming data [1]. It confirms a similar situation in data processing history analyzed by Stonebraker in his famous paper [14] in context of traditional relational DBMSs. He makes the argument that the relational DBMS cannot be extended ad infinitum, demonstrates how RDBMSs are inappropriate for several new applications, and argues that the DBMS market will fragment into a series of special-purpose engines. Thus a new wave of domain-specific systems for Big Data management has occurred in last years. They constitute a new generation of systems referred as *Big Data 2.0* processing systems [1, 12].

Bajaber et al. [1] distinguish four categories of Big Data 2.0 processing systems.

General Purpose Big Data Processing Systems. For example, Apache Spark[18], is an open source Big Data processing framework built around speed, ease of use, and sophisticated analytics. In a survey[19] nearly 70% of the respondents favoured Spark over dominating MapReduce, which is not appropriate to interactive applications or real-time stream processing.

---

[18] https://spark.apache.org/.

[19] http://www.syncsort.com/en/About/News-Center/Press-Release/New-Hadoop-Survey-Identifies-Big-Data-Trends.

Apache Spark provides programmers with an application programming interface centred on a data structure called the *resilient distributed dataset* (RDD), a read-only multiset of data items distributed over a cluster of machines that is maintained in a fault-tolerant way. It was developed in response to limitations in the M/R computing paradigm, which forces a particular linear dataflow structure on distributed programs. Spark's RDDs serve as a working set for distributed programs that offers a (deliberately) restricted form of distributed shared memory. Companies like ORACLE and SAP talk even about *Big Data Management Systems*.

Big SQL Processing Systems. SQL-on-Hadoop is a class of analytical application tools that combine established SQL-style querying with newer Hadoop data framework elements. Some examples of this technology:

- HadoopDB[20] is a hybrid combining a parallel database with Hadoop. It translates SQL queries into M/R jobs and optimizes query plans. It uses Postgres on a communication level and Hive on the translation level.
- HPE Vertica SQL on Apache Hadoop®[21] offers to perform SQL queries on Hadoop data.
- Splice Machine[22] is a Hadoop-relational DBMS. It uses HBase and HDFS as a file system. It supports real-time ACID transactions.
- BigSQL[23] is PostgresSQL implemented on Hadoop.

Most of the SQL-on-Hadoop solutions access directly HDFS, i.e. not through M/R jobs. Query accelerators based on SQL-on-Hadoop and OLAP-on-Hadoop technologies are blurring differences between traditional warehouses to the world of Big Data.

Big Graph Processing Systems. Although graph processing algorithms can be written with M/R, this approach is not appropriate for this purpose and leads to inefficient performance. Apache Giraph[24] is a graph-processing framework built on top of Hadoop. Giraph is based on the graph processing system Pregel [7] by Google.

Big Stream Processing Systems. Stream computing is a new paradigm occurring in context of scenarios like mobile devices, location services and sensor pervasiveness. Data is usually generated from multiple sources and are sent asynchronously to servers. Now, a new category of *Data Stream Management Systems* occurs. They are developed for real-time processing of data-in-motion, e.g. for analysis of data streams.

---

[20] http://db.cs.yale.edu/hadoopdb/hadoopdb.html.
[21] https://www.vertica.com/.
[22] https://www.splicemachine.com/.
[23] https://www.bigsql.org/.
[24] http://giraph.apache.org/.

6 Big Analytics

Big Analytics is the process of examining large data sets to uncover hidden patterns, unknown correlations, market trends, customer preferences and other useful business information. The analytical findings can lead to more effective marketing, better customer service, new revenue opportunities, improved operational efficiency, competitive advantages over rival organizations and other business benefits. This definition of Amazon Web Services[25] emphasises clearly a purpose such analytics. Authors of [16] talk about Big Analytics as of the execution of machine learning tasks on large data sets in cloud computing environments.

In the previous chapters, we saw that there are some technologies combining analytics of Big Data with Hadoop. But enterprises with complex, heterogeneous environments no longer want to adopt a BI access point just for one data source (Hadoop). Answers to their questions are buried in a host of sources ranging from systems of records to cloud warehouses, to structured and unstructured data from both Hadoop and non-Hadoop sources, as it is emphasized in trends Big Data formulated by Tableau[26]. Incidentally, even relational DBMSs are becoming Big Data-ready. SQL Server 2016, for instance, recently added JSON support.

As regards actual Hadoop software, Tableau also emphasizes that it is no longer just a batch-processing platform for some analytical tasks. Hadoop has become a multi-purpose engine for ad hoc analysis. It is even being used for operational reporting on day-to-day workloads—the kind traditionally handled by data warehouses. There is a growing trend of Hadoop becoming a core part of the enterprise IT landscape. Making Hadoop data accessible to business users is now one of the biggest challenges.

7 Problems with Big Data

Kushal Agraval[27] mentioned in his blog the following problems connected to Big Data technologies:

- Bigger data is not always better data. Quantity does not necessarily mean quality, see, e.g., data from social networks. Hence, the data filtering for useful information is a challenge in this context.
- Big Data is prone to data errors. Sometimes errors or bias are undetected owing to the size of the sample and thus produce inaccurate results [15].
- Big Analytics is often subjective. There can be multiple ways to look at the same information and to interpret it differently by different users.
- Not all the data is useful. It means, collecting data which is never used or which does not answer a particular question is relatively useless.

---

[25] http://searchbusinessanalytics.techtarget.com/definition/big-data-analytics.

[26] https://www.tableau.com/sites/default/files/media/Whitepapers/whitepaper_top_10_big_dat a_trends_2017.pdf.

[27] https://kushalagrawal.com/.

- Accessing Big Data raises ethical issues. Both in industry and in academics the issues of privacy and accountability with respect to Big Data have now raised important concerns.
- Big Data creates a new type of digital divide. Having access and knowledge of Big Data technologies gives companies and people a competitive edge in today's data driven world.

8   Conclusions

We conclude with the 10 hottest Big Data technologies based on Forrester's analysis from 2016[28]. They concern continuing development of NoSQL databases, distributed datastores, in-memory data fabric (dynamic random access memory, flash, or SSD), data preparation (sourcing, shaping, cleansing, and sharing diverse and messy data sets), and data quality. Data virtualization and data integration should contribute to delivering information from various data sources and to data orchestration across various exiting solutions (Hadoop, NoSQL, Spark, etc.). Additional technologies, i.e. predictive analysis, search and knowledge discovery, and stream analytics should support Big Analytics applications. On the other hand, the biggest challenge does not seem the technology itself. The more important problem is, how to have enough skills to make effective use of these technologies at disposal and make sense out of the data collected[29].

Acknowledgments. This work was supported by the Charles University project Q48.

References

1. Bajaber, F., Elshawi, R., Batarfi, O., Altalhi, A., Barnawi, A., Sakr, S.: Big data 2.0 processing systems: taxonomy and open challenges. J. Grid Comput. **14**, 379–405 (2016)
2. Borne, K.: Top 10 Big Data Challenges – A Serious Look at 10 Big Data V's. https://www.mapr.com/blog/top-10-big-data-challenges-serious-look-10-big-data-vs
3. Dean, J., Ghemawat, S.: MapReduce: simplified data processing on large clusters. Commun. ACM **51**(1), 107–113 (2008)
4. Gamble, M., Goble, C.: Quality, trust and utility of scientific data on the web: toward a joint model. In: Proceedings of WebSci 2011 Conference, Koblenz, Germany, Article No. 15. ACM (2011)
5. Gupta, R., Gupta, H., Mohania, M.: Cloud computing and big data analytics: what is new from databases perspective? In: Srinivasa, S., Bhatnagar, V. (eds.) BDA 2012. LNCS, vol. 7678, pp. 42–61. Springer, Heidelberg (2012). https://doi.org/10.1007/978-3-642-35542-4_5
6. Laney, D.: 3D data management: controlling data volume, velocity and variety. Meta Group, Gartner (2001). http://blogs.gartner.com/doug-laney/files/2012/01/ad949-3D-Data-Management-Controlling-Data-Volume-Velocity-and-Variety.pdf

---

[28] http://www.forbes.com/sites/gilpress/2016/03/14/top-10-hot-big-data-technologies/#5b66b0327f26.

[29] http://www.ebusinessbook.nl/185.

7. Malewicz, G., Austern, M.H., Bik, A.J.C., Dehnert, J.C., Horn, I., Leiser, N., Czajkowski, G.: Pregel: a system for large-scale graph processing. In: Proceedings of the 2010 ACM SIGMOD International Conference on Management of Data, SIGMOD 2010, pp. 135–146 (2010)
8. Nasser, T., Tariq, R.S.: Big data challenges. J. Comput. Eng. Inf. Technol. **4**(3), 1–6 (2015)
9. Pokorny, J.: Database technologies in the world of big data. In: Proceedings of the 16th International Conference on Computer Systems and Technologies, CompSysTech 2015. ACM International Conference Proceeding Series, vol. 1008, pp. 1–12. ACM, New York (2015)
10. Pokorný, J.: Graph databases: their power and limitations. In: Saeed, K., Homenda, W. (eds.) CISIM 2015. LNCS, vol. 9339, pp. 58–69. Springer, Cham (2015). https://doi.org/10.1007/978-3-319-24369-6_5
11. Pokorný, J., Stantic, B.: Challenges and opportunities in big data processing (Chapter 1). In: Ma, Z. (ed.) Managing Big Data in Cloud Computing Environments. IGI Global, Advances in Data Mining and Database Management (2016)
12. Sakr, S.: Big Data 2.0 Processing Systems - A Survey. Springer Briefs in Computer Science. Springer, Cham (2016). https://doi.org/10.1007/978-3-319-38776-5
13. Snow, D.: Dwaine Snow's Thoughts on Databases and Data Management (2012). http://dsnowondb2.blogspot.cz/2012/07/adding-4th-v-to-big-data-veracity.html
14. Stonebraker, M.: Technical perspective - one size fits all: an idea whose time has come and gone. Commun. ACM **51**(12), 76 (2008)
15. Tivari, S.: Professional NoSQL. Wiley/Wrox, Hoboken (2011)
16. Wu, C., Buyya, R., Ramamohanarao, K.: Big data analytics = machine learning + cloud computing. In: Buyya, R., Calheiros, R., Dastjerdi, A. (eds.) Big Data: Principles and Paradigms. Morgan Kaufmann, Burlington (2016)

Environmental Software Systems in National Park Monitoring and Management

Peter A. Fischer-Stabel[(✉)]

University of Applied Sciences Trier, 55761 Birkenfeld, Germany
p.fischer-stabel@umwelt-campus.de

Abstract. National Park (NP) Monitoring and Management is dealing with dozens of different data where the provenience of the data is as manifold as the fields covered in the monitoring process. International, national, and federal responsibility is found as well as NGO databases, crowd sourcing applications or dedicated field surveys in R&D – activities of single research groups. Environmental software systems are intelligent pencils to manage, analyse and visualize the environmental- but also the administrative data coming from the different sources mentioned. The paper emphazises different fields of activity in NP monitoring and management and is presenting software systems in use in the NP Hunsrück-Hochwald (Germany).

In general, the software systems used are mostly highly adopted to the individual needs of a NP. This depends on specific landscape, features, or the research focus in the park, to name but a few. The software solutions are realized as a customization of standard software products, or, as individual software packages, designed and developed according to the special requirements of the fields of activity in a dedicated park.

Regarding the future developments, there will be no significant changes: the heterogeneity of the data and software used will be similar as it was in the past or it is recently. Because of the long-lasting perspective in NP research and management, one important action the NP administration should focus on: a proper documentation of methods, datasets, publications and information systems targeting the NP, to make monitoring and management activities transparent, accessible and ready for future re-use.

Keywords: National park monitoring · Environmental software system
National park management

1 Introduction

The world network of nature reserves has remarkable high natural values (high ecological integrity, high biodiversity, limited human use, rather unstressed systems, resource management is not extraction-oriented, etc.) and often high cultural values in addition. Within this network, because of their large coverage, especially the National Parks (NP), but also the UNESCO MaB Biosphere reserves serve as sites for traditional environmental monitoring and, in addition, as laboratories for research and demonstration of

© IFIP International Federation for Information Processing 2017
Published by Springer International Publishing AG 2017. All Rights Reserved
J. Hřebíček et al. (Eds.): ISESS 2017, IFIP AICT 507, pp. 39–48, 2017.
https://doi.org/10.1007/978-3-319-89935-0_4

ways in progressing towards sustainability of human-environment interactions (including wise-use and economic development). Terabytes of data are collected in the different application domains in the long term monitoring programs of a national park, but also in single one shot data acquisitions, analysing and discussing highly specialized research topics.

This paper gives an overview about the very high diversity of data collected in national park monitoring and management and of the variety of software systems required to deal with all these data. The concrete setting is the youngest national park in Germany – the NP Hunsrück-Hochwald, inaugurated in 2015.

1.1 National Park Hunsrück-Hochwald

Behind all national parks worldwide, there is a common idea: the conservation of 'wild nature' for posterity [1]. The International Union for Conservation of Nature (IUCN) discusses the parameters defining a national park. In 1969, the IUCN declared a national park to be a relatively large area (>1000 ha) with the following defining characteristics [2]:

- One or several ecosystems not materially altered by human exploitation and occupation, where plant and animal species, geomorphological sites and habitats are of special scientific, educational, and recreational interest or which contain a natural landscape of great beauty;
- Highest competent authority of the country has taken steps to prevent or eliminate exploitation or occupation as soon as possible in the whole area and to effectively enforce the respect of ecological, geomorphological, or aesthetic features which have led to its establishment; and
- Visitors are allowed to enter, under special conditions, for inspirational, educative, cultural, and recreative purposes.

In addition, national parks can be used as laboratories for research and demonstrate ways to re-establish it's original, natural state.

"To Leave Nature Nature" – this principle shall be realized in the most recent national park in Germany. After several years of planning, the NP Hunsrück-Hochwald was officially opened in May 2015. It is a part of the nature park Saar-Hunsrück and comprises approximately 10,000 hectares, or more explicitly, 5% of the total area. The National Park Hunsrück-Hochwald is located in the southwest Germany and connects the federal states of Rhineland-Palatinate and Saarland (see Fig. 1). A low mountain range with an almost never-ending forest area characterizes the Hunsrück and differentiates the area from the surrounding best wine-growing regions of Germany: the Moselle, the Rhine, the Nahe and the Saar. The Federal Agency for Nature Conservation already counts the Hunsrück as a "hot spot region for biodiversity" [3]. Therefore, visitors can especially experience one thing: forest and wilderness.

Research plays, in accordance with the concept of the national park, an important role in the park. Nature conservation, forest development and ecology as well as local added value and the acceptance of the national park by the regional population are examined.

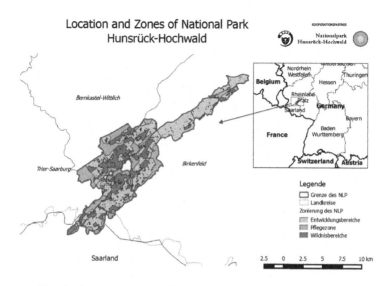

Fig. 1. Orientation map of the national park Hunsrück-Hochwald.

2 Data Sources

In national park monitoring, software systems are intelligent pencils to manage, analyse and visualize the environmental data coming from lots of different sources. Therefore, before discussing environmental software systems, we will have a deeper view to the data collected in national park monitoring and management. Figure 2 gives an overview to relevant subject fields in the national park monitoring process.

Thereby, the provenience of the data is as manifold as the fields covered in the monitoring process. International (e.g. earth observation), national (e.g. hydrologic network) and federal (e.g. air quality measurements) responsibility is found as well as NGO databases, crowd sourcing applications or dedicated field surveys in R&D – activities of single research groups.

On the other hand, looking at the data sources, NP management is not as diverse as it is in the field of environmental monitoring. Only limited new data is collected (e.g. by Ranger activities in park supervision). In this application domain, tasks are focused on the documentation of ongoing activities including the characterization of the collected data sets, on presentation of derived information e.g. for educational activities and on mapping or Web applications. Figure 3 gives an idea about some activities in NP – management.

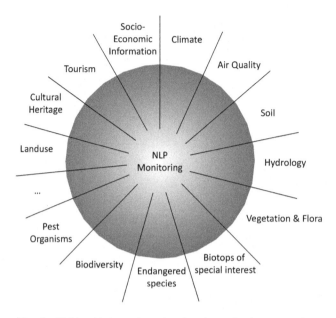

Fig. 2. Fields of interest in national park monitoring - overview.

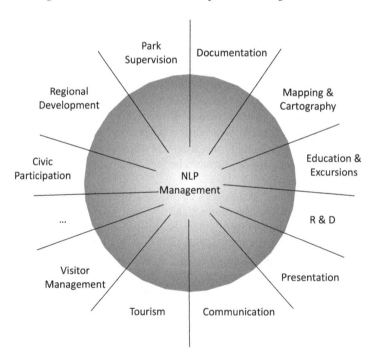

Fig. 3. Fields of activity in NP - management.

2.1 Data Quality Aspects

The data quality in data sets or in information systems becomes more and more important [4]. The quality of data is usually described by multiple dimensions, e.g. accuracy, completeness, consistency, relevance, accessibility and timeliness.

Quality defects during initial data acquisition lead to a huge additional effort to resolve. Practical experience showed that essential quality standards can easily be fulfilled by help of guidelines for data collection. Hence, corresponding guidelines should be worked out before the beginning of the collection, especially in long term monitoring programs. Additionally it must be defined how the data will be rechecked and actualised continuously.

Today, in national or federal monitoring programs, such as e.g. air quality monitoring, data quality aspects are addressed and appropriate actions are implemented [12]. On the other hand, with the installation of ad-hoc-networks or with some field surveys done by different research groups, aspects of data quality and representativeness often are not intensely discussed. In the worst case this can lead to data sets which are not usable in other context than the one focused on in the dedicated research.

3 Software Systems in NP Monitoring and Management

Because of the high diversity of the data in NP monitoring and management, there is no generic software available, dealing with all the different data in one shell. Beside some

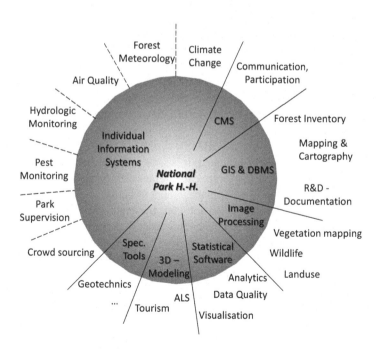

Fig. 4. Software in use in monitoring and management of the NP Hunsrück-Hochwald

typical standard tools as e.g. Geographic Information Systems, Database Management Systems or even Spreadsheet Software, highly specialized software is in use to support the requirements of a national park monitoring. Due to the high importance of the spatial information of the data in environmental monitoring, the ability to store and to deal with this kind of information is common to all software systems used in this context.

As shown in Fig. 4, there are a lot of individual software systems in use in the NP Hunsrück-Hochwald. Below, you will find a short description of these software systems. Because of the individual needs of the different national parks, the list below is without claim of completeness.

3.1 Standard Software

There are some standard software systems used in environmental monitoring programs in general. Below, some of them, which are in use in the NP Hunsrück-Hochwald, are listed:

- **Geographic Information Systems (GIS):** GIS are systems designed to capture, store, manipulate, analyze, manage, and present spatial or geographic data. Different technologies and methods are the foundation. Depending on the underlying functionality and the familiarity of the user with the system, GIS are in use for documentation, analyzing and mapping of mainly vector data as e.g. Biotopes, Permanent Observation Areas (e.g. matured forest cells) or the Forest Inventory. In addition, the use of standardized display- and download services (e.g. WMS, WFS, WCS) offered by third party data provider (e.g. land surveying agencies) via spatial data infrastructures (SDI) is a further important functionality.
- **Image Processing Software:** Processing of images using mathematical operations by using any form of signal processing for which the input is an image, a series of images, or a video, or a photograph. In NP-monitoring, main sources for image data are Earth Observation (Single spectral- /Multi spectral images in different spatial resolutions), Photo Traps (daylight or infrared photographs), Pass by imagery (daylight photographs), or even earth borne change detection photography systems (e.g. 360° recording).
- **Database Management System (DBMS):** A DBMS is the backbone in NP data management. If appropriately designed, it is able to integrate most of the different data gathered. In addition, the software can interact with further tools in use, such as GIS, statistical packages or content management systems.
- **Statistical Packages:** As specialized software for analysis in statistics, these tools are widely used to analyze and visualize e.g. sensor data regarding trends, in change detection analysis (e.g. climate change) but also in data quality management. Further applications are e.g. the estimation of population density of wildlife [5] or, with Geostatistics, focusing on spatial or spatiotemporal datasets.
- **Spreadsheet Software:** Widely used in field data collection, such as mapping of species including endangered or pest organisms, or as data sheets in vegetation or soil mapping.

- **Content Management Systems (CMS):** Software that supports the creation and modification of digital content, mainly used in Web content management to publish national park activities for the public, but also as Intranet for the staff. It is often used to support multiple users working in a collaborative environment.
- **3D-Modeling Software:** 3D modeling is the process of developing a mathematical representation of any three-dimensional surface of an object. With the event of Roomscale VR applications or interactive App guides, 3D – modeling starts it's career even in national parks. Especially cyber physical systems are now dealing with tourism promotion activities. In our case, some developments combining the recent earth's surface derived from laser scanning data with reconstructed ancient roman and celtic sites are under way and promoted because of their innovative aspects.
- **Geotechnical Software:** Because of the specific geomorphologic situation and the presence of endangered biotopes as peat bogs, 3D soil- and drilling profiles but also data coming from Palynology analyses have to be documented and analyzed in our reference national park. Specialized, commercial of the shelf software is supporting the scientists in this field of research.

3.2 Individual Software

Beside the standard software packages, there are some individual software and dedicated information systems in the monitoring and management of the NP Hunsrück-Hochwald in use. Configured and developed for the special needs in individual parks, each park will have its own individual software, depending on the natural resources (e.g. forest, grassland, maritime) and/or on the focus of the development of the park.

- **Documentation System of R&D-Activities:** In order to ensure central and efficient access to the literature and data of the NP for all scientists from the respective institutions and for a long-lasting period, in the NP Hunsrück-Hochwald a "research server" was established. The system serves future researchers as a scientific information portal. The goal is to avoid expensive, redundant data acquisition as well as time-consuming information retrieval for the individual teams. Furthermore, research becomes more transparent and allows better use of possible synergistic effects [6]. The system of the NP Hunsrück-Hochwald is accessible under: http://fs.nlphh.de/.
- **Pest Monitoring System:** Because of its special forest structure, the national park Hunsrück-Hochwald must be monitored regarding bark beetles calamities (mainly *Ips typographus*), to avoid significant damages in forests neighboring the park. This is done with a specific monitoring system collecting activity data of the beetles in traps, modeling the evolution of the population and resulting in an estimation of the damage risk for the forest. If there is a high damage risk for the forest, the NP administration has to take action to protect the forest outside the park. Further information can be found in [7]. The system is available under: http://ifff-riskanalyses.boku.ac.at/typo3/index.php?id=74.
- **Dedicated Apps:** With the intensive use of smartphones and field clients, there are dozens of Apps in use in NP-monitoring and management [8]. Combining the ability

to collect position information and link it with attribute data, Apps are supporting the rangers in park supervision, the collection of species data or are in use in crowd sourcing applications, e.g. monitoring the spread of invasive organisms. An example in the field of species data collection for the NP Hunsrück-Hochwald can be found under http://www.buergerschaffenwissen.de/projekt/artenfinder-rheinland-pfalz.

- **Laser Scanning Software:** Airborne Laser Scanning (ALS) data acquisitions are providing the scientific community with very high resolution 3D – data regarding the earth's surface. Starting with the raw point cloud data, specialized software tools are in use to derive high resolution elevation- but also surface models serving as input for many applications (e.g. vegetation analysis, erosion processes, micromorphological studies). In addition, the latter provide suitable information for 3D modeling applications.
- **Camera Trapping Software:** Camera trapping is increasingly becoming an important tool in ecological research. Capture-recapture surveys or the simple documentation of wildlife are nowadays common projects in national parks, collecting thousands of pictures. However, the organization of large collections of multimedia files and especially the efficient search for subsets of data is a challenging task. Camera trapping software makes classifying camera trap photos quick and easy, keeps track of camera trap, camera and species data and supports the management and retrieval of the photographs [9, 10].
- **Forest Meteorology and Climate Change Information System:** This information system is a cross-section task with the emphasis on data management, information, consulting, advanced training and contacts at the different levels of expertise. The central product of the climate change information system is a publicly accessible web portal, which is intended to appeal to a broad public. The user is offered detailed information on climate change and possible consequences for the Rhineland-Palatinate but also for the National Park. Further Information to the information system can be found under http://www.klimawandel-rlp.de/ or www.am.rlp.de/.
- **Immission Monitoring Network and Information System:** Since 1978, the agency for environment Rhineland-Palatinate has been operating the Central Immission Monitoring Network (ZIMEN) for Rhineland-Palatinate on behalf of the Ministry of Environment, Agriculture, Food, Viticulture and Forestry. This consists of 27 air measuring stations, which are telemetrically supervised by a measuring network in Mainz. It has the task to determine the long-term development of the air pollutants in cities and forest areas of the country by continuous measurements, in order to achieve a high protection level for human health and the environment [11, 12]. (www.luft-rlp.de/)
- **Hydrologic Monitoring Network and Information System:** On the one hand, the system is providing a quantitative measurement service on surface waters, precipitation and groundwater. Quantitative management of surface waters, management of groundwater and the protection of springs are tasks supported by the information system. Especially within, and in the surroundings of the NP Hunsrück-Hochwald, with its mineral springs and spa waters, there is a special focus on hydrologic monitoring. (www.quellenatlas.rlp.de/, geoportal-wasser.rlp.de/)

- **Tools for Communication, Civic Participation and local Governance:** Democracy relies on citizens participating in decision making, even or especially in national park regions with restricted use in landscape. Web 2.0 technology is enabling citizens to make their voices heard in new and innovative ways, important for civic participation and the decision making process in regional development. Some product examples can be found under [13, 14].

4 Summary and Outlook

Types of software systems used in NP monitoring are as manifold as the fields of scientific- and management activities are occurring in a park.

In general, software systems in NP monitoring and management are mostly highly adopted to the individual needs of a NP. This depends on specific landscape, features, or the research focus in the park, to name but a few. The software solutions are realized as a customization of standard software products, or, as individual software packages, designed and developed according to the special requirements of the fields of activity in a dedicated park. The case described in the paper was the NP Hunsrück-Hochwald (Germany).

In addition, the heterogeneity in software and information systems used in parks is strongly linked to the evolution process in environmental monitoring: Often, monitoring systems as e.g. air quality, hydrologic monitoring or forest inventory are implemented decades before the government decided, to install a national park in the region. Keeping this in mind, a mixture between historic and recently designed sensor networks and software systems is available. Especially with view to the long-term perspective, it is still difficult today, to combine and use all the information available in an integrated environmental monitoring in the park.

Regarding the future developments, it is the opinion of the author that there will be no significant changes: the heterogeneity of the data and software used will be similar as it was in the past or it is recently.

But, especially because of the long-lasting perspective in NP research and management, one important action the NP administration should focus on: a proper documentation of methods, datasets, publications and information systems targeting the NP, to make monitoring and management activities transparent, accessible and ready for future re-use.

References

1. EUROPARC Federation: Living Parks, 100 Years of National Parks in Europe, Oekom Verlag, Munchen (2009)
2. Gulez, S.: A method of evaluating areas for national park status. Environ. Manag. **16**(6), 811–818 (1992)
3. Ackermann, W., Sachteleben, J.: Identifizierung der Hotspots der Biologischen Vielfalt in Deutschland. BfN-Skripte 315, Bundesamt für Naturschutz (BfN), Bonn (2012)
4. Redman, T.C.: Data Quality – The Field Guide. Digital Press, Boston (2001)

5. Ebert, C., et al.: Estimating wild boar Sus scrofa population size using faecal DNA and capture-recapture modelling. Wildl. Biol. **18**(2), 142–152 (2012)
6. Fischer-Stabel, P., Mattern, M.: Scientific research documentation - an information server for the national park Hunsrück-Hochwald. In: International Environmental Modelling and Software Society (iEMSs), Proceedings of the 8th International Congress on Environmental Modelling and Software, Touluse, France (2016)
7. Delb, H., Pontuali, S. (eds.): Biotic risks and climate change in forests. In: Proceedings of the 10th Workshop on IUFRO Working Party 7.03.10 Methodology of Forest Insect and Disease Survey in Central Europe, Freiburg, Germany, 20th–23rd September 2010. Berichte Freiburger Forstliche Forschung Heft 89, FVA, 198 p. (2010)
8. Newman, G., et al.: The future of citizen science: emerging technologies and shifting paradigms. Front. Ecol. Environ. **10**(6), 298–304 (2012). https://doi.org/10.1890/110294
9. Bubnicki, J.W., Churski, M., Kuijper, D.P.J.: TRAPPER: an open source web-based application to manage camera trapping projects. Methods Ecol. Evol. **7**, 1209–1216 (2016). https://doi.org/10.1111/2041-210X.12571
10. Smeedley, R.: Snoopy. Portable software for capture-recapture surveys (2015). https://prezi.com/xqoogmni0ymu/snoopy/?utm_campaign=share&utm_medium=copy. Accessed 28 Feb 2017
11. Georgii, H.-W. (ed.): Atmospheric Pollutants in Forest Areas: Their Deposition and Interception. Kluwer Academic Publishers, Norwell (1982)
12. Federal Environmental Agency: Determination and Evaluation of Ambient Air Quality - Manual of Ambient Air Monitoring in Germany; Research report 200 42 261 UBA-FB (2004)
13. Platforms for civic engagement. http://www.shareable.net/blog/14-online-platforms-that-boost-civic-engagement. Accessed 28 Feb 2017
14. Software in civic participation. http://www.xpolitics.de/2013/01/24/update-software-anbieter-digitaler-burgerbeteiligung/. Accessed 28 Feb 2017

Air and Climate

Hough-Transform-Based Interpolation Scheme for Generating Accurate Dense Spatial Maps of Air Pollutants from Sparse Sensing

Asaf Nebenzal[1] and Barak Fishbain[2(✉)]

[1] Department of Mathematics, Technion – Israel Institute of Technology, Haifa, Israel
asaf.n@technion.ac.il
[2] Faculty of Civil and Environmental Engineering, Technion – Israel Institute of Technology, Haifa, Israel
fishbain@technion.ac.il

Abstract. Air pollution is a significant health risk factor and causes many negative effects on the environment. Thus, arises the need for studying and assessing air-quality. Today, air-pollution assessment is mostly based on data acquired from Air Quality Monitoring (AQM) stations. These AQM stations provide continuous measurements and considered to be accurate; however, they are expensive to build and operate, thus scattered sparingly. To cope with this limitation, typically, the information obtained from those measurements is generalized with interpolation methods such as IDW or Kriging. Yet, the mathematical basis of those schemes defines that pollution extremum values are obtained at the measuring points. In addition, they are not considering the location of the pollution source or any physicochemical characteristics of pollutant hence do not reveal the real spatial air-pollution patterns. This research introduces a new interpolation scheme which breaks the interpolation process into two stages. At the first stage, the source of pollution and its estimated emission rate are inferred through a detection procedure which is based on the Hough Transform. At the second stage, based on the detected source location and emission, spatial dense pollution maps are created. The method requires, for its computation, to assume a dispersion model. To this end, *any* model can be used as sophisticated as it may be. Spatial maps created with simplified dispersion models in a computational simulation, show that the suggested interpolation scheme manages to create more accurate and more physically reasonable maps than the state-of-the-art.

Keywords: Air-quality modeling · Spatial maps · Interpolation
Hough transform · Source detection

1 Introduction

Air pollution is a significant risk factor for multiple health situations including eye irritation, breathing difficulties, lung cancer, heart diseases and respiratory infections [1]. In addition, air-pollution causes many negative effects on the environment like decreased

J. Hřebíček et al. (Eds.): ISESS 2017, IFIP AICT 507, pp. 51–60, 2017.
https://doi.org/10.1007/978-3-319-89935-0_5

visibility, acid rain, global warming, climate change, water quality deterioration and ecosystems destruction [2]. Thus, arises the need for studying and assessing air-quality's characteristics, dispersion patterns and behavior.

Today, numerous air-pollution studies are based on data acquired from Air Quality Monitoring (AQM) Stations [3]. However, AQM are typically scattered sparingly, mainly near main roads, industrial factories, or near highly populated areas [4]. Thus, the AQM network has a limited ability to account for spatial variability of pollution levels in heterogeneous regions, such as urban areas, which in return, renders exposure assessment as a difficult task [5]. To cope with the measurements sparsity, the information obtained from those measurements is often generalized with mathematical methods to improve the spatio-temporal coverage. To this end, interpolation schemes are sought.

Interpolation is a mathematical method of constructing a continuous function that obtains the measured values (or close values) at the measuring point. Environmental interpolation is based on the assumption that data attributes are continuous over space and spatially dependent [6]. Grossly speaking, interpolation methods can be divided into deterministic and geostatistical methods. The first include Inverse Distance Weighted (IDW), Nearest Neighbor (NN) and radial basis functions [6], while the latter involve, for example, various types of Kriging methods [7]. Next, we focus on IDW and ordinary Kriging, owing to their frequent use in spatial maps creation.

There are many studies in the field of air pollution modeling that used IDW or Kriging for creating dense spatial map of air pollution. IDW, for example, was applied for examining the ratio between low birth weight and air pollution exposure during pregnancy [8]. In that research, the IDW interpolation was utilized for estimating PM10 levels at future mothers' home address. Clark et al. [9] examined the effect of early life exposure to air pollution on development of childhood asthma. For estimating the average exposure level of an area, IDW interpolation was applied. Trujillo-Ventura et al. [10] introduced multi-objective pollutant AQMs optimization. In their research, they applied a Kriging interpolation scheme for creating dense spatial maps. Sarigiannis and Saisana [11] used Kriging interpolation method to create pollution maps of CO and O3 as an additional input to their multi-objective optimization scheme, which was based on remote sensing satellites.

IDW and Ordinary Kriging are both well-known and widely used interpolation methods. However, these methods are not appropriate for creating air-pollution spatial dense maps for several reasons: The mathematical basis of those schemes defines that all interpolated values over the study area are essentially a weighted average of the measurements points, thus extremum values cannot be obtained at any other place than the measuring points. In addition, these methods do not consider the location of pollution sources or any physicochemical characteristics of pollution. Hence, the resulted dense pollution maps do fall short in describing accurately the real spatial patterns of pollution. Regarding these in the interpolation process is expected to result in better and more accurate interpolation methods.

This research introduces a Hough Transform-Based Interpolation (HTBI) method, which generates accurate dense pollution maps through finding sources' locations and the utilization of an air pollution dispersion model. The Hough Transform is a mathematical method, originated in image processing, used for detecting geometric shapes, like lines, circles or ellipses [12]. The main idea is converting from representing the shape in x, y coordinates (Cartesian) system to a parametric space, where the feature of interest is best represented. In this research, a feature space, which will represent best the source location is devised.

The method consists of two phases: at first, based on ambient concentration and assuming a dispersion model, the HTBI detects the sources' emission rates and locations. Then, using this information, the interpolation scheme builds the continuous pollution field. The suggested HTBI scheme applies no constraint on the assumed dispersion model. Hence, any dispersion model found in the literature (e.g., [13–15]), as sophisticated as it may be, can be incorporated into the suggested scheme.

2 Methodology

2.1 Notation

The following notation facilitate the description of the method. Let $\{S\}$ be a set of sources of a specific pollutant, with emission rates $\{Q\}$. Let A be the specific pollutant's continues signal generated by $\{S\}$, defined over a geographical area Ω. $\{S\}$ are located at $\{\gamma\} \in \Omega$. Let $\{a\}$ be a finite set of samples of signal A, taken in locations $\{\omega\} \subset \Omega$. Interpolation aims at estimating A over the entire space Ω, based on the set of samples $\{a\}$. This is achieved here by first finding sources' locations, $\{\gamma\}$. It is worthwhile noting that the discussion here is limited to a single pollutant interpolation, i.e., the generation of a dense map of the specific pollutant is based on a set of sparse measurements of the same pollutant.

2.2 Interpolation Scheme

Each sample $a_i \in \{a\}$, represents a measurement in ω_i. W.L.O.G, if we order $\{S\}$, and $\{Q\}$ so Q_i is the emission rate of source S_i; a_i is a weighted combination of the contributions from all the sources, $\{Q\}$. Assuming a dispersion model, M, so the kth element of the vector $\overrightarrow{M_i}$ is the decay coefficient of source k, Q_k, in location i; sensor i's measurement, a_i, is all sources contributions at i and is given by:

$$a_i = \overrightarrow{M_i} \cdot \overrightarrow{Q}^T \qquad (1)$$

Consequentially, forming the set $\{a\}$ as a vector, all sensors' measurements can be represented by the following matrices multiplication:

$$\vec{a} = M \cdot \overrightarrow{Q}^T \qquad (2)$$

Given $[M]$, we assume that there exists a matrix E, which satisfies:

$$\overrightarrow{Q} = [E] \cdot \vec{a}^T \qquad (3)$$

For finding Q and γ, a search on the entire Ω is suggested. To this end, Ω is divided into N disjoint catchments. We assume that each catchment, $C_n \subseteq \Omega$ is small enough so the pollution is uniform all over it. For each of the catchments an estimated emission rate $\hat{Q}_n^i$ is calculated, based on accepted measurements from single sample a_i; where e is a single row of E:

$$\hat{Q}_n^i = e_i \cdot a_i \tag{4}$$

Thus, $\hat{Q}_n^i$ introduces the estimated emission rate from the single source S, had it was located at C_n, based on the single measured sample at a_i.

The same process is applied for all C_n for each of the sensors:

$$\overrightarrow{\hat{Q}}_n = [E] \cdot \vec{a}^T \tag{5}$$

Applying Eq. (5), results in each C_n having its unique set of $\overrightarrow{\hat{Q}}_n$, one estimate for each sensor. Using the standard deviation (STD) of the estimates, the catchment with the lowest STD is the approximated location of S. Once the source location, γ, is obtained, the emission rate of S is estimated by the average of the catchment's estimates:

$$\hat{Q}_\gamma = \overline{\overrightarrow{\hat{Q}}_\gamma} \tag{6}$$

Having the estimated emission rate Q, of the source S, and its estimated location, γ, with the dispersion model M, we can now estimate the dense pollution map over Ω:

$$C_n = \overrightarrow{M} \cdot \hat{Q} \tag{7}$$

The process is illustrated in the simple example of Fig. 1, where three sensors are deployed in a region with one source (see Fig. 1a). While the catchments can assume any geographical region and shape, for the sake of simplicity, the region, Ω, is divided into squared catchments, forming a squared grid. Sensor 1, which measures a pollution level of 33 (i.e. $a_1 = 33$), is located at catchment (1, 3); Sensor 2, located at (2, 4), measures 29; and Sensor 3, at (3, 3) measures a level of 30. Keeping in mind the source's location, γ, is unknown, Fig. 1b demonstrates the execution of Eq. (4), where each catchment is assigned with the estimated source's emission rate if the source was located in this catchment, given Sensor 1's measurement, and an exponential isotropic decay dispersion model, with an extinction coefficient λ. i.e., for r, the Cartesian distance from the source, the pollution level at each location on the map is given by [16]:

$$a_i = Q \cdot e^{-\lambda|r|} \tag{8}$$

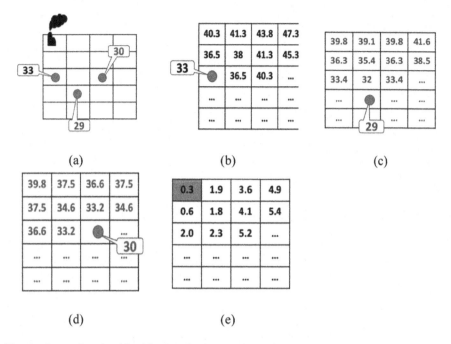

Fig. 1. Source location identification through HTBI assuming simple radial dispersion model.

If the source was located at $(2, 2)$, then the estimated emission rate, $\hat{Q}$, based on Sensor 1's measurement, should have been 38. If the source was located at $(1, 4)$, then $\hat{Q}$, according to Sensor 1, would be 47.3. Figures 1c and d are the estimation maps, generated in the same fashion as b, for Sensor 2 and Sensor 3 respectively.

Assuming the dense pollution maps are a collection of isolines, the estimated emission rate values of the three sensors should agree in one grid location [17]. To evaluate the agreement, we compute, in each C_n, the three sensors' estimates' standard deviation. The lower the STD, the higher the agreement. This is illustrated in Fig. 1e. The smallest STD, indeed is obtained at location $(1, 1)$, where, in this example the source is located.

3 Results and Discussion

3.1 Dispersion Models

As mentioned earlier, M represents the pollution decay function of the dispersion model. The suggested scheme, HTBI, does not apply any constraint on the dispersion model used. It can be any model, as long as it allows to compute the expected pollution on any given location on the map, given the emission rate Q and all other meteorological parameters required by the specific model in use. In this research, two models were used, the above isotropic decay dispersion model [16] (Eq. (8)), and the well-known Gaussian Plume Dispersion (GPD) model [18]:

$$a_i(x, y, z) = \frac{Q}{2\pi\sigma_y\sigma_z\bar{u}} \exp\left(-\frac{y^2}{2\sigma_y^2}\right)$$
$$\cdot \left[\exp(-\frac{(z-H)^2}{2\sigma_z^2}) + \exp(-\frac{(z+H)^2}{2\sigma_z^2})\right] \tag{9}$$

where x is the downwind, y is the crosswind and z is the vertical distances of a_i from the source; $\bar{u}$ is the time-averaged wind speed at the hight of release H; and σ_y and σ_z represent the standard deviations of the crosswind and vertical Gaussian distribution of the pollutant concentration, respectively. The model also assumes full reflection from the ground.

3.2   Computational Simulation

For generating a continuous pollution field, the two types of dispersion models, described above were used. Specifications of the models are: $Q = 8$ ton/h; wind speed (for the GPD model):4 m/h; wind direction (GPD model): 285°; effective stack-height: 120 m.

The continuous fields were sampled by the set of sensors described in Fig. 2. To simulate real conditions, additive white Gaussian noise with Signal to Noise Ratio (SNR) of 10% (10 dB) was added to the readings of the sensors. Each sensor is now reporting the ambient level in its location as derived from the dispersion model with noise added. See Table 1 for ambient data measured in each sensor, for the radial and the GPD models.

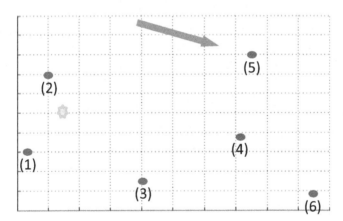

Fig. 2. A 20 km^2 geographical area, Ω. The sensors' locations are marked with pink circles, with a serial number below and the source (which typically its location is unknown) is marked by yellow star. Wind direction represented by red arrow. (Color figure online)

Table 1. Ambient data measured by the sensors (units are in µg/m³) for the radial and the GPD dispersion models

Sensor #	Radial	GPD
(1)	0.180	0
(2)	2.586	0
(3)	3.359*e−10	6.590*e−30
(4)	1.606*e−16	282.5981
(5)	1.659*e−20	6.20*e−17
(6)	1.233*e−30	1.1097

Using *only* the noisy readings obtained from the sensors, {a}, the source's location is estimated and then the dense pollution maps are created.

The results obtained for the radial dispersion model (Eq. (8)) are displayed in Fig. 3. The highest ambient pollution level is located at the source location and exponentially decay as moving away. However, both IDW and Kriging models create a pollution map in which the maximum pollution level is obtained at the closest sensor to the sources' location, and decay as the distance from the source decreases (Fig. 3(a) and (b) respectively). HTBI, on the other hand, find the accurate source's location and then computes the accurate dense pollution map (Fig. 3(c)).

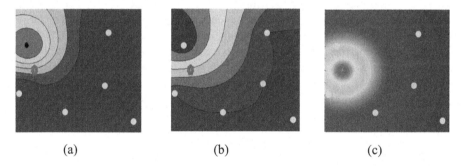

(a)   (b)   (c)

Fig. 3. Dense pollution maps based on the *radial dispersion model*: (a) IDW; (b) Ordinary Kriging; (c) HTBI. Sensors' locations are marked in pink and the source's location is marked with a yellow star. Pollution level is represented in a blue (low)- to red (high) color scale. (Color figure online)

The interpolation results for the GPD model are presents in Fig. 4. As both IDW and Kriging do not consider physicochemical characteristics nor atmospheric conditions, the maximum of the dense pollution maps is found at the closest sensor downwind from the sources' location (Fig. 4(a) and (b) respectively). Moreover, the created maps demonstrate a roughly radial dispersion around this point, which is not the true condition, due to the wind. HTBI, as presented in Fig. 4(c), does manage to create a dense spatial map which complies with the Gaussian plume behavior. This is attributed to the fact that the HTBI method does incorporates the Gaussian model, as it can incorporate any dispersion model.

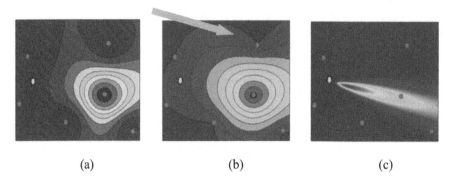

(a)   (b)   (c)

Fig. 4. Spatial maps based on the Gaussian dispersion model: (a) IDW; (b) Ordinary Kriging; (c) HTBI. Pollution level is represented in a blue (low)- to red (high) color scale. The red arrow represents the wind direction. (Color figure online)

The suggested algorithm is deterministic in nature, i.e., for the same input, the system will produce the same output. Therefore, the *uncertainty* in the system stems from the uncertainty of the measurements, i.e., measurements noise [19–22]. The results of Figs. 3 and 4 were obtained at a noise level of 10%. (SNR, of 10 dB). For evaluating the robustness of the algorithm, different noise levels were tested with the system. The radial model (Eq. (8)) showed stability even with up to 50% errors (SNR of 3 dB). The Gaussian model's (Eq. (7)) robustness showed dependency on the catchments size. For larger catchment sizes (e.g., cell size of 40 m^2), our algorithm showed stability up to 10% SNR. However, increasing the spatial resolution to a cell size of 20 m^2, the HTBI showed higher sensitivity to measurement noise and showed the correct source location and interpolation maps for noise levels of up to 5% (13 dB). For lower SNR values the algorithm faced difficulties in locating the source and consequentially generating the dense pollution maps.

4   Conclusions

IDW and Ordinary Kriging are well-known and commonly-used interpolation methods for creating dense spatial maps, however they are not considering the physicochemical properties of the pollution characteristics nor the source location, therefore not accurate for this task. In this research, we introduced the Hough Transform Based Interpolation (HTBI), a two-phase interpolation scheme, which addresses these limitations. At the first phase, the HTBI detects sources' locations and their estimated emission rate. Using this information, at the second phase, a dense pollution spatial map is built. The method incorporates an air-pollution dispersion model into its calculations. This may be *any* dispersion model that can be found in the literature. Comparing between the dense pollution maps created by the HTBI, IDW and Ordinary Kriging shows that the HTBI creates spatial maps, which represents the true pollution maps better and thus, is more accurate and sensible interpolation scheme. However, this work showed a computational simulation of a simple configuration with only one emission source. Implementing the method to a real-word situation is challenging. Air pollution emitted from many sources including industrial zones and transportation (line source). Hence, HTBI should be adjusted to face with this complex situation of multi sources detection.

Despite the above, HTBI indeed can be used in its current form, a single source detection. We can imagine at least two scenarios in which such configuration applies. The first is indeed when a single source can be identified. For example, when considering SO_2 which is emitted mainly from factories, and the study area contains only single industrial zone. The second is a case of leaks and we would like to identify the leak's source. In these cases, HTBI will be able to produce better and accurate spatial pollution maps than the existing methods.

Current work, carried out these days, is focusing on the implementation of HTBI in exactly such scenarios.

Another aspect this work sheds light on is the number of sensors and the way they scattered in the study area. It is obvious that the higher the number of sensors, the easier it will be to locate the source. There is a need for further research in finding the optimal number of sensors in a given area. The parameters that should be considered are the size of the study area, the characters of it (an open area is not the same as crowded urban area.), the coverage capacity and accuracy of the sensors and more.

References

1. Heroux, M.E., et al.: Quantifying the health impacts of ambient air pollutants: recommendations of a WHO/Europe project. Int. J. Publ. Health **60**(5), 619–627 (2015)
2. Venkatadri, M., Rao, P.S.: A survey on air quality forecasting techniques. Int. J. Comput. Sci. Inf. Technol. **5**(1), 103–107 (2014)
3. Özkaynak, H., Baxter, L., Dionisio, K.: Air pollution exposure prediction approaches used in air pollution epidemiology studies. J. Exp. Sci. Environ. Epidemiol. **23**, 566 (2013)
4. Goswami, E., Larson, T., Lumley, T.: Spatial characteristics of fine particulate matter: identifying representative monitoring locations in Seattle, Washington. J. Air Waste Manag. Assoc. **52**, 324–333 (2002)
5. Rao, et al.: Environmental modeling and methods for estimation of the global health impacts of air pollution. Environ. Model. Assess. **17**(6), 613–622 (2012)
6. Akkala, A., Devabhaktuni, V.: Interpolation techniques and associated software for environmental data. Environ. Prog. Sustain. Energy **29**(2), 134–141 (2010)
7. Li, J., Heap, A.D.: A Review of Spatial Interpolation Methods for Environmental Scientists (2008)
8. Xu, X., et al.: PM10 air pollution exposure during pregnancy and term low birth weight in Allegheny County, PA, 1994-2000. Int. Arch. Occup. Environ. Health **84**(3), 251–257 (2011)
9. Clark, N.A., et al.: Effect of early life exposure to air pollution on development of childhood asthma. Environ. Health Perspect. **118**(2), 284–290 (2010)
10. Trujillo-Ventura, A., Ellis, J.H.: Multiobjective air pollution monitoring network design. Atmos. Environ. Part A. Gen. Top. **25**(2), 469–479 (1991)
11. Sarigiannis, D.A., Saisana, M.: Multi-objective optimization of air quality monitoring. Environ. Monit. Assess. **136**(1–3), 87–99 (2008)
12. Hough, P.: Method and means for recognizing complex patterns. U.S. Patent, vol. 3,069,654 (1962)

13. Hystad, P., et al.: Creating national air pollution models for population exposure assessment in Canada. Environ. Health Perspect. **119**(8), 1123–1129 (2011)
14. Zannetti, P.: Air Pollution Modeling: Theories, Computational Methods and Available Software. Springer, New York (1990). https://doi.org/10.1007/978-1-4757-4465-1
15. Tominaga, Y., Stathopoulos, T.: CFD simulation of near-field pollutant dispersion in the urban environment: a review of current modeling techniques. Atmos. Environ. **79**, 716–730 (2013)
16. Buhmann, M.: Radial Basis Functions: Theory and Implementations. Cambridge Monographs on Applied and Computational Mathematics, vol. 12, pp. 147–165. Cambridge University Press, Cambridge (2003)
17. Ballard, D.H.: Generalizing the Hough transform to detect arbitrary shapes. Pattern Recogn. **13**(2), 111–122 (1981)
18. Ermak, D.: An analytical model for air pollutant transport and deposition from a point source. Atmos. Environ. (1967) **11**, 231–237 (1977)
19. Fishbain, B., et al.: An evaluation tool kit of air quality micro-sensing units (2015)
20. Fishbain, B., Moreno-Centeno, E.: Self calibrated wireless distributed environmental sensory networks. Sci. Rep. **6**, 24382 (2016)
21. Lerner, U., Yacobi, T., Levy, I., Moltchanov, S.A., Cole-Hunter, T., Fishbain, B.: The effect of ego-motion on environmental monitoring. Sci. Total Environ. **533**, 8–16 (2015)
22. Moltchanov, S., Levy, I., Etzion, Y., Lerner, U., Broday, D.M., Fishbain, B.: On the feasibility of measuring urban air pollution by wireless distributed sensor networks. Sci. Total Environ. **502**, 537–547 (2015)

A New Feature Selection Methodology
for Environmental Modelling Support:
The Case of Thessaloniki Air Quality

Nikos Katsifarakis[✉] and Kostas Karatzas

Department of Mechanical Engineering, Informatics Systems and Applications – Environmental
Informatics Research Group, Aristotle University, Thessaloniki, Greece
{nikolakk,kkara}@auth.gr

Abstract. Environmental systems status is described via a (usually big) set of
parameters. Therefore, relevant models employ a large feature space, thus making
feature selection a necessity towards better modelling results. Many methods have
been used in order to reduce the number of features, while safeguarding environmental model performance and resulting to low computational time. In this
study, a new feature selection methodology is presented, making use of the Self
Organizing Maps (SOM) method. SOM visualization values are used as a similarity measure between the parameter that is to be forecasted, and parameters of
the feature space. The method leads to the smallest set of parameters that surpass
a similarity threshold. Results obtained, for the case of Thessaloniki air quality
forecasting, are comparable to what feature selection methods offer.

Keywords: Air quality · Feature selection · Self-organizing maps

1 Introduction

Environmental systems are complex, in terms of the parameters required to describe
their status and spatiotemporal behavior. It is therefore expected that relevant models
are complex as well, involving a large number of features. In the case of urban air quality
systems [1] such parameters can be pollutant levels, meteorological conditions and any
other feature that describes the impact that the atmospheric environment poses on human
life [2]. Such features are commonly used as inputs to various data-driven environmental
models [3], while some of them contain very little or no valuable information for the
purposes of the model they are fed into. Therefore, it is necessary to select the most
appropriate ones and thus reduce their number, using feature prioritization and selection
methods [4]. In this paper, two well-established feature selection methods are used as a
reference, while a new feature selection method based on Self Organizing Maps (SOM)
is introduced. Methods are compared in terms of forecasting performance for a number
of Computational Intelligence (CI) oriented models, for the case of air quality forecasting in Thessaloniki, Greece.

© IFIP International Federation for Information Processing 2017
Published by Springer International Publishing AG 2017. All Rights Reserved
J. Hřebíček et al. (Eds.): ISESS 2017, IFIP AICT 507, pp. 61–70, 2017.
https://doi.org/10.1007/978-3-319-89935-0_6

2   The Case Study

The application domain of this study is urban air quality in the area of Thessaloniki. It is the second largest city of Greece, characterized by high urbanization and a heavily used traffic network. Its wider area covers approximately 93 km^2 and has a population density of around 16000 inhabitants per km^2. Thessaloniki is located in the inner part of the Thermaikos gulf and has Hortiatis mountain and the Seich Sou forest to its north and north – east respectively, while the industrial zone is situated on its western part [5]. Regarding its air quality, it is characterized by very high levels of PM$_{10}$ [6].

Available data include daily averages of air pollutant concentration levels (PM$_{10}$, CO, NO$_2$ and O$_3$ in μg/m^3), as monitored at seven stations located in different areas of the city, for the years 2000 to 2013 (a total of 17 features). In order to better evaluate the new proposed feature selection method, features with many missing values were omitted, this being the reason that the used dataset contains no meteorological parameters. A map of the city is presented in Fig. 1, where the seven stations (Agia Sofia, Aristotle University, Kalamaria, Kordelio, Panorama, Sindos and Neochorouda) are marked.

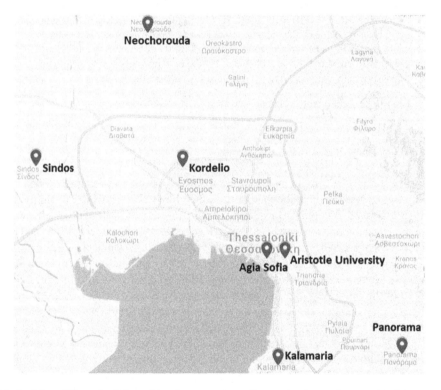

Fig. 1. Map of Thessaloniki, marking the seven air quality monitoring stations used in the current study.

3   The Proposed Methodology

With the aim of the study being the presentation and evaluation of a new feature selection methodology, two feature selection methods were rendered to be appropriate as reference methods, implemented in the WEKA computational environment [9]: (i) the Correlation - based feature selection (CfsSubsetEval) [7], and (ii) the ReliefFAttributeEval [8] The CfsSubsetEval method was chosen, as (a) it can be used in regression problems (i.e. the problem category where arithmetic values of feature(s) are forecasted), (b) it focuses on maximizing the forecasting ability of a model (our goal in this study), and (c) it employs features that demonstrate high predictive ability (i.e. lead to better forecasting statistics) and low intercorrelation [10]. The ReliefFAttributeEval method was chosen as it takes into account feature interrelationships by assigning a grade of relevance to each feature and then selecting those that are graded over a user given threshold [11].

The new feature selection method proposed makes use of the SOM method. SOMs are based on neural networks composed of a two-dimensional array of (initially) randomly weighted neurons [12]. All data points are passed through the neural network and are matched with a winning neuron, causing the network topology to adjust and eventually form clusters of similar attributes, while weights are updated to better fit into the process. The unified distance matrix (U-matrix) commonly used for SOM visualization, represents the Euclidean distance between neighboring neurons which is actually an expression of the relationship ("similarity") between neighboring neurons [13].

Here, the SOM Toolbox for Matlab [14] was used, as it offers a stable and commonly used implementation of the method. A typical example of the SOM representation, generated with the Matlab toolbox for the data used in this study is presented in Fig. 2 that contains a SOM for each parameter, as well as the U - matrix.

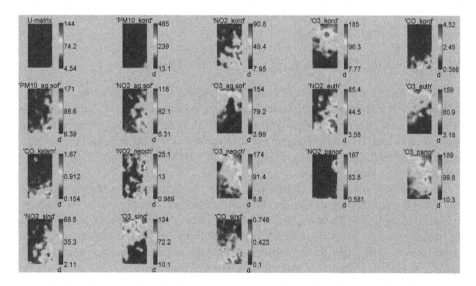

Fig. 2. A typical SOM representation of the case under study.

Each SOM visualizes the areas where the corresponding variables have high or low values (blue colors here correspond to low values and red to high), and the U – matrix indicates the distance between neighboring tiles (neurons). Thus, similarities between maps are indications of interrelationships between the corresponding parameters. For example, the maps of Ozone in the area of Agia Sofia (O3_ag.sof) and Ozone in the area of the Aristotle University of Thessaloniki (O3_auth) present with high values in their upper parts and low values in the lower parts, thus they look topologically similar. This indicates that there is strong relationship between these two features.

For each of the 17 parameters - features, the SOM method generates a topographic map presenting the weight values for the neurons in each of the SOM nodes. These values are stored in an M * N matrix, where M is the number on nodes that the afore-mentioned maps contain, and N is the number of the features. In this way, the values at each column represent the relevant weight ("importance") of each feature for the nodes within the SOM.

After one of the features is set as the parameter of interest (forecasting goal), the method aims at identifying the features that maximize the forecasting ability of the mode(s) to be used. For this purpose, we make use of the values of the M * N matrix W of the SOM weights. As the method is based on the weights of the existing features, we introduce a number of N random additional "features", so that the weight matrix doubles its columns becoming an M * 2 N matrix. This is done in order to enlarge the population of candidate features to be selected by introducing features that are not related whatso-ever with the problem under investigation, thus acting as indicators of "noise" and therefore be used as a selection threshold criterion as explained next. The weights matrix is then normalized, so that its values become (real) numbers between 0 and 1. In the next step, each feature column N is compared with that of the – parameter of interest, element by element, to determine how many values are either very similar, or complementary (i.e. have a sum close to 1), according to Eq. 1. An arbitrary parameter α is introduced, to quantitatively express the relationship between values being compared, α being a positive real number close to zero.

$$\left| Tar(j) - Feat_i(j) \right| \leq \alpha \quad \textbf{or} \quad \left| Tar(j) + Feat_i(j) - 1 \right| \leq \alpha \tag{1}$$

Here $Tar(j)$ is the j-th element of the target – parameter column and $Feat_i(j)$ is the j–th element of the column of the i-th feature. Thus, the initial M * 2 N matrix is trans-formed to a new one, S, with each column representing the same feature as the initial matrix, but with each element being equal to either one (when the original map's corre-sponding element is very similar or very complementary to the one of the target – parameter), or to zero otherwise.

With this new matrix, the feature that has the highest sum of values ("ones") is selected as the first feature of the current selection CL, and then the rest of the features are ranked accordingly. Then, a new ranking takes place, in which the remaining features are ranked again on the basis of Eq. 1, according to the amount of elements equal to "ones" they present, for element locations that the current selection demonstrates "zeros". Again, the feature that ranks first is selected, thus replacing the "zeros" of the current selection at the places where the newly selected feature had "ones". In this way, features are "completing" each other in order to be part of the population of the selected features, in an effort to maximize the amount of ones with the least possible features. This procedure also makes sure that there will be no redundancy, as similar features will have "ones" in similar places, therefore if one of them is selected, the rest will rank poorly in the next ranking round. The overall algorithm is presented in Table 1.

Table 1. The new feature selection algorithm based on SOM

```
Algorithm SOM_Feature_Selection

! N: the initial number of features
! M: the number of data rows (time stamps) in the data matrix
! Tar: the target parameter to be forecasted

  Get W;                      ! this is the SOM weights matrix
  CL := [];                   ! initialize current selection
  W := [W, rand(size(W))];    ! introduce N new random features
  NW := Normalized(W);        ! normalize the SOM weights matrix
  S := zeros(size(NW));
  S(|Tar(j) - Feat₁(j)| ≤ α or |Tar(j) + Feat₁(j) - 1| ≤ α) := 1;
  S2 := AddAllValuesPerLine(S) - ones(M,1);
  maxsim := (M - Sum(S2 == 0)) / M;
  R := Rank(features(feature != Tar)) ;
                        !Ranks according to Sum(S(:,i)), i = 1, …, 2N
  CL := [CL, R(1)];
  begin
    R := Rank(features(feature != Tar, feature not in CL)) ;
                        !Ranks according to
                        !Sum(S(:,i)), i ∈[1, 2N] and S(:,CL(i)) == 0

    CL := [CL, R(1)];
  until  Rank(1) > N or  Sum(CL(CL == 0)) == 0
  if CL(end) > N then
    CL := CL(1:end-1);
  end if
end
```

This process terminates once the maximum amount of ones is reached, or when one of the random "features" is selected, as this will indicate that the rest of the features offer little to no useful information for the parameter of interest. In this way, a set of features that describes the biggest part or the SOM concerning the parameter of interest is determined.

4   Results and Discussion

The parameter chosen to be forecasted as a test for the proposed methodology, was Ozone from the Panorama station (a typical inhabited urban area). The algorithms used for developing the forecasting models were Linear Regression (LR) [15] and Multilayer Perceptron (MLP) Artificial Neural Networks [16], since they are very commonly used in regression problems and have led to high AQ forecasting accuracy for the same geographic area [5]. Computations were again performed in WEKA [9].

Both LR and MLP were used for the cases of (a) the complete set of features, (b) the sets of features suggested by the CfsSubsetEval and ReliefFAttributeEval methods, and (c) the features resulting from the suggested methodology, for each value from 0.005 to 0.5, with a step of 0.005, for the parameter α. It should be noted that model development and training was made via the 10-fold cross validation method [17].

The comparison of the CI models' performance with the set of features presented in each case, as well as these of the CfsSubsetEval and ReliefFAtttributeEval methods are presented in Figs. 3, 4 and 5.

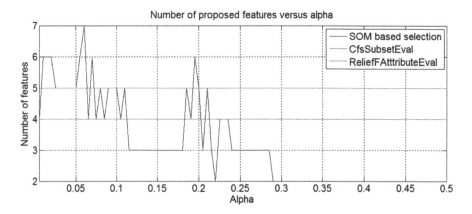

Fig. 3. Number of features of each feature set proposed by the SOM – based methodology, compared with these of the CfsSubsetEval and ReliefFAtttributeEval methods.

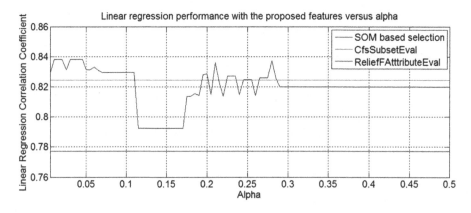

Fig. 4. Correlation coefficient of Linear Regression with each feature set proposed by the SOM – based methodology, compared with these of the CfsSubsetEval and ReliefFAtttributeEval methods.

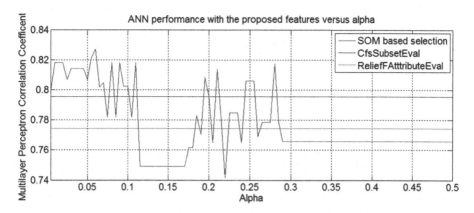

Fig. 5. Correlation coefficient of Multilayer Perceptron with each feature set proposed by the SOM – based methodology, compared with these of the CfsSubsetEval and ReliefFAttributeEval methods.

Results indicate that even a slight change in α can lead in different sets of features being selected. In more detail, for low values of α, (from 0.005 to 0.11), all the feature sets resulting from the new proposed method lead to better LR performance in comparison to the feature sets from both the reference methods (with 0.8382 being the highest value for correlation coefficient, 1.7% higher than the CfsSubsetEval method and 7.85% higher than ReliefFAttributeEval method), while regarding MLP, they all outperform the ReliefFAttributeEval method, and most outperform the CfsSubsetEval method as well (with 0.8332 being the highest value for correlation coefficient, 3.92% higher than the CfsSubsetEval method and 6.75% higher than ReliefFAttributeEval method). Values of 0.115 to 0.17 for α lead to the feature set with the poorest performance of all the sets offered by the new proposed method. Values of α between 0.175 and 0.295 lead to different sets that perform close to the set offered by the CfsSubsetEval method with LR and somewhere between the two reference methods with MLP. Finally, for α varying between 0.3 and 0.5, the feature set offered by the new proposed method does not change, and performs close to the set offered by the CfsSubsetEval method with LR and worse than the two reference methods with MLP, however, with only two features, as opposed to the four of the CfsSubsetEval method and the five of the ReliefFAttributeEval method.

The most popular features among all the offered feature sets are Ozone from the Kordelio station, which is also selected by the CfsSubsetEval method, and Ozone from the Neochorouda station, which is selected by both the reference methods as well. This selection seems very plausible, as it makes sense for the same pollutant from the other stations to be more correlated to our target – parameter than other atmospheric quality parameters.

Overall, the CI model's performance is comparable to this of the sets presented by the CfsSubsetEval and the ReliefFAttributeEval methods for each α. Table 2 presents the mean value and standard deviation of the CI models' performance for every α between 0.005 and 0.3 (as after 0.3 the results remain the same).

Table 2. Mean value and standard deviation of the CI models' performance for Ozone for the Panorama Station, with the sets of features from the suggested methodology, for α varying between 0.005 and 0.3.

	Mean	Standard deviation
Linear Regression	0.8202	0.0156
MLP	0.7848	0.0262

Table 2 indicates that even a poor choice of α will outperform the ReliefFAtttributeEval method, and perform close to the CfsSubsetEval method. The low standard deviation of the results, despite the number of different set of features offered, shows that the concept of complementarity of features with the aim of maximum similarity with the target – parameter will always lead to acceptable results for the case under investigation. It is also apparent that there are values of α that lead to sets of features which outperform both the ReliefFAtttributeEval and the CfsSubsetEval methods, as well some that lead to good performance with less features.

For reasons of further investigation, the same tests were also run for a different pollutant and monitoring station, namely NO_2 for the Sindos station. The mean value and standard deviation of both models' performance is presented in Table 3. It should be mentioned that in this case results did not change for any α greater than 0.27. Again low values for α lead to feature sets with better performance, at times superior to the two reference methods, with the maximum correlation coefficient for the LR model reaching 0.74 (for a = 0.11) while for the MLP model it was 0.67 (again for a = 0.11). Reference methods on the other hand led to the feature sets that correspond to the modelling results presented in Table 4, demonstrating better performance in comparison to the mean performance indicators of Table 3.

Table 3. Mean value and standard deviation of the CI models' performance for NO_2 for the Sindos Station, with the sets of features from the suggested methodology, for every α between 0.005 and 0.27.

	Mean	Standard deviation
Linear Regression	0.7049	0.0173
MLP	0.6261	0.0258

Table 4. Performance of the CI models with the feature sets offered by the two reference feature selection methods, for NO_2 and for the Sindos station.

	CfsSubsetEval	ReliefFAttributeEval
Linear Regression	0.7317	0.6931
MLP	0.6564	0.6286

5   Conclusions

In the present paper a new methodology for feature selection in data-driven air quality forecasting problems is presented and compared with two existing and commonly used feature selection methods, namely CfsSubsetEval and ReliefFAttributeEval. The new method is based on SOMs thus making use of additional information concerning feature interrelationship and cross-influence. Two air quality forecasting models were used for testing the performance of the feature selection methods, one being a standard multivariate Linear Regression model and the other being an Artificial Neural Network of the Multi-Layer Perceptron type. Model results show that the new feature selection method is comparable to the reference ones, while being also able to outperform them producing results up to +7.85% for the correlation coefficient, provided that computational experiments take place in order to determine the values for the selection parameter a (alpha). As such, this approach seems promising, and is offered for further investigation, involving testing additional cases while also improving the estimation of the alpha parameter.

References

1. Gulia, S., Nagendra, S., Khare, M., Khanna, I.: Urban air quality management-a review. Atmos. Pollut. Res. **6**(2), 286–304 (2015)
2. Chen, H., Goldberg, M.S., Villeneuve, P.J.: A systematic review of the relation between long-term exposure to ambient air pollution and chronic diseases. Rev. Environ. Health **23**(4), 243–297 (2008)
3. Araghinejad, S.: Data-Driven Modeling: Using MATLAB® in Water Resources and Environmental Engineering. WSTL, vol. 67. Springer, Dordrecht (2014). https://doi.org/10.1007/978-94-007-7506-0
4. Mesin, L., Orione, F., Taormina, R., Pasero, E.: A feature selection method for air quality forecasting. In: Diamantaras, K., Duch, W., Iliadis, L.S. (eds.) ICANN 2010. LNCS, vol. 6354, pp. 489–494. Springer, Heidelberg (2010). https://doi.org/10.1007/978-3-642-15825-4_66
5. Voukantsis, D., Karatzas, K., Kukkonen, J., Räsänen, T., Karppinen, A., Kolehmainen, M.: Intercomparison of air quality data using principal component analysis, and forecasting of PM10 and PM2.5 concentrations using artificial neural networks, in Thessaloniki and Helsinki. Sci. Total Environ. **409**, 1266–1276 (2011). https://doi.org/10.1016/j.scitotenv.2010.12.039
6. Moussiopoulos, N., Vlachokostas, Ch., Tsilingiridis, G., Douros, I., Hourdakis, E., Naneris, C., Sidiropoulos, C.: Air quality status in greater Thessaloniki area and the emission reductions needed for attaining the EU air quality legislation. Sci. Total Environ. **407**, 1268–1285 (2009)
7. Hall, M.A.: Correlation-based feature subset selection for machine learning. Ph.D. thesis, The University of Waikato (1998). http://www.cs.waikato.ac.nz/~ml/publications/1999/99MH-Thesis.pdf
8. Kira, K., Rendell, L.A.: A practical approach to feature selection. In: Ninth International Workshop on Machine Learning, pp. 249–256 (1992)

9. Hall, M.A., Frank, E., Holmes, G., Pfahringer, B., Reutemann, P., Witten, I.H.: The WEKA data mining software: an update. SIGKDD Explor. **11**(1) (2009). http://www.cs. waikato.ac.nz/ml/weka/

10. Cui, Y., Jin, J.S., Zhang, S., Luo, S., Tian, Q.: Correlation-based feature selection and regression. In: Qiu, G., Lam, K.M., Kiya, H., Xue, X.-Y., Kuo, C.-C.J., Lew, M.S. (eds.) PCM 2010. LNCS, vol. 6297, pp. 25–35. Springer, Heidelberg (2010). https://doi.org/10.1007/978-3-642-15702-8_3

11. Arauzo-Azofra, A., Benítez, J.M., Castro, J.L.: A feature set measure based on relief (2004)

12. Kohonen, T.: Self-organized formation of topologically correct feature maps. Biol. Cybern. **43**(1), 59–69 (1982)

13. Ultsch A., Siemon H.P.: Kohonen's self organizing feature maps for exploratory data analysis. In: Proceedings of International Neural Networks Conference (INNC), pp. 305–308 (1990)

14. http://www.cis.hut.fi/somtoolbox/

15. Rencher, A.C., Christensen, W.F.: Multivariate regression – Section 10.1, Introduction (Chap. 10). In: Methods of Multivariate Analysis, Wiley Series in Probability and Statistics, vol. 709, p. 19, 3rd edn. Wiley, Hoboken (2012)

16. Rumelhart, D.E., Hinton, G.E., Williams, R.J.: Learning internal representations by error propagation. In: Rumelhart, D.E., McClelland, J.L., The PDP Research Group (eds.) Parallel Distributed Processing: Explorations in the Microstructure of Cognition: Foundations, vol. 1. MIT Press, Cambridge (1986)

17. Kohavi, R.: A study of cross-validation and bootstrap for accuracy estimation and model selection. In: Proceedings of 14th International Joint Conference on Artificial Intelligence, vol. 2, no. 12, pp. 1137–1143. Morgan Kaufmann, San Mateo (1995)

Approaches to Fuse Fixed and Mobile Air Quality Sensors

Gerhard Dünnebeil[1(✉)], Martina Marjanović[2], and Ivana Podnar Žarko[2]

[1] AIT Austrian Institute of Technology GmbH, Vienna, Austria
gerhard.duennebeil@ait.ac.at
[2] Faculty of Electrical Engineering and Computing, University of Zagreb, Zagreb, Croatia
{martina.marjanovic,Ivana.podnar}@fer.hr

Abstract. Nowadays, air quality monitoring is identified as one of the key impacts in assessing the quality of life in urban areas. Traditional measuring procedures include expensive equipment in the fixed monitoring stations which is not suitable for urban areas because of the low spatio-temporal density of measurements. On the other hand, the technological development of small wearable sensor devices has created new opportunities for air pollution monitoring. Therefore, in this paper we discuss statistical approaches to fuse the data from fixed and mobile sensors for air quality monitoring.

Keywords: Air quality monitoring · Interpolation · Kriging · Mobile sensors

1 Introduction

Air pollution represents a serious threat in urban environments with a significant negative impact on human health. Therefore, the European Parliament and the Council of the European Union provided the Air Quality Directive to emphasize the importance of air quality monitoring in urban areas [1]. Also, scientists have proven that exposure to traffic-related air pollution can cause different respiratory problems [2]. Since heavy industry and vehicles are nowadays major producers of toxic gases, it is necessary to densely monitor air pollution in big cities, both in time and space, in order to identify contaminated areas promptly and devise appropriate actions.

Today Air Quality Monitoring is mostly done with stations that do long term monitoring at fixed location. Although the equipment often is mounted in containers which can be relocated (Figs. 1 and 2), there is a need to have undisturbed series of measurements over a long period of time that allow to exclude location based effects from the measurement campaign.

© IFIP International Federation for Information Processing 2017
Published by Springer International Publishing AG 2017. All Rights Reserved
J. Hřebíček et al. (Eds.): ISESS 2017, IFIP AICT 507, pp. 71–84, 2017.
https://doi.org/10.1007/978-3-319-89935-0_7

Fig. 1. A typical AQ monitoring fixed station (All images from fixed stations are courtesy of Authorities federal state of Upper Austria.)

Fig. 2. A set of analyzers as they are typically found in a fixed station

The traditional air quality measurement infrastructure can therefore be extended to obtain a higher spatial resolution by using a larger number of mobile wearable sensor nodes for environmental monitoring (Fig. 3).

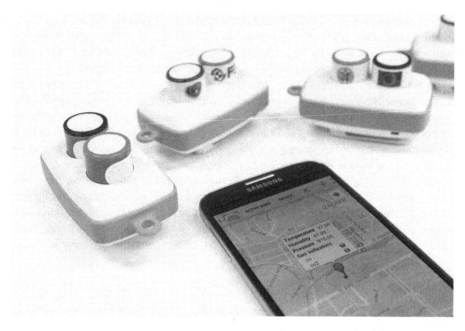

Fig. 3. Wearable sensors for air quality monitoring (Wearable sensors and smartphone application for air quality monitoring developed at University of Zagreb, Faculty of Electrical Engineering and Computing, Zagreb, Croatia.)

Although there is a significant discrepancy in the accuracy and sensitivity between the new mobile sensors and static meteorological stations, their affordability and simplicity have created the opportunity for wide usage of small and cheap sensor devices. Thus, we investigate how these two can coexist and benefit from each other. One of the major advantages of mobile sensors is the simplicity of taking samples on many locations. In this paper, we will focus on ideas how this wider coverage can be used to estimate the pollution at arbitrary points by exploiting the spatial and temporal coverage of mobile sensors in combination with the accuracy of fixed stations.

The rest of the paper is organized as follows: Sect. 2 introduces a model based sensor data interpolation with focus on the kriging method. In Sect. 3 we discuss the proposed model. We further introduce the problem of bogus sensor detection and determination of confidence factors in Sect. 4. Section 5 provides a brief overview of related work by addressing interpolation methods used in different areas of the environmental science. Finally, Sect. 6 concludes the paper and gives directions for future work.

2   Model-Based Sensor Interpolation

The mobility of sensors leads to a dynamic sensing coverage of geographical areas, which can potentially result in certain areas being redundantly covered, while other areas may suffer from lack of available sensor measurements. Obviously, it is not possible to cover all geographical points in a certain area of interest by actual sensor readings. Therefore, we need to use a finite number of sensor readings and estimate the actual values in between. Mathematically this requires an interpolation approach.

Interpolation is a method of constructing new data points from a set of previously known values. Basically, it makes some assumptions about the values at locations that have to be estimated by using some kind of a model. Classical interpolation approaches, like polynomial or spline interpolation, completely ignore the fact that sensor readings always come with a certain inaccuracy. Hereafter, we present and discuss other techniques that can be used to estimate missing values.

Interpolation can be done in space or in time or both. In this paper we implicitly restrict ourselves to interpolation in space. Our goal is to get subsequent maps of pollution for discrete points in time that incorporate as much information as possible to get the best accuracy. This includes not only information gained at or near the said points in time but also the knowledge about the involved sensors gained from the earlier maps.

2.1   Kriging Approach

One well known approach to interpolate sensor readings is kriging (originated by Krige in 1951 [3]). The basic idea of kriging is to estimate a value at a specific location by computing a weighted average of the known values in the neighborhood of that location. In other words, kriging takes into account the nearby sensor readings to eliminate to a certain degree the random errors inherent in every reading. The mathematical meaning of the term nearby is defined by the so called co-variance function $v(\vec{l})$ which defines the significance that a certain reading r has at location $\vec{l}$.

The estimated value at location $\vec{l}$ can be calculated as

$$Z(\vec{l}) = \sum_{\alpha=1}^{n(\vec{l})} \lambda_\alpha Z(\vec{l_\alpha}). \tag{1}$$

The factors λ_α describe how much a reading is relevant for the interpolated value. This is determined by the co-variance function.

There is a certain degree of freedom in choosing this function. Indeed, this is the model behind the kriging approach.

Usually one chooses a function that will have a value of 1 at the exact location $\vec{l}$ and will monotonically decrease with the distance from $\vec{l}$. Either this function will be zero at a certain distance from $\vec{l}$ or it will converge to zero with the distance reaching infinity. So the co-variance function typically has the form of a coefficient between 0 and 1 which defines the statistical weight of a reading r at the location $\vec{l}$. Figure 4 shows some typical curve forms for such function.

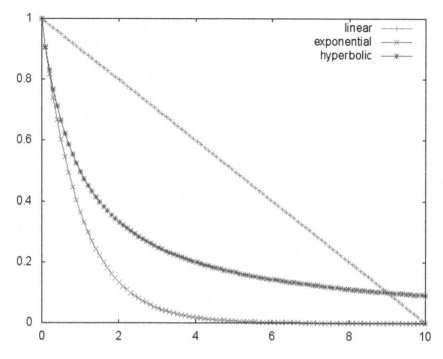

Fig. 4. Examples of different co-variance functions

This co-variance function gives an individual value for each sensor that is expected at a location $\vec{l}$. All these values usually differ from each other. The interpolated value is now calculated such that the individual errors are minimized (least mean square).

2.2 Taking Confidence into Account

Nowadays, mobile sensors typically have a much larger error than fixed stations. When trying to fuse the readings between fixed stations and mobile sensors we have to take this into account. Even though a mobile sensor takes measurements exactly at a sampling location, usually the readings collected by different sensors at the same location and point in time will not be the same. This will be the case even if both sensors are calibrated.

Since we want to model different confidence levels, we introduce a confidence coefficient cc which lies between 0 (not reliable at all) and 1 (completely reliable). Still we have to determine a method how to gain such confidence coefficients (which we show in the section below), but once they are available they simply attenuate the existing co-variance function $v(\vec{l})$ by defining a new one

$$v_1(\vec{l}) = v(\vec{l}) * cc. \tag{2}$$

This will result in a domination of a nearby fixed station in the interpolation process. But if multiple mobile sensors in the vicinity share the same reading, they can eventually dominate a fixed station.

2.3 Some Definitions

To keep the other chapters free from complex and repeated mathematics and definitions as much as possible, we introduce a few phrases here. We use the term physical sensor readings r_{phys} which indicates sensor readings without further corrections. We are aware though, that this concept is a bit problematic as this concept is not taking into account that real sensors suffer from cross sensitivity and similar effects. Certain compensations for these effects must still be applied to the raw sensor readings before they can be used in this context.

The most important function is the interpolation function I which gives us the interpolated value. I is a function of the location $\vec{l}$. An index of "F" will indicate that the interpolation is done only over the fixed stations, while an index of "M" will indicate the same only for mobile stations (i.e. I_F and I_M).

A function LMS means we use the least mean square fit on the data. The result of an LMS is a set of coefficients. Due to the lack of better models we assume a linear mean square fit throughout this paper so the result is a pair of numbers, amplification a and offset b so that the correction function is

$$r_{Fcorr} = f(r_{phys}) = ar_{phys} + b. \tag{3}$$

3 Model Discussion

The above described approach has a clear weakness as it assumes that only the distance between different sensors is important. This assumes an ideal situation where diffusion processes are not disturbed by wind or obstacles, neither natural nor artificial. The assumption does not hold in a typical urban environment where street canyons dominantly influence the spreading of pollutants. Further discussion of street canyon effects, their consequences and possible solutions is out of scope for this paper and it will be taken into account in future work.

3.1 Relating Mobile Sensors to Fixed Stations

Usually sensors tend to drift. Even though sensors are kept in a very controlled constant concentration of pollutants, the readings will still change over time. A lot of effort is taken to control and compensate the natural drift for fixed stations. The related analyzers are often calibrated and in many cases a so called function control procedure is performed once every 24 or 48 h. During the function control phase the analyzers are first exposed to gases with known concentrations, then the resulting error is recorded and all subsequent sensor readings are compensated numerically.

However, doing the same for mobile sensors would significantly devalue their advantages in mobility and costs. For that reason, it is necessary to find other ways of compensating the errors of mobile sensors. The first idea, to just compare readings between fixed and mobile sensors when a mobile sensor passes by a fixed station seems obvious but will not work. One reason is that mobile sensors typically measure one to four samples per minute as they have to operate on severely limited energy. If we assume that the sensor is moving with a bicycle or car, this means it will hardly measure at all within a distance close enough to a fixed station. Another reason is that mobile sensors typically measure at heights of 1 to 1.5 meters above ground level while fixed stations have their air inlet at least 4 meters high.

To compensate this errors, we first interpolate using only the fixed stations. This can usually be done easily as all fixed stations give their results for the same time. The result is a map that shows approximately the situation over the area for a given point in time.

The resulting interpolation function $I_F(\vec{l})$ is then used to calculate the deviation of each sensor reading to the related interpolated value. Of course, doing this for just one reading per sensor is still significantly influenced by different errors, some of them potentially huge. We need to gather enough of these (real reading, interpolated value) pairs to apply an LMS-function and get statistically significant coefficients for gain and offset to correct each sensor.

3.2 Relating Mobile Sensors to Each Other

The above described approach will only work when the probability of a mobile sensor to pass near a fixed station is high. However, the probability that two mobile sensors meet is much higher considering that only a certain (minimal) number of fixed sensors is in the field.

Doing an interpolation on the mobile sensors themselves and comparing individual sensor readings to the interpolated values can provide individual deviations for each sensor. When having sufficient deviations, a best-fit-line which will compensate individual sensors with respect to their companions can be calculated. When a network of mobile sensors is compensated, it is also possible to calculate compensation factors of certain sensors to the fixed stations. With this approach it is possible to adjust the complete set of sensors to the readings of fixed stations.

For this approach, we calculate the interpolation function for the mobile sensors, $I_M(\vec{l})$. Theoretically this is done for all sensor readings at a particular point in time. In praxis, it not possible to have this one point in time, instead we use a short time interval.

Subsequently all physical readings are paired with the interpolated readings at the same location. As singular readings are not sufficient to compute LMS statistics, these pairs are stored for later evaluation. A sufficiently large set of these pairs is then used to compute coefficients that correct sensors to be harmonized with the other sensors. This list of pairs must contain enough data to calculate a meaningful statistic. On the other hand, as the sensors tend to age and drift, it must not contain values too long. In practice, we found out that having a list length of a few hours is more than sufficient.

Next, for each fixed station n another pair $(I_M(\vec{l_n})$, station reading) is calculated. This dataset is subsequently used to compute an LMS. The resulting coefficients (a_F, b_F) are merged with the individual coefficients for each sensor.

$$r_{M,corr} = (a_F * (a_M * r_{phys} + b_M)) + b_F = a_F a_M r_{phys} + a_F b_M + b_F \qquad (4)$$

1. This can also be formulated as an algorithm:
2. Calculate the interpolation function IM for all mobile sensors.
3. Gather all pairs $(I_M(\vec{l}), r_{phys})$ for all locations where sensor readings are available and add those to the set of existing pairs for each sensor.
4. Calculate correction factors for each sensor.
5. Calculate the interpolation function IF for all fixed stations.
6. Gather all pairs $(I_F(\vec{l}), I_M(\vec{l}))$ for all locations of the fixed stations.
7. Calculate an LMS for all pairs and obtain the corrective coefficients a_F and b_F.
8. Apply both, individual and global, factors to each sensor reading to obtain harmonized readings.

3.3   Results and Discussion

To verify the proposed algorithm, we have used a real-world dataset acquired from the air quality measurement campaign "SenseZGAir" performed in the City of Zagreb, Croatia, in early July 2014 as part of the Smart City Zagreb initiative. The "SenseZGAir" dataset contains 151,000 data points, including temperature, humidity, pressure, concentrations of carbon monoxide (CO), and either nitrogen dioxide (NO2) or sulfur dioxide (SO2), obtained at 13,000 unique locations in Zagreb (according to GPS coordinates) in 3 days that the campaign lasted [4]. To evaluate our model, we have used CO measurements from mobile sensors and official gas concentrations from the Croatian Ministry of Environment and Energy on July 7, 2014.

Figure 5 shows individual paths which 8 of our sensors did during the field trial in the time span from 9:00 to 10:00 a.m, while the "zoom" part shows the sensors "near" one of the fixed monitoring stations in Zagreb (marked as red cross) which we have chosen for our experiments.

We have visualized individual sensor measurements together with the fixed station concentrations during the chosen time span, as shown on Fig. 6. It can be seen that CO values differ a lot between sensors which is obviously not only due to the measurement errors but also to local effects. Also, the figure shows the fixed station measurement value (hourly mean) for the same period.

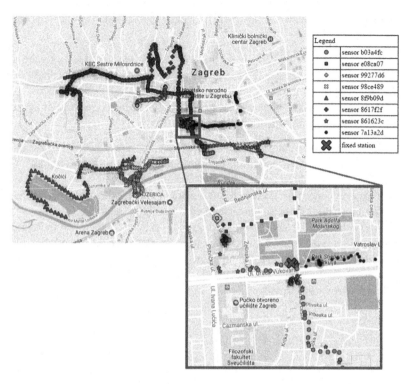

Fig. 5. Mobile sensor measurements in the City of Zagreb for July 7, 2014, from 9:00 to 10:00 a.m. (Visualized by the CopyPasteMap tool available at http://www.copypastemap.com/)

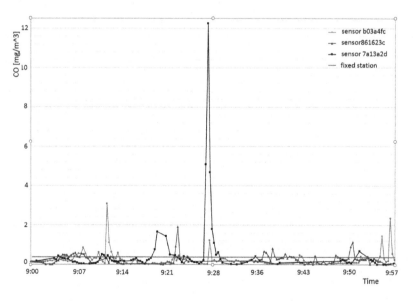

Fig. 6. All sensor measurements between 9:00 and 10:00 a.m. on July 7, 2014

Our initial experiments with real-world data have shown that the proposed procedure suffers from the following:

- Even if you restrict yourself to sensor measurements near fixed stations the mobile sensors show a lot of variance in the measurements which is most probably caused by the real changes in the local gas concentration.
- Fixed station data on the other hand is usually only published in form of aggregated (mean) values over a significant period of time.

Correlating these two datasets leads to the fact that many substantially different mobile measurements are compared to the same fixed station's measurement. This in return makes it impossible to calculate a least mean square fit.

In another experiment we tried to relate sensors to each other. For that we used the time slot from 9:00 to 9:10 from the same data set mentioned above.

We have visualized the sampling points in Fig. 7. It can be seen that there are quite some places where sensors are located close to each other. We have used those sensors to find correlations between them, i.e. to show whether the sensors deviate or not.

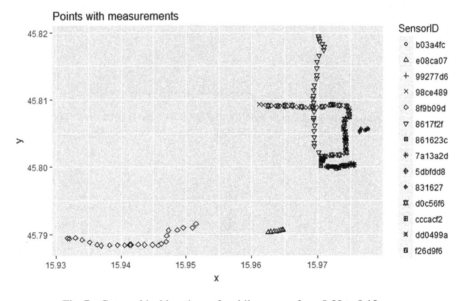

Fig. 7. Geographical locations of mobile sensors from 9:00 to 9:10 a.m.

The interpolation showed the small variations between sensor measurements in the observed area. It also showed that the overall concentration of CO is mostly low, except on the crossing of two big roads with heavy traffic where we observed slightly lower air quality depicted as a red area in Fig. 8. This is a well-known hot spot of lower air quality, so the public authorities have already placed the fixed station to continuously monitor the air quality as shown on Fig. 5.

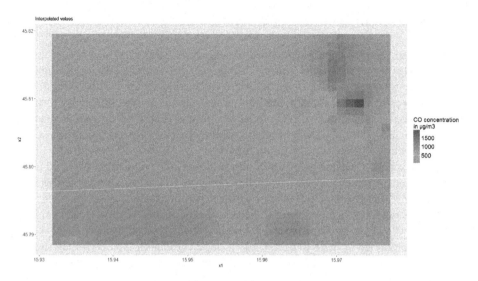

Fig. 8. Interpolated sensor measurements (Color figure online)

We have also compared the difference between the interpolated values and real sensor measurements as shown in Fig. 9. The comparison gave an interesting result as it showed very few deviations between sensors and their interpolated values. Most of interpolated values differ less than 500 $\mu g/m^3$ from the measured value, while few of them show a difference between 1000 and 1500 $\mu g/m^3$. Those readings from a sensor have the value of zero and are not valid anyway. The few sensors that show real deviations do not allow to make any useful statistic.

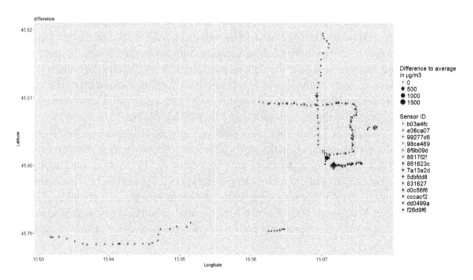

Fig. 9. Difference between real sensor measurements and their interpolated values

4   Bogus Sensor Detection and Determination of Confidence Factors

Mobile sensors tend to age and get unreliable over time. Detecting this effect is crucial for the evaluation of individual sensors. The procedures described above determine a best-fit-line for each sensor. Calculating the correlation factor for this best-fit-line provides an estimate of the quality of a sensor response to a given pollutant exposure. Sensors that occasionally give bad correlations most probably have severely changed their environment during the time window currently in focus, e.g. parts of the measurements are indoor while others are near a road.

A more sophisticated analysis may be able to classify these individual measurements and treat them as separate classes. We simply propose to use this correlation factor as the confidence factor, maybe scaled down with an additional fixed factor that describes the overall confidence in mobile sensor. Sensors that occasionally show a bad fit are not necessarily defective. There can be many reasons for small sets of measurements being "off". Therefore, we propose to keep track of these correlation factors. If they show a long-term degrading trend, the sensor will lose permanently influence to the complete system. A sensor that has less influence is not important anymore and can be removed from the network.

5   Related Work

There are several papers considering data interpolation in different areas of the environmental science. Gummadi [5] gives a short overview of conventional interpolation techniques and neural network approaches commonly used for modelling and estimation of radon concentrations in Ohio. Kravchenko et al. [6] evaluate different interpolation principles to determine the optimal method for mapping soil properties, similar as Li et al. [7] who compare the accuracy of spatial interpolation techniques to identify the best prediction method to illustrate the spatial variability of the studied soil properties.

Spatial interpolation is widely used for creating continuous data where estimation at any unobserved location is within the data boundary and it is spatially dependent [8, 9]. Vuran et al. have developed the theoretical framework for the spatio-temporal correlation in wireless sensor networks (WSN) and showed that correlation can be exploited to significantly improve the energy-efficiency in WSN [10]. Further, stochastic interpolation methods are used to predict the values at unmeasured locations based on the data spatial autocorrelation and to estimate the prediction accuracy. In particular, kriging has been used for the spatial analysis of soil bulk density [11], temperature mapping [12], estimation of rainfall [13], as well as air pollution [14]. Tyagi et al. [15] use ordinary kriging to estimate the pollution in areas without measurements in Agra (Dayalbagh) region, similar as Shad et al. [16] who use fuzzy spatial prediction techniques to determine pollution concentration areas in practical situations where observations are imprecise and vague.

6   Conclusion

This paper deals with the statistical approaches which can be used to estimate the pollution at arbitrary points by exploiting the spatial and temporal coverage of mobile sensors in combination with the accuracy of fixed stations. In particular, we discuss the model-based interpolation with a focus on the kriging approach. We have proposed an algorithm to fuse fixed and mobile air quality sensors and get harmonized sensor readings. However, due to the variance in the mobile sensor measurements together with the limited availability of fixed station data (note that this data is most often only available as aggregates over several minutes: Swiss – 10 min, Austria and Germany – 30 min, Croatia – 1 h time scale), the initial experiments did not provide usable results.

We also experimented with relating mobile sensors to each other. Interestingly this experiment showed that the often asserted inaccuracy of mobile sensors might be less than usually assumed. At least our finding was that we had no need for extensive compensation of the sensors.

We plan to repeat the experiment in a more controlled manner (like having some mobile sensors near the fixed station). Furthermore, we plan to simulate sensor networks combined from real stations and mobile sensors. Moreover, we want to integrate street canyon models into the system.

Acknowledgments. This work is supported in part by the H2020 symbIoTe project, which has received funding from the European Union's Horizon 2020 research and innovation program under grant agreement No. 688156. This work has been supported in part by Croatian Science Foundation under the project 8065 (Human-centric Communications in Smart Networks).

References

1. Directive 2008/50/EC of the European Parliament and the Council of 21 May 2008 on ambient air quality and cleaner air for Europe
2. HEI Panel on the Health Effects of Traffic-Related Air Pollution. Traffic-Related Air Pollution: A Critical Review of the Literature on Emissions, Exposure, and Health Effects; HEI Special Report, 17
3. Krige, D.G.: A statistical approach to some basic mine valuation problems on the Witwatersrand. J. Chem. Metall. Min. Soc. South Afr. **52**(6), 119–139 (1951)
4. Antonić, A., Bilas, V., Marjanović, M., Matijašević, M., Oletić, D., Pavelić, M., Podnar Žarko, I., Pripužić, K., Skorin-Kapov, L.: Urban crowd sensing demonstrator: sense the zagreb air. In: Proceedings of 22nd International Conference on Software, Telecommunications and Computer Networks, SoftCOM2014 (2014)
5. Gummadi, J.: A comparison of various interpolation techniques for modelling and estimation of radon concentrations in Ohio. Theses and Dissertations, Paper 86 (2013)
6. Kravchenko, A., Bullock, D.G.: A comparative study of interpolation methods for mapping soil properties. Agron. J. **91**(3), 393–400 (1999)
7. Li, J., Heap, A.D.: A Review of Spatial Interpolation Methods for Environmental Scientists, vol. 137. Geoscience Australia, Canberra (2008)

8. Robinson, T.P., Metternicht, G.: Testing the performance of spatial interpolation techniques for mapping soil properties. Comput. Electron. Agric. **50**(2), 97–108 (2006). Elsevier Science Publishers B. V.

9. Akkala, A., Devabhaktuni, V., Kumar, A.: Interpolation techniques and associated software for environmental data. Environ. Prog. Sustain. Energy **29**(2), 134–141 (2010)

10. Vuran, M.C., Akan, Z.B., Akyildiz, I.F.: Spatio-temporal correlation: theory and applications for wireless sensor networks. Comput. Netw. **45**(3), 245–259 (2004)

11. Sajid, A.H., Rudra, R.P., Parkin, G.: Systematic evaluation of Kriging and inverse distance weighting methods for spatial analysis of soil bulk density. Can. Biosyst. Eng. **55**, 1.1–1.13 (2013)

12. Hudson, G., Wackernagel, H.: Mapping temperature using Kriging with external drift: theory and an example from Scotland. Int. J. Climatol. **14**(1), 77–91 (1994)

13. Goovaerts, P.: Geostatistical approaches for incorporating elevation into the spatial interpolation of rainfall. J. Hydrol. **228**(1), 113–129 (2000)

14. Janssen, S., Dumont, G., Fierens, F., Mensink, C.: Spatial interpolation of air pollution measurements using CORINE land cover data. Atmos. Environ. **42**(20), 4884–4903 (2008)

15. Tyagi, A., Singh, P.: Applying Kriging approach on pollution data using GIS software. Int. J. Environ. Eng. Manag. **4**(3), 185–190 (2013)

16. Shad, R., Mesgari, M.S., Abkar, A., Shad, A.: Predicting air pollution using fuzzy genetic linear membership Kriging in GIS. Comput. Environ. Urban Syst. **33**(6), 472–481 (2009)

EO Big Data Connectors and Analytics for Understanding the Effects of Climate Change on Migratory Trends of Marine Wildlife

Z. A. Sabeur[1](✉) ⓘ, G. Correndo[1], G. Veres[1], B. Arbab-Zavar[1],
J. Lorenzo[2], T. Habib[3], A. Haugommard[3], F. Martin[3], J.-M. Zigna[4],
and G. Weller[4]

[1] Department of Electronics and Computer Science,
Faculty of Physical Sciences and Engineering, IT Innovation Centre,
University of Southampton, Southampton, UK
{zas,gc,gvv,baz}@it-innovation.soton.ac.uk
[2] Atos, Madrid, Spain
[3] Atos, Toulouse, France
[4] Collecte Localisation Satellite (CLS), Ramonville-Saint-Agne, France

Abstract. This paper describes the current ongoing research activities concerning the intelligent management and processing of Earth Observation (EO) big data together with the implementation of data connectors, advanced data analytics and Knowledge Base services to a Big Data platform in the EO4Wildlife project (www.eo4wildlife.eu). These components support on the discovery of marine wildlife migratory behaviours, some of which may be a direct consequence of the changing Met-Ocean resources and the globe climatic changes. In EO4wildlife, we specifically focus on the implementation of web-enabled advanced analytics web services which comply with OGC standards and make them accessible to a wide research community for investigating on trends of animal behaviour around specific marine regions of interest. Big data connectors and a catalogue service are being installed to enable access to COPERNICUS sentinels and ARGOS satellite big data together with other in situ heterogeneous sources. Furthermore, data mining services are being developed for knowledge extraction on species habitats and temporal behaviour trends. Also, high level fusion and reasoning services which process big data observations are deployed to forecast marine wildlife behaviour with estimated uncertainties. These will be tested and demonstrated under targeted thematic scenarios in EO4wildlife using a Big Data platform a cloud resources.

1 Introduction

EO4wildlife brings large number of multidisciplinary scientists such as marine biologists, ecologists and ornithologists around the world to collaborate closely together while using European Sentinel Copernicus Earth Observations more efficiently.

In order to reach such important capability, an open service platform and interoperable toolbox is being designed and implemented. It offers data processing services

© IFIP International Federation for Information Processing 2017
Published by Springer International Publishing AG 2017. All Rights Reserved
J. Hřebíček et al. (Eds.): ISESS 2017, IFIP AICT 507, pp. 85–94, 2017.
https://doi.org/10.1007/978-3-319-89935-0_8

that can be accessed by scientists to perform their respective research. The platform front end will be easy to use, access and it offers dedicated services that will enable scientists' process their geospatial environmental stimulations using Sentinel Earth Observation data and other observation sources. Specifically, the EO4wildlife platform will enable the integration of Sentinel data, ARGOS archive databases and real time thematic databank portals, including Wildlifetracking.org, Seabirdtracking.org, and other Earth Observation and MetOcean databases; locally or remotely, but simultaneously. EO4wildlife research specialises in the intelligent big data processing, advanced analytics and a Knowledge Base for wildlife migratory behaviour and trends forecasting. The research is leading to the development of web-enabled open services using OGC standards for sensor *Observation and Measurements* and data processing of heterogeneous geospatial observation data with estimated uncertainties. EO4wildlife designs, implements and validates various scenarios based on real operational use case requirements in the field of marine wildlife migrations, habitats and behaviour.

2   Global Architecture Overview

The EO4wildlife system is hosted in a SparkInData platform, which offers a set of core services for data discovery, data ingestion, process integration and execution. The SparkInData Platform, also known as *Smart Elastic Enriched Earth Data* (SEEED), is a generic platform which provides an EO data dedicated Cloud platform, infrastructure and services. Furthermore, the platform is organized under three functional zones, as shown in Fig. 1 below. These include: *1- Storage zone for mutualized storage capabilities; 2- Compute zone for mutualized intensive computing; and 3- Service zone for processing services.* Furthermore, the platform infrastructure services are provided by the Big Data Helix Nebula platform. Slipstream is used at a *Platform as a Service*

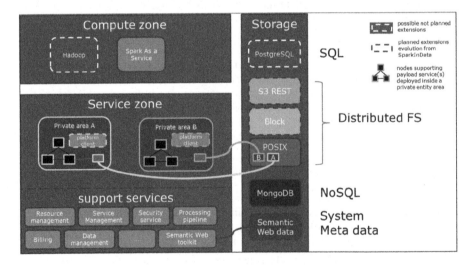

Fig. 1. Global Big data platform architecture overview

(PaaS) level. The PaaS is provided under a cloud computing services environment which enables developers run, test and manage their own applications while processing Big EO Data and analytics for extracting marine species migratory routes with respect to Ocean fronts geospatial and temporal trends. Specifically, PaaS is based on Google's Kubernetes (K8S) open software with an augmented dedicated SparkInData *Service Management Layer*. The latter is responsible for deploying applications on SaaS mode and managing them with auto-scaling, load balancing, monitoring or decommissioning upon request by application owners.

In addition to the above, the SparkInData platform components consist of the following:

Security Service: It registers users, their roles and rights to ensure their authentication and access control to the platform.

Processing Pipeline: It controls and monitors the chaining of the data analytics Web Processing Services (WPS).

Data management service: It ensures the "import" into the system of various data sets which are generated by data providers or new analytics into the system.

Service management: This enables the creation and control of applications deployment and their scalability of operations on the platform.

Resource Management: It controls resources deployment, their scalability and operations on the platform

Data Storage service: This service ensures and secures persistent data storage into the system.

Semantic Web Toolkit: It ensures linked data storage, access to RDF resources and mechanisms which define access control policies for graph stores.

Market Place: It provides a common place for information exchange for publishing application services outputs.

Billing service: It controls how application services can be purchased from the *Market Place* where payment can be performed.

Spark as a Service: It executes and controls Spark Jobs through a dedicated web service.

2.1 Knowledge Base and Big Data Analytics

The Knowledge Base services are being developed in support of the overall EO4wildlife platform architecture. They are integrated with it for the support of the deployment of the big data analytics services to the Platform. The overall aim of the Knowledge Base services is to enhance the meta-data support provided by OGC standards in order to employ data semantics and interoperability at the data access service level. The ontologies developed within this module aim at covering the gap between data producers (e.g. Argos, Copernicus or the animal tracks data owners) and the data consumers (e.g. the scientists which will develop the workflows).

This is achieved through the provision of a common overarching representation of the heterogeneous entities that access the Big EO data sources and analytics. The Knowledge Base architecture is made of various services functionalities which are exposed to the platform as REST services. The services are deployed as a separate

Docker container and it is supported by the Virtuoso triple store instance which is included in the SEEED platform.

2.2 Big Data Analytics

In order to provide proofs of concept of the EO4wildlife platform, a number of workflows based on specific domain studies of marine animal tracks are being developed. The more mature studies are presented in the following Sections.

2.2.1 Atlantic Bluefin Tuna Application Scenario

Atlantic Bluefin tuna (ABFT henceforth) is a highly migratory species which tolerates wide ranges of environmental conditions [1] in the Atlantic Ocean and Mediterranean Sea. In this section, we present initial attempts to correlate ABFT tracking data and environmental variables to identify different pattern of ABFT behaviour using Ecological Niche Modelling. The methodological steps undertaken to identify ABFT habitat preferences during different types of behaviour are inspired by [2] and depicted in Fig. 2.

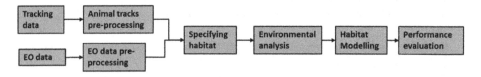

Fig. 2. Workflow of Atlantic Bluefin tuna application

For **animal tracks pre-processing** the following services are offered: animal tracks reconstruction, discarding the location on the land and redundancy filtering which removes duplications in the tracks and any relocation points on the same day separated by less than 2.3 km. **EO (Earth Observation) data pre-processing** includes bringing all environmental variables to the same spatial and temporal resolutions, smoothing filters to recover spatial missing data, calculating 3–7 days composites for variables with temporally missing data and performing additional operations on data such as gradients calculations.

Specifying Habitat of ABFT. Two patterns of behaviour can be observed for ABFT: spawning and feeding [1]. In the Mediterranean Sea, according to the literature spawning takes place between middle of May and middle of July months, while feeding is between mid-July and mid-September months, in the Mediterranean Sea or the North Atlantic Ocean. The following environmental variables were identified as relevant to influencing habitat utilization [2]: Daily sea surface temperatures (SST) and chlorophyll concentration (CHL) which can be used to calculate respective gradients and fronts; bathymetry; CO_2 net Primary Production (PP); daily sea surface height anomaly (SSHa), ocean currents (eddies) and wind speed at sea surface level. Additionally, several previous research papers [2] reported the specific environmental conditions which are favoured by ABFT for spawning and feeding activities.

For spawning habitat, Bluefin tuna prefers warm waters of the Mediterranean Sea (SST in the range 20 to 25.5 °C) with increasing SST over several weeks, relatively low levels of CHL, intermediate levels of Eddy Kinetic Energy (EKE) and preferable range for SSHa. While for feeding habitat, ABFT prefer to locate in the vicinity of chlorophyll frontal features and higher levels of concentrations, wide range of SST and immediate levels of PP. These observations and analyses show that it should be possible to distinguish between feeding and spawning behaviors of ABTF when environmental variables are added to modelling.

Environmental Analysis. Our environmental analyses started with investigating visual correlation between ABFT tracks and environmental variables. It could be visually observed that some mean values of environmental variables have different ranges for spawning and feeding such mean SST (Fig. 3) and CHL (Fig. 4). Additionally, environmental variables with different ranges for spawning and feeding are SSHa, CO_2 Net PP and Eddy Kinetic Energy (not shown due to space limitation). Note that though tracks for feeding (Adriatic Sea) and spawning (the Mediterranean Sea) do not cover exactly the same area, the difference in ranges between different behaviors are consistent with other findings in the Mediterranean Sea, i.e. This is due to different behavior of ABFT (spawning and feeding) to a large extent rather than due to different areas. However, further investigation will include more tracks from the Mediterranean Sea for both spawning and feeding to confirm these early findings.

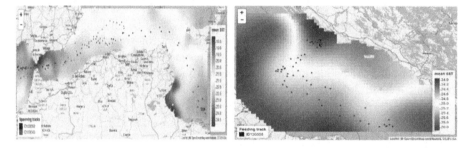

Fig. 3. Mean SST ranges for spawning (right) and feeding (left) tracks

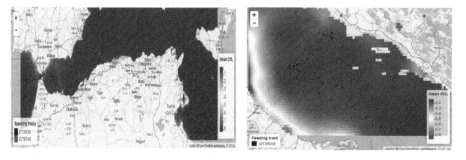

Fig. 4. Mean CHL for spawning (right) and feeding (left) tracks.

Further, the link between environmental variables and ABFT presence data will be analysed using a cluster analysis [5] and/or histogram approach. The cluster analysis is suitable for separating different behaviors that occur in distinct environments, for example feeding and spawning, or suitable and unsuitable habitats. K-means clustering can be explored for identifying the relevant thresholds for ecological variables (the most suitable for spawning), and overall environmental envelopes for feeding. When cluster analysis is used to define the relevant thresholds, the 15th and 85th percentile values can be used since they represent relatively extreme environmental boundaries while rejecting the potentially misclassified distribution tails [2]. Alternatively, a histogram approach may identify thresholds for environment variables with adding some uncertainty in the calculations due to the nature of tracking data. Since tracking devices report only where particular set of fish went, while we do not know the areas with no fish or indeed areas where other untracked fish went. We can overcome this difficulties to some extent by considering a presence/availability paradigm rather than a presence/absence model and generating potential tracks using a Null model movement paths based approach.

Habitat Modelling. Once the threshold values for environmental variables are set, the specific ecological niche of ABFT will be defined for feeding and spawning. An ecological niche model using environmental envelopes can be used to predict the daily suitability of cells within habitat for ABFT feeding and spawning on a given [0, 1] scale. The favorable habitat for each behavior are cells that meet all the suitable ranges of selected variables. This will be the next step of our services development.

Performance Evaluation. The performance evaluation can be challenging due to a small number of tracks available and observations covering only presence of fish tracked. However we can compare our potential results with findings reported in the literature and by computing the distance between the presence data and the closest favourable habitat (3-day composite) for available tracks.

2.2.2   Marine Turtle Application Scenario

Another exemplar data processing workflow which is being evaluated under the EO4wildlife platform as a proof of concept is the marine turtles application scenario. It is based on the workflow described by Pikesley et al. [3]. 21 female Olive ridley turtles are tracked between 2007 and 2010 in the south-east of the Atlantic ocean near the west-African coast [4]. The aim is to describe the observed and potential post-nesting habitat for these species in the region. This will also be important for the fishing industries in the region to become aware of areas with the presence of turtles that could potentially lead to their unnecessary bycatch. A similar approach is taken in [3], where 32 adult loggerhead turtles are tracked in the eastern part of the Atlantic. This work investigated how the predicted habitat may alter following climate change. Figure 5 depicts the workflow which is implemented within EO4wildlife's sea turtle scenario. It is based on the analysis described by Pikesley et al. in [3].

Other approaches describing the marine turtles' behaviour have also been considered and may be looked upon for further workflows in the marine turtle scenario. These workflows look at different sea turtle behaviors including: nesting activity and clutch

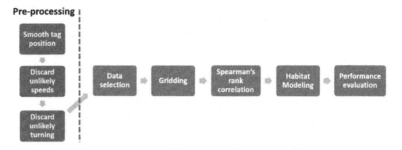

Fig. 5. Marine turtle workflow

frequency [5] and post-nesting migration and foraging behavior [6]. Habitat modelling via ecological niche modelling is one of the more systematic ways of analysing species distribution under climatic changes. Other climate change scenarios should be considered to make the causal projections of environmental variables. A Spearman's rank correlation test will then be calculated for each paired environmental variables. These environmental variables are sampled from long-term mean values at the location of track points. Twenty five tracks of adult loggerhead sea turtles are being evaluated during their post-nesting movements near the west coast of Africa. This data includes samples from Aug 2004 to Dec 2009, where in some of the turtles are tracked for a short time and some for longer periods. The considered environmental variables include: *(1) Sea Surface Temperature; (2) Bathymetry; (3) Sea surface Height (Absolute Dynamic Topography); (4) Net Primary Production; (5) Current Velocity; and 6) Eddies.* These environmental conditions were used and based on their previous reported correlations with marine turtle relocations [3, 4, 6]. Figure 6 shows the long-term mean of some of these variables that are superimposed with the species track points.

2.3 Web-Enabled Data Analytics Services

The data analytics based approaches of Sect. 2.2 are being wrapped as open web services. They have been specifically designed with fundamental capabilities that are exposed as OGC compliant WPS services [7]. This will also ease their integration in the overall SEEED big data platform architecture and increase their reusability between applications. These services have been implemented as Docker containers [8] whose instantiation is managed via the Kubernetes API. The adoption of Docker technologies ensures that the services' implementations are self-contained and their dependencies explicitly declared by means of Docker files. This is for the purpose of their invocation accordingly with respective to given input parameters to the data analytics processing algorithms. The deployment structure of such services in depicted in Fig. 7 below:

The data analytics based algorithms which are deployed in the platform primarily include mining, machine learning, data fusion and reasoning methods on marine species behaviour which correlates with geospatial and temporal trends of MetOcean fronts. The resulting open web processing services are grouped in three main categories: data pre-processing and aggregation, data mining services and high level fusion

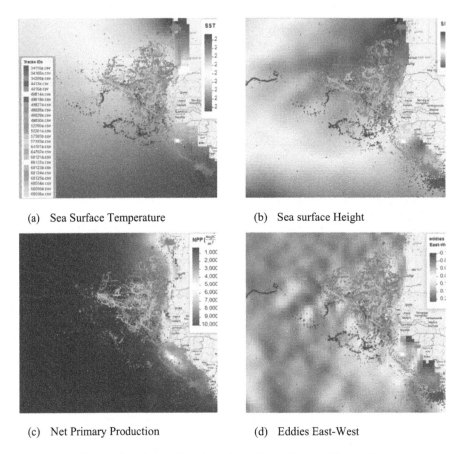

(a) Sea Surface Temperature

(b) Sea surface Height

(c) Net Primary Production

(d) Eddies East-West

Fig. 6. Superimposed tracks points with environmental variables

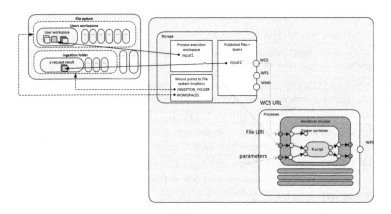

Fig. 7. Data analytics services deployment for the EO4wildlife big data platform architecture

services. The high level fusion services are those which group all the intelligent post-processing of data analytics, forecasting and reasoning through knowledge modelling.

2.4   Data Pre-processing and Aggregation

This category contains the services for the pre-processing, cleaning and aggregation of the data prior to data analytics. The pre-processing of geospatial data sets is an important step when dealing with potentially incorrect information such as non-plausible animal positions. These services allow the recognition and removal of all data elements which are clearly unrealistic given the knowledge of the domain (e.g. the animal is not capable of travelling at such velocities, or producing abrupt changes of directions or; again travelling inland). Moreover the pre-processing services allow the filling of missing data values and accommodation of different data grids using interpolations which are not directly collected and represented in the data sets. The aggregation service allows the reconciliation of data which represented with different spatial or temporal resolutions. It also provides functionalities to sample environmental observations and aggregate them into the required grid resolution for input to the niche modelling algorithms. Under this category, we also included services which process animal tracks to provide grouping of tracks in trips or gridding a number of tracks to compute and analyse species population distributions.

2.5   Data Mining Services

These services process animal tracks and satellite marine observations in order to model animals' use of space and correlate it with environmental observations. This is further subdivided in two sub-categories of services: Animal track based services and statistical environmental services. These respectively analyse animal tracks for estimating the species home range and foraging grounds; and the statistical relevance of environmental observations in modelling animals' presence.

2.6   High Level Fusion Services

This category contains services that make use of multiple data sources to better estimate animals' position, behaviour and modelling animals' habitats. This category includes the Track & Lock service which enables the estimation of submarine trajectories for animals equipped with pop-up or archival tags, Change-point Analysis and various Habitat modelling techniques.

Acknowledgements. This research is partly funded by the European Commission under H2020 Grant Agreement number 687275. We are also grateful to the European Commission for giving us access to Copernicus Satellite observation data in this project. Access to Argos satellite databases through our consortium partnership is also acknowledged.

References

1. Arrizabalaga, H., et al.: Global habitat preferences of commercially valuable tuna. Deep Sea Res. Part II **113**, 102–112 (2015)
2. Druon, J.-N., et al.: Habitat suitability of the Atlantic bluefin tuna by size class: an ecological niche approach. Prog. Oceanogr. **142**, 30–46 (2016)
3. Pikesley, S.K., et al.: Modelling the niche for a marine vertebrate: a case study incorporating behavioural plasticity, proximate threats and climate change. Ecography **38**(8), 803–812 (2015)
4. Pikesley, S.K., et al.: On the front line: integrated habitat mapping for olive ridley sea turtles in the southeast Atlantic. Divers. Distrib. **19**(12), 1518–1530 (2013)
5. Rees, A.F., Al-Kiyumi, A., Broderick, A.C., Papathanasopoulou, N., Godley, B.J.: Conservation related insights into the behaviour of the olive ridley sea turtle Lepidochelys olivacea nesting in Oman. In: Marine Ecology Progress Series, vol. 450, pp. 195–205 (2012)
6. Chambault, P., et al.: The influence of oceanographic features on the foraging behavior of the olive ridley sea turtle Lepidochelys olivacea along the Guiana coast. Prog. Oceanogr. **142**, 58–71 (2016)
7. Mueller, M., Pross, B.: OGC WPS 2.0 Interface Standard, pp. 14–65. OpenGeospatial Consortium Inc, OGC (2015)
8. Merkel, D.: Docker: lightweight Linux containers for consistent development and deployment. Linux J. **2014**(239), 2 (2014)

Water and Hydrosphere

Quick Scan Tool for Water Allocation in the Netherlands

P. J. A. Gijsbers[1,2(✉)], J. H. Baayen[2], and G. J. ter Maat[1]

[1] Department of Water Resources Management, Deltares,
P.O. Box 177, 2600 MH Delft, The Netherlands
peter.gijsbers@deltares.nl
[2] Department of Operational Water Management, Deltares,
P.O. Box 177, 2600 MH Delft, The Netherlands

Abstract. In the Netherlands, suitable water allocation decisions are required to ensure fresh water availability under dry conditions, now and in the future. A high-resolution integrated surface-and groundwater of the Netherlands, called the National Hydrological Model, exists to support water management decisions on a national scale. Given the run times of this model, it is less suited to accommodate screening of water allocation alternatives that deviate from the common practice. Therefore, policy makers and operational water managers within the Ministry of Infrastructure and Environment felt the need for a tool that can assist in the screening of alternative water allocation strategies. This Quick Scan Tool uses a coarse scale network model of the Netherlands water system to compute the water allocation pattern given water demands and boundary conditions as provided by the National Hydrological Model. To accommodate the priority based water allocation policies commonly used in the Netherlands, a lexicographic goal programming technique is used to solve the water allocation problem. The tool has been developed using RTC-Tools 2 as computation engine and Delft-FEWS as a front-end, where Delft-FEWS is also responsible for workflow and data management. This paper presents the Quick Scan Tool developed, including the mathematical techniques used and the validation of the results against the allocations computed by the National Hydrological Model.

Keywords: Water allocation · Netherlands · Quick scan tool
Goal programming

1 Introduction

1.1 Freshwater Availability in the Netherlands

The Netherlands is rich in water. In the current situation there is hardly any water scarcity, i.e. a situation in which usual consumption rates exceed the average water availability. However, the country has to cope with droughts, the natural phenomena in which there is temporarily decrease in fresh water availability, as occurred during extreme dry historical years 1976 and 2003.

© IFIP International Federation for Information Processing 2017
Published by Springer International Publishing AG 2017. All Rights Reserved
J. Hřebíček et al. (Eds.): ISESS 2017, IFIP AICT 507, pp. 97–109, 2017.
https://doi.org/10.1007/978-3-319-89935-0_9

The majority of the water system allows controlled redirection of water where most regions can be supplied from the national water system during dry periods, using the Rhine River and Meuse River as the main sources. After the Rhine and Meuse enters the Netherlands the water is distributed over the branches Waal, Nederrijn, and IJssel by means of a weir by Driel. In general, 2/3 of the inflow goes to the Waal, and 1/3 to the Nederrijn and IJssel. The IJssel supplies the Ijsselmeer and Markermeer lakes with fresh water. From the rivers and lakes, water is distributed to other parts of the country through an extensive network of ditches and canals [1].

Water is used for controlling levels, flushing and actual extractions (e.g. irrigation and drinking water). In the Netherlands there is no absolute shortage of water but a 'problem' of the right quality at the right time at the right place. Specific phenomena for the Netherlands as a low-lying country is the risk of salt water intrusion in the western part of the Netherlands; during low flow of rivers sea water enters the main water ways due to the lack of driving forces pressurizing the water supply of the western part of the Netherlands. As described above, in the north water can be stored in the IJsselmeer and Markermeer, a man-made lake (total 2000 ha), that was created in 1932 by building a large dike (the Afsluitdijk) and is fed by the River IJssel. The lake supplies the Northern provinces during summertime. Groundwater is the main water source in the elevated areas in the south and east, since these grounds cannot be reached by re-routed surface water from the rivers. Finally the islands and peninsulas in the south west have to deal with both saltwater intrusion and limited fresh water supply options due to their surrounding by salt water bodies.

Policy arrangements are in place and coordinated by the National Coordination Committee for Drought Conditions (LCW) to deal with reduced water availability conditions. Leading principle is the so-called *Verdringingsreeks*, a priority lists which puts infrastructure and nature integrity preservation purposes such as water level and water quality control (flushing) above extractions for drinking and industry water above irrigation for agriculture.

1.2 The Adaptation Challenge

Climate change scenarios provided by the Royal Netherlands Meteorological Institute [2] indicate that the Netherlands should expect both an increase in the number and extent of high flow events as well as low flow periods. It is expected that global climate change demands that various measures will be taken to guarantee the control of water levels and a supply of freshwater for the long term (at least until 2100). Socio-economic developments could raise water demands even further, beyond just climate change impacts. A quantitative assessment of both problems and solutions in collaboration with stakeholders should indicate if this expectation could come true and if yes, underpin to what extend one should expect.

In the previous phase of the policy process, the Dutch Deltaprogamme Phase 1, which ended in 2015, an adaptive pathways plan was presented to cope with droughts and water scarcity on the short term (until 2021), midterm (2050) and long term (2100). Funds were allocated for measures and on different levels: for the main water system, regional water system and for water users, that are agreed upon as implementation of the preferred pathway. For the short term it was also agreed upon to make the current system more flexible and robust by 'smart' operational water management.

1.3   The Need to Support Screening of Alternative Strategies

In 2008–2009 various Dutch institutes conducting water management research started a collaboration to jointly develop a National Hydrological Model [3]. This National Hydrological Model is a detailed integrated surface-groundwater system of the Netherlands, combining a 250×250 m grid model for groundwater (Modflow) and unsaturated zone (Metaswap) with a 8800 network elements based surface water balance and allocation model. This water allocation model uses a heuristic approach to allocate water to various prioritized purposes where the uses with high priority receive water before uses with lower priority. The National Hydrological Model is applied for policy analysis and for operational forecasting.

For the operational forecasting application, the National Hydrological Model is encapsulated in a Delft-FEWS based operational forecasting system call RWsOS-Waterbeheer [4]. Rijkswaterstaat, the Dutch National Authority responsible for the national waterways and water bodies uses RWsOS-Waterbeheer on a daily basis to produce a real-time forecast with a 10 day horizon using the National Hydrological Model. This operational system provides useful information to the National Coordination Committee for Drought Conditions to analyze the current water availability situation in the Netherlands. The Committee has the authority to change the water allocation at a national level if the drought situation is sufficient severe. For this purpose, it wants to be able to conduct what-if analysis runs such that trade-offs between different regions and sectors can be assessed when allocation patterns are changed. Since the runtime of the detailed National Hydrological Model is substantial, a need arose for a so-called Quick Scan Tool to accommodate this screening purpose. This operational tool will be referenced as the LCW-Quick Scan Tool.

In the policy analysis domain the National Hydrological Model is encapsulated in a larger modeling system called the National Water Model. The model is used for detailed policy analysis under future climate scenarios and socio-economic developments. Simulations, conducted for a 30–100 year time series targeted at a mid-term 21st century outlook (2050), take days to weeks. This makes it hard to use the model for an initial screening of interventions to address the issues that arise in terms of water supply and saline intrusion within a dynamic multi-stakeholder policy process. Also for these studies a need arose for a Quick Scan Tool that could be applied to analyze potential interventions for current or future bottlenecks in the water supply system. This policy analysis tool will be referenced as the PA-Quick Scan Tool. Once interesting interventions have been identified, they could be implemented in the National Hydrological Model of the Netherlands to conduct a detailed analysis.

1.4   Quick Scan Tool Requirements

While the two tools have different end users, they have also many similarities. The end users for the LCW-Quick Scan Tool are civil servants, namely the core members of the LCW itself. These people intend to use the tool as a preparation to the Committee meetings to investigate alternative water allocation strategies when hydrological conditions are becoming dry. Their tool needs to be based on the most recent datasets provided by RWsOS-Waterbeheer. The LCW-Quick Scan Tool must be easy and quick to use and provide insight in the current situation as well as the regional trade-off of water balance effects of alternative allocation strategies. The end users for the PA-Quick Scan Tool are Deltares experts conducting the policy analysis for different climate and socio-economic development scenarios. The input datasets for the PA-Quick Scan Tool will be 30 year time series of water demands and river discharge, provided by the National Water Model.

Both applications require a water balance model that can cope with priority based water management rules for extractions and management of lake levels. The challenge for the modeling the national Dutch water system, characterized by a high-density network of waterways, is to design a model schematization that represents the national water system with the main water delivery routes and storages appropriately while regional detail should be neglected when the issues at stake do not ask for those details. This network model has to accommodate regional trade-off analysis as well as analysis of the issues at stake, while potential interventions should transparently be facilitate in the parameterization of the model. Possible interventions can vary from changing requests (water demands for extraction and in-stream uses) to manipulation of the operating rules for the storages and modification of maximum intake capacities. To enable quick turnaround times in the analysis, all above interventions should be facilitated via a Graphical User Interface. Changing the order of water use priorities was left out of scope as reduction of water demands could be applied to accommodate analysis of the same intervention in water shortage conditions.

2   Methods and Techniques

The model underlying the Quick Scan Tool is composed of a coarse network of the Dutch water system including the major water storages, water distribution points and delivery routes to the various uses. Requests for water abstractions (agriculture, industry, drinking water, regional water systems) and instream flows for flushing are prioritized and assigned to the nodes and links in the network.

In the present section we discuss the methods and techniques used to develop a model for solving our water allocation problem.

The central design tenet of our tool is separation of concerns, i.e., implementation of conceptually disjunct functionalities in separate modules. In our case, the physical system model is kept separate from the specification of the water allocation goals. In the subsequent sections, we will discuss the methodologies underpinning the implementation of these two modules.

2.1   Modeling the Water System

The Dutch water system may be viewed as a network composed of elementary objects, such as

- storage nodes
- channel reaches
- weirs and pumping stations.

Objects of the same type share the same parameterized equations governing their dynamics. Storage nodes, for instance, are governed by the mass balance equation:

$$\frac{dV}{dt} = Q_I - Q_o \tag{1}$$

with storage volume V, inflow Q_I and outflow Q_o. This is a differential equation.

Instantaneous routing in a channel reach is governed by algebraic equations of type

$$Q_{down} = Q_{up} \tag{2}$$

with upstream inflow Q_{up} and downstream outflow Q_{down}.

Collecting the equations for all the network elements, results in a system of *differential-algebraic equations* (DAE). For the Quick Scan Tool a need was identified for a system to describe classes of model elements using DAE, and to combine instances of these classes into a network model. A modeling language that allows this is *Modelica* [5]. The Modelica objects used for the Quick Scan Tool are reaches with instantaneous routing with an extra term for a lateral flux (discharge/extraction), connection nodes for network confluences and diversions, and storage nodes.

2.2 Optimization with Prioritized Goals

The priority ordering of the control goals of the Dutch water system (the *Verdringings-reeks*) leads us to consider sequential optimization of the prioritized goals in order. In operations research, this technique is known as *lexicographic goal programming* (LGP) [6, 7]. The idea of LGP is to optimize the goal[1] functions f_i in a given order, prioritizing earlier goals over later goals. The goals are ordered by assigning each a non-negative integer priority value p_i. The goals are then solved in their priority order. Following the optimization of a goal f_i, its attainment level is fixed and added as a constraint to the optimization problem. The optimization of all following goals, in this way, will not worsen the attainment of any preceding goal. At each stage of LGP, optimization takes place within the degrees of freedom left open by the fixation of the attainment levels of the previous goals.

Solving Ordered Goals

Application of LGP to a multi-objective optimization problem results in a series of optimization problems. Let k be the priority level under consideration, and let the overall problem be constrained by the equation $g(x) \leq 0$. The k'th optimization problem is then

---

[1] Within this paper, the term *goal* and *objective* are interchangeable.

$$\min_{x} f_k(x) \text{ subject to}$$
$$g(x) \leq 0 \quad (3)$$
$$f_i(x) = \varepsilon_i \, \forall_i < k$$

with the attainment level of the ith goal

$$\varepsilon_i := f_i(x_{opt,i}) \quad (4)$$

and $x_{opt,i}$ being the optimal solution of the ith optimization problem.

LGP has been applied to decision support for the short-term operation of hydropower resources, e.g. [8], to surface water allocation, e.g. [9] and to water quality management.

Inequality Goals

In water systems, one often encounters the need to keep variables within a desired range. A channel reach is a typical case, where one aims to keep the water level within desired lower and upper bounds. It may not always be possible to keep the water level within the desired range, as in case of drought or flooding. Inequality, or range, goals are therefore an important ingredient in a multi-objective optimization framework.

Let h_i be a goal function and let $[m_i, M_i]$ be its desired range, with $m_i \in \mathbb{R} \cup \{-\infty\}$, $M_i \in \mathbb{R} \cup \{-\infty\}$ and $m_i \leq M_i$. Let k be the priority order level under consideration, and let the overall problem be constrained by the equation $g(x) \leq 0$. The k'th optimization problem is then

$$\min_{x, \delta_k} \| \delta_k \|_p \text{ subject to}$$
$$h_k(x) \geq m_k + \delta_k(\underline{h}_k - m_k)$$
$$h_k(x) \leq M_k + \delta_k(\overline{h}_k - M_k)$$
$$\delta_k \geq 0 \quad (5)$$
$$\delta_k \leq 1$$
$$g(x) \leq 0$$

with violation variable δ_k and goal function enclosure [11] $[\overline{h}_k, \overline{h}_k]$ such that $\underline{h}_k \leq h_k(x) \leq \overline{h}_k$ for all feasible x. The order $p \geq 1$ denotes the norm under consideration. One would select $p = 1$ for linear penalization, or $p = 2$ to penalize large violations disproportionately more than small ones. The concept of violation variables is illustrated in Fig. 1 (left). The goal function merely lies within its enclosure when $\delta_k = 1$, whereas the goal is fully satisfied when $\delta_k = 0$. Starting from a feasible seed value of $\delta_k = 1$, the objective is to minimize the value of δ_k.

In addition, for every $i < k$, the following constraint is added to fix the goal attainment level:

$$m_i + \delta_i(\underline{h}_i - m_i) \leq h_i(x) \leq M_i + \delta_i(\overline{h}_i - M_i) \quad (6)$$

When applying an inequality goal for every discretized time instance along the prediction horizon, the effect of an inequality goal is best described as a *soft constraint*. First, the optimizer will try to find a state trajectory that lies within the desired

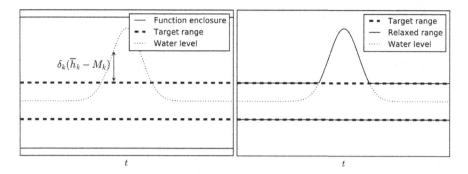

Fig. 1. Variable violation concept (left) and Relaxation of state beyond the target range (right)

range. All trajectories that lie within the range incur no penalty cost and are therefore equally preferable. If it is not possible to find a trajectory that fully lies within the desired range, the optimizer will select a trajectory that lies outside of it as little as possible. The desired range, relaxed just enough to accommodate the actual trajectory, is taken as a standard (hard) constraint for subsequent goals. This idea is illustrated in Fig. 1 (right).

LGP with inequality goals has been applied to decision support for the short-term operation of hydropower resources [8].

Multiple Goals per Priority Level
In the Quick Scan Tool, every priority level i may come with multiple goal functions $\{f_i^k\}_k$, each covering a different element of the model. These goals are assumed to be equally important, hence allowing the respective goal functions to be summed into a single objective function f_i:

$$f_i = \sum_k \bar{f}_i^k \tag{7}$$

Optimization Solver
The interior point solver IPOT [11] is used to solve the scalar optimization problems resulting from the lexicographic optimization procedure. IPOPT solves nonlinear problems, which is required for goals with order $p > 1$.

Software Suite
The techniques covered in the preceding sections are available as standard components in the environmental flow optimization software suite RTC-Tools 2.0 [7], which supports Modelica model formulations. RTC-Tools is available under a dual-licensing scheme. The open source version is available online under the terms of the GNU General Public License version 3 [12]. Precompiled binaries, source code, and documentation are available from the project website at: https://www.deltares.nl/en/software/rtc-tools/.

3   The Quick Scan Tool Application

The Quick Scan Tool application is a combination of two software products. Delft-FEWS provides the Graphical User Interface, the database and general data processing capabilities. The model component uses an internal model based on the RTC-Tools 2 model engine [7].

3.1   The Model Schematization

The Quick Scan Tool holds an internal network model for the water balance. The model, built in Modelica, is composed of model element of type branches, connection nodes, demand nodes, storages as well as boundary nodes (inflow and terminal). Each Modelica element holds its own water balance where flow enters via the 'in'-port and leaves via the 'out'-port. Lateral flows (extractions of discharges) can be applied to branches, demand nodes and storages.

The final network model schematization (Fig. 2) is the result of five collaborative design sessions with the end users. The challenge was to design a network which is as simple as possible while providing an appropriate representation of the main water system including the main water delivery routes. The network model should accommodate analysis of the issues at hand while potential interventions should be facilitated

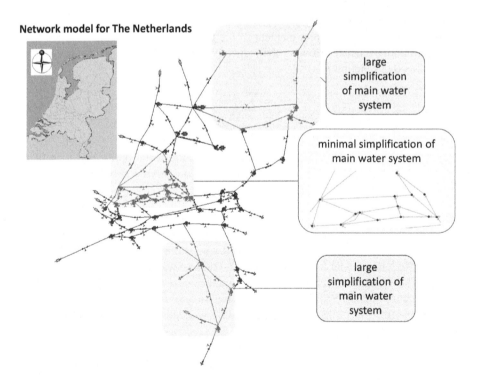

Fig. 2. QST network schematization of the main water delivery system in the Netherlands

transparently in the parameterization. The result is a schematization where areas in the north-east and in the south-east are grossly simplified compared to the actual water system as there are only few relevant water inlets. More network detail has been introduced in the west as many water delivery routes need to be analyzed in relation to saline intrusion of the most westward inlets. Capacities and management rule have been derived from the NHM.

3.2 The Work and Dataflow of the Application

The dataflow of the Quick Scan Tool is composed of the following steps:

1. acquire the input data sets (requests for extractions and flushing), river discharges and lake levels) from the National Hydrological Model
2. conduct a spatial assignment, using a coupling table, of all requests to a node or branch of the coarse network model
3. transform request by water use function to a request by priority
4. allocate the available water resources using the LGP method
5. The result is a water distribution over the network, with per element the inflow, the outflow and the lateral flux achieved. Since this lateral flux is the total flux for all extracting (and discharging) water uses functions, this flux need to be split
6. split the lateral flux into the portions allocated to each water use
7. aggregate the results by area for presentation purposes
8. compute a delivery rate percentage, broken up by water use, for presentation purposes.

Table 1 illustrates the order of priorities that is adopted in the PA-Quick Scan Tool.

Table 1. Ordering of goals as applied in the PA-Quick scan tool

Priority	Model variable	Lower bound	Upper bound
1	Lateral	Natural loss/contribution	Maximum extraction
2	Inflow	Min. capacity (physical)	Max. capacity (physical)
3	Level	Min. storage level (physical)	Max. storage level (physical)
4	Outflow	Request water level preservation	
5	Level	Min. storage (low priority)	Max. storage (low priority)
6	Lateral		Request utilities
7	Outflow	Request navigation locks	
8	Level	Min. storage (middle priority)	Max. storage (middle priority)
9	Lateral		Request rural water system
10	Level	Min. storage (high priority)	Max. storage (high priority)
11	Outflow	Request network flushing	
12	Level	Target storage level	Target storage level
13	Outflow		

The first three priorities are critical, i.e. similar to 'hard' constraints, as they intend to force the solution within the physical bounds of the water system. The remaining goals are water uses with their order prescribed by law and policies. As can be noted, the operating rules for the storages are divided in multiple goals such that lake levels can drop to meet high priority water demands. Target storage levels should be attained if sufficient water is available within the system. The goal with the last priority intends to minimize the outflow in a selected set of branches such that the water remains in the main rivers and only enters the water inlets to meet local water demands. All canal outlets that do not conduct a water delivery function to downstream uses should be included in this selection.

For in-stream flow requests (e.g. flushing and navigation locks), each new goal is identified by taking the maximum of all in-stream water use flow requests up till the priority at stake. For the lateral fluxes the LGP approach intends to squeeze the solution space with each priority such that the end result is at the desired request if the system is not under water shortage. The equations in the Fig. 3 indicate that the requested lateral fluxes for different water uses need to be stacked to obtain a series of goals that squeeze the solution space in the ordering of goals.

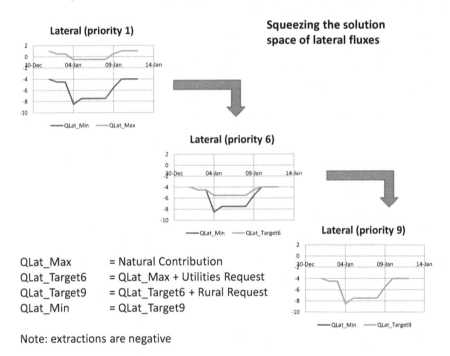

Fig. 3. Solution space squeezing and associated goal stacking for lateral fluxes

Once the LGP has completed its computation, the resulting flows need to be split according to the different water uses. For any in-stream flow request the request is fulfilled if the realized flow is larger than the request. For lateral flux requests, the delivery per water use needs to be based on the 'peeling off' the realized lateral flux by order of priority and allocating the remaining flux to a specific water use up to the request.

4   Validation of Model Results

The QST-model has been validated by comparison of the water allocation against the water allocation result computed in the detailed National Hydrological Model (NHM). Differences may partly be explained by the fact that the NHM uses a heuristic water allocation method. Important items checked are the distribution of the main river inflows, the behavior of the lakes, the flushing on the outlets and the main inlets for the rural area in the west. Figure 4 illustrates the water shortage for the flushing goal at the driest moment in the 30 year historical series, flushing being the goal with the lowest priority. In general the QST model results in fewer shortages. During the driest period, the difference with the NHM model result is 2–6% at this location, while most other network elements show hardly any difference. Also lake levels follow the same pattern between the two models if the QST is to lower the volume in order to meet in-stream flow requests.

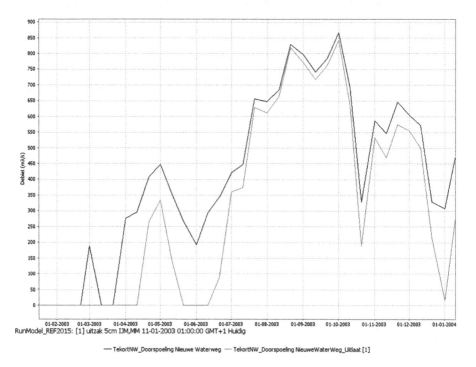

Fig. 4. Comparison of shortage at sea outlet between NHM (NieuweWaterWeg) and QST-model (NieuweWaterWeg_uitlaat)

5   Discussion and Conclusions

Within the Netherlands, a need arose at the national level to supplement the current high-resolution National Hydrological Model with a water allocation model to enable the screening of national water allocation decisions for their regional trade-offs. This paper illustrates how a so-called Quick Scan Tool has been developed for this purpose. The tool is composed of a water allocation model engine and a software component that offers a front end as well as pre and post-processing capabilities. The water allocation model is built with the RTC-Tools 2 software framework using a lexicographic goal programming approach to priority based water allocation rules. In the pilot version Excel was chosen as the front end offering pre and postprocessing capabilities. Data processing required extensive handling of lookup tables while conducting the necessary aggregations from detailed source data to coarse model input to aggregated output for presentation on areal scale. The prototype application showed that RTC-Tools 2 was meeting the model needs, while Excel was not the appropriate data processing platform. In the final version, the Delft-FEWS software framework was chosen as a data processing and visualization platform. This platform offered much more insight to debug the data flow from aggregating source data to model input data to the aggregation of results.

The resulting Quick Scan Tool has been validated against the detailed National Hydrological Model to confirm that the tool outcomes are sufficiently similar to this accepted model to support the policy process. The visualization capabilities Delft-FEWS, with its map based flow animations and graphs, were very beneficial while discussing model setup and validation results with the water management experts of Rijkswaterstaat, the governmental body who initiated the development of the tool.

At the time of writing, the first actual use of the tool is put in practice with preliminary analysis of a combination of additional flushing and water extraction requests under future conditions for the assessment years 2050 and 2085.

In the near term, functional extensions are foreseen using meta-relations to transform reduced river flows into impacts on salinity rates and navigation depths.

RTC-Tools 2 and Delft-FEWS are software platforms which initially were developed for near real-time water system operations. Based on this Quick Scan Tool, it can be concluded that the flexibility and customization capabilities of these platforms also allow development of decision support tools for strategic planning processes.

References

1. Haasnoot, M., van Deursen, W., Guillaume, J., Kwakkel, J., van Beek, E., Middelkoop, H.: Fit for purpose? Building and evaluating a fast, integrated model for exploring water policy pathways. Environ. Model Softw. **60**, 99–120 (2015). https://doi.org/10.1016/j.envsoft.2014.05.020
2. van den Hurk, B., Siegmund, P., Klein Tank, A. (eds.) KNMI 2014: Climate Change scenarios for the 21st Century – A Netherlands perspective KNMI scientific report WR 2014-01. http://bibliotheek.knmi.nl/knmipubWR/WR2014-01.pdf
3. De Lange, W., Prinsen, G., Hoogewoud, J., Veldhuizen, A., Verkaik, J., Oude Essink, G., van Walsum, P., Delsman, J., Hunink, J., Massop, H., Kroon, T.: An operational, multi-scale, multi-model system for consensus-based, integrated water management and policy analysis: the Netherlands Hydrological Instrument. Environ. Model Softw. **59**, 98–108 (2014). https://doi.org/10.1016/j.envsoft.2014.05.009
4. Weerts, A.H., Prinsen, G., Patzke, S., van Verseveld, W.J., Berger, H., Kroon, T.: Operational water resources forecasting system for the Netherlands. In: AGU Fall Meeting (2011). https://doi.org/10.13140/rg.2.2.17612.82568

5. Elmqvist, H.: Modelica – a unified object-oriented language for physical systems modeling. Simul. Practice Theory **5**(6), 32 (1997). https://doi.org/10.1016/s0928-4869(97)84257-7
6. Collette, Y., Siarry, P.: Multiobjective Optimization: Principles and Case Studies. Springer, Heidelberg (2003). https://doi.org/10.1007/978-3-662-08883-8
7. Baayen, J.H., den Toom, M., Gijsbers, P., van Duin, O., Vreeken, D.J., Schwanenberg, D.: Control and multi-objective convex optimization of environmental flow networks under predictive uncertainty. Environ. Model. Softw. (Submitted)
8. Eschenbach, E.A., Magee, T., Zagona, E., Goranflo, M., Shane, R.: Goal programming decision support system for multiobjective operation of reservoir systems. J. Water Resour. Plan. Manag. **127**(2), 108–120 (2001). https://doi.org/10.1061/(asce)0733-9496(2001)127:2(108)
9. McGregor, M.J., Dent, J.B.: An application of lexicographic goal programming to resolve the allocation of water from the Rakaia River (New Zealand). Agric. Syst. **41**(3), 349–367 (1993). https://doi.org/10.1016/0308-521x(93)90009-q
10. Moore, R.E., Bierbaum, F.: Methods and Applications of Interval Analysis, vol. 2. SIAM, Philadelphia (1979)
11. Wächter, A., Biegler, L.T.: On the implementation of an interior-point filter line-search algorithm for large-scale nonlinear programming. Math. Program. **106**(1), 25–57 (2006). https://doi.org/10.1007/s10107-004-0559-y
12. GNU General Public License. http://www.gnu.org/licenses/gpl.html

Information System as a Tool for Marine Spatial Planning: The SmartSea Vision and Prototype

Ari Jolma[1]([✉]) [iD], Ville Karvinen[1], Markku Viitasalo[1],
Riikka Venesjärvi[2], and Jari Haapala[3]

[1] Marine Research Centre, Finnish Environment Institute, Helsinki, Finland
ari.jolma@ymparisto.fi
[2] Fisheries and Environmental Management Group, University of Helsinki, Kotka, Finland
[3] Marine Research Unit, Finnish Meteorological Institute, Helsinki, Finland

Abstract. Planning the use of marine areas requires support in allocating space to particular activities, assessing impacts and cumulative effects of activities, and generic decision making. The SmartSea project studies the Gulf of Bothnia, the northernmost arm of the Baltic Sea, as resource for sustainable growth. One objective of the project is to provide an open source and open access toolbox for marine spatial planning. Here we present a vision for the toolbox and an initial prototype. The vision is based on a model of information system as a meeting point of users, information providers, and tasks. A central technical requirement for the system was found to be a data model and related database of spatial planning and a programmable map service. An initial prototype of the system exists comprising a database, data browser/editor, dynamic tile map service, web mapping application, and extensions for a desktop GIS.

Keywords: Marine spatial planning · Planning support system
Information environment · Web mapping · Dynamic tile service · WMTS

1 Introduction

Marine Spatial Planning (MSP) is a recently coined term for "a public process of analyzing and allocating the spatial and temporal distribution of human activities in marine areas to achieve ecological, economic, and social objectives that are usually specified through a political process" [1]. The aim and challenge of MSP is to manage both increasing and competing sectoral needs, especially for energy and natural resources, and increasing interest in maintaining biodiversity and conservation of nature [2]. The European Union (EU) has recently (2014) issued a Maritime Spatial Planning Framework Directive, which sets minimum common requirements for national MSP. EU has also launched a website for sharing experience and expertise in MSP[1].

---

[1] http://www.msp-platform.eu.

© IFIP International Federation for Information Processing 2017
Published by Springer International Publishing AG 2017. All Rights Reserved
J. Hřebíček et al. (Eds.): ISESS 2017, IFIP AICT 507, pp. 110–123, 2017.
https://doi.org/10.1007/978-3-319-89935-0_10

Effective MSP should be integrated and bring industries, such as fisheries, aquaculture, tourism, marine biotechnology, ocean or offshore energy, seabed mining, and commercial marine transportation, together to make coordinated decisions about how to use the sea and marine resources sustainably [1]. Some of these industries are strictly in competition, while some may co-exist in same space. There are also complex interactions between marine, coastal, and terrestrial industries and environment.

Several plans concerning sea areas have been carried out or are in progress in Europe. Jones et al. [2] describe 12 cases that were studied in the EU-FP7 project MES-MA. Stelzenmüller et al. [3] introduce a framework for monitoring and evaluation of spatially managed areas (SMAs), which was tested on nine of these case studies. Katsanevakis et al. [4] introduce and analyzes ecosystem based marine spatial management as a holistic approach that could be supported by MSP.

Stelzenmüller et al. [5] reviewed software tools that could have potential to support MSP and then developed a set of prototype tools to support MSP. They defined three categories of tasks that a practical MSP tool should support: (i) allocating space to particular activities, (ii) assessing impacts and cumulative effects of activities, and (iii) generic decision support. Zoning (partitioning the planning region into zones that are designed to allow or prohibit certain activities) is a popular method for managing both spatial interaction and cumulative effects [6]. However, in marine areas boundaries of zones are difficult to identify and enforce [5]. Also, zoning may result in a sectoral approach, which has been criticized [2].

Geodesign denotes a stated aim of developing plans, that is, synthesizing new geospatial data, with software tools [7]. Collaborative decision-making and networking is often emphasized in the development of geodesign tools [8–10]. For example, online tools like MarineMap[2] and SeaSketch[3] allow user participation and proposing of solutions, which can be compared. Merrifield et al. [8] describe a spatial decision support system that enables stake-holder participation in designing Marine Protected Areas (MPAs) and Janssen et al. [9] describe a method and a case of collaborative marine spatial planning involving the use of a decision support tool.

SmartSea is a research project (2015–2018), which aims to provide science-based guidance and new innovations for sustainable use of the marine resources of Finland. Finland is a Baltic Sea country and most of its foreign trade takes place by it. Finland is relatively poor on domestic energy sources and the shallow coastal waters of the Baltic Sea present an opportunity to develop offshore wind power. Due to its history, closedness, and current pressures, the Baltic Sea is a unique, fragile, and threatened sea area. Its environmental problems are, for example, eutrophication, lack of oxygen in the bottom layers, and the accumulation of environmental toxicants. The species diversity of the Baltic Sea is very low compared to oceans or lakes and rivers. Brackish water, young geological age of the basin, and the lack of certain habitats, such as tidal zone, cause the low biodiversity.

---

[2] www.marinemap.org.
[3] www.seasketch.org.

The SmartSea project will focus on Gulf of Bothnia (GoB), the northernmost arm of the Baltic Sea. GoB is divided into exclusive economic zones of Finland and Sweden. It is still a relatively undeveloped sea area with an area of 117 000 km^2.

The aim of this paper is to present the vision for the SmartSea MSP toolbox and describe its first prototype. The MSP toolbox will build on and be free and open source software and provide open access to existing and new information resources and tools.

2   SmartSea MSP Toolbox: The Context

The data that will provide input to marine spatial planning in GoB is extensive. A large amount of useful data already exists and a large portion of that is already openly available either as web mapping sites and/or downloadable datasets. The data is usually developed and maintained by national and international institutes. Especially, the Baltic Marine Environment Protection Commission (HELCOM), an intergovernmental cooperation body, collects, maintains, and provides a significant database on various aspects of the Baltic Sea. The data can broadly be divided into designated areas and boundaries; physical, chemical, biological, and ecological data describing the sea areas and species living there; and data about human activities.

An important data collection effort regarding the management of Finnish coasts and seas is the collaborative Finnish Inventory Programme for the Underwater Marine Environment (VELMU), where a large amount of data about underwater environment (e.g. abundance of keystone species and locations fish nursery grounds) has been collected since 2004. In VELMU, species specific data is extracted from the observations, such as underwater videos, and organized into geospatial layers, which are further used for species distribution modeling and other purposes. VELMU data is published on a web-mapping platform[4].

Other examples of data that is available or that is being collected and developed for the project are wind conditions[5], areas of importance for fisheries (surveys are being done by the Natural Resources Institute Finland), climate scenarios (developed by the Swedish Meteorological and Hydrological Institute), and the current and projected future oceanographic conditions (modeling and simulations carried out by the Finnish Meteorological Institute).

2.1   Spatial Data Infrastructure

Spatial Data Infrastructure (SDI) is a framework in which geographic data and metadata is made available for users and tools. When a connection between spatial data and its users is or is not a SDI is a debatable question but several characteristics has been given by researchers and practitioners. These include the use of specific technologies, such as the Internet, standards for data exchange and storage, policies for openness and other issues, and services for software applications and humans. The concept of Coastal/

---

[4] http://paikkatieto.ymparisto.fi/velmu.

[5] http://www.tuuliatlas.fi/en/index.html is a website based on the wind data. It provides maps of average wind speed and estimated wind power production.

Marine SDI has been studied and promoted by the Global Spatial Data Infrastructure Association (GSDI) and the recently established Open Geospatial Consortium (OGC) Marine Domain Working Group.

The public SDI in Finland is based on INSPIRE (an EU SDI initiative) and implemented for example as a generic catalog[6], a generic data browser[7], and services maintained by individual institutes. A good example of what even a private individual can do with open marine data is the website aaltopoiju.fi, which presents current and historical meteorological and oceanographic data on a map interface.

2.2 Collaborative Modeling

MSP requires collaborative modeling because its aim is to bring together relevant information from several sectors, and biological, geological, and oceanographic knowledge needs be integrated with information about human drivers. At each sector modeling is needed to produce data that is comprehensive and/or further developed/computed from the observation data. At the planning stage these data need to be integrated, which again requires modeling.

In SmartSea, the project partners bring in geological, oceanographic, biological, social, and economic models. The NEMO-Nordic ocean modeling framework [11] will be used to obtain water temperature, salinity, mean circulation, sea level, and ice extent scenarios in one nautical mile resolution. Simulations will be based on existing data from years 1980–2010 and the future conditions will be based on climate scenarios for the years 2030–2060.

3   An Information System for MSP

MSP is a series of undertakings by planners and eventually decision makers to organize human activities on a sea area. We shall call the planners and decision makers as the 'users' of the information system for MSP. Goals of MSP comprise conflict minimization, ensuring viability of businesses, maintaining sustainability of the marine environment, and achieving maximal social benefits. Users need data, information, and knowledge together with social values, criteria, and goals. We shall call these the 'materials' of the information system. The users obtain the materials from data providers, science community, and various stakeholders, who we shall collectively call 'providers'.

The information environment (Fig. 1) has been defined [12] as the aggregate of individuals, organizations, or systems that collect, process, or disseminate information; and the information itself. The users' information environment dictates how well they can carry out their planning and decision making tasks. The state-of-the-art information environment in MSP is multifaceted: use of diverse Internet sources, official organizational data channels, elicitation of expert knowledge and stakeholder values, and personal efforts. Organization of these materials for planning, so that they can be used

---

[6] http://www.paikkatietohakemisto.fi.
[7] http://www.paikkatietoikkuna.fi.

together in personal or organization information systems or software tools depends on they being in suitable formats. Otherwise manual data conversions and/or processing is required. Use of specific planning method tools usually requires lengthy data collection and preprocessing efforts. The private or local information environment can also greatly differ from the information environment shared among national, and especially international, MSP.

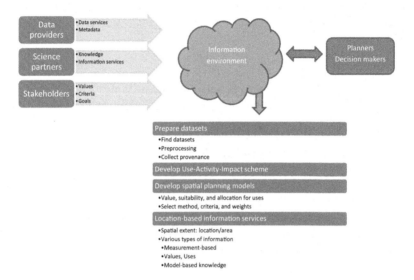

Fig. 1. Information environment as a place where data and information from providers become available for users with needs.

The promises and goals of spatial data infrastructures, such as the European INSPIRE, has been multiple [13]: datasets are collected and kept at one location, where it originates or where it can be maintained most effectively; different data can be combined seamlessly together; data can be obtained at varying scales and levels, depending on the type of investigation at hand; and information about availability, usability, and constraints of data is easily available. While there has been progress towards these goals, it is still a challenge to bring existing data into MSP information environment due to reasons such as data size and format; and lack of suitable data or other service.

Typically, MSP requires new, specific datasets to be developed. These can be original datasets obtained by field research, or created with models of natural systems or human preferences. We see challenges in bringing these into the MSP information environment due to semantic problems created by differences in the user and provider communities, data interpretation requirements, and the level of collaboration required.

There are typically several software systems available or in operation in an information environment. Software systems need, in order to work efficiently, interoperability, which may take various forms and is one of the aspects of software architecture. MSP is, like planning in general, an activity where information is continuously added and processed until the result is satisfactory. The information environment is unbounded in this sense. Thus flexibility towards new information sources, and support for provenance become key properties of the overall system.

4   A Vision for the SmartSea MSP Toolbox

MSP is a process that implements risk-averse ecosystem-based management of coastal and marine areas into practice, and enables integrated, forward-looking and consistent decision-making [1, 5]. In addition, it is an instrument whereby relevant stakeholder groups can be involved in a transparent manner. In MSP, planners assess the cumulative effects of human pressures and seek to make the use of marine resources more sustainable and proactively minimize the conflicts between sectors. SmartSea aims is to provide information to MSP and to develop scientifically sound tools for risk analysis and decision-making.

Gulf of Bothnia, the initial spatial context of the MSP toolbox spans six administrative regions in Finland. Regions are the first administrative division below the country itself. A region has a large autonomy in spatial planning, which adds a dimension to the overall national MSP.

Traditionally, MSP is based on static environmental data. However, considering ongoing climate change, any long-term plans should consider projected changes in the environmental parameters. In the GoB, the most apparent changes will be the increasing sea temperature, reducing ice cover, and decreasing salinity. All these will have considerable impacts on marine biota from plankton to fish species but they will also have an impact on fish farming and other marine related businesses and their possibilities.

The suitability of an off-shore location for activities depends on oceanographic, like wave height, sea level, sea surface temperature, and ice loads and geological conditions, like seabed substrate. A desirable feature of an MSP toolbox is thus to be able to consider return periods of extreme events and their characteristics.

The fundamental requirements for the SmartSea MSP toolbox have been identified as supporting identifying what could and what should not be done in various areas of the region, what would be the value and impacts of the activities, and where specific activities should be placed. These involve collection, analysis, and integration of spatial data that is relevant to possible uses of sea areas, information about gained benefits and ecological impacts of activities, and a consideration for shared use of areas.

Generic requirements for the SmartSea MSP toolbox are visualization of spatial data, both independently and as overlays to detect spatial competition. Modeling can be partially offline but for ad hoc type of queries and plans interactive use of some models will probably be needed. Design capabilities are needed for creating plans. Supporting collaborative and participatory planning requires tools for analyzing competing plans, capabilities for shared use, and visualization.

In a previous project[8] we developed a demonstration MSP tool. The tool was based on a workflow, where pressures from human activities and the current environmental

---

[8] Transboundary tools for spatial planning and conservation of the Gulf of Finland (TOPCONS) http://www.merikotka.fi/topcons/.

state were first coded on spatial rasters of the planning region. Second, the competing plans were devised and their local and spatially distributed impacts were computed and stored as compatible rasters. In the third and final step, valuation weights were computed for impacts and the plans could be ranked based on a resulting single indicator value for each plan. The local and spatial impact and valuation computations were based on models implemented as Bayesian Networks. The tool was implemented as a QGIS (community developed free and open source GIS)[9] plugin.

5   Components of the SmartSea MSP Toolbox

The SmartSea MSP toolbox is planned as a distributed application with one server and two types of clients. A work-in-progress setup of services has been developed on a server computer in a cloud infrastructure. The server hosts a database and services that build on it. The database comprises spatial data and data supporting the planning process. The services can provide data for desktop software such as QGIS and for applications running in a web browser. A simple web browser application for visualizing sectoral values, zoning plans, and competition was developed. Its core functionality is based on a WMTS service, which can dynamically compute spatial layers from existing layers based on simple rules. A goal is to be able to describe the logic of computing the value and impacts of, stimulating, allowing, and/or denying activities in areas as functions of the characteristics of those areas and activities as a set of sequentially applied rules.

The source code for the toolbox is available at github[10].

5.1   The Database

The database is implemented on a RDBMS (PostgreSQL+PostGIS) installation in addition to files in filesystem and it consists of three parts: the tool, the data catalog, and the datasets.

The tool part is based on a data model for planning, which consists of core classes Plan, Impact, Layer, and Rule (See Fig. 2). A *plan* is a comprehensive allocation of zones in the planning region. A zone is assumed to have a designed use, which is a realization of a designed use class, which may comprise several activities. An activity should be a well-defined description of a single enterprise or a ban of such[11]. Thus it is possible to compute both the benefits and the negative impacts of a use for an area. It is clear that the composition of this kind of uses is a large task in itself.

An (environmental) *impact* is something that an activity causes. The activity – impact mapping is done via an environmental pressure as the EU Marine Strategy Framework Directive instructs. In the quantitative assessment, an attempt is made to determine numerically the probabilities of different pressures and the likely extent of the losses under a particular pressure. Several alternatives can be used to define the probability

---

[9] http://qgis.org.

[10] https://github.com/ajolma/SmartSeaMSPTool.

[11] The description may, depending on what kind of MSP policy is adopted, include temporal and other conditions and thus be quite complex in the end.

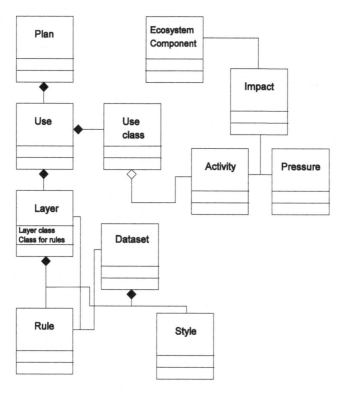

Fig. 2. A diagram of important classes and their relationships in the prototype MSP toolbox, see the text for explanations.

distributions attached to the pressures. These include, for example, statistical datasets, experimental data, modeling outputs, and expert knowledge. Expert assessments of relationships between activities, pressures, and impacts on ecosystem components have been obtained in other projects[12]. Structured expert judgement can be integrated into modeling approaches to improve predictions, and it can be particularly valuable if no relevant published data can be found. Further, as managers might believe that models do not result in better decisions than those supported by the opinions of experts, expert-informed modeling can contribute to bridging the gap between researchers and decision-makers [14, 15]. Experts give estimates for what pressures various activities create, what is their spatial range, how serious the impact of the generated pressure is to a range of ecological components, and how strongly the experts believe in their estimates. This data may be enough (assuming additional expert data is available, e.g., to account for cumulative impacts) to compute impacts of zoning proposals. However, this part of the project is still ongoing. Comprehensiveness of this kind of data is of course an issue since both the range of possible activities and ecological components is very wide. Based

---

[12] These are mostly projects done within the HELCOM collaboration and include projects HOLAS II, TAPAS, and MARISPLAN.

on the obtained results from the impact assessment, a decision analysis between the demand for marine resources and conservation of nature values will be performed.

A *layer* is a spatial dataset, prepared by the system as a 20 m × 20 m raster covering the planning region[13]. A layer represents an attribute (the layer class) associated with a use and it is obtained from a SDI or computed from datasets or other layers using *rules*. A rule is a mathematical expression for computing a layer from datasets or other layers. A rule consists of several elementary rules, which are combined in a specific way (the rule class). Rules can be combined exclusively, i.e., locations are deemed unsuitable for a use because of its characteristics; inclusively, i.e. locations are deemed suitable for some use because of its characteristics; multiplicatively, i.e., the value at a location is computed by multiplying values representing characteristics of it; or additively, i.e., the value at a location is computed by summing values representing characteristics of it.

A layer can depict the value or benefit obtained from a specific activity or use, depict areas designated for a specific use or the suitability of locations for the use, or it can describe the impact of a use. The style is information how a dataset or a layer is visualized.

The data catalog is a simple database of metadata and provenance information that describes the datasets used by the planning tool. Its purpose is to document the origin of data and the workflow that was applied to prepare the data for the tool. The MSP toolbox will contain several datasets obtained and/or derived both from the national SDI and from research projects within the SmartSea umbrella and elsewhere. In order to retain this information and possibly reapply the workflow in the case of new versions of the original data come available, the provenance of the datasets must be kept.

5.2 The Web Services

Since the data is maintained on a server in a cloud, it is natural to provide an API to it as web services besides the native database interface and raw file download. The web services are divided into non-spatial and spatial services. The spatial services are OGC services and the non-spatial services are custom services providing JSON for applications and HTML for human users.

The spatial data services focus on WMTS (a raster tile service), which is ideal for creating responsive web mapping applications that need to cover large areas but also provide detailed views (using graduated zoom levels). In this project we defined a use case, where WMTS should provide layers that could be computed from several original layers using several rules and optionally the user should be able to edit the rules online. This clearly is not feasible using pre-computed layers. It also requires the concept of user in the service providing code so that it can use the correct parameter values for the rules when preparing tiles to the respective users. The current solution skips the capability document (thus the list of the available layers is not provided and the client program of the service must know how the layer names are constructed) but is able to compute layers very flexibly. The computation is based on coded layer names, where the code specifies the plan, the use, the type of layer, and the rules to use.

---

[13] It is possible to create such a raster layer or input for one from a vector layer on-the-fly using rasterization.

Another type of spatial service is one that is used to provide information from a selected location/area. The client sends the selected location or polygon area as WKT and information that tells, which (spatial) data to use for the reply, and based on those, the service computes a reply.

The non-spatial data services has two purposes: (1) to provide a document for applications, which lists the plans, uses, layers, and rules, that is, data to populate the GUI and also to construct WMTS requests (the layer names); and (2) to provide an interface to construct the plans, uses, and rules. The importance and complexity of this API was a finding for us in this research. The API is still developing since the database is developing but the overall structure is already quite stable. The construct API is a simple CRUD (create, read, update, delete) API and currently focuses on direct interactive use by humans and thus HTML. With this API the user is able to manage the objects in the database and their relations. The relationships are either associations (for example a use class is associated with one or more activities), compositions (for example a plan is composed of uses), or multiplicity (for example a use can have only one use class but multiple associated layers). The document API is there for client applications to obtain the tree-like data structure of plans, uses in them, layers in the uses, and the rules that are used to create the layers.

The web services were developed as Perl modules using the Starman web server[14] and Perl modules related to it. The object–relational mapping is done using DBIx::Class[15]. The Perl Data Language (PDL) is used for raster computations and GDAL is used for spatial data access and management.

5.3   The Web Mapping Application

The focus of the user oriented development in the project has so far been on the web mapping application. The application is written in JavaScript using JQuery and Open-Layers libraries and it is according to the MVC design pattern[16]. The application presents the user an interface that relies of the plan–use–layer–rule model of the planning problem (See Fig. 3). Additionally, the GUI contains a select location/area – information tool.

The plan–use–layer–rule model upends the traditional GIS interface paradigm, which guides the user to construct maps from input data layers, which are presented. Here the result (the zoning or spatial allocation of uses) is what is presented to the user. Initially the whole region allocated for all uses and the paradigm is that the rules reduce (or add) the areas for uses.

The select location/area tool allows the user to select a location with a click or draw a polygon with a sequence of clicks. Once defined, the location or the polygon (as WKT) is sent to a server along with other selections made in the GUI, and the server reply is shown to the user. Currently this tool is a proof-of-concept only.

---

[14] http://search.cpan.org/dist/Starman.

[15] http://www.dbix-class.org.

[16] The code from https://alexatnet.com/articles/model-view-controller-mvc-javascript was used as a boilerplate.

Fig. 3. A screenshot of the web mapping application prototype showing a selected plan (SmartSea), a visualized and selected computed allocation of areas for offshore wind farms (essentially a suggestion for manual design), and a dialog box allowing the user to edit one rule.

5.4   The Desktop Tool

Some of the tasks in MSP are unstructured and require generic tools capable of analysis and providing decision support. A desktop GIS is a typical generic tool for tasks that involve a spatial dimension. SmartSea project will develop open and freely available tools and QGIS was selected as the desktop tool for the SmartSea MSP toolbox. The goal is to develop a QGIS plugin, which integrates with the other components of the toolbox. Currently very little has been done to further this task.

Python is the main programming language for developing QGIS plugins and it is relatively easy to create one. In an initial test it was possible with a few lines of Python code to download the main GUI document in JSON from the web service and construct a tree of layers in the QGIS layer list in its GUI and download the WMTS layers. This is the first requirement since the WMTS server does not provide a layer list to choose from.

6   Discussion

MSP, despite being a novel topic, is a variation of the general theme of spatial planning. Numerous examples of how spatial planning can be supported with information technology exist.

Our vision for the SmartSea MSP toolbox is based on examples found in literature and our previous work. The toolbox will be based on an existing SDI but specific support needs to be built for representing zoning plans, impact computations, and negotiating between competing plans and sectoral needs.

The development of the application has so far been carried out completely within the research institute and all discussions related to its requirements and design have been among researchers. A public seminar organized by the Ministry of Environment announcing MSP in Finland was held in November 2016. The seminar revealed that only the administrative structure of MSP has been decided upon. The SmartSea project is a key endeavor towards supporting the actual planning. A series of workshops and collaboration will be organized for transferring knowledge and tools from the research community to the planning community.

INSPIRE is the directive defining the European SDI. One of its principles is that "it should be possible to combine seamless spatial information from different sources... and share it with many users and applications" [16]. In our case the identified requirement to be able to dynamically compose planning proposals required us to download data from their sources to a dedicated server, which took care of the composition. This was in some cases necessary since the data was always not available as a service, or it needed some preprocessing. In those cases where the data was available as a service, moving it was considered a too fragile or slow operation to be a part of the MSP toolbox.

In a client–server environment for geospatial computing the map that is shown to the user can be rendered in the server or in the client from data sent by the server. If the data is dynamically changing, or, as in our case, the user has a great control over how the map is composed, the map needs to be generated dynamically. It is interesting that in the case of server side dynamically generated maps are usually considered only in relation to WMS and specifically not WMTS, which is seen as a set of statically rendered tiles[17]. In our case creating a plugin system for dynamically rendering raster tiles was easy since the WMTS code was developed by the main author.

MSP should be carried out with tools, which take account of uncertainties and are supported by a strong scientific background. We hope that the SmartSea MSP toolbox can eventually help to solve and structure complex and multidisciplinary problems, integrate knowledge and uncertainty, and communicate risks. Our approach identifies and quantifies explicit decisions among different objectives and represents spatial possibilities for sustainable blue growth. This work will be further developed to a decision analytic tool, which will provide a scientifically sound and consistent valuation method for evidence-based MSP.

---

[17] See for example the topic "Dynamically drawn map services" in the Penn State University course GEOG 585 at https://www.e-education.psu.edu/geog585/node/697.

Acknowledgements. We wish to acknowledge the funding received from the Strategic Research Council at Academy of Finland for the project SmartSea - Gulf of Bothnia as Resource for Sustainable Growth (Grant No: 292 985). We also acknowledge the editors of these proceedings and the anonymous reviewers for their work. Their comments significantly improved this paper.

References

1. Ehler, C., Douvere, F.: Marine Spatial Planning: a step-by-step approach toward ecosystem-based management, Intergovernmental Oceanographic Commission Manual and Guides No. 53, UNESCO, Paris, France (2011). http://unesdoc.unesco.org/images/0018/001865/186559e.pdf
2. Jones, P.J.S., Lieberknecht, L.M., Qiu, W.: Marine spatial planning in reality: introduction to case studies and discussion of findings. Mar. Policy **71**, 256–264 (2016). https://doi.org/10.1016/j.marpol.2016.04.026
3. Stelzenmüller, V., Breen, P., Stamford, T., Thomsen, F., Badalamenti, F., Borja, A., Buhl-Mortensen, L., Carlstöm, J., D'Anna, G., Dankers, N., Degraer, S., Dujin, M., Fiorentino, F., Galparsoro, I., Giakoumi, S., Gristina, M., Johnson, K., Jones, P.J.S., Katsanevakis, S., Knittweism, L., Kyriazi, Z., Pipitone, C., Piwowarczyk, J., Rabaut, M., Kirk Sørensen, T., van Dalfsen, J., Vassilopoulou, V., Vega Fernández, T., Vincx, M., Vöge, S., Weber, A., Wijkmark, N., Jak, R., Qiu, W., ter Hofstede, R.: Monitoring and evaluation of spatially managed areas: a generic framework for implementation of ecosystem based marine management and its application. Mar. Policy **37**, 149–164 (2013). https://doi.org/10.1016/j.marpol.2012.04.012
4. Katsanevakis, S., Stelzenmüller, V., South, A., Kirk Sørensen, T., Jones, P.J.S., Kerr, S., Badalamenti, F., Anagnostou, C., Breen, P., Chust, G., D'Anna, G., Duin, M., Filatova, T., Fiorentino, F., Hulsman, H., Johnson, K., Karageorgis, A.P., Krönke, I., Mirto, S., Pipitone, C., Portelli, S., Qiu, W., Reiss, H., Sakellariou, D., Salomidi, M., van Hoof, L., Vassilopoulou, V., Vega Fernández, T., Vöge, S., Weber, A., Zenetos, A., ter Hofstede, R.: Ecosystem-based marine spatial management: review of concepts, policies, tools, and critical issues. Ocean Coast. Manag. **54**, 807–820 (2011). https://doi.org/10.1016/j.ocecoaman.2011.09.002
5. Stelzenmüller, V., Lee, J., South, A., Foden, J., Rogers, S.I.: Practical tools to support marine spatial planning: a review and some prototype tools. Mar. Policy **37**, 149–164 (2013). https://doi.org/10.1016/j.marpol.2012.05.038
6. Halpern, B.S., McLeod, K.L., Rosenberg, A.A., Crowder, L.B.: Managing for cumulative impacts in ecosystem-based management through ocean zoning. Ocean Coast. Manag. **51**, 203–211 (2008). https://doi.org/10.1016/j.ocecoaman.2007.08.002
7. Dangermond, J.: GIS: Designing our Future. ArcNews (2009)
8. Mitsova, D., Wissinger, F., Esnard, A.-M., Shankar, R., Gies, P.: A collaborative geospatial shoreline inventory tool to guide coastal development and habitat conservation. ISPRS Int. J. Geo-Inf. **2**, 385–404 (2013). https://doi.org/10.3390/ijgi2020385
9. Merrifield, M.S., McClintock, W., Burt, C., Fox, E., Serpa, P., Steinback, C., Gleason, M.: MarineMap: a web-based platform for collaborative marine protected area planning. Ocean Coast. Manag. **74**, 67–76 (2013). https://doi.org/10.1016/j.ocecoaman.2012.06.011
10. Janssen, R., Arciniegas, G., Alexander, K.A.: Decision support tools for collaborative marine spatial planning: identifying potential sites for tidal energy devices around the Mull of Kintyre, Scotland. J. Environ. Plan. Manag. **58**(4), 719–737 (2015). https://doi.org/10.1080/09640568.2014.887561

11. Hordoir, R., Axell, L., Löptien, U., Dietze, H., Kuznetsov, I.: Influence of sea level rise on the dynamics of salt inflows in the Baltic Sea. J. Geophys. Res. Oceans **120**, 6653–6668 (2015). https://doi.org/10.1002/2014jc010642

12. Dictionary of Military and Associated Terms. S.v. "information environment". http://www.thefreedictionary.com/information+environment. Accessed 6 Mar 2017

13. Directive 2007/2/EC of the European Parliament and of the Council of 14 March 2007 establishing an Infrastructure for Spatial Information in the European Community (INSPIRE). http://eur-lex.europa.eu/eli/dir/2007/2/oj. Accessed 6 Mar 2017

14. Addison, P.F., Rumpff, L., Bau, S.S., Carey, J.M., Chee, Y.E., Jarrad, F.C., McBride, M.F., Burgman, M.A.: Practical solutions for making models indispensable in conservation decision-making. Divers. Distrib. **19**, 490–502 (2013). https://doi.org/10.1111/ddi.12054

15. Aizpurua, O., Cantú-Salazar, L., San Martin, G., Biver, G., Brotons, L., Titeux, N.: Reconciling expert judgement and habitat suitability models as tools for guiding sampling of threatened species. J. Appl. Ecol. **52**, 1608–1616 (2015). https://doi.org/10.1111/1365-2664.12515

16. INSPIRE what if? Call for position papers for an ad-hoc workshop at the OGC TC meeting in Delft 23 March 2017. http://inspire.ec.europa.eu/sites/default/files/inspire_what_if._call_for_position_papers.pdf. Accessed 28 Mar 2017

Mobile Crowd Sensing of Water Level to Improve Flood Forecasting in Small Drainage Areas

Simon Burkard[✉], Frank Fuchs-Kittowski[iD], and Anna O'Faolain de Bhroithe

HTW Berlin, Berlin, Germany
{s.burkard,frank.fuchs-kittowski,
Anna.OFaolaindeBhroithe}@htw-berlin.de

Abstract. Flood forecasting is particularly difficult and uncertain for small drainage basins. One reason for this is due to inadequate temporal and spatial hydrological input variables for model-based flood predictions. Incorporating additional information collected by volunteers with the help of their smartphones can improve flood forecasting systems. Data collected in this way is often referred to VGI data (*Volunteered Geographic Information* data). This paper discusses how this information can be incorporated into a flood forecasting system to support flood management in small drainage basins on the basis of mobile VGI data. It therefore outlines the main functional components involved in such a VGI-based flood forecasting platform while presenting the component for mobile data acquisition (mobile sensing) in more detail. In this context, relevant measurement variables are first introduced and then suitable methods for recording these data with mobile devices are described. The focus of the paper lies on discussing various methods for measuring the water level using inbuilt smartphone sensors. For this purpose, three different image-based methods for measuring the water level at the banks of small rivers using a mobile device and the inbuilt orientation and camera sensors are explained in detail. It is shown that performing the measurements with the user's help via appropriate user interaction and utilising known structures at the measuring points results in a rather robust image-based measurement of the water level. A preliminary evaluation of the methods under ideal conditions found that the developed measurement techniques can achieve both an accuracy and precision of less than 1 cm.

Keywords: Flood forecasting · Crowd sourcing · Mobile sensing · VGI
Water level

1 Improvement of Flood Forecasting in Small Drainage Basins Through Citizen Participation in Data Collection

Floods are one of the natural hazards that directly threaten the civilian population, regularly causing extensive material damage and costing many lives. Damage as a result of flooding has increased considerably in recent decades [1]. There is a very high

© IFIP International Federation for Information Processing 2017
Published by Springer International Publishing AG 2017. All Rights Reserved
J. Hřebíček et al. (Eds.): ISESS 2017, IFIP AICT 507, pp. 124–138, 2017.
https://doi.org/10.1007/978-3-319-89935-0_11

probability that this trend will continue and the intensity of floods will continue to increase [2]. This is due in particular to the increase in short-term, local flood events. In order to reduce the harmful impact of floods and to be able to take targeted protective measures, disaster relief forces and the affected population must be informed early and reliably of imminent threats through forecasting and early warning systems [3].

Hydrological and hydraulic forecasting models are used as the basis for decision-making for disaster relief measures. Model-based flood predictions are, however, often uncertain and error-prone. The reasons for this include uncertainties on the model and precipitation forecasts, as well as inadequate temporal and spatial hydrological input variables. Predictions are especially difficult for small bodies of water since very fast responses of the basin often occur, leaving very little warning time. There is often insufficient official data for these exceptional situations. However, extra information, such as additional water level measurements along a river, can be used to extend these important data sets and update the forecast models in order to reduce the uncertainties on the forecast [4].

Such additional hydrological data can also be voluntarily recorded and provided by citizens using the inbuilt sensors in their own devices (e.g., smartphones, tablets, etc.) via *mobile crowdsourcing and sensing* [5]. Location-specific data collected in this way is often referred to VGI data (*Volunteered Geographic Information* data) [6–8]. By incorporating VGI data, the amount of spatial and temporal input information for the prediction models can be increased, reducing uncertainties and therefore improving the predictions of flood forecasting systems. In addition, involving the population in the process raises awareness of flood hazards and citizens can actively contribute to improving flood forecasts and reducing flood damage [9].

In this article, methods for measuring the water level using smartphone sensors (mobile sensing) are presented. It is also discussed how this information can be incorporated into a flood forecasting system to support flood management in small drainage basins on the basis of mobile VGI data. The article is structured as follows: after an overview of the current status of the science and technology (Sect. 2), the conceptual architecture of such a VGI-based flood management platform is outlined and the functional components involved are described (Sect. 3). The component for mobile data acquisition (mobile sensing) is then presented in more detail. For this purpose, relevant measurement variables are first introduced and then suitable methods for recording these data with mobile devices are described (Sect. 4). Various methods for measuring the water level using inbuilt smartphone sensors are explained in detail and evaluated (Sect. 5). A final summary provides on outlook on future developments within the framework of the presented platform (Sect. 6).

2   Current Status of Research and Technology

2.1   Mobile Crowdsourcing and VGI in Disaster Management

Mobile crowdsourcing refers to the use of mobile devices to collect data as well as to coordinate volunteers involved in the data collection. The core concept is that ordinary citizens collect and share information about themselves or the surrounding environment using their own mobile devices. The participants contribute the data voluntarily, for their own benefit or for the benefit of a community. No task-specific special hardware is used, only normal mobile devices available on the mass market such as smartphones and tablets [5]. The required data is recorded using the built-in sensors in the mobile devices (mobile sensing). Volunteers can be proactively prompted to collect data, and their tasks can be coordinated (mobile tasking [10, 11]). The recorded data are known as VGI data [6] – usually geospatial measurements that are also often time-referenced.

Closely related to the notion of mobile crowdsourcing are concepts such as VGI [6–8], Public Participatory Geographic Information Systems (PPGIS [12]), and Participatory Sensing (PS [13]). Common to all concepts is the voluntary and collaborative nature of the data collection and data sharing process.

There are already many different crowdsourcing applications, especially in nature conservation, environmental protection, and disaster management [5]. In disaster management, mobile crowdsourcing can be used to great effect both during and after a catastrophe [11, 14]. For example, in a catastrophe, residents and rescue and emergency personnel can gather information about the current situation in the affected area so that aid and rescue workers can target the most critical zones. After a natural disaster (such as a flood, storm, or heavy rain), finding, documenting, and evaluating damage (such as fallen trees, flooded roads and paths, fallen power masts) is an important task that allows the limited resources to be deployed more quickly and accurately to begin clean-up and repairs. It also allows assessments of the total damage to be up-to-date and comprehensive [15].

Mobile crowdsourcing applications have already been successfully used in disaster situations, but the accuracy and quality of the information has been of minor importance. VGI data have been used, for example, during floods [16–18], wildfires [19], earthquakes [20], and even severe storms [21]. In the system presented in Sect. 3, VGI data is utilised, among other things, to update and validate forecast models. Therefore, there is a stronger focus on the accuracy and quality of the data recorded using mobile data collection methods.

2.2 Flow Measurement and Mobile Sensing for Flood Forecasting

Hydrological data which can be used to measure the water flow are of particular importance for flood prediction. Flow measurements in hydrometry are mostly indirect and rely on known flow cross sections and measurements of the flow speed and the water level [22]. Approaches to automatic flow measurement from images already exist. These are based on remote sensing methods which can be used to estimate the level of a body of water using aerial photographs [23], for example. Another example is the use of permanently installed cameras for the image-based measurement of the water level using markers or staff gauges [24–27]. The idea to have passers-by read off the water level at staff gauges was also successfully tested. The reading was sent via SMS [28] or an app [9] to a data server for evaluation.

The collection of data by mobile users does not necessarily involve manual data input, e.g., in a form, but can be automated by using the sensors already present in mobile devices. The term "mobile sensing" has been established to describe the acquisition and generation of data using the sensors installed in or connected to peoples' own mobile devices [5]. A mobile sensing application specifically for automatic image-based gauge monitoring has been developed by [29]. However, special staff gauges are required for robust measurements, as well as certain other factors such as sufficient brightness and a small distance between the camera and the indicator.

The sensor-based determination of water level lines by mobile devices can be facilitated by the knowledge of the device's exact position in 3D space. Therefore, research in the areas of mobile augmented reality and mobile 3D tracking for position determination is also of interest. These areas of research are still relatively new, but there are already several approaches and technologies for the image-based estimation of a device's own position in 3D space that are more accurate than the localisation provided by GPS signals [30]. There are currently no known existing applications that use such technologies for VGI-based determination of hydrological data.

While there are many mobile applications for information about water levels (e.g., Pegel[1], Pegelstand[2], Pegel-Online[3], Pegelstände[4], Meine Pegel[5]), very few mobile apps exist that allow users to measure the water level. For example, the MAGUN research project has developed mobile applications for the acquisition of current water levels and also historical high water marks [31], but these are not in widespread use. The goal of the WeSenseIt project is to design and test a complete platform for citizen-based documentation and monitoring of water levels and floods [32, 33]. Smartphones as well as various other cost-effective sensors are used for the measurement of hydrological data such as water levels and flow speeds in the project. Information on the robustness and quality of the measured data is, however, not documented. The measured data is also not intended to be directly embedded in a prediction model, i.e., the integration of the data (or the entire process) into a concrete operational scenario – such as flood management – is missing.

3   Conceptual Architecture of a VGI-Based Prediction System

In this section, the conceptual architecture of VGI-based flood forecasting system is proposed and described. This architecture is based on concepts of generic architectures for crowdsourcing [34] and crowdtasking applications [10], and has been specifically adapted for VGI-based flood forecasting systems. The functional components are illustrated in Fig. 1. In addition to an adapted classical flood forecasting system and central flood management software, the platform includes components for mobile tasking and mobile sensing.

---

[1] https://play.google.com/store/apps/details?id=de.posts.Pegel.

[2] https://play.google.com/store/apps/details?id=info.pegelstand.pegelstandnoebasic.

[3] https://play.google.com/store/apps/details?id=org.cirrus.mobi.pegel.

[4] https://play.google.com/store/apps/details?id=com.lifestream_creations.pegelmelder.

[5] https://play.google.com/store/apps/details?id=de.hochwasserzentralen.app&hl=de.

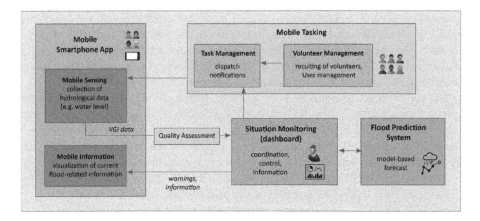

Fig. 1. Conceptual architecture of a VGI-based flood forecasting platform

3.1 Mobile Tasking and Mobile Smartphone Application

Volunteers should have the possibility to independently decide if, and in what form, they wish to record and provide measurements. With the help of smartphone notifications, volunteers can be additionally instructed to record and send data at certain times (mobile tasking). These notifications can be created and sent manually, but can also be sent automatically when coupled with an early warning system. For example, volunteers can be automatically notified and instructed to collect data when heavy rain and potential floods are forecast.

Hydrological data are collected via a smartphone application (mobile sensing) in the drainage basin(s) indicated in the flood forecast. The measured data can then be sent over the mobile network or a WLAN connection to a central server for further processing.

Ideally, the measurements should be made using the integrated sensors in mobile devices. These sensors include GPS sensors for rough positioning (accuracy up to 5–10 m) and tilt sensors (compass, accelerometers, magnetometers) for determining the viewing direction of the device as well as the integrated camera used to record images. The use of these sensors, in particular for the measurement of water levels, is explained in more detail in Sects. 4 and 5.

In addition to the ability to record and send user-generated data, the mobile application is also intended to provide users with relevant information about floods. With the help of flood risk maps and the representation of current water levels in the area, the user is kept informed about flood risks and the current flood situation.

3.2 Model-Assisted Flood Forecasting System

A problem of user-generated data is that the quality and accuracy of the data can vary considerably. Before the measured hydrological data are finally made available to the forecast system as input variables, an automatic quality and plausibility check of the incoming data is necessary. By means of a spatial and temporal comparison of the VGI data sets, erroneous input data (outliers) can be identified and eliminated. Based on a classical model-assisted prediction system, the system can subsequently supplement or validate the underlying model using the available VGI data in order to provide an improved flood forecast.

3.3 Situation Monitoring

A web-based user interface (dashboard) is used for situation monitoring. Incoming VGI data and flood forecasts are processed and appropriately visualised to enable an effective assessment of the flood situation. Besides the map-based representations and listings of current and historical VGI measurements and photographs, the hydrographs for the floods as well as official meteorological data such as radar images for precipitation forecasting are also displayed.

4 Mobile Sensing – Relevant Variables and Methods

With the help of the mobile smartphone application, certain parameters can be measured and made available by the volunteers. Relevant parameters are shown in Fig. 2. The selection of parameters that should ultimately be measured results from a consideration of the additional gain provided for the hydrological prediction model versus the technical feasibility of robust mobile measurement methods for these parameters.

Measurement Parameters	Manual Measurement	Automatic Measurement
Water Level	Estimate / reading of staff gauge	IMU-based or image-based detection (with/without user interaction)
Flow Velocity	Rough estimate („slow", „fast")	Image-based estimation of flow velocity
Precipitation Intensity	Rough estimate („no rain", „little rain", „heavy rain")	Image-based estimation
Depth of Snow	Rough estimate	
Photos & Videos (water levels, flood damages, etc.)	Capturing of images & videos via smartphone camera; location determination via GPS sensor	

Fig. 2. Relevant parameters and possible measurement methods

The water level and the flow speed of the water at defined measuring points are decisive inputs for the hydrological forecasting system as both parameters are relevant for the direct measurement of the flow rate. However, a meaningful measurement of the flow rate from smartphone measurements alone is very difficult. A rough estimate from the mobile user of the flow rate of the body of water is possible (e.g., "flow is very fast" or "flow is very slow") but an indication of the speed without a physical unit (e.g., meters per second) is not a useful input variable for the prediction system. An image-based estimate of the flow using a smartphone camera would be conceivable [35]. However, such an approach is quite complex and requires a fixed position from which to record as well as ideal external recording conditions (e.g., ideal lighting conditions). Additionally, it is only possible to roughly estimate the flow speed at the water's surface, but not the speed of currents below the surface. For the mobile measurement of the water level, however, there are several approaches. These techniques are presented in detail in Sect. 5.

Other relevant input parameters for the model are the current precipitation intensity and the depth of snow. However, robust automatic measurement methods using smartphones are difficult to implement for these parameters. Although an image-based estimate of the current rain intensity is possible [36], the result is often erroneous. Instead, a manual estimate of the intensity of precipitation can be provided directly by the volunteer. This rough estimate of the intensity ("no rain", "light rain", "heavy rain"), combined with the location of the user as determined by the GPS signal, is helpful for improving the localisation of strong precipitation cells.

The depth of snow can also be estimated by the volunteer. A rough knowledge of the snow conditions with high spatial resolution facilitates an estimate of the volume of water contained within the snow cover in the drainage basin. This estimate can be of great benefit as an input parameter for the prediction model.

In addition to these quantitatively measurable values, photographs and short video clips taken with the smartphone camera can be included. These recordings can be displayed on the dashboard map and aid the relief forces in assessing and documenting the flood situation in the field. Measured water levels can be augmented with additional images. This function can also be used to locate floods and flood damage. Volunteers can, for example, monitor critical locations in case of a flood threat to see if a flood has actually occurred and if so, take pictures to document and share its extent.

5   Methods for Water Level Measurement

The main focus of the development of the mobile sensing component is the implementation of suitable methods for measuring the water level with a smartphone. Measurements of the water level are not taken at arbitrary locations, but at fixed measuring points (e.g., bridges). There are several possible methods available to measure the water level with a smartphone, see Fig. 3. The functionality and suitability of these methods will be described in more detail in the following section. The focus of the current discussion is the presentation and evaluation of the methods for semi-automatic image-based measurements.

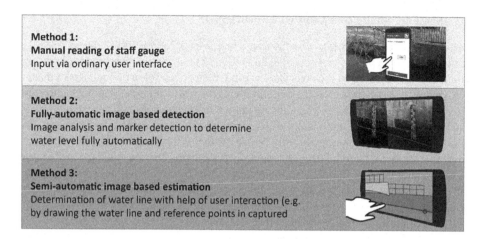

Method 1:
Manual reading of staff gauge
Input via ordinary user interface

Method 2:
Fully-automatic image based detection
Image analysis and marker detection to determine
water level fully automatically

Method 3:
Semi-automatic image based estimation
Determination of water line with help of user interaction (e.g.
by drawing the water line and reference points in captured

Fig. 3. Options for mobile water level measurement

5.1 Manual Reading of Staff Gauges

In the simplest case, the water level can be measured by simply reading it from an existing calibrated staff gauge and entering the value into the smartphone application via a classic interface (e.g., slider or text input field). This method is quite robust. It is independent of the smartphone sensor and is also possible under unfavourable lighting and weather conditions. However, visible and accessible staff gauges that have been calibrated and installed at the measuring points are a prerequisite for this method.

5.2 Fully Automatic Image-Based Water Level Measurement

Another option is a fully automatic image-based measurement of the water level. The general idea is that, after taking a photograph from a more variable position, an image analysis algorithm automatically determines the water level from the picture without further input from the user. A prerequisite for this method is the presence of an appropriate marker. This can be an easily-visible staff gauge or other artificial marker. The area of the marker still visible above the water line can be determined by means of classical image or text recognition algorithms in order to determine the water line and thus the water level. As the appearance of the markers is known in advance, the recognition algorithms can be specially trained and adapted for this particular application using test images.

Under ideal conditions, such a fully automatic procedure facilitates high-accuracy measurements, but the method is not always sufficiently robust and is often error-prone. The marker is often not sufficiently visible or the water line not sufficiently pronounced due to general light conditions (e.g., shadows or darkness) or close-by structures (e.g., walls with uneven surfaces). Other structures are often more prominent in the photograph and interfere with the algorithms' recognition of the marker or water line.

5.3   Semi-automatic Image-Based Measurement

Performing the measurements with the user's help via appropriate user interaction (e.g., drawing reference points on the image) and utilising known structures at the measuring points (e.g., a building on the river bank) results in a rather robust image-based measurement of the water level. As the measurements are made at predefined points and the flow cross section at these points must be known in advance of the flow calculation, it can be assumed that the dimensions of surrounding structures at these location are also known, e.g., the height and width of a bridge railing or the height of a wall beside the river relative to the riverbed (the zero-point of the gauge). This knowledge can be used in the development of the measurement method. In the following subsections, three different methods to measure the water level using the camera and orientation sensors of a smartphone, assuming the parameters mentioned above are known, are presented. The three variants are roughly sketched in Fig. 4.

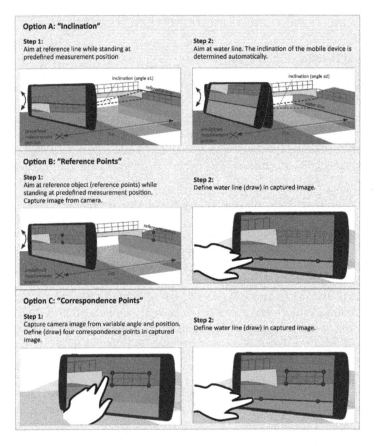

Fig. 4. Methods for semi-automatic image-based water level measurement

Variant A – Inclination. The general idea of this variant is that the inclination of the device with respect to a predefined reference line on the opposite bank of the river and the current water level is measured with the aid of the smartphone's rotational sensors (accelerometer and gyroscope). If the measurement is always preformed at a fixed measuring point, the current water level can be determined. A requirement for the procedure is that the reference line must be parallel to the horizontal water line and in a plane orthogonal to the water surface. Quay walls or boundary walls or railings are usually suitable for this purpose. The measuring point should be parallel to the reference line on the opposite side of the river. A horizontal line is overlaid in real time on the camera image. The user first aligns this displayed line with actual reference line by rotating the phone and confirming once both lines coincide. In the second step, the user performs an analogous process, this time aligning the displayed line with the water line. If the height of the reference line relative to the river bed (the zero level point) is known along with the orthogonal distance between the measuring point and the reference line, the water level can be calculated using trigonometry.

Variant B – Reference Points. This variant also assumes that the measurement is made from a fixed point. Additionally – analogous to variant A – a reference object or at least two reference points with a known position relative to the measuring point must be present on the opposite side of the river.

The position (3D coordinates) of the reference points are defined with respect to a predefined position of the smartphone camera (camera coordinate system) at the measuring point. The camera projection matrix (an intrinsic parameter of the camera) is used to calculate a projection of the points onto the camera image. This projection is displayed over the camera image. In calculating the projection, no rotation is taken into account, i.e., the identity matrix is defined as a fixed orientation. The orientation sensors are not used in this variant.

The user rotates the smartphone in the first step until the projected reference points are directly aligned with the actual reference points in the image. In this way, the rotation matrix of the device is forced fixed to be the identity matrix (i.e., zero rotation). From this camera position, the user then takes a high-resolution photograph. In the second step, the user indicates the water line in the photograph. This can be done, for example, by moving two points around on the picture, which when taken together, define the water line. The water level can then be derived in a simple manner given a knowledge of the position of the measuring point with respect to the reference points and the river bed (zero level point) and with the requirement that the water line and the reference points lie in the same plane.

Variant C – Correspondence Points. This last variant is based on the general idea that the measuring position can be determined if the user draws at least four points on the image that correspond to known reference points. In contrast to the former two variants, no fixed measuring position is required for this method. The user can take a photograph from any position provided that the defined reference points are located within the field of view of the camera. The chosen reference points must lie in the same plane as the water line on the opposite side of the river bank, as in the previous variants. Furthermore, it is assumed that the distances between the each of the reference points and the zero level point (river bed) are known. Following a manual selection by the user of the reference points in the photograph, a homographic relationship can be determined between the camera image plane P1 and the plane P2 on the opposite side of the river in which the reference points lie. In the second step, the water line is additionally drawn on the image by the user, that is to say in the plane P1, and this line can be projected onto P2 using the known homography. In this way, the water level can be directly determined in the coordinate system of P2.

5.4   Evaluation

The three variants for measuring the water level were implemented in a demo application for the Android platform. With this prototype, it was possible to test the accuracy and precision achieved by each method when measurements were taken under ideal conditions.

To perform the measurements, reference lines or a reference object (dimensions: 150 cm × 55 cm) as well as a fictitious water level were defined on a vertical wall in order to simulate an ideal measuring site on a small river. The imaginary water level was drawn at 95 cm above the ground (defined as the zero point). The water level was measured with each of the three methods using a Galaxy S4 (GT-I9515) as a test mobile device. For each method, the measurement was repeated 20 times. For variants A and B, which both require a fixed measuring point, the measurements were performed at a distance of 300 cm from the reference object. For variant B, a camera height of 150 cm was also defined. For variant C, the distance between the measuring point and the reference object varied from about 200 cm to 400 cm, and the viewing angle varied up to ± 45°. The results of the test measurements are shown in Fig. 5.

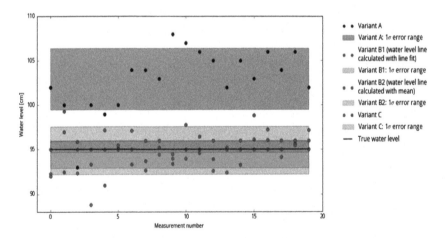

Fig. 5.   Results of the different measurement methods

The data sets corresponding to the different measurement variants are shown in different colours. The individual data points are represented by the coloured dots and the 1σ error range about the mean for each variant is shown by the filled areas. The results are also tabulated in Table 1.

Table 1. Results of the different measurement methods

Variant	A	B1	B2	C
Mean [cm]	102.95 ± 3.44	94.47 ± 1.51	94.88 ± 2.69	95.35 ± 0.67

It can be seen that Variant A consistently overestimates the water level. This is the most inaccurate method, and with the largest errors, also the most imprecise. Variants B and C determine the water level relatively accurately and the mean values of the data sets agree with the true water level within the calculated errors. Variant C achieves the highest precision of all the tested methods with a standard deviation of less than 1 cm. This variant also allows the greatest flexibility as the measuring point is not fixed. However, the measurements take longer to perform than with variant A or B as all four correspondence points must be input manually by the user. Variants A and B may there-fore be preferred if a quick measurement is important. It should be noted that the above results were achieved in an ideal environment. Under real conditions, appropriate refer-ence objects may only be available with certain limitations (e.g., the plane in which a reference object lies may not be completely identical to the plane in the water line is measured), introducing larger inaccuracies.

6 Conclusion and Outlook

In this article, methods for measuring the water level using the sensors integrated in smartphones (mobile sensing) have been presented. It has been described how mobile VGI data can be incorporated into a flood forecasting system to support flood manage-ment in small drainage basins. The use of such mobile techniques for measuring the water level or recording snow depth and precipitation intensity increases the density of available hydrological and meteorological data and can thus improve the accuracy of flood forecasts.

It has been shown that image-based measurement methods can be developed to determine the actual water level to within a few centimetres by using the built-in orientation and camera sensors in common mobile devices. The presented evaluation reveals that such high accuracies can be realised under ideal conditions. The chal-lenging task will be to achieve equally satisfying results when transferring the presented measurement techniques into real-world environments. In real-world situa-tions, further conditions and parameters have to be taken into account when performing measurements using the discussed techniques. An essential premise will be finding and surveying suitable measurement locations meeting the aforementioned requirements of the measurement methods (e.g., suitable reference objects, acces-sible fixed measurement positions, definable flow cross sections etc.). In addition, the identification and marking of such reference points and measurement positions as well as the usability and user friendliness of the mobile app will be an important role for the success of the mobile sensing methods. Only if the instructions and exact measurement procedures are clearly and unambiguously comprehensible to all user groups can the complex measurement methods be executed successfully.

In the next steps, the feasibility of the methods will therefore be tested more intensively under real-life conditions at selected locations along small rivers. Following this, a pilot phase involving a larger number of potential users will allow the evaluation of the proposed flood forecasting platform along with the general feasibility and efficiency of the VGI approach within the scope of flood management. Only after such field tests are complete, can the accuracy and efficiency of the presented water level measurement methods be evaluated conclusively.

References

1. Müller, U.: Hochwasserrisikomanagement - Theorie und Praxis. Vieweg+Teubner, Wiesbaden (2010)
2. Neumayer, E., Barthel, F.: Normalizing economic loss from natural disasters - a global analysis. Global Environ. Change **21**, 13–24 (2011)
3. Kundzewicz, Z.W.: Floods - lessons about early warning systems. In: Late Lessons from Early Warnings - Science, Precaution, Innovation. European Environment Agency, EEA Report, No. 1/2013, pp. 347–368 (2013)
4. Blöschl, G.: Flood warning - on the value of local information. Int. J. River Basin Manag. **6**(1), 41–50 (2008). https://doi.org/10.1080/15715124.2008.9635336
5. Fuchs-Kittowski, F.: Mobiles crowdsourcing und sensing. WISU **43**(9), 1031–1038 (2014)
6. Goodchild, M.F.: Citizens as voluntary sensors - spatial data infrastructure in the world of web 2.0. Int. J. Spatial Data Infrastruct. Res. **2**, 24–32 (2007)
7. Alcarria, R., Iturrioz, T.: Volunteered geographic information system design - project and participation guidelines. Int. J. Geo-Inf. **5**(5), 108 (2016). https://doi.org/10.3390/ijgi5070108
8. See, L., et al.: Crowdsourcing, citizen science or volunteered geographic information - the current state of crowdsourced geographic information. Int. J. Geo-Inf. **5**(5), 55 (2016). https://doi.org/10.3390/ijgi5050055
9. Fuchs-Kittowski, F., Bartusch, S., Pfützner, B., Fischer, F.: Mobile crowdsourcing of water level data. In: Wohlgemuth, V., Fuchs-Kittowski, F., Wittmann, J. (eds.) International Conference Environmental Information and Communication Technologies (EnviroInfo 2016), pp. 233–240. Shaker, Aachen (2016). ISBN 978-3-8440-4687-8
10. Neubauer, G., Nowak, A., Jager, B., Kloyber, C., Flachberger, C., Foitik, G., Schimak, G.: Crowdtasking – a new concept for volunteer management in disaster relief. In: Hřebíček, J., Schimak, G., Kubásek, M., Rizzoli, Andrea E. (eds.) ISESS 2013. IAICT, vol. 413, pp. 345–356. Springer, Heidelberg (2013). https://doi.org/10.1007/978-3-642-41151-9_33
11. Middelhoff, M., Widera, A., van den Berg, R., Hellingrath, B., Auferbauer, D., Pielorz, J., Havlik, D.: Crowdsourcing and crowdtasking in crisis management - lessons learned from a field experiment simulating a flooding in city of the Hague. In: International Conference on Information and Communication Technologies for Disaster Management (ICT-DM 2016) (2016)
12. Sieber, R.: Public participation geographic information systems: a literature review and framework. Ann. Assoc. Am. Geogr. **96**, 491–507 (2006)
13. Burke, J., Estrin, D., Hansen, M., Ramanathan, N., Reddy, S., Srivastava, M.B.: Participatory sensing. In: Workshop on World-Sensor-Web (WSW 2006): Mobile Device Centric Sensor Networks and Applications, pp. 117–134 (2006)

14. Schimak, G., Havlik, H., Pielorz, J.: Crowdsourcing in crisis and disaster management – challenges and considerations. In: Denzer, R., Argent, R.M., Schimak, G., Hřebíček, J. (eds.) ISESS 2015, vol. 448, pp. 56–70. Springer, Heidelberg (2015). https://doi.org/10.1007/978-3-319-15994-2_5

15. Abecker, A., Braun, S., Kazakos, W., Zacharias, V.: Participatory sensing for nature conservation and environment protection. In: Arndt, H.-K., Knetsch, G., Pillmann, W. (eds.) EnviroInfo 2012, pp. 393–401. Shaker, Aachen (2012). ISBN: 978-3-8440-1248-4

16. Kaewkitipong, L., Chen, C., Ractham, P.: Lessons learned from the use of social media in combating a crisis - a case study of 2011 Thailand fodding disaster. In: International Conference on Information Systems (ICIS 2012), pp. 1–17 (2012)

17. De Longueville, B., Annoni, A., Schade, S., Ostlaender, N., Whitmore, C.: Digital earth's nervous system for crisis events - real-time sensor web enablement of volunteered geographic information. Int. J. Digit. Earth 3(3), 242–259 (2010). https://doi.org/10.1080/17538947.2010.484869

18. Poser, K., Dransch, D.: Volunteered geographic information for disaster management with application to rapid flood damage estimation. Geomatica 64, 89–98 (2010)

19. Goodchild, M.F., Glennon, J.A.: Crowdsourcing geographic information for disaster response - a research frontier. Int. J. Digit. Earth 3(3), 231–241 (2010). https://doi.org/10.1080/17538941003759255

20. Yates, D., Paquette, S.: Emergency knowledge management and social media technologies - a case study of the 2010 Haitian earthquake. Int. J. Inf. Manag. 31, 6–13 (2011)

21. Huang, C.-M., Chan, E., Hyder, A.: Web 2.0 and internet social networking: a new tool for disaster management? - lessons from Taiwan. BMC Med. Inform. Decis. Making 10(1), 57 (2010). https://doi.org/10.1186/1472-6947-10-57

22. Herschy, R.W.: Streamflow Measurement, 3rd edn. CRC Press, Reading (2008)

23. Smith, L.C., Pavelsky, T.M.: Estimation of river discharge, propagation speed, and hydraulic geometry from space: Lena River, Siberia. Water Resour. Res. 44(3) (2008). https://doi.org/10.1029/2007wr006133

24. Iwahashi, M., Udomsiri, S., Imai, Y., Fukuma, S.: Water level detection for river surveillance utilizing JP2K wavelet transform. In: IEEE Asia-Pacific Conference on Circuits and Systems, Proceedings (APCCAS 2006), pp. 1741–1744 (2006)

25. Kim, Y., Park, H., Lee, C., Kim, D., Seo, M.: Development of a cloud-based image water level gauge development of river eye system. INPRA 2, 22–29 (2014)

26. Lo, S.W., Wu, J.H., Lin, F.P., Hsu, C.H.: Visual sensing for urban flood monitoring. Sensors 15(8), 20006–20029 (2015). https://doi.org/10.3390/s150820006

27. Royem, A.A., Mui, C.K., Fuka, D.R., Walter, M.T.: Technical note: proposing a low-tech, affordable, accurate stream stage monitoring system. Trans. ASABE 55, 2237–2242 (2012)

28. Lowry, C.S., Fienen, M.N.: CrowdHydrology: crowdsourcing hydrologic data and engaging citizen scientists. GroundWater 51, 151–156 (2013)

29. KISTERS: Einfach smart - App für Pegelmessung auf Knopfdruck. https://www.kisters.de/fileadmin/user_upload/Wasser/Produkte/WISKI/Produktblaetter/MobileWaterTracker_de_mail.pdf

30. Amin, D., Govilkar, S.: Comparative study of augmented reality SDK'S. Int. J. Comput. Sci. Appl. (IJCSA) 5(1), 11–26 (2015)

31. Fuchs-Kittowski, F., Simroth, S., Himberger, S., Fischer, F.: A content platform for smartphone-based mobile augmented reality. In: International Conference Informatics for Environmental Protection (EnviroInfo 2012), pp. 403–412. Shaker, Aachen (2012)

32. Lanfranchi, V., Wrigley, S., Ireson, N., Wehn, U., Ciravegna, F.: Citizens' observatories for situation awareness in flooding. In: International Conference Information Systems for Crisis Response and Management (ISCRAM 2014), p. 154 (2014)
33. WeSenseIt: Sensor Data - Sensors, Citizens, Information and Models. http://wesenseit.eu/wp-content/uploads/2014/12/data.pdf
34. Fuchs-Kittowski, F., Faust, D.: Architecture of mobile crowdsourcing systems. In: Baloian, N., Burstein, F., Ogata, H., Santoro, F., Zurita, G. (eds.) CRIWG 2014. LNCS, vol. 8658, pp. 121–136. Springer, Cham (2014). https://doi.org/10.1007/978-3-319-10166-8_12
35. Kwonkyu, Y., Byungman, Y., Seokmin, L.: Surface image velocity measurement system for wide rivers using smartphones. In: IAHR World Congress, E-Proceedings, pp. 1–3 (2015). http://89.31.100.18/~iahrpapers/81007.pdf
36. Garg, K., Nayar, S.K.: Vision and rain. Int. J. Comput. Vis. **75**(1), 3–27 (2007). https://doi.org/10.1007/s11263-006-0028-6

Flood Modelling and Visualizations of Floods Through 3D Open Data

Lukáš Herman[✉], Jan Russnák, and Tomáš Řezník

Department of Geography, Faculty of Science, Masaryk University,
Kotlářská 2, 611 37 Brno, Czech Republic
{herman.lu,russnak}@mail.muni.cz, tomas.reznik@sci.muni.cz

Abstract. This paper is devoted to 3D modelling at the city level from data sources considered as open. The open data presented in this paper enable free usage, modifications, and sharing by anyone for any purpose. The main motivation was to verify feasibility of a 3D visualization of floods purely based on open technologies and data. The presented state-of-the-art analysis comprises the evaluation of available 3D open data sources, including formats, Web-based technologies, and software used for visualizations of 3D models. A pilot Web application visualizing floods was developed to verify the applicability of discovered data sources. 3D visualizations of terrain models, 3D buildings, flood areas, flood walls and other related information are available in a pilot application for a selected part of the city of Prague. The management of different types of input data, the design of interactive functionality including navigation aids, and actual limitations and opportunities for future development are discussed in detail at the end.

Keywords: 3D modelling · 3D visualizations · Floods · Open data

1 Introduction

Nowadays, 3D geospatial data and technologies for 3D cartographic visualization are being used with increasing frequency in a variety of human activities. Crisis management is no different. Applications of 3D geospatial data and technologies can increase, for example, the awareness and understanding of flood-related issues [17, 26, 33, 35]. 3D visualization may be used by experts and laymen alike in the use case described below. 3D visualization also has the ability to assist in dealing with the problem of flooding on different scales – from the global and regional levels to the local level involving individual towns and cities [14]. Feasibility of a 3D visualization of floods purely based on open technologies and data was is the primary aim of this paper. Solely open data and technologies were used for this purpose; based on an analysis of available sources of open data for the case study area (a part of city of Prague, The Czech Republic).

J. Hřebíček et al. (Eds.): ISESS 2017, IFIP AICT 507, pp. 139–149, 2017.
https://doi.org/10.1007/978-3-319-89935-0_12

2   Open Data and Technologies

"Open Data and content can be freely used, modified, and shared by anyone for any purpose" [34]. This definition was initially derived from the Open Source Definition. Open data are available without access restrictions, licenses, copyright, patents, or charges for access or re-use. The main reasons, why data should be open, are:

- transparency,
- the release of social and commercial value,
- the release of participation,
- the release of engagement.

Because of the variability in open data, when, for example, one organization deploys PDF files while another deploys raw data, Tim Berners-Lee, the inventor of the Web and Open Data supporter, suggested a 5-star deployment scheme for Open Data. The scheme – from scanned tables in PDF, through XLS and CSV, to data that could be linked to other data (e.g. [24]) – is shown in Fig. 1.

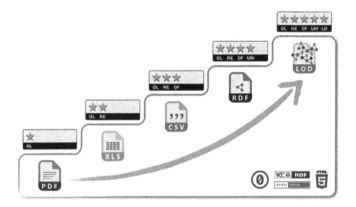

Fig. 1. 5-star schema of Open Data openness (source: [2])

2.1   Open Geospatial Data

There are various projects creating open geospatial data. Precise and detailed geospatial data are not usually open or distributed for free. National mapping agencies or commercial companies usually offer their geospatial data for a fee. Therefore because of such fees, open or free geospatial data are used whenever they are suitable enough. Free data could be licensed (e.g. for limited usage in educational context) unlike Open Data. Open geospatial data have potential uses and applications in various fields such as urban planning, urban studies or 3D city modelling [7, 18], transport analysis and navigation [11], precision farming [24, 25], environmental protection [16], sociology and socio-economic analysis [21], crime analysis [28], and also crisis management, which is the topic of this article. In the following paragraphs we present examples of various sources of open geospatial data, with an emphasis on data suitable for 3D modelling.

Open geospatial data, or open data in general, are often collected, managed, and then made available by an institution, organization or government. These providers should be responsible for the content. According to the provider, these open data can be termed open government data. The same should also hold for open geospatial data. The most commonly used freely available elevation data sets are derived from the SRTM (*Shuttle Radar Topography Mission*) and the ASTER GDEM (*Advanced Spaceborne Thermal Emission and Reflection Radiometer Global Digital Elevation Model*). **SRTM DEM** (*Digital Elevation Model*) is the result of a project spear-headed by NASA and NGA (*National Geospatial-Intelligence Agency*). The pixel size of the raw image represents 30 m over the USA and Australia. For the rest of the world, the ground resolution is 90 m. The elevation models obtained from SRTM data are freely available from the Internet. Up to 2009, SRTM DEM was the most complete high-resolution digital topographic database of the Earth. In 2009, the **ASTER GDEM** was released. Compared to SRTM DEM, ASTER GDEM covers a larger area of the Earth and the resolution is 30 m worldwide. By the end of 2015, all of the highest-resolution data generated from SRTM were also released. [3, 29, 32, 36] EU-DEM is another similar dataset for the pan European region, which is provided by the European Environmental Agency. For the European level, **EU-DEM** provides downloadable color-shaded relief data with values relating to actual elevations. The EU-DEM is a hybrid product based on SRTM and ASTER GDEM data fused by a weighted averaging approach. The resolution of EU-DEM is 25 m. [5]

Meanwhile, the currently most popular open geospatial data source, **Open-StreetMap** (OSM), is in the form of a Volunteered Geographic Information (VGI) project created by thousands of contributors, which are not responsible for the content or which cannot be held accountable for the content. OSM data can be both transformed from official sources and manually created by voluntary users. For this reason, OSM data should be used with caution, especially if the issue needs detailed (and precise) input data such as the 3D modelling of cities. Some 3D visualizations or 3D models have been created on the basis of OSM data. A basic extension for 3D modeling is **Simple 3D Buildings** based on the 3D attributes of buildings. On the basis of the heights of building outlines and building parts, 3D buildings are modeled or, for example, roof types are described. Another 3D application based on OSM data is the open source project **Open Earth View**. Its aim is full 3D web browsing of a world map. The base ground is built by OSM 2D tiles, which are extended by 3D tiles created essentially from SRTM and other accessible elevation data, or from OSM 2D data attributes like building elevation, number of floors, or roof elevation. For conversion from OSM data into a 3D model, **OSM2World** can also be used. The **OSM-3D** project combines OSM data and the SRTM DEM on a virtual globe. OSM-3D is a part of the development of a 3D Geodata Infrastructure for the entire World based on open web service standards of the Open Geospatial Consortium (OGC). The project aims to provide a Web-based inter-active 3D view of OSM data. OSM Buildings and F4map are two quite similar projects concerning also the 3D visualization of OSM data. [1, 19, 23, 30].

2.2 3D Data Formats

Both technologies and standards primarily designed for computer graphics and GIS formats are used to save 3D geospatial data. Probably the oldest most widespread format for interactive 3D computer graphics is VRML (*Virtual Reality Modelling Language*). VRML is a text file format in which 3D geometry can be specified along with surface colour, texture, transparency, and other properties. X3D (*Extensible 3D*) is an open standard file format based on XML for the description of spatial scenes. Essentially, it is recognized as the successor to VRML. COLLADA is designed to store 3D graphics; it has similar capabilities to X3D and also the XML structure [4]. There are many other 3D graphics formats besides the above mentioned technologies, and extensions of more conventional (2D) formats, such as 3D PDF, can also be used.

3D spatial objects are also stored through GIS technologies. For example, Multipatch is geometry used in ESRI geodatabases and in Shapefiles to represent 3D features. GML (*Geography Markup Language*) is an XML grammar defined by the OGC to express geographical features. GML was originally only 2D; however, since version 3.0, it has also been possible to manage 3D data. CityGML is an application schema for GML version 3.1.1 for the storage and exchange of virtual 3D city models. KML (*Keyhole Markup Language*) is primarily intended for the publication and distribution of geographic data. KML 2.2 was adopted in 2008 as an OGC standard [13].

3D formats can also be classified according to a 5-star scale of data openness. A 3D PDF or Shapefile (Multipatch geometry) can be classified under the 2-star class, other formats like COLLADA, KML, VRML, X3D, GML and CityGML under the 3-star class. An important issue for open data formats is their standardization. The most important standardization authority in geoinformatics is OGC. From the above mentioned, technologies standardized by OGC include CityGML, GML and KML. Formats from 3D computer graphics are standardized, for example, by ISO (*International Organization for Standardization*) or the Khronos Group. ISO standards are VRML and X3D. The Khronos group uses a standardized COLLADA format.

2.3 Freeware and Open Source Software for 3D Modelling

Software designed primarily for computer graphics, computer-aided drawing (CAD), photogrammetry, or GIS can be used when processing 3D geospatial data. Freely available 3D GIS software include the tools GRASS, LandSerf, 3DEM, and gvSIG with 3D extension. These software packages usually employ simple 3D visualization or 3D spatial analysis (in particular, GRASS). The 3D extension to gvSIG enables, for example, the extrusion of 2D geometry, the symbolisation of point layers, or the setting of stereo visualization. These tools also quite often allow the conversion of selected formats. Certain possibilities of 3D data processing are also provided through plug-ins (e.g. DEMto3D, Shp2D3, and Qgis2threejs) in the widespread open source software QGIS.

Trimble SketchUp, which is used regularly for the 3D modelling of buildings and other objects, is a CAD program working with 3D data. Regarding software for 3D computer graphics, commercial programs are often used. However, there are also the freeware applications MeshLab and View3DScene as well as the open source tools Blender and Wings 3D. The individual aforementioned applications are often combined in the process of creating 3D models. The key factor is then support for formats that are used to transfer data between applications. In these connections, it is appropriate to use standards (all formats specified in the previous section are standards). Price is also an important aspect when selecting 3D software, in addition to its functionality. In this study, we focus on non-commercially distributed applications (freeware and open source).

2.4   3D Rendering in a Web Browser

A broad spectrum of technologies is also available for rendering on the Web. In addition to thick clients, which are standalone applications such as Google Earth, there are a number of techniques for displaying 3D data using a simple web browser. Many of them use plug-ins. 3D models can be displayed in a web environment using Flash plug-in, version 11.0 or higher, or Microsoft Silverlight technology, version 3.0 or higher [4]. Plug-ins are also used for the implementation of virtual globes, for example NASA World Wind. Today, preference is given to technologies built on HTML5 and JavaScript library WebGL. These are, for example, SpiderGL, Three.js, XML3D and X3DOM. SpiderGL library is based on the COLLADA file structure [6]. Three.js was used for the implementation of 3D city model visualization by [38]. Practical aspects of the use of the X3DOM library for the 3D visualization of detailed models of cities are described, for example, by [8]. In addition to general 3D libraries, there are also a number of 3D virtual globes, e.g. OpenWebGlobe [20].

3   Pilot Study

The data and technologies described in this paper were tested in the area around the Vltava River in Prague, the Czech Republic. The floods in 2002 were the most destructive floods in the history of Prague. The flow of the Vltava River culminated at 5300 m^3/s. About 40 000 people were evacuated from immediate vicinity. The area around the Vltava was flooded again in 2013 (culmination at 3 200 m^3/s).

3.1   Open Geospatial Data in the Czech Republic

The Registry of Territorial Identification, Addresses and Real Estate (RUIAN) in the Czech Republic became a freely available online resource for geospatial data in 2012. Among other data and attributes, this registry also contains information about number of floors per each building. On the basis of this information, 3D models can be created from building footprints. The dataset is downloadable and includes also address points, streets, parcels, administrative units, and electoral districts [27].

There are also detail open data for city areas provided in the Czech Republic, e.g. Děčín, Plzeň and, above all, Prague. The Prague Institute of Planning and Development (IPR) manages and provides open data – specifically, open data for various purposes and analyses connected, for example, with power distribution, noise mapping, the climate, the environment, and flood protection. In addition to this kind of data, the datasets include 3D buildings, 3D towers, absolute and relative building heights, digital terrain models (DTM), or digital surface models (DSM). Similar data for 3D city models are also provided for cities around the world, e.g. Berlin, Hamburg, Montreal, Rotterdam and New York [10, 22].

3.2 Input Data

The following were used as input data for the creation of 3D models:

- The digital terrain model of the city Prague provided by IPR in TIFF format. This DTM was created from aerial photography in 2010 and designed for the level of detail commensurate with a map scale of 1:5 000.
- Building footprints from RUIAN that are available on-line as a Web Feature Service or as off-the-shelf GML files (data are compressed by the GZIP algorithm).
- Flood areas for various water levels (for 5-, 20- and 100-year floods) provided by IPR as Shapefiles with Polygon geometry. Alternatively, Shapefiles for identical water levels from the DIBAVOD (*Digital Base of Water Management Data*) database can also be used, but these do not have a clearly defined license.
- Flood walls provided by IPR as Shapefiles with Polyline geometry.
- Orthophoto Prague 2015 with a pixel resolution of 50 cm and in true colors. Data acquisition took place in August 2015. Orthophoto is stored in TIFF format.
- POI (*Points of Interest*) from OSM downloaded from Geofabrik Tools. We used POI as a Shapefile with Point geometry.

3.3 Processing of Open Data

These input data were processed in QGIS software (version 2.12) with the same plugins which are intended for the processing and visualization of 3D data. The QGIS program enables the use of functions important for 3D data pre-processing (interpolation and other techniques of virtual surfaces creation). Available 3D plug-ins for QGIS are: Shp2D3, CZML Generator, and Qgis2threejs. Shp2D3 transforms 2D vector data to 3D by the sampling of an elevation raster map. It works actually only with polylines. CZML Generator serves to export to form ready for virtual globe (for Cesium library). Qgis2threejs exports terrain data, map canvas images, and vector data to a web browser which supports WebGL. This plug-in uses the Three.js library; thus, in this study, final visualization was implemented through this library.

In this pilot study (see Fig. 2), we used mainly Qgis2threejs for visualization in a web browser. All data are loaded into QGIS as GML, Shapefiles, and TIFF files. Additional layer settings (e.g. color scales for terrain) can be set through QGIS. Other parameters of final visualization, like template of final web page, controls, and other parameters of individual layers (e.g. exaggeration, display of labels, transparency, background color, resampling of raster) are defined in the scope of the Qgis2threejs plug-in.

Fig. 2. Example of a web application for the 3D visualization of floods.

Three.js in final 3D visualization enables the basic functionality usually available in web map portals (see of Fig. 3 – left part). Users can switch between layers or set their transparency, because transparency avoids the occlusion of features or layers. One can create one's own "cut of plane" and simulate in this way the change of water level (shown in right part of Fig. 3).

Fig. 3. Interactive functionality of developed application (left – setting parameters of layers, right – "cut of plane")

4   Discussions

3D visualization in general has significant application potential, but it is affected by its properties, e.g. the UI (*User Interface*) or cartographic visualization methods. Regarding cartographic visualization, our approach is not directly dependent on the visualization(s) of underlying data. Cartographic visualization should be developed separately for each application and is not directly re-distributable since it is written directly in the Three.js code. We may define, for example, a standardized cartographic visualization for flood areas, flood walls, as well as POI using the developed software as shown in this paper. [15, 35] have focused on this issue.

The usability aspects of concrete UI are also important topics for future research. Some authors, e.g. [37], argue that 3D visualization is able to present geospatial data to wider audiences, including those with little or no cartographical or GIS experience. On the other hand, results of other previous studies [9, 12, 31] suggest that interactive 3D visualization will be more useful for users with previous experience with 3D visualization and for complex tasks in particular. It would be appropriate to validate created application through user testing.

When we focused on technological issues, we found that using Multipatch geometry for storing 3D open geodata limits the possibilities of 3D modeling in open source software which does not support this geometry (unlike Shapefiles with Point, Polyline or Polygon geometries). Multipatch geometry is supported only in commercial software (ESRI ArcGIS and FME), but not in QGIS or gvSIG. Buildings at the level of detail 1 (LoD 1) are modeled in the resulting application only. Web applications built with Three.js could be further tested in terms of capacity, availability and support in different Web browsers. Deployment in a form of daily service should be made after validations of above mentioned technological parameters.

5   Conclusion

The presented proof-of-concept application was established in order to demonstrate the possibility of open web-based 3D visualization. It should be emphasized that the openness relies on the data and software used, as well as on the final application. The developed proof-of-concept application is freely available to interested persons under a BSD license.

To sum up, the following major advantages of 3D visualization based on open data and Three.js library were identified:

- it represents (in this pilot study) an example of an open data application usable in flood impact analysis and crisis management;
- it enables user-friendly interactive 3D visualization, which is accessible to a broad spectrum of users (from the general public to experts);
- it does not require any new software or plug-ins to be installed on the client or server sides;

We also identified some limitations of available open source tools. The non-commercial software functionality needed for the creation of 3D visualizations is generally sufficient because, inter alia, programs primarily used in computer graphics can also be used for this purpose. Less commonly available is non-commercial software support for 3D analytical tools (3D equivalents of overlay algebra functions, calculations of surfaces or volumes of 3D elements).

We must also mention recommendations for the formats in which open ends are provided for 3D geospatial data. Multipatch geometry, which is used in the case of Prague open data for 3D models of buildings at the level of detail 2 (LoD 2), is not supported in open source tools such as QGIS. It is more suitable to transform these data into a standardized format like CityGML or into GML files formatted according to INSPIRE (*INfrastructure for SPatial InfoRmation in Europe*) data theme Buildings.

Acknowledgements. This research was funded by Grant No. MUNI/A/1419/2016, "Integrated research on environmental changes in the landscape sphere of Earth II" and Grant No. MUNI/M/ 0846/2015, "Influence of cartographic visualization methods on the success of solving practical and educational spatial tasks", both awarded by Masaryk University, Czech Republic.

References

1. 3D development. http://wiki.openstreetmap.org/wiki/3D_development
2. 5 ★ Open Data. http://5stardata.info/en/
3. ASTER Global Digital Elevation Map Announcement. https://asterweb.jpl.nasa.gov/gdem. asp
4. Behr, J., Eschler, P., Jung, Y., Zöllner, M.: X3DOM – a DOM-based HTML5/ X3D integration model. In: Proceedings of Web3D 2009: The 14th International Conference on Web3D Technology, Web3D 2011, pp. 127–135 (2009)
5. Copernicus. http://www.copernicus.eu
6. Di Benedetto, M., Corsini, M., Scopigno, R.: SpiderGL: a graphics library for 3D web applications. In: International Archives of the Photogrammetry, Remote Sensing and Spatial Information Sciences, vol. XXXVIII-5/W16, pp. 467–0474 (2011)
7. Goetz, M.: Towards generating highly detailed 3D CityGML models from OpenStreetMap. Int. J. Geogr. Inf. Sci. **27**(5), 845–865 (2013)
8. Herman, L., Reznik, T.: 3D web visualization of environmental information – integration of heterogeneous data sources when providing navigation and interaction. In: ISPRS Archives of the Photogrammetry, Remote Sensing and Spatial Information Sciences, vol. XL-3/W3, pp. 479–485 (2015)
9. Herman, L., Stachon, Z.: Comparison of user performance with interactive and static 3D visualization – pilot study. In: ISPRS Archives of the Photogrammetry, Remote Sensing and Spatial Information Sciences, vol. XLI-B2, pp. 655–661 (2016)
10. IPR Praha - Institut plánování a rozvoje hlavního města Prahy [IPR Praha - Prague Institute of Planning and Development]. http://www.iprpraha.cz/
11. Keler, A., Mazimpaka, J.D.: Safety-aware routing for motorised tourists based on open data and VGI. J. Locat. Based Serv. **10**(1), 64–77 (2016)
12. Jurik, V., Herman, L., Sasinka, C., Stachon, Z., Chmelik, J.: When the display matters: a multifaceted perspective on 3D geovisualizations. Open Geosci. **9**(1), 89–100 (2017)
13. Kolbe, T.H.: Representing and exchanging 3D city models with CityGML. In: Lee, J., Zlatanova, S. (eds.) 3D Geo-information Sciences. LNGC, pp. 15–31. Springer, Heidelberg (2009). https://doi.org/10.1007/978-3-540-87395-2_2
14. Konecny, M.: Cartography: challenges and potentials in virtual geographic environments era. Ann. GIS **17**(3), 135–146 (2011)
15. Konecny, M., Kubicek, P., Stachon, Z., Sasinka, C.: The usability of selected base maps for crises management - users' perspectives. Appl. Geomat. **3**(4), 189–198 (2011)
16. Kubásek, M.: Mapping of illegal dumps in the Czech Republic – using a crowd-sourcing approach. In: Hřebíček, J., Schimak, G., Kubásek, M., Rizzoli, Andrea E. (eds.) ISESS 2013. IAICT, vol. 413, pp. 177–187. Springer, Heidelberg (2013). https://doi.org/ 10.1007/978-3-642-41151-9_17

17. Kubíček, P., Muličková, E., Konečný, M., Kučerová, J.: Flood management and geoinformation support within the emergency cycle (EU example). In: Hřebíček, J., Schimak, G., Denzer, R. (eds.) ISESS 2011. IAICT, vol. 359, pp. 77–86. Springer, Heidelberg (2011). https://doi.org/10.1007/978-3-642-22285-6_9
18. Long, Y., Liu, L.: Transformations of urban studies and planning in the big/open data era: a review. Int. J. Image Data Fusion 7(4), 295–308 (2016)
19. Mooney, P., Corcoran, P.: Has OpenStreetMap a role in digital earth applications? Int. J. Digit. Earth 7(7), 534–553 (2014)
20. Netek, R., Loesch, B., Christen, M.: OpenWebGlobe - virtual globe in web browser. In: SGEM - Geoconference on Informatics, Geoinformatics and Remote Sensing – Conference Proceedings, vol. 1. pp. 497–503 (2013)
21. O'Brien, O., Cheshire, J.: Interactive mapping for large, open demographic data sets using familiar geographical features. J. Maps 12(4), 676–683 (2016)
22. Open Data Initiatives. http://www.citygmlwiki.org/index.php/Open_Data_Initiatives
23. OpenStreetMap. https://www.openstreetmap.org
24. Palma, R., Reznik, T., Esbri, M., Charvat, K., Mazurek, C.: An INSPIRE-based vocabulary for the publication of agricultural linked data. In 12th International Experiences and Directions Workshop on OWL, pp. 124–133 (2016)
25. Reznik, T., Lukas, V., Charvat, K., Charvat Jr., K, Horakova, S, Krivanek, Z., Herman, L.: Monitoring of in-field variability for site specific crop management through open geospatial information. In ISPRS Archives of the Photogrammetry, Remote Sensing and Spatial Information Sciences, vol. XLI-B8, pp. 1023–1028 (2016)
26. Roy, D.C., Coors, V.: 3D web-based GIS for flood visualization and emergency response. In: 73rd European Association of Geoscientists and Engineers Conference and Exhibition 2011: Unconventional Resources and the Role of Technology, vol. 2, pp. 1001–1005 (2011)
27. RÚIAN [RUIAN]. http://www.cuzk.cz/ruian/RUIAN.aspx
28. Russnak, J., Ondrejka, P., Herman, L., Kubicek, P., Mertel, A.: Visualization and spatial analysis of police open data as a part of community policing in the city of Pardubice (Czech Republic). Ann. GIS 22(3), 187–201 (2016)
29. Shuttle Radar Topography Mission. http://www2.jpl.nasa.gov/srtm/dataprod.htm
30. Simple 3D Buildings. http://wiki.openstreetmap.org/wiki/Simple_3D_buildings
31. Špriňarová, K., et al.: Human-computer interaction in real 3D and pseudo-3D cartographic visualization: a comparative study. In: Robbi Sluter, C., Madureira Cruz, C., Leal de Menezes, P. (eds.) Cartography - Maps Connecting the World. LNGC, pp. 59–73. Springer, Cham (2013). https://doi.org/10.1007/978-3-319-17738-0_5
32. SRTM DEM. http://www.gisat.cz/content/cz/produkty/digitalni-model-terenu/srtm-dem
33. Stachon, Z., Kubicek, P., Stampach, R., Herman, L., Russnak, J., Konecny, M.: Cartographic principles for standardized cartographic visualization for crisis management community. In: Proceedings of the 6th International Conference on Cartography and GIS, vol. 1 and 2, pp. 781–788 (2016)
34. The Open Definition. http://opendefinition.org
35. Van Ackere, S., Glas, H., Beullens, J., Deruyter, G., De Wulf, A., De Maeyer, P.: Development of a 3D dynamic flood WEB GIS visualisation tool. Int. J. Saf. Secur. Eng. 6(3), 560–569 (2016)
36. Vijith, H., Seling, L.W., Dodge-Wan, D.: Comparison and suitability of SRTM and ASTER digital elevation data for terrain analysis and geomorphometric parameters: case study of Sungai Patah subwatershed (Baram River, Sarawak, Malaysia). Environ. Res. Eng. Manag. 71(3), 23–35 (2015)

37. Vozenilek, V.: Cartography for GIS: Geovisualization and Map Communication. Univerzita Palackého, Olomouc (2005)
38. Wendel, J. Murshed, S.M., Sriramulu, A., Nichersu, A.: Development of a web-browser based interface for 3D data – a case study of a plug-in free approach for visualizing energy modelling results. In: Progress in Cartography, pp. 185–205 (2016)

Use of the Hydro-Salinity, Crop Production Optimization Model APSIDE to Validate Results from an Updated Regional Flow Model of the San Joaquin River Basin

Nigel W. T. Quinn[✉] and John Cronin

Lawrence Berkeley National Laboratory, Berkeley, CA, USA
nwquinn@lbl.gov

Abstract. APSIDE is an optimization model capable of simulating irrigation hydrology and agricultural production under saline conditions. The model has been used in the past to predict future agricultural production under future climate change in the San Joaquin River Basin of California (Quinn et al. 2004). In this study the model was used to query the results from a highly-regarded, published regional surface-groundwater flow model of the Central Valley of California – CVHM (Faunt et al. 2009) which includes the San Joaquin Basin. The APSIDE model was updated using recent aquifer and climate data and provided common initial conditions to allow a 53 year comparative simulation of the models. Model outputs for individual water districts for parameters such as deep percolation and upflux in APSIDE were compared to identical drained subareas within the CVHM model. The comparison showed that the APSIDE model produced lower values of deep percolation and upflux than CVHM. CVHM's deep percolation values were 18% higher in Panoche WD, 40% higher in Broadview WD, 68% higher in San Luis WD, and 46% higher in Pacheco WD. Unlike the CVHM model that assumes fixed levels of irrigation and drainage technology and static average water district irrigation efficiency APSIDE will substitute more cost effective irrigation and drainage technologies based on the calculated future benefit stream relative to the cost of production and impact of salinity on crop yields. An unpublished recent update to the current CVHM model (CVHM-2) which substitutes actual irrigation diversion records from delivery canals rather than usually-reliable Agency records - produced water district irrigation diversions that were approximately 50% of the previously provided diversion data. The new model produces water district aquifer recharge estimates that correlate closely with APSIDE model output. This study demonstrates the successful use of a complementary agricultural production optimization and hydro-salinity simulation model to help validate a radical and important update to a widely distributed and well-accepted regional flow groundwater model.

Keywords: Salinity · Crop production · Optimization · Drainage · Irrigation

© IFIP International Federation for Information Processing 2017
Published by Springer International Publishing AG 2017. All Rights Reserved
J. Hřebíček et al. (Eds.): ISESS 2017, IFIP AICT 507, pp. 150–162, 2017.
https://doi.org/10.1007/978-3-319-89935-0_13

1 Introduction

In California, agriculture is the largest user of water, an important source of employment and income for many regions, and source of tax revenues for the state. Statewide irrigated agriculture revenues are approximately $22 billion per year (www.opr.ca.gov) supporting 300,000 to 450,000 jobs. The population of California is forecast to exceed 65 million by 2050, implying significant increases in urban water demand and use. Further complicating the picture is an increasing awareness of the importance of the Sacramento-San Joaquin Delta as a key ecosystem for native fish and the importance of water quality, particularly salinity, in developing long-term sustainability plans for the Region. The use of surface and groundwater simulation models that incorporate economics can be useful for policy analysis and to help balance competing uses for water supply and protecting water quality. An ideal integrated modeling framework incorporates the dynamics of the interaction between the environment, urban and agricultural stakeholders providing a decision analysis tool for evaluating the economic benefits and costs of water policies and policy-induced changes to the current system (Howitt et al. 2010). This paper describes the use of a unique hydro-salinity and economic simulation tool APSIDE (**A**gricultural **P**roduction **S**alinity **I**rrigation **D**rainage **E**conomics), capable of simulating agricultural production and land use in the salinity-impacted western San Joaquin Valley of California, to query the results from a widely-accepted regional flow model of the Central Valley (Sacramento and San Joaquin Basins), developed by the US Geological Survey (USGS). This study also serves to validate preliminary results from a recent update to the USGS Central Valley Hydrologic Model (CVHM), based on raw diversion data obtained from the Water Authority charged with operating the water distribution system rather than the water agency traditionally charged with furnishing this data to the public.

Hydrological models used for planning, studies around the world often achieve legacy status – the datasets used to calibrate and validate these models are rarely questioned, especially when the models are developed by science-based institutions such as the US Geological Survey in the USA. Although subsequent studies by other agencies, universities and consultants may produce anomalous results – such is the inertia of the model development and review process that these models become a de-facto "gold standard" against which other modeling efforts are compared. Some datasets such as crop coefficients used for computation of crop-based evapotranspiration are based on experiments that are decades old and crop cultivars that have since been replaced by more robust and drought-tolerant strains. Similarly, methods for flow estimation in canals and at diversion structures have been replaced by more advanced acoustic Doppler technologies that provide more accurate accounting. Greater use of complementary modeling and simulation tools can help to challenge the validity of certain datasets and assumptions made in these important legacy models leading to improved outcomes.

2   Background

Technological innovation does not typically succeed without being cost effective – hence the consideration of economics is paramount to guide basin-scale water quality management. The most obvious technology solutions involve: (a) increasing irrigation efficiency by re-using drain water to blend with good irrigation water; (b) growing salt-tolerant crops; (c) improve on-farm drainage management. One can also fallow or retire the land and sell the water, or utilize the assimilative capacity of the San Joaquin River in a coordinated fashion to discharge limited amounts of salt load without exceeding salinity objectives. A changing climate can have an effect on water availability as well as temperature, which in turn can have an effect on plant yields.. Understanding water availability and water quality, in particular, is critical to understanding long-term agricultural production in the San Joaquin Valley.

The west-side of the San Joaquin River Basin (SJRB) receives limited rainfall and relies on additional water supply from the Delta to meet the needs of irrigated agriculture. Salts are imported with irrigation water - changing water availability and water salinity can have a direct effect on yields. Applied irrigation water is subject to the processes of direct evaporation from the soil surface and transpiration from the crop. Pure water is evaporated, leaving behind the salts in irrigation water. Over time, these salts can accumulate in the soil and groundwater and can affect agricultural yields. Excess water can leach out salts in soil profile - however excess water is limited in the SJRB to effect this leaching. Schoups et al. (2005) showed a steady cumulative increase in net salt in SJRB soils and groundwater – which has the potential to diminish irrigation sustainability.

To address salinization related problems on the west-side of the SJRB - drainage management measures have been suggested as follows:

- Reduction of deep percolation (the downward movement of water below the root zone, past drains to the local groundwater system) through the adoption of water conserving irrigation technologies and practices, better irrigation scheduling and changes in cropping practices (Grismer 1990).
- Reuse of drain water, through the use of salt-tolerant crops and agro-forestry.
- Manipulation of the water table to meet part of the crop evapotranspiration requirements.
- Conjunctive use of groundwater to meet a portion of crop needs.
- Improved instrumentation and monitoring systems to produce accurate and timely information and improve access to this information by growers.
- Development and installation of real-time monitoring systems to progressively evaluate changes in soil and water quality in the terrestrial and aquatic ecosystems over time.

High irrigation efficiencies may actually lead to higher concentrations of salt in deep percolation. Efficient irrigation methods are those with deep percolation of less than 10% of the irrigation applied water (Hanson et al. 2014). Doneen (1967) reported that in the SJRB the salinity of soils covered with native vegetation is generally lower than soils in irrigated areas. Irrigation water normally contains from 0.06 to 3.95 tons of salt per acre-ft of water (1 ton/acre-ft = 0.82 kg/m^3) and crop requirements are between 2.03 to

3.05 acre-ft/acre (1 acre-ft/acre = 3048 m^3/hectare) to fulfill evaporation requirements. Thus, this amount of irrigation water may add approximately from 0.12 to 1.29 tons of salts/acre (1 ton/acre = 2242 kg/ha) annually anywhere (Rhoades and Suarez 1977). Groundwater can become degraded by salinity through irrigated agricultural practices by three process (1) salt concentrated is due to the uptake of water by plant, (2) salt moves down from the unsaturated zone into groundwater (saturated zone) because of leaching and mixing of subsurface saline water with higher quality groundwater and (3) enhanced percolation of saline water into the lower zone as a result of groundwater pumping for irrigation. (Suarez 1989, Tanjii 1990).

3   Modeling of Hydrosalinity in West-Side Irrigated Agriculture

A state-of-the-art model known as the Central Valley Hydrologic Model, (CVHM) was developed by the US Geological Survey (USGS) and simulates the effects of hydraulic conductivity, irrigation, streamflow losses, wells, and other parameters on groundwater flow (Faunt et al. 2009). The CVHM model application uses the recently published FORTRAN hydrologic code, MODFLOW-OWHM which contains the Farm Management Process – a pre-processor that simulates agricultural irrigation hydrology (Hanson et al. 2014). This model was created and calibrated using historic observations, calculations, and measurements of the factors affecting hydrology, including geological and meteorological data from April 1961 until December 2013. Canal diversions to individual water districts were obtained from the Central Valley Operations Office of the US Bureau of Reclamation which has been providing this data to the public for many decades as is considered the most reliable source of this information. The model divides the valley into one- mile (1.6 km) square cells which form a grid 98 cells wide and 441 cells long. The grid is also 10 layers deep in the vertical dimension, enabling the user to analyze subsurface water flow separately from surface water flow.

Models such as CVHM have been used for long-term planning studies provided a suite of realistic future conditions can be developed including future hydrologic conditions, land use, agricultural production and regulatory constraints on agricultural production. However models such as CVHM assume static conditions for irrigation management and technology. Since detailed water district cropping data has typically only been publicly available in 5–7 year intervals (now available annually) models such as CVHM have typically also assumed static cropping mixes within each modeled subarea. More realistic tracking of agricultural production on the west-side of the SJRB requires a simulation tool that recognizes relationships between crop markets and costs of production, the impacts of investments in improved irrigation and drainage technologies on irrigation hydrology and soil salinity and the relationship between soil salinity and crop yield (Maas and Hoffman 1977) which can promote crop substitution over time to more salt tolerant crops and crop cultivars. The APSIDE (Agricultural Production-Salinity-Drainage-Economics) Model (Figs. 1a and 1b) fulfills this purpose allowing more realistic future irrigation hydrology projections to be made on the west-side of the SJRB. APSIDE was used in this study to develop comparative irrigation hydrology, drainage and aquifer recharge estimates over a 53 year simulation period.

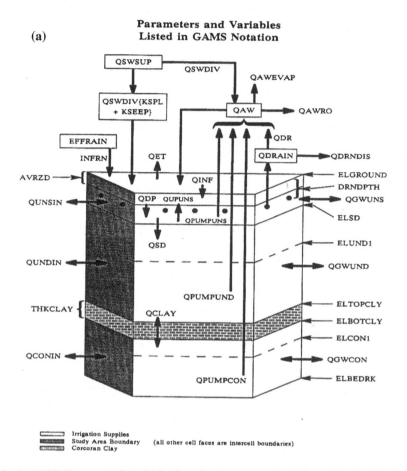

Fig. 1. (a) APSIDE conceptual model for flow showing parameters and variables listed in GAMS notation. Lateral flow between adjacent water districts are simulated as "equations of motion" or head-dependent fluxes between the centroids of each subarea.

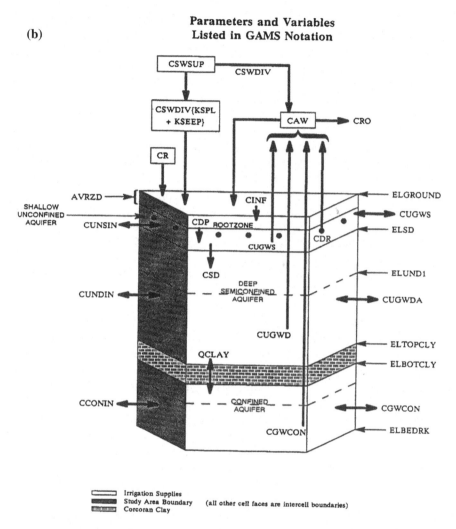

Fig. 1. (b) APSIDE conceptual models for salinity showing parameters and variables listed in GAMS notation. Lateral movement of salt between adjacent water districts is driven by the hydrology and hydraulic flux between the centroids of each area.

3.1 APSIDE Model Features

Resource analysts face a fundamental difficulty in modeling regional production activities: simplifications used to keep a model manageable by reducing computation and data requirements also prevent it from reproducing the variety and proportions of activities actually observed (Hatchett et al. 1989). These simplifications also often omit important cost differences that influence production patterns. Flexibility constraints can force regional activities to approximate observed levels, but then these constraints prevent the model from adjusting very much to policy changes.

APSIDE is an agricultural production optimization model, written in the GAMS language (GAMS 1998), that simulates hydrology and salinity (Figs. 1a and 1b) on the west-side of the SJRB. The model proved useful for understanding water resource utilization in the San Joaquin basin in response to potential future climate change and long term surface water allocations within the federal Central Valley Project service area (Quinn et al. 2004). The motivation for enhancing and updating the APSIDE model is to provide a decision tool that simulates long-term agricultural production taking into consideration the availability of groundwater resources, the cost of pumping and the impacts of salinity in groundwater pumpage. The genesis of the APSIDE model were two models - the Statewide Agricultural Production model (SWAP), which forecasts future agricultural production as a function of commodity price projections, anticipated changes in the costs of production and surface water supply availability and the Westside Agricultural Drainage Economics Model (WADE), which makes projections of future agricultural drainage and farm income resulting from policies that affect agricultural production and investments in irrigation and drainage technology (Hatchett et al. 1989). The agricultural production simulation algorithms utilize a technique known as Positive Mathematical Programming (PMP), which can reproduce observed activities quite precisely without a large increase in required data and without restricting the model's ability to shift activities as conditions change (Howitt 1995).

The PMP technique relies on the concept of dual variables, or shadow prices, to infer otherwise unobserved cost differences among activities. A PMP model of regional crop production is implemented in two stages. The first, or calibration, stage is a traditional programming model which restricts crop acreage to observed levels. The dual values associated with the acreage constraints are the marginal changes in the objective (usually net revenue) function from small changes in the constraints. The dual values are positive when the constraints force a lower acreage of a particular crop than an unrestricted model would calculate (and negative when the constraints force a higher acreage). The second stage of PMP re-solves the first stage model after making two important changes. First, the crop acreage constraints are removed. Then the dual values from the calibration stage are used to calculate a linear marginal cost function for each crop activity. Integrating the marginal cost gives a total cost quadratic in crop acreages. The quadratic form is then appended to the objective function. The cost function intercept and slope values for each crop and region, obtained for the PMP algorithm during calibration of the APSIDE model are used to estimate proxy crop activity levels at the beginning of each year simulated by the model. The PMP algorithm will duplicate the crop mix from the restricted calibration model and will also allow smooth changes in crop levels as conditions or policies change.

Five proxy crops were considered in the APM; alfalfa (including hay and seed crops, rice, irrigated pasture); trees, fruits and nuts (almonds, apples, apricots, olives, peaches, walnuts, pistachios, grapes, nectarines, oranges); row crops (cotton, sugarbeets, processing tomatoes, corn, sorghum); grain crops (wheat, barley, oats.) and vegetable crops (beans, melons, lettuce, spinach, onions, garlic, broccoli, peas). These proxy crops are assigned average hydrologic characteristics of the group they represent.

The PMP cost function were calculated separately for overspecialized and under-specialized crops grown in the study subareas. Overspecialized crops are those which are so profitable that greater quantities would be produced according to the model than would normally be observed. Hence an increment was added to the production costs of these crops to lower their activity to the observed marginal profitability levels. Conversely, incremental increases in revenue were added to the production of under-specialized crops in order to match the observed marginal values. The increments added are not fixed, but rather vary in quadratic fashion with crop acreage.

For the SWAP and WADE models - the agricultural production submodels considered the summer (irrigation) season and the winter (rain and pre-irrigation) season of each year, interacting sequentially with the hydrology and salinity models. In the APSIDE model the sequential seasonal hydrology and salinity models were transformed into a discrete monthly timestep hydrosalinity submodel that solves simultaneously in order to capture more of the complexity of irrigation hydrology and water quality within the SJRB - where water supply to agriculture is subject to frequent perturbations in water quality. This has allowed the APSIDE model to be used in the past in integrated model-based planning studies of the Basin that consider future potential climate change (Quinn et al. 2004).

3.2   Comparison of Model Simulations

The APSIDE model was run for a period of 53 years for four water districts in the Grasslands Subarea on the west-side of the SJRB (Fig. 2). The APSIDE model application used the same water table, cropping and irrigation water use efficiency initial conditions as the USGS CVHM (Faunt et al. 2009) model. In the APSIDE model aquifer characteristic data such as aquifer hydraulic conductivity, specific yield and storativity was averaged (lumped) for each water district in the study –whereas CVHM can assign unique values for each one mile square model cell.

The APSIDE and CVHM model outputs for deep percolation and upward capilliary flow were compared. These outputs are the most important factors impacting water tables, tile drainage, soil salinity and crop yield. The comparison showed that, on average, APSIDE produced lower values of deep percolation and groundwater upward capilliary flow (upflux) than CVHM (Fig. 3). On average, CVHM's deep percolation estimates were 26% higher in Panoche WD, 12.9% higher in Broadview WD, 45.3% higher in San Luis WD, and 51.3% higher in Pacheco WD (Fig. 4). (Broadview gets no surface water deliveries having sold their federal water rights to an adjacent water district more than a decade ago). Upflux estimates are similarly higher for the CVHM model (Fig. 5) – Pacheco WD shows the greatest difference between CVHM and APSIDE model estimates. Water deliveries (canal diversions) to each of these water districts were derived from publicly available US Bureau of Reclamation Central Valley Operations bulletins.

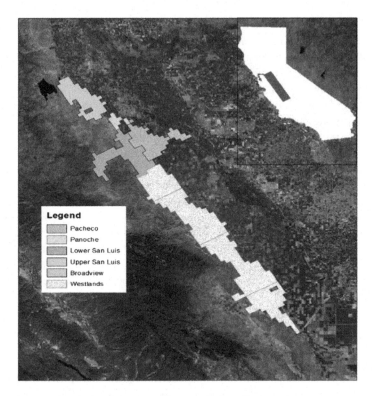

Fig. 2. Water districts within the salinity impacted study area on the west-side of the SJRB, California. Results from Panoche, Pacheco, Broadview and San Luis Water Dis-tricts are the subject of the analysis in this study.

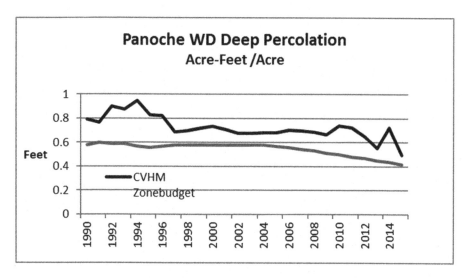

Fig. 3. Comparative results using APSIDE and CVHM models showing more real-istic deep percolation estimates using APSIDE agricultural production optimization algorithms using PMP.

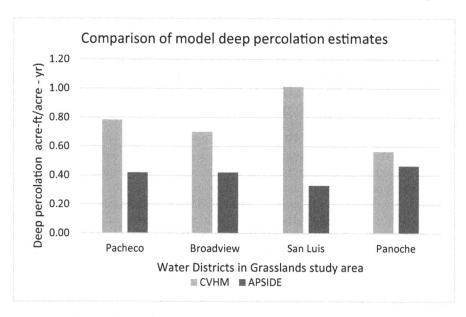

Fig. 4. Comparison of deep percolation estimates between CVHM and APSIDE models. Higher deep percolation rates raise water levels, increasing subsurface drain-age discharge production and salt load export to the San Joaquin River.

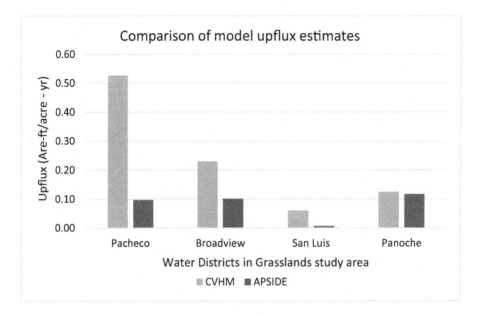

Fig. 5. Comparison of groundwater upflux estimates between CVHM and APSIDE models – higher groundwater upflux increases precipitation of salt in the crop root zone.

The APSIDE model bases water deliveries on water requirements which in turn are based on crop selection and irrigation management technology and practices. Hence differences in the APSIDE and CVHM model estimates can be ascribed either to the inability of the CVHM model to track changes in crop selection and irrigation water use efficiency resulting from changes in crop root zone salinity or to problems in the reported irrigation water deliveries (diversions) to each water district. One of the novel features of the APSIDE model is its ability to adapt irrigation and drainage technologies in response to production costs, the water saving potential of improved techniques and salt load discharge constraints that limit the export of salts to the San Joaquin River. As the cost of drainage disposal increases over time the APSIDE model substitutes more water conserving irrigation technologies such as sprinkler and drip irrigation for furrow and basin flooding techniques – improving irrigation water use efficiency over time. Using the same irrigation diversion data the APSIDE model still derived optimal yields and farm income by reducing irrigation application resulting in deep percolation rates that were as much as 50% lower than those produced by CVHM.

The deep percolation values in APSIDE and CVHM were further compared to reported data from Panoche and Pacheco Water Districts. Pacheco Water District reported year 2010 deep percolation values of 1770 acre-feet on 4080 acres of irrigated land (Panoche Water District 2015). This corresponds to a deep percolation of 0.43 acre-feet per acre. This aligns fairly closely to APSIDE's predicted value of 0.42 acre-feet per acre for Pacheco Water District (Westcot et al. 1994).

3.3 CVHM-2 Diversion Data Update

Difficulties in obtaining good model calibration for the west-side of the San Joaquin Valley in CVHM, particularly in the simulation of subsurface tile drainage, prompted the USGS to seek better quality data as part of the development of an updated simulation model of the Central Valley CVHM-2. The new model increased the number of vertical layers from 10 to 13, improved the accuracy of cropping data by incorporating data obtained directly from water districts and substituted public records from the US Bureau of Reclamation's Central Valley Operations office for raw canal turnout records compiled by the Water Authority responsible for daily operations along the Delta Mendota Canal – the main conveyance for federal water deliveries. These data had to be further processed to associate each irrigation turnout with a delivery point within each water district subarea. Preliminary (unpublished) model results shared by colleagues in the USGS have shown that average water diversions to the water districts that were the subject of this study decreased up almost 50%. Similarly the CVHM-2 model estimates of aquifer deep percolation were reduced by an equivalent amount. These same colleagues report that the CVHM-2 model achieved a better calibration for west-side San Joaquin Valley hydrology than the original CVHM model – much of it ascribed to the more realistic diversion data. These results correlate much more closely with the results from the APSIDE model.

4   Summary and Conclusions

The time and effort involved in developing comprehensive regional surface and ground-water simulation models often confers a legacy status to these models whereby they become the "gold standard" against which subsequent modeling studies are compared. This is accompanied by a reluctance or "inertia" to revisit model assumptions or the data used to develop the model – even though these further studies might suggest fundamental problems. The use of complementary simulation models and analytical tools to test assumptions and the conceptual hydrology underlying these legacy models has significant, unrealized potential to promote better outcomes and result in more accurate decision tools. This study has provided an exemplar of the use of a simple agricultural production optimization and hydro-salinity simulation model that utilizes a unique normative calibration technique to allow realistic simulation of future changes in agricultural land use and investments in irrigation and drainage technology over long-term planning horizons. The PMP algorithm allows substitution of irrigation and drainage technologies while calibrating crop production shifts to field observations – capturing some of the socioeconomic factors known to effect on-farm decision making. The APSIDE model can be applied to any problem involving irrigated crop production under saline conditions provided data are available for annual cropping and the costs of irrigation and drainage technology substitution are available. Soil and aquifer characteristic data including root zone and aquifer salinity data are also needed.

References

Doneen, L.D.: Quality of percolating waters, I. properties of deep substrata materials in the west side of the San Joaquin Valley, California. Hilgardia **38**(9), 285–305 (1967)

Faunt, C.C., Hanson, R.T., Belitz, K., Schmid, W., Predmore, S.P., Rewis, D.L., McPherson, K.R.: Numerical model of the hydrologic landscape and groundwater flow in California's Central Valley (Chapter C). In: Faunt, C.C. (ed.) Groundwater Availability of the Central Valley Aquifer, pp. 121–212. U.S. Geological Survey Professional Paper 1776, California (2009).

GAMS Inc., Brooks, A., Kendrick, D., Meerhaus, A., Raman, R.: GAMS: A User's Guide. GAMS Development Corp., Washington, DC (1998)

Grismer, M.E.: Leaching fraction, soil salinity, and drainage efficiency. Calif. Agric. **44**(6), 24 (1990)

Hanson, R.T., Boyce, S.E., Schmid, W., Hughs, J.D., Mehl, S.M., Leake, S.A., Maddock III, T., Niswonger, R.G.: One-Water Hydrologic Flow Model (MODFLOW-OWHM) (2014)

Hatchett, S.A., Quinn, N.W.T., Horner, G.L., Howitt, R.E.: A drainage economics model to evaluate policy options for management of selenium contaminated drainage. Toxic substances in agricultural water supply and drainage. In: Proceedings of the Second Pan American Regional Conference on Irrigation and Drainage, Ottawa, Ontario, 8–9 June 1989

Howitt, R.E.: Positive mathematical programming. Am. J. Agric. Econ, **77**, 329–342 (1995)

Howitt, R.E., et al.: Economic modeling of agriculture and water in California using the statewide agricultural production model. California Water Plan Update 2009, vol. 4, pp. 1–25 (2010). http://www.waterplan.water.ca.gov/docs/cwpu2009/0310final/v4c04a02_cwp2009.pdf

Maas, E.V., Hoffman, G.J.: Testing crops for salinity tolerance. Water Management Plan, U.S. Salinity Laboratory, USDA-ARS, Pacheco Water District, pp. 27–29 (1977)

Panoche Water District. Personal communication Marcos Hedrick, Panoche Water District. Panoche Water District keeps irrigation and drainage records for Pacheco Water District (2015)

Quinn, N.W.T., Brekke, L.D., Miller, N.L., Heinzer, T., Hidalgo, H., Dracup, J.A.: Model integration for assessing future hydroclimate impacts on water resources, agricultural production and environmental quality in the San Joaquin Basin. Calif. Environ. Model. Softw. **19**, 305–316 (2004)

Rhoades, J.D., Suarez, D.L.: Reducing water quality degradation through minimized leaching management. Agric. Water Manag. **1**(2), 127–142, 143, 305–316 (1977)

Suarez, D.L.: Impact of agricultural practices on groundwater salinity. Agric. Ecosyst. Environ. **26**, 215–227 (1989)

Schoups, G., Hopmans, J.W., Young, C.A., Vrugt, J.A., Wallender, W.W., Tanji, K.K., Panday, S.: Proc. Natl. Acad. Sci. **102**(43), 15352–15356 (2005)

Tanjii, K.K.: Nature and extent of agricultural drainage. In: Tanji, K.K. (ed.) Agricultural Salinity Assessment and Management. American Society of Civil Engineers Manuals and Reports of Engineering Practice, no. 71, pp. 1–17 (1990)

Westcot, D., Steensen, R., Styles, S., Ayars, J.: Grassland Basin Irrigation and Drainage Study. Irrigation Training and Research Center, San Luis Obispo (1994). Accessed 04 July 2015

Business Intelligence and Geographic Information System for Hydrogeology

Kamil Nešetřil[✉] ⓘ and Jan Šembera

Technical University of Liberec, Liberec, Czechia
kamil.nesetril@tul.cz

Abstract. We have developed the Hydrogeological Information System (HgIS). Its purpose is to load data from available data sources of any kind, to visualize and analyze data and to implement simple models. HgIS is mostly built upon the Pentaho business intelligence (BI) platform. HgIS uses only some components of BI in comparison to enterprise BI solutions. Adequacy and limitation of data warehousing and BI application for groundwater data is discussed. Data extraction, transformation and loading is focused on integration of wide variety of structured and semi-structured data. Data warehouse uses a hybrid snowflake/star schema. Inmon's paradigm is used because data semantics is known and the volume of data is limited. HgIS is data agnostic, database agnostic, scalable and interoperable. The architecture of the system corresponds to a spatial business intelligence solution (GeoBI) – a combination of BI and geographic information systems (GIS). Groundwater practitioners have worked with GIS software for decades but BI technologies and tools have not previously been applied to groundwater data.

Keywords: Hydrogeology · Groundwater · Environmental data management
Decision support system (DSS) · Business intelligence (BI)
Spatial business intelligence (GeoBI) · Data warehouse · Data model
Extract, transform and load (ETL) · Reporting · Pentaho

Environmental solutions often lack good analytics and reporting functionality – especially generic functionality that can be easily used for purposes that have not been foreseen at the design and development phase. Business intelligence (BI) and data warehousing is used mainly for integrating and analyzing corporate data. Groundwater data are very different from operational data of enterprises. This paper presents the Hydrogeological Information System HgIS that is based on business intelligence platform Pentaho. Adequacy of using data warehousing concepts and BI for groundwater data management, data analysis and for groundwater modelling is discussed.

1 Hydrogeological Information System HgIS

HgIS (Fig. 1) is an information system developed at the Technical University of Liberec (Czechia). Its purpose is to load data from the available data sources of any kind, to

© IFIP International Federation for Information Processing 2017
Published by Springer International Publishing AG 2017. All Rights Reserved
J. Hřebíček et al. (Eds.): ISESS 2017, IFIP AICT 507, pp. 163–170, 2017.
https://doi.org/10.1007/978-3-319-89935-0_14

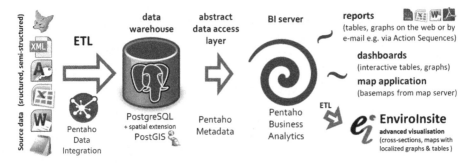

Fig. 1. Architecture of HgIS (arrows represent data flow)

visualize and analyze data (to support formulation of alternative conceptual models) and to implement simple models based on the data. Although it is focused on groundwater, it is also being used for broader range of environmental data.

The data are loaded to the database by the Extract, Transform and Load (ETL) tool Pentaho Data Integration. Data transformations can be implemented without coding through an intuitive graphical user interface and run also in command-line interface, on the ETL server Carte or on Pentaho Business Analytics Server. We implemented the loading data from a chemical laboratory (xBase files), Czech Geological Survey (MS Access), eEarth project (XML files) [9], legacy formats (MS Word documents created by a Geobanka software), specific flat text files, general cross-table (MS Excel) and formats from some other data vendors.

The database structure is based on the data model of the software EnviroInsite (enviroinsite.com) and on national and international standards. It contains 36 tables with data on: the observation objects*, characterization of the geological layers, technical construction of wells, definition of the observed quantities*, action levels, definition of the vertical intervals*, measurements tied to the vertical intervals (e.g. chemical analyses or head measurements)*, measurements tied to specific depth (e.g. geophysical logging) and sampling conditions. Tables containing data noted with asterisk (*) are organized to the snowflake schema. We are using the PostgreSQL (postgresql.org) database management system. Interpretations and non-point data (arcs, polygons etc.) are stored in the PostgreSQL due to the spatial extension PostGIS (postgis.net).

Ordinary users have access only to the online application Pentaho Business Analytics (Fig. 2). It is a BI server that provides dashboards (interactive visualization) and reports (optimized to be printed or saved to the format that the users are familiar to – MS Excel, MS Word or PDF). Reports can be visually designed in the Pentaho Report Designer tool. Community Dashboard Framework (JavaScript) was used to implement dashboards and a map application. The data model of HgIS is based on EnviroInsite software – therefore exporting data (by Pentaho Data Integration) for advanced hydrogeological visualization (in EnviroInsite) is straightforward. EnviroInsite has access via ODBC to the data stored in proprietary data model implemented in MS Access or MS Excel. The reports and the exported files can be downloaded from Pentaho Business Analytics web application or sent to the users by e-mail according to a schedule or an event (e.g. user login, new data or new data exceeding an action level).

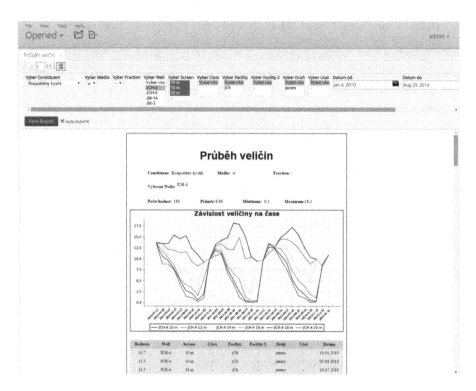

Fig. 2. Report example – a general-purpose report of time development of arbitrary quantities – graph and table

By some functionality HgIS belongs among "Environmental Data Management Systems" (EDMS). Some of these are EQuIS (earthsoft.com), SiteFX (earthfx.com), GW-Base (ribeka.com), WISKI (kisters.net), EnviroData (geotech.com), Oasis-montaj (geosoft.com), HydroManager (waterloohydrogeologic.com) or ESdat (esdat.net). Those tools usually have an excellent graphical user interface and are able to import dozens of data exchange formats. But they are not flexible enough to create new data imports because they do not contain an easy to use highly adaptable extract, transform and load (ETL) module. Without an ETL module they cannot efficiently combine data operations (e.g. aggregation), analyses and simple visualization (reporting). Those shortcomings are overcome by HgIS that takes advantage of the high-level universal BI tools.

The Hydrogeological Information System HgIS was previously presented at conferences as a tool for environmental data management [7] and for modelling [8]. This paper focuses on application of the concepts, technologies and tools of data warehousing and business intelligence in HgIS. Adequacy and limitation of such approach are discussed.

2   Data-Warehouse and BI Concepts for Groundwater Data

The architecture of the HgIS system corresponds to a spatial business intelligence solution (GeoBI) – a combination of business intelligence (Pentaho) and geographic information systems (PostGIS, the map application, EnviroInsite). BI technologies and tools have not previously been applied to groundwater data. However ESdat (esdat.net) integrates commercial reporting tools – SSRS, Telerik and Crystal Reports. Telerik is used also in EQuIS (earthsoft.com). MineRP (www.minerp.com) is based on Microsoft BI tools, but MineRP focuses on mining industry not on groundwater. Boulil et al. [2] analyzed quality of surface water (Online Analytical Processing) using Talend a PostgreSQL among others. Kingdon et al. [6] designed the data warehouse and the application PropBase from 10 operational databases of British Geological Survey.

The concept of data warehouse is suitable for environmental data because they contain temporal and spatial dimensions. Groundwater observations and measurements are usually not changed after they are recorded: HgIS is therefore both environmental data management software (operational) and decision support system (Online Analytical Processing).

Different BI components were used in HgIS. Corporate BI solutions use also other components. Selection is discussed in the Table 1. Processing of environmental data differs from processing of business data. We perceive that our approach of processing environmental data differs from the standard data-warehouse and BI applications. The differences are discussed in the following chapters.

Table 1. BI components

Component	Purpose	Used in HgIS
Operational system, operational databases, OLTP	Data source	Geofond, Geobanka, Lab-systém
Data staging area	Temporal storage of extracted data	No (not much data)
Operational data store	For data analyses	No (not much data)
ETL	Data integration	Yes: Pentaho Data Integration
Enterprise application integration	Integration of operational enterprise systems	No (HgIS is not utilizing operational enterprise systems)
Data warehouse	Principal data storage	Yes: PostgreSQL
Data mart	Problem-oriented data warehouse	No (Central data warehouse is sufficient)
On-line analytical processing cube	Data storage for analyses	Data warehouse is sufficient for HgIS
Reporting	Dedicated data display in the printable form	Yes: Pentaho Reporting
Dashboards, scorecards	Synoptic and interactive data representation	Yes (Pentaho Business Analytics)
Data mining		Weka – planned

2.1   Data Extraction, Transformation and Loading (ETL)

- HgIS is designed for practitioners to facilitate data management, data analysis and modelling. It is not intended for a countrywide or international data infrastructure. The source data for HgIS are nowadays not in the SQL databases but (purchased and) exported data from such systems. Groundwater data are available in common formats (exchange formats, flat files and reports) and also in legacy (xBase) and poorly structured formats (spreadsheets or even MS Word – in our case fortunately the Word files were generated by a software).
- HgIS benefits from using ETL tool by capturing diversity of source-data formats not by huge volume of data (big data) or real-time data (we deal mainly with broad data and long tail data [12]).

2.2   Data Warehouse

- HgIS uses a hybrid snowflake/star schema.
  - The spatial dimension is normalized – one observation object (e.g. well or borehole) has multiple monitored depth intervals (e.g. screens or sampled intervals).
  - The dimension of quantities is not normalized because quantities are of diverse nature and consistent sub-dimensions cannot be defined. A quantity is specified by a triad "constituent – media – fraction" (the same way as in the original EnviroInsite data model). This triad can be both "iron – in water – filtered (dissolved form)" and "precipitation – monthly – maximum".
  - The temporal dimension is a degenerated dimension (a column in the fact table). Timestamp column can represent both actual measurement and e.g. a center of the time interval for aggregated values (e.g. monthly average).
  - The dimension of samples contains metadata for a set of measurements (specimen, borehole logging of one quantity in one hole), sampling conditions, sample treating, methods etc.
  - Geology data do not fit to the snowflake/star schema at all.
- There are two major data warehousing concepts – by Inmon [4] (central data warehouse, top-down design) and Kimball [5] (data marts). We found Inmon's paradigm more suitable for groundwater data because its structure (semantics) is known in advance and the volume of data is limited.
  - Inmon defines data warehouse as a subject-oriented, integrated, nonvolatile, and time-variant collection of data in support of management's decisions [4]. The data warehouse of HgIS matches this definition with slight divergences:
    - *Integrated:* HgIS contains the data structure for unknown data due to the flexible design. The flexibility causes inconsistency if used across projects/sites.
    - *Nonvolatile:* The database of HgIS contains also:
      - Operational information that is not used for decision support (e.g. sample planning).
      - Some data structures in HgIS were developed to support planned functionality of an expert system. They contain the interpretation of the primary data (observations and measurements) imported by ETL. A hydrogeologist can

explore time series and label some values as background or natural condition not influenced by human activity. Those data can be used to compute
hydraulic head drawdown and quantify human influence. Primary data are
loaded by ETL but further interpretation is to be inserted by the user via
graphical user interface.

- Auxiliary tables (e.g. for renaming) of HgIS are the part of ETL (not of the
  data warehouse).

- *Time-variant:* Some descriptive attributes (e.g. well owner, water persistence
  or purpose) represent only the present state but the values can generally change
  in time. That information is used only for querying and reporting and not for
  tracking previous changes. However descriptive attributes can be defined as
  time-variant quantities – values are stored in the fact table then.

– HgIS diverges from Inmon's concept in following aspects:

- HgIS stores time-series on all levels of granularity (both original and aggregated) in one star/snowflake schema – because we use only small volume of
  data. Data of all levels of granularity are necessary for some kind of analysis.

- Observations and measurements are loaded directly to the snowflake/star
  schema. There is not separated data warehouse and dimensional database.

3   Advantages of the Used Concept

The approach applying data warehousing, BI tools (Pentaho platform) and geographic
information systems (GIS) brings many advantages. HgIS is easily extensible and therefore sustainable (maintainable). It can be easily used and even further developed by
business user/hydrogeologist. Moreover HgIS is:

- *Data agnostic* – The developed data model is a simple data structure that is still able
  to store all relevant data. It is able to store even unknown quantities (new quantities
  defined in the fact table).

- *Database agnostic* – HgIS is not dependent on a specific database management
  system because transformation can be performed in Pentaho Data Integration.
  Pentaho Data Integration is communicating with the database by a universal interface
  (JDBC, JNDI or ODBC).

- *Scalable* – HgIS is suitable for both local and server deployment. Data transformation
  can be parallelized by ETL server Carte (the part of Pentaho Data Integration).

- *Interoperable* – HgIS can be easily integrated with the data analysis tools and the
  data mining tools (using Pentaho Data Integration – steps: "Weka scoring", "ARFF
  output", "Tableau data extract" or "Execute R script"). Export routine to a specialized
  modeling software or implementation of special analysis can be easily developed
  (using Pentaho Data Integration, Report Designer and Pentaho Business Analytics).

4   Application and Impact

We have developed the following analyses and the models that are reusable because of their general purpose and connection to the database. Some analyses are utilizing Pentaho Data Integration. Results are stored directly in the database as separate quantities. One of them is computation of the hydrochemical type of water (based on major cations and anions) – e.g. Ca-Mg-HCO3.

Some analyses and a model are utilizing Pentaho Data Integration and formulas in Pentaho Reporting (OpenFormula). The results are depicted in the reports:

- Identifying redox processes in ground water from chemical composition (dissolved O_2, NO_3, Mn^{2+}, Fe^{2+}, SO_4^{2-} and sulfides) without measured Eh and pH [3].
- Multicriterial analysis assessing water quality trends in correspondence to eutrophication.

HgIS is used within 3 Czech national projects that deal with water quality evolution, predicting groundwater resources, water balance of mine pit lake, engineering geology and urban planning. HgIS is used as a part of a decision support system in a state enterprise.

5   Discussion

Since the previous versions of HgIS, presented in the conference papers [7, 8], following improvements were made: The architecture was refined and simplified. It is now more systematically based on the Pentaho platform. The first paper [7] was focused on data integration (ETL) while recent versions of HgIS take advantage of the whole BI stack. Recent versions do not include GeoKettle (spatially enabled fork of Pentaho Data Integration) because the latest version of GeoKettle is from the year 2013 and it is based on an outdated version of Pentaho Data Integration. Anyway GeoKettle does not provide precise conversion of spatial reference systems used in Czechia (WGS-84 and S-JTSK).

The original map application was implemented in PHP. It was rewritten for the Pentaho platform using Community Dashboard Framework [1].

The abstract business layer Pentaho Metadata is used as a data source for the reports, dashboards and the map application (instead of previous direct SQL access). Business user does not query physical data model but has access to e.g. denormalized business tables and columns with predefined format and language localization (similar to database views). Pentaho Metadata is based on the Common Warehouse Metamodel specification [10, 11].

The architecture of the system corresponds to a spatial business intelligence solution (GeoBI) – a combination of business intelligence (BI) and geographic information system (GIS). Therefore it can be used also for geographic analyses and management of big data sets. BI technologies and tools have not been applied for groundwater data before. Groundwater practitioners have worked with GIS software for decades but not with BI tools. Our effort is to introduce BI to the groundwater community. General concept of spatial BI for groundwater data is presented and can be applied using different BI stacks. HgIS is available commercially, upon request (contact the corresponding author).

Screenshots, documentation and background information is available at http://www.dataearth.cz.

Acknowledgments. The contribution was prepared with support of the Technology Agency of the Czech Republic via the project Nr. TH02030069 (GERIT «Expert system for monitoring, risk assessment and decision support in the field of land use»).

References

1. Alves, P., et al.: Community Dashboard Framework (2016). http://community.pentaho.com/ctools/cdf/
2. Boulil, K., Le Ber, F., Bimonte, S., et al.: Multidimensional modeling and analysis of large and complex watercourse data: an OLAP-based solution. Ecol. Inform. **24**, 90–106 (2014). https://doi.org/10.1016/j.ecoinf.2014.07.001
3. Chapelle, F.H., Bradley, P.M., Thomas, M.A., McMahon, P.B.: Distinguishing iron-reducing from sulfate-reducing conditions. Ground Water **47**(2), 300–305 (2009). https://doi.org/10.1111/j.1745-6584.2008.00536.x
4. Inmon, W.H.: Building the Data Warehouse, 4th edn. Wiley, Indianapolis (2005)
5. Kimball, R., Ross, M.: The Data Warehouse Toolkit: The Definitive Guide to Dimensional Modeling, 3rd edn. Wiley, Indianapolis (2013)
6. Kingdon, A., Nayembil, M.L., Richardson, A.E., Smith, A.G.: A geodata warehouse: using denormalisation techniques as a tool for delivering spatially enabled integrated geological information to geologists. Comput. Geosci. **96**, 87–97 (2016). https://doi.org/10.1016/j.cageo.2016.07.016
7. Nešetřil, K., Šembera, J.: Groundwater data management system. In: Gómez, J.M., Sonnenschein, M., Vogel, U., et al. (eds.) EnviroInfo 2014 – ICT for Energy Efficiency: Proceedings of the 28th International Conference on Informatics for Environmental Protection, 10–12 September 2014, Oldenburg, Germany, pp. 301–306. BIS-Verlag, Carl von Ossietzky University Oldenburg, Oldenburg (2014)
8. Nešetřil, K., Šembera, J.: An information system for groundwater data and modelling. In: Sauvage, S., Sánchez-Pérez, J.M., Rizzoli, A.E. (eds.) Proceedings of the 8th International Congress on Environmental Modelling and Software, 10–14 July, Toulouse, France, pp. 747–752 (2016)
9. Netherlands Institute of Applied Geoscience TNO - National Geological Survey 2005 Electronic Access to the Earth Through Boreholes, Project ID: 11142. http://www.cordis.europa.eu/project/rcn/78272_en.htmlml
10. Object Management Group, Inc.: Common Warehouse Metamodel (CWM) Specification. Version 1.1, vol. 1 (2003). http://www.omg.org/spec/CWM/
11. Poole, J., Chang, D., Tolbert, D., Mellor, D.: Common Warehouse Metamodel. Wiley, New York (2002)
12. Wallis, J.C., Rolando, E., Borgman, C.L.: If we share data, will anyone use them? Data sharing and reuse in the long tail of science and technology. PLoS One **8**, e67332 (2013). https://doi.org/10.1371/journal.pone.0067332

Health and Biosphere

A Pilot Interactive Data Viewer
for Cancer Screening

Ladislav Dušek, Jan Mužík, Matěj Karolyi, Michal Šalko, Denisa Malúšková,
and Martin Komenda(✉)

Faculty of Medicine, Institute of Biostatistics and Analyses, Masaryk University,
Brno, Czech Republic
komenda@iba.muni.cz

Abstract. The paper introduces processing, modelling, analysis and visualisation of data on cancer epidemiology and cancer care in compliance with a proven and validated methodology. We aim to provide online access to unique data on cancer care and cancer epidemiology, including an interactive visualisation of various analytical reports in order to provide relevant information to the general public as well as to experts, such as health care managers, environmental experts and risk assessors. The data viewer has been developed and implemented as a web-based application, making a very time-consuming process of data analysis fully automatic. The presented data contain dozens of validated epidemiological trends in the form of tables, graphs and maps.

Keywords: Cancer care · Epidemiology · Data analysis · Data visualisation
CRISP-DM · Czech Republic

1   Introduction

Health care reporting and overviews nowadays involve not only the distribution and availability of health care, but also the standardisation of diagnostic and treatment approaches [1]. The European health systems underwent a great deal of reorganisation in the last decade. There has been a tendency to facilitate the expanding involvement of the private and public health care sector, a process which has occurred mainly in the countries of Central and Eastern Europe [2]. Cancer care is a prime example of multidisciplinary medical service which requires integration and a certain degree of centralisation in order to ensure an optimal use of resources available and to achieve optimal treatment outcomes. Cancer surveillance holds a privileged position, compared to other diseases, in terms of sources for collecting data, rich experience and availability of data [1]. Various cancer monitoring systems aim to collect data on cancer occurrence and provide much more detailed information on cancer, including diagnostic criteria and therapeutic procedures at the level of individual patients. The Comprehensive Cancer Control (CanCon) initiative aims to improve the quality of cancer care in the European Union. Involved cancer experts from across Europe have joined forces to advance cancer care and reduce cancer incidence by: (i) identifying key elements and quality standards

© IFIP International Federation for Information Processing 2017
Published by Springer International Publishing AG 2017. All Rights Reserved
J. Hřebíček et al. (Eds.): ISESS 2017, IFIP AICT 507, pp. 173–183, 2017.
https://doi.org/10.1007/978-3-319-89935-0_15

for comprehensive cancer control in Europe and preparing an evidence-based European guide on quality improvement in comprehensive cancer control; (ii) facilitating cooperation and exchange of best practice between EU countries, to identify and define key elements to ensure optimal, comprehensive cancer care [3]. CanCon has been divided into nine work packages, of which three are horizontal (dealing with coordination, dissemination and evaluation), and six are core packages (focusing on developing the content of cancer control). The concept of Comprehensive Cancer Care Network (CCCN) has been introduced in the work package 6, providing synergy with all institutions that have complementary expertise. CCCN aims to: (i) promote the optimal use of advanced technologies; (ii) make innovative clinical trials accessible to the entire population in a certain area; (iii) identify the most suitable unit within the CCCN for the management of rare and complex cancers; (iv) promote common infrastructures within the CCCN; and (v) provide a forum for regular consultation among professionals. A pilot model of such CCCN has been set up in the Czech Republic, namely in the Vysočina Region and South Moravian Region. This model covers all components of cancer care: from cancer prevention and organised screening programmes through standard diagnostic and treatment procedures to follow-up plans; specialised care focused on rare cancers as well as palliative care are also included. This CCCN involves one highly specialised national comprehensive cancer centre, three regional cancer centres and four general hospitals. This consortium of core centres was at the very start of the pilot CCCN and took responsibility for the development of binding cancer care protocols, rules of multidisciplinary teams and quality assessment standards [4]. Beside the required organisation of cancer services in two specific regions (in order to provide the best possible care for their population), collecting data on cancer epidemiology, their processing, analysis, and visualisation is very important in order to summarise long-term trends in cancer burden and to provide up-to-date incidence and mortality overviews.

1.1 Problem Definition

The paper introduces the domain of epidemiological, clinical and demographic data aggregation, analysis and interactive visualisation. We started by research question formulation, which helped us clarify what exactly we wanted to achieve. We have defined the following issue focusing on a comprehensive and fully representative overview of analytical reports. Specifically, we aimed to investigate how to perform efficient modelling, storage and visualisation of data on cancer epidemiology from an area of Czech hospital network (the CCCN pilot model).

2   Methodological Background

The healthcare industry has continuously generated large amounts of data stored in various locations (e.g. national information systems and specialised registries) [5]. In general, processing, modelling and analysis of these data need to be in compliance with proven and validated methodologies. It allows the discovery of new knowledge and potential useful information based on data describing the particular domain of human interest [6]. In fact, analytical reports, overviews and visualisations should help plan, understand, work through and reduce cost by detailing procedures to be performed in each of the steps. For our purposes, we decided to use the CRoss-Industry Standard Process for Data Mining (CRISP-DM) reference model, which provides a life cycle overview of a given research question [7]. The CRISP-DM model serves mainly as the methodological standardised guideline in practice (Fig. 1).

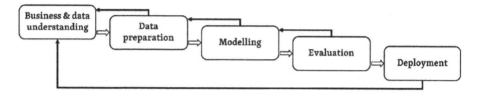

Fig. 1. CRISP-DM schema showing the relations between the different phases of the process.

(i) Business and data understanding introduces the defined objectives and requirements mapping from the research question perspective. It starts with initial data collection, identification of data quality problems, detection of interesting subsets regarding hidden and useful information. (ii) Data preparation covers construction of the final dataset from the initial raw data from various sources including table, record, and attribute selection, as well as data transformation and cleaning as pre-processed output files for modelling tools. (iii) Modelling represents a calibration of parametric values and the use of selected statistical and analytical techniques. (iv) Evaluation focuses on generating analytical reports (interactive data tables and graphs) assessing in terms of the usefulness, transparency and reliability. (v) Deployment phase consists of final reports implementation as well as testing and maintenance planning [8].

2.1 Business and Data Understanding

The Czech Republic is ranked among those countries with the highest cancer burden in Europe and worldwide [9]. Based on a thorough knowledge of the domain of cancer epidemiology, we needed to define the problem in the form of a research question corresponding to local regional estimates of incidence and mortality rates, which helps to choose the proper statistical and analytical methods and software tools selection. The main objective of our study entitled "CCCN pilot model: Interactive data views" was to design, to develop and to implement a web-based tool supporting scientific analytical reports on cancer data aggregated with demographic data from the Vysočina Region and the South Moravian Region. This stage also involved a more detailed fact-finding about all data sources. The Czech National Cancer Registry[1] provides fully representative long-term trends and consists of cases according to main risk factors and diagnostic descriptors including TNM classification of tumours in the following diagnostic groups [10]. These groups are presented in accordance with the 10th edition of the International Classification of Diseases (ICD-10) terminology [11], which is the standard diagnostic

---

[1] http://www.uzis.cz/en/registers/national-health-registers/czech-national-cancer-registry.

tool for epidemiology, health management and clinical purposes. We used only Chapter 2 (C00-D48 diagnoses), which classifies all neoplasms:

- I. Head and neck cancers;
- II. Digestive cancers;
- III. Cancers of the respiratory tract and intrathoracic organs;
- IV. Bone and soft tissue cancers;
- V. Skin cancers;
- VI. Breast cancers;
- VII. Gynaecological cancers;
- VIII. Genitourinary cancers;
- IX. Cancers of the central nervous system and eye;
- X. Malignant neoplasms of lymphoid, haematopoietic and related tissue;
- XI. Endocrine cancers;
- XII. Other malignant neoplasms;

Data describing the main demographic characteristics of the Czech population (such as the total population, age structure or life expectancy) were provided by the Czech Statistical Office[2].

2.2 Data Preparation and Modelling

We decided to use the data warehousing concept, which makes it possible to integrate information from heterogeneous databases and to query very large databases efficiently [12]. We aimed to synthesise available data on cancer care and to store them together in a single repository. First of all, a four-step process – extraction, transformation and load (ETL) – was performed.

Step 1: Stage. The first step includes data retrieval from the Czech National Cancer Registry and the Czech Statistical Office. Raw data are mined from both databases and further processing (data cleaning and transformation) is needed due to data format unification. Moreover, we discovered key dataset features and characteristics, which also include the tables, records (rows), and attributes (columns) selection. In case of a wrong format or syntax of the uploaded CSV file (syntactical and semantical check is performed), the transaction is aborted and the entire step has to be repeated. The output of the step is one table called <<import_nador>>.

Step 2: Operational data store. The second step is represented by the database table <<fact_primar>>. Data are syntactically and semantically checked by function f_restart_fact_primar() right before being stored to this table. If the check is not successful, the table <<import_nador>> has to be fixed and an attempt to transform it into a table <<fact_primar>> has to be made again.

Step 3: Primary Data Warehouse (PWD). The third step consists of fact tables and dimension tables. The fact tables are not directly connected to each other, but there are

---

[2] https://www.czso.cz/csu/czso/home.

relational links between them, depending on their dimensions contents. Dimension tables are simple tables which contain an abstract identifier as the primary key and columns with descriptive data; these are displayed on the screens of the data viewer. Based on the selection of one or more descriptive attributes, clustering of identifiers in the structure suitable for data selection from the dimension tables is performed. It is implemented through the re-start_dimensions_function() function, which firstly erases data from all the dimension tables and secondly inserts data to each dimension table by accumulation (implemented through GROUP BY clause) of <<fact_primar>>. In cases when the <<fact_primar>> table does not contain any descriptive attributes, data for the dimension table are inserted to it through SQL commands or manually from external sources. In contrast to the table <<fact_primar>>, fact tables do not contain atomic data providing the base for all data transformations, but contain aggregated data created by the count(*) function over all the appropriate dimensions. The data are cumulated in them. This means that the index over all dimensions in each fact table is unique and the measuring columns contain the numbers of specific cases that occur. Data selection is performed faster in this way. The only exception is the <<fact_demography>> table, which already contains aggregated data, and is imported directly from CSV file.

Step 4: Data Mart. This phase involves tables derived from the PDW data. These are so far represented only by the <<fact_agr_clinic_stage>> table. Data in the tables are derived from the fact tables <<fact_demography>> and <<fact_agr_patient_diag-nose>>. Again, the data in the fact table are arranged similarly to PWD based on aggregation over existing dimensions. The whole ETL process of selected entities is shown below (see Fig. 2). The external source (CSV file) is imported to the database entity <<import_nador>>, validated and transformed to the table <<fact_primar>>. At this point, several fact tables of PWD (e.g. table <<fact_agr_patient_diagnose>>) are created. The table <<fact_demography>> is created directly from the external source. The Data Mart includes one table entitled <<fact_agr_clinic_stage>>. The data for endpoint visualisations can be selected from all fact tables, but there are significant

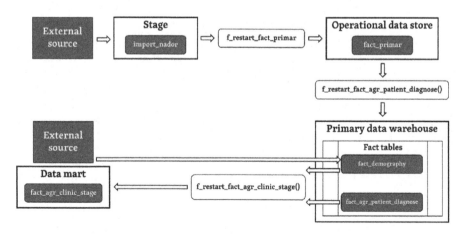

Fig. 2. Complete data flow in CCCN data warehouse subset.

performance differences (e.g. between the selection of the same information from the <<fact_primar>> and the <<fact_agr_clinic_stage>> tables).

The fact table <<fact_agr_clinic_stage>> (Fig. 3) is part of the CCCN Data Mart. This table is derived from fact tables included in the PDW and has the following dimensions, which correspond to the visualisation filters: dregion, dyear, dsex, dage_group, dage_group2 and ddiagnose_stage. The last dimension is a set of diagnoses and groups of diagnoses in accordance with ICD-10.

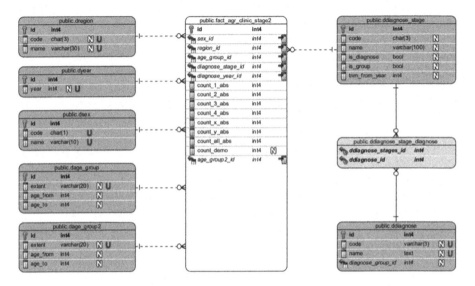

Fig. 3. Fact table of clinical stages where all relations between < <fact_agr_clinic_stage > > entity (white), parametric lists (grey) are shown.

2.3 Evaluation and Deployment

The evaluation phase assesses the degree to which the analytical reports meet the given objectives and seeks to determine if there are any imperfections or inaccuracies in terms of graphs, table validity and general user understanding. We made a detailed computational validation of the outputs presented by tables and graphs using standard epidemiological statistical methods [13]. This statistical validation was computed using the SPSS 24.0.0.0 software. The CCCN pilot interactive data viewer is a web-based application written in the Symfony framework[3] version 3.1. The data warehouse is implemented as a PostgreSQL[4] 9.5 database, which is hosted on the database server. The application core is divided into two parts:

- AppBundle (Symfony project) – the main application bundle which provides data access layer, PHP entity mapping and all processes connected to the Model-View-Controller (MVC) architecture.

---

[3] http://symfony.com/what-is-symfony.
[4] https://www.postgresql.org/about.

- VisualisationBundle – this bundle contains a functionality connected strictly with graphs, data tables and filters shown on all screens.

The Git[5] system was used for an efficient work with the code. All instances can be independently tested by a set of acceptance tests written in the integrated development environment for Selenium IDE[6] Mozilla Firefox plugin, which allows tests recording, editing, and debugging.

3   Results

The developed data viewer[7] allows the user to investigate general epidemiological trends for a particular diagnostic group. The viewer is divided into three individual modules, each of them containing a set of specific analytical reports visualised by interactive graphs and maps (Table 1).

Table 1. Modular structure of data viewer

Viewer module	Analytical report
Cancer epidemiology	Incidence and mortality trends over time
	Prevalence trend over time
	Age structure of incidence and mortality
	Age-specific incidence and mortality rate
Regional benchmarking	Incidence rates in regions
	Mortality rates in regions
Cancer diagnostics	Distribution of clinical stages
	Incidence trends by clinical stages
	Distribution of clinical stages by age
	Comparison of incidence of clinical stages by age

The user can access the analyses of each module through a module navigation homepage (Fig. 4).

The selection of individual analyses is at the top of the screen. The user has an overview of all provided data views in the current module, and can choose the one that interests him/her. The remaining part of the navigation page contains a selection of a particular diagnosis. The diagnoses are divided into twelve major cancer groups, which were defined in the domain and data understanding section. The groups can be freely expanded and browsed directly in the tree list (on the right) or by using the schematic picture of a human silhouette with tooltip elements and information about the part of human body being hovered over (on the left). After selecting a specific diagnosis – or a subgroup of diagnoses – the screen with the required analytical report appears again.

---

[5] https://git-scm.com.

[6] http://www.seleniumhq.org/projects/ide.

[7] http://cccn-viz.onconet.cz.

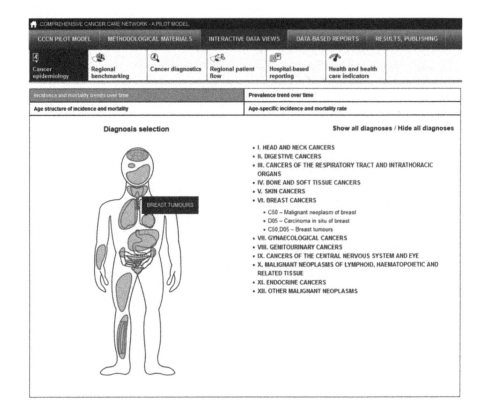

Fig. 4. Diagnosis selection page provides a human body interactive silhouette including tooltips (on the right) in combination with a complete list of all available diagnoses (on the left).

For illustrative purposes, four epidemiological views and analytical reports of the "Cancer epidemiology" viewer module are described as following.

- Incidence and mortality trends over time show annual incidence (newly diagnosed cases of a selected diagnosis) since 1977, and annual mortality (deaths caused by a selected diagnosis) since 1977 – absolute numbers or rate per 100,000 population.
- Prevalence trend over time shows annual prevalence (alive persons with disease or its history) since 1990 (point prevalence at 31 December of each year or interval prevalence during years) – absolute numbers or rate per 100,000 population.
- Age structure of incidence and mortality, and age-specific incidence and mortality rates show the numbers of new cases (incidence) or deaths caused by diagnosis (mortality) according to five-years age groups (absolute numbers, percentages or rate per 100,000 population).

When a user accesses the above-mentioned analyses in a standard way (there is also the option of proceeding through an URL with the already pre-filtered content), the graph and the table displays the complete information about all records in the registry. Additionally, we have provided a set of filters that correspond to fact table dimensions in the data warehouse. If the filter is disabled, the user is informed by the button's grey colour and the value is not included in the list of applied filters. The complete list of filters with analysis settings is on the right side of the screen (Fig. 5) and contains the following types of filters:

- Sex filter – men, women, both sexes.
- Age filter – five-year groups from 0 to 85+.
- Region filter – selection from 14 regions of Czech Republic plus the CCCN pilot model.
- Period filter – years from 1977 to 2014.
- TNM filter – extension of the primary tumour (T), regional lymph nodes (N), and distant metastases (M) [14].
- Clinical stage filter – combination of the TNM staging system, which determines the stage of cancer for each person (four stages: stages I to stage IV).

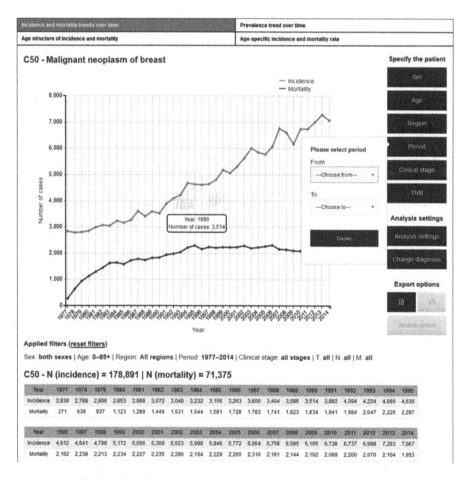

Fig. 5. Visualisation of incidence and morbidity trends over time.

4   Conclusion

We have designed, developed and implemented a prototype of interactive viewer of data on cancer care and cancer epidemiology, which shows the contemporary analytical overview of cancer incidence, prevalence and mortality, including the evidence on cancer care and cancer epidemiology in the CCCN pilot region and on the national level. In future, we might be able to extend the viewer in order to ensure regional and also international benchmarking analyses. Generally, the visual representation of cancer screening data is very heterogeneous (free text, parametric text, numerical and graphical format). The trend aims to show available data sources in a form of interactive visualisations, specifically graphs, maps and diagrams. Modern users want to easily understand aggregated information in a comprehensive and validated shape for further decision-making activities. The presented data visualisation concept heads towards data-driven approach, which is quite useful for health professionals in situations where a large amount of data must be presented in the most comprehensible way.

References

1. Azevedo, A.I.R.L.: KDD, SEMMA and CRISP-DM: a parallel overview (2008)
2. CanCon: official webpage [WWW Document]. http://www.cancercontrol.eu/. Accessed 2 Aug 2017
3. Comprehensive cancer care network: a pilot model [WWW Document]. http://cccn. onconet.cz/. Accessed 2 Aug 2017
4. Dušek, L.: Czech cancer care in numbers 2008–2009. Grada (2009)
5. Dušek, L., Mužík, J., Gelnarová, E., Fínek, J., Vyzula, R., Abrahámová, J.: Cancer incidence and mortality in the Czech Republic. Klin Onkol 23, 311–324 (2010)
6. Dušek, L., Mužík, J., Koptíková, J., Brabec, P., Žaloudík, J., Vyzula, R., Kubásek, M.: The national web portal for cancer epidemiology in the Czech Republic. In: Proceedings of the 19th International Conference Informatics for Environmental Protection (Enviroinfo 2005). Masaryk University, Brno (2005)
7. Edge, S.B., Compton, C.C.: The American joint committee on cancer: the 7th edition of the AJCC cancer staging manual and the future of TNM. Ann. Surg. Oncol. 17, 1471–1474 (2010)
8. Golfarelli, M., Maio, D., Rizzi, S.: The dimensional fact model: A conceptual model for data warehouses. Int. J. Coop. Inf. Syst. 7, 215–247 (1998)
9. Micheli, A., Coebergh, J.W., Mugno, E., Massimiliani, E., Sant, M., Oberaigner, W., Holub, J., Storm, H.H., Forman, D., Quinn, M., Aareleid, T., Sankila, R., Hakulinen, T., Faivre, J., Ziegler, H., Tryggvadòttir, L., Zanetti, R., Dalmas, M., Visser, O., Langmark, F., Bielska-Lasota, M., Wronkowski, Z., Pinheiro, P.S., Brewster, D.H., Plesko, I., Pompe-Kirn, V., Martinez-Garcia, C., Barlow, L., Möller, T., Lutz, J.M., André, M., Steward, J.A.: European health systems and cancer care. Ann. Oncol. Off. J. Eur. Soc. Med. Oncol. ESMO 14(Suppl 5), v41–v60 (2003)
10. World Health Organization: International statistical classification of diseases and related health problems. World Health Organization (2004)
11. Raghupathi, W., Raghupathi, V.: Big data analytics in healthcare: promise and potential. Health Inf. Sci. Syst. 2, 3 (2014)

12. Romero, C., Ventura, S., De Bra, P.: Knowledge discovery with genetic programming for providing feedback to courseware authors. User Model. User-Adapt. Interact. **14**, 425–464 (2004)
13. IARC Publications Website - Statistical Methods in Cancer Research Volume IV: Descriptive Epidemiology. http://publications.iarc.fr/Book-And-Report-Series/Iarc-Scientific-Publications/Statistical-Methods-In-Cancer-Research-Volume-Iv-Descriptive-Epidemiology-1994. Accessed 04 Apr 2017
14. Sastry, S.H., Babu, P., Prasada, M.S.: Implementation of CRISP Methodology for ERP Systems. arXiv Preprint arXiv:13122065 (2013)

GMP Data Warehouse – a Supporting Tool of Effectiveness Evaluation of the Stockholm Convention on Persistent Organic Pollutants

Jakub Gregor[1,2(✉)], Jana Borůvková[1], Richard Hůlek[1,2], Jiří Kalina[1,2], Kateřina Šebková[1], Jiří Jarkovský[2], Ladislav Dušek[2], and Jana Klánová[1]

[1] Research Centre for Toxic Compounds in the Environment, Masaryk University, Brno, Czech Republic
[2] Institute of Biostatistics and Analyses, Masaryk University, Brno, Czech Republic
gregor@iba.muni.cz

Abstract. The Stockholm Convention on Persistent Organic Pollutants is multilateral environmental agreement focused on selected persistent organic pollutants (POPs) for which the contracting Parties must adopt measures to eliminate or reduce their production and use or minimise the unintentional releases. One of the tools for the effectiveness evaluation of the Stockholm Convention is Global Monitoring Plan for Persistent Organic Pollutants (GMP) – a project that aims to collect global data on POPs concentrations in selected environmental matrices. This paper introduces an information system GMP Data Warehouse, which was developed in order to provide user-friendly tools for the collection, storage, analyses and visualisation of data from international POPs monitoring activities.

Keywords: Stockholm Convention · Global Monitoring Plan · POPs
Database · Data collection · Visualisation · Analysis · Standardisation
Data structure

1 Introduction

The Stockholm Convention on Persistent Organic Pollutants was adopted on 22 May 2001 in Stockholm, Sweden, and entered into force on 17 May 2004. The convention is focused on selected persistent organic pollutants (POPs) – chemicals that represent a significant risk for the environment and living organisms, including the humans.

Although POPs form a heterogeneous group from the chemical point of view, their common characteristics include acute or chronic toxicity and high resistance to transformation processes, which makes them capable of long-range transport and accumulation in tissues of the living organisms.

The Stockholm Convention (SC) and its annexes currently (2016) contain 26 selected POPs (or their groups), for which the contracting Parties must adopt measures to eliminate or reduce their production and use or minimise the unintentional releases. In other words, the list contains both chemicals that were or have been intentionally produced and used (e.g. DDT and other POP pesticides in agriculture, polychlorinated biphenyls

© IFIP International Federation for Information Processing 2017
Published by Springer International Publishing AG 2017. All Rights Reserved
J. Hřebíček et al. (Eds.): ISESS 2017, IFIP AICT 507, pp. 184–195, 2017.
https://doi.org/10.1007/978-3-319-89935-0_16

in industry) and chemicals that are unintentionally formed and released during anthropogenic processes (e.g. production of dioxins during combustion processes).

Naturally, adoption and application of (legal/technical) measures for the reduction of environmental burden by POPs is not the only step that should be implemented; these measures should be also continuously evaluated in terms of their feasibility and effectiveness. Effectiveness evaluation of the Stockholm Convention is defined in its Article 16. Among others, this article requires establishment and operation of the Global Monitoring Plan for Persistent Organic Pollutants (GMP) – a tool for the collection of global data on POPs levels, assessment of their spatial and temporal trends and thus generating information on whether the environmental burden by POPs decrease and measures adopted by the Convention are effective in reality.

2   Stockholm Convention's Global Monitoring Plan for POPs

GMP implementation was officially endorsed in 2007 by the decision. SC-3/19, of the 3rd meeting of the Conference of the Parties to the Stockholm Convention. Main objective of the GMP is global collection of available data on POPs concentrations in selected matrices – ambient air, human milk, human blood, and water (for hydrophilic substances). Article 16 of the SC expects collection of data from existing environmental monitoring programmes however it allows for capacity building assistance and establishment of new monitoring programmes only in those regions with data gaps.

Request for harmonised and standardised data collection framework and their assessment is set up in a document entitled "Guidance on the Global Monitoring Plan for Persistent Organic Pollutants" [1]. The first draft document was approved simultaneously with the establishment of the GMP framework in 2007 and has undergone several updates since then, due to the addition of several chemicals to annexes of the Convention and need for detailed updated data handling and assessment guidelines.

Data collection for GMP purposes is performed in a six-year interval and the results including interpretations, conclusions, and recommendations are published in five regional reports (UN regions) and one global monitoring report. The reports are prepared by Regional Organisation Groups (ROGs) and a Global Coordination Group (GCG). These bodies consist of experts, representatives nominated by the Parties to the SC, with a significant knowledge in environmental monitoring and data management.

3   GMP Data Warehouse Development and Tools

It is noteworthy that the collection of data from different sources (i.e. monitoring programmes) is not a trivial issue. Each national or international programme has a specific purpose, different design and methods of sampling and chemical analyses, the data are collected and stored in different forms and structures. Hence, their global comparison is a challenge that emerged immediately after the first data collection campaign in 2008. It is therefore necessary to set up a really robust and flexible methodology that allows merging such heterogeneous data together and performs their comparison, assessment and analysis. The published monitoring reports of 2008 showed that there is a strong need for a standardised electronic tool for both data collection and their presentation.

Establishment of a single data warehouse, in which all GMP data would be stored, is proposed in Chapter 6.5.2 of the GMP Guidance document. The GCG, ROGs, and Secretariat of the SC considered, supported and approved establishment of such at their meetings in 2011–2013. The concept and development of the electronic Global Monitoring Plan Data Warehouse (GMP DWH) was endorsed by the decision of the Conference of the Parties to the Stockholm Convention SC-6/23 at its 6th meeting in May 2013. Consequently, they authorised two research departments of the Masaryk University (Brno, Czech Republic) to design and develop a comprehensive information system for the collection, analysis and visualisation of GMP data in accordance with the following principles:

- fully electronic data processing
- standardised parametric data structure, standardised predefined code lists
- defined processes for the data input, validation, approval, and publication
- defined hierarchy of users and user rights with respect to access to the system and data processing
- connection of the database with visualisation and export tools
- online access to all tools and functions
- system of user support, help desk

Goal of the GMP DWH is to provide long-term reliable and cost-effective information and services to global community, support POPs monitoring activities and data management under the Stockholm Convention and offer tools for collection, storage, organisation, comparison, analysis, and evaluation of performance in relation to monitoring programmes on POPs. The objectives of the online GMP DWH are therefore twofold:

- provide user friendly tools for storage and analyses of data from international monitoring activities under the Global Monitoring Plan of the Stockholm Convention on Persistent Organic Pollutants and make POPs data visualisation available for regions and programmes that require support in data management, and
- contribute to the effectiveness evaluation of the Stockholm Convention by compiling and visualising results of global monitoring activities on POPs.

Development of the GMP DWH system was completed in 2014 and the system was handed over to the global community and main user (Secretariat of the Stockholm Convention). The GMP DWH structure has been designed to incorporate state of the art knowledge and expertise in building knowledge-based infrastructures. It encompasses data input, storage, processing (compiling and archiving) of both primary data as well as aggregated data, including supplementary data in cases where no primary data are made available. The system holds data on POPs in four core matrices: air, human milk, human blood, and water. By respecting the requirements of uniform and harmonised presentation of data, all outputs of the GMP DWH are shown on the visualisation portal (http://visualization.pops-gmp.org/2014/).

The GMP DWH architecture consists of three layers guiding the data flow from the initial upload to the final publication. Each layer is connected with appropriate tools and processes of the data flow, user administration, security, user support etc. (Fig. 1) Data repository and data visualisation are the main parts of the system accessible by a wider group of users. No additional software is required to use the system, because it is implemented fully online and is accessible through standard internet browsers (Internet Explorer, Mozilla Firefox, Google Chrome). It is highly recommended to use their recent versions, which are freely available and ensure proper functioning, particularly for visualisations and graphic outputs.

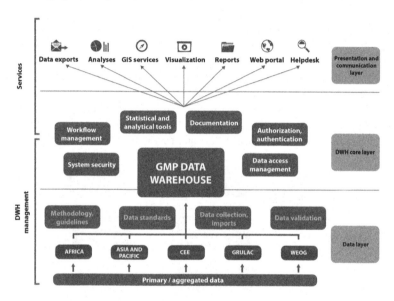

Fig. 1. GMP Data Warehouse architecture

3.1 Data Repository

The data repository refers to a database in which all data are stored and administered. Data are collected and inserted in a predefined structure, which is partly identical for all monitored environmental matrices (ambient air, human milk, human blood, water); however, it also reflects certain specificities of the individual matrices and nature of the data (primary vs aggregated). The individual items of data structure are logically grouped into three levels (Fig. 2). The top level ("Site") defines and describes the place in which sampling was performed. The middle level ("Sampling attributes") contains information about the sampling period and employed methods. The third level ("Measurement") provides data about measured chemical substances, their concentrations, statistical variability etc. Such predefined structure ensures a full comparability of collected data and also prevents gaps in their completeness.

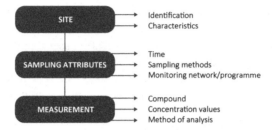

Fig. 2. Individual items of the GMP DWH data structure are grouped into three layers

The GMP DWH is designed to store aggregated data with one-year granularity. This consensus works under the assumption that a large part of data from the monitoring programmes are not available in their primary format and that POPs concentration show, particularly in temperate regions, fluctuations due to seasonal variations in the course of the year. However, data providers are allowed to send/upload both primary or aggregated data using online forms or MS Excel sheets of a predefined structure. The data sets are subsequently processed, validated and aggregated (where applicable) by the GMP DWH administrators. The data insertion process is shown in Fig. 3.

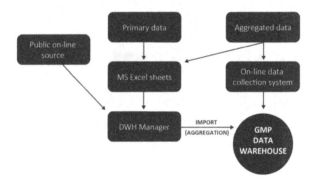

Fig. 3. The process of data insertion into the GMP DWH

Validated data are subject to approval process of the relevant geopolitical expert group ROGs; it is only relevant ROG members are allowed to approve particular data records for publication (in monitoring reports, online visualisation, data exports etc.) or reject any public use of these data in relation to the GMP.

The previous paragraphs imply that the system is accessed by various users and groups of users in terms of data management (data providers, administrators, ROG members) and geographical affiliation (individual UN Regional Groups). Management of users and user rights is therefore one of the crucial points in the system design. Access rights must be precisely defined for each individual user so that he/she could only view and process those data records that fall under his/her competence from both of the above-mentioned points of view. Data flow and the definition of user roles and rights are further complicated by the fact that the same user can be, for example, a representative of data-providing institution and a ROG member at the same time, or a European institution may provide data to ROG Africa etc. Development of the processes and rules for the management of users, their roles and rights (Fig. 4) was therefore another significant issue. This is closely linked to data security, which is guaranteed by a data security management certificate according to the ISO/IEC 27001:2014.

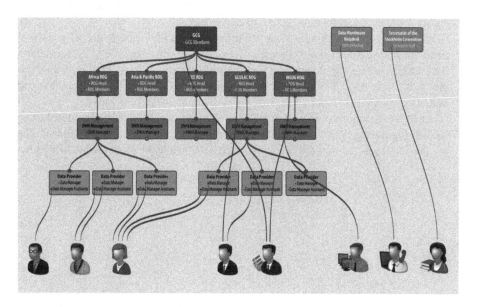

Fig. 4. Assignment of user roles and user rights in the GMP DWH

There are also other very important parts of the system, such as the statistical and analytical tools for data validation, correct aggregation, and last but not least, the assessment of time trends in POPs levels. For this purpose, a special R package [2] was developed in cooperation with the Environment Canada, which is able to perform all necessary steps. The software is described in details on a special website (http://www.genasis.cz/time-series/), which also provides a practical demonstration of the package [3]. See Sect. 3.3 for details.

3.2   Data Visualisation

Work with large data sets often requires some type of visualisation in order to understand their nature and distribution, to compare different data sets, or to identify outliers. The website http://visualization.pops-gmp.org/2014/ [4] was designed to provide such basic overview of data in the GMP DWH; moreover, it also offers advanced analytical and mapping tools that enable the user to browse and to analyse data from different points of view:

- "Spatial distribution" – a map overview of sites for which data are available. The sites can be stratified according to a set of criteria.

- "Data availability" – a plot describing data availability in time (years in which sampling ran) and for individual POPs (compounds that were analysed).
- "Summary statistics" – assessment of measured concentrations of a particular compound at individual sampling sites and years by means of descriptive statistics. The user can switch between various types of central value (mean, median) and variability (percentiles, min–max, standard deviation).
- "Time series" – three different views on time trends of POPs levels globally. Two of them are maps that display statistical assessment of long-term trends, i.e. whether the trend is increasing, decreasing, or statistically insignificant. The third tool is a plot that shows annual values of POPs concentrations in time, trend regression and outputs of statistical tests.
- "Data exports" – this provides an overall summary of selected dataset i.e. contributing monitoring programmes, sites, and analytical methods included in the current data set, and also tools for export of the dataset to files that may be processed in MS Excel.

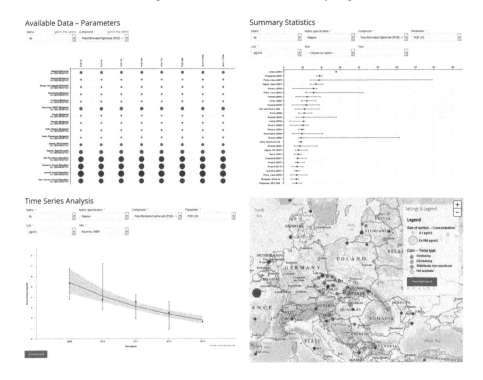

Fig. 5. Example of graphical outputs in the GMP DWH visualisation tool

The above-mentioned modules (Fig. 5) are further enriched by other functions to facilitate the work with the system. Graphical outputs can be directly adjusted according to user needs (ordering values, type of values) and they can also be exported into a PNG format in order to be used in further work. Each combination of filters and each view on the selected data set are defined by a unique code which is included in the URL of a particular view. This significantly enhances linking and sharing of information through various internet communication channels.

3.3 Employed Information Technologies and Approaches

The GENASIS system [5] was used as a platform for handling primary data and their transformation into the form and structure required by the GMP Guidance [1] and GMP DWH standards (see Sect. 3.1). An OpenCPU technology was used for integration of the R software environment into the GENASIS infrastructure [6]. The R package developed in cooperation between the Masaryk University and Environment Canada [2] ensured harmonisation of data on the level of data standards and metadata. In particular, this tool was used for the recalculation of air-passive sampling data to volume-based values, which ensured their comparability with data from the air-active monitoring programmes. Further steps involved the calculation of derived parameters required by the GMP Guidance (sums of related compounds, toxicity equivalents – TEQs) and the summation of individual sampled fractions (for air data). Another (unpublished) R package was used for the annual aggregation of primary data.

The data visualisation tool employs its own database layer, which is updated in 24-hour intervals on the basis of the central data warehouse content. The data and data views are partially pre-prepared and pre-calculated to enable a faster and more fluent operation, calculations and loading. Almost all charts displayed within the data visualisation are custom-made and have been implemented using the D3.js library, since common available visualisation libraries do not contain required types of charts.

Three different servers technologies are involved in the data visualisation: application/web server (Apache), ArcGIS Server and OpenCPU R-server. The application server provides web services and ensures the system security. The map server employs the ArcGIS for Server and ArcGIS for Javascript technologies to create map compositions that obtain information on sites from the database and display sites that correspond to the user's selection in map windows of the web application. The R-server performs real-time calculations of time trends for selected sites, compounds and period [7] (Fig. 6).

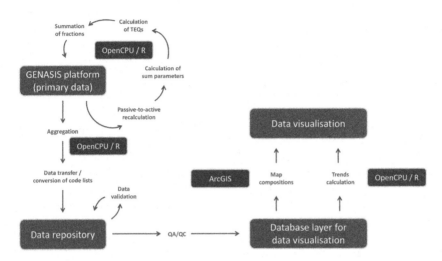

Fig. 6. Procedures and software tools employed in processing of the POPs data on their way from the primary database (GENASIS platform) to the GMP data visualisation

4   GMP DWH Operation and User Support

The final version of the GMP DWH was provided to the main user (Secretariat of the Stockholm Convention) in 2014, in which the second GMP data collection took place. In contrast to the first data collection period, these data were collected digitally in a parametric and structured form, which enabled both standardisation and comparability of outputs that were presented in regional monitoring reports. Monitoring reports were adopted and data visualisation was made publicly available at the 7th meeting of the Conference of the Parties to the Stockholm Convention in May 2015.

All tools and parts of the GMP DWH are accessible through the web portal www.pops-gmp.org/dwh. The website contains all important information about the system, links to individual tools, background information, user guides, overview of data structure and reporting spreadsheets (Fig. 7).

Fig. 7. Web portal of the GMP DWH (www.pops-gmp.org/dwh)

4.1 Providing User Support During Implementation of the GMP Data Tool

Help desk was introduced as soon as the first version of the GMP DWH emerged in 2013. This service supported all GMP DWH users and other relevant persons interested in the project. The service is available on weekdays from 8am to 4 pm CET via e-mail and phone. Help desk operators either immediately provide requested information or assistance, or in case of a more complicated request, allocate the task to another expert/ data manager. The help desk performance is in agreement with requirements of the international standard ISO/IEC 20000-1:2012 and guarantees that response will be provided within 24 h.

The main tasks of the service include:

- technical assistance to all GMP Data Warehouse (GMP DWH) users
- transfer of requests to appropriate DWH managers
- administration of user accounts and associated rights
- contact point for data files from the providers, their formal validation and transfer to DWH managers

- contact point for error reports and suggestions for further software and services development

The list below shows the range and types of requested hotline services and support in 2014 (a period in which the data collection, validation, and approval were carried out and the visualisation tool was not yet publicly available):

- Reception and validation of data files from the Environment Canada, communication with persons responsible for data transfer (3 persons). Most issues discussed were related to correct data format and terminology (~ 10 requests)
- Additional correction in data already provided and entered in the database (~ 10 requests)
- Providing ROG members and their consultants with access to the database and visualisation, preparation of instructions and user guides (43 user accounts)
- Support to users experiencing technical problems with the visualisation tool. These technical issues were caused by older versions of web browsers used by users. (~ 5 requests)
- Identification of bugs in the visualisation tool in cooperation with the Secretariat members and other users (~ 15 requests)

4.2 Attendance of the GMP Data Visualisation Website

Google Analytics were employed for the assessment of attendance of the GMP visualisation website. Table 1 summarises the main characteristics of users' behaviour when browsing the website during the first year from publication (from 1 May 2015 to 1 May 2016). The data indicate, among others, a relatively long duration of an average session and a high number of pages viewed. The highest attendance peaks were recorded on 11 June and 28 July 2016, when the GMP DWH was presented at the BRS Conventions' Twitter account and newsletter, respectively.

Table 1. Users' behaviour on the GMP data visualisation website in the first year of public operation (assessed by Google Analytics)

Parameter	Counts
Sessions	2,025
Users	818
Page views	30,012
Pages per session	14.82
Average session duration	11 min 8 s

4.3 Current Use of the GMP DWH

Functional and content updates of the system were temporarily discontinued on the date of its official publication and of publication of regional monitoring reports in May 2015. In the period preceding the final publication, the data visualisation module was mainly used by ROG members and consultants for data approval and compilation of the monitoring reports. It now serves as a supplementary and supporting tool to the monitoring reports that enhances browsing, viewing and analysing the global POPs data. It is also presented as a reference tool in the communication with new data providers and partners in order to identify new potential data sources worldwide.

5   Conclusion

A multimodular online GMP DWH was developed for data collection, processing and reporting for current and future GMP data collection rounds. The system is based on fully parametric data sheets to improve the quality of collected global data sets on POPs concentrations, to determine their fate in the environment over time and to strengthen the responsibility and visibility of data providers. The developed online tool for the Global Monitoring Plan is capable of visualising information available globally or from regional and country perspective. The GMP DWH is accessible for anyone with internet connection on a dedicated portal www.pops-gmp.org/dwh. The system is customised to function in all standard internet browsers (Internet Explorer, Mozilla Firefox, Google Chrome).

References

1. United Nations Environment Programme: Guidance on the Global Monitoring Plan for Persistent Organic Pollutants. Secretariat of the Stockholm Convention on Persistent Organic Pollutants, Geneva (2007)
2. Kalina, J., Klánová, J., Dušek, L., Harner, T., Borůvková, J., Jarkovský, J.: Genasis: Global ENvironmental ASsessment Information System (GENASIS) computational tools. Masaryk University, Brno (2014). https://cran.r-project.org/web/packages/genasis/index.html
3. Kalina, J., Jarkovský, J., Dušek, L., Klánová, J., Borůvková, J., Šnábl, I., Šmíd, R.: Time series assessment in the Era of Stockholm Convention & GMP. Masaryk University, Brno (2014). http://www.genasis.cz/time-series/
4. Hůlek, R., Borůvková, J., Gregor, J., Kalina, J., Bednářová, Z., Šebková, K., Melkes, O., Šalko, M., Novák, R., Jarkovský, J., Dušek, L., Klánová, J.: Global Monitoring Plan of the Stockholm Convention on Persistent Organic Pollutants: visualisation and on-line analysis of global levels of chemicals in air, water, breast milk and blood. Masaryk University, Brno (2014). http://visualization.pops-gmp.org/2014/
5. Hůlek, R., Jarkovský, J., Kubásek, M., Gregor, J., Hřebíček, J., Dušek, L., Klánová, J., Šebková, K., Borůvková, J., Holoubek, I.: GENASIS system architecture. In: Hřebíček, J., Schimak, G., Kubásek, M., Rizzoli, A.E. (eds.) ISESS 2013. IAICT, vol. 413, pp. 230–239. Springer, Heidelberg (2013). https://doi.org/10.1007/978-3-642-41151-9_22
6. Hůlek, R., Kalina, J., Dušek, L., Jarkovský, J.: Integration of R statistical environment into ICT infrastructure of GMP and GENASIS. In: Hřebíček, J., Schimak, G., Kubásek, M., Rizzoli, A.E. (eds.) ISESS 2013. IAICT, vol. 413, pp. 240–252. Springer, Heidelberg (2013). https://doi.org/10.1007/978-3-642-41151-9_23
7. Kalina, J., Hůlek, R., Borůvková, J., Jarkovský, J., Klánová, J., Dušek, L.: Three levels of R language involvement in global monitoring plan warehouse architecture. In: Hřebíček, J., Denzer, R., Schimak, G., Argentm, R.M. (eds.) IFIP AICT, vol. 448, pp. 426–433. Springer, Heidelberg (2015). https://doi.org/10.1007/978-3-319-15994-2_43

A Variable Length Chromosome Genetic Algorithm Approach to Identify Species Distribution Models Useful for Freshwater Ecosystem Management

Sacha Gobeyn$^{(\boxtimes)}$ and Peter L. M. Goethals

Laboratory of Environmental Toxicology and Aquatic Ecology,
Ghent University, Coupure Links 653, 9000 Ghent, Belgium
Sacha.Gobeyn@ugent.be

Abstract. Increasing pressure on freshwater ecosystems requires river managers and policy makers to take actions to protect ecosystem health. Species distribution models (SDMs) are identified as appropriate tools to assess the effect of pressures on ecosystems. A number of methods are available to model species distributions, however, it remains a challenge to identify well-performing models from a large set of candidate models. Metaheuristic search algorithms can aid to identify appropriate models by scanning possible combinations of explanatory model variables, model parameters and interaction functions. This large search space can be efficiently scanned with simple genetic algorithms (SGAs). In this paper, we test the potential of a variable length chromosome SGA to perform parameter estimation (PE) and input variable selection (IVS) for a macroinvertebrate SDM. We show that the SGA is an appropriate tool to identify fair to satisfying performing SDMs. In addition, we show that SGA performance and the uncertainty varies as a function of the chosen hyper parameters. The results can aid to further optimise the algorithm so models explaining species distributions can be identified and used for analysis in river management.

Keywords: Species distribution models · Model identification
Genetic algorithms · Freshwater management · Macroinvertebrate species
Input variable selection · Parameter estimation

1 Introduction

Freshwater ecologist and river managers are in need for system analysis techniques to investigate a wide range of ecological questions and support decision making. Species distribution models (SDMs) aiming to describe the species response to driving processes, have shown to be valuable tools in ecosystem health management. Many approaches to identify SDMs are available [17], however, the challenge remains to test a large set of candidate explanatory models.

Genetic algorithms (GAs) classified under evolutionary algorithms and inspired by various mechanisms observed in evolution (i.e. reproduction, mutation, selection) are promising approaches to evaluate a large search space [12, 15, 18]. Consequently, GAs

© IFIP International Federation for Information Processing 2017
Published by Springer International Publishing AG 2017. All Rights Reserved
J. Hřebíček et al. (Eds.): ISESS 2017, IFIP AICT 507, pp. 196–208, 2017.
https://doi.org/10.1007/978-3-319-89935-0_17

are used to select input variables (input variable selection, IVS) for SDMs by using them as a wrapper for data-driven approach [3]. They are also used to estimate parameter values (parameter estimation, PE) for fuzzy logic SDMs [5, 24]. PE and IVS are important aspects in SDM identification and it can hypothesized whether a joint approach can be encoded in GAs.

In this paper, we present the use of a simple genetic algorithm (SGA) for PE and IVS for an SDM. To do so, we encode the optimisation problem in a variable length chromosome. The approach is tested for a freshwater species, *cloeon dipterum*, with the Limnodata of the Netherlands. The acquired SDM performance, parameters and input variables are analysed. In addition, a sensitivity analysis is done to test the effect of the algorithm hyper parameters on the SGA performance (Sect. 3). The results of this approach are discussed in Sect. 4.

2   SDM Development

The SDM is developed by following a four step approach (Fig. 1). First, a number of ecological concepts are used to define the model. Second, the data are gathered and processed to construct the model (step 3). In a final step, a search algorithms is implemented and used to identify well-performing models.

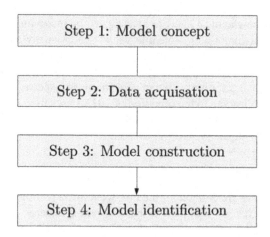

Fig. 1. Overview of methodology to develop SDMs (adapted after [2]).

2.1   Model Concept

Filter theory is used as basic concept for the SDM. In this theory, the realized species assemblage is explained by a number of hierarchical filters, i.e. dispersal, abiotic and biotic filters [14, 21]. Here, it is used because of its structural nature dividing the explanatory processes of species presence/absence in several filters. Only abiotic filtering is considered because the effect of pollutants on the species assemblage is assumed as the most relevant source of information for ecosystem health management.

Species response curves (or habitat preference curves) defining the biological response to abiotic gradients are used as to reflect the abiotic filters. The biological response can be expressed by many measures, i.e. species presence, abundance, density, usable area or volume. Species presence is used as a measure for biological response because it is assumed to be a robust measure for biological response [6].

In this paper, fine-scale and large-scale abiotic filters are considered. Fine-scale filters are filters acting at a local scale filtering species due to point specific pollution. In addition, the river typology characteristics (e.g. geology, river/catchment slope,..) are considered to be large-scale filters which act on a river or catchment scale [21].

2.2   Data

The Limnology Neerlandica database (http://www.stowa.nl/) and information on the river typology [4] are processed and compiled to a coupled database. The Limnodata is a database containing observations of the biology (macroinvertebrates, fish and macroflora) and physical-chemical state over 20 years in the Netherlands. The river typology is defined as a function of river catchment characteristics, i.e. average river slope, water source, average river width, catchment area, tidal influence, catchment geology [22].

The observations of the macroinvertebrate species *cloeon dipterum* are extracted from the Limnodata. The records are transformed from abundance to presence/absence in order to get an insight in the spatial and temporal distribution patterns of the species. Outliers in the physico-chemical data are investigated by inspecting summary statistics (mean, minimum, maximum and percentile values) and visually analysing box plots, histograms and dot plots. A number of variables are tested to physical boundaries. For instance, the width and depth of rivers are assessed as a function of the river type. In addition, the mass balance for nitrogen and phosphorus is inspected. In total 133 values are inspected in-depth leading to the omission of 102 records from the data. Finally, the correlation between variables is calculated so to exclude highly correlated variables and reduce dimensionality of the problem (Table 1).

2.3   Model Construction

Species response curves are defined for the fine-scale filters (continuous variables). The species response curves are assumed to have a non-symmetric unimodal trapezoid shape chosen as a simplification of a bell-shaped curve [1, 13]. The curves are allowed to be asymmetric so they can skew from extreme (heavy polluted) conditions [1, 16]. Four parameters (a_1, a_2, a_3 and a_4) are used to define the trapezoid curve:

$$SI_f\left(x_i^j\right) = \begin{cases} 0 & \text{if} & x_i^j < a_1 \\ \frac{(x_i^j - a_1)}{(a_2 - a_1)} & \text{if} & x_i^j \in [a_1, a_2[\\ 1 & \text{if} & x_i^j \in [a_2, a_3] \\ \frac{(a_4 - x_i^j)}{(a_4 - a_3)} & \text{if} & x_i^j \in]a_3, a_4] \\ 0 & \text{if} & a_4 < x_i^j \end{cases} \tag{1}$$

Table 1. Overview of physico-chemical variables. #n: not included because of insufficient samples after coupling with biological data. ex. = excluded, corr. = correlated to, r = spearman rank correlation, min. = minimum, $\tilde{X}$ = median, $\bar{X}$ = mean, max. = maximum, Chlor. a = chlorophyll a, Cond. = conductivity, Transp. = transparency, Kjel. N = kjeldahl N, R. = river, Temp. = temperature.

Variable	ex.	Reason	min.	$\tilde{X}$	$\bar{X}$	max.
%DO	x	Corr. DO (r = 0.89)	0.00	80.00	78.07	277.00
BOD_2	x	#n	10.00	10.00	92.87	2000.00
BOD_5			0.05	2.00	3.55	360.00
Chloride			1.00	40.00	56.99	1250.00
Chlor. a	x	#n	0.10	9.00	19.51	1170.00
COD	x	#n	2.00	26.00	32.57	200.00
Cond.	x	Corr. Chloride (r = 0.79)	0.50	50.00	52.48	542.00
DO			0.00	8.80	8.64	29.00
Transp.			0.00	0.50	0.50	3.00
Flow	x	#n	0.00	0.10	0.69	33.34
Kjel. N	x	Corr. NH_4 (r = 0.91)	0.00	1.70	2.60	70.00
NH_3-N			0.00	0.01	0.03	6.10
NH_4-N			0.00	0.40	1.13	80.00
NO_2-N			0.00	0.06	0.10	6.30
NO_3-N			0.00	3.50	4.89	64.00
PO_4-P			0.00	0.07	0.28	26.00
pH			3.60	7.40	7.33	10.40
R. depth	x	#n	0.00	0.40	0.66	5.00
R. width	x	#n	0.02	3.00	5.94	135.00
SO_4			1.00	62.00	68.15	6200.00
Temp.			−1.00	11.50	11.73	32.00
Total N	x	Corr. NO_3-N (r = 0.93)	0.05	5.56	7.07	66.30
Total P	x	Corr. to PO_4-P (r = 0.92)	0.00	0.20	0.47	29.00
Velocity	x	#n	0.00	20.00	24.15	300.00

With SI_f, the suitability index for the fine-scale filters, x_i^j, the input value i ($\in \{0, 1, .., N\}$, n data points) for variable j ($\in \{0, 1, .., M\}$, m variables). The parameters a_1 and a_4 describe the range of the conditions in which a species is able to survive. The parameters a_2 and a_3 describe the preferable range of conditions for the species (i.e. $SI = 1$). The values of a_1 and a_4 are set by the minimum and maximum values of the observations for which the species is observed. For the large-scale abiotic filters, suitability indices are defined based on a set of parameters (a_1, a_2,..., and a_r) and the class (categorical):

$$SI_l(x_i^k) = \begin{cases} a_1 & \text{if } x_i^k = C_1^k \\ a_2 & \text{if } x_i^k = C_2^k \\ \quad \dots \\ a_r & \text{if } x_i^k = C_r^k \end{cases} \tag{2}$$

With SI_l, the suitability index for the large-scale filter, x_i^k, the input value i ($\in \{0, 1, .., N\}$, n data points) for categorical variable k ($\in \{0, 1, .., O\}$, o variables). The habitat suitability index (HSI) for a point i is calculated by multiplying the geometric mean for the fine and large-scale filters:

$$HSI_i = \left(\prod_{j=1}^{m} SI(x_i^j)\right)^{\frac{1}{m}} * \left(\prod_{k=1}^{o} SI(x_i^k)\right)^{\frac{1}{o}} \tag{3}$$

2.4   Model Identification with Simple Genetic Algorithms

The aim of the model identification tool is to identify a number of input variables and coupled species response curve parameters with an optimisation algorithm. This algorithm has to be able to efficiently search a large unconstrained space since it is difficult to a priori define the shape of a species response (skewed, Gaussian, …). In addition, a number of solutions is possibly more informative than one solution. Therefore, it is preferred to obtain an ensemble. The tool should be compatible with high performance computing to facilitate repeated runs for uncertainty analysis. Even more, it is required to be an open source package, available freely online, so to increase code and approach transparency (Fig. 2).

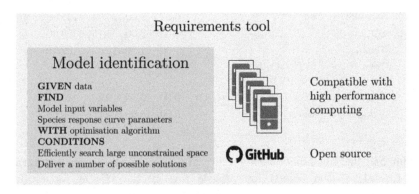

Fig. 2. Requirements for model identification tool for species distribution models.

An SGA with three operators, i.e. selection, crossover and mutation is implemented and used as optimisation algorithm. An SGA requires the encoding of the phenotype, i.e. the model, in a genotype. This genotype is typically coded as a binary string. This string is then translated to a model in a genotype-phenotype mapper. A list of lists is programmed to implement a variable length chromosome (Fig. 3). The genome is defined by a second order binary string when a bit in the first order binary string has a value of one. The first order binary string is translated in a mapper by either in- or excluding the variable (one = present, zero = absent). The second order binary string is translated to parameter values of a_2 and a_3 in the mapper function by transforming every three bit sequence to an integer representation which is used to define the values for a_2 and a_3 (Eq. 1) and a_r (Eq. 2).

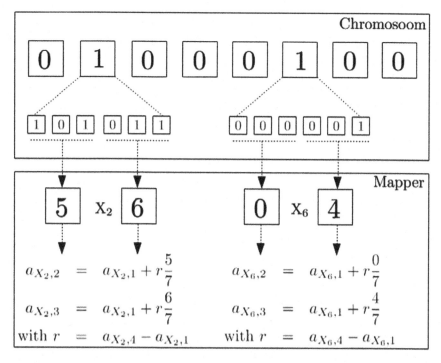

Fig. 3. Definition of chromosome and mapper function. The genome is programmed as a list of lists, where a second order binary string is defined when a bit of the first order string has the value of one. Every three bits of this second order string are translated to an integer which is used to define the values of the parameters a_2, a_3 and a_r. In this example, the second and sixth variable are considered in the model. The parameters for the species response curves are defined by second order binary strings (six bits). The first three bits for variable X_2 are used to define $a_{X2,2}$ and the last three bits to define $a_{X2,3}$. A binary coding is used to define a fraction (i.e. 5/7 and 6/7) of the total range r ($a_4 - a_1$) which is added to the parameter a_1 to obtain values for a_2 and a_3. Parameters a_2 and a_3 are respectively bounded by the range [a_1, a_3] and [a_2, a_4]. For the categorical variables, the parameters a_r are bounded by zero and one.

The tournament selection method is used to select the fittest individuals from a population as parents [11]. The selection rate defined as the fraction of the population that survives for the next step of mating is multiplied with the population size to obtain a number of parents. In the crossover operator, the parents are randomly paired to mate and produce offspring with a certain rate, i.e. crossover rate. If mating does not occur, the parents are replaced in the population. The last operator, mutation, is defined as the probability that a random gene is assigned a new value ($0 \rightarrow 1$ or $1 \rightarrow 0$). The fitness of the chromosomes is the sum of squared errors (SSE) calculated with the HSI_i values and the observed presence or absence Pr_i:

$$SSE = \sum_{i=1}^{n} (Pr_i - HSI_i)^2 \tag{4}$$

3   Results

The SGA is implemented and used to identify near-optimal models for the species *cloeon dipterum*. In the first part of this section, a set of hyper parameters (mutation and crossover rate) for the SGA are tested so to estimate the effect of hyper parameter choice on the algorithm performance. In the second part, the results found with the SGA and near-optimal hyper parameters are used to analyse the acquired model structure and performance.

3.1   Sensitivity of SGA

The SGA sensitivity as a function of the hyper parameter values are shown in Fig. 4. For this experiment, an initial near-optimal set of parameters is determined by following the guidelines of [12]. The required number of chromosomes P are estimated by applying Eq. 5:

$$\frac{FE}{P} \log_{10}\left(1 - \frac{1}{P}\right) = -M - \log_{10}(\sqrt{\frac{l}{12}}) \tag{5}$$

With M equal to three, FE, the number function evaluations determined by dividing the computational time available by the average runtime of one simulation and l, the chromosome length. For l, the maximum possible length of the chromosome is used (= 111 = three bits * (two parameters * 12 continues variables + 13 parameters for categorical variables)). With Eq. 5, 100 is found as a value for P. The mutation rate is calculated by dividing five by P (pm = 0.05 * 100%) and the crossover rate (pc) is set to 100% [12]. It is assumed that the performance of the SGA is near-optimal with these values. In order to verify the choice of the values, the sensitivity of the SGA performance to the values is checked by assessing the effect of the surrounding values of the found near-optimal values for the crossover and mutation rate (nine point grid with pc = {60, 85, 100} and pm = {1, 5, 10}).

The best found solution follows a similar evolution for the nine sets of hyper parameters with a varying convergence and performance. When inspecting the effect of the mutation rate (pm) on the performance of the algorithm, one observes that the SGA analysis with a mutation rate of 1% gives on average the best solutions (Fig. 4, left panel). The evolution of the best solution found with a mutation rate of 5% is similar whereas a higher mutation rate (10%) leads to less optimal solutions. The initial speed with which these solutions are found is highest for a mutation rate of 5%, however, the

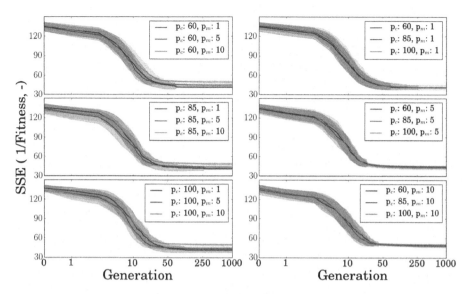

Fig. 4. Evolution of SSE (inverse of fitness) as a function of the number of generations. On the left, the results are shown for varying mutation rates and constant crossover rates. On the right, the results are shown for constant mutation rates and varying crossover rates. The uncertainty on the analysis is acquired by repeating the SGA a number of times with different initial conditions and preserving the best solution every generation.

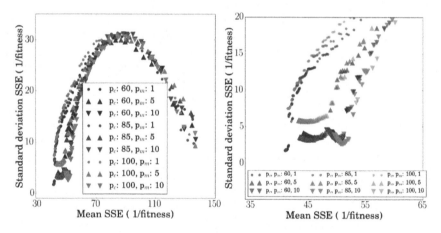

Fig. 5. Standard deviation on SSE as a function of the mean value of the SSE, for varying values of the hyper parameters (%). The right panel zooms in a narrower range of the left panel.

population converges - on average - earlier. For the crossover rate (Fig. 4, right panel), one observes that the sensitivity of the performance is lower than for the mutation rate.

One observes that a varying degree of uncertainty is observed for different hyper parameter values (Figs. 4 and 5). The uncertainty is estimated by repeatedly running the SGA with a number of initial conditions and preserving the best solution over the generations for every SGA run. The variation of this uncertainty follows a hyperbole as a function of the mean SSE (and thus the generation) (Fig. 5, left panel). At the point of convergence (low SSE, Fig. 5, right panel), the uncertainty on the found near-optimal solutions for a crossover rate of 85% is lower than for a crossover rate of 100%. This seems to suggest that the crossover rate of 85% is an appropriate choice to reduce SGA analysis uncertainty.

3.2   Analysis of Identified SDMs

The acquired models with the SGA (pm = 1%, pc = 85%) are evaluated by calculating the Cohen's Kappa (Kappa) and area under the receiver operator curve (AUC) (see [20] for mathematical description). The acquired models are assessed to have a fair to satisfying performance. The mean Kappa is equal to 0.33 ± 0.03 which is assessed as fair (Kappa $\in [0.2, 0.4]$, see [8]). The mean AUC is equal to 0.7 ± 0.03 which is assessed as satisfying (AUC > 0.7, see [19]). In Fig. 6, the model structure and accompanied uncertainty found by repeatedly running the SGA is shown. The support (%) for a model variable is calculated as a measure of variable importance by dividing the number of times a variable is selected by the SGA by the total number of SGA analysis. The support for the variable pH is very high (99%) whereas the support for the river slope, catchment area, tides and geology is lower and uncertain.

In Fig. 7, the species response curves and the accompanied uncertainty for the variable pH is shown. Either a response with very steep boundaries or a triangular response is observed. The uncertainty is shown for three values of the mutation rate (constant crossover rate). It is observed that the uncertainty on the acquired curves increases for higher mutation rate. This patterns is similar to the increase of uncertainty in the convergence of the objective function (Fig. 5, right panel). When inspecting the uncertainty on the parameters of the categorical variables (not shown here), one observes a rather high uncertainty. In conclusion, the uncertainty in the objective function is reflected in the uncertainty of the model structure.

4   Discussion and Outlook

In this paper, a variable length chromosome SGA is implemented and used to jointly perform IVS and PE. The implemented algorithm is able to identify fair to satisfying models. The uncertainty on the acquired species response curve parameters is rather low, at least for the variable with a high support. In addition, it is observed that the uncertainty on the acquired near-optimal solution is not equal over different values of the mutation and crossover rate.

The accuracy of the models could be improved by increasing the precision of the binary encoding used for the algorithm. In the current implementation every three bits code one parameter of the species response curves (see Fig. 3). This allows to encode eight discrete values for every parameter. The representation restricts the possible parameter values to a limited set defined by the lower and upper boundary of the parameter interval and the number of bits [24]. Increasing the number of bits for the binary encoding might increase the precision but will also increase the length of the

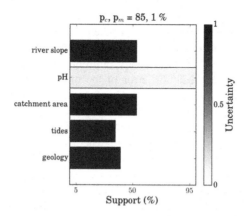

Fig. 6. Support for variable inclusion for repeated SGA analysis ($p_c = 85\%$, $p_m = 1\%$). The support is calculated by dividing the number of times a variable is selected by the SGA by the total number of analysis (i.e. 100). The uncertainty is estimated with the Shannon entropy [22].

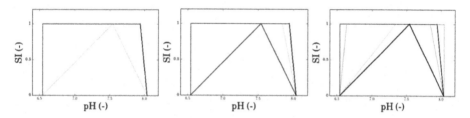

Fig. 7. Uncertainty on acquired species response curves with the repeated SGA analysis. From left to right, a mutation rate of 1, 5 and 10% is used (constant crossover rate = 85%).

chromosome. Consequently, different near-optimal values for the hyper parameters will be obtained with Eq. 5. When testing the required number of chromosomes, for a fixed number of *FE*, one observes that the found number of chromosomes (and thus mutation rate, see [12]) is almost equal for higher chromosome lengths. For example, for a bit length of three, a maximum chromosomes length of 111 (three bits * (two parameters * 12 continues variables + 13 parameter for categorical variables)) leads to a population size of 112, whereas for a four and six bit problem ($l = 148$, $l = 185$) a number of 111 and 110 chromosomes is found. Since the determined near-optimal values for the hyper parameters for varying chromosome lengths does not vary, it is expected that the performance and uncertainty of the SGA will not vary as a function of the length used to encode the optimisation. This suggests that increasing the precision of the binary encoding will not influence the performance and uncertainty of the SGA analysis. Additional experiments with the SGA should confirm this hypothesis.

A hyperbolic relation is found between the uncertainty on the SGA analysis and the found near-optimal solution. At the start of the analysis, the uncertainty is rather small, and increases with the number of generations to finally converge to a value as the SGA converges. There are differences in the amount of uncertainty at convergence for varying values of mutation and crossover rate. For low mutation rates, the uncertainty on the found near-optimal solution declines as the crossover rate is lowered. For higher mutation rates, this relation is inverse but less apparent. In general the guidelines by [12] are assessed as appropriate for these type of problems, since with these settings the SGA is able to reduce the prediction error of the models (mean SSE declines from approximately 140 to 40). Options to further improve the algorithm performance can be to improve the exploitive character of the algorithm by combing the genetic algorithm with a hill climbing (HC) approach or to vary the mutation and crossover rates over the generations. Further research can investigate whether these implementation have a significant added value for SDM identification and whether they can reduce the uncertainty of the analysis.

Genetic algorithms have shown to be valuable for PE and IVS in species distribution modelling [3, 5]. In this study, a variable length chromosome implementation of an SGA is presented to jointly perform PE and IVS. The results tested for one species are promising, however, it should be further investigated how the performance of the algorithm varies as function of the algorithm settings. In addition, the approach should be validated by applying the SGA for different species.

The current available software is an open source package implemented in the Python programming language [9, 10]. Many other packages are available (Generalized Linear Models, GLM, in the R programming language or Genetic Algorithm for Rule set Production/Prediction (GARP) software [23]). For instance, the GLM R package is an user-friendly package useful for ecologist, however, automated running a number of analysis to estimate uncertainty is difficult. Even more, the statistical approaches present a number of boundary conditions to the shape of the species response. In the developed approach, these boundary conditions are relaxed as is the case for GARP. The difference with GARP is that the SDMIT approach is designed to run on high performance clusters whereas GARP was initially designed for single-run analysis in a graphical user interface environment. In addition, machine learning approaches like decision trees and support vector machines are available [7]), however, the disadvantage of these approaches is that the tools are not implemented specifically for the optimisation of SDMs and thus often lack the ecological theoretical background. Consequently they are used as data mining approaches rather than model optimisation algorithms. The SDMIT packages is an answer to these limitations. With this, SDMs can obtained that improve the insight in species and community response to environmental changes.

Acknowledgments. Sacha Gobeyn is supported by a Bijzonder Onderzoeksfonds (BOF) project related to the Ecuador Biodiversity Network of the Vlaamse Interuniversitaire Raad-Universitaire Ontwikkelingssamenwerking (VLIR-UOS). This research was performed in the context of the VLIR Ecuador Biodiversity Network project. The computational resources (Stevin Supercomputer Infrastructure) and services used in this work were provided by the VSC (Flemish Supercomputer Center), funded by Ghent University, the Hercules Foundation and the Flemish Government - department EW.

References

1. Austin, M.P.: Species distribution models and ecological theory: a critical assessment and some possible new approaches. Ecol. Model. **200**, 1–19 (2007). https://doi.org/10.1016/j.ecolmodel.2006.07.005
2. Bennetsen, E., Gobeyn, S., Goethals, P.L.M.: Species distribution models grounded in ecological theory for decision support in river management. Ecol. Model. **325**, 1–12 (2016). https://doi.org/10.1016/j.ecolmodel.2015.12.016
3. D'heygere, T., Goethals, P.L.M., De Pauw, N.: Use of genetic algorithms to select input variables in decision tree models for the prediction of benthic macroinvertebrates. Ecol. Model. **160**, 291–300 (2003). https://doi.org/10.1016/S0304-3800(02)00260-0
4. Elbersen, J.W.H., Verdonschot, P.F.M., Roels, B., Hartholt, J.G.: Definitiestudie kader-richtlijn water (KRW) I. Typologie nederlandse oppervlaktewateren. Alterra, Research Instituut voor de Groene Ruimte, Wageningen (2003)
5. Fukuda, S., De Baets, B., Mouton, A.M., et al.: Effect of model formulation on the optimization of a genetic Takagi-Sugeno fuzzy system for fish habitat suitability evaluation. Ecol Modell **222**, 1401–1413 (2011). https://doi.org/10.1016/j.ecolmodel.2011.01.023
6. Fukuda, S., Mouton, A.M., De Baets, B.: Abundance versus presence/absence data for modelling fish habitat preference with a genetic Takagi-Sugeno fuzzy system. Environ. Monit. Assess. **184**, 6159–6171 (2012). https://doi.org/10.1007/s10661-011-2410-2
7. Fukuda, S., De Baets, B., Waegeman, W., Verwaeren, J., Mouton, A.M.: Habitat prediction and knowledge extraction for spawning European grayling (Thymallus thymallus L.) using a broad range of species distribution models. Environ. Model Softw. **47**, 1–6 (2013). https://doi.org/10.1016/j.envsoft.2013.04.005
8. Gabriels, W., Goethals, P.L.M., Dedecker, A.P., Lek, S., De Pauw, N.: Analysis of macrobenthic communities in Flanders, Belgium, using a stepwise input variable selection procedure with artificial neural networks. Aquat. Ecol. **41**, 427–441 (2007). https://doi.org/10.1007/s10452-007-9081-7
9. Gobeyn, S.: Species distribution model identification tool (SDMIT). https://doi.org/10.5281/zenodo.998046. https://sachagobeyn.github.io/SDMIT/
10. Gobeyn, S., Volk, M., Dominguez-Granda, L., Goethals, P.L.M.: Input variable selection with a simple genetic algorithm for conceptual species distribution models: a case study of river pollution in Ecuador. Environ. Model Softw. **92**, 269–316 (2017). https://doi.org/10.1016/j.envsoft.2017.02.012
11. Goldberg, D.E., Deb, K.: A comparative analysis of selection schemes used in genetic algorithms. Found. Genet. Algorithms **1**, 69–93 (1991). 10.1.1.101.9494
12. Gibbs, M.S., Dandy, G.C., Maier, H.R.: A genetic algorithm calibration method based on convergence due to genetic drift. Inf. Sci. **178**, 2857–2869 (2008). https://doi.org/10.1016/j.ins.2008.03.012
13. Guisan, A., Zimmermann, N.E.: Predictive habitat distribution models in ecology. Ecol. Model. **135**, 147–186 (2000). https://doi.org/10.1016/S0304-3800(00)00354-9
14. Guisan, A., Rahbek, C.: SESAM – a new framework integrating macroecological and species distribution models for predicting spatio-temporal patterns of species assemblages. J. Biogeogr. **38**, 1433–1444 (2011). https://doi.org/10.1111/j.1365-2699.2011.02550.x
15. Hamblin, S.: On the practical usage of genetic algorithms in ecology and evolution. Methods Ecol. Evol. **4**, 184–194 (2013). https://doi.org/10.1111/2041-210X.12000
16. Hirzel, A.H., Le Lay, G.: Habitat suitability modelling and Niche theory. J. Appl. Ecol. **45**, 1372–1381 (2008). https://doi.org/10.1111/j.1365-2664.2008.01524.x

17. Li, X., Wang, Y.: Applying various algorithms for species distribution modelling. Integr. Zool. **8**, 124–135 (2013). https://doi.org/10.1111/1749-4877.12000

18. Maier, H.R., Kapelan, Z., Kasprzyk, J., et al.: Evolutionary algorithms and other metaheuristics in water resources: current status, research challenges and future directions. Environ. Model Softw. **62**, 271–299 (2014). https://doi.org/10.1016/j.envsoft.2014.09.013

19. Manel, S., Ceri, W.H., Ormerod, S.J.: Evaluating presence-absence models in ecology: the need to account for prevalence. J. Appl. Ecol. **38**, 921–931 (2001). https://doi.org/10.1046/j.1365-2664.2001.00647.x

20. Mouton, A.M., De Baets, B., Goethals, P.L.M.: Ecological relevance of performance criteria for species distribution models. Ecol. Model. **221**, 1995–2002 (2010). https://doi.org/10.1016/j.ecolmodel.2010.04.017

21. Poff, N.L.: Landscape filters and species traits: towards mechanistic understanding and prediction in stream ecology. J. North Am. Benthol. Soc. **16**, 391–409 (1997). https://doi.org/10.2307/1468026

22. Sandin, L., Verdonschot, P.F.M.: Stream and river typologies - major results and conclusions from the STAR project. Hydrobiologia **566**, 33–37 (2006). https://doi.org/10.1007/s10750-006-0072-9

23. Shannon, C.E.: A mathematical theory of communication. Bell Syst. Tech. J. **27**, 379–423 (1948). https://doi.org/10.1145/584091.584093

24. Stockwell, D.: The GARP modelling system: problems and solutions to automated spatial prediction. Int. J. Geogr. Inf. Sci. **13**, 143–158 (1999). https://doi.org/10.1080/136588199241391

25. Van Broekhoven, E., Adriaenssens, V., De Baets, B.: Interpretability-preserving genetic optimization of linguistic terms in fuzzy models for fuzzy ordered classification: an ecological case study. Int. J. Approx. Reason **44**, 65–90 (2007). https://doi.org/10.1016/j.ijar.2006.03.003

Conceptual Design of a Software Tool
for Management of Biological Invasion

Peter A. Khaiter[(✉)] and Marina G. Erechtchoukova

Faculty of Liberal Arts and Professional Studies, School of Information Technology,
York University, 4700 Keele Street, Toronto, ON M3J 1P3, Canada
{pkhaiter,marina}@yorku.ca

Abstract. Invasion of alien species is recognized as one of the most pressing
global challenges altering the composition, structure and functioning of invaded
ecosystems as well as the services they generated before the invasion. We
consider the case of Norway maple (*Acer platanoides*) which was intentionally
introduced to North America as an ornamental street shade tree, but now has been
viewed as a serious threat to native forest ecosystems in the United States and
Canada. Decisions about the management of invasive cases are inherently difficult
because of the multifactorial and multiattribute scope of the problem. To facilitate
management efforts, decision-makers and environmental practitioners require a
software tool integrating relevant knowledge and acting as a supporting expert.
The underlying methodology, conceptual design of the tool and its main modules
are discussed in the paper. In particular, we argue for an approach taking into
account the entire ecosystem purview of the problem, phases of invasion process,
tree development stages and driving mechanisms underlying the cases of biological invasion. Functional architecture of a software tool for environmental modelling and decision-making in managing of invasive cases (EMDMIC) is presented.
Largely, the EMDMIC consists of the three main modules: "Factors", "Ecosystem
Modelling" and "Management". Functionality of each module is articulated in
the paper. At the current stage of architectural design, the principles of multi-
layered designs and platform independence have been applied. The latter enable
to keep the options for future implementations of the tool open and also makes it
potentially suitable for various targeting environments.

Keywords: Invasive species · Ecosystem · Norway maple · Software tool
Functional architecture · Decision-making

1 Introduction

Biological invasion of nonnative species is considered as one of the major threats to
sustainable development and as a major danger to marine and terrestrial biodiversity
(Molnar et al. [24]; Hughes and Worland [12]). Alien species are seen as one of the
primary means for human-accelerated global change: they pose a threat to biodiversity,
re-work ecosystem arrangements, tasks and services, and induce huge economic costs
and serious health complications to humans (Mazza et al. [23]). The effects of having

© IFIP International Federation for Information Processing 2017
Published by Springer International Publishing AG 2017. All Rights Reserved
J. Hřebíček et al. (Eds.): ISESS 2017, IFIP AICT 507, pp. 209–220, 2017.
https://doi.org/10.1007/978-3-319-89935-0_18

no control in place for invasion species could be costly in terms of both direct monetary values and the negative consequences for human life (Andersen et al. [1]).

In the present study, we focus on the case of Norway maple (*Acer platanoides*). This plant species was introduced intentionally from continental Europe during the mid-1700s to eastern North America (initially to Philadelphia around 1760) as an ornamental shade tree and then widely planted during the latter half of 20th century (Webb et al. [39]; Wangen and Webster [38]). Nowadays, it has invaded northeastern forests of the United States and the riparian and mesic montane forests of the northern Rocky Mountains (Reinhart et al. [31]). *A. platanoides* has been recognized as a serious threat to native forest ecosystems in the United States and Canada.

The scales of invasive spread call for managerial actions aimed at the protection and restoration of native ecosystems (e.g., removal of *A. platanoides* from invaded areas, Webb et al. [39]) which are associated with considerable difficulty and expense and whose effect is not easily foreseeable due to the complexity and substantial non-linearity of the contributing factors and processes. To facilitate the management efforts, decision-makers and environmental practitioners should be equipped with a software tool integrating relevant knowledge and acting as a supporting expert.

2   Methodology

Biological invasion is a complex phenomenon making decisions about management of invasive cases inherently difficult because of the multifactorial and multiattribute scope of the problem, a great level of uncertainty regarding the outcomes of possible management actions, multiple, sometimes conflicting, objectives and numerous parties involved in the process (Maguire [19]). In the sub-sections below, we discuss some important aspects of the problem.

2.1   Phases of Invasion Process

The process of plant invasion comprises certain stages (Fig. 1). Thus, Radosevich et al. [30] defined three phases: introduction, colonization and naturalization. Wangen and Webster [38] paralleled them with the phases of stratified diffusion by Shigesada et al. [34]. Andersen et al. [1] argued for four phases of entry, establishment, spread and impact. In the latter classification, the entry phase marks the arrival of a non-indigenous species into a new environment; the establishment phase occurs where this arriving population begins to reproduce *in situ* and escapes immediate danger of local extinction; in the spread phase, the species disperses from its initial site of establishment and occupies available habitat within its new environment; and in the impact phase, an established species persists and competes in its new geographical range (Andersen et al. [1]).

Introduction	Colonization	Naturalization	
Entry	Establishment	Spread	Impact

Fig. 1. Phases of invasion process (after Radosevich et al. [30]; Andersen et al. [1])

2.2 Tree Development Stages

The starting point in the tree life history is seed planting (Fig. 2). Surviving seeds will germinate and establish the seedlings. Seedlings are defined as trees whose height does not exceed the maximum seedling height for a given species (e.g., 1.00 m, Wyckoff and Webb [41]; 1.35 m, Murphy [26]). Accordingly, seedlings have no diameter at breast height (DBH); their primary size measurement is the diameter at a height of 10 cm (diam10). When a seedling reaches the maximum seedling height, it becomes a sapling, for which a DBH is greater than 0 and less than the minimum adult DBH (Murphy [26]). The sampling phase continues until the tree reaches a specific threshold height (e.g., 3 m; Senbeta and Teketay [33]) or the minimum adult DBH (e.g., 2.5 cm, Wyckoff and Webb [41]), after which it becomes adult. Snags are standing dead trees which are produced when either saplings or adults die due to normal tree mortality or a disturbance event, such as disease. Fallen snags form woody debris.

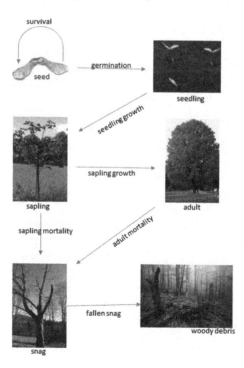

Fig. 2. Tree development stages

2.3 Ecosystem Scope

It is commonly accepted that alien species produce substantial negative effects on the composition, structure and functioning of the invaded ecosystems (e.g., Higgins et al. [10]; Wangen and Webster [38]). Therefore, the ecosystem scope needs to be taken into consideration in the analysis for decision-making associated with invasive cases. The introduction of nonnative species is a stress onto invaded ecosystems, and this stress, in most of the cases, will be compounded with, and possibly amplified by, other natural and anthropogenic influences. The impacted ecosystem, its components and functions will react to stress in different ways. A typology of ecosystem stresses (*sensu* Khaiter and Erechtchoukova [15]; Gutiérrez et al. [8]) enables differentiation between specific categories of stress, on the one hand, and the distinct functions and ecosystem components (biotic and abiotic) being influenced, on the other.

Furthermore, it is important for practical environmental management to predict the persistence capacity and probable transformations in invaded ecosystems. It has been demonstrated (Khaiter and Erechtchoukova [14]) that there are common patterns in the behaviour of ecosystems as they respond to exogenous disturbances, and the following five scenarios in ecosystem stress dynamics have been determined: (1) resistance; (2) deformation; (3) resilience; (4) degradation; and (5) shift. To predict a particular scenario, a good understanding of the impact mechanisms driving the changes is necessary, but by far, it remains rather limited (Reinhart et al. [31]).

2.4 Driving Mechanisms

From the ecosystem perspectives, persistence to invasion occurs in the form of competition from the native communities (Martin and Marks [22]), and a dominating concept since seminal paper by Elton [6] has been that resistance to invasion is greater in intact or undisturbed communities. However, recent studies are not so definitely supportive of this paradigm (e.g., Webb et al. [39]) and rather unveil a more complicated interplay of biotic and environmental drivers in the resulting ecosystem resistance to biological invasion.

In addition, competition with resident species can take on multiple forms – e.g., in the cases of woody invasion in forest ecosystems, for light, soil nutrient resources, as allelopathic interference and disruption of mycorrhizal associations (Urgenson et al. [35]). However, invasive plant species may bring novel symbiotic mutualisms into the ecosystem (Vitousek et al. [36]). The resistance to invasion in forest ecosystems can be modified by environmental factors, such as soil moisture and nutrient levels (e.g., nitrogen, Walters and Reich [37]) or soil pH. Strongly acidic soils offer the highest resistance to invasion, while base-rich soils can significantly reduce invasion resistance (Martin and Marks [22]). The outcome of this competition can affect critical functional roles in both terrestrial and adjacent aquatic habitats: regulating microclimate, stabilizing stream banks and water flow and providing energy and nutrients to soil and aquatic food webs (Urgenson et al. [35]), i.e., ecosystem services.

3   EMDMIC Design

In this section, the development of a software tool for environmental modelling and decision-making in managing of invasive cases (EMDMIC) is presented. Following its introduction (Khaiter et al. [16]), architectural design and detailed aspects are considered in the paper. Though the motivation for the study has been the case of *Acer platanoides*, there are good reasons to believe that the suggested software tool is suitable for a broader range of biological invasions in forest ecosystems. The tool consists of the three main modules (Fig. 3): "Factors", "Ecosystem Modelling" and "Management" which are discussed in the corresponding sub-sections below.

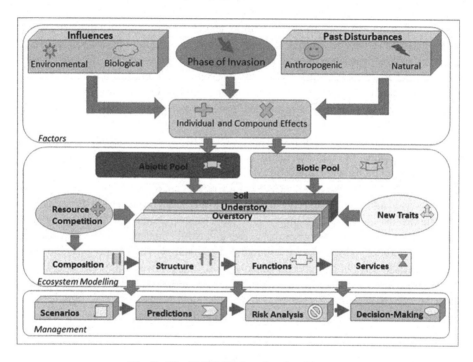

Fig. 3.   The EMDMIC functional architecture

3.1   Module "Factors"

The "Factors" module specifies a particular stage of the invasion process (see Subsect. 2.1) as well as environmental factors (e.g., topology, geology, soil composition, hydrology and meteorology, including the annual insolation above the forest canopy, Botkin et al. [3]) and biological factors (e.g., shade tolerance, soil nutrient cycling, phenotypical plasticity, animal and plant parasites and pollinating insects, etc.) creating traits for invasion. In particular, studies on *A. platanoides* unveiled such invasive advantages of this tree species as:

- high shade tolerance and adaptation;
- light interception that reduces light availability (both quantitatively and qualitatively) for native communities (e.g., Reinhart et al. [31]);
- physiological mechanisms including early leaf expansion and late leaf drop for a longer growth season compared to native species (Webb et al. [39]);
- allocation plasticity (Urgenson et al. [35]) changing patterns of dominance due to higher inherent growth rate, by increasing nutrient availability (i.e., Ca, Mg, K, N) and their recycling rates (Gómez-Aparicio et al. [7]).

Ultimately, these specific properties of *A. platanoides* form important drivers of native suppression, leading to decreased survival and growth of native species (e.g., Reinhart et al. [31]). The module "Factors" will take into account the history of past disturbances experienced by the ecosystem under consideration, both natural (e.g., fire, flooding, extreme weather events, diseases, herbivory, etc.) and anthropogenic (e.g., pollution, habitat destruction, introduced pets and pathogens, logging, climate change, dam and road construction, etc.). As the outcome, the module implements an assessment of individual and compound effects of the contributing factors from the perspective of potential drivers creating favourable conditions for successful invasion of nonnative species (e.g., Reinhart et al. [31]).

The entry phase of invasion is characterized by the native tree canopies and exotic invaders attempting to establish themselves in the understory. The dynamics of the process may vary with a particular tree development stage. For example, the establishment of seedlings is viewed as a key phase in forest succession (Martin and Canham [20]; Morrison and Mauck [25]) during which closely related species are more likely to compete against each other on the basis of their shared characteristics (Lapointe and Brisson [17]). Comparing very similar native and exotic congeners (e.g., *A. sacharum* and *A. platanoides*) *in situ*, it is recommended to identify which traits promote invasiveness (Mack [18]). In particular, while observing that Norway maple is highly shade-tolerant, it was reported that this species is more shade-tolerant as a seedling than as a maturing tree (Nowak and Rowntree [27]; Wyckoff and Webb [41]), thus, conferring it invasive advantages by enabling to dominate in the understory and displace or diminish the native *A. sacharum* during the seedling stage.

3.2 Module "Ecosystem Modelling"

The "Ecosystem Modelling" module provides a formalized description of the invaded ecosystem. The abiotic (or non-living) pool includes physical factors (e.g., temperature, light, pressure, energy, acidity measure, soil depth, soil moisture-retention capacity, etc.) and chemical factors (e.g., oxygen, carbon, phosphorus, nitrogen, sulphur, calcium, etc. levels and availability). The biotic (or living) pool is organized in hierarchical structures of organisms depending on their roles in the energetic and metabolic processes at the overstory, understory and soil levels. Invaders will compete with native species for resources (e.g., light, space, mineral nutrients, etc.), and new traits in the ecosystem can be formed as a result (e.g., novel symbiotic mutualisms, means of acquiring resources, adaptation plasticity, allelopathic compounds, amplifying of native traits, etc.).

The invasion of alien species will alter the composition, structure and functioning of the invaded ecosystem as well as the services it generated before the invasion occurred. The ultimate task of this module is to predict any such transformations. Some of the computational formulae are shown in (1)–(6). Seed germination is estimated as:

$$NSG = \%G * NSP, \tag{1}$$

where NSP, NSG are number of seeds planted and germinated, respectively; $\%G$ is germination rate, as defined by Ologundudu et al. [28]. The cumulative growth of biological organisms at the juvenile phase occurs with the accelerating rate, at the mature phase – with the constant rate and at the senescent phase – with the decelerating rate. The lifespan cumulative growth curve (CGC) is, thus, sigmoidal, and a growth variable (e.g., DBH, height, volume, etc.) can be found from the following formula (Brack and Wood [4]):

$$DBH = \exp\left(a + \frac{b}{TA}\right), \tag{2}$$

where TA is the tree age; a and b are species-specific regression parameters. Non-linear (sigmoidal) growth functions are widely used in developing tree height-diameter relationships (Huang et al. [11]). Zhang [43] investigated the performance of six functions and concluded that each growth function was equally well-fitted to data of ten species collected in the inland Northwest of the United States with a minor superiority of three functions, one of which is the Weibull-type formula (Yang et al. [42]):

$$TH = 1.37 + c * \left[1 - \exp\left(-d * DBH^f\right)\right], \tag{3}$$

where TH is the total tree height; c, d and f are species-specific parameters. Crown width (CW) can also be estimated as a function of DBH (Peper et al. [29]):

$$CW = \exp\left\{\frac{MSE}{2} * \left[g + h * \log\left(\log\left(DBH + 1\right)\right)\right]\right\}, \tag{4}$$

where MSE is the mean standard error; g and h are species-specific parameters. Light regime in forest is largely determined by the overstory canopy gaps (CG), which can be predicted from:

$$CG = D_{i,j} - (CW_i + CW_j)/2, \tag{5}$$

where $D_{i,j}$ is the distance between two neighbouring trees; CW_i and CW_j are their respective crown widths. Then, the light level ($\%L$) will be found as:

$$\%L = \frac{CG}{D_{i,j}} * 100\%. \tag{6}$$

In the open, $\%L = 100\%$ (i.e., full sun regime) while for the closed canopies, $\%L = 0\%$. Formulas (5) and (6) are a simplified version of the gap light index by Canham [5].

Dependant variables (Table 1) in formulas (1)–(6) are computed under the assumption of optimal (i.e., most favourable) conditions for the dynamics of contributing processes. In reality, they will be affected by environmental, biological and anthropogenic influences which can be factored through the corresponding transformation functions for each affected state variable and for each type of the influence (Khaiter [13]), i.e.:

$$x_i^A = TF_{i,k} * x_i^U, 0 \le TF_{i,k} \le 1, \forall i = 1, .., n, \forall k = 1, ..K, \tag{7}$$

where x_i^U and x_i^A are the ith state variable before and after the influence of the kth type factor, respectively; $TF_{i,k}$ is the transformation function of the kth type factor on ith state variable. A compound effect of multiple factors can be expressed through the resulting transformation function (TFR) built either from the ecological Liebig's law of the minimum of limiting factors (8) or in the multiplicative form (9):

$$TFR = \min_{k=1,...,r} \{TF_k\}, \tag{8}$$

$$TFR = \prod_{k=1}^{r} \{TF_k\}. \tag{9}$$

Table 1. Characteristics of the variables and parameters in (1)–(6).

Variable symbol	Description	Unit
NSP, NSG	Number of seeds planted and germinated	
%G	Germination rate	%
TA	Tree age	years
DBH	Diameter at breast height	m
TH	Total tree height	m
CW	Crown width	m
D	Distance between two neighbouring trees	m
CG	Canopy gap	m
%L	Light level	%
a, b, c, d, f, g, h	Species-specific parameters	

3.3 Module "Management"

The "Management" module generates possible scenarios of management interventions to cope with the invasiveness. It should be noted that measures can be taken at different decision-making levels, which can be divided into three categories: (1) decisions about preventing the entry of potentially invasive species (through existing laws, agreements on ballast water and shipping, etc.); (2) decisions about targeted control of invasive species after they have been introduced, whether purposely or accidentally; and (3) restoration of invaded habitats and ecosystems. For example, to restore an old-growth oak forest at the Washington Grove in Rochester, NY to its original and native state,

Rogers [32] recommended a two-step approach. The first step foresees the removal of mature *A. platanoides* trees from the forest area, along with other invasive species, which would also create open canopy conditions. By also removing *A. platanoides* trees from the streets near the Grove and replacing them with stress-resistant native trees, the propagule pressure of invaders will be reduced. The second step of the management plan would encourage native species diversity and oak recruitment by installing physical barriers inhibiting disruption of the leaf layer.

Once the set of scenarios is formed, the module executes predictions of ecosystem components, their short- and long-term dynamics, ecosystem persistence capacity and restoration capabilities in response to each potential managerial effort. It takes into account the mechanisms of invasion, typology of stresses and the common patterns in the ecosystem stress behaviour. As it was mentioned above, a high level of uncertainty concerns each phase of the invasion and also when controls are being applied (Maguire [19]). Thus, woody plant invasion of shade-tolerant species can endure periods of suppressed growth before reaching the canopy layer, which, in combination with the long generation time of trees, makes it difficult to perceive as it unfolds, and, hence, difficult to manage in its early stages (Herron et al. [9]; Lapointe and Brisson [17]; Martin et al. [21]; Wangen and Webster [38]; Webster et al. [40]).

The resilience limits of invaded ecosystems also remain unclear. Theoretical ecologists question the ability of a forest ecosystem to fully recover to the original, pre-invaded state in the face of complex interactions among anthropogenic impacts: forest fragmentation, climate change and the introduction of invasive species (Webb et al. [39]).

Given various sources of uncertainty and likely significant cost associated with the implementation of controls in view of scarce budgeting resources, a risk analysis becomes a necessary step of the decision-making process. Specific features of risk analysis in application to the cases of biological invasion have been examined by Andersen et al. [1] and Bartell and Nair [2]. The outcome of this module and the entire tool will be a set of recommended measures aimed at addressing the intervention of alien species in the most efficient way and suggesting resilient solutions for the impacted ecosystems.

4   Discussion and Conclusions

In this paper, we presented functional architecture of the software tool and its internal structural logic, focusing on the modelling module as a backbone of the framework. The principles of multi-layered designs and platform independence have been applied at this stage. The latter enable future implementations of the framework suitable for various targeting environments. At the same time, the transition from the current stage of architectural design to detailed design and further to implementation phase of the software tool described above will require the following groups of models:

- models of pre-invaded dynamics of native species and the ecosystem as a whole;
- models of invasive dynamics of the alien species, including mechanisms underlying their invasive success;

- models of invasive-resident species interactions (e.g., competition for light, space, nutrient resources; possible symbiotic mutualisms, etc.) and their modification by biotic and environmental drivers;
- models of persistence capabilities to sustain the invasion and probable transformations in invaded ecosystems;
- models of effect of invasion on critical functions of the ecosystem; that is, ecosystem services;
- models predicting ecosystem components, their short- and long-term dynamics, ecosystem persistence capacity and restoration capabilities in response to each potential managerial effort or scenario;
- models aimed at selection of the best possible scenario for managing the invasion.

Prior to the realization of the tool, a number of non-trivial issues should also be addressed. This includes, e.g., predictions of the invasive stress dynamics of the ecosystems. It appears that prediction of the invasive potential of a certain alien species to invade a given environment can be viewed as a problem of machine learning and solved by classification algorithms, provided that sufficient volumes of relevant empirical data are accumulated and available. Prediction of endogenous ecosystem dynamics caused by biological invasion and resulting in compositional, structural and functional transformations most likely calls for process-based models.

There is a view that an integrated ecosystem perspective of invasive species is amenable to mathematical formalization and system dynamic modelling (Gutiérrez et al. [8]), and it is shared by the authors. It also is a subject of our ongoing endeavours on the topic of decision-making and management of biological invasion.

Acknowledgements. The authors would like to express appreciation to all researchers whose publications are referred to in this paper for their field studies and theoretical generalizations on invasive species which inspired our interest towards the topic. The authors are thankful to the editor and anonymous reviewers for their helpful suggestions and comments on the early versions of the manuscript which helped to improve the quality.

References

1. Andersen, M.C., Adams, H., Hope, B., Powell, M.: Risk analysis for invasive species: general framework and research needs. Risk Anal. **24**(4), 893–900 (2004)
2. Bartell, S.M., Nair, S.K.: Establishment risk for invasive species. Risk Anal. **24**(4), 833–845 (2004)
3. Botkin, D.B., Janak, J.F., Walls, J.R.: Some ecological consequences of a computer model of forest growth. J. Ecol. **60**(3), 849–872 (1972)
4. Brack, C.L., Wood, G.B.: Forest mensuration - measuring trees, stands and forests for effective forest management (1998). http://fennerschool-associated.anu.edu.au/mensuration/BrackandWood1998/T_GROWTH.HTM
5. Canham, C.D.: An index for understory light levels in and around canopy gaps. Ecology **69**, 1634–1638 (1988)
6. Elton, C.S.: The Ecology of Invasions by Animals and Plants. Methuen, London (1958)

7. Gómez-Aparicio, L., Canham, C.D., Martin, P.H.: Neighbourhood models of the effect of the invasive *Acer platanoides* on the tree seedling dynamics: linking impact on communities and ecosystems. J. Ecol. **96**, 78–90 (2008)
8. Gutiérrez, J., Jones, C.G., Sousa, R.: Toward an integrated ecosystem perspective of invasive species impact. Acta Oecol. **54**, 131–138 (2014)
9. Herron, P.M., Martine, C.T., Latimer, A.M., Leicht-Young, S.A.: Invasive plants and their ecological strategies: prediction and explanation of woody plant invasion in New England. Divers. Distrib. **13**, 633–644 (2007)
10. Higgins, S.I., Richardson, D.M., Cowling, R.M.: Modeling invasive plant spread: the role of plant-environment interactions and model structure. Ecology **77**(7), 2043–2054 (1996)
11. Huang, S., Titus, S.J., Wiens, D.P.: Comparison of nonlinear height-diameter functions for major Alberta tree species. Can. J. For. Res. **22**, 1297–1304 (1992)
12. Hughes, K.A., Worland, M.R.: Spatial distribution, habitat preference and colonization status of two alien terrestrial invertebrate species in Antarctica. Antarct. Sci. **22**(3), 221–231 (2010)
13. Khaiter, P.A.: Modelling of Anthropogenic Dynamics of Forest Biogeocenoses. Znaniye, Kiev (1991)
14. Khaiter, P.A., Erechtchoukova, M.G.: Environmental assessment of anthropogenic impact through the patterns of ecosystem stress reactions. Int. J. Environ. Cult. Econ. Soc. Sustain. **3**(4), 179–189 (2007)
15. Khaiter, P.A., Erechtchoukova, M.G.: The notion of stability in mathematics, biology, ecology and environmental sustainability. In: Anderssen, B. et al. (eds.), Proceedings of the 18th IMACS World Congress – MODSIM 2009 International Congress on Modelling and Simulation, Cairns, Australia, pp. 2265–2271 (2009)
16. Khaiter, P.A., Erechtchoukova, M.G., Roushan, S.: A Framework for decision-making in cases of invasive species. In: Sauvage, S., Sánchez-Pérez, J.M., Rizzoli, A.E. (eds.), Proceedings of the 8th International Congress on Environmental Modelling and Software, 10–14 July, Toulouse, France, pp. 1210–1217 (2016)
17. Lapointe, M., Brisson, J.: A comparison of invasive *Acer platanoides* and native *A. Saccharum* first-year seedlings: growth, biomass distribution and the influence of ecological factors in a forest understory. Forests **3**, 190–206 (2012). https://doi.org/10.3390/f3020190
18. Mack, R.N.: Predicting the identity and fate of plant invaders: emergent and emerging approaches. Biol. Conserv. **78**, 107–121 (1996)
19. Maguire, L.A.: What can decision analysis do for invasive species management? Risk Anal. **24**(4), 859–868 (2004)
20. Martin, P.H., Canham, C.D.: Dispersal and recruitment limitation in native versus exotic tree species: life-history strategies and Janzen-Connell effects. Oikos **119**, 807–824 (2010)
21. Martin, P.H., Canham, C.D., Marks, P.L.: Why forests appear resistant to exotic plant invasion: intentional introductions, stand dynamics, and the role of shade tolerance. Front. Ecol. Environ. **6**, 142–149 (2008)
22. Martin, P.H., Marks, P.: Intact forests provide only weak resistance to a shade-tolerant invasive Norway maple (*Acer platanoides* L.). J. Ecol. **94**, 1070–1079 (2006)
23. Mazza, G., Tricarico, E., Genovesi, P., Gherardi, F.: Biological invaders are threats to human health: an overview. Ethol. Ecol. Evol. **26**(2–3), 112–129 (2014)
24. Molnar, J.L., Gamboa, R.L., Revenga, C., Spalding, M.D.: Assessing the global threat of invasive species to marine biodiversity. Front. Ecol. Environ. **6**(9), 485–492 (2008)
25. Morrison, J.A., Mauck, K.: Experimental field comparison of native and non-native maple seedlings: natural enemies, ecophysiology, growth and survival. J. Ecol. **95**, 1036–1049 (2007)

26. Murphy, L.E.: SORTIE-ND user manual, version 6.11. Institute of Ecosystem Studies, Millbrook, NY (2011). http://www.sortie-nd.org/software/index.html
27. Nowak, D.J., Rowntree, R.A.: History and range of Norway maple. J. Arboric. **16**, 291–296 (1990)
28. Ologundudu, A.F., Adelusi, A.A., Adekoya, K.P.: Effect of light stress on germination and growth parameters of *Corchorus olitorius, Celosia argentea, Amaranthus cruentus, Abelmoschus esculentus* and *Delonix regia*. Not. Sci. Biol. **5**(4), 468–475 (2013)
29. Peper, P.J., McPherson, E.G., Mori, S.M.: Equations for predicting diameter, height, crown width, and leaf area of San Joaquin Valley street trees. J. Arboric. **27**(6), 306–317 (2001)
30. Radosevich, S.R., Stubbs, M.M., Ghersa, C.M.: Plant invasions: process and patterns. Weed Sci. **51**(2), 254–259 (2003)
31. Reinhart, K.O., Gurnee, J., Tirado, R., Callaway, R.M.: Invasion through quantitative effects: intense shade drives native decline and invasive success. Ecol. Appl. **16**(5), 1821–1831 (2006)
32. Rogers, J.P.: Invasion ecology of *Acer platanoides* in an old-growth urban forest. In: Environmental Science and Biology Theses, pp. 1–74 (2013)
33. Senbeta, F., Teketay, D.: Regeneration of indigenous tree species under the canopies of the tree plantations in central Ethiopia. J. Trop. Ecol. **42**, 175–185 (2001)
34. Shigesada, N., Kawasaki, K., Takeda, Y.: Modelling stratified diffusion in biological invasion. Am. Nat. **146**, 229–251 (1995)
35. Urgenson, L.S., Reichard, S.H., Halpern, C.B.: Multiple competitive mechanisms underlie the effects of strong invader on early-to late-seral tree seedlings. J. Ecol. **100**, 1204–1215 (2012)
36. Vitousek, P.M., Walker, L.R., Whiteaker, L.D., Mueller-Dombois, D., Matson, P.A.: Biological invasion by Myrica faya alters ecosystem development in Hawaii. Science **238**, 802–804 (1987)
37. Walters, M.B., Reich, P.B.: Are shade tolerance, survival, and growth linked? Low light and nitrogen effects on hardwood seedlings. Ecology **77**(3), 841–853 (1996)
38. Wangen, S.R., Webster, C.R.: Potential for multiple lag phases during biotic invasions: reconstructing an invasion of the exotic tree *Acer platanoides*. J. Appl. Ecol. **43**, 258–268 (2006)
39. Webb, S.L., Dwyer, M., Kaunzinger, C.K., Wyckoff, P.H.: The myth of the resilient forest: case study of the invasive Norway maple (*Acer platanoides*). Rhodora **102**(911), 332–354 (2000)
40. Webster, C.R., Jenkins, M., Jose, S.: Woody invaders and the challenges they pose to forest ecosystems in the eastern United States. J. For. **104**, 366–374 (2006)
41. Wyckoff, P.H., Webb, S.L.: Understory influence of the invasive Norway maple (*Acer platanoides*). Bull. Torrey Bot. Club **123**(3), 197–205 (1996)
42. Yang, R.C., Kozak, A., Smith, J.H.G.: The potential of Weibull-type functions as a flexible growth curves. Can. J. For. Res. **8**, 424–431 (1978)
43. Zhang, L.: Cross-validation of non-linear growth functions for modelling tree height-diameter relationships. Ann. Bot. **79**, 251–257 (1997)

Open Farm Management Information System Supporting Ecological and Economical Tasks

Tomáš Řezník[1(✉)], Karel Charvát[2], Vojtěch Lukas[3], Karel Charvát Junior[4], Michal Kepka[5], Šárka Horáková[2], Zbyněk Křivánek[2], and Helena Řezníková[2]

[1] Laboratory on Geoinformatics and Cartography (LGC), Department of Geography, Faculty of Science, Masaryk University, Kotlářská 2, 611 37 Brno, Czech Republic
tomas.reznik@sci.muni.cz
[2] Lesprojekt – Služby, s.r.o., Martinov 197, Záryby, Czech Republic
{charvat,charvat_junior1,horakova,krivanek, reznikova}@lesprojekt.cz
[3] Department of Agrosystems and Bioclimatology, Faculty of Agronomy, Mendel University, Brno, Czech Republic
vojtech.lukas@mendelu.cz
[4] Baltic Open Solutions Centre, Rīga, Latvia
Charvat_junior@bosc.cz
[5] Department of Mathematics, Faculty of Applied Science, University of West Bohemia, Pilsen, Czech Republic
kepka@ccss.cz

Abstract. A Farm Management Information System (FMIS) is a sophisticated tool managing geospatial data and functionalities as it provides answers to two basic questions: what has happened and where. The presented FOODIE (Farm-Oriented Open Data in Europe) and DataBio (Data-Driven Bioeconomy) approach may be recognized as an OpenFMIS, where environmental and reference geospatial data for precision agriculture are provided free of charge. On the other hand, added-value services like yield potential, sensor monitoring, and/or machinery fleet monitoring are provided on a paid basis through standardised Web services due to the costs of hardware and non-trivial computations. Results, i.e. reference, environmental and farm-oriented geospatial data, may be obtained from the FOODIE platform. All such results of whatever kind are used in the European DataBio project in order to minimise the environmental burden while maximising the economic benefits.

Keywords: Open data · Precision agriculture · Geospatial services · FMIS
Yield potential · Machinery monitoring

1 Introduction

The importance of the agricultural sector is evident due its strategic importance around the world. The different groups of stakeholders involved in agricultural activities have to manage many different and heterogeneous sources of information that need to be

© IFIP International Federation for Information Processing 2017
Published by Springer International Publishing AG 2017. All Rights Reserved
J. Hřebíček et al. (Eds.): ISESS 2017, IFIP AICT 507, pp. 221–233, 2017.
https://doi.org/10.1007/978-3-319-89935-0_19

combined in order to make economically and environmentally sound decisions, which include (among others) the definition of policies (with respect to subsidies, standardisation and regulation, national strategies for rural development, climate change), the development of sustainable agriculture, crop recollection timing and pricing, and plague detection, etc.

In the agriculture domain, the period of the past 20 years may be characterized by a shift from (conventional) farming to precision farming. This shift is caused by increased demand for higher yield on one hand but increased concern for loss of biodiversity which is quite significant in agricultural regions [1, 2] and might be also one of the driving forces in using precision farming. Even though precision farming is in general considered as a form of intensive agriculture [3] due to the fact that it enables using exact necessary amount of fertilizers or pesticides in explicitly spatially delineated plots it could be considered as an additional tool in so called ecological intensification [4] or conservation agriculture [5].

Precision farming relies on geospatial data and functionality that are available through a Farm Management Information System (FMIS). Any FMIS may also be considered as a kind of Geographic Information System (GIS) as it provides answers to two basic questions: what has happened and where. FMIS effectiveness from the geospatial point of view is limited chiefly by a lack of accurate data.

This is a paradoxical situation, since there are proprietary FMIS's on the one hand and requests for open data and services to power proprietary FMISs on the other. A way out may be found in the form of an Open Farm Management Information System (OpenFMIS). We would like to emphasize that an OpenFMIS also uses both open and proprietary data. Open data are used as inputs into an OpenFMIS, geospatial data being the best example; e.g. starting from satellite and aerial images through cadastre to zones where the usage of nitrogen is forbidden. Proprietary data typically comprise sensitive economic information like the turnover of a farm, the consumption of fertilizers/pesticides/fuels, the wages of employees etc. Proprietary data remain in the system, no matter whether it is an FMIS or an OpenFMIS. The greatest difference between an FMIS and OpenFMIS lies in the presence of open application programming interfaces that allow (mostly) the (re)use of data and/or the functionality offered by other open applications. An OpenFMIS is also capable of exporting non-protected data, such as the better geometrical representation of a field. An OpenFMIS also offers modularity, i.e. any component with reference to geospatial/information technology standards may be added or taken away.

Moreover, world-wide concepts like the Digital Earth and Global Earth Observation System of Systems (GEOSS) are the ideal candidates for the integration of such agricultural pollution data from around the world.

The European project "Farm-Oriented Open Data in Europe" (FOODIE), funded between the years 2014 and 2017, addresses the above-mentioned issues. The FOODIE project aims at building an open and interoperable specialized agricultural platform hub on the cloud for the management of spatial and non-spatial data relevant for farming production, for the discovery of spatial and non-spatial agriculture-related data from heterogeneous sources, for the integration of existing and valuable European open datasets related to agriculture, and for data publication and the data linking of external agriculture data sources contributed by different public and private stakeholders allowing for the provision of specific and high-value applications and services to support the planning and decision-making processes of different stakeholder groups related to the agricultural and environmental domains.

2   Functionalities Provided by the Platform

The FOODIE approach supports the better adoption of Information and Communication Technologies (ICT) and also enables better collaboration between different stakeholders across the agri-food chain. It supports trusted software models as services for the farming sector. This will help farmers employ new types of solutions without the necessary investment and also allow the easy integration of existing platform through interoperable interfaces. This approach also incorporates the support of mobility platforms – the accessing of information and knowledge everywhere, and also the integration of different devices into all systems – as well as guarantees the accessibility of different types of information.

The FOODIE platform aims at being the "glue" in-between the public and private sectors by acting as a central platform (e.g., a Land Parcel Identification System) ICT system combined with intelligent and underlying hardware and software infrastructure that allows the storage of farmers' data (unique land parcel ids inside a region, farming activities performed), landowners, land use, orthoimages, satellite data etc. An open data model for (precision) agriculture was defined as the backbone of the FOODIE platform, as described by [6, 7]. Portions of these datasets would remain private (e.g., famer data) whereas others like orthoimages and satellite data plus derived data from all European Member States and other open datasets could be accessed and used by all other user groups besides the Ministry of a Member State. The EU Directive concerning the re-use of public sector information sets down the legal framework in this respect. This would definitely transform ICT use in agriculture and forestry. As seen in the previous section, the INSPIRE Directive also goes in the same direction; that is, to establish an infrastructure for spatial information in Europe for the purposes of EC environmental policies or activities which might have an impact on the environment (see also [8]).

In order to implement the FOODIE concept and the associated service platform hub, the project aims at accomplishing the following technological objectives:

- to make use of the existing spatial information resources and services for various domains coming from different initiatives like INSPIRE (INfrastructure for SPatial InfoRmation in Europe; see [9]), Copernicus, GNSS, Galileo, GEOSS (Global Earth Observation System of Systems); GBIF (Global Biodiversity Information Facility), and EUNIS (European Nature Information System) etc., in which the European Commission and the Member States have invested heavily over the past decade;
- to design and provide an open and interoperable geospatial platform hub on the cloud based on existing software components derived from research results and available solutions in the market (mostly open-source). These include:
- the integration of external agriculture production and food market data using the principles of Open Linked Data,

- the creation of an open and flexible lightweight Application Programming Interface (API) that allows private and public stakeholders in the agricultural and environmental area to publish their own datasets (e.g., datasets provided by local sensor networks deployed *in situ* in farms, and knowledge from farm communities and agricultural services companies, etc.) and make them available via the platform hub as open linked data (enabling them to be subject to further processing),
- the creation of specific and high-value applications and services to support the planning and decision-making processes of different stakeholder groups,
- the provision of security mechanisms to prevent the unauthorised access and use of the platform users' personal information as well as the data published by them,
- the establishment of a marketplace where data can be discovered and exchanged but where external companies can also publish their own agricultural applications based on the data, services and applications provided by FOODIE.

The FOODIE platform offers two levels of functionality as defined in its business and exploitation model:

- open data relevant for (precision) farming in the most advanced exchangeable form possible;
- added value services built on the top of open data to provide advice to the end users (such as farmers, consultant companies, environmentalists, policy makers, researchers, or citizens).

The first level functionality also includes a catalogue inventorying all available datasets and services to discover whether a FOODIE platform contains the desired data/services or not. The discovery concept originates from the INSPIRE domain [10], including the structure as well as the exchange format of metadata. Searching for data/services in the FOODIE catalogue is provided free of charge for all kinds of users. The FOODIE Catalogue respects the standards designed to publish and access digital metadata for geospatial data, services, and related (semantic) resource information as defined by [11–16]. The same also applies to the downloading of data, unless the particular owner of the data has imposed some restriction or condition on data sharing. The first level functionality is intended for users who are searching for European spatial data related to agriculture and would like to process data themselves.

Licenses are open for the first level functionality; Creative Commons Attribution Share Alike 4.0 [**Chyba! Nenalezen zdroj odkazů.**] for data components like data models and Open Data Commons Open Database License (ODbL) for databases [**Chyba! Nenalezen zdroj odkazů.**]. Searching and previewing capabilities are also available free of charge. Licenses are explicitly mentioned at each product (e.g. component, database) description typically at GitHub repository [**Chyba! Nenalezen zdroj odkazů.**] like [**Chyba! Nenalezen zdroj odkazů.**].

In concert with its five star rating, the FOODIE platform offers relevant data in one place at the highest possible level of data openness (see [**Chyba! Nenalezen zdroj odkazů.**]). For example, the Open Transport Network, which also includes unpaved rural roads, is being offered in the RDF through the SPARQL endpoint; meanwhile, satellite data from the Copernicus programme are in a machine readable georeferenced (TIFF) format.

Meanwhile, the second level functionality brings added value services derived from open (and sometimes also proprietary) data. For instance, an 8-year series of satellite images combined with other data allows the computation of yield potential, see Fig. 1. The yield potential concept of the FOODIE platform aims at establishing a general model for predicting yield potential zones for almost any kind of crop. Such added value services are being offered on the basis of payment through standardised Web interfaces, e.g. Open Geospatial Consortium's Web Processing Service.

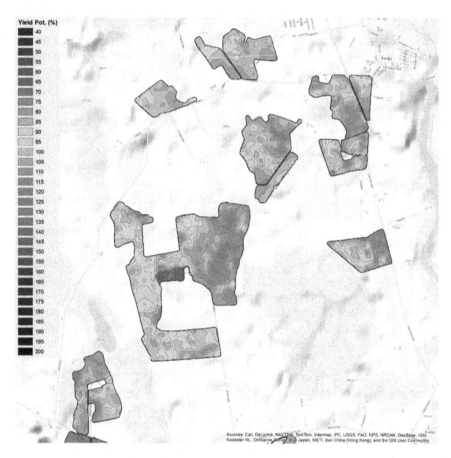

Fig. 1. Yield potential map for one farm as a reference for ecologically and economically sound decisions

Licenses are commercial for the second level functionality; individually set according to the purpose(s) of use, number of end users, included/excluded maintenance etc. The functionality of added value services is described in the following sub-sections. The FOODIE architecture follows the so-called Service-Oriented Architecture, which enables orchestration between and beyond the FOODIE platform through standardized services. Open interfaces and formats, as defined by the Open Geospatial Consortium [**Chyba! Nenalezen zdroj odkazů.**], [**Chyba! Nenalezen zdroj odkazů.**], [24] as well as [25] and/or World Wide Web Consortium [26] as well as [27] enable connections to various (external) systems (services) as well as to other layers of the FOODIE platform.

2.1 Yield Potential

Yield potential zones are areas with the same yield level within fields. Yield is the integrator of landscape and climatic variability and, as such, it provides useful information for identifying management zones as defined by [28, 29]. This represents the basic delineation of management zones for site-specific crop management, which is usually based on yield maps for the past few years. The presence of complete series of yield maps for all fields is rare; thus, remotely sensed data are analysed to determine the field variability of crops through vegetation indices.

The yield potential concept of the FOODIE platform aims at establishing a general model for yield potential zones for almost any kind of crop. However, such universality comes at a price. The model is capable of expressing significant spatial variations for a given crop yield on a plot by distinguishing three kinds of values: below average, average, and above average. However, the model depicts spatial variations within a plot, and therefore it may be misleading when trying to compare yield zones between plots. Altogether, we may conclude that some areas in a plot have significantly lower productivity than others and take such information into the decision making process. However, we cannot determine that it is better to produce a crop on plot A or plot B.

So far, the ESPA (United States Geological Survey's Earth Resources Observation and Science Center Science Processing Architecture repository) of LANDSAT satellite images [30] is being used as the main data source, which offers surface reflectance products, main vegetation indices (NDVI, EVI; for details see [31]), and cloud identification by the CFmask algorithm. A selection of scenes from the past eight years was made for a particular farm area in order to collect cloud-free data related to the second half of the vegetation period. Yield potential was calculated for separate scenes as the relation of each pixel to the mean value of the whole field. In the last step, all scenes were combined and the median value of yield potential was calculated. After the full operation of Sentinel 2A/B satellites, the calculation of yield potential will be enhanced by these vegetation products.

The concept of yield potential was successfully validated. It was proven that the whole evaluated farm, Tršická zemědělská in the Czech Republic, has the spatial variation of a yield potential equal to 80% when comparing yield results with estimations of the yield potential. The evaluated farm has acreage about 1,284 hectares. Ongoing research follows two main directions. The first one aims at optimising the algorithm to increase the probability of yield prediction up to 90%. Another direction of the current research focuses on the implementation of yield potential calculation as an open Web service, namely as an OGC Web Processing Service [24].

2.2 Sensor Monitoring

It goes without saying that the most precise data will always be the data gained through observations and measurements performed directly on the farm. This is partly true in the contemporary practices of precision agriculture. Sensor networks for atmospheric and meteorological conditions such as aerial and ground thermometers, anemometers, hygrometers etc. are available on farms [32]. Similar sensor networks for collecting information on soil conditions [33] or ground water levels can also be established directly on farms. However, information on the application of treatments in certain places and at certain times may often be of significantly lower quality (see Sect. 2.3 for details). The best data source in this respect is the tractor and its application machine. Issues related to the manual and aerial application of treatments are, however, beyond the scope of this paper. Sensor data collected on farms by different sensor networks are stored and managed by the SensLog application.

SensLog is a complex component of the FOODIE platform for collecting, storing, processing, analysing and publishing sensor data. SensLog receives observations and measurements from individual gateways deployed in farm fields by means of a system of Web services to the repositories of the FOODIE platform. The internet connections for deployed gateways can be realized by a number of methods; therefore, SensLog provides for variable usage. SensLog is capable of storing the observations and positions of mobile sensors in same way as for static sensors. Additional data sets can be provided by storing data in the database in different schemas. SensLog provides processing procedures and analytical functions to pre-process raw collected data or to detect alert events in operating sensor networks. Additional data sources can be involved in these analytical functions (e.g. the geometries of plots from LPIS, hydrography geometries, statistical data, zone pricing etc.). Such additional data sources are stored in the FOODIE platform and/or in external repositories.

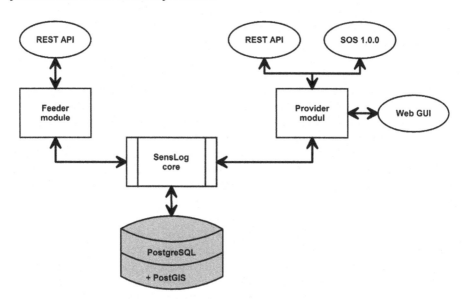

Fig. 2. Overview diagram of SensLog application and communication interfaces

The database schema of SensLog follows the ISO 19156 Observations and Measurements concept [34]. Extended functionality was implemented in the database model to fulfil all farmer requirements. Data are stored in a PostgreSQL (open source) database in version 9.3.6 together with its spatial extension PostGIS in version 2.1.0. In addition, the developed database schema has been replicated in the Cloud (Infrastructure as a Service) provided by the Poznań Supercomputing and Networking Center (in Poland) using OpenStack as an Open Source Cloud Computing Software.

A system of Web services in several forms was developed to provide a variety of methods of data publishing. RESTful services publishing data in JSON format are used for operational usage and communication between FOODIE platform components. Services based on OGC Sensor Observation Service 1.0.0 core methods are used for the standardised publishing of data. An overview diagram of the SensLog application is shown in Fig. 2 above.

2.3 Machinery Fleet Monitoring

Machinery fleet monitoring, abbreviated as MapLogAgri, is an extension of the SensLog component intended for collecting, storing, processing, analysing and publishing (near) real-time measurements of tractors and their application machines like spreaders or sprayers. Especially collecting, processing and analysing capabilities differ the most from the SensLog solution due to amount of data measured within one time frame.

As depicted in Fig. 3, a tractor contains a monitoring unit that is the centralised point from which it is possible to configure which data will be collected and how. A monitoring unit is connected to a GPS receiver to obtain the position of the tractor over the whole course of an agricultural intervention. The position of the application machine is computed from the position of the tractor and the size of the application machine. Communication between the tractor and the application machine is achieved through RFID (Radio Frequency Identification). The RFID interface enables the whole solution to be set as a modular one. It is then easy to combine any tractor with any application machine as far as they follow the same standards. The same applies to the ECU CAN/BUS (Electronic Control Unit Controlled Area Network) interface as a mediator between the monitoring unit and the software of the tractor.

To summarize, the whole solution consists in a set of hardware (e.g. the monitoring unit, GPS receiver) and software (e.g. ECU CAN/BUS and RFID interfaces as well as the user application). MapLogAgri may be understood as a hardware and software solution offering data for an OpenFMIS. The FOODIE system as a whole is then an example of an OpenFMIS.

Standardised communication exists also on the level of machinery sensor monitoring. ECU/CAN (Electronic Control Unit/Controlled Area Network) BUS represents a robust vehicle bus used in car industry, no matter whether it is a personal car or a bus [35]. On the contrary, so called ISO BUS is a specific definition of a universal protocol for electronic communication between tractors and computers originating from ISO 11783 standard – "Tractors and machinery for agriculture and forestry - Serial control and communications data network" [36]. So far (June 2017), ISO BUS is understood as a part of the Internet of Things concept [37], however beyond the Industrial Internet

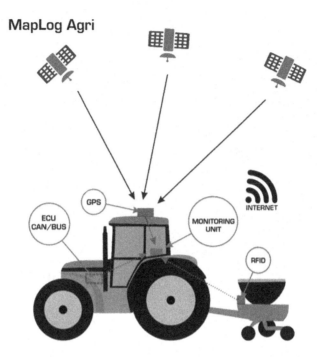

Fig. 3. Communication scheme between a tractor and its application machine

Consortium (IIC [38]) activities. ISO BUS and ECU/CAN BUS are used for communication on the sensor level. Note that the latest versions of ISO BUS do not offer straightforward open communication as their predecessors did. It is an open question whether this is a consequence of a changing policy on the part of agricultural machine producers. Some of them have recently introduced a new business model where the farmer only rents agricultural machines. The license agreement prohibits the farmer from buying the machine. As a result, all the data measured remain the property of the agricultural machine producer. We have identified this change as a threat to the openness of machinery sensor monitoring.

In total, 9 tractors and 23 machines were monitored second by second on the "Tršice" farm in the Czech Republic from March 2015 till the end of 2016. Such monitoring has proven the need for a robust cloud-based geospatial solution since, in this case, ten megabytes of data were generated each day, i.e. when operating on a real commercial farm with almost 1,300 hectares. Geospatial data revealed significant differences between economic (e.g. fuel consumption or time needed to perform the same operation) and ecological characteristics (e.g. the number of fertilizer or pesticide applications as a result of an inappropriate trajectory); see also Fig. 4. The discovered differences are the subject of ongoing analyses.

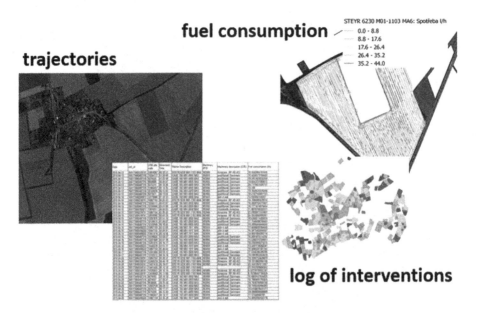

Fig. 4. Environmental, economic and geospatial results of machinery sensor monitoring

2.4   Conclusions

The three presented modules, i.e. yield potential, sensor measurement, and machinery fleet monitoring, were developed to minimize the environmental burden arising from agricultural activities. All the modules aim to reduce the amount of fertilizer or pesticide applied during agricultural production, and thus to ensure that lower amounts of nutrients or chemical residues such as nitrogen appear in soil and/or (ground) water. That is, they should help to reduce the eutrophication of natural water sources. Therefore, the integration of these modules was adopted as part of the GEOSS AIP-8 (Global Earth Observation System of Systems' Architecture Implementation Pilot 8) targeting agricultural and water pollution.

The presented geospatial technologies focus on the environment during the agricultural planning phase, i.e. via yield potential monitoring, as well as during the application phase, where near real-time monitoring is supported by means of meteorological and hydrological sensors as well as by the machinery fleet monitoring module. The machinery fleet monitoring module was developed as a crowdsourcing extension of the sensor network concept (SensLog). In addition, an alerting service with an open (REST, Representation State Transfer) API was developed in order to forward notifications to environmental information systems and/or to iOS and Android based mobile devices.

The first discovered bottleneck lies in the general lack of farms producing yield results in the form of maps with sufficient detail (i.e. details of management zones within a plot). So far, only two such farms out of a possible thousand have been identified. Without such maps, spatial correlation between the theoretically computed yield potential on the one hand and yield results on the other is not feasible.

The second discovered bottleneck lies in the technological and licencing limitations relating to machinery fleet monitoring. Technological limitations arise from the various implementations of vague ISO/CAN bus standards by different machine manufacturers and from the need for tractors to have on-board computers. Licensing agreements prohibit farmers from buying machines. As a result, all data measured remain the property of the agricultural machine producer.

The third discovered bottleneck lies in Big Data processing. For instance, yield potential was computed for the country of Luxembourg (an area of about 2'500 km2, i.e. 1'000 sq mi, comprising some 92'000 plots) in order to verify the concept of transferability. The computation of yield potential through the Empirical Bayesian Kriging interpolation of Landsat 8, Sentinel 2, and MODIS (Moderate Resolution Imaging Spectroradiometer) satellite data, together with smoothing to a spatial resolution of 5 meters, took two weeks at the Poznań Supercomputing and Networking Center (64 computer nodes in the cloud, each node with two E5 2670 v2 / 2697 v3 @ 2.6 GHz processors, an operational memory of 256 GB, and a storage capacity of 40 TB, connected via Fibre Channel, 50 TB Ceph via 10 Gbit ethernet). PostgreSQL XL (Structured Query Language, eXtra Large), i.e. a version for cloud-based solutions, was found to be insufficient for the storage and processing of computed yield potential zones.

Ongoing research of the DataBio project focuses on the development of more efficient storage and processing capabilities in order to increase the performance of the provided yield potential-, sensor-, and machinery monitoring-related open Web services for environmental information systems. The improvement of yield potential computation is also a subject of further research.

Acknowledgement. This project has received funding from the European Union's Horizon 2020 research and innovation programme under grant agreement No 732064 called "Data-Driven Bioeconomy" (DataBio), from the European Union's Seventh Framework Programme for research, technological development and demonstration under grant agreement No. 621074 titled "Farm-Oriented Open Data in Europe" (FOODIE); from the Horizon 2020 research and innovation programme under grant agreement No. 633945 designated "Farming Tools for external nutrient Inputs and water Management" (FATIMa); and from Grant No. MUNI/A/1419/2016, the "Integrated research of environmental changes in Earth's sphere II", awarded by Masaryk University, the Czech Republic.

References

1. Tscharntke, T., Klein, A.M., Kruess, A., Steffan-Dewenter, I., Thies, C.: Landscape perspectives on agricultural intensification and biodiversity – ecosystem service management. Ecol. Lett. **8**, 857–874 (2005). https://doi.org/10.1111/j.1461-0248.2005.00782.x
2. Skokanová, H., Havlíček, M., Unar, P., Janík, D., Šimeček, K.: Changes of ortolan bunting (Emberiza hortulana L.) habitats and implications for the species presence in SE Moravia, Czech Republic. Pol. J. Ecol. **64**, 98–112 (2016). https://doi.org/10.3161/15052249PJE2016.64.1.009
3. Tilman, D., Cassman, K.G., Matson, P.A., Naylor, R., Polasky, S.: Agricultural sustainability and intensive production practices. Nature **418**, 671–677 (2002). https://doi.org/10.1038/nature01014

4. Cassman, K.G.: Ecological intensification of cereal production systems: yield potential, soil quality, and precision agriculture. Proc. Nat. Acad. Sci. USA **96**(11), 5952–5959 (1999)
5. Kassam, A., Firedrich, T.: Conservation agriculture: global perspectives and developments. In: Proceedings of Regional Conservation Agriculture Symposium, 8–10 February 2011, Johannesburg, South Africa (2011)
6. Reznik, T., Charvat, K. Jr., Charvat, K., Horakova, S., Lukas, V., Kepka, M.: Open data model for (precision) agriculture applications and agricultural pollution monitoring. In: Johannsen, V.K., Jensen, S., Wohlgemuth, V., Preist, C., Eriksson, E. (eds.) Proceedings of Enviroinfo and ICT for Sustainability 2015. ACSR, vol. 22, pp. 97–107. Atlantis Press, Paris (2015)
7. Palma, R., Reznik, T., Esbrí, M., Charvat, K., Mazurek, C.: An INSPIRE-based vocabulary for the publication of agricultural linked data. In: Tamma, V., Dragoni, M., Gonçalves, R., Ławrynowicz, A. (eds.) OWLED 2015. LNCS, vol. 9557, pp. 124–133. Springer, Cham (2016). https://doi.org/10.1007/978-3-319-33245-1_13
8. Skokanova, H.: Can we combine structural functionality and landscape services assessments in order to estimate the impact of landscape structure on landscape services? Moravian Geogr. Rep. **21**, 2–14 (2013). https://doi.org/10.2478/mgr-2013-0016
9. Reznik, T.: Geographic information in the age of the INSPIRE Directive: discovery, download and use for geographical research. Geografie **118**, 77–93 (2013)
10. Reznik, T., Chudy, R., Micietova, E.: Normalized evaluation of the performance, capacity and availability of catalogue services: a pilot study based on INfrastruture for SPatial InfoRmation in Europe. Int. J. Digit. Earth **9**, 325–341 (2016). https://doi.org/10.1080/17538947.2015.1019581
11. ISO 15836-1:2017 Information and documentation – The Dublin Core metadata element set – Part 1: Core elements. International Organization for Standardization
12. ISO 19115:2003 Geographic information – Metadata. International Organization for Standardization
13. ISO 19119:2016 Geographic information – Services. International Organization for Standardization
14. ISO/TS 19139:2007 Geographic information – Metadata – XML schema implementation. International Organization for Standardization
15. Nebert, D., Whiteside, A., Vretaonos, P.: OpenGIS catalogue services specification – version 2.0.2. http://portal.opengeospatial.org/files/?artifact_id=20555
16. DCAT application profile for data portals in Europe. https://joinup.ec.europa.eu/asset/dcat_application_profile/asset_release/geodcat-ap-v10
17. Creative Commons Attribution/ShareAlike 4.0 International. https://creativecommons.org/licenses/by-sa/4.0/
18. Open data commons open database license (ODbL). https://opendatacommons.org/licenses/odbl
19. GitHub. https://github.com/
20. FOODIE data model license. https://github.com/Wirelessinfo/FOODIE-data-model/blob/master/LICENSE.TXT
21. Berners-Lee, T.: Linked data. https://www.w3.org/DesignIssues/LinkedData.html, 2006
22. Beaujardiere, J. (ed.): OpenGIS web map server implementation specification. http://portal.opengeospatial.org/files/?artifact_id=14416
23. Vretanos, P.A. (ed.): OpenGIS web feature service 2.0 interface standard. http://portal.opengeospatial.org/files/?artifact_id=39967
24. Schut, P., Whiteside, A. (eds.): OpenGIS web processing service implementation specification. http://portal.opengeospatial.org/files/?artifact_id=24151

25. Senkler, K., Voges, U. (eds.): OpenGIS catalogue service specification – ISO metadata application profile. http://portal.opengeospatial.org/files/?artifact_id=20555
26. RDF – resource description format. https://www.w3.org/RDF/
27. SPARQL query language for RDF. https://www.w3.org/TR/rdf-sparql-query/
28. Evans, L.T., Fischer, R.A.: Yield potential: its definition, measurement, and significance. Crop Sci. **39**, 1544–1551 (1999)
29. Kleinjan, J., Clyde, D.E., Carlson, C.G., Clay, S.A.: Productivity zones from multiple years of yield monitor data. In: Pierce, F.J., Clay, D. (eds.): GIS Applications in Agriculture, pp. 65–70. CRC Press, Boca Raton (2007)
30. USGS ups ease of use for landsat data. https://www.usgs.gov/news/usgs-ups-ease-use-landsat-data
31. Measuring   vegetation   (NDVI&EVI).   https://earthobservatory.nasa.gov/Features/MeasuringVegetation/measuring_vegetation_2.php
32. Kubicek, P., Kozel, J., Stampach, R., Lukas, V.: Prototyping the visualization of geographic and sensor data for agriculture. Comput. Electron. Agric. **97**, 83–91 (2013). https://doi.org/10.1016/j.compag.2013.07.007
33. Feiden, K., Kruse, F., Řezník, T., Kubíček, P., Schentz, H., Eberhardt, E., Baritz, R.: Best practice network GS SOIL promoting access to european, interoperable and INSPIRE compliant soil information. In: Hřebíček, J., Schimak, G., Denzer, R. (eds.) ISESS 2011. IAICT, vol. 359, pp. 226–234. Springer, Heidelberg (2011). https://doi.org/10.1007/978-3-642-22285-6_25
34. ISO 19156:2011 Geographic information – Observations and measurements. International Organization for Standardization, Geneva, 2011
35. CAN bus. https://www.kth.se/social/upload/526eab8ef2765479ddbd9131/CAN
36. ISO 11783 (parts 1 to 14). Tractors and machinery for agriculture and forestry – Serial control and communications data network
37. Tervonen, J., Mikhaylov, K., Pieskä, S., Jämsä, J., Heikkilä, M.: Cognitive internet-of-things solutions enabled by wireless sensor and actuator networks. In: Proceedings of 5th IEEE International Conference on Cognitive Infocommunications (CogInfoCom), pp. 97–102 (2014)
38. Industrial Internet Consortium. http://www.iiconsortium.org/index.htm

Risk and Disaster Management

Large Scale Surveillance, Detection and Alerts Information Management System for Critical Infrastructure

Z. Sabeur[1]([⊠]) [iD], Z. Zlatev[1], P. Melas[1], G. Veres[1], B. Arbab-Zavar[1], L. Middleton[1], and N. Museux[2]

[1] Department of Electronics and Computer Science, University of Southampton IT Innovation Centre, Southampton, UK
{zas,zdz,pm,gvv,baz,ljm}@it-innovation.soton.ac.uk
[2] THALES Research and Technology, Palaiseau, France
nicolas.museux@thalesgroup.com

Abstract. A proof-of-concept system for large scale surveillance, detection and alerts information management (SDAIM) is presented in this paper. Various aspects of building the SDAIM software system for large scale critical infrastructure monitoring and decision support are described. The work is currently developped in the large collaborative ZONeSEC project (www.zonesec.eu). ZONeSEC specializes in the monitoring of so-called Wide-zones. These are large critical infrastructure which require 24/7 monitoring for safety and security. It involves integrated in situ and remote sensing together with large scale stationary sensor networks, that are supported by cross-border communication. In ZONeSEC, the specific deployed sensors around the critical infrastructure may include: Accelerometers that are mounted on perimeter fences; Underground acoustic sensors; Optical, thermal and hyperspectral video cameras or radar systems mounted on strategic areas or on airborne UAVs for mission exploration. The SDAIM system design supports the ingestion of the various types of sensors platform wide-zones' environmental observations and provide large scale distributed data fusion and reasoning with near-real-time messaging and alerts for critical decision-support. On a functional level, the system design is founded on the JDL/DFIG (Joint Directors of Laboratories/Data Fusion Information Group) data and information fusion model. Further, it is technologically underpinned by proven Big Data technologies for distributed data storage and processing as well as on-demand access to intelligent data analytics modules. The SDAIM system development will be piloted and alidated at various selected ZONeSEC project wide-zones [1]. These include water, oil and transnational gas pipelines and motorway conveyed in six European countries.

Keywords: Big data · Data fusion · Information systems
Surveillance of critical infrastructure

© IFIP International Federation for Information Processing 2017
Published by Springer International Publishing AG 2017. All Rights Reserved
J. Hřebíček et al. (Eds.): ISESS 2017, IFIP AICT 507, pp. 237–246, 2017.
https://doi.org/10.1007/978-3-319-89935-0_20

1   Introduction

The SDAIM functional objectives specialize in the enablement of the intelligent fusion of data and information processing and reasoning from heterogeneous observation data sources. These are generated from a high variety of sensor observation platforms and processing components. Currently, the SDAIM considers observation data sources from 3D accelerometers, underground acoustic sensors, CCTV cameras, thermal and hyperspectral cameras, radars, SCADA (Supervisory Control and Data Acquisition) systems and human observers. This is achieved by undertaking sources, data and information modelling through the creation of metadata for such sources, in order to automate the system and data processing configurations. The aim is to achieve sensors platforms "plug-and-play" and the automatic on-demand access to fusion processes, their configuration and execution. Furthermore, open standards are used for fetching sensor data and processing metadata such as OGC Sensor Web Enablement using SensorML, JSON and RDF; and OWL for metadata description and modelling.

In addition to the above, the SDAIM system encounters high big data velocities for processing under the fusion resources. This is the case because of high data transmission volumes from thousands of sensors mounted at various platforms. This challenging problem is addressed through combining of advanced system's architecture design solutions with the adoption of specialized Big Data technologies. Specifically, the SDAIM advanced architecture is based on the de-facto functional data and information fusion model, the JDL/DFIG generic model [2–4]. This modelling framework provides highly structured functionalities of the SDAIM data processing modules, while adopting the current Google approach for scalable big data processing workloads. The latter uses concepts of Dockers for creating lightweight virtualized containers for the processing modules, and Kubernetes for scalable deployment and execution of processing components. This approach enables the SDAIM to be deployed and executed in a distributed fashion over a high variety of operating systems, ranging from lightweight embedded platforms to heavy-duty servers.

2   SDAIM Scalable Data Fusion Approaches

An important aspect with regards to the scaling of the SDAIM data fusion and processing is our structured approach for achieving a scalable high level data and information fusion. This particularly needs to be addressed at the JDL fusion level 3 on Situation Assessment. In the SDAIM, level 3 fusion components generate, what we call, 'alerts' and these needs to be critically achieved through an intelligent processing of big data for messaging them into a distributed system with effective action and mitigation on detected illicit activities at wide-zones. The JDL framework, see Fig. 1, is defined as follows[1]:

---

[1]   At this stage, only the first four levels of the JDL/DFIG framework are described. The full extended level will be described in the full paper as defined in Fig. 1.

Level 0 → Fusion components generate signals, e.g. raw signal, co-registered signals with early data pre-processing, harmonisation and aggregations

Level 1 → Fusion components which specialise in the identification of background low level feature within a scene of interest

Level 2 → Fusion components which detect events concerning objects of targeted types; and/or critical state transitions within a given sensory signal; and/or specific behaviours which may be qualified as unusual

Level 3 → Fusion components which generate alerts on the detected objects, events or behaviour of critical status that may compromise the security and safety of the wide-zone of interest. These fusion components work on the level of reasoning on objects and behaviours relations.

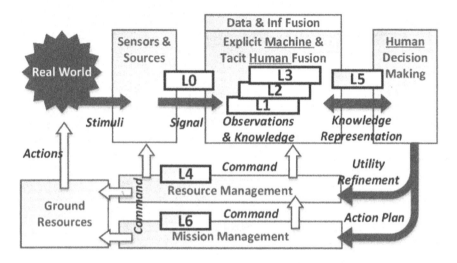

Fig. 1. The JDL/DFIG data and information fusion model

Alerts are consequently disseminated for consideration for decision-support to the security practitioners' operations via an online accessible graphical user interface. It will represent the Common Operational Picture (COP) of the wide-zone specific scene of interest. Depending on the COP diagnosis, the security practitioners could potentially raise a level of alert to a specified hierarchy of decision-makers and first responders.

Based on the JDL/DFIG information model, the logical architecture of the SDAIM is depicted on Fig. 2. In it, the central components are the data and information fusion algorithms. These components, as per the JDL/DFIG model, fulfil fusion functions at different logical levels, e.g. signal processing, event or object detection, multiple classifications with various levels of confidence to high level extracted knowledge through fusion and reasoning on the wide-zone operational spatial and temporal contexts.

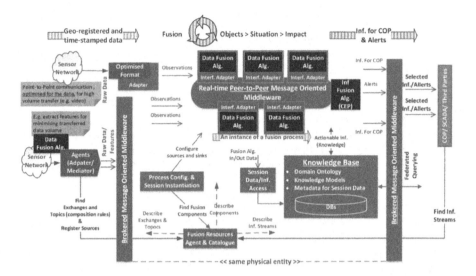

Fig. 2. SDAIM architecture logical view

Finally, Fig. 3 depicts a simplified deployment case of the SDAIM. The SDAIM is deployed for a Wide-zone with 3 sub-regions and their respective sub-regional and global regional control centers.

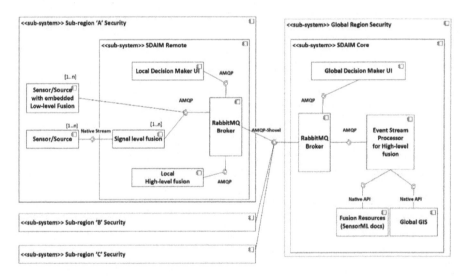

Fig. 3. SDAIM deployment for a wide-zone with 3 sub-regions and sub-regional and a global regional control centres

3 Applications on Surveillance, Detection and Alerts of Illicit Behaviour in Wide-Zones

In this section, we present early specific applications concerning surveillance, automated detection and alerts of illicit behaviour in wide-zones. The use of multiple type of sensing methods enable the automated detection and interpretation of potential illicit events occurring at wide zones. These approaches scale to large geospatial coverages and potential enable reasoning on detected events accordingly for establishing advanced situation awareness for safety and security management practitioners.

3.1 Physical Disturbance Event Detections at Fences of Critical Areas

Perimeter fences are widely used to protect Critical Areas such as water treatment plants, oil refinery, construction sites etc. Fence structures help to prevent only part of potential intrusions or postpone them. Therefore a high level of security is needed to monitor and investigate activities on and around fences. Accelerometers are relatively reliable tools which can be used for monitoring non rigid fences. While monitoring perimeter fences, two problems have to be addressed (1) Detect unusual events; and (2) classify these events to help with decision making and security related actions. Below, we present solutions to both of these problems using vibration sensors which are mounted on fences.

To efficiently detect unusual events along a perimeter fence, the developed event detection algorithm has to have the following properties: Fast, simple, and online; little or no interference of the user; data passed in small packets (1 or 2s of data); training stage enabled. Taking into consideration such requirements, an event detector based on Median Absolute Deviation (MAD) of signal and confidence interval method was adopted [5]. For each sensor directional axis, $y(N)$ will be a packet of data with specified window size N pass. The Median Absolute Deviation is a robust measure of data variability that can be calculated as follows:

$$MAD(y(N)) = median|y(N) - median(y(N))|$$

Then the median of this packet of data should be inside a confidence interval with a selected value range. The lower and upper bounds of the confidence interval are calculated as:

$$D(N)_{low} = median(y(N)) - \gamma * \sigma_y, D(N)_{up} = median(y(N)) + \gamma * \sigma_y$$

Where, the standard deviation of the signal in the given window is estimated as

$$\sigma_y = \frac{MAD(y(N))}{0.6745 * \sqrt{2}}$$

γ was selected to be equal to 4 in order to guarantee more than 99.7% of confidence in the samples to be within these bounds.

Then an event for a given axis is detected if $D(N)_{up} - D(N)_{low} >$ threshold. The latter is estimated using packets of data when no-activities take place. The threshold indicates an allowed deviation from the confidence interval when the packet of data will be considered while associated to no-activities. The quality of the MAD event detector is assessed using precision and recall measures. It was shown in the literature that such events as rattle, kick, climb or lean can be successfully classified for detecting security fence breaching under certain conditions [6]. In this paper, we will classify kick (K), shake (S) and no-activity (NA) events for each packet of data using a Bagging algorithm (Bag of decision trees) [7]. Cascade classification is also suggested in this paper. At the first stage, a packet of data is classified as Activity (A), No-activity (NA), Start (St) and End (E). If Activity (A) was classified, then this packet is classified as either kick (K) or shake (S). If the classifier returns Start event, then it is classified as a transition from no-activity to kick (NAK) or shake (NAS). The End event is classified as transition from kick or shake to no-activity (KNA, SNA). The initial investigation showed that mis-classifications of K and S occur quite often during transition periods due to damping effects of the vibration signal. The quality of classification is assessed using Correct Classification Rate (CCR) for each state detection.

Experiments were performed using fence structure, as shown in Fig. 4. Each fence section 2 m high and 3 m wide. S1 and S2 indicate the locations of the vibration sensors.

Fig. 4. Schematic presentation of non-rigid fence and vibration sensors

Six tests were performed with 2 persons who kicked and shook various sections of the fence at different times. Overall, 30 kicks and 31 shakes were experimented and recorded. The sensors were left on the fence for 15 min to record no-activities which used to calculate a threshold for event detection (it was 0 in this case for both sensors). The sampling rate of sensors were at 100 Hz, and packets of 200 samples (2s of data) was passed to the MAD event detector and classifier. The start and end of events were manually labelled with some bias for the end of event due to the damping effect of the signal. For the training stage of the detector and classifier, 70% data was used for training (21 kicks and 22 shakes) while the rest of the data was used for testing (9 kicks and 9 shakes). In this paper, we consider High Level Event detection, i.e. an event is detected if the alarm was raised at least for one packet of data when the event takes place. Such event is marked as TP (True Positive). If the MAD event detector sets the alarm when no events took place, such event was marked as FP (False Positive). False Negative (FN) is counted when a whole event was missed. Table 1, below, shows recall and precision for individual tests and overall. Although all events were detected, some FPs occur usually in the end of an event. Examples of MAD event detector performances are shown in Fig. 5.

Table 1. Performance evaluation of MAD event detector

Test	Test1	Test2	Test3	Test4	Test5	Test6
Recall	100%	100%	100%	100%	100%	100%
Precision	93.3%	72.7%	100%	84.2%	88.9%	90%

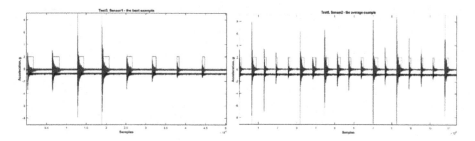

Fig. 5. Performance of the MAD event detector: the best and average examples

		Predicted						
		K	KNA	NA	NAK	S	SNA	NAS
Actual	K	**87.01**	0	0	0	11.69	1.3	0
	KNA	17.07	**65.85**	0	0	2.44	14.63	0
	NA	0	0.6	**98.68**	0	0	0.48	0.24
	NAK	9.09	0	0	**63.64**	0	9.09	18.18
	S	9.4	0.85	0	0	**88.03**	1.71	0
	SNA	6.52	13.04	6.5	0	10.89	**63.04**	0
	NAS	0	0	16.67	8.33	0	0	**75**

Fig. 6. Confusion Matrix for event classifications

A Cascade classifier which was suggested earlier achieved correct classification rate (CCR) at 93.75% overall. The Confusion Matrix for all detected events is given in Fig. 6.

NA is almost always classified correctly, the mis-classification usually occur during transition from K/S to NA which is expected due the nature of the vibration signals. NA is mis-classified as transition NAS sometimes when a packet of data contains more than 60% of NA samples. CCRs for both K and S exceed rates of 85%.

The results above showed that MAD event detector can be used to detect event reliably in Critical areas fences using vibration sensors, while the Cascade classifier can identify the nature of events taking place for further decision-support.

3.2   Unusual Behaviour Detection at a Toll Motorway

Automatic detection of incidents and unusual traffic events in motorways from visible spectrum videos is a challenging problem. These incidents range from: traffic collisions between vehicles and between vehicles and road structures, cars driving in the opposite direction or reversing, pedestrians and animals crossing the motorway, and more. Two main approaches are considered for this problem. First approach is through learning the environment and thus learning which motions and behaviours are usual in this environment [8–11]. The second possibility is the direct approach of detecting the specific objects and further detecting their motion and appearance and finally classifying these in terms of behaviours and events. Works on object classification and tracking [12], human detection and tracking [13–15] and human behaviour recognition [16] falls into this category.

Given the diversity of incident types, we have initially opted for the more generic approach of learning the usual behaviour/motions of the scene. Please note that this choice is often a trade-off between the flexibility and accuracy of the detector. Furthermore, the number of training examples are often limited and this would hinder the design of specialized detectors. A hybrid approach has since been developed to handle a specific case of stationary cars in a tunnel and a more generic detector for the non-roofed areas.

Detecting Unusual Behaviour via Learning the Usual Flow

The approach here is similar to the method introduced by Adam et al. [8] where a grid of local monitors learn the low-level local statistics of physical motions. A monitor will produce a local alert if the observed motion does not conform with the usual patterns of motion in that neighbourhood. These alerts are then fused across spatio-temporal windows to make the decision regarding the existence of an unusual event. The hypothesis states that incidents are events that disrupt the usual traffic flow in a motorway; and therefore can be detected as samples that do not fit the modelled usual flow. Figure 7 summarizes this method. Two examples of detected unusual behaviour are also shown, where the area with unusualness has been highlighted automatically. These two examples show a car driving in opposite direction and a dog crossing the motorway.

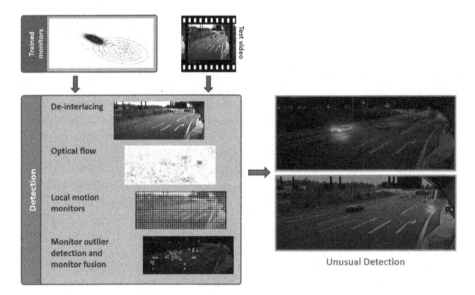

Fig. 7. Unusualness detection on traffic flow in motorways

Detecting Stationary Vehicles in a Tunnel

The specific problem considered here concerns the detection of a stationary car and a pedestrian on the pavement in a tunnel while the traffic is in a one-way flow. The placement of the camera is such that the images of the vehicles are captured from a side/frontal view. It was found that the accuracy of detection using the above method is low due to some inherent difficulties of the set. These difficulties include: (i) The specific pose and car headlights, which give rise to a significant amount of erroneous motion detections using optical flow; (ii) Motion of cars in the left lane of the road are near to parallel to the camera's principal axis, due to direction of travel and the placement of the camera.

As a result, the optical flow values of the stationary car do not produce the required signal to noise ratio for detection. A combination of background subtraction methods and a blob tracker is used to detect the stationary car and the person on the pavement. In this, the temporal variance-based method introduced by Joo and Zheng [17] and the median background subtraction are combined to obtain the robustness of temporal variance and capability of the median model to detect stationary objects. Further morphological transforms are used to clean the foreground, in order to assist the detection of distinctive blobs in the foreground. The detected foreground blobs are compared between two consecutive frames based on the size and motion of the blobs using a Kalman filter. The outcome of tracking is shown in Fig. 8.

Fig. 8. Blob tracking based on foreground detection

4   On Site Integration Pilot (OIP) and Future Development

In December 2016, a prototype demonstrator was implemented on-site at an ATTIKES toll motorway, Athens, Greece. This prototype consisted of the major elements with reliable messaging using RabbitMQ and algorithm processing codes which were implemented within linux containers (Docker). The processing was then passed to a reasoning engine which performed event stream processing and high level fusion to make final assertions about the sensor processing and detected events in real-time. Several days of testing were performed along with a final live exercise evaluated by end-users. The use of containers made fixing and redeploying the detection algorithms very efficient. The aim was for the Motorway Traffic Management Centre at Attikes to be enabled with automated detection of unusual events in their motorways sections. With tens of surveillance cameras in place at the Centre, staff cannot efficiently detect all unusual events with rapid response. The SDAIM consequently provides real-time alerts to events for staff which will reduce their response time lags by 50% according to the discussion which we conducted with Attikes staff. Additionally, and due to the flexible nature of the

SDAIM architecture, we will deploy further performing algorithms for unusual event detection. The final version of the SDAIM system will be tested and validated at the Traffic Management Centre for Attikes Motorway in May 2018.

Acknowledgement. The authors would like to thank partners TEKNIKER and Attikes for the acquisition of experimental data using accelerometers and CCTV respectively. The ZoneSEC research project is partly funded by the European Union under contract Number: EC_FP7 607292.

References

1. ZONeSEC: Towards an EU framework for the security of wide-zones (2014–2018). http://www.zonesec.eu/
2. Lambert, D.: A blueprint for higher level fusion systems. Inf. Fusion **10**(1), 6–24 (2009)
3. Sabeur, Z.: Structured multi-level data fusion and modelling of heterogeneous environmental data for future internet applications. In: Geophysical Research Abstracts. EGU General Assembly 2013, vol. 15 (2013)
4. Zlatev, Z., Veres, G., Sabeur, Z.: Agile data fusion and knowledge base architecture for critical decision support. Int. J. Decision Support Syst. Technol. (IJDSST) **5**(2), 1–20 (2013)
5. Barat, V., Grishin, D., Rostovtsev, M.: Detection of AE signals against background friction. J. Acoust. Emission **29**, 133–141 (2011)
6. Yousefi, A., Dibazar, A., Berger, T.: Application of non-homogeneous HMM on detecting security fence breaching. In: Proceedings of the ICASSP (2010)
7. Meinshausen, N.: Quantile regression forests. J. Mach. Learn. Res. **7**, 983–999 (2006)
8. Adam, A., Rivlin, E., Shimshoni, I., Reinitz, D.: Robust real-time unusual event detection using multiple fixed-location monitors. PAMI **30**(3), 555–560 (2008)
9. Breitenstein, M.D., Grabner, H., Van Gool, L.: Hunting nessie-real-time abnormality detection from webcams. In: IEEE 12th International Conference on Computer Vision (ICCV) Workshops (2009)
10. Saligrama, V., Chen, Z.: Video anomaly detection based on local statistical aggregates. In: Computer Vision and Pattern Recognition (CVPR) (2012)
11. Yun, K., Kim, J., Kim, S.W., Jeong, H., Choi, J.Y.: Learning with adaptive rate for online detection of unusual appearance. In: Bebis, G., Boyle, R., Parvin, B., Koracin, D., McMahan, R., Jerald, J., Zhang, H., Drucker, Steven M., Kambhamettu, C., El Choubassi, M., Deng, Z., Carlson, M. (eds.) ISVC 2014. LNCS, vol. 8887, pp. 698–707. Springer, Cham (2014). https://doi.org/10.1007/978-3-319-14249-4_67
12. Shah, M., Javed, O., Shafique, K.: Automated visual surveillance in realistic scenarios. IEEE MultiMed. **14**(1), 30–39 (2007)
13. Dalal, N., Triggs, B.: Histograms of oriented gradients for human detection. In: IEEE Computer Vision and Pattern Recognition (2005)
14. Bouchrika, I., Carter, J.N., Nixon, M.S., Morzinger, R., Thallinger, G.: Using gait features for improving walking people detection. In: International Conference on Pattern Recognition (2010)
15. Niebles, J.C., Han, B., Fei-Fei, L.: Efficient extraction of human motion volumes by tracking. In: IEEE Computer Vision and Pattern Recognition (2010)
16. Chaquet, J.M., Carmona, E.J., Fernández-Caballero, A.: A survey of video datasets for human action and activity recognition. Comput. Vis. Image Underst. **117**(6), 633–659 (2013)
17. Joo, S., Zheng, Q.: A temporal variance-based moving target detector. In: IEEE International Workshop on Performance Evaluation of Tracking and Surveillance (PETS) (2005)

ENSURE - Integration of Volunteers in Disaster Management

Frank Fuchs-Kittowski[1,2]([✉]) [iD], Michael Jendreck[1], Ulrich Meissen[1,2], Michel Rösler[1], Eridy Lukau[1], Stefan Pfennigschmidt[1], and Markus Hardt[1]

[1] Fraunhofer FOKUS, CC ESPRI, Berlin, Germany
{Frank.Fuchs-Kittowski,Michael.Jendreck,
Ulrich.Meissen,michel.matthias.roesler,eridy.lukau,
stefan.pfennigschmidt,markus.hardt}@fokus.fraunhofer.de
[2] HTW Berlin, Berlin, Germany
{Frank.Fuchs-Kittowski,Ulrich.Meissen}@htw-berlin.de

Abstract. Volunteers can be a valuable support for disaster management. Disaster management must be able to coordinate volunteers in order to benefit from their support. Interactive, collaborative, and mobile technologies have the potential to overcome the challenges involved in integrating volunteers into crisis and disaster management. This paper presents the ENSURE system, designed to effectively integrate volunteers for an improved approach to disaster management. The system supports the aid forces in recruiting, managing, activating, and coordinating volunteers in the event of a large-scale emergency. To achieve this, ENSURE provides necessary functions such as volunteer registration, volunteer profiles, sending alerts, and volunteer activation (via the mobile app). The system uses a subscription-based approach in which the volunteers agree to take part in an emergency operation by responding to an alert. The system architecture provides technical insights into how to implement crowdtasking systems. It contains seven logical components to provide the necessary features. It was designed to ensure scalability, performance, and availability. The results of a first comprehensive evaluation of ENSURE, which was performed as a large-scale exercise directed by the disaster relief forces in Berlin, were, without exception, positive in all three evaluation areas: efficiency & security, clarity & usability, reliability & availability.

Keywords: ENSURE · Volunteers · Crowd tasking · Disaster management

1 Introduction

In recent years, more and more citizens are willing to actively help during crises and disasters [1], such as during the flood in 2013 in Saxony-Anhalt [2]. The engagement of so-called "unbound volunteers" can be a valuable contribution while coping with a disaster [3]. Nevertheless, this kind of support can be problematic if it is not coordinated by emergency personnel. The lack of efficient coordination can result in the support being ineffective, with overcrowded or understaffed operation sites. This can lead to

© IFIP International Federation for Information Processing 2017
Published by Springer International Publishing AG 2017. All Rights Reserved
J. Hřebíček et al. (Eds.): ISESS 2017, IFIP AICT 507, pp. 247–262, 2017.
https://doi.org/10.1007/978-3-319-89935-0_21

frustration among the volunteers [4] and can hinder the actions of the emergency personnel or may even result in unintentional damages [5].

Modern (i.e., interactive, collaborative, and mobile) technologies can help to effectively involve spontaneous unbound volunteers in disaster management in case of an emergency [6]. Web 2.0 has created concepts of participation, such as crowdsourcing [7], which facilitate the engagement of volunteers and which have successfully been used in crisis management [8, 9]. In addition, the widespread use of mobile devices among the population offers a high potential to change the means of communicating with citizens in the event of a disaster, and to simplify the participation of the citizens as active volunteers [10]. With the help of mobile applications, crisis management can provide current on-site information via mobile devices in real time as well as organize and coordinate the activities of the volunteers at specific locations.

This paper presents the ENSURE system, designed to effectively integrate volunteers for an improved approach to crisis management. The system enables the registration, coordination, and notification of volunteers. The paper is structured as follows: Sect. 2 provides a brief introduction into crowdsourcing and crowdtasking in the context of disaster management and the conceptual architecture of crowdtasking systems is presented. In Sect. 3, the ENSURE system is considered from a user's perspective by discussing the functions it provides. Details on the technical system architecture are presented in Sect. 4. A brief overview about implementation and evaluation of the system is provided in Sect. 5. Related work is discussed in Sect. 6. A summary of the paper is given in Sect. 7.

2   Mobile Crowd Sourcing and Tasking in Disaster Management

2.1   Existing Approaches and Concepts

There is a variety of approaches to mobile IT systems for the integration of volunteers into crisis management. The majority of these systems are primarily designed for users to collect or assess information on their mobile devices, e.g., CrisisTrackers, Ushahidi, GeoChat, Mobile4D, Cross, Diadem, CrowdHelp, RE-ACTA. This type of involvement, in which simple, digital tasks are performed on-site by volunteers, can be described as "Mobile Crowdsourcing" [11] (or "Mobile Crowdsensing", if data are captured using the built-in sensors of the mobile devices). A sub-form of mobile crowdsourcing is "Mobile Crowdtasking", in which volunteers undertake special physical tasks (such as filling sandbags, providing first aid to injured people, protecting cultural assets, securing dangerous places, etc.) and report on them if appropriate.

Two forms of mobile crowdtasking can be distinguished based on the task distribution scheme [11], with one approach being independent, autonomous task selection and the other coordinated task assignment. In the first case, the volunteers choose their own tasks from a pool of globally available tasks. In the second case, qualified volunteers are efficiently given appropriate tasks with the aim of fulfilling the objectives of the application as best as possible. In a narrower sense of the term, only the subcategory in which the volunteers are not addressed as a group, but rather assigned individual tasks, is referred to as crowdtasking [16].

The potential of crowdtasking systems remains largely untapped with only a few examples of such systems currently in use to assign real, physical tasks to volunteers (e.g., filling sandbags). Scientific approaches and projects for such integration of unbound volunteers are Hands2Help [12], AHA [13], and KOKOS [14]. In addition to these scientific approaches, there are already some projects based on practical experience, such as ZUKS [15], and Team Österreich [16], aimed at the coordinated involvement of volunteers. Other helpful systems such as Mobile Retter, instantHelp, FirstAED, or Pulsepoint (which notifies a registered user of an accident in the area according to the user's skills) are also aimed at involving and coordinating volunteers, but they are mainly used for *ad hoc* lifesaving, i.e., they are specifically designed for first aid, and not common tasks in crisis management.

All the approaches to mobile crowdtasking mentioned so far have the following points in common: they provide methods and tools to recruit a greater number of volunteers, mobilize and activate them when needed, and coordinate their activities. To achieve this, a specific control system is required in order to distribute the tasks to suitable volunteers. A mobile app is also necessary for the volunteer to receive the tasks, coordinate with others, get involved, and capture and send data or reports to the control system. Additionally, the data captured and the reports sent (e.g. about task fulfilment) by the volunteers have to be analysed and evaluated by the control centre to gain a better awareness of the situation and to support campaign and crisis management.

2.2   Conceptual Architecture for Mobile Crowdtasking Systems

Based on these application examples as well as proposals for a general architecture for crowdsourcing applications [11], volunteer management systems [16], and a general process of crowdtasking [17–19], we identify the following components of a general architecture for crowdtasking systems (see Fig. 1).

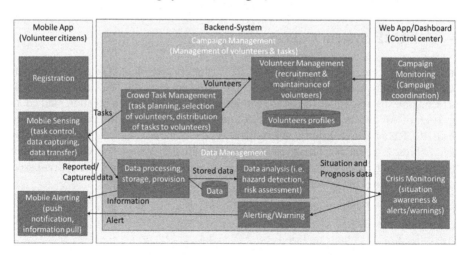

Fig. 1. Conceptual architecture of crowdtasking systems

Typical *roles* within this architecture are "campaign manager", "crisis manager" (both within the control centre), and "volunteer (citizen)".

- **Campaign manager (control centre):** initiates and monitors the crowdtasking campaign, including the definition of the campaign as well as recruitment, control, and coordination of well-suited volunteers.
- **Volunteer (citizen):** contributes to the crowdtasking campaign by (voluntarily) accepting and fulfilling tasks using his/her own mobile device. Often volunteers are members of the general public ("unbound volunteers"), but they can also be in a formal relation to the organizer ("formal voluntary engagement", see [16]).
- **Crisis manager (control centre):** accesses and processes the data captured or reports sent by the volunteers for better situational awareness and crisis management.

The conceptual architecture is divided into three independent *runtime systems*:

- Backend system (server) with two main components: (1) **Campaign Management** provides subcomponents for **Crowd** or **Volunteer Management** (campaign planning, volunteer management, recruiting and maintenance of volunteers), and **Crowd Task Management** (task planning, selection of volunteers, distribution of tasks to volunteers). (2) **Data Management** contains components for data processing (preprocessing, storage, processing, and provisioning), data analysis (i.e. hazard detection, risk assessment), and notification/warning.
- Mobile App (mobile client) for the volunteers with the components for **Registration** (motivation of volunteers, creation and maintenance of a volunteer profile), **Mobile Notification** (push notification, pull information), and **Mobile Sensing** (task control, data capturing, and data transfer).
- Web App (web client) for the control centre providing dashboard features for **Campaign Monitoring** (campaign coordination, monitoring of task fulfilment), and **Crisis Monitoring** (situational awareness, decision support).

3   ENSURE System Concept

In this section, the concept of the ENSURE system is presented. The most important functions of the system are discussed from the users' perspective. The aim of the system is to support disaster relief forces in recruitment, administration, activation, and coordination of volunteers in urban spaces in case of disasters. From the user perspective, the ENSURE system distributes help requests or alerts in the event of a hazard or emergency (Figs. 2, 3, and 4). These requests or alerts are delivered to the volunteers via a mobile app (Fig. 5). Volunteers agree to receive requests through a subscription-based system. Therefore, the system provides certain functionalities such as

- Registration of volunteers,
- Profiling of volunteers,
- Notification of volunteers (see Figs. 2, 3, and 4),
- Activation of volunteers (see Fig. 5)

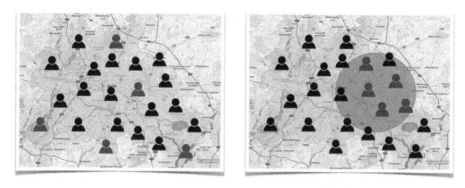

Fig. 2. Alerting of volunteers: coordination system (left: topic-based alert, right: regional alert)

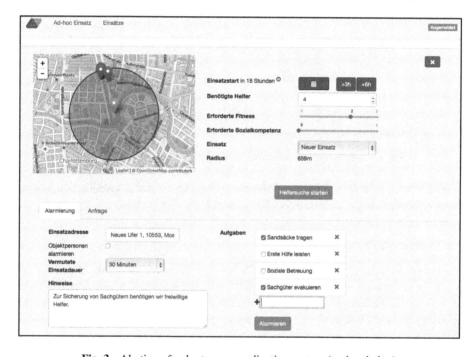

Fig. 3. Alerting of volunteers: coordination system (regional alert)

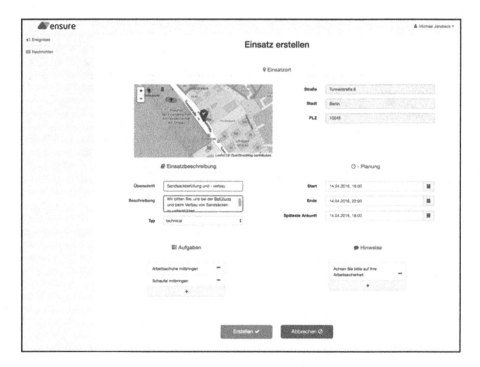

Fig. 4. Alerting of volunteers: coordination system (topic-based alert)

by means of a mobile app for the volunteers (see Fig. 5) and a coordination system (control centre) for the disaster relief forces (see Figs. 2, 3, and 4).

3.1 Volunteer Registration

Volunteers must first register via the mobile app in order to receive alerts. When the app is run for the first time, the user is presented with a project guide to encourage him/her to "join in". If the user decides to take part, this is technically equivalent to registering and is taken as implicit consent to create a user profile.

3.2 Volunteer Profiles

One of the basic principles of data protection is data minimization. The ENSURE system implements this as much as possible. Only the following information is stored (anonymously) in the base profile of a user:

- *Current location:* It is necessary to know the approximate current location of the volunteer in order to send regional alerts. With regard to data protection and informational self-determination, a volunteer must actively agree, after registration, to receive regional alerts and accept that their location is therefore always recorded by the system.

- *Fitness level and social skills:* In order to effectively activate volunteers in the event of a hazard or emergency, it should be possible to filter volunteers based on some properties. Information (subjective assessments) regarding physical fitness and social skills are stored in the base profile of the volunteer. This information is based on answers supplied by the volunteer to questions posed during the app setup.

In addition to the base profile, the system allows volunteers to add so-called "profile extensions". These profile extensions can provide information such as third-party verified qualifications (e.g., first aid), driving license class, technical expertise, etc.

3.3 Alerts

The help requests (or alerts) sent by the system to the volunteers are created by the app control centre by means of a web-based control system.

Filtering and alerting of volunteers is a multistep process and proceeds as follows:

- *Alert type:* It must first be established whether to send a regional alert or a topic-based alert.
- *Filtering:* Volunteers are chosen based on the location and time of the emergency, the number of volunteers needed, and any special skills that may be required.
- *Alert details:* Additional information such as specific tasks, estimated duration of the emergency operation, instructions, etc., can be added to the alert.

Volunteers can be alerted in one of two ways:

- The control system can trigger a *regional alert* to all volunteers in a given area (Fig. 2, right and Fig. 3). With this type of alert, volunteers receive a request if they are in the immediate vicinity of the emergency based on their current location.
- Alternatively, volunteers can receive *topic-based alerts* by subscribing to a certain topic, e.g., "Flooding 2013 – Dresden" (Fig. 2, left and Fig. 4). The location of the volunteer does not play a role in this type of alert, and so does not need to be known. The volunteer can freely select which type of alerts to receive in the mobile app.

In addition to regional and topic-based alerts, alerts can be further classified as early warning alerts and *ad hoc* alerts:

- *Early warning alerts:* If the warning period is sufficiently long, the potential volunteers can be requested to confirm their willingness to participate in advance. This procedure can be used for both regional and topic-based alerts and is particularly beneficial for improving planning. A questionnaire can also be sent to the volunteers in order to collect information about special skills that may be required during the emergency operation. The results of the questionnaire are stored as profile extensions in the system and can be used as filtering criteria.
- *Ad hoc alerts:* These alerts do not have a warning period or a planning phase. The idea is that volunteers in the immediate vicinity of an emergency (e.g., a medical emergency) arrive as soon as possible and provide first aid. In order to not lose time creating the alert, only the location and the emergency operation code must be given. If the emergency is assigned an address, this is set automatically as the target location.

Extra details can be entered in a free-text field in the creation form for the alert. As the control system is web-based, all fields of the alert form can be filled with URL parameters. Specialized procedures can pass pre-existing information to the control system via a URL link.

Other functions that are available on the control system include:

- Sending updates to all users,
- Sending additional information about an emergency operation to all users taking part in that operation,
- A detailed view of ongoing emergency operations (including volunteer feedback).

3.4 Volunteer Activation

For activation (Fig. 5), the selected volunteers receive a message via push notification on their smartphones. The users are shown all the information about the emergency operation in the app and can decide whether to accept or reject the request. They can also respond to a questionnaire regarding special skills for the emergency operation if one was sent with the alert.

Fig. 5. Volunteer activation via the mobile app

4   System Architecture

In this section, the architecture of the ENSURE system is presented (see Fig. 6).

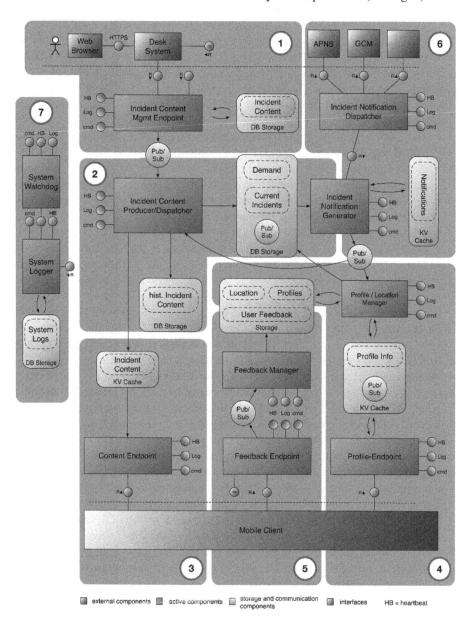

Fig. 6. ENSURE – system architecture (mobile app, web app, backend)

4.1 Components

The components of this system can be divided in seven logical parts (subsystems).

- **Accepting and managing events (1).** The *Incident Content Management Endpoint* is responsible for managing incoming events (alerts or requests from the control system). It accepts event messages (raw events) via different external interfaces and saves them in the Incident *Content Storage*. New or updated events are forwarded to the *Incident Content Producer/Dispatcher* and thus to the distribution system.
- **Distribution system (2).** The *Incident Content Producer/Dispatcher* has two main tasks: it prepares the raw data of the incoming events and is responsible for the distribution system.
  - The processing is performed according to how the information will be further distributed. The system stores the data required for sending the notifications in the *Demand/Incident Storage* and informs the *Incident Notification Generator* about the new or updated event. It also generates the data required by the end users for the textual and graphical processing on their devices. These data are made available for retrieval via the *Incident Content Cache*.
  - The *Incident Content Cache* serves as a buffer for content to be delivered (e.g., events such as alerts or inquiries, additional information). The *Demand/Incident Storage* maps subscriptions from system users and event messages in a high-performance runtime model that facilitates efficient matching between both types of information.
- **Content retrieval (3).** The *Content Endpoint* provides the interface through which content may be queried. This includes queries of processed events and relevant additional information. The data are taken from the *Incident Content Cache*. The *Content Endpoint* is designed for maximum scalability and employs dynamic load distribution.
- **Management of personal and device information (4).** The *Profile Endpoint* presents the interface through which the user can query, add, or modify profile information. Similar to the *Content Endpoint*, the *Profile Endpoint* uses a dynamic load distribution in order to enable, among other things, multiple profile updates within a short period of time. The *Profile Endpoint* retrieves answers to queries from the *Profile Info Cache*, which holds frequently requested data as well as current profile information in a high-performance key-value cache. The *Profile/Location Manager* is responsible for managing all profile-related data in the system. User inquiries are forwarded to the manager if they cannot be answered directly from the *Profile Info Cache*. All data are persistently stored in the *Location/Profile/Feedback Storage*. Changes to subscriptions are also send to the *Demand/Incident Storage* and forwarded to the *Incident Notification Generator* to check if a notification is required.
- **Notification service (6).** The *Incident Notification Generator* is responsible for matching subscriptions (current position) and events.
  - The service has access to the *Demand/Incident Storage*, a special runtime database in which the subscription and event data have already been combined. The main task is to retrieve the mailing addresses of the relevant volunteers for each of the event messages and send these data to the *Incident Notification Dispatcher*. In addition,

this component has a store in which the notification statuses of the individual devices/users are held.

- The *Incident Notification Generator* also informs other system components of which devices are expected to send queries in the near future before triggering the notification delivery. This makes it possible to prepare the system so that requested information is more readily available.
- The *Incident Notification Dispatcher* is responsible for sending the notifications over different channels. It receives the event messages generated by the *Incident Notification Generator* along with the corresponding mailing addresses and sends the notifications.

- **User feedback (5).** The *Feedback Endpoint* allows all user feedback (task accepted/ rejected, feedback after completion of a task, as well as feedback regarding the basic profiling) to be received and forwarded to the *Feedback Storage*. Furthermore, the content management system can access all feedback information via this endpoint and prepare it for the dispatchers or use it as filter parameters (profile extensions) for the volunteer search.

- **System monitoring (7).** The *System Watchdog* is an instance of a checking system that checks to see if all active components are working properly within a given timeframe.
- The so-called *Heartbeat* is a complex object that is regularly sent by each active component to the *System Watchdog*. This object contains, among other things, information on the current status, errors, processed objects, as well as environment variables (such as required memory). With these data, the *System Watchdog* can react in the case of faulty behaviour and take control using the *Command Interface*.
- The *System Logger* receives log entries from all active components, prepares this information, and stores it in the System Logs Storage. Furthermore, it offers a request interface for retrieving log entries from both internal and external components, e.g., for support.

4.2   Performance, Scalability, and Data Security

The system architecture was designed to ensure scalability, load balancing, performance, and availability. In order to realise the performance and scalability of the system, the following design decisions were consistently applied within the architecture and later in the implementation:

- *Key-value caches* are used to quickly respond to queries. These are designed for the purpose of load distribution using multiple distributable instances. The number of instances can be dynamically adjusted depending on the expected or actual load. Additionally, key-value storage instances provide advantages over relational storage instances in terms of scalability.
- All data are persistently stored in databases. This means that all cache instances have persistent data storage. If an (unexpected) restart occurs, the information in the caches can be restored.
- Communication between the individual components in the system backend is asynchronous.

5   Implementation and Evaluation

The ENSURE system has been developed in an iterative process. In each iteration, new functionality is added to the system and evaluated. For the evaluation of the system, several alerting exercises as well as two large-scale field tests directed by the disaster relief forces in Berlin (Berlin fire brigade and red cross) are carried out. The results of evaluations are used for improvement of the existing system, which will be evaluated in the next iteration.

The **implementation** of the system is based on the following technologies:

- The **mobile client**, used by the volunteers, was implemented as a native mobile app for the mobile platforms iOS and Android.
- The **control system**, used by the control centre, was implemented as a single-page web application using the client-side JavaScript framework AngularJS.
- The **backend**, providing the functionality for the two clients and ensuring satisfaction of non-functional requirements like performance, robustness, and scalability, was implemented using server-side JavaScript technology included in the MEAN stack (MongoDB, Express.js, AngularJS, and Node.js) as well as Redis as a key value store.

A comprehensive **evaluation** of the system was performed as a large-scale exercise directed by the disaster relief forces in Berlin. In total, 24 volunteers and 120 aid workers took part in this exercise. Volunteers had to fulfil 14 different tasks before the arrival of the aid forces as well as simultaneously with the work of the disaster relief forces.

The evaluation criteria concentrated on the three established requirements on software applications in disaster management [6]: efficiency & security, clarity & usability, reliability & availability. The evaluation results were, without exception, positive in all three evaluation areas. In particular, the app was found to be very usable (SUS score: 90 points), highly stable, and had short response time as well a good success rate when storing a personal profile. First aid tasks were especially well performed (observation) and the volunteers followed instructions very accurately (clearing vehicle access routes, etc.) (See [20] for details.)

Currently, another large-scale field-test of ENSURE is taking place in Berlin under the name "Support the Berlin fire brigade". The ENSURE app is available in app stores (iOS and Android) for the field test so that anyone can participate as a volunteer in the exercise.

6   Related Work

Overall, the ENSURE approach described above has a number of similarities with existing concepts and systems (see Sect. 2.1), but it also shows significant differences.

The aim of the ZUKS project (Zivile Unterstützung im Katastrophenschutz) is to acquire helpers and to organise and deploy them. Similar to the ENSURE project, notification, organisation, and coordination is carried out using a control system. Activating previously registered helpers and sending task details is done analogously to a smartphone app. However, there is a considerable divergence in the integration of both systems. ENSURE provides the technical platform to the emergency and rescue services for free use; in contrast, the ZUKS project integrates the separate organisations into the existing system, and then the system manages the helpers. Furthermore, ENSURE is defined by anonymous registration and the continued organisation and coordination of helpers on the ground (including food and accommodation).

Similar to ENSURE, the Hands2Help project offers an app-based coordination and notification system that is designed to support emergency and rescue services in coordinating volunteers. Control centres can define a request for help by filling out a form. Volunteers can offer help and indicate their abilities through the app. If the system detects a match between an offer and a request, the relevant users are automatically contacted. This continues until the appropriate number of suitable volunteers is found. In contrast to ENSURE, no control system is provided for manual notification of volunteers by a control centre since the matching between offers and requests as well as the notification is automatically taken care of by system algorithms. The fact that every user can publish a request for help also differentiates both projects. In addition, Hands2Help requires compulsory data on the availability of the users with regard to time and location. ENSURE, in addition to notifying volunteers based on their location, offers topic-based notifications that do not require the location data of the volunteers.

The AHA project (Automatisiertes Helferangebot bei Großschadensereignissen) and the KOKOS project (Kooperation mit freiwilligen Helfern in komplexen Schadenslagen) both run parallel to the basic idea of ENSURE and also have the goal of involving the population in dealing with damage. However, there are differences in the concrete implementation of this objective. The KOKOS project focusses on integrating the public into crisis management. In addition to the volunteers themselves, the AHA project especially considers the technical equipment of the volunteers to be a useful resource, and it requests and registers availability.

In the Team Österreich project, volunteers can be registered with the Red Cross Austria as helpers and can be notified via various channels (SMS, email, etc.) in case of an emergency. Suitable volunteers are identified for a task, taking into account their place of residence as well as distance to the task location, so that enough volunteers with the right skill set are automatically notified. ENSURE relies on a content management system, which allows control centres to notify a certain number of volunteers and if necessary, request more help. The ENSURE app also offers users the possibility to report a delay in arriving at the task site so that the "non-appearance" of helpers can be taken into account by the control centre and included in the planning and coordination.

7   Conclusions

Disaster management is currently changing. On the one hand, citizens are very willing to actively help during crises and catastrophes and support the local emergency services. On the other hand, citizens are also increasingly seen as major players and a key resource in disaster relief. Nevertheless, the integration of volunteers into disaster management is still in its infancy.

There are a variety of approaches to implementing mobile IT systems for integrating citizens into crisis management. However, the potential of crowdtasking systems remains largely untapped with only a few examples of such systems in existence and a low level of interest and consideration in the research community.

This paper presents the ENSURE system. The goal of ENSURE is to effectively integrate volunteers for an improved approach to disaster management. The system enables the registration, coordination, and alerting of spontaneous volunteers. The functionality and architecture of the system are described in detail. ENSURE provides a concrete example that mobile crowdtasking applications can contribute to the effective involvement of volunteers in disaster relief.

A general, conceptual architecture for mobile crowdtasking systems was also proposed in this paper. The characterisation of mobile crowdtasking systems helped to understand the individual components and their attributes as well as the existing relationships and interdependency among the components, as determined by the system as a whole. The generic system architecture allows specific applications to be designed, classified, and evaluated, e.g., the ENSURE system.

The system architecture of ENSURE is not only an example of the use of the conceptual architecture. It is also an example of a system architecture that ensures scalability, load balancing, performance, and availability. It demonstrates the feasibility of developing robust crowdtasking applications. Identifying variables and features that affect the scalability and performance of a system is helpful when planning its design or making improvements to it once it is in operation.

The great potential, but also the associated difficulties, are only slowly coming to light. Questions regarding the validation and quality of the services provided by the volunteers as well as the handling of data protection issues arising from the use of personal data are currently being discussed. In addition, volunteer motivation and incentive systems for volunteer participation are important issues. In the end, evaluations of emergency operations must show how much the operations could be improved by the participation of the volunteers.

The systems that are known so far for the successful integration of the population into disaster relief show the starting points for the necessary change: citizens should not only be seen as recipients, but as an important resource in disaster management. Even though there may already be some examples of citizen integration in crisis management, these are always isolated and individual cases. So far, there is no unified, integrated concept covering all phases of disaster management, in which the different parties – professional forces, volunteer forces, and citizens – are well coordinated.

References

1. Ohder, C., Röpcke, J.: Hilfebedarf, Hilfeerwartung und Hilfebereitschaft bei einem Stromausfall. Ergebnisse einer Bürgerbefragung in Berlin. Crisis Prev. **2**, 33–35 (2014)
2. Geißler, S., Sticher, B.: Hilfeverhalten in Katastrophen und die Folgen für das Katastrophenmanagement - am Beispiel des Hochwassers 2013 in Magdeburg. Poliz. Wiss. **4**, 53–70 (2014)
3. Reuter, C., Heger, O., Pipek, V.: Social media for supporting emergent groups in crisis management. In: Proceedings of CSCW 2012 Workshop on Collaboration and Crisis Informatics, International Reports on Socio-Informatics (IRSI), vol. 9, no. 2, pp. 84–92 (2012)
4. Kircher, F.: Ungebundene Helfer im Katastrophenschutz. In: BrandSchutz, vol. 68, no. 8, pp. 593–597. Kohlhammer, Stuttgart (2014)
5. Schorr, C., Biergert, A., Weber, T., Max, M., Schulze, M.: Die Rolle der ungebundenen HelferInnen bei der Bewältigung von Schadensereignissen. Dt. Rotes Kreuz, Berlin (2014)
6. Mauthner, J., Engelbach, W., Engel, K.: Informationstechnologien für das Freiwilligenmanagement in Katastrophenschutz und Krisenmanagement. In: Engagiert im Katastrophenschutz - Impulse für ein zukunftsfähiges Freiwilligenmanagement, pp. 165–178. Wochenschau Verlag, Schwalbach (2015)
7. Howe, J.: The rise of crowdsourcing. Wired **14** (2006). www.wired.com/wired/archive/14.06/crowds.html
8. Kaufhold, M.A., Reuter, C.: Vernetzte Selbsthilfe in Sozialen Medien am Beispiel des Hochwassers 2013. i-com **13**(1), 20–28 (2014)
9. Schimak, G., Havlik, D., Pielorz, J.: Crowdsourcing in crisis and disaster management – challenges and considerations. In: Denzer, R., Argent, R.M., Schimak, G., Hřebíček, J. (eds.) Environmental Software Systems, vol. 448, pp. 56–70. Springer, Cham (2015). https://doi.org/10.1007/978-3-319-15994-2_5
10. Reuter, C., Ludwig, T., Pipek, V.: Ad hoc participation in situation assessment - supporting mobile collaboration in emergencies. ACM Trans. Comput.-Hum. Interact. **21**(5), article 26 (2014)
11. Fuchs-Kittowski, F., Faust, D.: Architecture of mobile crowdsourcing systems. In: Baloian, N., Burstein, F., Ogata, H., Santoro, F., Zurita, G. (eds.) CRIWG 2014. LNCS, vol. 8658, pp. 121–136. Springer, Cham (2014). https://doi.org/10.1007/978-3-319-10166-8_12
12. Hofmann, M., Betke, H., Sackmann, S.: Hands2Help – Ein App-basiertes Konzept zur Koordination freiwilliger Helfer. i-com **13**(1), 36–45 (2014)
13. Detjen, H., Geisler, S., Bumiller, G.: Nutzeranforderungen eines Systems zur automatischen Helferbereitstellung. In: Weibecker, M. Burmeister, A. Schmidt (eds.): Mensch und Computer 2015, pp. 11–18. Oldenbourg, Stuttgart (2015)
14. KOKOS: Project-Website, 31 March 2017. http://kokos-projekt.de/
15. ZUKS e.V.: ZUKS – Zivile Unterstützung im Katastrophenschutz – Konzept im Juni 2015, 31 March 2017. https://www.zuks.org/static/files/Konzept_1.2.pdf
16. Neubauer, G., Nowak, A., Jager, B., Kloyber, C., Flachberger, C., Foitik, G., Schimak, G.: Crowdtasking – a new concept for volunteer management in disaster relief. In: Hřebíček, J., Schimak, G., Kubásek, M., Rizzoli, Andrea E. (eds.) ISESS 2013. IAICT, vol. 413, pp. 345–356. Springer, Heidelberg (2013). https://doi.org/10.1007/978-3-642-41151-9_33
17. Auferbauer, D., Ganhör, R., Tellioạlu, H.: Moving towards crowd tasking for disaster mitigation. In: ISCRAM 2015 - Proceedings of the 12th International Conference on Information Systems for Crisis Response and Management (2015)

18. Middelhoff, M., Widera, A., van den Berg, R., Hellingrath, B., Auferbauer, D., Pielorz, J., Havlik, D.: Crowdsourcing and crowdtasking in crisis management: lessons learned from a field experiment simulating a flooding in city of the Hague. In: ICTDM2016- International Conference on Information and Communication Technologies for Disaster Management (2016)
19. Auferbauer, D., Ganhör, R., Pielorz, J., Tellioɪlu, H.: Crowdtasking: field study on a crowdsourcing solution for practitioners in crisis management. In: ISCRAM 2016 - Proceedings of the 13th International Conference on Information Systems for Crisis Response and Management (2016)
20. Jendreck, M., Meissen, U., Rösler, M., Lukau, E., Fuchs-Kittowski, F.: ENSURE - increasing resilience by integration of volunteers in disaster management. In: Environmental Informatics – Stability, Continuity, Innovation: Current trends and future perspectives based on 30 years of history, Shaker, Aachen, pp. 131–140 (2016)

C2-SENSE – Pilot Scenario for Interoperability Testing in Command & Control Systems for Crises and Disaster Management: Apulia Example

Marco Di Ciano[1(✉)], Agostino Palmitessa[1], Domenico Morgese[1(✉)], Denis Havlik[2(✉)], and Gerald Schimak[2(✉)]

[1] InnovaPuglia, Valenzano, Italy
{m.diciano,a.palmitessa,d.morgese}@innova.puglia.it
[2] AIT, Vienna, Austria
{denis.havlik,gerald.schimak}@ait.ac.at

Abstract. Different organizations with their Command & Control (C2) and Sensing Systems have to cooperate and constantly exchange and share data and information in order to manage emergencies, crises and disasters. Although individual standards and specifications are usually adopted in C2 and Sensing Systems separately, there is no common, unified interoperability specification to be adopted in an emergency situation, which creates a crucial interoperability challenge for all the involved organizations. To address this challenge, we introduce a novel and practical profiling approach, which aims at achieving seamless interoperability of C2 and Sensing Systems in emergency management. At the end of this interoperability challenge a Pilot Application is set up and will be tested in the field to demonstrate the advantages resulting from this effort. This paper gives an overview about the involved entities in the pilot application scenario and the testing of the system functionality by using predefined microscenarios suitable for the pilot region in Apulia.

Keywords: Command and Control · Interoperability
Crises-, disaster- and emergency management

1 Introduction

C2-SENSE system is an environmental application for crises and disaster management. It allows alignment and cooperation between all entities involved in emergency management assuring interoperability between them. To address this challenge, C2-SENSE introduces a novel and practical profiling approach [1] that, unlike the conventional profiling approach, which addresses only the first three layers of the interoperability stack [2], involves all the layers of the communication stack in the security field. The work presented in this paper examines in particular the aspects relating to the testing of a pilot application in the region of Apulia (Italy) and the interfacing with information systems of local authorities.

© IFIP International Federation for Information Processing 2017
Published by Springer International Publishing AG 2017. All Rights Reserved
J. Hřebíček et al. (Eds.): ISESS 2017, IFIP AICT 507, pp. 263–278, 2017.
https://doi.org/10.1007/978-3-319-89935-0_22

2   C2-SENSE Overview

2.1   Profiling Approach for Interoperability

An innovative and technological solution to the mentioned problems is represented by profiles that allow you to improve the interoperability between the entities involved in emergency management. The C2-SENSE project develops a profile-based Interoperability Framework [1] by integrating existing standards and semantically enriched web services to expose the functionalities of Command & Control (C2) Systems and Sensing Systems involved in the prevention and management of disasters and emergency situations. In a typical C2-SENSE scenario, two main interoperability challenges need to be addressed: the vertical interoperability between Sensing and C2 Systems and the horizontal interoperability among different organizations involved in the prevention and governance of emergency situations. To address the challenge profiling is offered as a practical approach in achieving seamless interoperability by addressing all the layers of the communication stack in the security field. The profile concept aims to eliminate the need for a prior bilateral agreement between any two information exchange partners by defining a standard set of messages/documents, choreographies, business rules and constraints. The profile compliant partners are able to exchange information and services among themselves. This is in contrast to the bilateral agreements that have to be settled between partners for each new exchange partner. Considering the nature of emergency management, in which the responding organizations can change at run time (especially in an international intervention case), these generic profiles provide the needed coordination flexibility in order to deal with the unexpected circumstances and prevent chaotic response in a crisis situation.

3   Regional Involved Institutions/Organizations

In the following we will give a short overview about the most important organizations, authorities and institutions involved in the Pilot Scenario.

3.1   Prefecture

The prefecture of Foggia is the organization that represents the national government in the territory. It has the task of coordinating all the operations related to emergency management and decision-making at the highest level. During emergencies, it inter-acts with all the involved organizations, in particular with Civil Protection.

3.2   Provinces

The test takes place in the area of the Province of Foggia. In general the role of the province is critical in terms of methodological support and governance for local authorities. The improvements made by a modern information system for Civil Protection are important, as they allow local authorities in the Province of Foggia to prepare, adopt and publish plans for Civil Protection that are fully integrated with the risk management process.

The C2-SENSE system will be able to ensure access and proper use of the functional system for all organizations involved in the province, providing all the information (static and dynamic) and visual support necessary to represent and describe the land, resources available and the population.

In summary, the information system will strengthen the operational structure of the Civil Protection of the Province of Foggia through an integrated system of information on risk scenarios to be developed and updated in "non-emergency periods". This system will be articulated according to various intervention models for the emergency management, in order to enable the timely response of the province, also in the management and coordination of resources (personnel, materials and means).

3.3 Municipalities

The municipalities involved in the tests of the pilot application (as described in Sect. 6) are belonging to the Province of Foggia which has several thousand inhabitants. According to the survey carried out at the beginning of the project, these municipalities replied that they currently do not have an electronic system for handling emergencies, thus we need to simulate these systems adequately.

3.4 Regional Civil Protection Department

The Civil Protection department has the task to be prepared and handle risk management in accordance with national guidelines.

It has a control system (SOIR) "Integrated Regional Control Room" that plays a major role in the coordination and management of emergencies, particularly for all risks affecting the Apulia region.

The SOIR is appointed to handle all the technical decisions, communications and control actions, and, as such, must ensure the continuity, activate procedures and count the occurrence of emergency situations, taking into account the received re-quests for assistance.

The CFD (Decentralized Functional Centre) monitors the area using specific pluvio-metric sensors installed in the Region.

3.5 Voluntary Associations

The high number of criticalities following an event requires a huge deployment of volunteer forces across the entire region.

The activation of voluntary associations is carried out by the SOIR. The business activities of the volunteers associations are shared with CFD (Civil Protection) and are related to sensor monitoring tasks on the territory and collaboration during emergency situation.

3.6 Fire Brigade

The Fire Brigade from 2011 adopts the CAP Profile, a simple and flexible format for the exchange of digital data, open and non-proprietary, for the collection and distribution of notifications and emergency alerts. All Entities/Organizations will be equipped with instruments for standardized data exchange with the operating rooms.

4 Stakeholders Interactions

4.1 Roles for Emergency Management

The entities and their roles involved in an emergency or crises event are different and heterogeneous. The envisaged flood emergency scenario involves multiple organizations having different roles and providing different services (e.g. police, medical care, rescue forces, fire fighters, etc.) and interacting vertically (i.e. with components of the same organization).

Figure 1 shows the institutions and actors involved in emergency situations and illustrates the role of the parties involved as described above. Analyzing this figure shows that the Prefecture has a central role. It is the party that coordinates the operations of emergency management. Furthermore, the Civil Protection plays a key role as it handles operations between SOIR and CFDs.

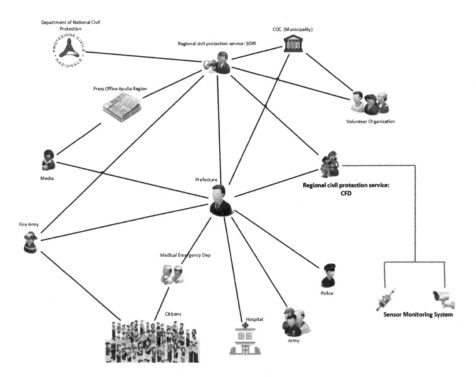

Fig. 1. Institutions and actors involved in emergency situations

A CFD in particular retrieves important information like rainfall data directly from the sensor system within the region. Finally an increasingly important role is played by citizens. In fact, they become participants in a triple role: first, an active role to inform the organizations responsible when an emergency situation occurs; second, a passive role, which allows them to be informed in real time following the occurrence of an emergency situation in their area, and third, the possibility of being easily located on the territory and therefore being properly tasked or informed in case they are needed.

Actually most of the communication is done by phone or fax which of course is highly error prone in crisis situations and not state of the art anymore. Existing plans or organizational information is outdated or invalid this can quickly lead to confusion and wrong decisions. C2-SENSE system intends to overcome this unsatisfying situation and provide interoperable means (e.g. tools, adapters, applications) to the stakeholders involved in the Pilot Scenario.

Interoperability is important because it enables different components to work together across organizational and system boundaries. The ability representing the system as a set of components and to combine the various components is essential for the construction of complex systems. Without interoperability this becomes almost impossible - as in the myth of the Tower of Babel, where the inability to communicate (and interoperate) results in a systemic failure in the construction of the tower.

Thus, there is an urgent need to improve mechanisms for crisis management information and communication technologies that can keep track of the many details involved in all phases of disaster management. ICT enabled collaboration and related tools that support interoperability have become a must today for all task involved in emergency management.

The purpose of the C2-SENSE project is to ensure a proper management and coordination of all activities and tasks supported by a set of components and tools [4]. The envisaged organizational structure for the scenario allows a seamless coordination of all technical and administrative activities respecting all the interest of the involved stakeholders (e.g. authorities, organizations, institutes, project partners, and external environments) in the project.

4.2   Criticalities

As a result of a survey done at the beginning of the project several critical issues have been identified in relation to activities carried out by the Regional Civil Protection Department. They are mainly related to notification and communication management as well as to data and information sharing. This also relates to activities and processes of the alert management, situation monitoring and/or management of emergency meteorological, hydrological and hydraulic risks.

As already mentioned before, during an emergency situation, currently all information are managed through telephone communications (mainly), email, radio and fax machines that are simultaneously collected by involved stakeholders; which leads to huge challenge and considerable difficulties in managing all the diverse and heterogeneous information.

Therefore we put our focus in the pilot application respectively scenario on these issues and challenges in order to provide a better understanding of IT supported emergency management solutions.

5   Pilot Application

5.1   Functions

The Pilot Application respectively the Scenario has three main features to be tested: data sharing, notification management and communication management.

Data Sharing as one of the important aspects to be tested. Key is the capability to share data and information about the actual situation but also about available resources with multiple applications and/or users.

In fact, to deal successfully with critical (crises/emergency) situations, it is crucial for all the involved systems (of different organization) to have all necessary information at their disposal. C2-SENSE has to guarantee to operate on an actual dataset that is coherent with the data provided by the involved organization. Thus, mutual interactions between organizations will imply information sharing between different systems. Consequently C2-SENSE will provide necessary data integration between different datasets in a transparent way with respect to the underlying technical systems and to their input specific sources.

Notification management, in any emergency situation, is one of the most important critical factors. Independent of the event (e.g. natural hazards, such as floods, tsunamis, etc. or from man-made accidents and threats) it is essential to be notified as fast as possible.

C2-SENSE shall provide a timely communication that is able to supply detailed and meaningful information, about an evolving emergency, to be exchanged among the involved institutional and non-institutional actors.

Communication management is one of the fundamental activities of emergency management. It becomes crucial when there are different subjects responding to an emergency and even more complex when we have to deal with different public information channels. Social media, especially Facebook and Twitter, but also WhatsApp, Telegram, YouTube, Instagram and Google Plus, are taking a very important part in the emergency response today. During emergencies, they are used by disaster responders, governments and non-governmental organizations, as an integrative information tool for crisis management.

The involved stakeholders can be grouped into three categories: control base, on field points and command stations.

The *control base* is made up of civil protection systems which are considered the main user of the C2-SENSE system. As described in the previous paragraphs, it is divided into a Functional Center and a Control Room.

For *field points* we can find actuators such as alarms or automatic barrier systems, voluntary organizations occurring in the territory to meet the most varied events and emergencies, and citizens that can interact with the C2-SENSE system either to communicate an emergency situation or to receive information related to the evolution of the event and risk situations.

Command stations are command and control points such as prefectures and municipalities, but also others like the fire brigade and the medical centers involved in the territory where the emergency occurs.

Finally Fig. 2 shows the data inputs that enrich the system with information needed to manage the emergency. This information is introduced by sensors installed in the region, or is information shared by systems that are involved in emergency management.

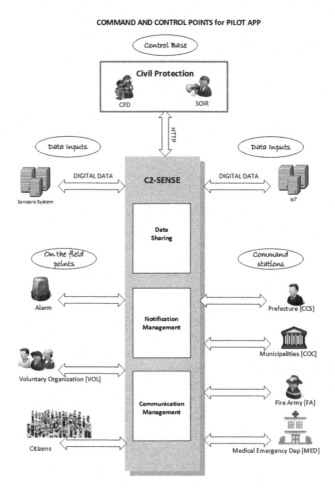

Fig. 2. Pilot application functions

5.2   C2-SENSE Pilot Application Environment

In Fig. 3 the pilot environment is shown. It is divided into two different logical ecosystems: C2-SENSE test environment (on the top) and end-users systems (second half).

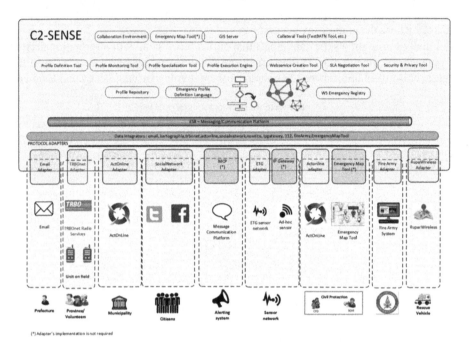

Fig. 3. Pilot application environment

C2-SENSE test environment is a digital ecosystem composed of various C2-SENSE tools having specific tasks: tools for definition and specialization of integration profiles, tools for communications management between the different C2-SENSE systems, and tools for performance monitoring. This ecosystem interacts with another ecosystem consisting of all systems of the local end users involved in emergency management and taking part in the pilot application testing. The interaction between the two ecosystems is done via different interfacing modules, called adapters, implemented between end-user's system and the C2-SENSE tools. Data used by the *end-user system* is translated by the adapter to make it C2-SENSE compliant; then, this information is processed and transmitted to the end-user recipient according to his local understanding or standards. The integration profiles define the way in which such integration has to be done.

5.3   Pilot Scenario

C2-SENSE will assess its outcomes in a realistic pilot "Flood Scenario in Italy" to ensure that the developed profiling approach is generic enough but also applicable in real life situations [3]. The pilot territory chosen is located in the north of Apulia, and in particular in the Province of Foggia, forming the border with the region of Molise. The Pilot Scenario covers a period of two days and describes step by step what could happen, before and during a flooding along the Fortore River as well as the evolution of the event.

This area (Fig. 4) is characterized by the terrain of the Gargano promontory, and the flat plains of Tavoliere.

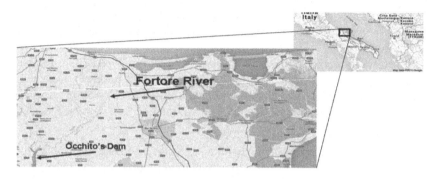

Fig. 4. Test area

In this area, there are many rivers present, and for the trial river Fortore (Fig. 5) was selected. It crosses the territory from south to north, and collects the waters of four other rivers; The Occhito dam meets along the way, and flows into the Adriatic Sea, not far from Lake Lesina.

Fig. 5. Fortore river

During the first day, the Pilot Scenario describes what are the institutions involved in the "Forecasting Phase" and what are the documents produced. In particular:

- The National Weather Service (CFN) announces bad weather conditions for the next 24–36 h;
- The Regional Functional Center (CFD) issues a Bulletin about the regional criticality.

- The manager of the Regional Civil Protection publishes and sends an alert message to Prefectures, Municipalities, and other organization as far as they are concerned.

For the second day, the Pilot Scenario describes what happens during the flooding along the Fortore River, and the institutions and organizations involved including their roles and responsibilities. In particular:

- CFD (Regional Functional Center) follows the evolution of the situation through the regional monitoring network installed in the territory (monitoring and surveillance activities).
- SOIR ensures emergency operations and H24 service to update the information related to the activities carried out, the type and amount of resources needed.
- The Prefecture opens its Assistance Coordination Center (CCS) at the provincial level with the presence of Healthcare Service, Police Department, Fire Brigade, Red Cross, etc.

Municipalities, the responsible body in their territory, activate its own emergency procedures and keep in contact with the voluntary organizations and other involved organizations.

The events described in the Pilot Scenario are grouped into micro-scenarios (MS 1–10 in following tables). They are used to describe in detail the interactions between two or more involved end-users. In particular: what is the event, which are the triggering systems, which are the target systems, what has to be tested, and what the positive/negative evaluation criteria are. In the following there is an overview about the proposed micro-scenarios used for the pilot:

Official Sensor Value Display
Decentralized Functional Centre (CFD) wants to show all the regional official sensors connected. They activate 'Emergency Map Tool (EMT)' [4] and start the sensor data acquisition. The Emergency Map Tool acquires sensor data using the C2-SENSE system and displays them on the map. In this case all existing sensor networks are connected directly to C2-SENSE (Fig. 6).

MS01 – Sensor values display			
Interaction Step	Initiator	Target	Test Modality
1	Sensor network (ETG sensors)	CFD (EMT)	Activate the function (or the layer) on the emergency Map Tool.

Fig. 6. Official sensor value display: pilot steps

AdHoc Sensor Adding
Decentralized Functional Centre (CFD) decides to put additional sensor(s) in the field. They use the ActOnline[1] (AOL) application to ask a volunteer organization to install (an) ad-hoc sensor(s) and activate them. ActOnline adapter catches this request and forwards it to the Enterprise Service Bus (ESB), further on another service catches it on

---

[1] ActOnline is a tool used for events and communications management during an emergency event. It is used by Civil Protection and municipalities.

ESB and forwards it to volunteers using TRBOnet[2] application. Sensors are connected to the IP based gateway. They communicate with C2-SENSE using mobile phone network. Once activated, the sensor(s) immediately start sending data, and the data becomes visible in Emergency Map Tool (Fig. 7).

MS02 – AdHoc sensor adding			
Interaction Step	Initiator	Target	Test Modality
1	CFD (AOL)	Volunteers (TRBOnet devices)	Insert a new request about ad-hoc sensor to Volunteers of Foggia.
2	Ad-hoc sensor (new sensor)	CFD (EMT)	New values are displayed on Map Tool.

Fig. 7. AdHoc sensor adding: pilot steps

COC Opening

Operating Room of Civil Protection (SOIR) asks to the involved municipality to apply their Emergency Plan. This request will be performed using ActOnLine. The Message Communication Platform (MCP) will distribute the messages to the alert responsible persons in the municipality. At the same time the message will arrive via ActOnLine in the Municipality Emergency Control Room (COC) system. COC reads the message from ActOnLine and send a 'read notification' to SOIR using the C2-SENSE environment in order to acknowledge that the message was read by the COC (Fig. 8).

MS03 – COC opening			
Interaction Step	Initiator	Target	Test Modality
1	SOIR (AOL)	Alerting system (MCP), COC (AOL)	SOIR operator sends a specific message to 'municipality of province of Foggia' in order to apply their emergency plan.
2	COC (AOL)	SOIR (AOL)	COC operator reads the message and marks it as read.

Fig. 8. COC opening: pilot steps

Volunteers' Involvement

The volunteers of Foggia start the operation and activate their radio terminal. Then the radio terminal starts to send its GPS position using a specific TRBOnet function. The position is displayed on the Emergency Map Tool used in the Regional Civil Protection Operating Room (SOIR) (Fig. 9).

The Municipality Emergency Control Room (COC) requests the volunteer organization in order to start the foreseen operation as defined in the plan. The COC gives feedback to the Regional Civil Protection Operating Room (SOIR). SOIR reads the message and the notification of having read the message is sent to the COC.

The Regional Civil Protection Operating Room (SOIR) sends a message to a voluntary group and the Municipality Emergency Control Room (COC) in order to 'follow the situation on field' taking care about certain specific river points. The message is something like 'Attention, it is very important to follow the river 'abc' near the point 'xyz'. COC reads the message using ActOnLine which sends a 'read notification' to

---

[2] TRBOnet is a tool installed on radio device used by volunteers in the Province of Foggia.

MS04 – Volunteers Involvement			
Interaction Step	Initiator	Target	Test Modality
1	Volunteers (TRBOnet)	SOIR (EMT)	Volunteers' position is geo-localized on Map Tool.
2	COC (AOL)	SOIR (AOL)	COC sends an update message to SOIR about involved volunteers.
3	SOIR (AOL)	COC (AOL)	SOIR operator reads the message and marks it as read.
4	SOIR (AOL)	COC (AOL), Volunteers (TRBOnet devices)	SOIR sends a message to COC and volunteers to follow situation on field.
5	COC (AOL)	SOIR (AOL)	COC operator reads the message and mark it as read.

Fig. 9. Volunteers' involvement: pilot steps

SOIR using the C2-SENSE environment. And also the volunteers' group receives the message directly on their radio device.

Risk Detection

Volunteers of Foggia report a dangerous flooding situation to the Municipality Emergency Operating Room (COC) using TRBOnet radio devices. The COC informs the SOIR (Regional Civil Protection Operating Room about the evolving situation (ActOn-Line of COC sends a reply message to SOIR). SOIR reads the message and using its ActOnLine (AOL) that sends a 'read notification' to the COC (Fig. 10).

MS05 – Risk detection			
Interaction Step	Initiator	Target	Test Modality
1	Volunteers (TRBOnet devices)	COC (AOL)	Volunteers send a message to COC
2	COC (AOL)	SOIR (AOL)	COC operator sends message to SOIR to communicate the risk.
3	SOIR (AOL)	COC (AOL)	SOIR operator reads the message and mark it as read.

Fig. 10. Risk detection: pilot steps

Internal Civil Protection Communication

See Fig. 11.

MS06 – Internal civil protection communication			
Interaction Step	Initiator	Target	Test Modality
1	SOIR (AOL)	CFD (AOL)	SOIR sends information about flood situation
2	CFD (AOL)	SOIR (AOL)	CFD operator reads the message and mark it as read.

Fig. 11. Internal civil protection communication: pilot steps

Closure of Main Roads

Province of Foggia closes some main roads. They use the Message Communication Platform (MCP) to perform this step. A new updated ' road map' will be displayed in the Emergency Map Tool (EMT) at the Regional Civil Protection Operating Room (SOIR) (Fig. 12).

MS07 – Closure of main roads			
Interaction Step	Initiator	Target	Test Modality
1	SOIR (EMT)	COC (AOL)	Closed provincial road is displayed on Map Tool

Fig. 12. Closure of main roads: pilot steps

Alert Messages

Under the responsibility of the Regional President of Regione Puglia the SOIR (Regional Civil Protection Operating Room) needs to alert the population via different channels using the Message Communication Platform (MCP): SMS, email, Twitter, Facebook (municipality page). SOIR prepares a message on ActOnLine (AOL) and the C2-SENSE system pushes the messages through the different channels, using a combination of the MCP, twitter and Facebook. The Social Network Adapters produce a reply message to inform the SOIR that the message was correctly delivered to Facebook and/or twitter (Fig. 13).

MS8 – Alert message			
Interaction Step	Initiator	Target	Test Modality
1	SOIR (AOL)	Message Communication Platform	SOIR sends an alert message to all alerting system users.
2	SOIR (AOL)	Citizens (SocialNetworks)	SOIR posts a message on its own social network page.
3	Citizens (SocialNetwork)	SOIR (AOL)	Social network sends a reply message to confirm operation.

Fig. 13. Closure of main roads: pilot steps

Unique Emergency Number Involvement

The Municipality Emergency Control Room (COC) requests healthcare services and equipment to provide first aid to the citizen. They ask this request to CSS (prefecture) and SOIR (Regional Civil Protection Operating Room) using its ActOnLine (AOL). C2-SENSE delivers the request to CSS by email (read notify is required) and to SOIR with ActOnLine. SOIR takes the request into account and sends 'mobile column' to the municipality. When COC receives the equipment it communicates the delivery of the 'mobile column' using ActOnLine (the message will be delivered to the SOIR and the Prefecture hat use ActOnLine and email) (Fig. 14).

MS09 – Unique emergency number involvement			
Interaction Step	Initiator	Target	Test Modality
1	COC (AOL)	SOIR (AOL), Prefecture (Email)	COC sends a request for means to SOIR and Prefecture
2	SOIR (AOL), Prefecture (Email)	COC (AOL)	SOIR and Prefecture mark the message as read.
3	SOIR (AOL)	COC (AOL), Prefecture (Email)	SOIR takes the request into account and informs COC and prefecture
4	COC (AOL), Prefecture (Email)	SOIR (AOL)	COC and Prefecture mark the message as read.
5	SOIR (EMT)	Rescue Vehicle (RuparWireless)	SOIR asks to Rescue Vehicle to go to a specific place.
6	Rescue Vehicle (RuparWireless)	SOIR (EMT)	Vehicle transmits its position to EMT
7	COC (AOL)	SOIR (AOL), Prefecture (Email)	COC sends an update message to SOIR and Prefecture
8	SOIR (AOL), Prefecture (Email)	COC (AOL)	SOIR and Prefecture mark the message as read.

Fig. 14. Unique emergency number involvement: pilot steps

Fire Brigade Involvement

Municipality discovers a fire accident at a big fuel station. So they send a request to the Fire Department and they accomplish the request. During their intervention SOIR (Regional Civil Protection Operating Room) is updated continuously (C2-SENSE is involved to allow message exchange from/to fire department using CAP (Common Alerting Protocol) protocol and to update SOIR on via the ActOnLine system). SOIR operator reads the message and ActOnLine with C2-SENSE is used to provide a notification to COC (Municipality Emergency Operating Room) (Fig. 15).

MS10 – Fire Army involvement			
Interaction Step	Initiator	Target	Test Modality
1	COC (AOL)	Fire Department (CAP System), SOIR (AOL)	COC requires service to Fire Department
2	Fire Department (CAP System), SOIR (AOL)	COC (AOL)	Fire Department and SOIR mark the message as read.
3	Fire Department (CAP System)	COC (AOL), SOIR (AOL, EMT)	Fire Department sends update about situation to COC and SOIR and intervention is geo-localized

Fig. 15. Fire brigade involvement: pilot steps

6   Pilot Test

6.1   Test Phases and Procedures

At the end of the deployment phase of the Pilot Application, the C2-SENSE system will be tested in order to demonstrate the effectiveness and feasibility of the project. In this test phase the main components of C2-SENSE and interfacing with the local end-users systems will be tested. The test procedure is divided into three phases: Phase 0, Phase 1 and Phase 2.

In *phase 0* the C2-SENSE system is configured and made ready to be used in an emergency situation. In this phase, the Emergency Interoperability Profiles will be created. As stated above the Emergency Interoperability Profiles will address all the layers of interoperability stack, i.e. physical layer, protocol layer, data/object model layer, information layer, knowledge layer. In this phase all profiles created for the different layer are generic, meaning that they are not specific to any country, organization or incident.

Phase 1 is located between before and during emergency situations. It can be regarded as a transition phase. In this phase, the generic Emergency Interoperability Profiles will be specialized for the Apulia region according to organizational structure and emergency procedures of this region. By using the Profile Specialization Tool, it will be possible to specialize and combine the profiles accordingly. To be more specific, they will be able to illustrate the Pilot Scenario through the GUI of Profile Specialization Tool and assign organizations, emergency teams, and emergency systems as actors of the scenario. By doing so, they will enable the execution and monitoring of the Pilot Scenario by the C2-SENSE system.

In *phase 2* the C2-SENSE system is used in a real life emergency situation, e.g. flood in Apulia region. The profiles specialized for Apulia region will be executed through Profile Execution Engine. Execution of the specialized profiles means that organizations taking part in the emergency plan of Apulia region will exchange information among themselves according to the specifications in the profiles. C2-SENSE system will control, monitor and track these operations and display the progress through Profile Monitoring Tool.

7 Summary

This paper described applicative aspects related to the project C2-SENSE, with the aim of providing valuable and assessable instruments with regards to effective emergency management and interoperability among the information systems of the involved stakeholders.

In order to ensure that the developed profiles are appropriate in real life, they are being assessed in a realistic flood scenario in Apulia region of Italy.

The Pilot Scenario represents an attempt to apply the C2-SENSE system to a real situation in which the involved stakeholders will use IT technology to enable them to interact and communicate in way they could not do before.

Furthermore the designed Pilot Scenario, demonstrates interoperability between the regional civil protection system and government agencies (Prefecture, Province, Municipalities), the other organizations like the fire brigade, the police, the medical rescue, and last but not least the citizens. Therefore the functional tests and results of different micro-scenarios presented in this paper shows that it is possible to adapt specific information technologies to a real emergency scenario, improving the interaction between the different organization and optimizing the response time during emergencies.

Acknowledgements. The research leading to these results has received funding from the European Community's Seventh Framework Programme (FP7/2007-2013) under grant agreement nr. 607729.

References

1. Gençtürk, M., Arisi, R., Toscano, L., Kabak, Y., Di Ciano, M., Palmitessa, A.: Profiling approach for the interoperability of command & control systems with sensing systems in emergency management. In: Proceedings of the 6th Workshop on Enterprise Interoperability, Nîmes, France (2015)
2. Duro, R., Schimak, G., Bojan Božić, B.. C2-SENSE: the emergency interoperability framework and knowledge management. In: Geospatial World Forum INSPIRE Conference (INSPIRE 2015), Lisbon, Portugal (2015). http://c2-sense.eu/wp-content/uploads/2014/07/Refiz-Duro.pdf
3. Di Ciano, M., Palmitessa, A., Cavone, M., Caputo, I., Bufi, A., Redaelli, M.: Profiling approach for the interoperability of command & control systems with sensing systems in emergency management: an applicable scenario. In: Interoperability for Enterprise System and Applications, Guimaraes, Portugal (2016)
4. Schimak, G., Kutschera, P., Duro, R., Kutschera, K.: EMERGENCY MAPS TOOL – facilitating collaboration and decision making during emergency & crises situations. In: Sauvage, S., Sánchez-Pérez, J.-M., Rizzoli, A. (eds.) Proceedings of the International Environmental Modelling and Software Society (iEMSs), 8th International Congress on Environmental Modelling and Software, Toulouse, France (2016). http://scholarsarchive.byu.edu/cgi/viewcontent.cgi?article=1511&context=iemssconference

Achieving Semantic Interoperability in Emergency Management Domain

Mert Gençtürk[1,2(✉)], Enver Evci[1,2], Arda Guney[1,2], Yildiray Kabak[1], and Gokce B. Laleci Erturkmen[1]

[1] SRDC Software Research and Development
and Consultancy Corp., Ankara, Turkey
mert@srdc.com.tr
[2] Department of Computer Engineering, Middle East Technical
University, Ankara, Turkey

Abstract. This paper describes how semantic interoperability can be achieved in emergency management domain where different organizations in different domains should communicate through a number of distinct standards to manage crises and disasters effectively. To achieve this goal, a common ontology is defined as lingua franca and standard content models are mapped one by one to the ontology. Then, information represented in one standard is converted to another according to the mappings and exchanged between parties.

Keywords: Semantic interoperability · Semantic web · Ontology
Emergency management

1 Introduction

Common standard interfaces allow data communication among disparate systems. By complying with a standard interface, each system can exchange data with every other compliant system. Otherwise the interoperability of the systems can be quite challenging, technologically complex, time consuming and expensive. Emergency management is a multi-discipline domain where effective management of crises and disasters requires communication of different organizations in different domains such as government, health, media, and military. Although each of these domains has its own well-established standards, not all emergency responding parties conform to the same set of standards, which creates a crucial interoperability challenge. Furthermore, standards have many optional fields and different versions. Even if only one standard is used by two different systems, interoperability of them can still be problematic due to misinterpretation of optional fields or usage of different versions [1].

Semantic Interoperability has been an active research and development area in various domains such as eHealth and eBusiness. There are several completed and ongoing work in these domains for the semantic interoperability of electronic documents. OASIS Semantic Support for Electronic Business Document Interoperability (SET) TC [2] is one of them and its basic idea is to explicate the semantics of different

© IFIP International Federation for Information Processing 2017
Published by Springer International Publishing AG 2017. All Rights Reserved
J. Hřebíček et al. (Eds.): ISESS 2017, IFIP AICT 507, pp. 279–289, 2017.
https://doi.org/10.1007/978-3-319-89935-0_23

but overlapping electronic business document standards as ontologies and then provide semantic mediation among these ontologies. OASIS SET TC approach has been proven to be useful and effective in several studies such as iSURF project, where a Semantic Interoperability Service Utility were developed by following this approach for the exchange of supply chain planning information documents [3].

In order to solve the interoperability problem, in European Commission supported C2-SENSE project [4] which aims to develop a profile based Emergency Interoperability Framework by the use of existing standards and semantically enriched Web services, we take this engineering approach and apply it to the emergency management domain to implement semantic mediation mechanisms to be able to harmonize information conforming to different but overlapping emergency standards. In this regard, in this paper, we present a Semantic Interoperability Suite which enables the information exchange between emergency management domain applications through a central layer instead of one-to-one transformations between several different content models, by developing a common ontology. Common Data Elements (CDEs) that have been elicited within this study underpin the common ontology which can be considered as the semantic dictionary of the interoperating applications.

2 Technology Description

2.1 Standards

The Emergency Data Exchange Language (EDXL), developed by OASIS International Open Standards Consortium, is a suite of XML-based messaging standards that facilitate emergency information sharing between government entities and the full range of emergency-related organizations [5]. EDXL standardizes messaging formats for communications between these parties. EDXL includes several individual standards, that are Common Alerting Protocol (EDXL-CAP), Distribution Element (EDXL-DE), Hospital AVailability Exchange (EDXL-HAVE), Resource Messaging (EDXL-RM), Reference Information Model (EDXL-RIM), Situation Reporting (EDXL-SitRep), Tracking Emergency Patients (EDXL-SitRep).

The Common Alerting Protocol [6] is an XML-based data format for exchanging public warnings and emergencies between alerting technologies. CAP allows a warning message to be disseminated simultaneously over many warning systems to many applications.

Distribution Element [7] is used as a container that facilitate the routing of any properly formatted XML emergency message to recipients.

EDXL-HAVE [8] is a document format for exchanging information on status of a hospital, its services, and its resources such as bed capacity, service availability etc.

Resource Messaging [9] defines specific message types supporting the major communication requirements for allocation of resources across the emergency incident life-cycle.

EDXL-SitRep [10] is an XML-based data format for transmitting timely available situation reports, incident or event information, and operational picture.

In much the same way that HTML and HTTP standards enable the exchange of any type of information on the Web, The Open Geospatial Consortium's (OGC) Sensor Web Enablement Initiative (SWE) [11] is focused on developing standards to enable the discovery of sensors and corresponding observations, exchange, and processing of sensor observations, as well as the tasking of sensors and sensor systems.

2.2   ISO/IEC 11179, Semantic Metadata Registry and IHE Data Element Exchange

ISO/IEC 11179 is an international standard developed with the aim of providing a metadata-driven data exchange in heterogeneous environments. Combining principles of semantic theory and data modelling, the standard defines the representation of metadata in a metadata registry [12].

In our study, we employ an ISO/IEC 11179 compliant Semantic Metadata Registry (MDR) to maintain metadata of data elements (e.g. location, alert, observation) and communicate with it via the IHE Data Element Exchange (DEX) profile, which we authored [13]. DEX provides a standardized way of querying data element metadata, and allows dynamic mappings between data elements such as EDXL data elements to their OGC equivalents when complemented with extraction specifications (e.g. XPATH, SQL scripts) maintained in Semantic MDR.

3   Methodology and Implementation

During the implementation of Semantic Interoperability Suite, first information domain has been carefully analysed and following standards corresponding to emergency management have been identified as relevant [14].

- EDXL-SitRep (Situation Reporting)
- EDXL-RM (Resource Messaging)
- EDXL-HAVE (Hospital Availability Exchange)
- EDXL-TEP (Tracking of Patients)
- EDXL-CAP (Common Alerting Protocol)
- OGC SensorML (Sensor Modeling Language)
- OGC O&M (Observations and Measurements).

The common ontology has been created based on the knowledge that was gained as a result of this analysis. In this regard, first a number of Common Data Elements (CDEs) which can be considered as ontology resources have been defined and stored in Semantic MDR. CDEs are the smallest meaningful data container in a context. They can be regarded as the semantic dictionary of the interoperating application.

Figure 1 illustrates an example decomposition of a CDE which refers to birth date information of a person. As shown in the figure, the concept of the CDE and the representation are separate in the metamodel. In the given example, "Person" is the Object Class and "Date of Birth" is the property together which constitute the concept of "Person.DateOfBirth". This is the concept of the data element regardless of its representation. The other main concepts for which CDEs are defined can be listed as address, location, resource, report, alert, and observation (sensor measurement). After CDEs are defined, a common ontology in OWL (Web Ontology Language) format is generated by following the OASIS SET TC approach.

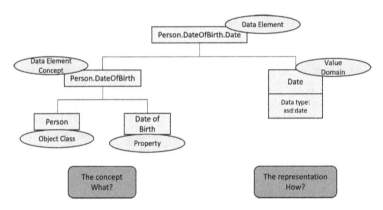

Fig. 1. An example of decomposition of a Common Data Element: Person.DateOfBirth.Date

In the next step, standard content models listed above have been mapped to the common ontology via extraction specifications so that data represented in one standard format can be converted to another. Extraction specifications are for locating relevant data element in the corresponding standard content model. As all current standards are XML based, extraction specifications are defined as XPATH queries in our system. Table 1 below presents three different extraction specifications of EDXL-SitRep, EDXL-CAP and OGC-O&M standards for "LocationByCoordinates.Latitude" data element.

Table 1. Data element and extraction specifications

Data element	
Property	LocationByCoordinates.Latitude
Data type	characterstring
Definition	Measure of the latitude of the coordinate in degrees
Extraction specification	
EDXL-SitRep	/element(*,ResourceDetailType)/reportToLocation/ct: EDXLGeoPoliticalLocation/ct:geoCode/ct:value
EDXL-CAP	/cap:alert/cap:info/cap:area/cap:circle
OGC-O&M	/om:featureOfInterest/gml:AbstractFeature/gml:boundedBy/gml: Envelope/gml:coordinates

C2-SENSE Semantic Interoperability Suite enables domain experts to define extraction specifications only once, then the conversion between content models is done automatically according to these specifications. It is possible to define extraction specifications for any number of standard content models. There is no need to make an update on the system, when specifications for a new content model is going to be added.

Overall architecture of C2-SENSE Semantic Interoperability Suite is illustrated in Fig. 2. In Semantic Interoperability Suite, a Semantic MDR Tool is provided to users

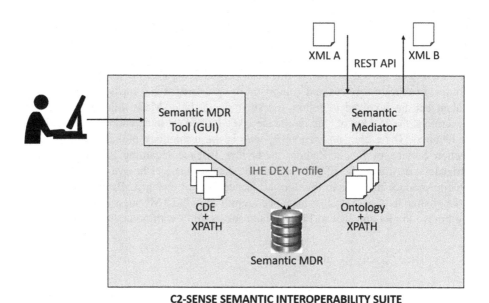

Fig. 2. Architecture of C2-SENSE Semantic Interoperability Suite

as a graphical user interface (GUI) to facilitate the definition of CDEs and extraction specifications. Semantic MDR Tool can be considered a web-based metadata management and data modelling tool to create and maintain CDEs collaboratively either based on imported standard content models or from scratch [15]. Given a standard format, it is able to list the data elements included in it; given the data element list, it can also provide mappings of elements to a specified target standard format.

Semantic Mediator is the component in Semantic Interoperability Suite fulfilling the duty of converting data represented in one standard to a data represented in another standard. This functionality is satisfied thanks to Semantic MDR and IHE DEX profile. When the system receives a request of conversion, it fetches common ontology (in other words CDEs) and corresponding extractions specifications from Semantic MDR using DEX profile. If the source and target content models are available in the registry, e.g. EDXL-SitRep as the source and OGC-O&M as the target, conversion is done automatically by Semantic Mediator according to pre-defined extraction specifications. Semantic Mediator is provided to outside world through a RESTful API.

4 Example Usage

In C2-SENSE project, an Emergency Domain Interoperability Framework, which Semantic Interoperability Suite is part of, has been developed. This framework has been validated by a realistic flood scenario in Puglia region of Italy. In this section, we present an example usage of Semantic Interoperability Suite in this scenario.

It has been raining in Puglia region for several days and the sensors located near Fortore river measures the water level exceeding the threshold value. Therefore, Regional Functional Center of Puglia is alerted and emergency plan for flood situation is started to be applied. As part of this plan, people living near flood area is evacuated, houses, healthcare services and equipment are provided, some roads are blocked and volunteers are involved to follow the situation on field. Meanwhile, a car accident occurred at the 15th km of "Strada Statale 100". Immediate intervention of Fire Brigade is required. Therefore, Innova Puglia, who is the technology provider of Civil Protection Service of Puglia Region, alerts Fire Brigade regarding the accident. Fire Brigade system uses the EDXL-CAP as the data format and Innova Puglia system is able to produce message in this format. Hence, the following XML message (for the sake of simplicity, namespaces have been removed in the XML messages) is generated by Innova Puglia and sent to Fire Brigade successfully with no additional effort.

```xml
<?xml version="1.0" encoding="UTF-8" standalone="yes"?>
<alert xmlns="urn:oasis:names:tc:emergency:cap:1.2">
    <identifier>20161206.2.71.1</identifier>
    <sender>mailaddress@mailaddress.com</sender>
    <sent>2016-12-06T10:45:40+01:00</sent>
    <status>Actual</status>
    <msgType>Alert</msgType>
    <scope>Private</scope>
    <code>CAP-IT-VF:0.1</code>
    <info>
        <language>it-IT</language>
        <category>Transport</category>
        <event>Car accident with rollover</event>
        <urgency>Immediate</urgency>
        <severity>Unknown</severity>
        <certainty>Unknown</certainty>
        <effective>2016-12-06T10:45:40+01:00</effective>
        <senderName>INNOVAPUGLIA</senderName>
        <headline>Road vehicle fuel transport acci-
dent</headline>
        <description>Traffic accident caused by the com-
bination of vehicles overturning tractor with registra-
tion numbers AA00AA and BB11BB. Dangerous goods: UN num-
ber 33, Kemler code 1203.</description>
        <instruction>Prompted intervention by the local
fire brigade command</instruction>
        <area>
            <areaDesc>Strada Statale 100, km
15</areaDesc>
            <circle>41.003822,16.913184 0.01</circle>
        </area>
    </info>
</alert>
```

After Fire Brigade receives the alert message, it needs to inform corresponding local authorities about the situation, and this message should be sent in EDXL-SitRep format. However, Fire Brigade system is only able to produce and retrieve messages in EDXL-CAP format. A solution to this problem could be updating the Fire Brigade system so that it can support exchanging documents in EDXL-SitRep format as well. However, this requires a lot of work and is impossible to do during the emergency situation. Instead of this, Fire Brigade uses the Semantic Interoperability Suite of C2-SENSE system to convert the EDXL-CAP message presented above to EDXL-SitRep message automatically. The result of this operation is the following XML.

```xml
<?xml version="1.0" encoding="UTF-8"?>
<sitRep
xmlns="urn:oasis:names:tc:emergency:EDXL:SitRep:1.0">
  <messageID>20161206.2.71.1</messageID>
  <preparedBy>
    <personDetails>
      <personName>
        <nameEl-
ement>mailaddress@mailaddress.com</nameElement>
      </personName>
      <addresses>
        <address>
          <locality>
            <nameElement>it-IT</nameElement>
          </locality>
        </address>
      </addresses>
    </personDetails>
    <timeValue>2016-12-06T10:45:40+01:00</timeValue>
  </preparedBy>

  <authorizedBy>
    <personDetails>
      <personName>
        <nameElement>INNOVAPUGLIA</nameElement>
      </personName>
    </personDetails>
    <timeValue>2016-12-06T10:45:40+01:00</timeValue>
  </authorizedBy>
  <reportPurpose>Alert</reportPurpose>
  <reportNumber>1</reportNumber>
  <reportVersion>Final</reportVersion>
  <forTimePeriod>
    <fromDateTime>2016-12-
06T10:45:40+01:00</fromDateTime>
    <toDateTime>2016-12-06T10:45:40+01:00</toDateTime>
  </forTimePeriod>
  <reportTitle>Road vehicle fuel transport acci-
dent</reportTitle>
  <incidentID>T20161206.2.71.1</incidentID>
  <originatingMessageID>CAP-IT-
VF:0.1</originatingMessageID>
  <urgency>Immediate</urgency>
  <reportConfidence>NoConfidence</reportConfidence>
  <severity>Unknown</severity>
  <actionPlan>Transport</actionPlan>
```

```xml
<report xsi:type="SituationInformationType">
  <primaryIncidentInformation>
    <incidentName>Strada Statale 100, km
15</incidentName>
    <geographicSize>
      <size>1</size>
    </geographicSize>
    <incidentLocation>
      <EDXLGeoPoliticalLocation>
        <geoCode>
          <valueListURI>circle</valueListURI>
          <value>41.003822,16.913184 0.01</value>
        </geoCode>
      </EDXLGeoPoliticalLocation>
    </incidentLocation>
  </primaryIncidentInformation>
  <extension>
    <parameter>
      <nameURI>description</nameURI>
      <value>Traffic accident caused by the combination
of vehicles overturning tractor with registration numbers
AA00AA and BB11BB. Dangerous goods: UN number 33, Kemler
code 1203.</value>
    </parameter>
  </extension>
  <extension>
    <parameter>
      <nameURI>instruction</nameURI>
      <value>Prompted intervention by the local fire
brigade command</value>
    </parameter>
  </extension>
  <extension>
    <parameter>
      <nameURI>event</nameURI>
      <value>Car accident with rollover</value>
    </parameter>
  </extension>
  <extension>
    <parameter>
      <nameURI>status</nameURI>
      <value>Actual</value>
    </parameter>
  </extension>
  <extension>
    <parameter>
```

```
      <nameURI>scope</nameURI>
      <value>Private</value>
    </parameter>
  </extension>
  <extension>
    <parameter>
      <nameURI>certainty</nameURI>
      <value>Unknown</value>
    </parameter>
  </extension>
 </report>
</sitRep>
```

In technical point of view, for instance, in CAP message, latitude and longitude information is provided in *"/cap:alert/cap:info/cap:area/cap:circle"* element (see Table 1). In order to present this information in SitRep message, Semantic Mediator of Semantic Interoperability Suite performs following actions:

1. Retrieve CDEs and extraction specifications from Semantic MDR.
2. Find the corresponding Common Data Element for the XPATH *"/cap:alert/cap: info/cap:area/cap:circle"*, that is *LocationByCoordinates.Latitude.characterstring*.
3. Find the corresponding XPATH definition of SitRep for this Common Data Element, that is *"/element(*,ResourceDetailType)/reportToLocation/ct:EDXLGeoPoliticalLocation/ct:geoCode/ct:value"*.
4. Place the information.

5   Conclusion

In order to manage crises effectively, interoperability of different systems using dispersed standards is crucial. One way to provide interoperability among these systems is to update the existing software so that one system can generate messages in all the desired formats. It is obvious that this requires a lot of work and should be done for every single system. In this regard, C2-SENSE Semantic Interoperability Suite is a powerful mechanism since it enables organizations to make such conversions between emergency domain standards automatically without making any updates on their own systems.

Currently, C2-SENSE Semantic Interoperability Suite is able to make conversion among EDXL-SitRep, EDXL-RM, EDXL-HAVE, EDXL-CAP, OGC SensorML and O&M standards. Feasibility and usability of the system is currently being tested in a realistic flood scenario in Puglia Region of Italy within the scope of C2-SENSE Project.

Acknowledgements. The work presented in this paper is achieved in the scope of C2-SENSE project [4] supported by the European Community's Seventh Framework Programme (FP7/2007-2013) under grant agreement number 607729.

References

1. Chen, D., Daclin, N.: Framework for enterprise interoperability. In: Proceedings of IFAC Workshop EI2 N, pp. 77–88, March 2006
2. OASIS Semantic Support for Electronic Business Document Interoperability (SET) Technical Committee (n.d.). https://www.oasis-open.org/committees/set/charter.php. Accessed 16 Jan 2017
3. Kabak, Y., Dogac, A., Ocalan, C., Cimen, S., Laleci, G.B.: iSURF semantic interoperability service utility for collaborative planning, forecasting and replenishment. In: The Proceedings of the eChallanges 2009 Conference, October 2009
4. C2-SENSE Project - Interoperability Profiles for Command/Control Systems and Sensor Systems in Emergency Management. http://c2-sense.eu/. Accessed 16 Jan 2017
5. Emergency Data Exchange Language (EDXL). https://en.wikipedia.org/wiki/EDXL. Accessed 16 Jan 2017
6. EDXL Common Alerting Protocol (EDXL-CAP) Specification. http://docs.oasis-open.org/emergency/cap/v1.2/CAP-v1.2-os.html. Accessed 16 Jan 2017
7. EDXL Distribution Element (EDXL-DE) Specification. http://docs.oasis-open.org/emergency/edxl-de/v1.0/EDXL-DE_Spec_v1.0.pdf. Accessed 16 Jan 2017
8. EDXL Hospital AVailability Exchange (EDXL-HAVE) Specification. http://docs.oasis-open.org/emergency/edxl-have/os/emergency_edxl_have-1.0-spec-os.pdf. Accessed 16 Jan 2017
9. EDXL Resource Messaging (EDXL-RM) Specification. http://docs.oasis-open.org/emergency/edxl-rm/v1.0/os/EDXL-RM-v1.0-OS.pdf. Accessed 16 Jan 2017
10. EDXL Situation Reporting (EDXL-SitRep) Specification. https://docs.oasis-open.org/emergency/edxl-sitrep/v1.0/cs01/edxl-sitrep-v1.0-cs01.html. Accessed 16 Jan 2017
11. OGC Sensor Web Enablement (SWE). http://www.opengeospatial.org/ogc/markets-technologies/swe. Accessed 16 Jan 2017
12. ISO/IEC 11179-3, Information technology – Metadata registries (MDR) – Registry metamodel and basic attributes. http://metadata-standards.org. Accessed 16 Jan 2017
13. IHE Quality, Research and Public Health Technical Framework Supplement Data Element Exchange (DEX). http://ihe.net. Accessed 16 Jan 2017
14. Božić, B., Gençtürk, M., Duro, R., Kabak, Y., Schimak, G.: Requirements engineering for semantic sensors in crisis and disaster management. In: Denzer, R., Argent, R.M., Schimak, G., Hřebíček, J. (eds.) ISESS 2015. IFIP Advances in Information and Communication Technology, vol. 448, pp. 397–406. Springer, Cham (2015). https://doi.org/10.1007/978-3-319-15994-2_40
15. Semantic MDR Tool. http://www.srdc.com.tr/semantic-mdr/. Accessed 16 Jan 2017

Framework for Enabling Technical and Organizational Interoperability in the Management of Environmental Crises and Disasters

Refiz Duro[1]([⊠]), Mert Gençtürk[2], Gerald Schimak[1], Peter Kutschera[1], Denis Havlik[1], and Katharina Kutschera[1]

[1] Austrian Institute of Technology GmbH, Vienna, Austria
refiz.duro@ait.ac.at
[2] Software Research and Development and Consultancy Corp., Ankara, Turkey

Abstract. Interoperability is a core component in management of crises and disasters. Crises require interoperability on several different levels: physical (communication, devices and tools), operational (crisis response procedures and protocols) and document level (information exchange). Here we present the Framework that facilitates interoperability on a level that relieves a crisis manager from most burdens related to crisis response (e.g., being available to access sensor data or communicate with other responders). The software components in the Framework are described, as well as the profiling approach that is necessitated for functioning interoperability at such a demanding level. The Framework can be implemented for dealing with environmental challenges through real-time monitoring and response. The frequency of disasters is expected to increase in the forthcoming future mostly due to environmental changes, thus emphasizing the need for interoperability approaches as the one presented in this paper.

Keywords: Interoperability · Crisis mapping · Crisis management

1 Introduction

The lack of interoperability among systems, sensor networks and in communication is one of the major obstacles for effective crisis and disaster management (CDM), especially in heterogeneous and multi-user environments. Accessing data provided by the first responders in the field, having a joint operational picture of a crisis by accessing sensor data and maps, and having a possibility of real-time effective communication with other crisis managers (organizations) are all examples of needs and activities a crisis responder experiences. However, the presence of significant diversity in the CDM domain in general creates barriers halting the efficient cooperation. Typical issues include usage of different hardware and software solutions, conforming to different (or incompatible) data and communication standards, not fully adjusting to the legal and administrative policies and procedures of involved organizations and responders, or considering the defined (data) security requirements. An example is a

© IFIP International Federation for Information Processing 2017
Published by Springer International Publishing AG 2017. All Rights Reserved
J. Hřebíček et al. (Eds.): ISESS 2017, IFIP AICT 507, pp. 290–301, 2017.
https://doi.org/10.1007/978-3-319-89935-0_24

response to the Haiti earthquake in 2010, where lack of interoperability of equipment and procedures among the European field hospitals caused less efficient cooperation and response [1]. Similar story goes for Hurricane Katrina in 2005, in which a higher level of data interoperability would have enhanced evacuation cooperation between the governmental and voluntary organizations in matching parents with missing children [2]. Moreover, the frequency of disasters is expected to increase in the forthcoming future mostly due to environmental changes [3]. Floods are just one type of a crisis that in its nature often is transboundary, spanning several neighbouring countries or regions. For example, the Danube River is known for flooding Central and Eastern Europe regions for centuries, and several times in the recent two decades only [4], bringing devastation and loss of lives, together with an economic burden on the affected population and governments. Such situation calls for an enhanced level of cooperation, where linguistic, law and information exchange barriers are no longer an obstacle [5].

These are just some examples among a myriad implying a necessity for a solution involving *"the capability to communicate, execute programs, or transfer data among various functional units in a manner that requires the user to have little or no knowledge of the unique characteristics of those units"* (OGC's definition for interoperability[1]). In other words, in a fully interoperable response, every organization would have the possibility to use any software, data and communication formats and language that best suits their procedures and methods of operation while maintaining their independence, and at the same being able to take part in a joint crisis response.

The currently ongoing C2-SENSE[2] project [6] is meeting this demand by developing a framework where all relevant entities (organizations, rescue services, etc.) that need to cooperate during crises are collaborating. Collaboration means facilitating communication, information, and data exchange among actors, regardless if their systems are proprietary, or open. This reduces reaction time, increases the effectiveness of the management, and thereby saves lives and resources. The C2-SENSE Framework encompasses two parts:

(1) components related to the physical nature of the Framework meaning software and hardware, and
(2) the profiling approach, i.e., incorporation of rules orchestrating the functionalities of those components and rules for achieving interoperability.

The methodology and the approach in the second part are flexible enough to allow for implementation not only in crisis and disaster domain, but also in other domains where such functionality is required.

We present the Framework and its Collaboration Environment in Sect. 2, where the main software components necessary for interoperability processes are described in detail. In Sect. 3, the profiling approach is described, while an example of implementation is given in Sect. 4. The discussion and conclusion on the still ongoing work is provided in the Sect. 5.

---

2   The Framework and Collaboration Environment

Collaboration occurs whenever humans and/or computer applications work together to accomplish a common goal. In the domain of crisis and emergency management, it is critical that a sufficient level of collaborative effort and alignment between the crisis responders is achieved. In order to process and align the activities and procedures performed by the responders, applications and different Command and Control and Sensor Systems, the C2-SENSE Framework provides *Collaboration Environment*. It allows for critical functionalities and activities such as real-time data and information exchange, communication between entities involved in response activities, and alignment of operations and procedures during crises.

Collaboration Environment incorporates a set of software components. One group of these components are intended for decision making activities, covering functionalities such as GUI for crisis mapping, or data and sensor management. The second group of components are developed with the sole purpose of managing profiles, thus allowing for functionalities to achieve the interoperability at the level of seamless information and data exchange and procedure alignment, a process more described in Sect. 3.

2.1   Components and Applications for Decision Making

The following software components and tools are part of the Collaboration Environment important for the decision making in critical situations, as well as in the preparation phases.

Emergency Maps Tool (EMT): The main purpose of the Emergency Maps Tool is to provide the end user or the network of users (e.g., crisis managers, responders in the field) with a collaboration tool for representation and sharing available geo-referenced data and information. This tool mashes up the emergency geospatial data from the C2-SENSE data repository, map layers and data from external Map Services. The tool displays the emergency area geographically to the related authorized users.

The EMT is, however, not only about data on maps, but it also includes widgets that are useful and required in emergencies. These are widgets for displaying timeseries sensor data (e.g., water level development for the last 24 h), monitoring exchanged messages among the C2-SENSE responders, or monitoring the latest incoming values regardless of their source (temperature data, showing the last position of an ambulance, etc.). The EMT tool is easily expandable to include new widgets and features. A screenshot is given in Fig. 1.

Object of Interest Data Repository (OOI): All the relevant data that have to be available to other Collaboration Environment components are stored in the Object of Interest Data Repository [7]. Fast response times are required during crises, implying quick data access and repository response and tight coupling between the OOI repository and technologies for reliable and fast data access and exchange by using the available technologies (e.g., Apache Kafka[3]). The sources of data can be anything from

---

[3] https://kafka.apache.org/.

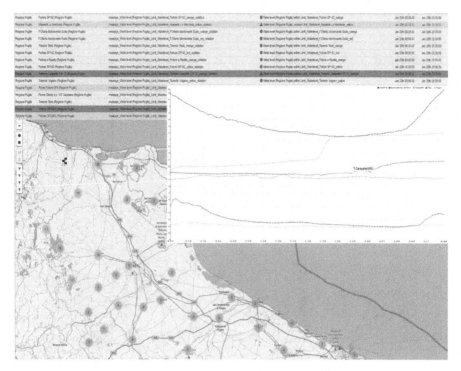

Fig. 1. Emergency maps tool with the map, line graph, and last values table

sensors measuring environmental parameters (air quality, temperature), to sensors tracking location of ambulances. To allow for effective and accurate applications of the OOI data, the data can be further enriched with meta-information (e.g., data are geo-referenced). Moreover, other type of sources, as are texts in exchanged messages or in social media can also be stored as relevant data in the OOI data repository. The component is working in the background without any direct interaction with the end user (e.g., crisis responder).

Sensor Management Tool (SMT): The purpose of the Sensor Management Tool is to provide an overview over available sensors in the field to crisis mangers and to allow them some basic configuration in a generic way without the need to know all the details about the sensors. As the configuration needs to be agnostic in respect to the sensor type, the possibilities of the tool are intentionally limited to very basic and generic commands. These include sending information on sensor identification (ID), capabilities and location, controlling and adjusting the data-sampling rate (off, low, medium and high), or re-locating a sensor (in case of autonomous sensor platforms).

SMT encompasses a GUI for sending commands and for visualizing responses (see Fig. 2). Visualization functionalities can also be done with the EMT. The component defines messages for the ESB, and information/data on how sensors can react by providing a reference implementation. This is an optional implementation of the interface to sensors and sensor network adapters. Finally, SMT is not planned as a

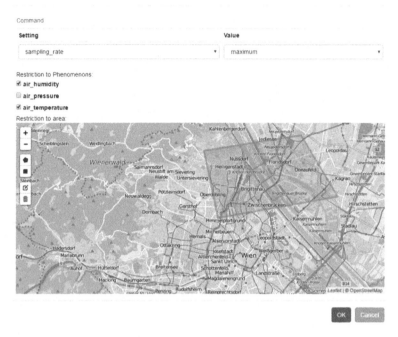

Fig. 2. Sensor management tool user interface for sending commands

replacement for any sensor specific configuration tools, but as a complementary tool to be used without any prior knowledge of the actual sensors used.

GIS Server: The GIS Server is used to provide the data from the OOI in a standard conform way to clients already used within a specific organization. The clients range from dedicated GIS solutions (e.g., QGIS) to broadly used applications (e.g., Google Earth). The component primarily makes the data available to the end users who are connected to the C2-SENSE Framework and authorized to access the data. The data, however, can also be made available to end users in case the data are open. Moreover, by using the GIS Server, it is possible to visualize crisis related data on standard GIS clients making the information available to everyone without the need to use a specialized tool like EMT.

LimitChecker: Crisis responders require automatic provision of warnings and alarms during crises. This is specifically important when many events occur simultaneously, and when there are large amounts of data coming in, making having an overview of the crisis very hard. LimitChecker provides automatic monitoring functionality. This C2-SENSE component monitors relevant sensor data (i.e., water levels) that are streamlined in the C2-SENSE data repository, and compares them to pre-defined threshold values. In the case of exceedance, a warning or an alarm are sent to the system and relevant end users. Moreover, the LimitChecker component also provides data modelling functionality, where timeseries sensor data for a chosen period are analysed to predict the development of, e.g., water levels, for the next few hours.

Due to the flexible component architecture, which includes free statistical software R sub-component, LimitChecker can easily be used and extended to serve other, more complex, data analysis tasks (e.g., combining ground-based sensor data with weather forecast).

2.2   Components and Applications for Profile Management

Management of profiles defined in Sect. 3 is done by four software components described in the following. The management process is given in Fig. 3.

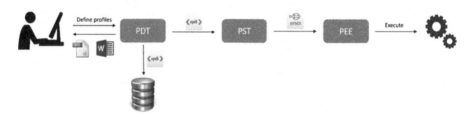

Fig. 3. Profile management process

Profile Definition Tool (PDT): The main purpose is to provide users with an online tool to create, to update and maintain profiles in an easy way. It provides users a graphical user interface to define a profile as an ad hoc workflow describing the order of the tasks, messages to be exchanged within tasks, and documents that constitute the message content. The aim is to lighten the workload of domain experts and help them to handle complex tasks easily. After profiles are defined, PDT produces automatically both human readable Word documents, which addresses the versioning problem and helps to keep documents always up-to-date; and machine processable XML documents, which enables software systems to understand the profiles. The schema definition of this XML document (XSD) is referred as Emergency Profile Definition Language (EPDL).

Profile Specialization Tool (PST): Profiles defined through PST are generic and independent from organizations and specific incidents. These generic profiles contain enough structure to prevent chaotic response to crises situations such as the initial activities, control and data flow structure, and resources needed to start managing a variety of crisis situations. Profile Specialization Tool is used to customize the generic profiles to specific organizations and specific incidents by considering the existing procedures and operations of the organizations involved. It is used to create a machine readable and executable process definition from the graphical definition by using a business process specification language, namely BPMN[4]. The BPMN documents created by the tool are then sent to Profile Execution Engine for execution.

---

[4] BPMN, Business Process Model and Notation.

Profile Execution Engine (PEE): This is a tool built on Alfresco Activiti, which is an enterprise Business Process Management (BPM) solution targeted at business people and developers. PEE is used to execute emergency web processes defined as business rules in BPMN format by invoking corresponding Web services automatically.

Profile Monitoring Tool (PMT): Profile Monitoring Tool, a graphical user interface, makes it possible to visually trace the execution of a specific instance of profiles by PEE. The aim is to enable users to track the status, bottlenecks and incomplete tasks to take necessary measures.

3 Profiling Approach

The second part of the C2-SENSE framework is the application of profiles. Profiles define a standard set of messages and documents, business rules, processes, constraints and choreographies that allow even a new entity to join an already existing response network, without any additional integration efforts, as long as the entity conforms to one or more predefined profiles. In cases where entities do not conform to any profile or standard specification (meaning that they have their own proprietary document formats, workflows, business rules, etc.), adapters should be implemented for every two entities so that they can be interoperable. This operation should be repeated every time a new entity joins the network. In this regard, profiling approach helps in improving interoperability as it eliminates the need for prior bilateral agreements between entities involved in crisis response, and who wish to exchange information and data by defining standard specifications for achieving specific goals. In other words, these are sets of rules orchestrating the functionalities of the Framework.

A profile-based approach has already been successfully implemented in domains such as eHealth [8] addressing three layers of the Interoperability Stack. "Communication Layer" covers the transport and communication layer protocols, "Document Layer" addresses the content format of the messages and documents exchanged among the applications, while the "Business Process Layer" addresses the choreography of the activities to be executed by the participants [9]. For the CDM domain, however, organizational aspects including policies, procedures, strategies and operations are critical. Therefore, the Interoperability Stack shown in Fig. 4 has been proposed for the domain [10].

The first full implementation of the Stack is deployed through the C2-SENSE Emergency Interoperability Framework [11]. The profiles developed in the project are addressing all the layers, exposing available applications and implementing the missing technologies, and making them available to the crisis response community. In the following, we provided details on profiles currently available in the Framework, while keeping in mind that the new ones can be added upon the need and purpose of the collaboration (e.g., data exchange for environmental monitoring, maritime surveillance [12], etc.).

Emergency Situation Map profile: This profile describes how a user or an organization is provided with a common operational picture of the emergency area using a real-time data and geographical maps. It describes how to get the data, maps and

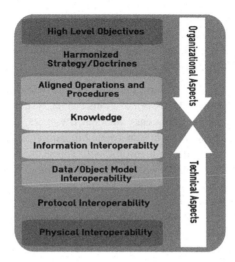

Fig. 4. Interoperability stack for emergency management

mash-ups. The objectives of implementing this profile are: 1. Getting the overview of the current situation in the emergency area. 2. Identifying emergency characteristics/ attributes/hallmarks. 3. Identifying the critical emergency areas. 4. Identifying location and information related to emergency resources. 5. Identifying location and information related to rescue targets. 6. Comparing different information related to maps (e.g., elevation) or data (water levels at different locations). 7. Communicating the findings to other C2-SENSE and local parties.

The profile supports a process of providing C2-SENSE users with a common operational picture with maps and/or data with access determined by the Service Level Agreements (SLA). The intended scope for this profile includes pre-emergency, during and after emergency on-site coordination centres, local organizations, national organizations and non-governmental organizations. The activities specified in this profile are intended to provide a common ground for a decision support between organizations taking part in emergency operations. It is expected that all parties have necessary infrastructure/devices, to enable them to acquire maps and data, and to view them.

Situation Analysis profile: This profile describes how a user or an organization is provided with a possibility to simulate the situation on the ground for a given set of data. The profile describes how to get the data, maps, mash-ups and simulation results. The objectives of implementing this profile are: 1. Acquiring an overview of the possible situations based on the current situation (data) in the emergency area. 2. Identifying the potentially critical emergency areas. 3. Identifying the potentially critical events. 4. Communicating the findings to other parties.

This profile supports a process of providing users with a common operational picture with maps and/or data. The intended scope for this profile includes: pre-emergency, during and after emergency situations on-site coordination centres, local organizations, national organizations and non-governmental organizations The activities specified in this profile are intended to provide a common ground for a decision support between organizations taking part in emergency operations. It is expected that the parties have necessary infrastructure/devices, to enable them to acquire maps and data, to view them and to run simulations on them. The access is determined by the SLA agreements.

Sensor Measurement Profile: The profile describes how sensors transmit their measurements to the C2 Systems, where organizations can analyse the observations. This is important across the complete emergency incident life cycle, including preparedness, initial and on-going response, recovery and demobilization/release of sensors.

The objective of implementing this profile is to expect that all sensors are sending measurements of their observations according to their configuration.

This profile supports the process of sensors that send measurements to C2 Systems. The intended scope for this profile includes (during and after emergencies) emergency managers among on-site coordination centres, local organizations, national organizations and non-governmental organizations. It is assumed, (1) that the sensor infrastructure is ready to run and (2) that sensors can send their measurements. That means that configuration (including type of protocol, physical connection, etc.) is a prerequisite and thus not part of this profile.

Sensor Management Profile: This one describes how organizations can configure sensors to gain observations from areas of interest. This is important across the complete emergency incident life cycle, including preparedness, pre-staging of sensors, initial and on-going response, recovery and demobilization/release of sensors. The objective of implementing this profile is to expect that sensors are available and that they need to respond and adapt to emergency incidents, such as querying and finding out about available sensors, and configuring sensors to send the requested observations (data).

The profile supports a process of discovering, ordering and deploying sensors, which are needed in emergencies. The intended scope for this profile includes (during and after emergencies) emergency managers among on-site coordination centres, local organizations, national organizations and non-governmental organizations. It is assumed, that the sensor infrastructure is ready to run, i.e., low-level configuration (including type of protocol, physical connection, etc.) is a prerequisite and thus not part of this profile.

4   Collaboration Environment in a Real Life Example

We show here a simplified example in order to see how the physical components and the profiling approach harmonize the data exchange among two or more entities (organizations, responders, etc.). The example is a part of a larger crisis scenario involving floods.

Entity A has only limited overview of the situation in field: reports from police and firefighters provide last measurements on water levels and the extent of flooding, which can be mapped into their Geographical Information System (GIS). These are, however, not real-time and can be obsolete due to rapidly changing situation on the ground. Besides reports, Entity A can have direct access to water level measurements provided by the sensors in-situ owned by Entity B. Accessing sensor data would provide real-time situation data and an overview of the situation that would manifold the effectiveness of decision making for Entity A. The obstacles are, however, which protocols to use in order to access the data, how to get the correct permissions, and finally, how to align the data formats to be embedded into their GIS system. Since the data are in the possession of Entity B, some kind of exchange and alignment rules and agreements need to be put in place in order to bypass the mentioned obstacles. The following process is applied when exchanging the data between Entities A and B (Fig. 5):

(1) Register as a new organization (in the C2-SENSE system),
(2) Choose a *default* profile for data exchange (i.e., *Emergency Situation Map profile*).

The profile defines the needed input, such as the data format and communication protocol. Normally (without profiles), Entity A and Entity B are supposed to first understand their proprietary formats, protocols, rules etc., update their internal systems according to specifications of the other, and then exchange information. However, with the profiles, they just either update their internal system according to standard specifications in the profile, or use some adapters in C2-SENSE framework, which makes them profile compliant.

(3) Specialize the chosen profile by providing the network access point (e.g., URL) of the receiver/sender of the data,
(4) Activate the *specialized* profile.

After the final step, it is possible for Entity A to receive the data from Entity B based on the specifications defined in business process model and notation, and apply further functionalities provided by the components in Collaboration Environment (e.g., decision making, etc.) The process of specializing a chosen profile, however, needs to be executed by both actors for their respective specifications. Entity B sends the data in JSON format, while Entity A can only treat XML formats. The Framework would then consider this and make the appropriate transformations needed for these two actors to exchange data and information. Transformation can be done at semantic level as well. The framework provides a semantic interoperability suite allowing for semantic transformation for organizations using different data models, or the same standard but different versions. What this example shows is the interaction between the physical components that offer data integration and transformation and the rules governing the data exchange between these components. Without the profiles, the system would not know which format is received, nor which format is accepted and used by the receiving actor.

Very similar actions are planned as a part of the real flood scenario in the C2-SENSE project's pilot due in 2017 [11]. The results will be reported in a subsequent publication.

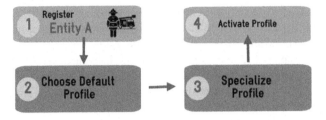

Fig. 5. Steps in the alignment process in the profiling approach for one entity

5   Discussion and Conclusion

The novel profiling approach presented here is based on the successful application of the conventional profiling approach in eHealth domain [8]. However, the conventional one addresses only the first three layers of the Interoperability Stack, covering the transport and communication layer protocols, addressing the content format of the messages and documents exchanged among the applications, and addressing the choreography of the activities to be executed by the participants [9]. For the emergency management domain, however, organizational aspects, such as policies, procedures, operations and strategies are as important as technical aspects of interoperability. Absence of those can result in loss of time and resources, and potential wrong decision-making.

The C2-SENSE Framework offers a solution in form of its software components and profiles. The defined and developed profiles in C2-SENSE are addressing additional layers of the Interoperability Stack defined in [10], thus covering these lacking aspects. The solution is flexible enough to be applied for the Emergency Management domain, or to be adjusted for any other domain that incorporates sensor and sensor network data, data exchanges, crisis mapping, and collaboration in multi-user environments. One such domain is Maritime Surveillance where illegal activities such as smuggling or piracy, or maritime vessel traffic management and protection are of critical importance for law enforcement. Implementing the identified profiles in such scenarios can serve for their improvement [12].

This implies potential for introducing the Framework in domains dealing with environmental challenges, being that of real-time monitoring, or mitigating. Since the world today awaits more disasters related to climate changes (e.g., floods, droughts, landslides, air pollution), it is important to provide necessary tools for not only treating the crises when they occur, but also for monitoring the events leading to a disastrous situations. Moreover, such solutions need to have the strength of being easily implementable, adjustable to all the needs of different end-users (e.g., crisis responder, police, volunteer [13]), adjustable to new research and technological approaches (e.g., citizen science [14], crowdtasking [15]), and potentially globally affordable and available. It is expected that the profiling approach of the C2-SENSE Framework, with its provided software components in combination with the set of rules orchestrating the functionalities of those components and rules for achieving interoperability, is a solution fulfilling those needs.

Acknowledgement. The research leading to this paper has been performed in the scope of the C2-SENSE project. C2-SENSE has received funding from the European Community's Seven Framework Programme (FP7/2007-2013) under grant agreement number 607729.

References

1. Alexander, D., Masini, E., Mugnai, L.: Integrated emergency management for mass casualty emergencies. In: Proceedings of the NATO Advanced Training Course on Integrated Emergency Management for Mass Casualty Emergencies organized by CESPRO, Florence (2013)
2. Lent, B.: Facing the Challenge of Data Interoperability. https://tinyurl.com/ltlcelp. Accessed 15 Mar 2017
3. Alfieri, L., Burek, P., Feyen, L., Forzieri, G.: Global warming increases the frequency of river floods in Europe. Hydrol. Earth Syst. Sci. 14 (2015). https://doi.org/10.5194/hess-19-2247-2015
4. Blöschl, G., Nester, T., Komma, J., Parajka, J., Perdigão, R.A.: The June 2013 flood in the Upper Danube Basin, and comparisons with the 2002, 1954 and 1899 floods. Hydrol. Earth Syst. Sci. **17**, 5197–5212 (2013). https://doi.org/10.5194/hess-17-5197-2013x
5. Ansell, C., Boin, A., Keller, A.: Managing transboundary crises: identifying the building blocks of an effective response system. J. Contigencies Crisis Manag. **18**(4), 13 (2010). https://doi.org/10.1111/j.1468-5973.2010.00620
6. C2-SENSE project web site. http://c2-sense.eu/. Accessed 14 Jan 2017
7. Havlik, D., et al.: Training support for crisis managers with elements of serious gaming. In: Denzer, R., Argent, R.M., Schimak, G., Hřebíček, J. (eds.) ISESS 2015., vol. 448, pp. 217–225. Springer, Cham (2015). https://doi.org/10.1007/978-3-319-15994-2_21
8. Integrating the Healthcare Enterprise Profiles. http://www.ihe.net/profiles/index.cfm. Accessed 14 Jan 2017
9. Namli, T., Dogac, A.: Testing conformance and interoperability of eHealth applications. Methods Inf. Med. **49**, 281–289 (2010). https://doi.org/10.3414/me09-02-002
10. Tolk, A.: Introducing a reference model for measures of merit for coalition interoperability. In: Command and Control Research and Technology Symposium, Washington, D.C. (2003)
11. Gençtürk, M., Arisi, R., Toscano, L., Kabak, Y., Di Ciano, M., Palmitessa, A.: Profiling approach for the interoperability of command and control systems with sensing systems in emergency management. In: 6th International IFIP Working Conference on Enterprise Interoperability, Nîmes (2016)
12. Gençtürk, M., Duro, R., Kabak, Y., Božić, B., Kahveci, K., Yilmaz, B.: Interoperability profiles for disaster management and maritime surveillance. In: eChallenges, Vilnius (2015). https://doi.org/10.1109/echallenges.2015.7441073
13. Whittaker, J., McLennan, B., Handmer, J.: A review of informal volunteerism in emergencies and disasters: definition, opportunities and challenges. Int. J. Disaster Risk Reduct. **13**, 358–368 (2015)
14. Mazumdar, S., Wringley, S., Ciravegna, F.: Citizen science and crowdsourcing for earth observations: an analysis of stakeholder opinions on the present and future. Remote Sens. **9**, 87 (2017)
15. Middelhoff, M., Widera, A., van den Berg, R.P., Hellingrath, R., Auferbauer, D., Havlik, D., Pielorz, J.: Crowdsourcing and crowdtasking in crisis management: lessons learned from a field experiment simulating a flooding in the city of the Hague. In: 3rd International Conference on Information and Communication Technologies for Disaster Management (ICT-DM), Vienna (2017)

An Integrated Decision-Support Information System on the Impact of Extreme Natural Hazards on Critical Infrastructure

Z. A. Sabeur[1]([✉]) [iD], P. Melas[1], K. Meacham[1], R. Corbally[2], D. D'Ayala[3], and B. Adey[4]

[1] Department of Electronics and Computer Science,
University of Southampton IT Innovation Centre, Southampton, UK
{zas,pm,kem}@it-innovation.soton.ac.uk
[2] Roughan and Donovan Innovative Solutions, Dublin, Ireland
[3] Department of Civil, Environmental and Geomatic Engineering,
University College London, London, UK
[4] ETHZ, Zurich, Switzerland

Abstract. In this paper, we introduce an Integrated Decision-Support Tool (IDST v2.0) which was developed as part of the INFRARISK project (https://www.infrarisk-fp7.eu/). The IDST is an online tool which demonstrates the implementation of a risk-based stress testing methodology for analyzing the potential impact of natural hazards on transport infrastructure networks. The IDST is enabled with a set of software workflow processes that allow the definition of multiple cascading natural hazards, geospatial coverage and impact on important large infrastructure, including those which are critical to transport networks in Europe. Stress tests on these infrastructure are consequently performed together with the automated generation of useful case study reports for practitioners. An exemplar stress test study using the IDST is provided in this paper. In this study, risks and consequences of an earthquake-triggered landslide scenario in Northern Italy is described. Further, it provides a step-by-step account of the developed stress testing overarching methodology which is applied to the impact on a road network of the region of interest.

Keywords: Environmental decision support systems · Data analytics
Crisis management · Critical infrastructure · Natural hazards · Risk management
Climate change · Black swans · Stress testing

1 Introduction

The INFRARISK Decision Support Tool (IDST) version 2.0 [1] is an information system tool that allows urban planners, civil engineers, crisis managers, urban development agencies and enterprise consortia to assess potential multiple risks from natural hazards to which critical infrastructure may be exposed. These may include earthquakes, landslides, floods or a combination of all. The IDST hosts specialized databases with supporting scenario simulations derived from models of a number of natural hazards

© IFIP International Federation for Information Processing 2017
Published by Springer International Publishing AG 2017. All Rights Reserved
J. Hřebíček et al. (Eds.): ISESS 2017, IFIP AICT 507, pp. 302–314, 2017.
https://doi.org/10.1007/978-3-319-89935-0_25

allowing their likelihood of occurrence and intensity levels for different statistical return periods to be estimated at the locations of critical infrastructure elements. Two exemplar case studies have been considered using the IDST. These consist of two large European transport networks (road and rail), located in Italy and Croatia respectively. They demonstrate the use of the adopted generic and overarching INFRARISK methodology for the evaluation of risks which are engendered by natural hazards on critical infrastructure. The IDST has options for applying the risk methodology to other transport networks of interest, provided that the necessary input data is uploaded into the system. The development of the IDST required the deployment of phase driven software development tasks using an agile approach. The first version [2] of the IDST specification was initially developed through consultation with a large number of domain knowledge experts and end-users, both within the project partnership and externally. The IDST specification v1.0 was focused on capturing the functionality requirements for the IDST decision-support system. This exercise has led to the development of the IDST System [3] with its basic functionalities. Version 2.0 of the IDST was then extended to include more advanced functionalities of the IDST [4]. Specifically, it includes the following modules:

1. Web Framework technologies;
2. Database engines;
3. User authentication and authorization, management functionalities;
4. GIS Map Engine; and
5. Visualization and Reporting tools.

The following sections, highlight the agile IDST architecture design and implementation of IDST v2.0 [1].

2 Agile IDST System Design and Development

The IDST has been specified to integrate tools, databases and user interfaces in consultation with end users and knowledge experts in crisis management under INFRARISK. It is primarily a web-based system (or portal) which is user-accessible via a web browser on multiple client platforms (laptop, tablet, etc.) and operating systems (Windows, Linux, etc.). For the IDST v2.0, commonly used browsers are supported (e.g. Internet Explorer, Firefox), and run on Windows or Linux operation systems. The design of the graphical user interface (GUI) took into account multiple platforms, by exploiting the latest platform independent user interface (UI) toolkits.

The IDST software system is deployed on a central server, which has secure remote access available for registered users and selected stakeholders. Access is enabled via HTTPS and, for the main IDST pages, the user will be required to be logged in using their existing user account information. The initial welcome page of the IDST is available to all users, therefore providing some background information about INFRARISK and the IDST while providing links to the secure parts of the portal. The IDST system is modular, i.e. based on multiple autonomous and interacting components. These include:

- Database (local or remote, PostgreSQL, with PostGIS modules)
- Flat files (e.g. shape files, OpenStreetMap data)
- Software module (e.g. Python code)
- Application (e.g. a command line executable)
- Remote web service
- Client-side tool (e.g. JavaScript jQuery, Bootstrap)

The IDST uses the Django framework which allows multiple components to be incorporated easily, while we integrated the GUI features of these modules concurrently. Certain components were included as modules (or executables) and launched by the main IDST component (i.e. IDST Process Workflow Engine). The components were executed with their required inputs and the results returned either by direct visual display or indeed as input to a subsequent module within the workflow. Certain components were deployed as a web service, either on the same host as the IDST or another remote server. Modules which require significant processing time (e.g. greater than one minute) were made available as results in a pre-populated database since it would not be appropriate for the user to practically experience running these simulations dynamically. Some components have been included as look-up tables and provide fast access to pre-run simulation results. In any case, the GUI made use of Ajax calls to the IDST server for any browser requests (e.g. page updates) that require more than a few seconds to perform. The agile development of the IDST system scaled successfully by supporting a large number of concurrent users. Its databases are also scalable since they can handle a mix of structured and unstructured data. Additionally, the data is made available to authorized users, so that they can extract information for their own specific applications.

2.1 High Level Architecture Design Architecture

Figure 1 below, presents a high level conceptual view of the IDST modular architecture. This shows the main components in the system and how they fit together and interact. The IDST system consist of three layers. These are: (1) Presentation Layer; (2) Data Processing Layer; and (3) Data Storage Layer. The Presentation Layer is responsible for the creation of all of the content (as HTML) for the user's browser. It consists of a main component called the 'Portal', which handles user requests and delegates to various sub-components within the 'Visualisation Engine' to create specific pieces of content for the requested IDST page. The Data Processing Layer contains any computational components that are required in the IDST system. This includes the Process Workflow Engine (PWE) module (for evaluating multiple risks), as well as the various associated computational modules. These are: (a) Domain Computation (e.g. fragility functions); and (b) Data Analysis (e.g. analytics algorithms). The Data Storage Layer is responsible for handling all access to and from all databases within the IDST system. The computation and presentation components communicate with this layer via a GeoDjango Data Access Layer (ORM). It provides user-friendly APIs to the underlying data which encapsulate lower level database access statements (e.g. SQL).

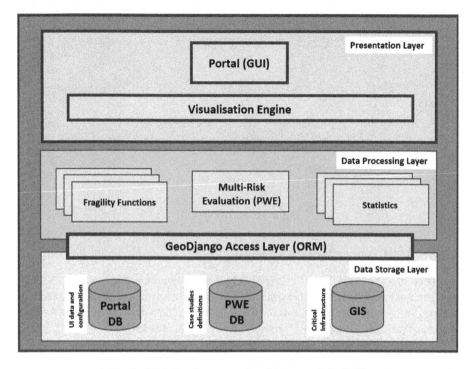

Fig. 1. High level conceptual architecture of the IDST

3 The IDST Information System

3.1 Authentication Services

The authentication of access of users in the IDST is based on the following services: *1- Local user account authentication (exclusive for administrators); and 2- Third party authentication services (for other users), e.g. Google, Yahoo, LinkedIn.* Once the authentication mechanism is selected, the user is redirected to the respective site for login in. After a successful login, users access the IDST portal profile. The full profile information is required for completing user authentication. If permission is given by the administrator, then the IDST portal associates the user's profile with the provided account details and enabled access to the portal.

3.2 IDST Dashboard

After a successful login, the user is presented with the IDST Dashboard page (Fig. 2). The dashboard enables the users to create and manage their own stress tests data, as well as access to exemplar case studies.

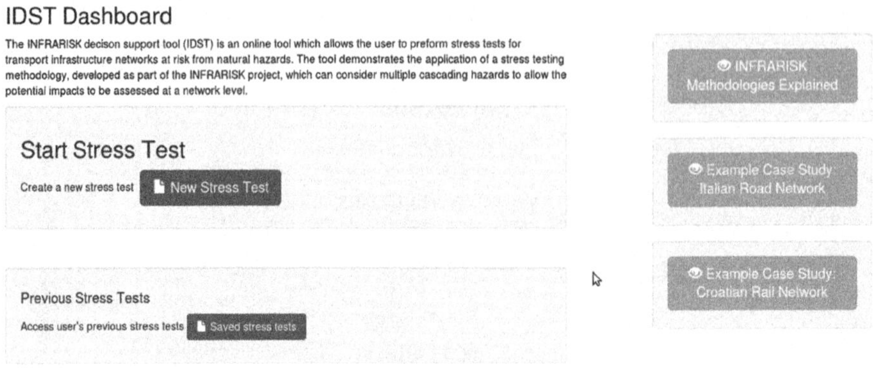

IDST Dashboard

The INFRARISK decison support tool (IDST) is an online tool which allows the user to preform stress tests for transport infrastructure networks at risk from natural hazards. The tool demonstrates the application of a stress testing methodology, developed as part of the INFRARISK project, which can consider multiple cascading hazards to allow the potential impacts to be assessed at a network level.

Start Stress Test

Create a new stress test   New Stress Test

Previous Stress Tests

Access user's previous stress tests   Saved stress tests

INFRARISK
Methodologies Explained

Example Case Study:
Italian Road Network

Example Case Study:
Croatian Rail Network

Fig. 2. IDST Dashboard

3.3 The IDST Process Workflow Engine

The IDST Process Workflow Engine (PWE) is designed around the Overarching Risk Management Framework (ORMF) concept [5, 6]. The ORMF describes the various steps involved in carrying out a stress tests for an infrastructure network [7]. The ORMF consists of the following enacting steps as shown in Fig. 3 below:

3.4 IDST Data Storage

The IDST stores various datasets in its database system. The database system is preloaded with datasets to support the basic case studies, e.g. geometry and characteristics of the Northern Italian road network. In addition, users can upload the necessary datasets in order to run their own stress tests. Generated results for stress tests can be also exported and used outside the IDST workflow for further analysis. The type of datasets the IDST system supports are:

- Infrastructure element characteristics such as road, rail lines, bridges, tunnels, embankments, intersections, etc.
- Hazard models/maps (e.g. seismic, landslide, flooding)
- Simulation results from stress tests
- Analysis results.

3.5 IDST Models

The risk evaluation in the IDST is based on specialized models which are pluggable modules that compute transport network elements of various stages of the IDST workflow. These are classified into (a) hazard and (b) vulnerability models. **Hazard Models** provide information derived from numerical models of different hazards. This information specifies the relevant intensity levels, depending on the model inputs specified by the user for a particular scenario. **Network Models** estimate the probability of the various infrastructure elements experiencing different levels of damage, given the

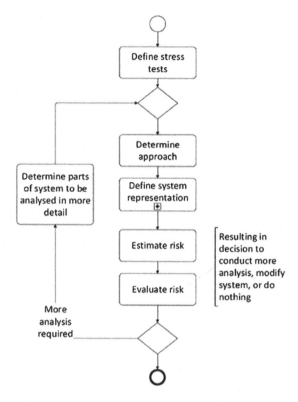

Fig. 3. IDST Workflow

occurrence of a particular hazard scenario. During this step, fragility curves (Fig. 4) are assigned to the network elements. Fragility curves, specific to a particular infrastructure element (e.g. bridge, tunnel, road segment, etc.), describe the vulnerability of that element to a particular hazard [8]. In order to estimate the probability of having a defined Damage State (DS) in any given network element, these fragility curves are used, in combination with the information from the hazard models, to estimate the likelihood of experiencing different levels of damage. Table 1 provides an overview of the typical damages states considered.

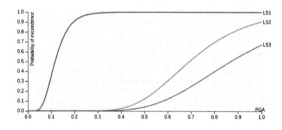

Fig. 4. Illustrative bridge element fragility curves

Table 1. Damage state (DS)

	Damage state	Description
0	DS0	No damage
1	DS1	Slight/minor damage
2	DS2	Moderate damage
3	DS3	Extensive/major/severe damage
4	DS4	Complete damage/collapse/failure

3.6 Network Element Characteristics

The user must define the individual characteristics for each type of element being considered within the stress test. These characteristics must be defined for each hazard that is deemed to affect the different types of elements on the network (hazards will affect different types of elements in different ways). For example, the user might choose to consider the effect of ground acceleration (from an earthquake) on bridges, or the effect of landslides on road segments. In each case, the appropriate hazard models and vulnerability models must be available within the IDST. Once the characteristics have been defined the user proceeds by clicking the "Upload Network Elements" button.

3.6.1 The IDST Hazard Scenario

The IDST hazard scenario is used to define a set of cascading hazard events to be considered for a particular stress test. In particular, a hazard event is the combination of (a) a hazard source, e.g. an earthquake; (b) a hazard event, e.g. a ground shaking caused by the earthquake; and (c) a model that describes that hazard event. In most cases the hazard model will require a detailed configuration and a dataset to operate upon, depending on the complexity of the model used. The hazard source in the first hazard event is considered as the primary hazard source which can trigger secondary hazard events, e.g. a landslide caused by the occurrence of an earthquake.

3.6.2 The IDST Network Scenario

The IDST network scenario allows the user to define multiple sets of network events. A network event is defined by a combination of a network type, e.g. a road network, a hazard event deemed to impact that element type, and a network model that assigns fragility functions to that element type. For each network event a dataset of network elements (bridges, road segments, tunnels, etc.) has to be considered. That set of network elements can be selected from the pre-populated IDST datasets for the case study regions which are confined by stress the test boundary polygon, or uploaded directly from the user, e.g. as a shape file. Risk estimation, i.e. damage state calculation, for each network event is carried out by using the appropriate hazard model along with the vulnerability models for each of the network elements to estimate the potential damage to each of the associated infrastructure elements. Risk evaluation can then be carried out considering the calculated damage state for each infrastructure element.

4   Case Study Using the IDST

In this section, a case study is presented which comprises a road network around Bologna in Northern Italy, see Fig. 5 below. Full details of this case study can be found in [9]. The region covers approximately 990 km^2 and is located around the city of Bologna.

Fig. 5. Northern Italy case study borders

For this road network, the hazard source was an earthquake, with ground acceleration considered as the primary hazard event. In addition, earthquake-triggered landslides were considered as a secondary, cascading, hazard for this stress test hazard scenario. Figure 6 shows the hazard scenario as defined through the IDST. The primary hazard event is a ground motion event which has assigned the INFRARISK GM hazard model [10] assigned to it to allow the ground acceleration within the case study region to be calculated at the location of the various road infrastructure elements. An earthquake-triggered landslide hazard event is defined as a secondary event which utilizes a pre-loaded model for calculating locations where landslides may occur due to ground shaking.

Hazard Source
Choose the hazard source for this stress test.
Hazard source:
Earthquake
Store Hazard Source
The IDST does not currently support other hazard sources, please contact us for further information on how these should be considered.
Hazard Events
Add hazard events to your hazard scenario.
Associated hazard event list:
Hazard Type
Primary/Secondary
Model
Action
Ground Motion
primary
INFRARISK GM MODEL
Change model
Delete
Landslide
secondary
N/A
Void
Delete
Add Hazard Event

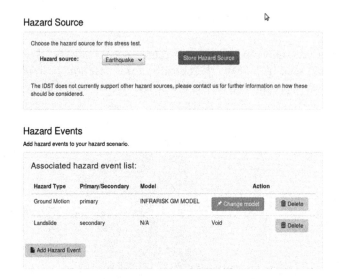

Fig. 6. Northern Italy case study hazard scenario

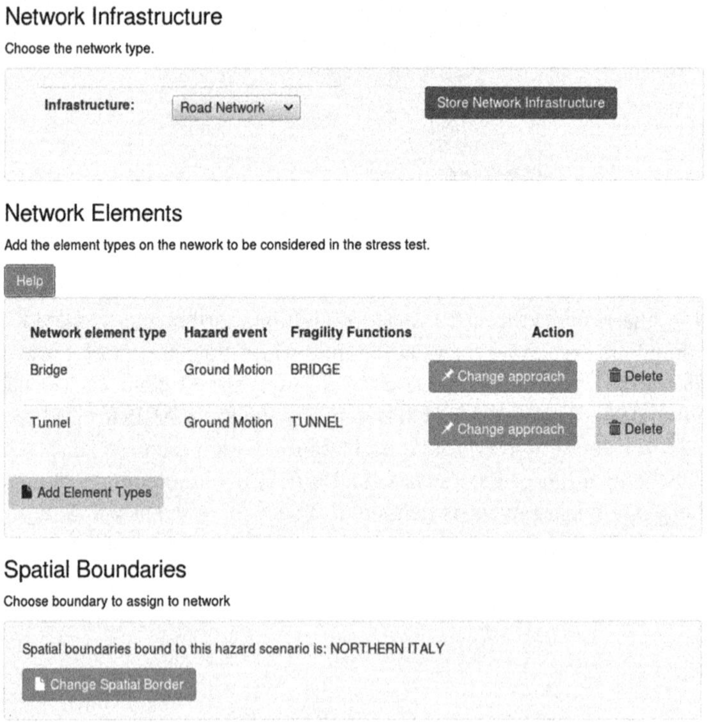

Network Infrastructure
Choose the network type.
Infrastructure:
Road Network
Store Network Infrastructure
Network Elements
Add the element types on the nework to be considered in the stress test.
Help
Network element type
Hazard event
Fragility Functions
Action
Bridge
Ground Motion
BRIDGE
Change approach
Delete
Tunnel
Ground Motion
TUNNEL
Change approach
Delete
Add Element Types
Spatial Boundaries
Choose boundary to assign to network
Spatial boundaries bound to this hazard scenario is: NORTHERN ITALY
Change Spatial Border

Fig. 7. Northern Italy case study network scenario

The impact of ground motion on bridges and tunnels is considered along with the effects of earthquake-triggered landslides on road sections. Figure 7 shows the network scenario for this stress test. The targeted infrastructure is the road network. Selected network element types are bridges and tunnels, where the associated hazard event is the ground motion and the assigned vulnerability models are bridge and tunnel fragility functions. The whole area around Bologna shown in Fig. 7 is defined as the spatial boundary.

The network element datasets used for this case study are selected from the IDST case study database which has been pre-populated with relevant characteristics for the elements in the region of the Italian case study. As shown in Fig. 8, the system has identified 328 bridges and 30 tunnels included within the spatial borders of the region considered for this stress test. Figure 9 shows the locations of each of these elements, a heat map of ground acceleration values which correspond to the ground motion for an earthquake scenario considered for the stress test.

Network Element Datasets

Dataset elements for the Bridge event:

Dataset Type	Name	Num of elements	Action
IDST Case Study Database	IDST DB	328	

Dataset elements for the Tunnel event:

Dataset Type	Name	Num of elements	Action
IDST Case Study Database	IDST DB	30	

Fig. 8. Stress test infrastructure datasets

At this point the system proceeds with risk estimation for this stress test. The appropriate fragility functions are assigned to each identified network element, i.e. tunnels and bridges and the likelihood of each element experiencing different levels of damage is calculated. This information can then be used to calculate direct and indirect consequences associated with the earthquake. Figure 10 shows the levels of Damage States and the statistical aspects of some of the respective direct consequences by the IDST.

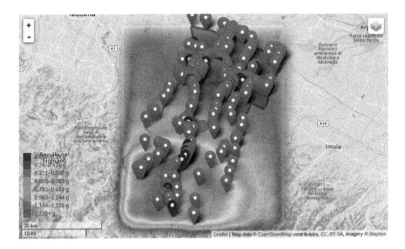

Fig. 9. Stress test PGA map with marked infrastructure elements

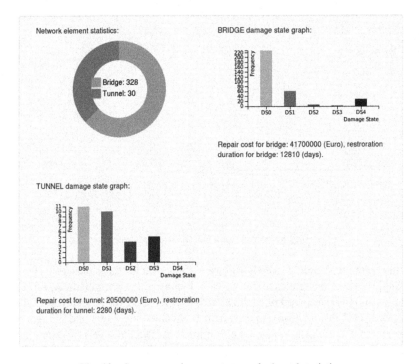

Fig. 10. Stress tests damage state analysis and statistics

5   Conclusion and Future Work

The IDST as a decision-support tool has concretely enabled civil engineers and critical infrastructure management stakeholders set up cascading risk scenarios with low probabilities of occurrence and high impact on and damages to Critical Infrastructure (CI). The IDST was successfully demonstrated to the referred communities of specialised CI engineering firms and stakeholders at a large scale INFRARISK project conference [11]. The integration of the heterogeneous data sources, information and outputs under specialised databases and modelling tools in the IDST gives a unique common operational picture for the engineering communities who specialise in the management of CIs. Furthermore, the overarching risk assessment methodology which provides an automated Process Workflow Engine in the IDST clearly enables crisis management experts to usefully set "what if" scenarios on exposure of urban CIs to extreme natural hazards. The next step of this research and development work is for testing the scalability the IDST system towards architectures for supporting very large spatial coverages, mining of big data sources and extreme analytics for the computation of highly complex cascading risks of extreme and rare natural events on CIs. This is clearly a big data problem and challenge which can be met with supporting cloud and high performance computing infrastructure in the future. This will be our research goal for advancing our understanding and quantification of the socio-economic impact of very complex cascading natural hazards on CIs in Europe and beyond.

Acknowledgements. INTRARISK is funded by the European Commission's FP7 programme, Grant Agreement No. 603960. Further information can be found at www.infrarisk-fp7.eu. The authors gratefully acknowledge the contributions of the other INFRARISK consortium partners: Draga-dos SA, Gavin and Doherty Geosolutions Ltd., Probabilistic Solutions Consult and Training BV, the Spanish National Research Council, PSJ, Stiftelsen SINTEF and Ritchey Consulting AB.

References

1. Melas, P., Sabeur, Z.: IDST system v2.0. INFRARISK project deliverable D7.4 (2016). https://www.infrarisk-fp7.eu/deliverables
2. Meacham, K., Sabeur, Z.: IDST system specification v1.0. INFRARISK project deliverable D7.1 (2014). https://www.infrarisk-fp7.eu/deliverables
3. Melas, P., Sabeur, Z.: IDST system v1.0. INFRARISK project deliverable D7.3 (2015). https://www.infrarisk-fp7.eu/deliverables
4. Melas, P., Sabeur, Z.: IDST system specification v2.0. INFRARISK Deliverable D7.2 (2015). https://www.infrarisk-fp7.eu/deliverables
5. Adey, B., Hackl, J., Heitzler, M., Iosifescu, I.: Preliminary model, methodology and information exchange. INFRARISK EU project deliverable D4.1 (2014). https://www.infrarisk-fp7.eu/deliverables
6. Hackl, J., Heitzler, M., Lam, J.C., Abey, B., Hurni, L.: Final model methodology and information exchange. INFRARISK project deliverable D4.2 (2016). https://www.infrarisk-fp7.eu/deliverables

7. van Gelder, P., van Erp, N.: Stress test framework for systems INFRARISK project deliverable D6.2 (2016). https://www.infrarisk-fp7.eu/deliverables
8. D'Ayala, D., Gehl, P.: Fragility functions matrix. INFRARISK project deliverable D3.2 (2015). https://www.infrarisk-fp7.eu/deliverables
9. Clarke, J., Corbally, R., OBrien, E.: Case study results. INFRARISK project deliverable D8.2 (2016). https://www.infrarisk-fp7.eu/deliverables
10. Jimenez, J.M., Garcia-Fernandez, M.: INFRARISK Technical Report Development of Seismic Hazard Modelling for Low-Probability Extreme Ground Motions (2016). https://www.infrarisk-fp7.eu/deliverables
11. Sabeur, Z., et al.: The Integrated Decision Support Tool. In: INFRARISK Project Final Conference, Dragados, Madrid, 29th September 2016. https://www.youtube.com/watch?v=nK2li3t8NU4

UNISDR Global Assessment Report - Current and Emerging Data and Compute Challenges

Nils gentschen Felde[1], Mabel Cristina Marulanda Fraume[2],
Matti Heikkurinen[1(✉)], Dieter Kranzlmüller[3], and Julio Serje[2]

[1] Ludwig-Maximilians-Universität München (LMU), Munich, Germany
{felde,heikku}@nm.ifi.lmu.de
[2] The United Nations Office for Disaster Risk Reduction (UNISDR),
Geneva, Switzerland
{marulandafraume,serje}@un.org
[3] Leibniz Supercomputing Centre of the Bavarian Academy of Sciences
and Humanities, Garching bei München, Germany
Dieter.Kranzlmueller@lrz.de

Abstract. This paper discusses the data and compute challenges of the global collaboration producing the UNISDR Global Assessment Report on Disaster Risk Reduction. The assessment produces estimates – such as the "Probable Maximum Loss" – of the annual disaster losses due to natural hazards. The data is produced by multi-disciplinary teams in different organisations and countries that need to manage their compute and data challenges in a coherent and consistent manner.

The compute challenge can be broken down into two phases: hazard modelling and loss calculation. The modelling is based on production of datasets describing flood, earthquake, storm etc. scenarios, typically thousands or tens of thousands scenarios per country. Transferring these datasets for the loss calculation presents a challenge – already at the current resolution used in the simulations. The loss calculation analyses the likely impact of these scenarios based on the location of the population and assets, and the risk reduction mechanisms (such as early warning systems or zoning regulations) in place. As the loss calculation is the final stage in the production of the assessment report, the algorithms were optimised to minimise risks of delays. This also paves the way for a more dynamic assessment approach, allowing refining national or regional analysis "on demand".

The most obvious driver of the future compute and data challenges will be the increased spatial resolution of the assessment that is needed to more accurately reflect the impact of natural disasters. However, the changes in the production model mentioned above and changing policy frameworks will also play a role. In parallel to these developments, aligning the current community engagement approaches (such as the open data portal) with the internal data management practices holds considerable promise for further improvements.

Keywords: Hazard and loss modelling · Probabilistic modelling
Disaster risk · Distributed data management

J. Hřebíček et al. (Eds.): ISESS 2017, IFIP AICT 507, pp. 315–326, 2017.
https://doi.org/10.1007/978-3-319-89935-0_26

1   Introduction

This paper describes the data and compute challenges related to the production of the biennial Global Assessment Reports (GAR) [1], key documents providing high-level overviews of the status of the disaster risk reduction activities on the global level. The production of the data these documents are based on – hazard scenarios, exposure information and vulnerability modelling – is performed by distributed collaborations and coordinated by UN Office for Disaster Risk Reduction (UNISDR). The risk calculation that provides estimates of the likely annual losses due to natural disasters represents a time-critical challenge, both in terms of organising the necessary computational processes to produce and verify the results, and in terms of managing the data sets in a consistent way. In parallel to the GAR-specific analysis, making the modelling data available as an open data service could support numerous additional research activities. These issues and goals form the context of the ongoing collaboration between UNISDR, LMU and LRZ.

While the type of large-scale disaster risk modelling GAR represents is most likely unique, we can see similarities with overall process and organisation as well as technical approaches with certain initiatives in other research domains. For example, the overall organisational structure resembles the approach used by global High-Energy Physics (HEP) collaborations. However, managing the complex, interdependent evolution of the interfaces (both physical and software ones) between thousands of components in a typical HEP project has necessitating developing relatively rigid and formalised organisational processes. This makes most of the tools developed to support HEP collaborations (ranging from document management systems - such as EDMS [2] - to global data/compute systems such as Worldwide LHC Computing Grid [3]) developed for HEP collaborations not optimal for the GAR process.

Perhaps the closest analogue can be found from the earth observation domain. The Group on Earth Observations (GEO) has launched the GEO-DARMA [4] initiative with a goal of bringing earth observation data into disaster risk management. The effort builds on earlier initiatives focusing on specific hazards (floods, volcanoes) and aims to extend the focus from supporting the immediate, acute response to supporting preparedness and risk reduction. However, at the time of writing the initiative is still in its early stages.

2   Global Assessment Report - GAR

2.1   Background

UNISDR was established in 1999 and its role in the UN system is to serve as the focal point for disaster risk reduction activities to ensure coordination and synergies between UN organisations, and regional and national activities. The two major UN policy documents bringing all this guidance together into top-level policy documents are the 2005 Hyogo Framework for Action [5] and the 2015 Sendai Framework for Disaster Risk Reduction [6]. The GAR process played a key role in implementing the Hyogo Framework and in the preparations of the Sendai Framework. It provided concrete data and examples of how the policies implemented (or to be implemented), changing natural conditions (e.g. climate change), population movements and major infrastructure projects are influencing the likely consequences (lives lost and direct economic losses) of natural hazards.

On the abstract level, the Global Risk Assessment processes of GAR 13 and GAR 15 are based on building three datasets used to generate risk metrics such as the "Loss Exceedance Curve" (LEC), the "Average Annual Loss" (AAL) and the Probable Maximum Loss (PML) plot the for the different hazards considered for each country. The data necessary for performing the global risk assessment of the GAR15report are:

- Hazard data, consisting of groups of simulated scenarios for each of the natural hazards for each of the natural hazard (earthquake, tsunami, riverine flood, cyclonic wind, storm surge and so on) used in the analysis. Each set of simulated scenarios must comply with the certain key requirements, such as being mutually exclusive, collectively exhaustive and having an annual frequency of occurrence associated with them.
- Exposure data, describing each exposed asset with a set of attributes such as their geographical location, structural characteristics, construction material type, economic value (among others).
- Vulnerability data, characterising the exposed asset with a set of attributes describing their relevant characteristics that determine how sensitive they are to different hazards at different intensities.

Current GAR information linked to other datasets allow further evaluations and analysis. For example, risk associated to hydrometeorological hazards are strongly influenced by climate change, hence the IPCC data IPCC [7] data and reports used as an input for simulation of new hazard scenarios considering climate change. Similarly, the exposure data used includes contributions collected using crowdsourcing approach based on OpenStreetmap [8] and the vulnerability data can be improved by counting with better information of exposed assets. Additional data sources, such as OECD macroeconomic data, are used to conceptualise the disaster risk metrics. These dependencies are a partial rationale for the relatively frequent releases of the GAR.

The key output of the analysis are the country-level summaries presented in the Global Assessment report (a typical view of the online version is presented in Fig. 1). This distils a complex and multi-faceted analysis into a summary with few key indicators that are suitable for steering policy-level decision making in the UN member states.

As a result, the environmental modelling behind GAR can have a major societal impact. While not legally binding, the GAR recommendations have an impact on national legislation and e.g. zoning decisions – both areas that unavoidably have an impact on economic situations and prospects of both public and private sector entities. In the long-term it has been shown that most of the investments in risk reduction are "profitable" in the sense that investments will eventually prevent direct economic losses that would have been several times higher than the money spent on protection (as an example, analysis of government-funded flood defence schemes in the UK showed an average benefit–cost ratio or 9.5:1 [9]). However, statistically major natural hazards usually have several decades between each occurrence, complicating the benefit-cost

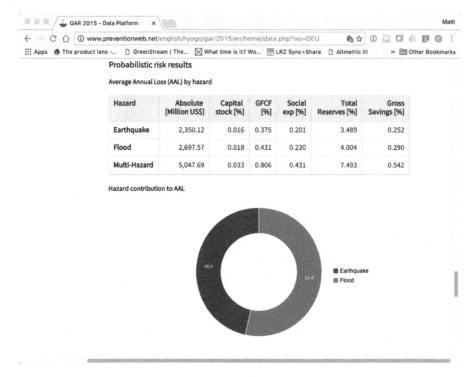

Fig. 1. A small sample of some of the risk results of Germany as presented in the online version of the GAR. The average annual losses are put in the context of key macroeconomic indicators of the country, such as the Gross Fixed Capital Formation (GFCF) that measures the annual net increase of fixed assets owned by business sector, government and households and Social Expenditure. This contextualisation illustrates the load on the society natural disasters represent more effectively than mere average annual loss figures would.

calculations. Justifying the immediate costs (loss of revenue or increased tax burden) by increased resilience in situations that statistically occur e.g. once every 50 years can be politically challenging.

For reasons outlined above, the results of the modelling can be expected to be under more scrutiny than a typical peer-review process for an academic publication. This pressure is further increased by the fact that the scale of the problem necessitates limiting the granularity of the analysis from what would be possible on local or regional analysis. Thus, the modelling software, loss calculation process and all the related data management practices need to be monitored very carefully.

2.2 GAR Contents

As outlined earlier, the GAR analysis process needs to take into an account changes in the hazards themselves (e.g. increased frequency of extreme weather events), the developments in the distribution of population and infrastructure (e.g. urbanisation) and the impact of the policies implemented so far (e.g. changes in building codes, flood barriers, early warning systems and so on). Based on input data from UN member states and from other sources (such as WMO and IPCC), a large-scale simulation effort will produce tens of thousands to millions of hazard-specific scenarios (e.g. flood, seismic, tropical storms etc.) describing the location and intensity of the natural hazard. The hazard- specific scenarios are put together with the country-specific exposure (geographical location and physical attributes) and their associated vulnerability corresponding to each hazard in order to perform probabilistic calculation of risk (likely losses).

The resulting risk metrics such as the AAL and PML for different return periods are put into context, e.g. by comparing the average direct economic losses to key macroeconomic indicators (see Figs. 1 and 2). This can be used to gain a quick overview of the risks on the global scale (see Fig. 3). An interactive viewer [10] is also available online.

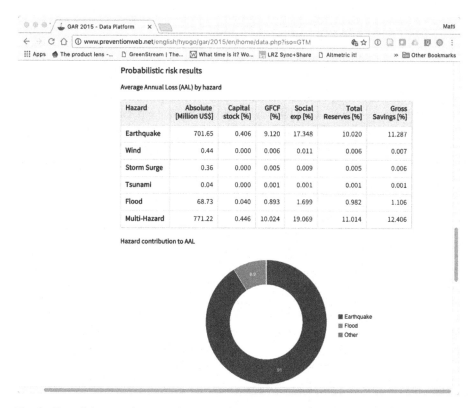

Fig. 2. Part of the annual average loss data of Guatemala illustrate how the impact on society is considerably more severe despite the absolute losses being lower than the German ones (Fig. 1)

The implementation of the Sendai framework for disaster risk reduction will increase the interest on both the GAR reports themselves, as well as the underlying data. The new framework for disaster risk reduction calls for more ambitious

Global multi-hazard average annual loss in relation to capital investment[11]

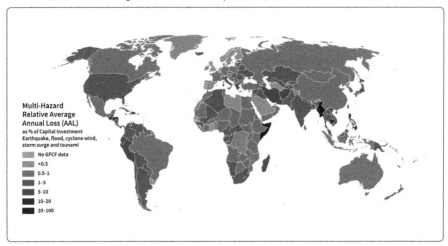

Fig. 3. A global summary of the proportional impact of the AAL to national economies

monitoring and modelling of risk. The plans to move into a "on demand" approach for risk modelling – as well as related policy developments that e.g. call for taking disaster risk into account when planning any investments – increase the demands on the assessment process. In addition, they make the provision of direct access to hazard, exposure and vulnerability data an important tool for increasing synergies between these activities.

3   The GAR Compute Challenge

The GAR compute challenge can be broken into two parts: generating the hazard scenarios and combining them with the exposure database and the associated vulnerability functions to calculate the potential losses. The main dependencies between these steps are presented in Fig. 4. The tools used in this process are heterogeneous, usually developed independently by the teams who are responsible for specific subtasks. Thus, the mode of operations is both globally distributed and very heterogeneous. On the technical level the CAPRA-GIS [11] toolkit plays an important integrating role: it provides the common formats for presenting hazard scenarios, as well as providing foundations for the overall loss calculation process. Hence the computational challenges have a clear interface between them.

3.1   Production of Hazard Scenario Files

The hazard scenarios are produced using a wide variety of methods, ranging from models running on powerful desktop computers to ones using computer clusters to perform the work. The basic probabilistic process is similar: the hazards scenarios are

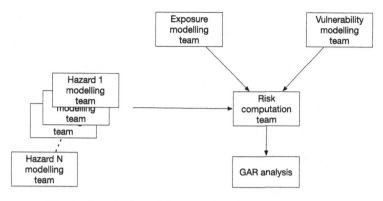

Fig. 4. Organisation of the teams involved in GAR analysis

produced independent from each other and can thus be considered trivially paral-lelisable processes. The implementation tools range from software developed completely in-house to models that run on platforms such as Matlab. However, despite the considerable computing resources needed, this step is rarely a time critical issue, as the schedule for producing the data is known well in advance and due to lack of dependencies between individual calculations any additional resources that can be brought in will speed up the process.

This situation may well change if the anticipated move to a more dynamic GAR process will be extended to the production of scenario files. For example, the overview document describing the latest approach to the production of the flood model data [12] lists 19 different external datasets used to initiate and fine-tune models, which represents a part of the process that is inherently serial in nature, representing an execution step that will not benefit from additional computing resources.

3.2   Loss Calculation

The performance of the loss calculation step tends to be the most time critical part of the Global Risk Assessment process – already with the 2-year publication cycle. Any unanticipated delay in the generation of the hazard scenarios will delay the overall loss calculation. Furthermore, due to the importance of presenting the data on per-country basis, summarising the loss estimates of large countries (such as China) can take a very long time.

Development of the CAPRA framework needs also to ensure that any new versions of the software produce same results as the original reference software versions. Hence, short-term developments tend to be incremental in nature. However, this incremental approach may face challenges with increased resolution (a uniform 1 km × 1 km grid instead of the current approach using resolutions ranging from 1 km × 1 km to 30 km × 30 km, depending on the hazard and geography of the region) and especially more dynamic production schedule of the GAR.

At the moment, the risk calculations are performed using two different versions of the CAPRA software: the original, single-threaded version (implemented in Visual

Basic and available as part of the overall CAPRA-GIS package [11]) is used for most of the risks, as it is sufficiently powerful for risks where high-resolution modelling is not needed (e.g. modelling of droughts). A version of the risk calculation engine that has been parallelised and ported to Java (by the UNISDR team in collaboration with LMU and LRZ) is currently the reference implementation for flood modelling and is planned to be taken into use for the assessment of earthquakes in the near future. The Java version is already capable of exploiting shared memory parallelism and achieving close to a factor 50 speed up compared to single-threaded version. It is likely that further, incremental development of this version of the software will be sufficient to cope with the increase in resolution in the major publications (with the 2-year production cycle). However, additional optimisation is likely needed for the on-demand production of the reports (some potential approaches are discussed in chapter 6 of this paper).

4   The GAR Data Challenge

The current GAR data challenge can be broken down into two main phases: the hazard scenario stage and the data transfer to UNISDR. The vulnerability and exposure datasets are very small in comparison, and produced in more centralised manner. In either of the cases the amount of data is not a major problem per se, but rather the latencies introduced by the data production and transfer. While the hazard scenario development may in some cases need considerable resources, even the largest global hazard dataset will be of the order of few Terabytes. The situation might change slightly in the future due to higher resolutions used in the risk modelling. However, as the information is transmitted in compression format move from "5 km × 5 km" to "1 km × 1 km" resolution will not mean that the amount of data would automatically grow by factor of 25.

A bigger issue is moving the data to the loss calculation team in an efficient and coherent manner. While the current datasets are not excessively large (of the order of few Terabytes), limitations of the network infrastructure available to some of the partners in the collaboration necessitates moving the data by sending physical hard drives through postal or courier services. This approach is unlikely to cause insurmountable problems in the near future, as long as the resolution of the analysis will not be increased dramatically. It is likely that the capacities of commodity hard drives will grow at sufficient rate to match the increase of the data volume.

However, the approach is not without its issues: copying the data from the original storage system to a transient media may introduce issues with consistency, especially if there will be additional versions of the data that complement the biannual GAR process. Developing processes and metadata approaches to handle these issues are relatively straightforward to manage in setting where the data processing is done by a relatively small, established collaboration. However, turning the hazard, vulnerability and exposure datasets into open data products and services used by a broader research community will likely bring up additional issues that GAR collaboration needs to address e.g. through additional documentation or training activities.

4.1   Impact of the on-Demand Process

Traditionally the GAR process has required storing only a complete, global dataset for each of the biannual publications. This means that even considerable increase in resolution will not increase storage capacity needed beyond what is possible to handle using commodity solutions. The two-year cycle will also create a framework for managing versions of the datasets in a very intuitive manner: even a directory structure that is based on the production year of GAR is sufficient in most cases.

The on-demand process will create additional challenges. When parts of the analysis will complement the main GAR dataset with updated information related to a country or a region, the consistency of the data management and the ability of the metadata system to maintain link between a publication and the corresponding dataset will need to be reassessed. With the increased resolution it is also possible that – if these additional model executions and subsequent versioning of the result datasets are a frequent occurrence – the size of the overall dataset grows to a level that makes moving it challenging. This may create a need to re-examine the current distributed computing model, as in more and more cases performing the computation in the same computing centre that holds the relevant datasets are stored will be advantageous or even necessary from the performance point of view.

5   Open Data Prototype and Pilot

The motivation for investigating the feasibility of an open data approach are manifold, ranging from principles related to transparency of the GAR process to catalysing and supporting open innovation ecosystem that could also uncover novel approaches to disaster risk reduction. The data is already shared on request and used actively by third parties (e.g. by insurance companies to support their internal risk assessment processes). However, providing potential new users instant access is seen as a key method for removing barriers to new research and innovation activities.

The technical approach chosen for the open data pilot can be characterised as a "Minimal Viable Product" approach. The starting point is simple: a download portal addressing the key requirements of the GAR team and the external parties participating in the "beta phase" of the open data pilot:

- Download functionality: browse and download individual files or directories
- Mechanisms for branding and ensuring that users are aware of the licensing issues and key disclaimers related to interpretation of the data.
- Basic mechanisms for linking metadata to the data itself
- To be considered: upload/updates through the web interface – maintain consistency between different copies and with metadata.

The first versions of the portal were developed at LMU in fall 2016, and will be used to refine the requirements of the production version that may eventually become part of the formal LRZ service portfolio (Fig. 5).

Once sufficiently mature, the solution will most likely be merged with the current, download functionality [13] that is included in online version of the GAR, providing

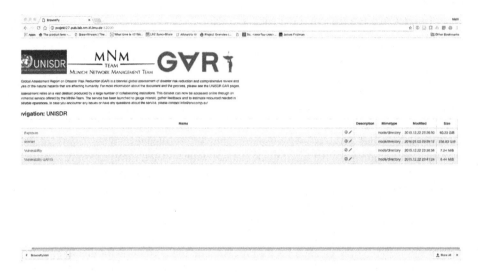

Fig. 5. A screenshot of an early version of the download portal (proof of concept) used to gather feedback related to the functionality.

access to a limited subset of the information. The immediate needs for further development are mainly related to supporting archive file formats that are commonly used by the intended user community (possibly zip or rar formats in addition to tar.gz). In the longer term, aligning the data download functionality with the online visualisation tools and the Risk Atlas will also need to be considered.

Outside the purely technical issues, the open data pilot may bring up new requirements in terms of engaging with the community. Making the data available in a way that decouples it from the interpretations made by the experts (either in GAR or by the groups who developed the hazard models) may bring up situations where the interpretation – or misinterpretation – of the data outside the strict UNISDR scope should at least be brought to the attention of the original experts. Thus, supporting functionality such as social media integration may be deemed a useful complement to the download functionality itself.

6   Future Directions

The open data portal will most likely play a role in the launch of the 2017 version of the Risk Atlas that provides a consistent geographical view of the disaster risk information, allowing business, investors and international organisations assess and compare the risks and resilience to the occurrence of natural hazard events in different countries more intuitively. Linking the GAR data organically to such an overview document will most likely increase interest in both. Thus, determining methods to discover and support new use cases emerging from the use of Risk Atlas and GAR data will proceed in parallel with the implementation of the first version of the open data service.

We foresee that the data management back-end will need additional functionality as the dynamic, on-demand approach to the production of GAR and country reports will be adapted. In the absence of a clear two-year cycle of report production, issues such as persistent identifiers, versioning of the data and metadata need to be reviewed. Initial assessment of solutions such as KIT Datamanger [14] and CKAN [15] as tools to meet these new requirements is already ongoing.

In response to the computing challenges related to risk calculation outlined in the chapter 4.1, more advanced parallelisation approaches are already being studied by the collaboration. For example, both MapReduce [16] and MPI [17] based approaches could allow parallelisation beyond the limitations of the shared memory space and – with sufficient resources – even allow in-memory processing of the data.

The new data management approaches and tools discussed will obviously also have an impact on the processes that are internal to GAR collaboration manages the data. They may also influence the interfaces the GAR data services can support for the third-party analysis. As an example of a potential explorative research topic, investigating approaches where the analysis of the data could be performed at the storage location in a flexible manner (e.g. by shipping the analysis code embedded in a virtual machine or software container to data) could support more efficient and flexible management and use of growing and increasingly dynamic GAR data.

References

1. UNISDR: Global Assessment Report on Disaster Risk Reduction (GAR) 2015. http://www.preventionweb.net/english/hyogo/gar/2015/en/home/index.html
2. The CERN Engineering and Equipment Data Management Service. https://espace.cern.ch/edms-services/default.aspx
3. Worldwide LHC Computing Grid. http://wlcg.web.cern.ch/
4. GEO-DARMA = Data Access for Risk Management, Group on Earth Observations. https://www.earthobservations.org/activity.php?id=49
5. UN-ISDR: Hyogo Framework for Action 2005–2015: Building Resilience of Nations and Communities to Disasters. United Nations – International Strategy for Disaster Reduction, UN/ISDR-07-2007
6. United Nations General Assembly: Sendai Framework for Disaster Risk Reduction 2015 – 2030, A/CONF.224/L.2
7. Intergovernmental Panel on Climate Change. https://www.ipcc.ch/
8. OpenStreetMap Foundation, OpenStreetmap Project. https://www.openstreetmap.org/
9. UK National Audit Office report: Strategic Flood Risk Management, p. 38, paragraph 2.26, ISBN 9781904219460
10. UNISDR: Global Assessment Report on Disaster Risk Reduction 2015, Risk Data Platform CAPRAViewer. http://risk.preventionweb.net/capraviewer/
11. CAPRA Probabilistic Risk Assessment Program, CAPRA-GIS. http://www.ecapra.org/capra-gis
12. Rudari, R., et al.: Improvement of the Global Flood Model for the GAR 2015, Input Paper prepared for the Global Assessment Report on Disaster Risk Reduction (2015). http://www.preventionweb.net/english/hyogo/gar/2015/en/bgdocs/risk-section/CIMAFoundation, ImprovementoftheGlobalFloodModelfortheGAR15.pdf

13. UNISDR: Risk Data and Software Download Facility. http://risk.preventionweb.net/capraviewer/download.jsp
14. WM, KIT – Universität des Landes Baden-Württemberg and nationales Forschungszentrum in der Helmholtz-Gemeinschaft: Kit Data Manager – The Research Data Repository Platform. http://datamanager.kit.edu/
15. CKAN Association: CKAN – The open source data portal software. http://ckan.org/
16. Dean, J., Ghemawat, S.: MapReduce: simplified data processing on large clusters. In: OSDI 2004: Sixth Symposium on Operating System Design and Implementation, San Francisco, CA, December 2004. https://research.google.com/archive/mapreduce.html
17. MPI Forum, MPI Documents. http://mpi-forum.org/docs/

Information Systems

netCDF-LD SKOS: Demonstrating Linked Data Vocabulary Use Within netCDF-Compliant Files

Nicholas J. Car[1]([⊠]), Alex Ip[1] [iD], and Kelsey Druken[2]

[1] Geoscience Australia, Symonston, ACT, Australia
{nicholas.car,alex.ip}@ga.gov.au
[2] Australian National Computational Infrastructure, Acton, ACT, Australia
kelsey.druken@anu.edu.au

Abstract. netCDF, the widely-used array-oriented data container file format, has previously been extended in an initiative called netCDF-LD, to include Linked Data metadata elements. In this paper, we build on that initiative with demonstrations of a Simple Knowledge Organization System (SKOS)-aware file format and associated tooling. First, we discuss a very simple way to reference SKOS vocabulary data stored online in netCDF files via Linked Data. Second, we describe our prototype *ncskos* tools, including '*ncskosdump*', which wraps the well-known '*ncdump*' tool used to print out netCDF headers and data. Our tools utilize some of the features of Linked Data and SKOS vocabularies to enhance the metadata of netCDF files by allowing: multilingual metadata label retrieval; alternate term name retrieval; and hierarchical vocabulary relationship navigation. In doing this, *ncskosdump* preserves the *ncdump* practice of writing output in standard CDL (network Common Data Language). For the demonstration of theses formats and tools, we relate how we have included URI links in netCDF files to SKOS concepts within a demonstration vocabulary and how the *ncskos* tools can be used to manage these files in ways that are not possible using only regular netCDF metadata. We also discuss problems we perceived in scaling Linked Data functionality when applying it to large numbers of netCDF files or in multiple file management sessions, and how we have catered for these. Finally, we indicate some future work in the area of more comprehensive Linked Data representation in netCDF files.

Keywords: netCDF · netCDF-LD · Linked data · Inference · Vocabularies
SKOS

1 Introduction

NetCDF files [1] are containers that include both data – usually array-oriented scientific data – and metadata. The intention of the metadata inclusion is that netCDF files should be 'self-describing' meaning the metadata (usually referred to as being in a 'header') describes the rest of the file (the data), as well as an arbitrary number of name/value attributes which together allow for accurate interpretations of the data and thus sensible use of it. Some communities, such as the Climate and Forecasting (CF) Conventions [2],

© IFIP International Federation for Information Processing 2017
Published by Springer International Publishing AG 2017. All Rights Reserved
J. Hřebíček et al. (Eds.): ISESS 2017, IFIP AICT 507, pp. 329–337, 2017.
https://doi.org/10.1007/978-3-319-89935-0_27

use standardized name/value attributes to enhance metadata understanding between different parties leading towards interoperability of netCDF data. In most cases, those communities achieve interoperability by constraining the metadata values, potentially reducing its richness.

The Semantic Web [3] is a set of extensions to Web standards that allow for data exchange and, ultimately, knowledge representation. Collections of terms (vocabularies) and knowledge graphs (ontologies) can be codified and, through Linked Data principles [4], be published and accessed. The ability for Linked Data links in any Internet-connected system to give live access to rich vocabulary and ontology information published on Web is potentially very useful for netCDF data. Such links in file metadata allow associations with further, more detailed, metadata, meaning that not all of the metadata relevant to a netCDF file needs to be contained within the netCDF container itself. While this may seem to break with the netCDF aim of the format being self-describing, we believe that conventions that maintain any information externally to netCDF files, such as the CF Convention's relations between terms given in a website hierarchy, have already broken with this (what we believe to be impossible) aim.

Agreed systems of knowledge representation (ontologies) can be used to define the type (classes) of knowledge within a domain. One such ontology is the Simple Knowledge Organization System (SKOS) [5] which has been made to represent items within vocabularies and thesauri. Rather than constraining the metadata values of netCDF files to achieve interoperability, Semantic Web and Linked Data methodologies can be used to constrain the mechanisms for describing and accessing metadata without constraining the content itself. In addition to achieving interoperability via the use of SKOS, since it is a standardized and a well-known ontology, SKOS use also instantly provides netCDF file makers with access to a large number of already published SKOS vocabularies and their content, such as those employed by Geoscience Australia[1] and several versions of the CF Conventions' terms which have recently been published[2].

Sophisticated methods for the inclusion of Linked Data within netCDF files have been demonstrated at a previous ISESS conference called 'netCDF-LD' [6] and an example of netCDF-LD using Linked Data reasoning has also been given recently [7]. This paper is both a 'next step' to those bodies of work and also a step back with respect to the complexity of implementation. We present a simplified mechanism for referencing SKOS data within a netCDF file (Sect. 2) which, we believe, is easily understood by users of regular netCDF data, and yet which delivers at least some the benefits that a fully-fledged combination of netCDF and Linked Data offer. Due to the simple nature of our encoding mechanism, we can demonstrate a simple wrapper for the well-known *ncdump* command line tool, which we call *ncskosdump*, which prints out netCDF data and metadata. Details of this tool are given in Sect. 3. In Sect. 4, we describe a test deployment of SKOS data to netCDF files that references a demonstration SKOS

---

[1] http://pid.geoscience.gov.au/def/voc/.

[2] http://vocab.nerc.ac.uk/collection/P07/current/. The same SKOS vocabulary is republished at http://auscope-services-test.arrc.csiro.au/elda-demo/nerc/resource?_view=skos&uri=http://vocab.nerc.ac.uk/collection/P07/current/.

vocabulary that we have built. Vocabularies like this are to be used in place of community-agreed conventions for the classification of those files, using features of the vocabulary, using *ncskos* tools. In Sect. 5, we discuss how the netCDF combined with the Linked Data and Semantic Web methodologies and *ncskos* tools we have presented here might be made more efficient when used at scale. Finally, in Sect. 6, we indicate a few areas of future work regarding more comprehensive linked data representation in netCDF files.

2 Simple Linked Data Encoding

While Yu et al. [5] proposed and Baird et al. [6] have demonstrated sophisticated integration of Linked Data into netCDF files, we have tested simples of integrations only whereby we place Universal Resource Indicator (URI) links [8] to SKOS concepts within attribute metadata in netCDF files. Our reason for taking this very simple approach is to enable the demonstration, and ultimately the adoption, of some limited Linked Data and Semantic Web functionality with the lowest possible barrier to uptake. This link inclusion approach delivers files that very closely resemble 'normal' netCDF files that conform with the netCDF4 specification. Figure 1 shows some basic netCDF metadata taken from a file used by the Unidata community for the demonstration of metadata extraction using the *ncdump* tool.

Figure 2 shows this same header metadata with the standard_name key/value pair replaced with a URI link (key: skos_concept_uri) to a segment of a SKOS vocabulary; the entry for the concept of "sea surface temperature". This linking allows a whole set of SKOS data – the entire vocabulary the concept is drawn from – to be associated with the netCDF file containing the link via link look-up ("dereferencing"), rather than just the single textual value of "sea_surface_temperature" which may have further information associated with it which is not discoverable in any standardized way. The link in this example is to data in a demonstration vocabulary that we have built to replicate a small portion of the CF Conventions' [2] terms, with some of our own additions for testing purposes, relating to surface temperature using the SKOS ontology.

3 The *ncskosdump* Tool

The netCDF specification includes a set of software tools used to manipulate netCDF files [6]. These tools allow people to view netCDF metadata and data, create netCDF files and view visual representations of netCDF's gridded arrays. Some examples of tools, their developers and their usages are given in Table 1.

In order to make our simple SKOS-only deployment of netCDF-LD usable by people without detailed knowledge of Linked Data, we have created a prototype Python[3] utility called *ncskosdump* which wraps the *ncdump* tool (see Table 1) and adds

---

[3] The Python programming language, v2.7: https://www.python.org/download/releases/2.7/.

```
float tos(time, lat, lon) ;
   tos:standard_name = "sea_surface_temperature" ;
   tos:long_name = "Sea Surface Temperature" ;
   tos:units = "K" ;
   tos:cell_methods = "time: mean (interval: 30 minutes)" ;
   tos:_FillValue = 1.e+20f ;
   tos:missing_value = 1.e+20f ;
   tos:original_name = "sosstsst" ;
   tos:original_units = "degC" ;
```

Fig. 1. A sample of normal netCDF metadata for the time variable within an example file. (http://www.unidata.ucar.edu/software/netcdf/examples/files.html), see table "Sample files following CF conventions"

```
float tos(time, lat, lon) ;
   tos:skos__concept_uri =
"http://pid.geoscience.gov.au/def/voc/netCDF-
LD/sea_surface_temperature";
   tos:units = "K" ;
   tos:cell_methods = "time: mean (interval: 30 minutes)" ;
   tos:_FillValue = 1.e+20f ;
   tos:missing_value = 1.e+20f ;
   tos:original_units = "degC" ;
```

Fig. 2. Similar netCDF metadata to Fig. 1 with key/value pairs removed and a `skos_concept_uri` key/value pair added with the URI of a concept in a demonstration vocabulary (Demo vocabulary online at http://pid.geoscience.gov.au/def/voc/netCDF-LD-st-demo).

Table 1. Several netCDF tools

Name	Creators	Purpose
ncdump[a]	Unidata, the makers of netCDF	Command-line utility converts netCDF data to human-readable text form (CDL or XML)
ncgen[b]	Unidata	A program that creates a netCDF dataset fro CDL input
ncview[c]	Scripps institution of oceanography	A netCDF visual browser
The netCDF operators toolkit[d]	A community of developers	Command-line programs that take netCDF, HDF, and/or DAP files and derive new data, compute statistics, print or otherwise manipulate them

[a] http://www.unidata.ucar.edu/software/netcdf/netcdf-4/newdocs/ncdump-man-1.html.

[b] http://www.unidata.ucar.edu/software/netcdf/netcdf-4/newdocs/ncgen-man-1.html.

[c] http://meteora.ucsd.edu/ ~ pierce/ncview_home_page.html.

[d] http://nco.sourceforge.net/.

a series of options for the retrieval and display of Linked Data that the tool is able to extract from a netCDF file, including links to vocabulary terms as described in Sect. 2.

ncskosdump finds and dereferences SKOS concept URIs to access vocabulary metadata and uses a series of SPARQL queries [9] on that data to present requested subsets of it to users.

The tool is presented as a Git[4]-based code repository online which is catalogued at http://pid.geoscience.gov.au/dataset/103620 (repository version 1.0). That repository contains comprehensive documentation and test code & data for the tool, including all examples used in this paper. The vocabulary used for testing is online at http://pid. geoscience.gov.au/def/voc/netCDF-LD-eg-ToS (version 1.1) and a copy of its content is stored within the repository in the file examples/tos.ttl.

4   A Deployment Scenario

A series of small netCDF test files (included in the data directory of the code repository) has been created to test and demonstrate the Linked Data functionality of the *ncskos* tools, including *ncskosdump*. One file was created for each valid concept in the test vocabulary, and a "*skos__concept_uri*" variable attribute in the file set to the URI of the Concept. In addition, one file was created with its "*skos__concept_uri*" variable attribute value set to an un-resolveable ("non-dereferenceable", in Linked Data jargon), dummy URI; another with a valid global "*skos__concept_uri*" attribute (as opposed to an attribute of a variable); and yet another with no "*skos__concept_uri*" global or variable attribute value defined for error case testing.

The *ncskosdump* command, like its ancestor, *ncdump*, could be invoked within a script for each netCDF file, and its Common Data Language (CDL) or eXtensible Markup Language (XML) output parsed to infer relationships between concepts. This approach would, however, be extremely inefficient, so Python classes (*ConceptHierarchy* and *NCConceptHierarchy*) have been implemented in order to facilitate efficient programmatic handling of large numbers of files and the resolution of their URIs using the same Linked Data mechanisms implemented for *ncskosdump*.

The script *skos_inferencing_demo.py* inspects each of the specified netCDF files, resolves its URI(s), where possible, and then displays the file paths and variable names grouped hierarchically by Concept as indented lists, as shown in Fig. 3. The Concept hierarchies are inferred from the broader/narrower results of the SKOS queries. The Concepts are cached in memory within a session, so each Concept is resolved only once across multiple files, and cached on persistent storage between sessions by using YAML[5] files of concept retrieval results. By default, the concept hierarchies are populated recursively from each linked Concept all the way up to the Top Concept(s) of the vocabulary to provide the full context of the Concepts in the files. It is also possible to recursively build the full Concept hierarchy downward to the narrowest Concepts by specifying the "–narrower" command line option.

---

[4] Git is a distributed version control system: https://git-scm.com/.

[5] YAML is a human-readable data serialization language: https://en.wikipedia.org/wiki/YAML.

```
> python skos_inferencing_demo.py --lang=pl C:\data
...
temperatura powierzchni
  C:\data\sst.ltm.1999-2000_skos_surface_temperature.nc:sst
        temperatura powierzchni morza
          C:\data\sst.ltm.1999-2000_skos_sea_surface_temperature.nc:sst
                sea surface skin temperature (English)
                  C:\data\sst.ltm.1999-
2000_skos_sea_surface_skin_temperature.nc:sst
                sea surface subskin temperature (English)
                  C:\data\sst.ltm.1999-
2000_skos_sea_surface_subskin_temperature.nc:sst
                temperatura powierzchni morza do kwadratu
                  C:\data\sst.ltm.1999-
2000_skos_square_of_sea_surface_temperature.nc:sst

Unresolved URI dummy_uri
  C:\data\sst.ltm.1999-2000_skos_dummy_uri.nc:sst

Uncategorised (Missing URI)
  C:\data\sst.ltm.1999-2000_skos.nc
```

Fig. 3. Sample output from *skos_inferencing_demo.py* showing netCDF files and variables in hierarchical groupings with polish language labels. Note the fallback to English where Polish prefLabels are not defined.

In order to cater for another practical application of SKOS, the script skos_inferencing_demo.py also takes an optional command line argument "–altlabels = <altLabels>", where <altLabels> is a comma-separated list of case-sensitive altLabels (alternative names for a label) for which netCDF files and variables matching a corresponding or narrower Concept are listed. Sample output is shown in Fig. 4.

Current command line options for skos_inferencing_demo.py are as follows:

–verbose to enable verbose output

–lang = <lang_code> where *<lang_code>* is a two-character ISO 639-1:200 code for the language in which the results are sought

–narrower to recursively create complete tree of narrower concepts, not just ones resolved directly from URIs

–altLabels = <altLabel_list> where *<altLabel_list>* is a comma-separated list of altLabels to match in order to list their associated datasets

–retries = <max_retries> where *<max_retries>* is the maximum number of retries to attempt for unresolved URIs. Default retries = 0

–delay = <retry_delay_seconds> where *<retry_delay_seconds>* is the number of seconds to wait before each retry. Default delay = 2 s

–refresh to discard current file cache and repopulate the cache from scratch

```
> python skos_inferencing_demo.py --lang=pl -altlabels=SST,sst C:\data
…
altLabel matches

Concepts and datasets with altLabel "SST":
temperatura powierzchni morza
  C:\Users\Alex\git\ncskosdump\data\sst.ltm.1999-
2000_skos_sea_surface_temperature.nc:sst
        Narrower Concepts:
        sea surface skin temperature (English)
            C:\Users\Alex\git\ncskosdump\data\sst.ltm.1999-
2000_skos_sea_surface_skin_temperature.nc:sst
        sea surface subskin temperature (English)
            C:\Users\Alex\git\ncskosdump\data\sst.ltm.1999-
2000_skos_sea_surface_subskin_temperature.nc:sst
        temperatura powierzchni morza do kwadratu
            C:\Users\Alex\git\ncskosdump\data\sst.ltm.1999-
2000_skos_square_of_sea_surface_temperature.nc:sst

No concepts found with altLabel "sst"
```

Fig. 4. Sample output from *skos_inferencing_demo.py* showing search results using two altLabels "SST" & "sst". NetCDF files which match the corresponding concept, or its narrower concepts, are shown in hierarchical groupings with Polish language labels (where available).

5   Consideration of Scaling and Retrieval Strategies

The *ncskos* Python classes used in the current version of *skos_inferencing_demo.py* utilize in-memory caching of Concepts retrieved via SKOS queries within a single session and caches whole Concept hierarchies and their information on disk in YAML for use between equivalent sessions (i.e. sessions with the same SKOS options). This means that for most operations, the *ncskos* Python classes need only resolve (dereference) each Concept URI once which, for large numbers of files with the same URIs, greatly reduces network overheads and thus improves program performance.

   As with any client-side caching system, care needs to be taken to ensure that cached data is kept consistent with the point of truth (i.e. the source vocabulary online), hence the command matching and the ability for users to refresh the file cache. The current version of *skos_inferencing_demo.py* also resolves concept URIs recursively as required.

6   Future Work

Resolution strategy changes are likely with a better understanding of the tool's usage patterns, as indicated above. An alternative approach for efficient URI resolution might be to read all URIs within netCDF files and then resolve the multiple URIs in bulk using a much smaller number of queries. Where a complete concept hierarchy is required and the source(s) is/are resolvable, it may also be better to retrieve the entire concept hierarchy from each relevant vocabulary before matching individual URIs. The decision as to which approach is best for given scenarios cannot be determined until a larger number of community uses of this tool are available for analysis.

Additionally, extensions to the tool's ability to handle more forms of Linked Data encoded in netCDF files will surely be considered. Already the potential for handling multiple URIs per global or variable attribute (as a comma-separated list) has been implemented and tested during development, but was deemed to be problematic at this stage because of the potential for inconsistent or nonsensical user-defined combinations of URIs. This remains an area open to further investigation, since it may be very useful to be able to reference multiple, independent concept URIs if appropriate validation can be undertaken.

Current work being undertaken by the authors and members of a larger "netCDF-LD working group" are looking in to methods of full Linked Data representation within netCDF files, as indicated in [7]. Results from this work make prompt changes to SKOS Concept URI representation within netCDF files, perhaps through the use of URI and URI prefix (the "*skos__concept_uri*" key) aliasing that is more akin to Linked Data conventions.

7 Conclusions

Metadata "bloat" is a very real issue for many of today's scientific datasets, and it can be difficult to maintain consistency where metadata is replicated within data files. For example, complex hierarchical relationships are difficult to represent in metadata encapsulated within netCDF files and where such information is stored externally to the files, such as the CF Conventions community has done, that information may not be either easily discoverable or machine-readable. Linked Data provides a mechanism which can address these issues.

The simple Linked Data functionality demonstrated in our *ncskos* implementation can reference much richer metadata for netCDF files in standardized ways, including alternate language representations and the complete broader/narrower context of concepts as required. The attribute containing URIs to SKOS Concepts can coexist with existing netCDF metadata conventions such as the Climate and Forecasting (CF) [2] or Attribute Convention for Data Discovery (ACDD) [10] so that backwards-compatibility with 'normal' netCDF files and file use can be maintained. In addition, at least some of the well-known conventions (CF) have already been represented in SKOS vocabularies thus we expect that many of those initiatives will come to publish their term lists in ways compatible with this approach.

Our code has been written expressly to handle large numbers of netCDF files with multiple Linked Data concepts, and we are looking to move to real-world implementation in the very near future.

Acknowledgements. The authors thank the members of the netCDF-LD Working Group for their stimulation of work in this area and their thoughts around Linked Data representation in netCDF.

This paper is published with the permission of the CEO, Geoscience Australia.

References

1. UCAR: Network Common Data Form (NetCDF). http://www.unidata.ucar.edu/software/netcdf/. Accessed 29 Sept 2016
2. Eaton, B., Gregory, J., Drach, B., Taylor, K., Hankin, S.: NetCDF Climate and Forecast (CF) Metadata Conventions (2011). http://cfconventions.org/cf-conventions/v1.6.0/cf-conventions.html. Accessed 09 Jan 2017
3. Berners-Lee, T., Hendler, J., Lassila, O.: The Semantic Web. Scientific American Magazine, 17 May 2001. http://www.scientificamerican.com/article/the-semantic-web/. Accessed 29 Sept 2016
4. Berners-Lee, T.: Linked Data. Design Issues, W3C. https://www.w3.org/DesignIssues/LinkedData.html. Accessed 29 Sept 2016
5. Miles, A., Bechhofer, S. (eds.): SKOS Simple Knowledge Organization System Reference. W3C Recommendation, 18 August 2009. https://www.w3.org/TR/skos-reference/. Accessed 29 Sept 2016
6. Yu, J., Car, N.J., Leadbetter, A., Simons, B.A., Cox, S.J.D.: Towards linked data conventions for delivery of environmental data using netCDF. In: Denzer, R., Argent, R.M., Schimak, G., Hřebíček, J. (eds.) Environmental Software Systems. Infrastructures, Services and Applications. ISESS 2015, vol. 448, pp. 102–112. Springer, Cham (2015). https://doi.org/10.1007/978-3-319-15994-2_9
7. Biard, J.C., Yu, J., Hedley, M., Cox, S.J.D., Leadbetter, A., Car, N.J., Druken, K.A., Nativi, S., Davis, E.: Linking netCDF data with the semantic web - enhancing data discovery across domain. In: AGU Fall Meeting Advancing netCDF-CF for the Geoscience Community, San Francisco (2015)
8. Joint W3C/IETF URI Planning Interest Group: URIs, URLs, and URNs: Clarifications and Recommendations 1.0. Report from the joint W3C/IETF URI Planning Interest Group, W3C Note, 21 September 2001. https://www.w3.org/TR/uri-clarification/. Accessed 29 Sept 2016
9. Prud, E., Seaborne, A. (eds.): SPARQL Query Language for RDF. W3C Recommendation, 15 January 2008. https://www.w3.org/TR/rdf-sparql-query/. Accessed 29 Sept 2016
10. ESIP Federation. Category: Attribute Conventions Dataset Discovery, January 2015. http://wiki.esipfed.org/index.php?title=Category:Attribute_Conventions_Dataset_Discovery. Accessed 05 Jan 2017

Evolution of Environmental Information Models

Reusable Properties Bound to a Persistent URI

Katharina Schleidt[(✉)]

DataCove, Vienna, Austria
Kathi@datacove.eu

Abstract. Reusability of environmental data is essential for environmental research and control; standardized data models are being created by various organizations to facilitate this process. Due to the evolving nature of environmental science, these data models must be continuously extended for the support of new concepts, thus rapidly breaking the level of standardization achieved. The definition of reusable properties would allow for standardization of this extension process. In this paper, we first analyze the requirements to reusable properties, and explain the rational for the decision that reusable properties tightly bound to a URI would be the most apt solution; the following list of requirements was defined in order to compare the viability of the options proposed: URI Coupling, DataType Coupling, Semantics Coupling and Persistence. We then go on to explore possible avenues for implementation of reusable URI-Properties, whereby the following approaches where analysed for applicability: Data Types, Interfaces, MOF level adjustment of UML and a solution utilizing stereotypes for the definition and use of reusable URI-Properties. Of these approaches, all were deemed feasible except for the MOF level adjustment of UML; MOF level adjustment is not possible due to cardinality constraints within the MOF definition. Examples were created for the other 3 possibilities, including serialization options towards XML Schema. These examples were then compared with the requirements defined for URI-Properties; based on this analysis, the UML Stereotype based solution for the specification and use of reusable URI-Properties was deemed as most viable and is described in further detail.

1 Introduction

Access to environmental data is necessary for environmental research and control. Due to the complexity of environmental concerns, this task often requires the reuse of data originating from various sources. Triggered by this requirement, organizations from various environmental domains have started initiatives aimed at the provision of standardized access to environmental data; standardized data models for the exchange of various types of environmental data are now available, together with the required service definitions for discovery and access.

© IFIP International Federation for Information Processing 2017
Published by Springer International Publishing AG 2017. All Rights Reserved
J. Hřebíček et al. (Eds.): ISESS 2017, IFIP AICT 507, pp. 338–348, 2017.
https://doi.org/10.1007/978-3-319-89935-0_28

These developments should guarantee easy access to standardized and harmonized environmental data. However, many standardized data models cover only common concepts pertaining to a wide range of usage areas; thematic extensions are required for the support of specific community's requirements. As the thematic extensions develop, domains with similar requirements create parallel extensions; while these may be semantically identical, this fact cannot be simply verified [1]. Thus, after much effort, we find ourselves dangerously close to the starting point.

After discussions with various stakeholder representatives, the conclusion was reached that the most efficient mechanism to allow for flexible extension in a complex environment as described would be the introduction of reusable properties, such as commonly used within semantic technologies. An overview of implementation options for reusable properties is provided, together with an analysis of their viability.

2   Background and State of the Art

Various initiatives have been launched in the last years aimed at providing easy access to relevant data stemming from various environmental sub-domains through the standardization of data models and service specifications. While data standards are provided for core concepts, there is always a need to extend these concepts in order to support new or alternative requirements.

2.1   Background

In this paper, we use the European INSPIRE Initiative [2] as an illustrative example, and thus focus on the first approach.

The INSPIRE Directive

The INSPIRE Directive (2007/2/EC), specifying an Infrastructure for Spatial Information in the European Community, entered into force on the 15th of May 2007 with the aim to assure easy availability of high quality spatial data as required for the definition and enforcement of European Community environmental policy. 34 spatial data themes are covered by INSPIRE; data models and service specifications have been created accordingly. While aiming to be technology agnostic through flexibility in the serialization technology, the data modelling process was solely based on the ISO/OGC Suite of Spatial Standards together with its inherent data modelling requirements.

ISO/OGC Suite of Spatial Standards

As environmental data almost invariably has a spatial component, the International Standards Organisation (ISO) & Open Geospatial Consortium (OGC) Suite of Spatial Standards is increasingly being used for the creation of thematic application schemas. This trend has in turn led to the creation of various standards beyond the classical spatial domain, including data and service standards covering the provision of measurement data, be they individual observations, time-series or multidimensional coverages.

2.2 State of the Art

The technological basis both for the creation of the underlying data models defining the structure of the data as well as the formats and technologies used for data provision varies across initiatives; the following approaches have been identified:

1. Definition of individual defined concepts that can be combined to data structures. Examples:
   (a) Clinical Data Interchange Standards Consortium (CDISC) foundational standards supporting clinical and non-clinical research processes;[1]
   (b) Darwin Core standard for biodiversity observations.[2]
2. Definition of data structures in Unified Modelling Language(UML), provision Extendible Markup Language (XML), sometimes JSON. Examples:
   (a) Most ISO/OGC standards and extensions, i.e. INSPIRE;
   (b) American National Information Exchange Model (NIEM).[3]
3. Definition of data structures directly in XML. Examples:
   (a) Geography Markup Language (GML; ISO 19136)
4. Definition of data structures using semantic technologies (Resource Description Framework (RDF) and Web Ontology Language (OWL))
   (a) Open Biomedical Ontology (OBO);[4]
   (b) The Extensible Observation Ontology (OBOE).[5]

3 Methodology

Based on an analysis of existing approaches as well as a workshop ISESS 2015, the requirements for harmonized data model extension were analyzed; URI-Properties, defined as reusable properties bound to a persistent Uniform Resource Identifier (URI) [3], were identified as a potential solution. A set of requirements that must be fulfilled by URI-Properties was defined:

1. A URI-Property must be uniquely identifiable through an URI
2. The datatype of a URI-Property must be tightly coupled with its definition
3. The semantics of a URI-Property must be tightly coupled with its definition
4. A URI-Property must be persistent. We shall define persistence in analog manner to the definition used for Global Unique Identifiers (GUIDs) referencing data: A URI-Property may not be redefined with different semantics while retaining the same URI; while the definition of a URI-Property may at some point no longer be available, the reuse of the URI is not allowed.

---

[1] https://www.cdisc.org/.

[2] http://rs.tdwg.org/dwc/.

[3] https://www.niem.gov/.

[4] https://www.bioontology.org/.

[5] https://github.com/NCEAS/oboe/.

The following sections describe the viability of the options identified for the provision of reusable properties within UML, as well as their conformance to the requirements defined above.

3.1 Data Types

Defining the semantics of data types via derivation hierarchies is state-of-the art. However, pushing the complexity of semantics into data type definition could cause difficulties, as a complex derivation hierarchy must be created and maintained; should this approach be pursued methods of coupling required data types with a formal ontology, i.e. formulated in OWL, should be explored [4]. In addition, while base semantics are defined, the usage of these concepts as data types allows for definition of class attributes using the same data type but with subtly different meanings. Such differentiation could be as simple as the provision of a preferred concept together with an alternative concept, with no additional information on the subtle difference between these two concepts.

Finally, as XML Schema doesn't currently support multiple inheritance, while the semantics stemming from the derivation hierarchy are available within the UML data model, no indication of this additional information is available within the XML Schema.

3.2 Interfaces

Interfaces are state of the art for provision of reusable attributes. However we encounter problems due to the fact that XML doesn't support multiple inheritance. While GML MIXIN overcomes this shortcoming by copying attributes and associations (copy down), this technique provides no information as to the source of these attributes and associations in the final XML Schema. Further, the utilization of interfaces for the representation of reusable properties would break a great deal of the visual clarity of UML; the properties provided by the interface are not visible in the class inheriting from the interface, nor for classes derived from this class. Thus, while the benefits of reusable properties would be valuable, the cost for both the creation as well as the interpretation of the model would be a great deal higher than with normal methodologies.

3.3 MOF Level Adjustment of UML

Initially, the approach of defining reusable URI-Properties at the Meta Object Facility (MOF) level seemed the most promising, as this would integrate the concept at the UML definition level. However, this proved not to be possible, as both attributes and associations have a minimal cardinality of 1 in the MOF definition. Thus a property cannot be defined without it being directly used.

3.4 Stereotypes

Stereotypes are well suited for the definition of reusable URI-Properties. Through the tight binding of the URI-Property to the URI, the semantics of the URI-Property can be provided through an external ontology referencing this URI. This URI is visible within the XML Schema defining the URI-Property via the appinfo element, allowing applications encountering this property to resolve the URI for more information on this attribute. In the final schema, the element name and data type are automatically supplied through the element reference. The schema encoding rules are in alignment with the requirements of the underlying GML and ISO standards, and should be easy to implement.

The only problems currently identified with to this solution pertain to its integration in UML development tools. At present the use of URI-Properties requires discipline from the data modelers, as the constraints on URI-Properties are not checked by the UML tools, and thus inconsistencies will only be flagged during the schema generation process. In addition, registries of reusable URI-Properties would need to be developed and ideally integrated within the UML tools.

A final advantage of the use of URI-Properties is the fact that the definition is agnostic of the final serialization form. While well suited to serialization in XML, the logic behind the URI-Properties is also in alignment with the requirements ensuing from semantic serialization technologies such as RDF.

3.5 Analysis Against Requirements

The following table shows the approaches analyzed against the individual requirements identified (Table 1).

Table 1. Analysis approaches against requirements

Requirement approach	URI coupling	DataType coupling	Semantics coupling	Persistence
Data types	✗	~	~	✗
Interfaces	✗	~	~	✗
MOF adjustment	✗	✗	✗	✗
Stereotypes	✓	✓	✓	✓

4   Stereotype Solution

Based on the insights presented above, UML Stereotypes were selected for the implementation of reusable URI-Properties is the use of UML Stereotypes. In the following section this is illustrated through the creation of the URIProp Stereotype.

4.1 UML Example

The URIProp stereotype, defined on both attributes and associations, adds the following tags to the attributes and associations it is applied to:

- URI: a unique URI for this property
- Name: the name of the attribute or association role
- Datatype: the datatype of the attribute or of the target of the association

In addition, the following three constraints are added to the URIProp stereotype:

- Property unique per class: A URI property can only occur once per class
- Name aligned: The attribute name must be the same as the Name tag of the attribute, which must in turn be the same as that stored for the specified URI Property under the referenced URI
- Datatype aligned: The attribute datatype must be the same as the Datatype tag of the attribute, which must in turn be the same as that stored for the specified URI Property under the referenced URI

For the definition of reusable URI-Properties, the stereotype must first be applied to the definition of the URI-Property, be it for an attribute or for an association role. In the example below, we define two URI-Properties:

- euStationName: this URI-Property provides an attribute named euStationName referencing the data type CharacterString. The following Tagged Values are added through the URIProp stereotype:
  - URI: http://www.props.eu/euStationName.
  - name: euStationName
  - dataType: CharacterString
- euStationNameAss: this URI-Property provides an association named euStationNameAss referencing the data type GeographicalName. The following Tagged Values are added through the URIProp stereotype:
  - URI: http://www.props.eu/euStationNameAss.
  - name: euStationNameAss
  - dataType: GeographicalName

The following diagram shows the UML Encoding of the URI-Properties:

As part of the definition process for URI-Properties, the Tagged Values from the URIProp stereotype must be provided (Fig. 1). This stereotype must then be added to the class attributes or associations that are utilizing an URI-Property as shown in the following diagrams (Fig. 2).

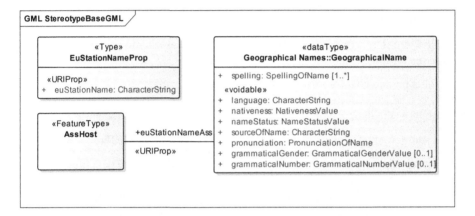

Fig. 1. Definition of URI-properties using stereotypes

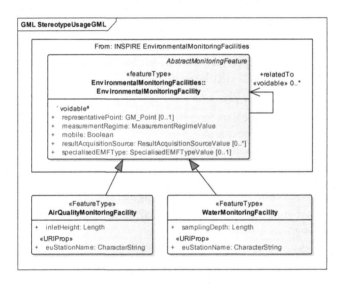

Fig. 2. Usage of attribute URI-properties using stereotypes

The same tagged values as defined above for the definition of the URI-Properties must also be provided for each usage instance. The constraints defined for URI-Properties must be complied with, assuring alignment to the original URI-Property definition (Fig. 3).

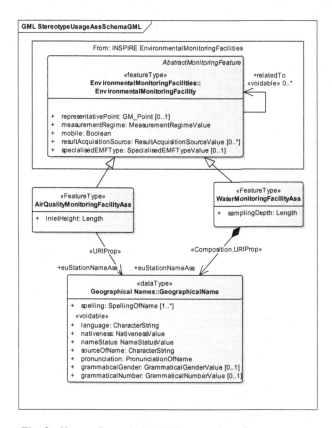

Fig. 3. Usage of association URI-properties using stereotypes

4.2 Serialization

While the schema encoding rules for data types and interfaces are specified in the GML and ISO standards, we must first define encoding rules for the use the URIProp Stereotype.

For the definition of URI-Properties, we will make use of the XML Schema option of defining an element by reference. The URI defining the URI property is provided within the appinfo section of the annotation element.

The element declarations for the URI-Properties pertaining to attributes are as follows:

```
<xs:element name="euStationName" type="xs:string">
  <xs:annotation>
    <xs:appinfo
source="http://www.props.eu/euStationName">URI-
Property</xs:appinfo>
  </xs:annotation>
</xs:element>
```

A similar pattern is utilized in the element declaration for URI-Properties pertaining to associations, taking into account the encoding requirements stemming from the GML and ISO standards:

```
<xs:element name="euStationNameAss" >
  <xs:annotation>
    <xs:appinfo
source="http://www.props.eu/euStationNameAss">URI-
Property</xs:appinfo>
  </xs:annotation>
  <xs:complexType>
    <xs:complexContent>
      <xs:extension base="gml:AbstractMemberType">
        <xs:sequence minOccurs="0">
          <xs:element ref="gn:GeographicalName"/>
        </xs:sequence>
        <xs:attributeGroup
ref="gml:AssociationAttributeGroup"/>
      </xs:extension>
    </xs:complexContent>
  </xs:complexType>
</xs:element>
```

Once the URI-Property has been defined, it can then be referenced from the XML Schemas reusing this property as follows:

```
<xs:element ref="st:euStationName"/>
```

The same pattern can also be used pertaining to associations:

```
<xs:element ref="st:euStationNameAss"/>
```

The following XML snippet shows the serialization of the AirQualityMonitoring-Facility station name attribute using stereotypes:

```
<st:euStationName>AT_AQ_Station1</st:euStationName>
```

Namespaces:

- st: interface property schema

When the URI-Property is defined as an association, it is possible to provide the information either inline, or via xlink to an external instance.

4.3 Reflection

Stereotypes are well suited for the definition of reusable URI-Properties. Through the tight binding of the URI-Property to the URI, the semantics of the URI-Property can be provided through an external ontology referencing this URI. This URI is visible within the XML Schema defining the URI-Property via the appinfo element, allowing applications encountering this property to resolve the URI for more information on this attribute. In the final schema, the element name and data type are automatically supplied through the element reference. The schema encoding rules are in alignment with the requirements of the underlying GML and ISO standards, and should be easy to implement.

The only problems currently identified with to this solution pertain to its integration in UML development tools. At present the use of URI-Properties requires discipline from the data modelers, as the constraints on URI-Properties are not checked by the UML tools, and thus inconsistencies will only be flagged during the schema generation process. In addition, registries of reusable URI-Properties would need to be developed and ideally integrated within the UML tools.

A final advantage of the use of URI-Properties is the fact that the definition is agnostic of the final serialization form. While well suited to serialization in XML, the logic behind the URI-Properties is also in alignment with the requirements ensuing from semantic serialization technologies such as RDF.

5 Conclusion and Outlook

Based on the analysis of the implementation options, the current best candidate for the implementation of URI-Properties is the stereotype solution.

Further analyzing the potential of the stereotype solution, it becomes apparent that the addition of URI-Properties via stereotypes serves to bring traditional UML data modelling closer to emerging semantic technologies, where properties are traditionally first class citizens. If an alignment between URI-Properties within a UML model and predicates as utilized within RDF and OWL is provided, it becomes possible to easily traverse between UML based data models and semantic data models. This would be beneficial, as the spatial data community is progressively moving towards semantic technologies, while wishing to retain as much as possible of the existing data model standards. Thus, by properly utilizing URI-Properties, it is possible to reuse the UML based data models for data serialization both via semi-structured technologies such as XML as well as semantic technologies such as RDF and OWL, opening up the scope of potential end users for the data provided.

References

1. Tóth, K., Portele, C., Illert A., Lutz, M., de Lima, M.A.: A conceptual model for developing interoperability specifications in spatial data infra-structures, JRC reference report (2012). http://inspire.ec.europa.eu/documents/Data_Specifications/IES_Spatial_Data_Infrastruct ures_(online).pdf
2. Schleidt, K.: Evolution of Environmental Information Models. In: Denzer, R., Argent, R.M., Schimak, G., Hřebíček, J. (eds.) Environmental Software Systems. Infrastructures, Services and Applications, vol. 448, pp. 71–80. Springer, Cham (2015). https://doi.org/ 10.1007/978-3-319-15994-2_6
3. Schleidt K.: Evolution of Environmental Information Models. Workshop Outcomes (2015). http://datacove.eu/data/documents/EIM_WS_Outcomes.pdf
4. Janssen, S., Andersen, E., Athanasiadis, I.N., van Ittersum, M.K.: A database for integrated assessment of European agricultural systems. Environ. Sci. Policy **12**(5), 573–587 (2009)

Semantic BMS: Ontology for Analysis of Building Operation Efficiency

Adam Kučera[✉] and Tomáš Pitner

Faculty of Informatics, Masaryk University, Botanická 68a, 602 00 Brno, Czech Republic
akucera@mail.muni.cz, tomp@fi.muni.cz

Abstract. Building construction has gone through a significant change with the emerging spread of ICT during last decades. Intelligent buildings are equipped with building automation systems (BAS) that can be remotely controlled and programmed. However, such systems lack convenient tools for data inspection, making building performance and efficiency analysis demanding on large sites. The paper presents an adaptation of Semantic Sensor Network ontology for use in the field of building operation analysis. The proposed Semantic BMS ontology enriches the SSN with a model of building automation data points and describes relations between BAS and physical properties of a building. Proposed ontology allows facility managers to conveniently query BAS systems, providing decision support for tactical and strategic level planning.

Keywords: Facility management · Building automation systems
Semantic sensor network ontology · Decision support · Energy efficiency
Operation efficiency

1 Introduction

Each organization needs to ensure various aspects of its operation that are not directly involved in reaching its primary goal (e.g. providing service to a customer or sell its products). Such tasks are the core part of the Facility Management discipline. In recent years, environmental aspects of facility operation gain attention in the eyes of facility managers, both because of the legislative requirements and a close relation to sustainability and low operation costs.

We can distinguish several systems and/or data sources that can be utilized to support and simplify tasks of facility management staff.

Computer Aided Facility Management (CAFM) systems facilitate tasks such as assignment of employees to rooms, a log of maintenance plans, requests, and tasks, or energy consumption data. A Building Information Model (BIM) contains spatial information about building constructions, parts, and technologies installed in them. Modern ("intelligent") buildings are equipped with a variety of sensors and controllable devices (e.g. HVAC, security systems). The devices are integrated into the Building Automation System (BAS), also referred as Building Management System (BMS). The devices incorporated in BAS can be remotely controlled, monitored, and queried. Individual

© IFIP International Federation for Information Processing 2017
Published by Springer International Publishing AG 2017. All Rights Reserved
J. Hřebíček et al. (Eds.): ISESS 2017, IFIP AICT 507, pp. 349–359, 2017.
https://doi.org/10.1007/978-3-319-89935-0_29

information objects (such as current temperature in particular room measured by a sensor) accessible in the BAS network are referred to as "data points" further in the paper.

A crucial part of sustainable and effective facility operation is benchmarking. Benchmarking methods in facility management are covered in EN 15221-7 standard, including environmental awareness. Requirements placed on benchmarking Key Performance Indicators (KPIs) are summarized in [1]. Among others, the authors mention flexibility, the quantitative nature of the KPIs and simplicity of use. BMS data satisfy the first three requirements, the simplicity of use is a downside of current BAS solutions.

The BAS contains a large amount of a precise, up-to-date, and detailed data that are valuable for a building operation analysis and cannot be obtained any other way. However, data points of the BAS are described by their location in the network topology, not by the role that algorithms, sensors, and actuators fulfill in the building operation. Using BACnet protocol as an example, data point representing temperature sensor is identified by the network address of the device that reads the value, data type of the input (Analog input) and ID of the input within the device. Besides this identification of data point, BACnet provides only several free-form string attributes such as Name or Description, which are intended to be easily readable by human operators.

The absence of structured semantic information prevents efficient querying of the data points for analytical purposes, as it is not possible to select and filter the data based on criteria such as a type of a source device, location of a measurement or measured quantity kind. If the data from data points are required (e.g. electricity consumption for last month for each of the buildings on the site which will be later compared), the operators of the system must manually gather the data point addresses by inspecting the building plans or user interface of the BAS.

The above-mentioned problem clearly emerges when operating large BAS system. Masaryk University utilizes BAS network consisting of approximately 1500 devices communicating using BACnet automation protocol with hundreds of thousands of data points available. The network covers 35 buildings with the overall area of 120 000 m^2 at the site of University Campus Bohunice in Brno, Czech Republic and several more over the whole Brno city. Previous attempts of data coming from the BMS of the university have been published in [2] and [3]. The requirements of effective operation of large-scale installations of automation technologies are discussed in [4].

This paper presents Semantic BMS ontology that aims to provide a semantic description of the building automation systems. Such description can be easily queriedfor building operation data needed for benchmarking, providing decision support in tasks such as improving facility efficiency, sustainability and increasing organizations' environmental awareness.

2   Related Work

The semantic description of sensor networks is a subject of ongoing research, as it combines two significant trends in computer and information science – Semantic Web (Open Linked Data) and Internet of Things. Furthermore, the trend towards "Smart

Cities" stimulates research on the integration of automation systems and building auto-mation data analysis.

The Open Geospatial Consortium (OGC) provides Sensor Web Enablement (SWE) suite of standards, ensuring syntactic model of sensor networks (SensorML) as well as interfaces and protocols for data exchange. OGC's Observation&Measurements (O&M) provides a limited semantic description of sensor networks. The SWE however does not covera domain specific semantics.

Probably the most notable ontological description of sensor networks is Semantic Sensor Network Ontology (SSN) developed and maintained by W3C Consortium [5], which adopts the scheme of Observations&Measurements Model.

In architecture, engineering and construction industry, integration of different Building Information Model solutions is facilitated by Industry Foundation Classes standard in current version IFC 4 (ISO 16739:2013). The object-based data model together with the provided file formats ensure data exchange between BIM systems and can be viewed as a source of semantic information that can be used for analysis of building performance, as shown in [6]. However, the IFC does not aim to model complex semantic information concerning data points available in the building automation systems. In [7] and [8], direct mapping of data points to IFC entities is used for building operation analysis. As noted by the authors of [8], the IFC itself does not provide built-in capabilities for describing features of interest and properties observed by sensors.

Standardized building automation protocols such as BACnet (ISO 16484-5), LonWorks (ISO 14908-1), KNX (ISO 14543), or ZigBee generally cover the operation of building automation devices, providing specifications for physical communication layer, data link and networking layer and application layer on the highest level. Auto-mation protocols focus on communication interfaces and do not provide tools for the complex and structured description of the semantics of the data points.

The MOST project presented in [9] provides a framework for building operation analysis. The MOST uses a relational database for storing basic semantic information about operation data.

In [10], the SSN is extended by a model of physical processes occurring in the building (e.g. adjacent room exchanging energy) to provide tool for building operation diagnosis and anomaly detection.

The Open Linked Data approach for building automation data streams is facilitated by EDWH Ontology proposed in [11]. The aim of the EDWH ontology is to provide a bridge between the SSN ontology and the W3C RDF Data Cube vocabulary, as the data are meant to be analyzed by OLAP data cube techniques.

In [12–14] the authors use a SSN-based ontology for energy management based on sensor data using OLAP and Complex Event Processing. The semantically described BAS data help to establish situation awareness at the strategy level and allow multi-level evaluation of energy consumption (from organization level to the level of individual appliances).

In general, existing ontologies either aims to describe different aspects of BAS than data analysis, use proprietary/ad-hoc structures for storing semantic data, ignore inte-gration with BIM systems or do not provide a domain-specific mapping of BAS systems to the SSN ontology.

3   Semantic BMS Ontology

The goal of presented research is to provide a BAS-protocol-independent model of intelligent building systems. The Building automation system can be viewed as a sensor and actuator network for the purposes of data analysis. A semantic description of sensor networks is a subject of extensive research, resulting in frameworks and tools such as SensorML language, Observations & Measurements (O&M) model or Semantic Sensor Network ontology (SSN). However, for the use in the domain of building automation, certain differences have to be taken into account.

The Semantic BMS Ontology (SBMS) proposed in this paper is thus an extension of the SSN ontology, addressing domain-specific requirements of building automation data analysis. The SBMS remains "fully backward compatible" with the SSN ontology (meaning no modification were made in the SSN itself, it was only extended) and at the same time provide greater semantic description strength for the target domain that "pure" SSN.

The proposed ontology aims to represent information (data) available for operation analysis. It does not aim to describe physical topology of the BAS network or physical properties of the sensors and actuators such as operating range. Standardized building automation protocols themselves also provide limited metadata description of the system as well as other services such as a data store. Similarly, the BIM and CAFM provides additional sources of semantic information. As a result, the semantic description of the BMS is not required to contain some information that would be a duplicate (copy) of data available in the BAS, BIM or CAFM systems. The aim of the presented research is to enrich the BAS/BMS with semantic links to entities present in other systems (BIM, CAFM) and add a new layer of semantic metadata that are not available elsewhere.

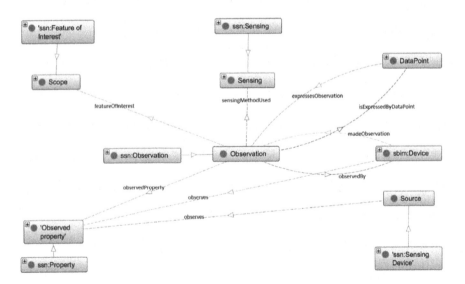

Fig. 1. Overview of the SBMS ontology

The SBMS ontology enriches the SSN by adding the concept of a datapoint, which is distinct from a sensing device. While a sensing device is a source of data presented by a datapoint, a datapoint conceptualizes a measured value available in an automation system. It describes a representation of measured data in building automation software.

Figure 1 presents standard components of the SSN ontology together with their specializations defined in the SBMS ontology. The center point of the SSN is the *ssn:Observation* concept. The observation connects all actors and objects that take part in the process of obtaining measurement data, and thus provide all available semantic information via its properties. The specialized *sbms:Observation* as well as properties defined in the SBMS limits domains and ranges to those concepts that are usable in the domain of building automation. The changes affect the definition of the feature of interest, observed property, sensing methods and sensing devices.

Key concepts for accurate semantic annotation of sensor/actuator data are "Observed property" (OP) and "Feature of Interest" (FoI). The concepts were defined in O&M framework and adapted by the SSN ontology. The FoI represents an object of measurement. The OP represents specific information that we observe. In the domain of building automation, we can demonstrate the concepts on examples such as energy consumption (OP) of a specific building (FoI) or speed (OP) of a specific fan (FoI). The SBMS ontology further specializes the concepts for use in the domain of building automation.

The *ssn:Feature of Interest* is restricted by the subclass *sbms:Scope* to be site, building, floor, room, or device further described in the BIM database. This restriction reflects a nature of a data available in BAS. Since BAS ensure operation of the building, every piece of information available in the system can be related to specific part of a facility or to a piece of installed equipment. Class and property definitions are restricted so as validFoI can be either a device (e.g. valve, pump, engine, or PLC) or a location (site, building, floor, or room).

A similar restriction is applied to the *ssn:Sensing Device* by the subclass *sbms:Source*. Every piece of information available in the BAS must be measured by some device connected to the BAS network. Such devices are naturally present in the BIM database. As a result, each individual of *sbms:Source* has to be a device described in the BIM database, represented by *sbim:Device* class.

The SBMS ontology contains a simplified model of selected elements from the BIM systems. Such concepts reside in dedicated namespace sbim. Namely, it contains concepts describing locations and parts of the facilities (sbim:Site, sbim:Building, sbim:Floor, sbim:Room), and devices (sbim:Device and its descendants) that provide sensor data or that are observed by the building automation system. Classes representing specific types of building equipment are adapted from the IFC 4 specification.

3.1   Semantic Description of BMS Addresses

The SBMS ontology adds a representation of an address that publishes observed data in the BAS. Identification of a sensing device is not sufficient in case we need to obtain the data from the BAS system. The sensing device is identified by ID in the BIM. The BIM ID, however, cannot be used for accessing data in the BAS, since certain sensors are represented in the BIM as independent devices, but they are primitive and do not directly communicate within the BAS. An example of such device is a temperature sensor, which is a simple thermistor in a casing, connected to a PLC. The sensor is represented in the BIM as a separate entity, but the data is accessible via the PLC.

The *sbms:Address* class defines several subclasses, most important are *sbsms:Input* and *sbms:Output*, representing sensor reading and actuator command.

4 Results

The presented ontology is designed to model the data sources available in the BAS and provide additional semantic information regarding relationsof respective data points to a physical environment of the building. The newly added semantic information can be used by developers of new analytical applications for the domain of building operation analysis. Such applications will provide decision support for improving building performance and efficiency.

Typical environment-related tasks for such applications are related to energy consumption and workplace temperature conditions.

In case of energy consumption, the ontology can be easily used for selecting data points containing electric consumption. The combination of appropriate parameters defines desired data points: *Source* device type – Energy meter, "Input" *data point type* and *Property domain* "Electricity"). The *Scope* attribute in the result set then describes facilities that are responsible for a consumption measured by a given data point.

Another use case of the ontology related to environmental responsibility searches for rooms that are cooled or heated ineffectively. The ontology allows for easy selection of room temperature data. Data selection is very similar to the previous use case, finding data originating from temperature sensors measuring air temperature with *Scope* type of "Room". The data then can be gathered and outliers – rooms with unreasonably high temperatures in winter on low temperatures during warm periods – can be identified and inefficient behavior can be addressed and removed.

The novelty of the ontology allows selecting data according to mentioned criteria. Current building automation systems do not provide querying mechanism and do not annotate the data by desired attributes, such as *Scope* or *Property domain*.

In order to facilitate the development of analytical applications to maximal extent, the Semantic BMS framework is being developed (see Fig. 2). The framework is divided into two main parts – Data providers and Semantic providers. Data providers are used for accessing measurement data. The Semantic providers present data available in the SBMS ontology. The rest of this section will be focused on the Semantic provider.

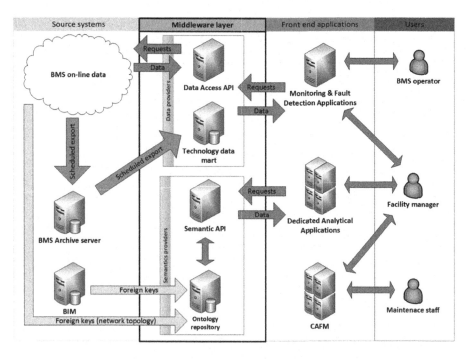

Fig. 2. Semantic BMS framework overview

As an ontology repository, Apache Jena TDB is used. The repository can be queried directly (using SPARQL) or via the Semantic API.

SPARQL Query that collects all the available data about a data point has following structure (in this case, the datapoint has BMS ID "1600.AV4":

```
 1    SELECT * WHERE { values ?bmsId { "1600.AV4" }
 2    ?dataPoint sbms:hasBMSId ?bmsId.
 3    ?dataPoint a ?dataPointClass.
 4    ?dataPointClass rdfs:subClassOf sbms:DataPoint.
 5    ?dataPoint sbms:expressesObservation ?observation.
 6    ?observation sbms:observedBy ?source.
 7    ?source sbim:hasBIMId ?sourceBIMId.
 8    ?source a ?sourceClass.
 9    ?sourceClass rdfs:subClassOf* sbim:Device.
10    FILTER (not exists {?subtype rdfs:subClassOf
11    ?sourceClass.
12    FILTER (?subtype != ?sourceClass) }
13    && ?sourceClass != sbms:Source).
14    ?observation sbms:featureOfInterest ?scope.
15    ?scope sbim:hasBIMId ?scopeBIMId.
16    ?scope a ?scopeClass.
17    ?scopeClass rdfs:subClassOf* dul:PhysicalObject.
18    FILTER (not exists {?subtype rdfs:subClassOf
19    ?scopeClass.
20    FILTER (?subtype != ?scopeClass) }
21    && ?scopeClass != sbms:Scope).
22    ?observation sbms:observedProperty ?property.
23    ?property sbms:hasPhysicalQuality ?quality.
24    ?property sbms:hasPropertyDomain ?propDomain.
25    ?observation sbms:sensingMethodUsed ?sensing.
26    ?sensing a ?sensingClass.
27    ?sensingClass rdfs:subClassOf* sbms:Sensing.
28    FILTER not exists {?subtype rdfs:subClassOf
29    ?sensingClass.
30    FILTER (?subtype != ?sensingClass) }.
31    OPTIONAL { ?sensing sbms:hasAggregationTimeWindow
32    ?timeWindow }
33    }
```

The segments of SPARQL query are ensure retrieval of different data point semantic descriptors. Lines 1–2 ensure selection of the desired data point. Line 3 retrieves a type of the data point (e.g. input or output). Line 5 gets the Observation individual that connects the data point to other semantic metadata. Lines from 6 to 13 retrieve information related to the source of the data – BIM id and type of source device. Similarly, lines 14–21 gather data about scope of the data point. Lines from 22 to 24 are related to the Observed property parameter. Lines 25–32 are intended to retrieve information regarding sensing type and possibly time window if applicable for given sensing. Often repeated FILTER statement deals with type hierarchy in ontology language. The query selects only leaf, most specialized subclass of given individual.

Results of such query are then returned in various serialization formats, such as SPARQL JSON.

Due to the complexity of SPARQL queries and generic SPARQL-JSON responses, semantic API was developed as a RESTful service providing semantic data using JSON format. The API uses Jersey framework ensuring RESTful capabilities and Apache Jena API for communication with the ontology repository.

As an example of API goals and capabilities, the "data points" endpoint will be discussed. The endpoint allows a consumer to query the ontology repository for data point semantic description based on given semantic criteria.

Example of JSON response payload:

```
{ "dataPoints":[
  {"bmsId":"1600.AV4",
    "dataPointType":"Input",
    "property":{"domain":"Electricity",
                "quality":"energy"},
    "scope":{"bimId":"Building:A1","type":"Building"},
    "source":{"bimId":"ElectricMeter-A1",
              "type":"FlowMeter"},
    "sensing":{"type":"AggregateSumSensing",
               "window":"Months01"}
  }]}
```

The API provides following information about the data point with BMS ID "1600.AV4":

- Datapoint type – Specifies a role of the datapoint in the BAS.
- Physical quality and property domain – Specifies physical quality represented by the data point (e.g. temperature, humidity, energy, or output power).
- Scope (Feature of Interest) – A scope specifies object the data point value is related to. Possible scopes are the location (e.g. building when measuring energy consumption) or device (e.g. fan in the case of data point representing fan speed).
- Data source – Specifies the device that provides the BAS with the data.
- Source device type – Describes the type of the source device (e.g. Flow meter).
- Sensing method and time window – The simplest case is direct sensing (e.g. room temperature). Other (indirect) sensing methods employ computation or aggregation over some period (e.g. energy consumption total for the last month).

Presented examples of the Semantic API capabilities aim to show how the data stored in Semantic BMS ontology can be queried using convenient and easy to implement methods, thus significantly simplifying development of various analytical and decision support application for the field of building operation analysis.

5   Conclusions

The presented ontology aims to provide additional semantics to datapoints available in building automation systems. The ontology is designed to be automation protocol independent and describes available data in a way that can be utilized during decision support tasks needed for building performance analysis, evaluation, and improvement, which are crucial tasks to achieve energy efficient and environment-friendly operation of facilities.

Using additional semantic layer, the process of obtaining and inspecting key performance indicator data is significantly simplified. Ontology design was based on long term experience with the operation of University Campus of Masaryk University as site equipped with hundredths of automation devices.

At the moment, the ontology is populated with sample data representing several typical components of building automation systems. Further steps contain the development of proof-of-the-concept Data provider for the BACnet protocol. The ontology will be populated with information describing an actual building. Next, methods described in the "EN 15221-7 Facility Management - Part 7: Guidelines for Performance Benchmarking" standard will be used for evaluation of the ontology and API usability. Assessment of query retrieval performance is also planned in this step, leading to possible optimization of ontology model or query composition.

References

1. Alwaer, H., Clements-Croome, D.J.: Key performance indicators (KPIs) and priority setting in using the multi-attribute approach for assessing sustainable intelligent buildings. Build. Environ. **45**(4), 799–807 (2010)
2. Kriksciuniene, D., Pitner, T., Kučera, A., Sakalauskas, V.: Sensor network analytics for intelligent facility management. In: Tsihrintzis, et al. (eds.) Proceedings of the 6th International Conference on Intelligent Interactive Multimedia Systems and Services (IIMSS2013), pp. 212–221. IOS Press, Amsterdam (2013)
3. Kriksciuniene, D., Pitner, T., Kučera, A., Sakalauskas, V.: Data analysis in the intelligent building environment. Int. J. Comput. Sci. Appl. **11**, 1–17 (2014)
4. Kučera, A., Pitner, T.: Intelligent facility management for sustainability and risk management. In: Hřebíček, J., Schimak, G., Kubásek, M., Rizzoli, Andrea E. (eds.) ISESS 2013. IAICT, vol. 413, pp. 608–617. Springer, Heidelberg (2013). https://doi.org/10.1007/978-3-642-41151-9_57
5. Compton, M.E.A.: The SSN ontology of the W3C semantic sensor network incubator group. Web Semant.: Sci. Serv. Agents World Wide Web **17**, 25–32 (2012)
6. Menzel, K., Weise, M., Liebich, T., Valmaseda, C.: Capabilities of IFC 4 for advanced building performance management. In: Proceedings of the 2nd Central European Symposium on Building Physics, vol. 2013, pp. 467–474. Vienna University of Technology - Faculty of Architecture and Regional Planning, Vienna, Austria, Sep 2013
7. Schuelke, A., et al.: A middleware platform for integrated building performance management. In: Proceedings of the 2nd Central European Symposium on Building Physics, vol. 2013, pp. 459–466 (2013)

8. Wang, H., et al.: Integration of BIM and Live Sensing Information to Monitor Building Energy Performance. In: Proceedings of the 30th International Conference of CIB W78. pp. 344–352, Beijing, China, Oct 2013

9. Zach, R., et al.: MOST: an opensource, vendor and technology independent toolkit for building monitoring, datapreprocessing, and visualization (2012)

10. Ploennigs, J., Schumann, A., Lécué, F.: Adapting semantic sensor networks for smart building diagnosis. In: Mika, P., Tudorache, T., Bernstein, A., Welty, C., Knoblock, C., Vrandečić, D., Groth, P., Noy, N., Janowicz, K., Goble, C. (eds.) ISWC 2014. LNCS, vol. 8797, pp. 308–323. Springer, Cham (2014). https://doi.org/10.1007/978-3-319-11915-1_20

11. Mehdi, M., Sahay, R., Derguech, W., Curry, E.: On-the-fly generation of multidimensional data cubes for web of things. In: Proceedings of the 17th International Database Engineering and Applications Symposium. pp. 28–37. IDEAS 2013. ACM, New York (2013)

12. Curry, E., Hasan, S., O'Riain, S.: Enterprise energy management using a linked dataspace for energy intelligence. In: Sustainable Internet and ICT for Sustainability (SustainIT), pp. 1–6 (2012)

13. Curry, E., et al.: Linking building data in the cloud: integrating cross-domain building data using linked data. Adv. Eng. Inform. 27(2), 206–219 (2013)

14. Hasan, S., Curry, E., Banduk, M., O'Riain, S.: Toward situation awareness for the semantic sensor web: complex event processing with dynamic linked data enrichment

A Generic Web Cache Infrastructure for the Provision of Multifarious Environmental Data

Thorsten Schlachter[1](✉), Eric Braun[1], Clemens Düpmeier[1],
Christian Schmitt[1], and Wolfgang Schillinger[2]

[1] Karlsruhe Institute of Technology, Karlsruhe, Germany
{thorsten.schlachter,eric.braun2,clemens.duepmeier,
christian.schmitt}@kit.edu
[2] Baden-Wuerttemberg State Institute for Environment, Measurements,
and Nature Conservation, Karlsruhe, Germany
wolfgang.schillinger@lubw.bwl.de

Abstract. As a basis for the efficient data supply for web portals, web-based and mobile applications of several German environmental authorities, a microservice-based infrastructure is being used. It consists of a generic data model and a series of corresponding generic services, e.g. for the provision of master data, metrics, spatial data, digital assets, metadata, and links between them. The main objectives are the efficient provision of data as well as the use of the same data by a wide range of applications. In addition, the used technologies and services should enable data supplyasopen (government) data or as linked data in the sense of the Semantic Web. In a first version, these services are used exclusively for read access to the data. For this purpose, the data are usually extracted from their original systems, possibly processed and then stored redundantly in powerful backend systems ("Web Cache"). Generic microservices provide uniform REST interfaces to access the data. Each service can use different backend systems connected via adapters. In this way, consuming components such as frontend modules in a Web portal can transparently access various backend systems via stable interfaces, which can therefore be selected optimally for each application. A number of tools and workflows ensure the updating and consistency of the data in the Web Cache. Microservices and backend systems are operated on the basis of container virtualization using flexible cloud infrastructures.

Keywords: Environmental information systems · Generic data model
Master data · Time series · Spatial data · Semantics · Schema
Microservices · REST · Web portals · Mobile apps
Container-based virtualization · Cloud computing · Open government data
Linked data · Semantic web

1 Introduction

A direct consequence of the Aarhus Convention was the adoption of the EU directive 2003/4/EG [1]. This directive, respectively its implementation into national law, e.g. the Environmental Information Act in Germany [2], regulates access to environmental

© IFIP International Federation for Information Processing 2017
Published by Springer International Publishing AG 2017. All Rights Reserved
J. Hřebíček et al. (Eds.): ISESS 2017, IFIP AICT 507, pp. 360–371, 2017.
https://doi.org/10.1007/978-3-319-89935-0_30

information for the public. Authorities are obliged to the active dissemination of environmental information [2, Sect. 7]. The Internet provides a perfect platform for this purpose. Therefore, a lot of environmental information, as well as (raw) data in the sense of open (government) data [3], are already made available using Internet based applications, e.g. websites, portals, mobile applications [4].

Nevertheless, even today, 15 years after the Aarhus Convention entered into force, much environmental information are not yet or only partially available online. The reasons are manifold and correspond with the challenges of providing open government data [4, pp. 30–39]: political, technical, legal, organizational, cultural, and economic reasons are hindering the free dissemination of environmental information. The majority of these barriers cannot be broken down technically, but modern technologies can help in reducing them.

In some cases, however, long-term processes must lead to a rethinking and rerouting of people and institutions in politics and administration. With the concept of a Web Cache presented in this paper, we want to give an impulse how more environmental information can be made accessible to a wider public by addressing at least some of the inhibitory causes.

2 Idea and Basic Concepts

Starting point of our considerations is that environmental information is made available through central entry points such as Web portals and mobile applications. Most of these applications ultimately use data that have been arisen in the daily work of environmental agencies. Mostly the primary purpose of this (original) data is not information for the public, which leads to the problems and challenges listed above. For example, environmental information include personal data, are subject to licenses, consist of large amounts of information, require appropriate user rights, are stored in special data formats, are not accessible via the Internet, are incomprehensible to lay people, aren't available around the clock, etc.

Our basic idea is to provide "Internet-enabled" copies[1] of the original data on a "Web Cache" (Fig. 1). The information is being extracted automatically from the original systems (data sources), e.g. professional databases and specialist applications, then being processed (data ingestion) and provided in redundant systems (data management). The avoidance of direct access to original data sources allows for better availability and usage-based scaling of services (data services and data management), and offers security benefits by strict separation of internal and external/public requests. Data flow is designed unidirectional from data sources to the Web Cache. So the Web Cache represents a read-only copy of the data. Consistency or coherence conditions are set for each data type and any data source influencing the nature and frequency of synchronization between data source and Web Cache.

Limited to mainly unidirectional data flows, the Web Cache application is ideally suited to be implemented as a horizontally scalable microservice-based framework. In

---

[1] An excerpt of the original data meeting all the conditions for publication on the Internet.

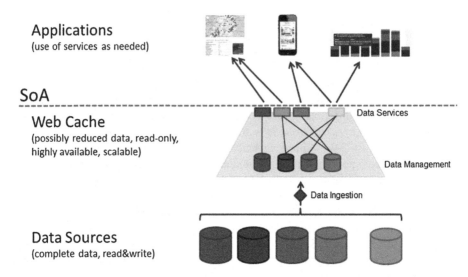

Fig. 1. Web Cache architecture at a glance

general, however, the framework provides the full range of functionality for data management, i.e. functions for adding, updating and deleting data are also available (known as CRUD for create, read, update, delete), also including mechanisms for authentication and authorization, which do not apply for the Web Cache, which exclusively contains public data and does not have any access restrictions for reading.

3 Architecture and Components

In order to keep efforts of setting up the Web Cache on an acceptable level, it is an essential objective of the project to provide the entire information by means of a limited number of generic services which have to be able to handle a large variety of data semantics. For this purpose, a small set of generic data services and their functionality have been defined allowing the storage of multifarious kinds of data as well as additional semantic metadata in order to provide applications with strongly typed data where necessary. Depending on the application, in addition to newly developed services the use of cloud services off the shelf is eligible[2].

For the implementation of environmental portals, e.g. the LUPO environmental portal family [5], a total of 8 generic services has been identified:

- Master Data Service
- Schema Service
- Time Series Service
- (Media and) Digital Asset Service

---

[2] Since they may not meet all future requirements, such standard cloud services are rather regarded as interim solutions.

- (Full Text) Search Service
- Geo Data Service
- Metadata Service
- Link Service

These 8 core services are supplemented by two additional services supporting configuration management of (and therefore rather belonging to) consuming applications:

- Application Configuration Service
- Data Discovery Service

These services are described in more detail in Sect. 5.

In a microservice-oriented architecture all services should be independently deployable and usable, and only being coupled loosely. This requirement corresponds to the term "functional decomposition" being used for microservices [6]. Therefore, each data service provides functionality for managing one single generic type of data.

Packed in runtime containers such as Docker[3], the services can be operated without any additional effort on a variety of possible infrastructures, like dedicated servers, clusters, or in the cloud [7]. Using runtime infrastructures like Kubernetes[4], operational aspects such as (rolling) updates, monitoring, horizontal scalability and load balancing are just a matter of configuration – assumed an appropriate computing infrastructure and software design.

All services use suitable backend systems, which in particular ensure the persistence of the data. Here, again, the architecture is abstracted from concrete systems, so that backend systems can easily be replaced by others, or different backend systems can be used simultaneously. The selection of suitable backend systems, e.g. various NoSQL technologies, also ensures dynamic properties such as load balancing, scalability, etc. at this level. All services provide their functionality through versioned RESTful interfaces via content negotiation [8]. This facilitates the development, maintenance, and replacement of individual services.

The postulated independence of services must not lead to a loss of possible functionality, for example by a lack of inter-service interaction. For this purpose, a microservice-based architecture provides a messaging infrastructure (channels) for loose asynchronous coupling of services. However, unlike Gartner's microservice architecture [9], in applications similar to the Web Cache the functionality of the messaging layer "below" the microservices may be delegated to the data ingestion phase and/or to consuming applications using an event bus [5], a simplification, which is sufficient for a wide range of given use cases with unidirectional data flow.

---

[3] https://www.docker.com.

[4] http://kubernetes.io.

4   Generic Data Model

The services mentioned in Sect. 3 are the basic elements of a well-considered generic data model resulting from a use case analysis in different application domains beyond the environmentalfield. However, we do not claim it to be completely universal. Although the model implements generic data types, it compensates the loss of a strong (relational) schema by using additional semantic services which add missing semantics back into the service-oriented data management infrastructure (like it is done for the Semantic Web). One main advantage of the external provision of semantic information bymeans of dedicated services is that schema information is not hard-coded anymore, so it can easily be shared between applications.

The core data type of the generic data model is the master data object. A master data object may be a digital model of any entity (of the application-relevant part) of the real world, e.g. anature protection area, a measuring station, a wind turbine, or a legal document. Each master data object is described by a set of structured properties identifiable by a certain key attribute. This structure can be formalized in a data schema. Objects of the same type use the same schema and belong to the same class of objects (master data). This classification stepis of great importance as it directly assigns particular semantics to classes and the respective objects. Relationships between master data objects (or between master data types) can be expressed in various ways, e.g. a composition within a schema (an object consisting of sub-objects), or by the explicit provision of a certain relation between two objects. In general, relations can be typed, directed or undirected, and may have properties as well.

A number of master data types need special consideration. Environmental monitoring often consists of measured values, e.g. time series describing the concentration of ozone on a certain location or the performance of a wind turbine over time. In addition, most environmental objects do have a spatial reference, i.e. (at a certain time) they are located at a specific place in the world and may have specific geometry. Thegeneric data model takes this into account and therefore provides generic data types (and respective services) for time series and spatial data. Digital assets can also be viewed as a special case. Just like other "real world objects", they are usually assigned properties (metadata). In addition, however, the concrete digital object may be provided as well, e.g. as image file, HTML snippet, PDF document or audio/video stream. The generic data types mentioned thus form the basis for specialized services, which offer specific access (service interfaces) to the respective data type.

5   Data Services

The services are divided into data services, which form the core of the framework, and supplementary services, which focus on the support of consuming applications. For the Web Cache, the following sections only describe the core data services. Further services, e.g. Link Service and Data Discovery Service, are described in the conference paper by Braun et al. [10].

5.1   Master Data Service and Schema Service

Almost all real-world objects have properties which can be expressed in a corresponding data model. In general, this is not only static or structured data, but there are also dynamic or unstructured parts, e.g. objects can contain components which can be regarded as independent objects, too (subobjects or compositions).

The Master Data Service considered here represents a simplification in comparison to such a general master data model since it essentially stores static and structured data. Other properties, in particular dynamic parts, compositions and relationships, are stored by means of references which can refer to both master data and various data types from other services.

For example, the master data of an air measurement station (id, name, location, references to multiple measurement series, etc.) are stored in the Master Data Service (Fig. 2). A measurement series is also stored in the Master Data Service (id, substance, unit, accuracy, references to the measured values, etc.), while the actual measured values are stored in the Time Series Service. The reference type "timeSeries" defines a custom data type not shown here (timeSeries $\sim$ array of measurement).

The Master Data Service primarily provides a service facade, which guarantees a uniform and stable interface to applications. The actual persistent storage of the data takes place in different backend systems, which are each connected to the MasterData Service via adapters. This allows the connection and exchange of various backend systems (e.g. relational or NoSQL databases, search engines) depending on the specific requirements or applications.

In order to store and provide different data types using a generic service, a structural as well as a semantic description of the data is required. The descriptions of all data types are provided via a Schema Service. Since data types can change over time, schemas have to be versioned. Schemas do not only refer to the data types used in the Master Data Service, but also to the contents of all data services within the framework. Services and consuming applications may use these schemas, e.g. to validate incoming data or to use the structure when visualizing the data. The Schema Service and its implementation based on JSON schema[5] are described in more detail in [10].

Using schemas, the Master Data Service and other services may resolve references, i.e. replace references by the corresponding data, or provide references as URLs/HTTP URIs[6]. Using server-side communication via message channels, the former can lead to a considerable performance gain and possibly reduce complexity in the client or the consuming application.

On the code base of the Master Data Service, specialized content-specific variants can be set up, e.g. a service for storing and providing metadata. Another possible use is described as "Application Configuration Service" below.

---

[5] http://json-schema.org.

[6] The use of HTTP URIs as references between objects applies to the core ideas of Linked Data.

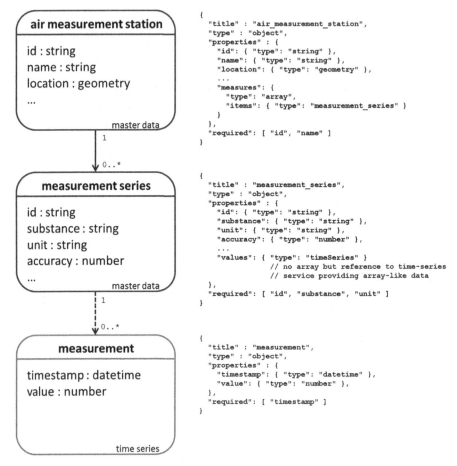

Fig. 2. Example of master data using a composition (measurement series as sub-objects of air measurement station) and references to actual measurement values in the time series service shown as UML-like diagram and JSONschema

5.2 Time Series Service

Since the corresponding master data is already stored in the Master Data Service, the Time Series Service simply stores the actual measured values (time stamp and value per measurement). This again corresponds to the paradigm of the single responsibility per microservice[7]. In the sense of this single responsibility, the Time Series Service, with the aid of the underlying specialized time series databases, is capable of performing specific, timeseries-related tasks, e.g. filtering of data, data aggregation or unit transformations.

---

[7] As known from Unix as "Do one thing and do it well.".

5.3   Geo Data Service

The Geo Data Service is used to store and provide spatial data. In many cases, these data correspond to masterdata, whereby one or more attributes describe the position and/or the geometry of the objects. Therefore, depending on the application, e.g. if no complex spatial operations are required, it is possible to provide spatial data exclusively via the MasterData Service, e.g. using the GeoJSON format.

However, if specific spatial operations or special data formats are required, the provision of the data on the spatial data service is useful and necessary.

Since the requirements for the Geo Data Service are still fully supported by a (Cloud-based) solution off the shelf (CARTO[8]), the implementation of this service is currently postponed. For some applications, data is stored redundantly in both the Geo Data Service and the Master Data Service and synchronized automatically.

5.4   Digital Asset Service

Digital assets have the special characteristic that in addition to the descriptive properties (depending on the context called master data or metadata), the object itself can be accessed as binary data stream. Depending on the application, sometimes a link (HTTP URI) on the original asset may be sufficient, in other cases the provision of a copy may be useful or necessary.

Although the range of types of digital assets, their formats, and use cases is significant, the service just considers them as binary data with a certain format (MIME type) and different properties. In other words, the Digital Assets Service generally does not look into the digital assets. If necessary e.g. the Search Service can be used for that.

A digital asset may exist in several variants and/or formats, e.g. images may be available in different resolutions, or a text document either in MS Word or PDF format. According to the mechanisms of content negotiation the client application usually determines required format.

The Digital Asset Service can be connected to different backend systems via adapters, e.g. document management systems providing a CMIS[9] interface. Using suitable backend systems, streaming services (e.g. for videos) can be applied as digital assets, too.

5.5   Search Service

The last actual data service presented here is the Search Service. It provides index information related to unstructured data, often in the form of text documents. To be more specific, it provides access to full-text indexes, which usually provide relevant excerpts (snippets) from as well as references on the entire document.

The Search Service serves as a uniform interface for connecting various full-text search engines, again connected using adapters. The Search Service can also be used in

---

[8] https://carto.com.

[9] https://www.oasis-open.org/committees/tc_home.php?wg_abbrev=cmis.

conjunction with the Digital Asset Service, e.g. if an application needs to search the actual content of a document in addition to its metadata.

However, the Search Service can also provide structured data, e.g. when structured and unstructured search results have to be presented in a single view, or when the search engine provides structured information for a facetted search.

The use of the Search Service also simplifies the replacement of a search engine product, usually by creation of an additional adapter. Many search engines can be connected via the existing Open Search[10] adapter, and web catalogues using the CSW[11] interface.

5.6   Application Configuration Service

The Application Configuration Service allows applications to store structured information. The service focusses on the reuse of information beyond application boundaries, e.g. complex visualization configurations, map configurations (a map as a compilation of several specific layers), or cross-system settings for individual users.

Technically the Application Configuration Service shares most of its code with the Master Data Service, but there exist some specific extensions, e.g. relaxations with regard to the use of schemas, extended multi-tenant capabilities, vastly limited access, and the use of special service-accounts for authentication and authorization.

6   Technologies

The diversity of services directly implies the use of different technologies for data management, e.g. geographic information systems, different types of NoSQL databases, time series databases, document management systems, full-text search engines, structured search engines, etc. to match the specific requirements of each case. Services can implement facades accessing underlying (Cloud) services, such as Google Cloud SQL, Bigtable, DataStore, storage, etc.

In addition, tools for data ingestion are required, for example Apache Flume[12], Logstash[13] or FME[14]. These tools are essential to ensure the necessary degree of automation for the management of large and diverse data sets, and to be able to control workflows easily and transparently. In addition, they already offer many prefabricated interfaces for the processing of standard data formats, or for adding further interfaces by configuration or by programming of small additional modules.

All services are implemented as microservices based on Java using the "Spring Boot" framework[15], are packaged in Docker containers, and operated on a Kubernetes

---

[10] http://www.opensearch.org/Home.

[11] http://www.opengeospatial.org/standards/cat.

[12] https://flume.apache.org.

[13] https://www.elastic.co/products/logstash.

[14] http://www.safe.com.

[15] http://projects.spring.io/spring-boot/.

infrastructure in the Cloud (Google Container Engine). Development instances run on dedicated servers and on a (local) computer cluster, also based on Kubernetes.

Table 1 gives a brief overview of the data services, used frameworks for implementation and runtime environment, and a selection of connectable backend systems.

Table 1. Services, their underlying frameworks, and backend systems

Service	Implementation and runtime environment	Persistence layer
Master Data Service	Spring Boot, Docker, Kubernetes	Elasticsearch[a] MongoDB[b] Google Cloud SQL[c]
Master Data Service (Interim version)	Google App Engine	Google Cloud SQL
Schema Service	Spring Boot, Docker, Kubernetes	Elasticsearch, MongoDB
Time Series Service	Spring Boot, Docker, Kubernetes	OpenTSDB[d] InfluxDB[e] Elasticsearch
Geo Data Service	CARTO (Cloud)	CARTO
Digital Asset Service *experimental*	Spring Boot Docker, Kubernetes	Alfresco[f] (CMIS-Interface)
Search Service	Spring Boot, Docker, Kubernetes	Google Search Appliance[g] Elasticsearch OpenSearch (Atom)
Application Configuration Service *experimental*	Spring Boot, Docker, Kubernetes	Elasticsearch MongoDB
Link Service *experimental*	Spring Boot, Docker, Kubernetes	neo4j[h]

[a] https://www.elastic.co/de/products/elasticsearch.
[b] https://www.mongodb.com.
[c] https://cloud.google.com/sql/.
[d] http://opentsdb.net.
[e] https://www.influxdata.com.
[f] https://www.alfresco.com.
[g] https://enterprise.google.com/search/products/gsa.html.
[h] https://neo4j.com.

7   Experiences

The Web Cache has gradually grown and the presented architecture is in operation since the beginning of 2016. Some precursors of individual services were based on other technologies (Servlets, Google App Engine). With the general idea of the microservice-based architecture in mind during their development, those services could be refactored to "real" microservices.

Experiences in development and operation are very positive. Because of the independence and loose coupling of services a gradual start-up was possible. The development of individual services is straightforward and requires relatively short periods of time.

Nowadays, significantly more data are available for more applications than ever before. Data that previously haven't been available, or have been hidden in business applications, now can be used in many ways, for example, by other special applications, websites, portals and mobile apps. Rising requirements in operation, for example a growing number of accesses, can easily be scaled out on the fly using the horizontal scaling capabilities of the container virtualization infrastructure. The use of container technologies allows a greater independence in the selection of infrastructure operators. Also, the relocation of single or several services is easily possible.

Within consuming applications the use of a generic family of services enables the implementation and reuse of generic, highly configurable frontend components. This additionally simplifies the work of online editors and increases the recognition value for users.

Existing generic services are suitable for many new applications and use cases, usually implemented just by configuration.

By abstracting the (versioned) interfaces (REST APIs) from the underlying internal modules, components or even whole services can be exchanged transparently for consuming applications, depending on the infrastructure even without interrupting operations.

For the synchronization of data sources and services, a high level of automation is possible.

The Web Cache has some positive side effects: With the help of its generic services, it is possible to combine data from different sources, or to create comprehensive views on (disjoint) databases, e.g. from different federal states.

Drawbacks can be seen as opportunities, depending on the approach. The fundamental problem of redundancy (dual operation and redundant data storage with the corresponding additional expenses) generates operational flexibility, and facilitates the provision of "Internet-enabled" data. The necessity of concepts for legal issues, operations, consistency, data schemas and formats, provides opportunities to clarify issues, responsibilities and the (re-)definition of (operational) processes.

Although the provision of data for a wide range of users creates transparency, it also reveals poor data quality in some cases.

8 Conclusion and Outlook

The Web Cache concept presented in this paper defines a complete architecture for the dissemination of environmental information. The keystone of this architecture is the provision of multifarious types of data by a limited number of generic microservices. Consistent implementation of these services with (versioned) RESTful APIs, and use of container virtualization offer the greatest possible degree of flexibility in the (further) development and operation. In contrast to the development of monolithic applications, individual services or data containers can be provided very quickly. This leads to a gradual improvement of the consuming applications, allowing the "release early, release often" philosophy in the development of modern (mobile) applications.

The development of individual services is not yet completed. Existing APIs have to be partly replaced by new, unified, and more powerful versions. This entails a better automatic processing of data, with the aim of being able to provide information according to the ideas of the Semantic Web [10], e.g. using relevant standard formats such as RDF. This also includes, for example, information on provenance of data as well as usage and exploitation rights.

Currently, only freely accessible data is stored in the Web Cache. In order to provide data with limited access via the Web Cache the existing mechanisms for authentication and authorization have to be instrumented.

References

1. European Union: Directive 2003/4/EG" (2003). http://eur-lex.europa.eu/legal-content/DE/ALL/?uri=CELEX:32003L0004
2. Bundesrepublik Deutschland: Umweltinformationsgesetz (2004). https://www.bgbl.de/xaver/bgbl/start.xav?jumpTo=bgbl104s3704.pdf
3. Ubaldi, B.: Open government data - towards empirical analysis of open government data initiatives. In: OECD Working Papers on Public Governance, No. 22. OECD Publishing (2013). ISSN 1993-435. https://doi.org/10.1787/5k46bj4f03s7-en http://www.oecd-ilibrary.org/governance/open-government-data_5k46bj4f03s7-en
4. Schlachter, T., Düpmeier, C., Weidemann, R., Schillinger, W., Bayer, N.: "My environment" – a dashboard for environmental information on mobile devices. In: Hřebíček, J., Schimak, G., Kubásek, M., Rizzoli, A.E. (eds.) ISESS 2013. IAICT, vol. 413, pp. 196–203. Springer, Heidelberg (2013). https://doi.org/10.1007/978-3-642-41151-9_19
5. Schlachter, T., et al.: LUPO Umsetzung einer (micro-)serviceorientierten Architektur (SOA) für Landesumweltportale. In: Weissenbach, K., Schillinger, W., Weidemann, R. (Eds.) F + E-Vorhaben INOVUM - Innovative Umweltinformationssysteme - Phase I 2014/2016, KIT Scientific reports 7715, pp. 25–38 (2016)
6. Fowler, M., Lewis, J.: Microservices – definition of this new architectural term. http://martinfowler.com/articles/microservices.html. Accessed 31 August 2016
7. Cohen, U.: Containers, microservices, and orchestrating the whole symphony open-source.com. https://opensource.com/business/14/12/containers-microservices-and-orchestrating-whole-symphony. Accessed 31 August 2016
8. Seemann, M.: REST implies Content Negotiation. http://blog.ploeh.dk/2015/06/22/rest-implies-content-negotiation/. Accessed 31 August 2016
9. Olliffe, G.: Microservices: Building Services with the Guts on the Outside. Gartner Blog Network. http://blogs.gartner.com/gary-olliffe/2015/01/30/microservices-guts-on-the-outside/ Accessed 31 August 2016
10. Braun, E., et al.: A Generic Microservice Architecture for Environmental Data Management, submitted to ISESS (2017)

The SensLog Platform – A Solution for Sensors and Citizen Observatories

Michal Kepka[1], Karel Charvát[2(✉)], Marek Šplíchal[3], Zbyněk Křivánek[3], Marek Musil[3], Šimon Leitgeb[4], Dmitrij Kožuch[4], and Raitis Bērziņš[5]

[1] Department of Geomatics, Faculty of Applied Sciences, University of West Bohemia, Pilsen, Czech Republic
mkepka@kgm.zcu.cz
[2] Wirelessinfo, Cholinská 19, Litovel, Czech Republic
charvat@wirelessinfo.cz
[3] Czech Centre for Science and Society, Radlicka 28, 150 00 Praha 5, Czech Republic
{splichal,krivanek,musil}@ccss.cz
[4] Help Service Remote Sensing, Husova 2117, 256 01 Benešov, Czech Republic
leitgeb.simon@gmail.com, dmitrii@hsrs.cz
[5] Baltic Open Solution Center, Krišjāņa Barona iela 32-7, Rīga, 1011, Latvia
raitisbe@gmail.com

Abstract. SensLog is an integrated server side Web based solution for sensor data management. SensLog consists of a data model and a server-side application which is capable of storing, analyzing and publishing sensor data in various ways. This paper describes the technical advancements of the SensLog platform. SensLog receives measured data from nodes and/or gateways, stores data in a database, pre-processes data for easier queries if desired and then publishes data through the system of web-services. SensLog is suitable for sensor networks with static sensors (e.g. meteorological stations) as well as for mobile sensors (e.g. tracking of vehicles, human-as-sensor). The database model is based on the standardized data model for observations from OGC Observations & Measurements. The model was extended to provide more functionalities, especially in the field of users' hierarchy, alerts and tracking of mobile sensors. The latest SensLog improvements include a new version of the database model and an API supporting citizen observatories. Examples of pilot applications using SensLog services are described in the paper.

Keywords: Sensors · VGI · SensLog · Citizen observatories · Open data

1 Introduction

Sensors are an important part of data producers, especially in the field of spatial data. There are large number of sensor data available on the Web in variety of formats encoding. Wide-ranging services and solutions for sensor data publishing for different type of sensors are usually very complex and complicated for non-expert users. The authors address this problem by designing tools and processes for effortless and

J. Hřebíček et al. (Eds.): ISESS 2017, IFIP AICT 507, pp. 372–382, 2017.
https://doi.org/10.1007/978-3-319-89935-0_31

straightforward utilization of existing sensors available on the Web. This work has been done in the scope of the Open Sensors Network pilot as part of the SDI4Apps project[1].

Reusing existing sensors operated by third-party providers is currently problematic. The problems range from initial search of services through metadata description of sensors to filtering of found sensor candidates. It could be understood as searching for suitable repairman company in yellow pages. In the same way, it would be useful to find some "yellow pages" for searching appropriate sensors and sensor data producers on the Web. A good starting point for reusing sensors is to find the rate between usability and complexity of sensor services and providing them straightforwardly. The SensLog application described in following paper can be given as an example of sensor data management for small and medium sensor networks [1–4]. SensLog serves a data provider as a tool for collecting, processing and publishing of sensor data on the Web. SensLog allows to receive measurements from sensor networks (from sensors, gateways or by intermediate daemons) through defined web services. Received data are processed and stored in a data storage. Stored data can be published for data consumers by different web services in various formats and metadata of registered sensors can be exported to semantic sensor catalogues together with the endpoint description [5, 6].

2 SensLog

SensLog is a software component for sensor data management on the Web. SensLog receives sensor data by requests over HTTP protocol and stores them in a database. SensLog publishes raw and/or processed sensor data using several interfaces. One of the communication interfaces is proprietary-defined but extensive RESTful API [9] publishing data mostly in the JSON format. Another interface is based on the core methods of the OGC Sensor Observation Service[2] version 1.0.0 standard [8]. SensLog has also a simple graphical user interface (GUI) with several functions to visualize data. However, the application is intended to be used in combination with other standalone clients.

The SensLog application was designed as a modular solution from the very beginning. New modules were developed and tested during contemporary projects including SDI4Apps, FOODIE[3] and OTN[4]). A module for collecting volunteered geographic information (VGI) was designed and developed with the emphasis on character and properties of such type of data. The expansion of precision farming utilization has affected the design and development of another SensLog module for telemetry of agricultural machinery. Both new modules are based on the SensLog core functions, methods and modules providing extensions to the current interfaces. The server-side part of SensLog is written in the Java programming language. The database part is written in the PL/SQL language and the Web GUI uses the JavaScript jQuery library.

---

[1] SDI4Apps – Uptake of Open Geographic Information through Innovative Services Based on Linked Data (http://sdi4apps.eu/).

[2] Open Geospatial Consortium standard Sensor Observation Service (http://www.opengeospatial.org/standards/sos).

[3] FOODIE – Farm-Oriented Open Data In Europe (http://www.foodie-project.eu/).

[4] OTN – Open Transport Net (http://opentnet.eu/).

2.1   The SensLog Data Model

The SensLog data model is based on the OGC Observations & Measurements 1.0 standard [7]. The model was further extended based on requirements provided by the SDI4Apps, FOODIE and OTN projects. The SensLog data model is used for storage of raw sensor data and results of data analyses. A diagram of the last version of the SensLog data model is shown in Fig. 1. The core tables of the model include *units, sensors, phenomenons, observations* and *units_positions*. The object unit represents a physical device that has got one or more connected sensors which are producing observations. A unit can be equipped with a GNSS chip to periodically determine its own position (e.g. in case of mobile devices monitoring), or the position of the unit can be defined by another method (e.g. in case of static in-situ monitoring).

The SensLog data model was recently improved especially for potentially large tables. The *observations* and *units_positions* tables are the largest ones. Their volume is growing in coherence with continuous data monitoring. These tables were supplemented with a table partitioning mechanism (shown as series of tables in Fig. 1). The core SensLog model was extended by tables defined by the new VGI and telemetry modules. The consistency of stored data is ensured not only by the referential integrity but also by the system of triggers and stored functions. The consistency is ensured especially in the case that extension tables are stored in separate database schemas. In this way, child tables of partitioned observations and unit positions allow better querying, backing up and maintenance. The SensLog data model was implemented in RDBMS PostgreSQL 9.x+ with spatial extension PostGIS 2.x+.

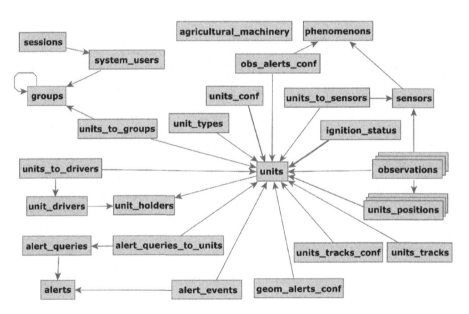

Fig. 1. Diagram of the SensLog data model

2.2 SensLog VGI Module

The importance of VGI is growing in present days and current projects brought requirements on incorporating this type of data into SensLog. The character of VGI does not allow to store such type of data directly to the present SensLog data model without loss of information. Therefore, a new module for VGI was designed and implemented. This VGI module contains new services for receiving and publishing data over the Web. The SensLog data model was extended with new tables with emphasis on variability of VGI. A VGI observation is characterized by several mandatory attributes and can be enriched with additional attributes. It's not necessary to define the final number and names of additional attributes before starting collecting VGI. The datatype of an additional attribute is only limited to data types which values can be stored in the JSON format. A VGI observation can include a list of multimedia files that are also stored in the data model. A schema of tables of the VGI module is shown in Fig. 2. A common type of VGI is a point of interest (POI). The concept of POI is similar to the general observation concept. The implemented scenario defined by the SDI4Apps project considers a POI as a spatially and temporally localized observation with several attributes and an array of connected multimedia files. Each POI is classified into one of the predefined categories and is sorted as a user-defined dataset.

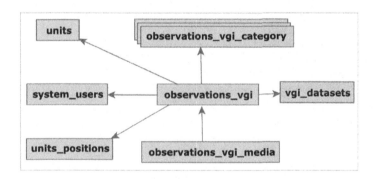

Fig. 2. The data model of the SensLog VGI module

The tables added by the VGI module include:

- *observations_vgi* – this is the main table that stores VGI observations with all attributes except for multimedia content,
- *observations_vgi_media* – this table stores multimedia files connected to VGI observations,
- *observations_vgi_category* – this table stores categories of VGI observations, the table uses a partitioning mechanism to sort categories,
- *vgi_datasets* – this table stores user-defined datasets with dataset metadata.

The VGI observation has got relations to some core tables of the SensLog model. The information about the device that produced the VGI observation is stored in the *units* table. The information about the user is stored in the *system_users* table. The main VGI geometry is a type of point and it is stored in the *units_positions* table. The geometry of VGI represents the point where the VGI observation was localized. An additional geometry of different type can be stored as an additional attribute. The categories of POIs can be stored in tables inherited from the master table *observations_vgi_category*. This enables to store different kinds of categories in a hierarchical order.

2.3 SensLog RDF Export of VGI

In order to publish data according to the Open Linked Data best practices and with a self-describing data structure, the Virtuoso graph model engine is used. The data are stored in quads, which consist of a graph name describing a dataset and a triple which maps an attribute value (object) to POI (subject). The mapping is done by using a property which is in the best case scenario defined in some public ontology thus making it easier to integrate data with other systems. The data can be queried and inserted into the quad-store through the SPARQL [11] endpoint at http://data.plan4all.eu/sparql or uploaded and parsed on the server via RDF [10] files if the amount in one batch exceeds 100 megabytes. An insert operation for one POI can be seen in the following example:

```
INSERT DATA {
GRAPH <http://www.sdi4apps.eu/poi.rdf> {
<http://www.sdi4apps.eu/new_poi/c72cf4a7>
<http://purl.org/dc/elements/1.1/identifier>
"http://www.sdi4apps.eu/new_poi/c72cf4a7".
<http://www.sdi4apps.eu/new_poi/c72cf4a7>
<http://www.opengis.net/ont/geosparql#asWKT>"POINT(13.431
49.741)"^^virtrdf:Geometry.
<http://www.sdi4apps.eu/new_poi/c72cf4a7>
<http://www.openvoc.eu/poi#class>
<http://gis.zcu.cz/SPOI/Ontology#bus_stop>.
<http://www.sdi4apps.eu/new_poi/c72cf4a7>
<http://purl.org/dc/elements/1.1/title>"New point"
}}
```

The data visualization is performed through a web-based map client based on the HSLayers-NG library (Fig. 3). Map layers are dynamically generated for each graph (dataset) and category (http://gis.zcu.cz/SPOI/Ontology#bus_stop in the above mentioned example in Fig. 3) which can be found in a particular dataset. Displaying of the triples is based on principle that each subject in a triple is displayed as a new vector (point) feature in the map. Likewise each property and object is converted to the feature's attribute and value in GIS terms. Styling of the features such as choosing an icon and color is based on attribute (category) values and is application specific.

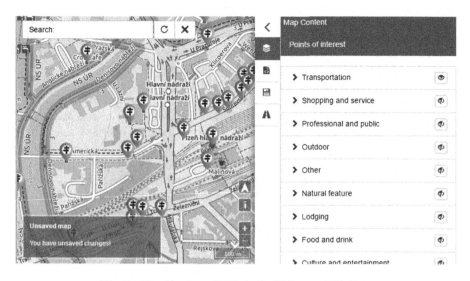

Fig. 3. Visualization of POIs in the HSLayers-NG client

2.4 SensLog Interfaces

The publication of stored data is provided by the system of web services. The system of web services allows publication of stored data in different levels of detail and in various export formats. The modularity of SensLog allows to have a different interface for each module with specific web services according to the character of the following application. The diagram in Fig. 4 shows the structure of SensLog modules along with the corresponding interfaces and formats provided by each module.

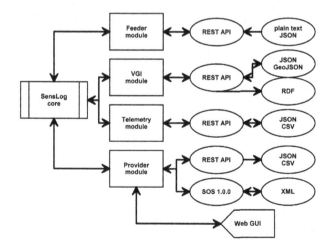

Fig. 4. Diagram of the structure of the SensLog modules

On the one side, there is the feeder module for inserting new observations and positions through methods of the HTTP protocol. The feeder module is independent from other modules which enables having an allocated database connection for continuous insertion. Only authenticated clients are allowed to insert new objects.

On the other side, there is provider module that contains the system of web services via methods of the HTTP protocol to publish stored data. The provider module uses mainly the RESTful interface publishing data in the JSON format in a proprietary-defined form. The provider module contains also a standardized interface based on the core methods of OGC SOS 1.0.0. The proprietary interface contains a wider range of services with a variety of data formats.

The VGI module has also the RESTful interface defined with an emphasis on character of the VGI observation object. A VGI observation can be inserted encoded in the JSON format or as a multipart form of data. The insertion of a new VGI observation is variable due to the possibility of pushing VGI observations from mobile applications. There is an option to store a plain VGI observation with mandatory attributes and to add multimedia contents afterwards (e.g. while having a better Internet connection). The stored VGI observations can be published encoded in the JSON format in a proprietary form or in the GeoJSON[5] format as the Feature or FeatureCollection object. The connected multimedia files are addressed in a form of a direct URL. An exporting web service according to the requirements from the SDI4Apps project was designed. This exporting service publishes stored VGI observations encoded in the RDF format to be further processed in the Virtuoso system.

The telemetry module uses mainly the previously described feeder module for inserting observations and positions. The telemetry module defines only standalone web services for publishing analysis results on utilization of machinery and farm fields. The data are provided in the JSON format in a proprietary form or in case of any listings, data are provided in the textual CSV format.

The import of sensor data to SensLog is provided by the services of the feeder module in most cases. The pattern of services of the feeder module is straightforward without the necessity of any specially object mapping. An ordinary scenario is to insert data to SensLog when the data are observed. In exceptional cases, especially when the data connection is lost for longer time and observations are restored from flash memory of gateway, data can be pushed into the SensLog storage by a script in a batch. In case of very long time series that need to be imported, it is possible to import data directly to the database model by PL/SQL scripts.

3   SensLog Applications

The modularity of SensLog allows its use in a variety of applications. Currently, the authors are supporting three types of sensors as pilots including the monitoring of the level and quality of ground water, utilization of a wide spectrum of sensors in precision farming and utilization of SensLog as a gateway for collecting VGI directly by users.

---

[5] http://geojson.org.

3.1 Groundwater Monitoring

The water quality is dependent on several aspects including the crop type, irrigation method, soil types, groundwater levels, soil and water chemistry, nutrient loads, limits on chemicals, salt tolerance of crops, leaching of salts and management of drainage water. There are several barriers to the reuse of wastewater in agriculture. The key barrier is that many stakeholders do not view wastewater as a resource, even if adequately treated. The stakeholders see the energy costs for treating wastewater to an adequate standard as being prohibitively expensive. One of the aims of the project pilot is to utilize recent innovations to turn wastewater reuse into a profitable, socially beneficiary and environmentally safe solution. A number of phenomena are monitored in this pilot including chemical and physical properties of the surface and underground water.

The observations are produced by sensors deployed in shallow wells and they are sent by gateway stations on the ground in defined intervals. The observations are processed and user-defined analyses are run. There is a system of alerts that is triggered in case of reaching some defined thresholds. The services of the provider module are publishing not only measured data but also results of analyses and alerts.

3.2 Agrometeorological Monitoring

Agriculture requires collecting, storing, sharing and analyzing large quantities of spatially referenced data. Such type of data, to be used effectively, must be transferred between different hardware, software and organizations. These data flows present a hurdle to uptake of precision agriculture. The use of multitude of data models, formats, interfaces and reference systems is resulting in incompatibilities. The management of huge amounts of data is a challenge. Spatio-temporal data is increasingly collected by remote or in-situ sensors rather than by field campaigns. Wireless communications have several benefits, but also pose challenges to the data exchange reliability and power supply. Sensor calibration and deployment as well as the maintenance of sensors need resources and technical skills and increase the costs of data acquisition. The increasing of both the data amount and the data quality awareness issue highlighted importance.

An important part of using sensors in agriculture is represented by tracking of agriculture machinery to provide analyses oriented not only on utilization of monitoring of particular machinery but also on intervention monitoring of a particular field. The combination of machinery data together with field information provides a higher level of economic evaluation. The screenshot in Fig. 5 shows a client application visualizing results of analyses provided by the SensLog telemetry module.

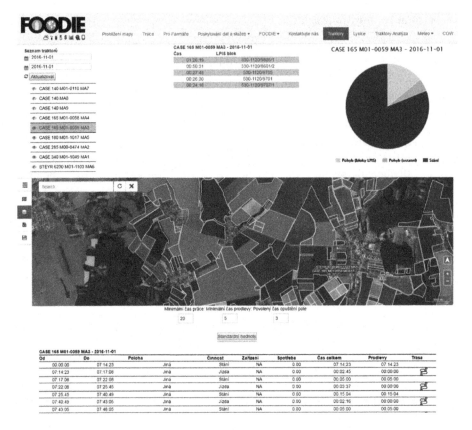

Fig. 5. Client application for visualization of analysis results

3.3 VGI and Citizen Observatories

A human as a sensor, also referred to as VGI monitoring, represents collecting measurements and observations by users by portable devices. It is a typical way of collecting spatially referenced thematic data in the domain of Earth observations. The characteristics of such type of observations include high variability of attributes of not only primitive data types and an uncertainty in data accuracy. An example of collaboration between pilots is shown by collecting of POIs. The Smart Points of Interest[6] (SPOI) [5] data set was developed in the frame of the SDI4Apps project providing information as linked data [6]. SensLog became a segment in the chain of collecting and updating user-defined POIs. SensLog provides services to push new POIs collected by users in the database on the one side and it provides export services to pull sets of POIs to final storage based on the Virtuoso server[7] on the other side. Screenshots of client mobile application for collecting POIs is shown in Fig. 6.

---

[6] SPOI – Smart Points of Interest (http://www.sdi4apps.eu/spoi/).
[7] Virtuoso Universal Server (https://virtuoso.openlinksw.com/).

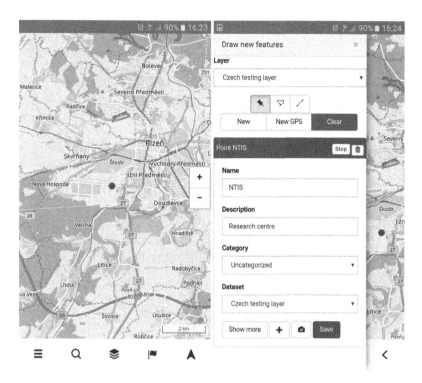

Fig. 6. Mobile application for collecting POIs. Main screen on the right and attributes of the selected POI on the left side.

4 Conclusions

SensLog is an application for sensor data management and it is used operationally in a number of solutions and pilots. SensLog provides a system of web services for both data producers and data consumers. A stress was put on finding a good ratio between the usability and generality of these web services during the design and the development phases of the solution. SensLog is an effective way how to combine the OGC standards [7, 8] with a light API for development of subsequent applications. The SensLog data model was designed to store observations produced by variety of sensor types. Extensibility of SensLog by additional modules was confirmed during pilot applications in the current projects. Additional modules for agricultural machinery telemetry and for collecting POIs by smart devices were developed.

The authors plan to add an additional module that will be oriented on devices from the Internet of things domain. One of the main tasks will be to implement the OMA[8] NGSI[9] specification which is a primary interface for Generic Enablers in FIWARE.

---

[8] OMA – Open Mobile Alliance (http://openmobilealliance.org/).
[9] NGSI – Next Generation Services Interface.

Acknowledgement. This paper was supported by the SDI4Apps project (CIP-ICT-PSP-PB 621129) which has received funding from the EU ICT Policy Support Program as part of the Competitiveness and Innovation Framework Program. This paper was supported by the European Union Research and Innovation programme H2020 under the grant agreement No 732064 "Data-Driven Bioeconomy" (DataBio). The author Michal Kepka was supported by the Grant No. SGS-2016-004 "Využití matematiky a infromatiky v geomatice III," awarded by the University of West Bohemia.

References

1. Kepka, M., Ježek, J.: Server-side solution for sensor data. In: ICT for Agriculture, Rural Development and Environment Where we are? Where we will go? Czech Centre for Science and Society, Praha, pp. 264–274 (2012). ISBN 978-80-904830-9-5
2. Kepka, M., Ježek, J., Charvát, K., Musil, M.: Complex solution for sensor network in precision farming. In: IST-Africa 2013 Conference Proceedings. International Information Management Corporation, Nairobi, pp. 1–7 (2013). ISBN 978-1-905824-38-0
3. Reznik, T., Charvat Jr., K., Charvat, K., Horakova, S., Lukas, V., Kepka, M.: Open data model for (Precision) agriculture applications and agricultural pollution monitoring. In: Johannsen, V.K., Jensen, S., Wohlgemuth, V., Preist, C., Eriksson, E. (eds.) Proceedings of Enviroinfo and ICT for Sustainability 2015, ACSR, vol. 22, pp. 97–107. Atlantis Press, Paris (2015)
4. Krivanek, Z., Musil, M., Jezek, J., Kepka, M., Vohnout, P., Alberts, M., Charvat, K.: Alert system in case of excess drawing of ground water. In: IST-Africa 2012 Conference Proceedings. International Information Management Corporation (2012)
5. Cerba, O., Mildorf, T.: Smart points of interest: big, linked and harmonized spatial data. In: EGU General Assembly Conference Abstracts (2016)
6. Berners-Lee, T.: Linked Data (2006). https://www.w3.org/DesignIssues/LinkedData.html
7. ISO 19156:2011 Geographic information - Observations and measurements, International Organization for Standardization, Geneva (2011)
8. OGC 06-009r6 OpenGIS Sensor Observation Service, Open Geospatial Consortium, Inc. (2007)
9. Fielding, R.T.: Architectural styles and the design of network-based software architectures. Ph.D. University of California, Irvine (2000)
10. RDF – Resource Description Format. https://www.w3.org/RDF/
11. SPARQL Query Language for RDF. https://www.w3.org/TR/rdf-sparql-query/

A Generic Microservice Architecture
for Environmental Data Management

Eric Braun[✉], Thorsten Schlachter, Clemens Düpmeier, Karl-Uwe Stucky,
and Wolfgang Suess

Karlsruhe Institute of Technology, Karlsruhe, Germany
{eric.braun2,thorsten.schlachter,clemens.duepmeier,
karl-uwe.stucky,wolfgang.suess}@kit.edu

Abstract. The growing popularity of Web applications and the Internet of Things cause an urgent need for modern scalable data management to cope with large amounts of data. In the environmental domain these problems also need a solution because of big data coming from a large amount of sensors or users (e.g. crowdsourcing applications). This paper presents an architecture that uses a microservice approach to create a data management backend for the mentioned applications. The main concept shows that microservices can be used to define separate services for different data types and management tasks. This separation leads to many advantages such as better scalability and low coupling between different features. Two prototypes, which are already implemented, are evaluated in this paper.

Keywords: Microservices · Data management
Environmental information systems (EIS) · Databases · Time series · REST
Semantic Web · Linked data · Big data

1   Introduction

Nowadays the Internet of Things and modern Internet infrastructures lead to a massive amount of data stored in data centers all around the globe. In the field of environment, the sensorization of the environment and new crowdsourcing applications will also produce large amounts of data which have to be stored, managed and analyzed timely in order to provide early input for decision makers and the general public. Often, the acquired data in such applications consists of a mixture of measurement data, more general time series data, structured master data or unstructured text or binary assets. The most useful tools to get an insight into this data are visualizations and data analysis. However, classical information system architectures and desktop data analysis and visualization tools have severe problems in handling large amounts of data and new techniques are needed to manage these amounts of data in a scalable way. Therefore, the Web based Information Systems (WebIS) and Data Life Cycle Lab Energy (DLLE) groups at KIT/IAI work on a new data management runtime environment based on microservices [1], which can be easily integrated with Big Data infrastructures, and scalable data analysis and web based visualization tools.

© IFIP International Federation for Information Processing 2017
Published by Springer International Publishing AG 2017. All Rights Reserved
J. Hřebíček et al. (Eds.): ISESS 2017, IFIP AICT 507, pp. 383–394, 2017.
https://doi.org/10.1007/978-3-319-89935-0_32

Based on the microservice reference architecture introduced by Gartner[1] a new modular set of distributed services instrumenting a polyglot distributed data management model on top of an underlying Big Data environment was implemented. These services can be used with additional infrastructure services to provide a very generic and flexible scalable data management infrastructure with all the features needed by modern large scale web based information system applications. Based on these services, existing environmental backend applications for data management, such as the environmental information system applications within the LUBW[2], can be brought to a state-of-the-art level of technology to provide a future-proof way of managing the massive amounts of data which will be gathered and analyzed by future Web and mobile environmental information system applications. This paper describes the chosen basic architectural approach and then focuses on the mentioned collection of basic microservices that were conceptualized and implemented to create a generic solution for an efficient large-scale (environmental) data management. Further papers will describe other aspects of the architecture and specific microservices.

2   Basic Concepts and Main Goals

Data management is needed in many application domains other than the environmental domain. For example, the research groups at the KIT are also involved in several smart grid projects in which it is critical to gather and analyze large amounts of data for future energy system solutions. Therefore, the KIT was looking for a data management solution which not only applies to the environmental but also to the smart grid domain. The architecture described in this paper fulfills this requirement and is conceptualized based on very generic data type notions that enable data management for nearly any domain. Current information system applications in the environmental area are often still implemented as big monoliths using a standard multitier architecture, in which the data tier is concentrated in one relational database model and access layer. The resulting data model has a very strong structure but ties the whole data management to one application or application domain and does not scale horizontally to meet performance needs in a world of big data. A microservice based architecture can replace this monolithic data management concept by providing a set of modular and low coupled data services whereas each service defines its own data management tier based on a more generic and reusable data model and the most adequate database technology underneath which is not necessarily a relational database system. Microservices in general can be defined as follows:

> "In short, the microservice architectural style is an approach to developing a single application as **a suite of small services**, each **running in its own process** and communicating with lightweight mechanisms, often an HTTP resource API. These services are **built around business capabilities and independently deployable** by fully automated deployment machinery. There is a **bare minimum of centralized management** of these services, which may be written in different programming languages and use different data storage technologies."
> James Lewis and Martin Fowler, 2014 [emphasis added]

---

[1] http://blogs.gartner.com/gary-olliffe/2015/01/30/microservices-guts-on-the-outside.
[2] Baden-Wuerttemberg State Institute for Environment, Measurements, and Nature Conservation, Karlsruhe, Germany.

Microservices are typically designed to scale horizontally to meet the currently needed performance. Since microservices separate functionalities into distinct services, each functionality can be scaled independently from each other according to the need. This advantage directly applies to data management because often scaling is not needed for the whole data model, e.g. for some rather static or seldomly used parts, but only for providing access to highly frequented parts of the data.

In a polyglot data model different data services use different database technologies to provide a more generic data handling and data access. For example, a document oriented database can be used to implement a very generic model of structured master data storage without tying the implementation too much to a specific master data schema. Nonetheless, a separate schema service which describes specific types of master data more precisely can provide all benefits of having a strong schema without hard-coding the data type schemas into the implementation of the master data service.

Another advantage of microservices is the more modular development approach allowing projects to be performed by smaller independent development groups, each of them having to manage just one or a few microservices. The communication between microservices is often realized using REST over HTTP(S). This communication interface is the only component of a microservice that is visible from the outside. Everything else, like application and data logic, is hidden within the service. Therefore, the REST API is the only interface that has to be standardized across development teams. This has the benefit that all technical interfaces between the otherwise separate projects are externalized. However, this also makes it crucial to define a proper API with an appropriate documentation and manage these APIs application or enterprise wide (called API management) in order to guarantee long term stable interaction between microservices and clients.

This paper will demonstrate how dedicated microservices can be conceptualized which allows the management of large amounts of different types of data by instrumenting a polyglot data model. The different services follow a common philosophy which leads to a REST API that is similar in its core for all services. A first prototypical implementation that proves this concept and solves first development challenges is discussed.

3 Architectural Overview

The microservice based architecture used is inspired by the reference architecture of Gartner [2]. Figure 1 shows this reference architecture.

The architecture can be split into three main functional areas: microservice management capabilities, actual microservices and operational capabilities. In the following only the second part is of major importance. Although management and operational capabilities are crucial for operating and maintaining a microservice architecture, this paper mainly focuses on which microservices are needed as part of the inner architecture to provide a scalable data management functionality for large scale information system applications.

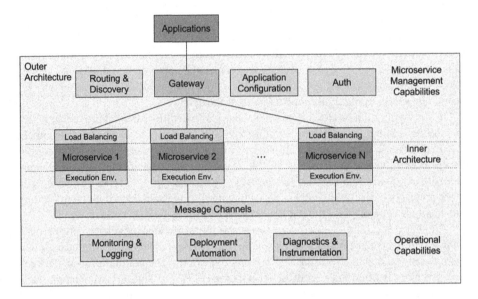

Fig. 1. Overview of microservice based architecture

Typically, microservices are designed to be load balanceable which leads to a (horizontally) scalable system. Therefore, the management layer of the Microservice Architecture contains an API gateway which distributes incoming client calls with the help of a discovery and routing service onto different instances of the inner services. Communication with the management layer and clients is generally achieved by using REST over HTTP(s) or WebSockets[3]. The communication between different microservices is implemented using a message channel (e.g. Apache Kafka[4]) to realize asynchronous messaging. This leads to more autonomous services because there are no synchronous and therefore blocking dependencies. Each microservice has its own execution environment which enables a service to be deployed as a container using container virtualization technologies (e.g. Docker[5]). This enables services to be automatically deployed, updated, and to run on many different platforms. Container automated services can also be scaled by increasing or decreasing the number of replicated instances. Service instances are registered with the discovery service and a heartbeat detection checks if instances are still alive. The execution environment of a service instance may also include a private, internal database system but usually the database systems are separated from the microservices in order to keep the latter stateless. This enables databases to scale independently from the used services. As already mentioned for operating such microservice based applications a computing cluster with support for container virtualization is needed (this is typically the case in modern cloud environments). If the cluster or cloud environment also supports a Big Data stack (such as Apache Hadoop[6]), then

---

[3] https://tools.ietf.org/html/rfc6455.

[4] https://kafka.apache.org.

[5] https://www.docker.com.

[6] http://hadoop.apache.org.

Big Data tools, like NoSQL database technologies, can be used and integrated with the inner architecture microservices. As already explained the term polyglot data model means that each service is supposed to use the database technologies which are optimized for the data type managed by the service.

Figure 2 displays a more detailed architecture of the data management services. It shows the gateway as the single access point for client applications which allows to use a single harmonized URL space as well as a single REST API pattern to access the different services. This harmonized URL space and single API is key for the integration of the otherwise on several services distributed data. Each data object stored in a data management service is represented by a unique URI and URIs can be linked to each other to implement relations. Additionally, semantic services define the structure and interrelationship of the otherwise distributed data and provide this knowledge to the application and/or other services.

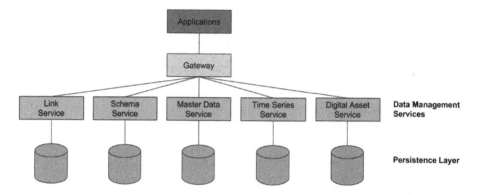

Fig. 2. Data management architecture

The inner architecture for data management consists of five microservices which are briefly described as follows:

- Link Service: a semantic service that is used internally to create relations between data. This service is crucial to create semantic links between different data objects. The service follows the concepts of linked data and semantic Web [3].
- Schema Service: a semantic service that manages schema descriptions (format, data types, etc.) of data objects stored in the different services.
- Master Data Service: manages structured data describing specific objects, i.e. master data.
- Time Series Service: manages time series data. Persistence is usually achieved using a time series database. The separation of time series data into a separate service has many advantages as already depicted in [4].
- Digital Asset Service: manages digital assets similar to systems like Alfresco[7] that feature a CMIS[8] interface.

---

[7] https://www.alfresco.com.

[8] http://docs.oasis-open.org/cmis/CMIS/v1.1/cs01/CMIS-v1.1-cs01.html.

Another important feature of the architecture is shown in Fig. 3 using e.g. the Time Series Service. Each of the data management services is connected to the persistence layer through one or more specific adapters that create a mapping between a concrete database technology used to implement a persistence layer and the respective service. This enables the independent development of persistent layers using different database technologies. The service itself is completely generic and has no dependencies on the underlying database technologies.

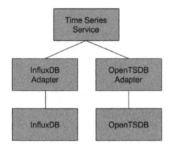

Fig. 3. Abstraction layer between the Time Series Service and time series databases

4   Services in Detail

This chapter focusses on the following services: Schema Service, Link Service and data discovery. The other services mentioned in the previous chapter are discussed in more detail in Schlachter et al. [6].

The Schema Service stores the structure, data types and other semantic information of the data stored in the basic data services. The Master Data Service benefits most from the Schema Service because master data is meant to be of a specific structure using specific data types. The main exchange format for the different services is JSON. Therefore, the Schema Service uses JSON schema[9] as default format to store and exchange schema information. An example for such a schema is depicted in Fig. 4. It is a schema for an air measurement station. Beside the required attributes id and name this example contains two attributes that hold information about the particulate matter limit and current value. Additionally, the attribute *timeSeries* is a complex type that is not part of the official JSON schema standard. Such a complex type usually has an own schema also described in the Schema Service. The service itself uses a document oriented database to store the JSON schemas efficiently.

The service is meant to be used internally mainly by the Master Data Service to validate incoming data and to add schema information to the data to implement linked data. The concept of linked data [5] can be used by applications that consume both; master data and their semantics.

---

[9] http://json-schema.org.

Furthermore, the Schema Service can also be directly accessed from clients (through the gateway) to request a specific schema. This feature is used by applications that generate generic inputs and need the structure of the different fields to do so.

An additional requirement for the Schema Service is the support of different versions and namespaces. The structure of data can change over time which leads to an updated schema for the data. With introduced versions, the schema can exist in more versions and the Master Data Service can associate the data to the appropriate version depending on the changes. The namespace can be used to use the same schema name in different contexts.

```
{
  "title": "Air Measurement Station",
  "type": "object",
  "properties": {
    "id": { "type": "string" },
    "name": { "type": "string" },
    "pm10Limit": { "type": "number" }
    "pm10Current": { "type": "number" }
    ...
    "timeSeries": { "type": "timeSeries" }
  },
  "required": ["id", "name"]
}
```

Fig. 4. JSON schema of an air measurement station

Simple applications only need one of the services because they process a single type of data but more complex applications might need multiple data sets and most probably data sets that are related to each other. Using a microservice architecture, the data is distributed among different services which means that there is a need for a service that defines relationships between different data sets and objects. This service is called Link Service in our architecture. It allows to fully support linked data. The Master Data Service can only support the linked data concept for one data object but with the help of the link service data, corresponding schema information and relationships between data objects can be aggregated into one linked data description of complex interrelated data.

Links are implemented using URIs that point to the data. Additionally, relationships can define additional properties. Applications have the possibility to get a data object with all their links as URIs or with resolved links which lead to nested data objects. Figure 5 presents an example with both options in a pseudo format that is not part of the specification but only to explain the link resolving concept. The first option is the master data object for the air station mentioned above that contains two links that point to time series data for the measurements of air pollutants NO2 and PM10. These links have to be fetched separately from the application in order to get the actual time series data. The second option contains the same master data object but the links are already replaced by the data. Additionally, both objects have a PM10 limit and a current value that obviously matches the last value of the time series.

Object 1   Object 2

```
{                                    {
  "id": "DEBW019",                     "id": "DEBW019",
  "name": "air station Ulm",           "name": "air station Ulm",
    "pm10Limit": 50,                     "pm10Limit": 50,
    "pm10Current": 20,                   "pm10Current": 20,
  ...                                  ...
  "timeSeries": [                      "timeSeries": [
    timeseries/DEBW019/no2,              [26, 22, 21, 23, 31, 58],
    timeseries/DEBW019/pm10              [26, 14, 11, 15, 26, 20]
  ]                                    ]
}                                    }
```

Fig. 5. Time series link resolving

A third concept that will be discussed in this chapter is data discovery. Unlike the described services, the Data Discovery Service will only be used internally and has no external API. It closes the gap between data services (e.g. Master Data Service, Time Series Service) and a specific adapter. As discussed in the previous chapter, data services are implemented by internally using an abstract persistence interface which decouples them from specific implementations of the persistence layer using a certain database technology. One data service can use more than one persistence layer implementation. This abstraction leads to the requirement that a data service needs a way to find out in what persistence layer a specific data set (e.g. master data object or time series) is stored, and this information is provided by the Data Discovery Service. Figure 6 depicts an example for the Time Series Service. The Time Series Service gets the storage location of data using the identifier that is externally communicated as lookup key to the Discovery Service which returns the storage location. The request can then be forwarded to the appropriate adapter. This separation of core services and their underlying persistence layers allows the services to be much more flexible and generic. The Data Discovery Service can be used by every service that stores data in a location that is not known by this service itself.

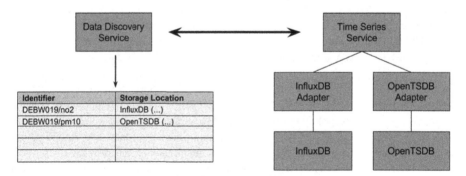

Fig. 6. Time series service and Data Discovery Service interaction

5 Prototype and Evaluation

The generic microservice based architecture was implemented as a prototype and evaluated in context of concrete information system applications, such as environmental information systems and smart energy systems control center software. The Gateway Service is implemented manually in the current prototype environment omitting load balancing features for the moment. In the future, it will likely be replaced by gateway tools like Netflix Zuul[10] for more complete operation. The data management services except the Digital Asset Service are already implemented to some extent. All microservices are implemented using the Java Framework Spring Boot[11] as implementation framework. The Schema Service and the Master Data Service use the document-oriented MongoDB NoSQL database as one persistence layer option by using specific adapters as described above. The Time Series Service is implemented with an OpenTSDB adapter. The adapters are implemented as own microservices which convert the HTTPS requests from database specific requests into abstract requests and vice versa. The communication between microservices as well as between the gateway and the client applications is realized using REST over HTTP(S). The asynchronous messaging channel mentioned while describing the architecture will be used in the future version to lower the synchronous coupling between services. Instead, services will cache data from other internal services. Decoupling and data actualization of cached data will be instrumented via the message channel. An appropriate solution using spring cloud stream and RabbitMQ was already tested in a separate prototype.

The Link Service is implemented using the Neo4j graph database[12] to model the different relations. To connect two data objects only their URI and a relation key are stored. Data can be fetched using the unique URI. The relation key can be used to further filter data by relation type. Such a relation key can describe the multiplicity of the relation or its semantic context.

The first prototype using the generic microservice architecture was implemented as background data service infrastructure for a showcase of the environmental information system "Umweltnavigator Bayern" of the "Bayerisches Staatsministerium für Umwelt und Verbraucherschutz". As shown in Fig. 7, a web page of the Umweltnavigator displays a map of different air measurement stations. A specific station can be selected within the map resulting in the display of more information about the selected station in the right panel and the display of the related measurement data within the bottom visualization. Multiple backend services are accessed in parallel to aggregate this page. The map is filled with information from a geo service that contains the location and icon information of each measuring station. The panel to the right shows more detailed information about the station which is fetched from the Master Data Service. The visualization at the bottom uses the same master data object and fetches the different available time series datasets referenced by the master data object. The URIs pointing to the time series datasets are resolved by the Master Data Service using the Link Service which

---

[10] https://github.com/Netflix/zuul/wiki.

[11] http://projects.spring.io/spring-boot.

[12] https://neo4j.com.

contains the relationship information between measuring station and the measured time series. This example shows the interaction of the basic data services and more complex services like the Link Service or the Geo Service.

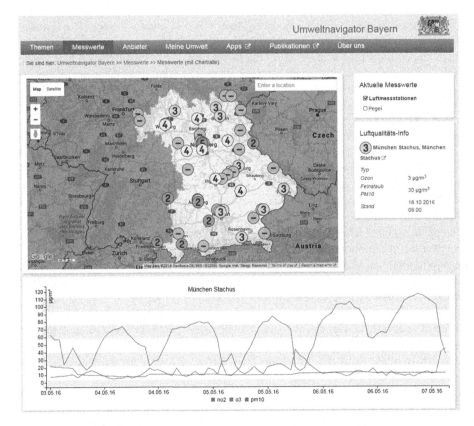

Fig. 7. Environmental information system Umweltnavigator

The second prototype (Fig. 8) is used as a background data service infrastructure for a web based dashboard solution that displays the energy consumption of buildings. The prototype of the dashboard solution beside the backend services was developed in a diploma thesis [8]. The following description explains the usage of the web page from the point of view of a user and of a dashboard manager who creates and customizes pages. An end user accessing the dashboard web page with his browser can select a building on the map which then changes the visualizations of the measurement data accordingly to data that belong to that building. Similar to the previous prototype the visualization uses the master data and the Time Series Service to display the data. Furthermore, the dashboard solution offers additional functionality to customize the structure of the dashboard web page. A dashboard manager can change the information that is shown based on what the master data object that is displayed (in this case: a building) offers. The Schema Service provides this information for the dashboard configuration dialog. Therefore, the dashboard manager sees the different properties that a building can have, including the time series datasets. This allows him to customize every block of the dashboard page that can display information of an arbitrary master data object of a certain type (e.g. a building). In contrast, using a less generic solution, each building needs a manually customized page which does not scale for a large amount of buildings. This more complex scenario shows that the additional use of the Schema Service allows the development of smart applications that provide generic features.

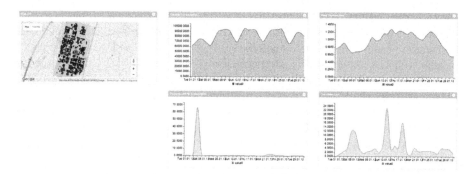

Fig. 8. Dashboard solution using the service infrastructure

Both prototypical implementations present first proofs of the concept and already show the great potential of the envisioned solution. The generic data service infrastructure is used in both use cases to provide application specific data to web applications belonging to different application domains. Both applications directly use the REST API of the different services which result in an easy and lightweight communication. The scalability of the backend was not tested yet but overall the architecture is scalable because every microservice can be deployed multiple times behind the gateway without changes to the implementation of the prototypes. Furthermore, although the data services work with a very generic data model, the Link Service and the Schema Service can be used to implement applications that use additional meta information like relationships or schemas to fulfill very specific and more complex requirements regarding the data semantics of the stored data objects. This information is not hard coded within the implementing data services but can be configured as needed by using the semantic services.

6   Conclusion and Outlook

This paper shows a concept for a generic service oriented data management infrastructure for managing a large variety of data which can be implemented with state-of-the-art microservice frameworks and database technologies. The framework uses a polyglot data model and provides distinct services for managing large amounts of heterogeneous data in a generic way. Especially the separation of schemas, master data, time series data and digital assets was discussed in detail. An additional feature of the architecture discussed is the abstraction from database technologies. This enables the microservice architecture to be even more generic because the exposed interface is completely independent from underlying technologies. A prototype was implemented and used for an evaluation of the concepts with two web applications belonging to different application domains. The evaluation showed that the presented microservice architecture can be used in many application domains that have to deal with heterogeneous data, different databases, and that need a high performance and scalability which can be provided by horizontal scaling of the microservices.

The concept and the prototype can and will be extended in various ways. Firstly, the Gateway Service will be replaced by a tool like Netflix Zuul or NGINX Plus which is more reliable and has more features than the service implemented in the prototype. Secondly, an upcoming version of the prototype will also provide an additional binary and therefore faster communication interface than a pure REST API (e.g. by using web sockets). Tools like RabbitMQ[13] and Apache Kafka[14] can and will be used as messaging systems implementing a publish/subscribe protocol for decoupling clients and services which makes the whole system more elastic. Additionally, they will support distributing data to other services beside the Data Management Service, like dedicated data analytics pipelines. Another step towards the compatibility with more Web applications is to add services that can provide data in generic ways (e.g. in feed formats). Such services can be full text search or geo services (see [6]). Furthermore, the generic web visualization framework [7], which is also developed by the WebIS research group, is already integrated with the microservice architecture and it is already implemented using a microservice backend. This will allow to easily explore data by using advanced visualizations.

References

1. Fowler, M., Lewis, J.: Microservices – definition of this new architectural term. http://martinfowler.com/articles/microservices.html. Accessed 26 Sept 2016
2. Gartner Blog Network: Microservices: Building Services with the Guts on the Outside. http://blogs.gartner.com/gary-olliffe/2015/01/30/microservices-guts-on-the-outside/. Accessed 26 Sept 2016
3. Bizer, C., et al.: Linked data – the story so far. Int. J. Semant. Web Inf. Syst. 5(3), 1–22 (2009). https://doi.org/10.4018/jswis.2009081901
4. Leighton, B., et al.: A best of both worlds approach to complex, efficient, time series data delivery. In: Environmental Software Systems. Infrastructures, Services and Applications, ISESS 2015, Melbourne, VIC, Australia, 25–27 March 2015, pp. 371–379 (2015). https://doi.org/10.1007/978-3-319-15994-2_37
5. W3C: JSON-LD 1.0 W3C Recommendation. https://www.w3.org/TR/json-ld/. Accessed 26 Sept 2016
6. Schlachter, T., et al.: A generic web cache infrastructure for the provision of multifarious environmental data. In: Extended Abstract Submitted ISESS 2017 (2017)
7. Braun, E., Düpmeier, C., Kimmig, D., Schillinger, W., Weissenbach, K.: Generic web framework for environmental data visualization. In: Wohlgemuth, V., Fuchs-Kittowski, F., Wittmann, J. (eds.) Advances and New Trends in Environmental Informatics. PROIS, pp. 289–299. Springer, Cham (2017). https://doi.org/10.1007/978-3-319-44711-7_23
8. Pathomkeerati, K.: A new generic approach for web based dashboard solutions in a microservice architecture. Diploma thesis (2016)

How to Start an Environmental Software Project

Ioannis N. Athanasiadis[(⊠)] iD

Wageningen University, Wageningen, The Netherlands
ioannis@athanasiadis.info

Abstract. How to lay the grounds for interdisciplinary teams to start communicating and collaborating effectively remains an obstacle for many environmental software efforts. In this work, a structured, participatory interactive method is introduced: The Inception Workshop aims to assist interdisciplinary teams at the start-up stage of an environmental software project, with the goal to explore the solution space and for early requirements analysis. It is an ice-breaker event to engage heterogeneous actors to open up, express their interests, and start working together to identify and solve common problems. Two installations of the workshop were conducted, and participant familiarity to the problem and technologies involved were captured with pre- and post-workshop questionnaires. Participant responses proved statistical significance in increasing participant confidence with concepts across disciplines.

1 Introduction

Environmental software projects are intensive research collaboration projects, where research challenges go beyond a single discipline. Collaboration projects are typically characterised by heterogeneous actors with collective responsibilities and accountabilities, organised in geographically dispersed teams [6]. Those aspects imply challenges for conventional project management approaches, and involve uncertainties about working and collaboration methods. A clear *big picture* of the project, where heterogeneous actors identify their roles and communicate effectively is the key for successfully managing collaborative projects. To this end, it is essential that actors involved develop early in the project a common language to share their ideas, and shape a common vision.

Voinov and Shugart suggested that we need more creativity in integrated modelling, instead of mechanistically plugging modules together [13]. However, there has been little reported ever since, on how environmental software projects are set up in order to foster creativity. On the contrary, most interdisciplinary environmental modelling and software projects today are still organized in complex disciplinary hierarchies.

While this paper does not address the problem in its entirety, it introduces and evaluates a modus operandi for starting with an environmental software projects. It presents a single day workshop format that intends to lay the grounds for interdisciplinary teams to start communicating and collaborating effectively in integrated

© IFIP International Federation for Information Processing 2017
Published by Springer International Publishing AG 2017. All Rights Reserved
J. Hřebíček et al. (Eds.): ISESS 2017, IFIP AICT 507, pp. 395–407, 2017.
https://doi.org/10.1007/978-3-319-89935-0_33

environmental software teams. The *Inception Workshop* is a participatory method to be applied at the start up stage of a project to explore the solution space or for early requirements analysis. The intention is to start a project with an event that allows for creativity, to charge heterogeneous actors involved, to start communicating effectively about their disciplinary interests, and work together beyond disciplinary barriers to identify and solve common problems.

The rest of this paper is structured as follows. Section 2 debriefs common attitudes in interdisciplinary projects and introduces the *Inception Workshop* objectives and participant roles. Section 3 presents implementation guidelines and Sect. 4 details an experimental setup, involving the two workshop installations, along with lessons learned in practice. Section 5 presents the workshop evaluation results, and conclusions are drawn in Sect. 6.

2 Materials and Methods

2.1 Domain Understanding and Common Attitudes in Environmental Software

Domain understanding is generally acknowledged as a prerequisite for successful projects that involves information technology innovations, however it is often neglected. Software developers seem not to appreciate domain modelling, nor to recognize its importance in effective requirements engineering and risk management [10]. A common attitude observed in several occasions in environmental software projects is that information engineers overestimate the capabilities of their solutions, while underplay the complexity of environmental systems. At the same time, environmental experts tend to underestimate the burden of technological solution deployment and system integration, they typically pass on the shoulders of the IT team. Both sides seem to spin a vicious cycle that creates great expectations on software solutions and drives projects to failure. In environmental software projects we observe the same, recurring motif: *Environmental modelling problems are convoluted for the IT experts, and information technology innovations are arcane for environmental scientists.* The result is the *illusion of the magic wand for environmental modelling*: Information technology experts believe that they have one, while environmental experts expect that is going to work!

Model integration and integrated modelling in environmental software projects is a challenging task for several reasons. Janssen viewed integration in interdisciplinary modelling projects as a multi-headed Hydra snake, due to the many different types of integration that have to be achieved in parallel, and to the important role of communication [9].

For an environmental scientist it is costly to be involved in an interdisciplinary project, as it entails extra effort, for which there is not always appropriate academic credit, and the development of new skills. Rhoten [11] notes that interdisciplinary research requires *sharing existing information through "collegial" interactions*, confirming that interdisciplinary science needs effective and active communication across disciplines.

Environmental software projects are also challenging for software experts. Software curricula cover a handful of application areas, and most textbooks have examples from the most common ones, let it be retail, finance, or entertainment. In this respect, IT experts are less prepared for science applications, and even less for interdisciplinary ones. With practicing the profession, software engineers become more experienced with certain application areas, and switching to a new one can be a very stressful experience. Bjørner estimates that "*to establish a reasonably trustworthy and believable theory of a domain may take years, possibly 10–15!*" [5].

Environmental software projects are by definition interdisciplinary, and interdisciplinary science is founded on communication. This comes together with current practice in requirements engineering, as requirements gathering and agreement process has shifted from a documentation to a communication effort [15]. Traditional methods for requirement analysis as via detailed specification documents, questionnaires or interviews are not suited for environmental software projects. More agile approaches are better suited, as those using less formal means for team building, engaging with stakeholders, gathering requirements, and possibly involve rapid prototyping in small increments to verify them continuously with the end-users.

2.2 The Inception Workshop Approach: Purpose and Objectives

Effective communication requires heterogeneous teams to speak the same language. In most environmental software projects this means that they need to invent it. To facilitate this goal, the *Inception Workshop* is proposed, an event that is expected to be the first meet-up of experts within an integrated project. At project starting phase, communication between team members is difficult. Each discipline has its own value systems, models of work, communication patterns, terminology and jargon. They look like knowledge islands with not much in common. Domain understanding is the bridge that will make these worlds collaborate effectively. Focusing early on building domain knowledge is essential for the success of an environmental software project, as it will help scientists to get out of their disciplinary safe house and foster collaboration. Interdisciplinary science can be achieved only by understanding better each other's scientific niche, while tackling together well-defined problems. This goes beyond superficial coexistence that is founded on short-lived meetups. Consilience is the key to interdisciplinary projects, as scientists not only need to interact with each other, but also have to engage in seeing the *big picture*.

In the case of environmental software projects, the more environmental scientists are exposed to innovative IT technologies, the easier it becomes to build confidence with IT processes and tools, and to engage actively in technical integration tasks. Similarly, there are benefits for IT scientists involved, as a dialogue with environmental scientists allows to identify early critical system aspects. In an environmental software project, IT experts need to get out of their cubicles and the tools they are locked-in with, and start working on interdisciplinary integration from the start of the project.

The *Inception Workshop* aims to establish communication bridges across heterogeneous team members in an environmental software project. It is intended for early project stages, for problem clarification and early requirements analysis. The goal of the workshop is to identify initial user stories, which will be further considered in the project.

The main tool is to give the floor to scientists, members of a heterogeneous team to present their own expertise in an informal, open fashion. Team members interact intensively for a day, collaborate, and make their first achievements together.

When setting up the *Inception Workshop* format, it was assumed that time allotted is restricted. As integrated projects typically involve geographically distributed teams, we assume that there is available only one full day (or two half ones) which seems already too much for facetime in many collaboration environments. However, more time may be allotted, if conditions allow. Spontaneous, informal communications (that resemble standup meetings of agile programming) were intentionally preferred as opposed to structured formats preferred in academic fora.

In terms of preparation, team members are invited to come with no prepackaged content as presentation slideshows, or marketing pamphlets. All discussions are intentionally unpremeditated, unrehearsed. The invitation only sets the overall workshop goal in the form of a question, that does not impose any particular solution. It can be phrased as "*How to improve the domain-specific system X (with technology offering Y)?*". During the workshop, there is no speaker agenda, only a general structure for the discussion (see Table 1 below), with a single goal which is to identify one or more interesting *user stories*.

Table 1. *Inception Workshop* typical agenda

Duration	Topic	Lead participant
30'	Welcome - The workshop process and introductions	Facilitator
90'	'*Storytelling*' (Domain understanding session)	Domain experts
30'	Short Break	
90'	'*Technology roadshow*' (Explore technology opportunities)	IT experts
60'	Long Break	
60'	*Synthesis* (Define first user stories)	All
30'	Short Break	
60'	*Synthesis* (*cont.*) (Set priorities and identify risks)	All

The general flow of the workshop is as follows. First, domain (environmental) experts get the floor to present their current (or intended) activity in a storytelling fashion, and altogether try to identify *hotspots* which are interesting or challenging, (or weak and tedious), and improvements seem needed. This identifies a first list of open problems that call for interdisciplinary intervention. Then, the team reflects on technologies and solutions that could potentially address some of the open problems. This is a spontaneous reaction in the form of sharing anecdotes or experience from previous projects from other fields. The final step is that the team tries to match *hotspots* with *tools available* to put together solutions and formulate them as *user stories*. Last but not least, priorities and risks are estimated for each user story.

2.3   Participants and Roles

There are three types of participants involved. Team members may have the role of environmental expert, IT expert and a facilitator. As interdisciplinary projects involve big teams, it remains a challenge to select the right people to invite. Readers may be refer to literature for stakeholder identification [8, 12].

The **facilitator** is responsible for running the workshop according to the general schedule and to keep discussions focused. Experts tend to get excited with their work and thus dive fast into details, or divert the discussion to irrelevant topics. The facilitator is the one to give pace to the discussion, ensure that everyone gets the opportunity to contribute with their ideas and encourage participants to stand up. She should not be the one that needs to deliver the final outcome of the workshop, in the sense that the stress should not be on her shoulders. Her role is rather to stimulate critical thinking in a Socratic way, than that of the interrogator, and she is not expected publicly interview the experts in a panel discussion. She is not required to have a very deep understanding of the domains or the technologies presented, rather than appreciating the various disciplines involved, interdisciplinarity and the process of integrated modelling. She should be very experienced in discussion facilitation.

Environmental experts participate in order to represent their disciplines, and present obstacles in their everyday work practice, which they want to solve with environmental software. When invited they are asked to bring to the workshop documents, tools, photographs or other artifacts from their practice they thing they would like to show, and share with the rest team. While this sound odd, in practice it was proved a nice way to start the discussion. In the start of the workshop most participants feel a bit odd, so "*What have you brought?*" is a nice line to start with, though certainly this may not be working with all disciplines or cases.

IT experts come to the workshop to better understand the problem at hand, and do their first step in requirements elicitation, together with the rest of the team. The composition of the IT team is not restricted to analysts or designers, and certainly developers are welcomed. Our assumption is that IT scientists not directly involved may contribute. IT team members have a lot to gain in terms of domain understanding, and from engaging with disciplinary scientists. They are expected to show creativity and forward thinking and try to exemplify their technologies to the rest team. This is a crucial step for building confidence among the team members. Note that IT experts from different backgrounds may be less open to change, as new technologies may be disruptive to their routine.

The participation model is founded on open, democratic principles. While each organization involved in an environmental software project has its own structure and hierarchy, for this workshop participants are asked to contribute freely, directly, and simply. The facilitator needs to clarify from the beginning that the workshop is exploratory without formalities, and encourage participants to contribute. The facilitator is to protect the group from insisting participants that may slow down the discussion. At the same time, he makes clear that everyone has the right to speak, and he needs to accommodate time for all, while decisions are taken by the majority.

3   Implementation

3.1   Preparation and Agenda

The workshop is intended to run for one or two days in a room with a round table. The equipment needed is a white-board or a flip-chart, pens, post-it notes and *stuff* brought by the participants. Part of the preparation is to provide food and beverages for coffee and lunch breaks. Table 1 presents a typical agenda. The workshop starts with a welcome from the facilitator and a short introduction round of the participants. The facilitator presents the workshop agenda and main question, and may give a couple of examples of user stories, if asked by the participants.

3.2   Part I: Storytelling

The first session focuses on *domain understanding*. The goal is to follow the current or future processes and increase the understanding of team members. Team share their knowledge across environmental domains involved in a **storytelling** fashion: They communicate their knowledge by sharing experiences and anecdotes. In a collaborative team environment, experts stand up to share their views of the system, while rest team members may intervene with clarifying questions. If needed, environmental experts may start drawing on flip charts to illustrate their claims. In other cases, they might show the stuff brought, that could be equipment, documents, or other exhibits of their practice. Each contributes with a partial view of the integrated system to be developed, undoubtedly biased by her own disciplinary background and intentions.

While the flip chart starts to fill up, and artifacts are on the table, participants are instructed to use post-it notes and identify "*hotspots*" that need intervention. These could be processes or activities that are popular, crucial or bottlenecks that are shared by team members. Discussions should not run into solutions at this stage, and participants are encouraged to flag hotspots, but reserve solution ideas for later. The facilitator needs to keep the storyline progressing, and prevent the team from diving into details.

3.3   Part II: Technology Roadshow

The second session, called **technology roadshow**, focus is on familiarizing the team with IT opportunities and identify possible solutions. This is achieved by working with examples and learning by analogy. This supports two objectives: First objective is to increase team awareness of IT tool capabilities, as potential options to adopt for certain problems. This will build interest in the beginning, and hopefully confidence at a later stage to (new) technologies for environmental software. Second objective is to identify via brainstorming possible solutions for the "*hotspots*" flagged in the previous session. Team members take turns and '*put guns on the table*', i.e. they exemplify how technical solutions might be used for tackling the problems presented before. Existing or new solutions are presented informally, in the form of examples. Solutions do not need necessarily be related to the problem at hand, but may come from other disciplines as well. Simplifications are encouraged so that team members with different backgrounds get a grasp of how a solution works and which are the potential benefits. Participants are encouraged to ask questions, and the facilitator is responsible for moderating jargon language and reminding technical experts to use simple examples from applications known to the rest team members.

3.4   Part III: Synthesis of User Stories and Risks

The final session aim is to produce a **synthesis** of the two previous sessions. In a collaborative team environment, participants are challenged to interpret *together* the identified hotspots and the tools presented in order to form *initial user stories*. Agile requirements methodology considers user stories as very high-level definition of requirements, containing just enough information so that the developers can produce a reasonable estimate of the effort to implement it [7]. In our case, initial user stories aim to produce high-level requirements of an environmental software system, often called *epic* in agile methodology.

The first part of this session is to identify user stories. Any workshop participant is free to summarize a solution of the equation *hotspot + tool = user story*. While a story is presented others may contribute to clarify or extend it. User stories at this stage are given short names and listed on the flipchart, so that participants may refer to them later on.

The second part of this session is to go through the user story list and set priorities in terms of effectiveness, risk and cost. While these are rough estimates, it is also interesting from a team building point of view, as it reveals the different priorities and perception of difficulty from heterogeneous team members.

4   Application

The *Inception Workshop* method presented above has been applied in two projects that the author has been involved in, and are shortly described below.

4.1   Workshop #1

The AITOLOS project aimed to identify smart ICT solutions to be incorporated into the everyday work of national forest protection services [1, 3]. The project team consisted of forest service officers with several years of field work in forest protection, but from different functions, and software experts with varying expertise (business analysts, telecommunications, GIS, image processing, remote sensing, semantic web). In this team environment forest service officers were not proficient users of IT, and software experts had no prior experience in forestry applications. In order to identify potential solutions, a bidirectional knowledge shift between team members was needed, so that they develop a common language and achieve consensus.

The AITOLOS inception workshop took place in Thessaloniki, Greece, on January 25, 2013, with the participation of 12 environmental experts from the forest services of Kilkis and Goumenissa, in Greece, and 7 software experts from the Information Technologies Institute (CERTH), and the Surveying and Geomatics Department of TEI of Central Macedonia. The project was in the initial problem identification phase, and the main goal of the workshop was to answer the question: *"How smart ICT solutions may be applied in forest service practice to combat illegal logging and timber trade?"*. After a single day of intensive discussions, the team concluded with seven user stories, spanning the whole lifecycle of logging and timber trade. The workshop findings are detailed in separate reports [2, 3].

4.2   Workshop #2

The ALPINE project aimed to develop an intelligent, low-power sensor network architecture for environmental management. One of the two pilots is concerned with wildlife management, and specifically was concerned with how sensor networks can be used to improve the current situation with large carnivore monitoring and protection in the study area. Though the case study was different from the previous workshop, again the situation was similar: IT experts from industry and academia had very poor understanding of large carnivore protection domain, and wildlife scientists were not up to date with recent advances in IT. While the project was not in a very early stage, communication between the two sides was very slow and ineffective. Based on the first workshop experience, we decided to organize an event with the same structure, and monitor if it will help improving communications among the interdisciplinary team, and achieve some progress with the test case.

The ALPINE/Wildlife Inception Workshop was held in Xanthi, Greece, on February 13, 2014. We invited two wildlife scientists, working with different species and six IT experts. The main goal of the workshop was to answer the question: *"How intelligent sensor network technology and applications can be used for bear and wolf monitoring and management?"*. After a single day of intensive discussions, the team concluded with four user stories, three related to bear and one related to wolf management. One of those epics has been actually implemented in the project [4].

5   Evaluation

5.1   Methodology

In order to evaluate the effectiveness of the proposed method, in both experimental workshops we conducted a survey. The survey was done in two stages, with pre- and post- workshop questionnaires. Both questionnaires included the same set of questions, in which the respondents were asked to evaluate their familiarity with environmental domain concepts and procedures, and IT tools and technologies. Half of the questions were related to the application domain and the rest related to technology. All participants were asked to respond to all questions independently of their expertise. The level of familiarity was measured using a five-point Likert scale. A portion of the two questionnaires is presented in Table 2. The post-workshop evaluation form included questions to evaluate workshop performance and organization, adapted from [14]. Workshop participants gave their oral consent to process their answers, given that no personal information are disclosed. In the first workshop, 14 out of 19 participants returned the questionnaire forms. In the second workshop, all seven participants returned the questionnaire forms.

Table 2. Questionnaires for the two workshops. The question was How familiar are you with...

	Workshop #1		Workshop #2
1	Forest value	1	Value of ecosystems
2	Forest office organization	2	Wildlife in Greece
3	Forest management plans	3	Large carnivore movement patterns
4	Forest products	4	Human-wildlife coexistance conflicts
5	Legal logging processes	5	Wolf damages on livestock
6	Forest product market	6	Human effect on wildlife habitat
7	Taxes on loggers permits	7	Spotting wildlife
8	Legal timber trade cycle	8	Trap and drug a bear
9	Illegal timber trade cycle	9	Bear identification collars
10	Cross-border illegal logging	10	GIS and maps
11	GPS applications	11	Ecosystem population models
12	GIS and maps	12	GPS applications
13	Remote sensing	13	Delay tolerant networks
14	Digital signatures	14	Knowledge modelling
15	RFID tags	15	RFID tags
16	Office applications	16	Barcode, QR code
17	Barcode, QR codes	17	Software development
18	Software development	18	Sensor networks
19	e-governance	19	Low power sensors
20	Social networks		

5.2   Ethics Statement

Voluntary feedback evaluation forms are commonly distributed in workshops. Participants of the two pilot workshops evaluation were exposed to no risk; there were no vulnerable populations involved; and no sensitive data were collected. For these reasons, no approval from an ethics committee/IRB was asked. Participants were informed briefly before the start of the workshop about the goals of this research and were given the option to fill in the pre-workshop questionnaire that was included in their folder. The same happened with post- workshop questionnaires. The questionnaire forms included information about the researcher who conducted the study. The questionnaire forms included a written outline of the research purpose and contained a statement that completion and return of the questionnaire indicates consent to participate in the study.

Written consent was not obtained as there was no risk for the participants; to ensure anonymity of the responses; and the involved procedures would not normally require written consent outside the purposes of this study. Completed questionnaire forms were returned in a box, while the researcher was not present. No private information has been disclosed. No penalty or consequences was implied by not filling in the questionnaire. No benefits or long term engagement was associated with participating to this study. Written responses were digitized, and original forms destroyed. Participants had the option to mention their name, a common practice for workshop feedback forms to build engagement and trust with a team. However, responses were treated anonymously. Anonymized responses of the questions relevant for reproducing the results presented in this manuscript have been archived on Zenodo [16].

5.3 Results

Answers to pre- and post-workshop questions suggest that most participants felt more familiar with the domain concepts and related technologies after the workshop end. This can be considered as a sign of effective communication towards the development of a common language in a heterogeneous team.

We performed the *Wilcoxon matched-pairs* signed-rank test, a nonparametric method to compare before-after (or matched) questionnaires. The test was conducted to each participant matched responses before and after the workshop, to determine whether there was a statistical difference in their reported *familiarity* with the domains and technologies involved. The results are reported in Table 3, and indicate that in the vast majority of the participants, in both workshops, there was a statistically significant difference in their responses. For *Workshop #1*, the Wilcoxon analysis yielded with $p < 0.05$ for 10 out of 14 participants. The difference in average response was not due to chance for the majority of both domain and IT experts. For *Workshop #2*, the Wilcoxon tests reveals that shift in respondents' *familiarity* is statistically significant for five out of seven participants with $p < 0.05$.

5.4 Lessons Learned

Both workshops concluded with valuable outcomes for each project, and participants in principle were satisfied with the workshop goals, structure, and process. However, the two workshops were executed in different ways.

In the first one, discussion went deep in operational detailed, which crunched the time available for risk estimation. However, this allowed us to identify many high-level user stories, and satisfied the project need for identification of alternative solutions. At the same time, the large number of participants made discussions last longer, and some of the domain experts had no opportunity to participate actively, rather they participated as observers. This was considered as a significant organizational drawback as it is commonly acknowledged that engaging with experts is hard to achieve, and their time shouldn't be wasted. Thus, in the second *Inception Workshop*, the same process was repeated with less number of participants. However, due to an emergency we missed one of the two domain experts, to our disappointment.

In the second workshop we experienced a better balance of time allocation between 'storytelling' and 'technology roadshow' sessions. The four user stories we concluded with were more detailed, tailored to the needs of the participants. In this respect, the workshop was less exploratory. Risk analysis and prioritization was done in more detail, also taking under account the limitations of the project. The take-home message from this installation was to host the workshop in the vicinity of the customer headquarters, if possible.

In both cases, the user stories were epic, in the sense that they can be broken down to smaller, more targeted stories [7]. However, this was rather expected as the goal of

Table 3. Questionnaire statistics (Wilcoxon p-value) from the two workshops. The perception of each participant is evaluated with respect to her confidence to domain concepts and technology topics. Participants are identified with a letter and a number. The letter encodes the discipline of the participant - D for domain scientists and S for software experts.

Workshop #1			Workshop #2		
ID	p value	p < 0.05	ID	p value	p < 0.05
D1	0.002	*	D1	1.000	
D2	0.009	*	S1	0.070	
D3	0.009	*	S2	0.001	*
D4	0.025	*	S3	0.001	*
D5	1.000		S4	0.033	*
D6	0.033	*	S5	0.000	*
D7	0.057		S6	0.009	*
S1	0.554				
S2	0.000	*			
S3	0.001	*			
S4	0.018	*			
S5	0.001	*			
S6	0.530				
S7	0.020	*			

these workshops was not to identify specific features to be implemented, rather it was to identify solutions to be subsequently specified in detail.

6 Conclusions

Domain knowledge is essential for heterogeneous teams that are challenged with integrated projects, as limited or no familiarity with a domain increases the risks for project failure. Domain knowledge is even more critical with increasing agility of the software development process. As interdisciplinary teams move from bureaucratic, plan-based processes to more iterative and less structured methods, requirements elicitation is transformed from an understanding and documentation activity to a learning and communication one.

This paper argues that at the beginning of environmental software projects, more effective communication is required. While agile methods are well suited for ill-defined needs and ever-changing requirements, they assume effective communication among heterogeneous teams. This is certainly not the case in environmental software. As a remedy to this problem we presented the *Inception Workshop* to establish effective communication between team members, early in the project. With the *Inception Workshop*, a team of heterogeneous actors is challenged to collaborate for identifying user stories and associated risks for an interdisciplinary environmental software project. The method has been applied twice, and lessons were reported about the number of the participants, time allocation, specificity of the user stories. In both installations participant found the process stimulating and helped them to engage with each other.

Participants of both inception workshops were satisfied; and this is attributed to the fact that all had gains from the process. Some familiarized themselves with new domains, others with certain technologies. All participants learned new things, and had their say in the project start. A set of user stories to further develop in the project is a tangible result for everyone satisfaction. The workshops were also helpful in building team spirit due to the participatory sessions, where interactions brought participants closer. Questionnaire analysis of the two pilot workshops suggests statistical significance of the participant responses after the workshop. Though, participant enthusiasm and long-standing engagement to their project success is the stronger evidence of success.

Acknowledgments. Author was partially supported by the Greek Secretariat of Research and Technology Collaboration (ALPINE grant 11SYN-6-411), and the IPA cross-border programme (AITOLOS grant IPA/2010/DN022619/CN314 294) which is co-funded by the EU and by national funds of the participating countries. The funders had no role in study design, data collection and analysis, decision to publish, or preparation of the manuscript. The author would like to thank the participants of both workshops for their encouraging comments.

References

1. AITOLOS Consortium, Project website (2012). http://www.aitolos.eu
2. Anastasiadou, D., Koulinas, K., Kiourtsis, F., Athanasiadis, I.N.: Complementary software solutions for efficient timber logging and trade management. In: Gomez, J.M., et al. (eds.) Proceedings of 28th International Conference on Informatics for Environmental Protection (Enviroinfo 2014), University of Oldenburg BIS Verlag, Oldenburg, Germany, 2014, pp. 783–788 (2014)
3. Athanasiadis, I.N., Anastasiadou, D., Koulinas, K., Kiourtsis, F.: Identifying smart solutions for fighting illegal logging and timber trade. In: Hřebíček, J., Schimak, G., Kubásek, M., Rizzoli, A.E. (eds.) ISESS 2013. IAICT, vol. 413, pp. 143–153. Springer, Heidelberg (2013). https://doi.org/10.1007/978-3-642-41151-9_14
4. Athanasiadis, I.N., Villa, F., Examiliotou, G., Iliopoulos, Y., Mertzanis, Y.: Towards a semantic framework for wildlife modeling. In: Gomez, J.M., et al. (eds.) Proceedings of 28th International Conference on Informatics for Environmental Protection (Enviroinfo 2014), University of Oldenburg BIS Verlag, Oldenburg, Germany, pp. 287–292 (2014)
5. Bjørner, D.: Domain engineering. In: Boca, P., Bowen, J., Siddiqi, J. (eds.) Formal Methods: State of the Art and New Directions. Springer, London (2010). https://doi.org/10.1007/978-1-84882-736-3_1
6. vom Brocke, J., Lippe, S.: Managing collaborative research projects: a synthesis of project management literature and directives for future research. Int. J. Proj. Manag. **33**, 1022–1039 (2015)
7. Cobb, C.G.: Making Sense of Agile Project Management. Wiley, Hoboken (2011)
8. Glinz, M., Wieringa, R.J.: Guest editors' introduction: stakeholders in requirements engineering. IEEE Softw. **24**, 18–20 (2007)
9. Janssen, S.J.: Managing the hydra in integration: developing an integrated assessment tool for agricultural systems. Wageningen University (2009)

10. Offen, R.: Domain understanding is the key to successful system development. Requir. Eng. **7**, 172–175 (2002)
11. Rhoten, D.: Interdisciplinary research: trend or transition. Items Issues **5**, 6–11 (2004)
12. Sharp, H., Finkelstein, A., Galal, G.: Stakeholder identification in the requirements engineering process. pp. 387–391 (1999)
13. Voinov, A., Shugart, H.H.: 'Integronsters', integral and integrated modeling. Environ. Model Softw. **39**, 149–158 (2013)
14. WGBH: Enhancing Education: A Producer's Guide (2004)
15. Zhang, Z., Arvela, M., Berki, E., Muhonen, M., Nummenmaa, J., Poranen, T.: Towards lightweight requirements documentation. J. Softw. Eng. App. **3**, 882–889 (2010)
16. Athanasiadis, I.N.: Anonymized survey responses from two Inception Workshops [Data set]. Zenodo (2017). http://doi.org/10.5281/zenodo.1041743

Modelling, Visualization and Decision Support

Environmental Modelling with Reverse Combinatorial Auctions: CRAB Software Modification for Sensitivity Analysis

Petr Fiala$^{(\boxtimes)}$ and Petr Šauer

University of Economics, Prague, Czech Republic
{pfiala, sauer}@vse.cz

Abstract. This paper builds on reverse combinatorial auctions theory and its selected environmental applications, which were presented at ISESS 2013 and ISESS 2015. It provides an approach for calculating the sensitivity and proposals for necessary adjustments of CombinatoRial Auction Body Software System (CRAB), which makes its use for the relevant decision-making tasks more user friendly. Two possibilities are suggested. The first approach is appropriate for cases with relatively small numbers of subjects, where it is possible to compute all feasible solutions ordered by total cost. In such cases it is possible to analyse changes of coalition structures with increasing the cost. The second one suggests modification of the CRAB software, which would make it possible to analyse cases with high numbers of feasible coalition structures located between the optimal coalition (i.e. the cost-effective one) and the structure consisting of individual projects. This approach is appropriate for complex real applications involving setting of cost levels.

Keywords: Environmental management · Decision-making
Sensitivity analysis · Reverse combinatorial auctions

1 Introduction

The paper builds on work published in ISESS 2013 [1] and in ISESS 2015 [2], where the general model of the theory of reverse combinatorial auctions and its selected environmental applications were presented. At the same time, we presented the results of laboratory experiments showing whether and to what extent the negotiating parties at auctions are able to approach the optimal result. The main practical goal of the paper was to contribute to increased cost-effectiveness of waste water cleaning projects [3, 4] in conditions where coalition solutions are possible.

The previous research results [1, 2, 5] have shown the need to deepen our research into sensitivity analysis of the resulting optimal solutions. Specifically, in terms of understanding how to study coalition structures in the space between the optimal solution and solutions in the form of individual projects, and how the change of feasible coalition structures changes achieved cost. This paper provides an approach for calculating the sensitivity and proposals for necessary adjustments of CRAB software, which makes its use for the relevant decision-making tasks more user friendly.

© IFIP International Federation for Information Processing 2017
Published by Springer International Publishing AG 2017. All Rights Reserved
J. Hřebíček et al. (Eds.): ISESS 2017, IFIP AICT 507, pp. 411–419, 2017.
https://doi.org/10.1007/978-3-319-89935-0_34

2 Models of Reverse Combinatorial Auctions in Environmental Applications

Before explaining the nature of the proposed approach of sensitivity analysis, we provide the basic model of reverse combinatorial auctions.

Supposed that m potential sellers S_1, S_2, ..., S_m offer a set R of r items, $j = 1, 2, ..., r$, to one buyer B; a bid made by the seller S_h, $h = 1, 2, ..., m$, would be defined as

$$b_h = \{C, c_h(C)\}, \tag{1}$$

where

$C \subseteq R$, is a combination of items,

$c_h(C)$ is the price offered by the seller S_h for the combination of items C.

The constraints ensure that the procurement provides at least one set of all items. The objective is to minimise the buyer's cost, given the bids made by the sellers.

Binary variables are introduced for the model formulation:

$y_h(C)$ is a binary variable specifying whether the combination C is bought from the seller $S_h(y_h(C) = 1)$.

The basic reverse combinatorial auctions model can be formulated as follows [6]:

$$\sum_{h=1}^{m} c_h(C)y_h(C) \rightarrow min \tag{2}$$

subject to

$$\sum_{h=1}^{m} \sum_{C \subseteq R} y_h(C) \geq 1, \forall j \in R, \tag{3}$$

$$y_h(C) \in \{0, 1\}, \quad \forall C \subseteq R, \quad \forall h, h = 1, 2, ..., m. \tag{4}$$

This basic model only considers the minimisation of costs, which is complemented by restrictions on environmental standards. In terms of mathematical formulations, inequalities are added that compare the pollution reduction achieved with the required limit values for five specific environmental parameters (5).

$$\sum_{h=1}^{m} \sum_{C \subseteq R} e_{hi}(C)y_h(C) \geq E_i. \tag{5}$$

where e_{hi} are pollution parameters of the projects and Ei are the prescribed environmental standards for the parameters.

3 Sensitivity Analysis

For further decision-making about the investment program that is realised in practice, it is important to learn how sensitive deviations from the optimised coalition structure would be to other feasible structures.

For small examples it is possible to compute and relatively easily analyse all solutions, with coalition structures from the first best (optimal) solution ranked by increasing cost. The optimal solution is computed by solving the problems (2)–(4). As a result, we get the so-called first-best solution. The optimal costs are denoted Z1. Generally, we get the i-th solution by solving the problems (2)–(4) with an added constraint

$$\sum_{h=1}^{m} \sum_{C \subseteq R} c_h(C) y_h(C) \geq Z_{i-1} + \varepsilon, \tag{6}$$

where ε is a small positive number.

In typical practical cases, the number of feasible coalition structures is huge. For this reason, it is not possible to analyse all of them individually, i.e. to follow the order of the second-best, third-best, etc. solutions.

We propose that sensitivity analysis, based on analysing coalition structures for specific cost levels, can still provide support for decision-making about the projects in such cases. The difference between costs for individual project structures and costs for the first best solution could be divided to several levels corresponding to politically acceptable deviations of the practical program from the first best solution. It is possible to work with quartiles, quintiles etc. in the space of all feasible solutions.

The solutions for the cost levels could be computed from the basic model (see formulas (2), (3), and (4)) adding constraints:

$$\sum_{h=1}^{m} \sum_{C \subseteq R} c_h(C) y_h(C) \geq L_i, i = 1, 2, \ldots, n, \tag{7}$$

where n is number of levels and L_i are cost levels.

4 Suggestions for CRAB Software Modification

We have developed our own software tool, CRAB (CombinatoRial Auction Body Software System) [7]. CRAB is a non-commercial software system for generating, solving, and testing combinatorial auction problems. The system solves problems using Balas' method or the primal-dual algorithm [8]. CRAB has several advantages over CATS software [9], in particular, CRAB generates problems faster; combinations are generated in a more predictable way and only in given subset of all items; CSV is used as the primary data format; there is fine-grained control over the generated problem; a linear problem solver is a part of CRAB; and it provides multiple output formats. CRAB is implemented in Ruby, which enables us to quickly experiment with different approaches.

In the first phase of analysis, all combinations of goods in each package are generated (except empty set). This step is done for every package. In the second phase, the file is transformed into the binary programming problem. The bundles correspond to variables and bids correspond to prices of the objective function that is maximised. The problem consists of automatic constraints for each good (each good can be sold only once) and each buyer (buyer cannot get over his budget). The user of CRAB software can change automatically generated constraints and add or remove additional ones. The problem can be passed to the built-in binary programming solver to find out the optimal solution for a given combinatorial auction. Afterwards, the transformed model is passed to the Balas algorithm [8].

The CRAB architecture provides the possibility of extending the system, especially with respect to the implemented models and algorithms. For the sensitivity analyses, we modified the CRAB software according to the approaches for sensitivity analysis, (6) and (7), above.

A problem occurs when entering data for complex applications in optimisation of coalition solutions, such as in the construction of a waste water treatment plant (WWTP). This is particularly the case when appropriate variable names for multiple coalitions derive from the encoding of individual municipalities entering into these multiple coalitions. Experts generating sets of "promising" coalitions progress by identifying coalition-names on maps and not by the order of the municipalities in their list. Clarity is lost by this encoding, but this sequence has its own logic, because two coalitions comprising the same set of municipalities, but in a different order, may provide different solutions, for example, with a different location of the common WWTP. The software compares the same combination and warns the user in the report.

Currently we are working on improving user comfort when loading large data describing the real situation in the river basins and reservoirs, where there is a large number of "promising" coalitions entering the optimisation calculations. The new version should communicate better with conventional spreadsheets than is currently the case.

5   Sensitivity Analysis by CRAB Software

Imagine a situation where four municipalities discharge their wastewater into a small river that flows into the reservoir intended for bathing (e.g. may be ranked in so called Bathing Water by the Directive 2006/7/EC [10]). If we want to restore the quality of water for bathing, it is necessary that all four municipalities built waste water treatment plant (WWTP). This can be done by each building an individual WWTP or, alternatively, it is possible to try to merge the villages into so-called multiple coalitions to build a common WWTP either for all or some of them.

We let the experts estimate the necessary costs for the construction of the WWTP for the "promising projects". These data are contained in Table 1.

The optimal solution for the numerical example given by the CRAB software, see Table 2:

Table 1. Estimated costs for the "promising projects"

Project	Participated municipalities	Project costs
Individual projects		
1.	A	7500
2.	B	18000
3.	C	31000
4.	D	28000
Coalition projects		
1.	AB	27750
2.	BC	41750
5.	BD	59000
3.	CD	65000
4.	ABC	45000
6.	BCD	69000
7.	ABCD	82750

Table 2. Optimal solution computed by CRAB software

```
OPTIMAL SOLUTION
Total cost:
73000.00
Coalition structure:
1-member coalition: D
3-member coalition: ABC
```

Sensitivity analysis can be performed for the above example. The analysis is described above by the model (6). The problem has 9 solutions in our case. For the results, see Table 3.

In practical cases, there are a large number of polluters, thus creating more complex models and calculations. In such cases, there are a large amount of feasible solutions. These situations can be solved in two ways:

1. In some cases, the solution of the entire case is divided into optimisation problems of sub-segments of river basin. A typical example is in a mountainous area, where it is possible to optimise the construction of wastewater treatment plants for each valley. For this situation, see the above numerical example.
2. If this is not possible, then one can work with "levels" between the cost of first best (optimal) solution and the cost of individual projects.

Table 3. Sensitivity analysis computed by CRAB software

```
1st Solution (=first best)
Total cost: 73000.00
Coalition structure:
One 1-member coalitions: D
One 3-members coalitions: ABC
```

| ```
2nd solution
Total cost: 76500.00
Coalition structure:
1-member coalitions: A
3-member coalitions: BCD
``` | ```
6th Solution
Total cost: 86750.00
Coalition structure:
1-member coalitions: C,D
2-member coalitions: AB
``` |
|---|---|
| ```
3rd Solution
Total cost: 77250.00
Coalition structure:
1-member coalitions: A,D
2-member coalitions: BC
``` | ```
7th Solution
Total cost: 90500.00
Coalition structure:
1-member coalitions: A,B
2-member coalitions: CD
``` |
| ```
4th Solution
Total cost: 82750.00
Coalition structure:
4-member coalitions: ABCD
``` | ```
8th Solution
Total cost: 92750.00
Coalition structure:
2-member coalitions: AB, CD
``` |
| ```
5th Solution
Total cost: 84500.00
Coalition structure:
1-member coalitions:
A,B,C,D
``` | ```
9th Solution (least
efficient solution)
Total cost: 97500.00
Coalition structure:
1-member coalitions: A,C
2-member coalitions: BD
``` |

As a demonstration of the second case, we provide two practical applications from recreation lakes in the Czech Republic. Bathing water quality is an important issue in the EU (see Directive 2006/7/EC concerning the management of bathing water quality [10]). In both cases, multiple small municipalities should build their own WWTP or join one or more other municipalities and build a common WWTP. Solving these problems in small municipalities is quite costly in comparison to building and operating WWTPs in larger cities and requires support from public financial sources. Calculating the (theoretically) optimal solution could support political decision making about allocation of public funds in this area. In the case of cleaning phosphorus from water in a recreation lake, it is important that all polluters contribute to the project. In practice, they negotiate a common project proposal and apply for financial support. For assessing these proposals, it is useful to have the sensitivity analysis results available.

Lake Rozkoš is the first case. It is located in the Elbe River basin in Bohemia [11–13]. Two scenarios for achieving environmental targets (required status of the lake water) were formulated by specialists, together with an assessment of the investment and operating costs of the projects. The optimal solution (investment program) for 41 polluter-municipalities, where 166 coalitions were considered (41 individual WWTPs and 125 joint WWTPs), was computed. The results of the optimisation modelling presented in this paper have shown that over 20% of the costs could be saved where selected joint WWTPs are realised.

A sensitivity analysis was performed. Since the number of feasible coalition structures is huge (there are 2^{166} of them in the case of Rozkoš Lake), it would not be practical to analyse all of them (as it is done in our illustration presented above). For this reason, the difference ("space") between costs for individual projects and costs for the first best (optimal) solution was initially divided into six levels corresponding to policy decisions about potential (politically acceptable) deviation of the practical program from the (theoretical) first best solution. The levels create borders of quintiles in the space of all potential (feasible) solutions. Level 1 was defined as the cost for the first best solution, level 6 as the cost for individual projects. Other levels are always about 20 percent higher than the previous level, where the second level was suggested as the politically acceptable one. These calculations provided a useful picture for better assessment of potential projects submitted in the region. For more details, see [5].

Lake Pastviny is the second case. This lake is located in east Bohemia, near the Polish border [14, 15]. The initial set of projects aimed at achieving the environmental standards required for bathing water in Lake Pastviny consists of 24 individual projects (WWTPs) and 131 multiple-coalition projects. These included 32 two-member coalitions, 38 three-member coalitions, 38 four-member coalitions, and 22 five-to-eight-member coalitions. The abatement costs, in the form of investment and operating costs, were assessed by the specialists for all of these projects. The analysis indicated a potential saving of annualised abatement costs of 6% in the case where half of the municipalities located in the lake watershed join specific coalitions and the rest build an individual WWTP.

In this case, the initial sensitivity analysis works with 4 costs levels. Level 1 was defined as the cost for the first best (optimal) solution, level 4 as the cost for individual projects. Other levels are always about 33% higher than the previous level. Moreover, here, the results provide a picture of how changing the coalition structure by decreasing of the number of multiple-member coalitions leads to an increase of the costs. For more details, see [16].

6 Conclusion

The paper is devoted to modification of the CRAB software for sensitivity analysis of solutions to combinatorial auction problems. The modification is used for analyses of coalition projects for the building of WWTPs.

We propose two possibilities. The first approach is appropriate for small examples, where it is possible to compute all feasible solutions ordered by total cost. In such cases, it is possible to analyse changes of coalition structures in terms of their increasing cost.

The second suggested modification of the CRAB software makes it possible to analyse a high number of feasible coalition structures located between the optimal coalition (i.e. the cost-effective one) and the structure consisting of individual projects. This approach is appropriate for setting of cost levels in complex real applications, including multiple-round subsidy negotiations (see [17]). The proposed approach of sensitivity analysis can be used not only in the case of reverse combinatorial auctioning in cleaning waste waters; the waste water treatment issue was used as a typical practical application.

Two practical applications are presented in the paper, together with a discussion of their contribution to relevant decision-making processes. In both cases, it is possible to continue to more detailed sensitivity analysis, according to the concrete requirements of participants in the decision making process. This could be particularly useful when the projects are multiple-round negotiated with the authority and other stakeholders.

Acknowledgement. The paper was developed with the support of the Czech Science Foundation, GACR č. 16-01687S: "Novel approach to seeking cost/effective water pollution abatement: Developing reverse combinatorial auctions theory".

References

1. Šauer, P., Fiala, P., Dvořák, A.: Modelling of environmental risk management under information asymmetry. In: Hřebíček, J., Schimak, G., Kubásek, M., Rizzoli, A.E. (eds.) ISESS 2013. IAICT, vol. 413, pp. 391–402. Springer, Heidelberg (2013). https://doi.org/10.1007/978-3-642-41151-9_37
2. Šauer, P., Fiala, P., Dvořák, A.: Water pollution reduction: reverse combinatorial auctions modelling supporting decision-making processes. In: Denzer, R., Argent, R.M., Schimak, G., Hřebíček, J. (eds.) ISESS 2015. IFIP IAICT, vol. 448, pp. 196–206. Springer, Cham (2015). https://doi.org/10.1007/978-3-319-15994-2_19
3. Berbel, J., Martin-Ortega, J., Mesa, P.: A cost-effectiveness analysis of water-saving measures for the water framework directive: the case of the Guadalquivir river basin in southern Spain. Water Resour. Manag. **25**(2), 623–640 (2011)
4. CzGOV: Czech Government Regulation No. 401/2015 Coll., amending GR No. 61/2003 Coll., on Indicators and Values of Acceptable Pollution of Surface Water and Wastewater, Mandatory Elements of Permits for Discharging Wastewater into Surface Water and Sewerage Systems, and on Sensitive Areas (as amended by GR No. 229/2007 Coll.) (2011)
5. Šauer, P., Fiala, P., Dvořák, A., Kolínský, O.: Coalition projects to cut back costs of cleaning recreational water bodies: the case of the Bohemian lake Rozkoš. Polish J. Environ. Stud. **26**(4), 1701–1714 (2017)
6. Cramton, P., Shoham, Y., Steinberg, R. (eds.): Combinatorial Auctions. MIT Press, Cambridge (2006)
7. Fiala, P., Kalčevová, J., Vraný, J.: CRAB—combinatorial auction body software system. J. Softw. Eng. Appl. **3**(7), 718–722 (2010)
8. Balas, E.: An additive algorithm for solving linear programs with zero-one variables. Oper. Res. **13**, 517–546 (1965)
9. Leyton-Brown, K., Pearson, M., Shoham, Y.: Towards a universal test suite for combinatorial auction algorithms. In: The Proceedings of ACM Conference on Electronic Commerce, EC-00, Minneapolis, pp. 448–457 (2000)

10. Directive 2006/7/EC of the European Parliament and of the Council of 15 February 2006 concerning the management of bathing water quality
11. PL: Limnological dindings and possibilities to improve current condition in the Lake Rozkoš (in Czech), Povodí Labe, s.p. Hradec Králové (1999)
12. PL: Control order at the waterwork Rozkoš (in Czech), Povodí Labe, s.p. Hradec Králové (2007)
13. VRV/PL: An Analysis of Importance of Impact of Eutrophication Pollution Sources at the River Basin of Water Lake Rozkoš (in Czech), Vodohospodářský rozvoj a výstavba a.s. nad Povodí Labe, s.p. Praha (2013)
14. PL: Process Rules for Hydraulic Structure on the Divoká Orlice - Pastviny I. (in Czech), Povodí Labe s.p., Hradec Králové (2009)
15. VIS: Basic strategy for attaining water quality for recreational purposes at Pastviny water reservoir (in Czech), Vodohospodářsko-inženýrské služby spol. s r.o. study for Povodí Labe, s.p., Hradec Králové (2014)
16. Šauer, P., Dvořák, A., Fiala, P.: Improvement to green in-country tourism conditions: a case of the Czech recreation lake Pastviny. J. Environ. Prot. Ecol. **17**(4), 1434–1442 (2016)
17. Šauer, P., Dvořák, A., Fiala, P.: Negotiation between authority and polluters - model for support of decision making in environmental policy. Politická ekonomie **46**(6), 772–787 (1998)

A Domain Specific Language to Simplify the Creation of Large Scale Federated Model Sets

Zachary T. Reinhart, Sunil Suram, and Kenneth M. Bryden[(✉)]

Iowa State University, Ames, IA, USA
{zrein, sunils, kmbryden}@iastate.edu

Abstract. This paper presents an attempt to address the challenge of modeling complex systems in which people, energy, and the environment meet. This challenge is met by developing a simple domain specific language for building systems models in a federated modeling environment. The language and its support infrastructure are designed for simplicity and ease of use. This language is demonstrated using a thermodynamic model of a biomass cookstove for the developing world as an example, and the use of the tools described in this paper to further extend that cookstove model into an end-to-end design tool for cookstoves and other energy systems for the developing world is discussed.

Keywords: Federated modeling · Integrated modeling · Complex systems

1 Introduction

Sustainability is the challenge of the future. Understanding systems in which people, energy, and the environment intersect will be critical in meeting this challenge. Modeling these large-scale complex systems will be key in gaining this understanding. However, creating these complex, integrated models is challenging. Traditionally, models for each of these domains have been built independently by researchers working in different, often unconnected fields. Integrating these disparate models to create a holistic systems model and that accurately represents these systems in which people, energy, and the environment intersect is difficult, time consuming, and expensive with conventional approaches. One approach to this model integration challenge is the development of federated model sets [1].

2 Background

Integrated modeling has largely been developed by the environmental modeling community as an answer to the challenge of modeling large, complex systems. The goal of integrated modeling is to take a variety of components, be they mathematical models, databases, or other data sources, and combine them together into an integrated systems model [2]. A model integration framework is often utilized to achieve this integration. Various open- and closed-source model integration frameworks have been

© IFIP International Federation for Information Processing 2017
Published by Springer International Publishing AG 2017. All Rights Reserved
J. Hřebíček et al. (Eds.): ISESS 2017, IFIP AICT 507, pp. 420–432, 2017.
https://doi.org/10.1007/978-3-319-89935-0_35

created, each with slightly different goals. For example, SCIRun [3] and OpenDX [4] have a visualization focus, while others focus on providing a component-based approach to model integration, such as the Object Modeling System (OMS) [5], The Invisible Modeling Environment (TIME) [6], and the Community Surface Dynamics Modeling System (CSDMS) [7]. Others, such as VE-Suite [8], seek to be general purpose model integration tools. Closed source packages such as Matlab™, Simulink™, [9] and Aspen Plus™ [10] can be considered as model integration tools, though they tend to be less flexible and are often focused on a specific domain, such as process plant simulation in the case of Aspen Plus.

The drawback of most integrated modeling frameworks is that they require significant effort in project management and software development to create the desired integrated model, and in some cases they lack the ability to utilize and manage large-scale, high-fidelity models needed for detailed analysis. Typically, full access to the source code of all constituent models is required, and the system builder or team must develop a global ontology that connects all models. This approach tends to produce a well-integrated product, but the challenges of management, software development, and global ontology development can become unwieldy when modeling large systems with myriad component models.

There have been attempts to address this shortcoming. The CSDMS implements a component-based programming model that is intended to minimize invasive changes to component models. This is achieved through a pair of software interfaces, the Basic Model Interface (BMI) and the Component Model Interface (CMI) [7, 11, 12]. The BMI is the interface to the component model, and the CMI is the corresponding interface that connects to the integration framework. Once the code of a component model has been modified to implement the BMI, it can be registered as a usable component model within the CSDMS framework [7, 12]. While this approach was originally created for large-scale geological modeling, Antonelli et al. [13] have adapted the BMI to link a molecular dynamics simulation with a lattice Boltzmann solver to form a concurrent multi-scale model of fluid flow, demonstrating the applicability of the BMI concept to other types of models and systems.

Another approach is the development of federated model sets [1]. Federated model sets have been envisioned to take advantage of cloud-based independent models and to enable rapid construction of complex system models from these cloud-based independent modeling components. Specifically, in a federated model set, component models are implemented as independent information services with self-documenting interfaces. Information transfer between models is brokered, allowing for the creation of peer-to-peer ontologies instead of a global ontology for the integrated model. Component models can maintain a high level of autonomy and independence while still being members of a larger system model. This independence streamlines component and system model development and project management through a clear separation of roles.

In a federated modeling system, there are three primary user roles: the component modeler, the system builder, and the end user. The component modeler provides the constituent component models that can be utilized to build systems models. The system builder selects component models and composes a systems model. The end user utilizes the systems model to answer questions or gain insight into the modeled system. While these roles may overlap, they can be totally independent. The component modeler need not coordinate development with the system builder; they need only to provide their model in the required format with proper library entries and message contracts for inclusion in the federated modeling system. System builders may choose freely from these component models to construct systems models.

Suram et al. [14] have implemented a proof-of-concept federated model set based on a heat-transfer model of a small, shielded-fire cookstove for the developing world developed by MacCarty and Bryden [15]. This model was decomposed into seven independent information services, each implemented as a stateless web microservice [14, 16]. These microservices fulfill requests for computation; each request must contain all information necessary to fulfill the request, and after the results of the computation are returned, all state is discarded. As currently implemented by Suram et al. [14], a federated modeling system has the following characteristics.

- Models as stateless microservices
- Message broker for communication between microservices and infrastructure services
- A programmable federation management system (FMS)
- Simple message contracts
- Web-based front-end server.

These characteristics can be leveraged to create a system model that is accessible as a dynamic web service, but to do so the system builder must write code in Java that coordinates with the FMS to route data through the selected system of models. Any translation that is necessary between adjacent models must be handled manually by the system builder. Creating, modifying, and utilizing a federated modeling system as it exists now requires the system builder to be an expert in cloud computing and app development. However, by creating a domain specific language (DSL) and supporting infrastructure, we can substantially simplify the process of creating a federated model set, making it approachable for many more users.

A DSL is a custom programming language designed for a specific problem domain, built using the idioms and concepts of that domain [17]. The advantages of DSLs over general purpose languages include increased productivity and more readable, maintainable, and reusable code, among others. One of the chief advantages of a DSL for complex system modeling is that it enables clear communication with domain experts [17, 18]. Since a DSL natively uses the concepts and idioms of the domain in question, code in that language is easily read, understood, and written by domain experts even with limited programming experience [17, 18]. DSLs strive for fluent translation between mental models and code. This is a significant advantage when building models of complex systems, and is our primary motivation in designing a DSL for federated modeling.

3 Language Discussion

To create a working federated model set, four pieces of information are necessary:

- A list of constituent models,
- A list of connections between models,
- A list of input parameters,
- A list of desired output variables.

The desired component models and system level inputs and outputs are usually straightforward to define. The connections between models are generally much more complex to define fully. However, many of these connections can be determined automatically by the DSL tools by leveraging the self-describing interfaces of the constituent models along with supporting infrastructure. Therefore, the focus of the DSL is to allow the system builder to specify the constituent models, inputs, and outputs in a straightforward manner, with less emphasis on fully defining detailed connections between models. By removing this burden of complexity, the syntax of the language can be made readable and intuitive, even to those users who have limited programming experience. To that end, we have laid out a simple syntax that consists of three types of text blocks: input blocks, output blocks, and system blocks, illustrated in Fig. 1. These blocks may appear in any order in a system script. The input and output blocks do not need to be placed ahead of the system block, for example. The syntax avoids the use of brackets, braces, and other symbols whose purpose may not be obvious to new users.

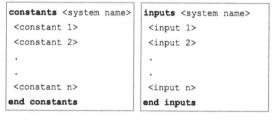

Input blocks:

```
constants <system name>
   <constant 1>
   <constant 2>
   .
   .
   <constant n>
end constants
```

```
inputs <system name>
   <input 1>
   <input 2>
   .
   .
   <input n>
end inputs
```

Output block:

```
outputs <system name>
   <output 1>
   <output 2>
   .
   .
   <output n>
end outputs
```

System block:

```
system <system name> from library <library address>
   <model 1 name>
   <model 2 name>
   .
   .
   <model n name>
end system
```

Fig. 1. Brief syntax for code blocks.

There are two types of input blocks, user inputs and constants. User inputs are passed in by the end users of a model. Since a federated model set is implemented as a web service, inputs will be uploaded to a specific web location. Constants are specified by the system builder, either in the code they write or in a file. The file location may be specified as a valid uniform resource locator (URL). Output blocks simply specify the output variables of interest. These outputs will be available for download at a specified URL upon completion of the requested modeling job. The system block contains a list of the models that constitute the system, along with the address of the model library from which these models are drawn. In many cases, these models can just be listed by their unique names as looked up in the component library. They do not need to be listed in any defined order. In cases where it is necessary for the user to define some of the connections between models, the following syntax is used:

```
model_a, model_b -> model_d
```

where `model_a` and `model_b` represent the names of two models that are providing inputs to a third model, named `model_d`. This syntax could be extended to allow the system builder to specify specific variables from source and destination models if needed.

To maintain this level of simplicity, supporting software infrastructure within the federated modeling environment is required. The critical enabling infrastructure services are the model library services and the message contract database. The DSL interpreter will rely on these services to determine possible workflows for solving the specified models [19]. These services and their use will be discussed in the next section.

4   Support Infrastructure Discussion

As mentioned above, the model library service and the message contract database are the key infrastructure services for enabling the simplicity of our DSL. The model library service is straightforward. It is a database that stores information about each component model available in a federated modeling system. Each record in the database corresponds to one component model, and will have information such as a unique name, a network address for the model microservice, a human-readable description, and other relevant data and metadata. Among this data is a full list of required and optional inputs and outputs in the form of message contract references.

All data transfer between models in a federated model set is governed by a system of "snappers" [1] or message contracts [14]. Taken together, these message contracts and their corresponding connections on component models form an extensible system of complex composite data types that enables peer-to-peer ontologies to be negotiated between adjacent communicating models [1]. A message contract takes the form of a document or database record that contains the following fields:

- A globally unique identifier (GUID),
- A list of variables, including name, data type, and description for each,
- A human-readable name,
- A brief description.

This information is used as the basis for a mediated negotiation between two models, with the FMS serving as the mediator. First, the FMS checks that the output of the source model and the input of the destination model are referencing the same message contract GUID. This ensures a basic shared vocabulary of variable names and data types. The interfaces of the models also incorporate questions and answers, or constraints, that are used to further negotiate data exchange. At minimum, these constraints should define the units for all variables. Simple, scalar unit conversions will be performed by the FMS. In addition, other optional constraints can be imposed by component modelers, such as valid input and output ranges, ranges of accuracy or stability, invalid inputs due to discontinuities, etc. If acceptable answers are found to all required question/answer pairs between two models, a peer-to-peer ontology is defined and the models may communicate freely.

This process is most easily understood by examining an example. Consider the following two component models drawn from MacCarty and Bryden's [20] village energy model, which is being modularized for use in a federated modeling system. The model presented in [20] is an integrated model of the comprehensive energy use of a small African village composed of smaller component models. We will select two models that are used internally, the fuel collection model and the fuel cost model. The fuel collection model takes several inputs and provides an output of the number of annual hours of a given fuel type. The fuel cost model takes the annual hours of a given fuel type as an input, among others, and produces the annual cost of fuel collection time for a given fuel as an output.

We define a message contract to facilitate this connection. The contract is assigned a GUID by which it will be referenced. It defines a data interchange containing two variables: a floating-point variable named hours containing the time quantity, and a string variable named type containing the fuel type. Each model would reference the GUID and have a set of constraints, which would be the unit for time, hours, a constraint that values be positive, and the requirement that the fuel be of a known type. The two models and their message contract are illustrated in Fig. 2.

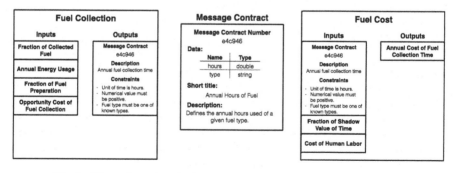

Fig. 2. Illustration of model input/output and matching message contract.

Once the model library and the message contract system are in place, the DSL tools can utilize the data within both systems to infer connections within model sets and calculate computational workflows to solve model sets. The inputs and outputs of a given component model together with the referenced message contracts allow the system to create a list of possible connections that are valid. That is, for any given input or output of a model, a list of compatible other models can be created. In some cases, there will be a unique set of compatible connections between the component models listed in the DSL script. In this case, the system builder will not have to explicitly specify any connections between models. When there are multiple valid sets of connections between specified component models, the DSL tools will provide detailed feedback on the points of ambiguity to the system builder. The system builder can then use the syntax defined in the previous section to select one among the possible valid connections where the ambiguity exists. In this way, the DSL tools and the system builder form a partnership, with the system builder offering clarifying information when necessary instead of having to be concerned with the details of every connection between the cloud-based component model microservices in a model set. In the next section, we will explore how all this will work with a real system by applying these tools to the cookstove model used by Suram et al. in [14].

5   Example and Discussion

5.1   Cookstove Model Example

Most of the energy requirements for families in the developing world are currently met by three stone fires [21, 22]. However, three stone fires are inefficient, dangerous, and have significant negative environmental impact [23, 24]. Improve biomass cookstoves have been developed to address the shortcomings of the three stone fire. Such a cookstove typically consists of a combustion chamber, a grate to elevate the fuel for better airflow, and geometric features to direct the flow of hot gases from the fire around the pot, improving heat transfer [15]. Figure 3 shows a representation of this type of cookstove. Improved biomass cookstoves are key components of energy interventions in the developing world, but there is a dearth of modeling and design tools for such cookstoves. MacCarty and Bryden's model [15] seeks to address this shortage, providing a tool for designers to experiment with materials and geometry while receiving immediate feedback on the thermal efficiency of their notional stove.

This model breaks the cookstove into three coupled zones: the fuel bed zone, the flame zone, and the heat transfer zone, as shown in Fig. 3(A). Solid phase combustion is modeled in the fuel bed zone, gas phase combustion in the flame zone, and heat transfer to the pot and the environment is modeled in the heat transfer zone. Buoyancy driven fluid flow is modeled throughout the coupled zones [15]. This model has been implemented in [14] as seven component model microservices, which are summarized in Table 1.

Originally these models were federated manually with custom Java code. To leverage our proposed domain specific language, model library entries would be created for each model, along with an appropriate system of message contracts. For brevity's sake, the

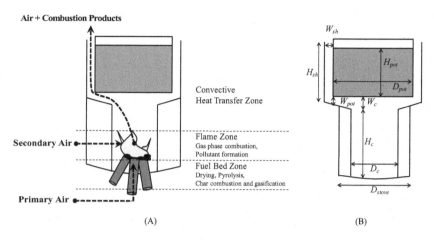

Fig. 3. (A) Biomass cookstove with modeling zones. Adapted from [25]. (B) Geometric stove design parameters. Adapted from [15].

Table 1. Constituent models of cookstove federated model set, after [14].

Model name	Description
Mesh	Initializes geometry and allocates variables
Bed	Calculates rate of burning, production of fuel moisture and combustion products, and fuelbed and exit gas
Flame	Calculates rate of burning volatiles and exit gas temperature from the flame zone
Heat transfer	Calculates exit temperature through each control
Flow	Calculates velocity and pressure drop through each control volume in the flow path
L2 norm	Calculates L2 norm between mass flow rates
Convergence	Set a flag if the system of models has converged

creation of the various message contracts will not be discussed in depth here. The strategy is to create a single message contract for each interacting pair of models. The connections in this system are simple, so only a handful of message contracts are necessary. As discussed earlier, the creation of the model library entries and message contracts is the responsibility of the component model builder, not the system builder. The system builder should find all those things in place and validated for any component model that is listed as ready to use.

With the library entries and message contracts in place, we can now represent this system in the domain specific language. Since message contracts were constructed specifically for the connections necessary in this system, there is only one valid set of possible connections, and the system builder will not need to explicitly specify any connections. Thus, the code representing the system model becomes:

```
inputs stove_model
  H_sh
  W_sh
  W_pot
  W_c
  H_c
  D_c
  D_stove
  D_pot
  H_pot
end inputs

constants stove_model
  http://10.10.10.10/stovemodel/constants.json
end constants

outputs stove_model
  stove_efficiency
end outputs

system stove_model from library stove_library
  stove_mesh
  bed_model
  flame_model
  heat_model
  flow_model
  l2_norm
  convergence_check
end system
```

In the above code, the inputs block contains the specified input variables. These are geometric parameters for the stove. Briefly, they are the height of the pot shield, H_sh; the width between the pot shield and the pot, W_sh; the width of the gap between the pot and stove at the corner of the pot, W_pot; the distance from the bottom of the pot to the top of the combustion chamber, W_c; the height of the combustion chamber, H_c; the inner and outer diameters of the combustion chamber, D_c and D_stove; the diameter of the pot, D_pot; and the height of the pot, H_pot. These correspond to the geometric parameters show in Fig. 3(B). The constants block contains a URL that points to a data file in JavaScript Object Notation (JSON) format. This file lists all necessary constants to run the model. The outputs block specifies the output of interest, thermal efficiency. The system block simply lists the seven component models shown in Table 1 that make up the cookstove model.

In a federated modeling environment, this would be the only code necessary to create the cookstove model as a web service. When run, the system would check the code, instantiate model microservices as necessary, create appropriate URLs for inputs and outputs, and provide those addresses along with status messages to the end user. The set of input and output URLs form an application programming interface (API) to the systems model, as used in web app development. An intuitive graphical user interface for modifying geometric stove parameters and visualizing the resulting performance of the stove could be built around this API.

5.2   Extensibility Discussion

The above model allows users to design cookstoves based on thermal efficiency. However, cookstoves for the developing world are intended to improve quality of life through better health outcomes and reduced environmental impact. The current cookstove model does not account for any of these factors, but it could form part of a systems design tool that does. By utilizing models from domain experts in energy systems for the developing world and sustainable agricultural and integrating these models with the cookstove model, a design tool that provides feedback in terms of health outcomes and environmental impact could be created.

MacCarty and Bryden [20] have identified the following factors as significant in prediction the adoption and impact of any energy device in the developing world:

- Desirability – perceived quality and aesthetic benefit
- Disruption – ability of stove to fit existing cooking patterns
- Convenience – ease of use and amount of attention required
- Safety – safety of the device for the user and family

have developed an integrated systems model [20] that accounts for these factors encompasses all the common energy needs in rural villages in the developing world. This model takes as input a set of energy components such as cookstoves, lighting equipment, water heating systems, etc., and performs a Monte Carlo simulation to predict the outcomes for a village, including energy access, environmental effects, health impact, cost, quality of life.

Of major concern when considering any energy intervention in the developing world is environmental impact. While this impact occurs in many forms, including CO_2 and black carbon emissions, deforestation [20] and its impact on local agriculture should also be considered. Muth and Bryden [26] have developed an integrated systems model to predict sustainable levels of agricultural residue removal. This integrated model incorporates several existing models for soil erosion and agricultural databases to create a tool that can predict the sustainability of a given farming practice at a high resolution anywhere in the United States. This model is becoming the standard for modeling sustainable agricultural processes in the United States, and it could be easily adapted for other places in the world.

By modularizing both the village energy model and the sustainable agricultural residue model and implementing them in a federated modeling environment, it becomes simple to modify them and integrate them into a new design model. The thermal efficiency from the cookstove model would become an input to the village energy model, and biomass remove rates from village energy model would become inputs into the sustainable agriculture model. The sustainable agriculture model would be modified with the appropriate databases to predict soil erosion and conditions in the developing world.

This would yield an end-to-end design tool that could predict health, environmental, agricultural, and energy outcomes for the developing world based on material and geometric design changes to the cookstove being designed. It would also be straightforward to extend this design tool with physical models of other energy devices being considered for the developing world, giving designers, aid workers, and policy makers a powerful tool to predict the real-world impact of holistic, village-wide energy systems design in a way that has not been possible before. A conceptual representation of this is shown in Fig. 4.

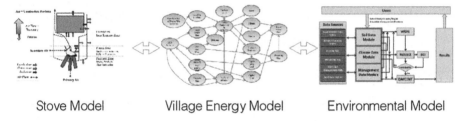

Stove Model   Village Energy Model   Environmental Model

Fig. 4. Model integration example

Since each component and subcomponent would exist as an independent web microservice, each model could be maintained and updated by domain experts. The domain experts in each field could retain ownership of their models, even as those models become constituent parts of the integrated end-to-end stove design model. Further, the stove design model will automatically benefit from improvements in the performance, capability, and accuracy of the underlying constituent models.

6 Conclusion and Future Work

This paper presents a proposed domain specific language and supporting infrastructure for rapidly and fluently creating systems models in a federated modeling environment. This not only simplifies model development and team management, but also enables more informed decision making based on rapidly developed end-to-end models of complex systems in which people, energy, and the environment meet. Further research is needed to demonstrate the capabilities envisioned here and integrate the set of environmental and other models needed to create the stove design tool as presented.

References

1. Bryden, K.M.: A proposed approach to the development of federated model sets. In: Ames, D.P., Quinn, N.W.T., Rizzoli, A.E. (eds.) International Environmental Modeling and Society 7th International Congress on Environment Modeling and Software, San Diego, CA (2014)
2. Arnold, T.R.: Procedural knowledge for integrated modelling: towards the modelling playground. Environ. Model. Softw. **39**, 135–148 (2013). https://doi.org/10.1016/j.envsoft. 2012.04.015

3. Scientific Computing and Imaging Institute: SCIRun. http://www.scirun.org
4. OpenDX. http://www.opendx.org
5. David, O., Ascough, J.C., Lloyd, W., Green, T.R., Rojas, K.W., Leavesley, G.H., Ahuja, L. R.: A software engineering perspective on environmental modeling framework design: the object modeling system. Environ. Model. Softw. **39**, 201–213 (2013). https://doi.org/10. 1016/j.envsoft.2012.03.006
6. Rahman, J.M., Seaton, S.P., Perraud, J.-M., Hotham, H., Verrelli, D.I., Coleman, J.R.: It's TIME for a new environmental modelling framework. In: MODSIM 2004 International Congress on Modelling and Simulation. Modeling and Simulation Society of Australia and New Zealand, pp. 1727–1732 (2003)
7. Peckham, S.D., Hutton, E.W.H., Norris, B.: A component-based approach to integrated modeling in the geosciences: the design of CSDMS. Comput. Geosci. **53**, 3–12 (2013). https://doi.org/10.1016/j.cageo.2012.04.002
8. McCorkle, D.S., Bryden, K.M.: Using the semantic web technologies in virtual engineering tools to create extensible interfaces. Virtual Real. **11**, 253–260 (2007). https://doi.org/10. 1007/s10055-007-0077-3
9. Mathworks. http://www.mathworks.com
10. AspenTech. http://www.aspentech.com
11. Community Surface Dynamics Modeling System Basic Model Interface (BMI). https:// csdms.colorado.edu/wiki/BMI_Description
12. Community Surface Dynamics Modeling System Component Model Interface (CMI). https://csdms.colorado.edu/wiki/CMI_Description
13. Antonelli, P.E., Bryden, K.M., LeSar, R.: A model-to-model interface for concurrent multiscale simulations. Comput. Mater. Sci. **123**, 244–251 (2016). https://doi.org/10.1016/j. commatsci.2016.06.031
14. Suram, S., MacCarty, N.A., Bryden, K.M.: A distributed systems approach to engineering modeling. To be Submitted to: Advances in Engineering Software (2016)
15. MacCarty, N.A., Bryden, K.M.: A generalized heat-transfer model for shielded-fire household cookstoves. Energy Sustain. Dev. **33**, 96–107 (2016). https://doi.org/10.1016/j. esd.2016.03.003
16. Thönes, J.: Microservices. IEEE Softw. **32**, 113–116 (2015)
17. van Deursen, A., Klint, P., Visser, J.: Domain-specific languages: an annotated bibliography. ACM Sigplan Not. **35**, 26–36 (2000). https://doi.org/10.1145/352029.352035
18. Fowler, M.: Domain-Specific Languages/Martin Fowler. Addison-Wesley, Upper Saddle River (2011)
19. McNunn, G.S., Bryden, K.M.: A proposed implementation of Tarjan's algorithm for scheduling the solution sequence of systems of federated models. Procedia Comput. Sci. **20**, 223–228 (2013)
20. MacCarty, N.A., Bryden, K.M.: An integrated systems model for energy services in rural developing communities. Energy **113**, 536–557 (2016). https://doi.org/10.1016/j.energy. 2016.06.145
21. International Energy Agency: Energy poverty: how to make modern energy access universal? Special Early Excerpt of the World Energy Outlook 2010 for the UN General Assembly on the Millennium Development Goals. Paris (2010)
22. Johnson, N.G., Bryden, K.M.: Energy supply and use in a rural West African village. Energy **43**, 283–292 (2012). https://doi.org/10.1016/j.energy.2012.04.028
23. Lim, S.S., Vos, T., Flaxman, A.D., Danaei, G., Shibuya, K., Adair-Rohani, H., AlMazroa,

M.A., Amann, M., Anderson, H.R., Andrews, K.G., et al.: A comparative risk assessment of burden of disease and injury attributable to 67 risk factors and risk factor clusters in 21 regions, 1990–2010: a systematic analysis for the Global Burden of Disease Study 2010. Lancet **380**, 2224–2260 (2013)

24. Bond, T.C., Sun, H.: Can reducing black carbon emissions counteract global warming? Environ. Sci. Technol. **39**, 5921–5926 (2005). https://doi.org/10.1021/es0480421

25. MacCarty, N.A., Bryden, K.M.: Modeling of household biomass cookstoves: a review. Energy Sustain. Dev. **26**, 1–13 (2015)

26. Muth, D.J., Bryden, K.M.: An integrated model for assessment of sustainable agricultural residue removal limits for bioenergy systems. Environ. Model. Softw. **39**, 50–69 (2013). https://doi.org/10.1016/j.envsoft.2012.04.006

Modelling and Forecasting Waste Generation – DECWASTE Information System

Jiří Hřebíček[1]([⊠]), Jiří Kalina[1], Jana Soukopová[2], Eva Horáková[3], Jan Prášek[3], and Jiří Valta[3]

[1] Institute of Biostatistics and Analyses, Masaryk University, Kamenice 126/3, 625 00 Brno, Czech Republic
hrebicek@iba.muni.cz, kalina@mail.muni.cz
[2] Faculty of Economics and Administration, Masaryk University, Lipová 507/41a, 602 00 Brno, Czech Republic
soukopova@econ.muni.cz
[3] Czech Environmental Information Agency, Vršovická 1442/65, 100 10 Prague 10, Czech Republic
{eva.horakova, jan.prasek, jiri.valta}@cenia.cz

Abstract. The DECWASTE forecasting waste generation information system is presented. It is based on Annexes I, II and III of Regulation (EC) No 849/2010 amending Regulation (EC) No 2150/2002 of the European Parliament and of the European Council on waste (WSR). DECWASTE forecasts the quantity of waste generated for each waste category listed in Section 2(1) of Annex I of the WSR at the Czech national level. Its multi-linear regression forecasting model is based on environmental as well as economic and social predictors. These models use historical data of the waste information system (ISOH) of the Czech Environmental Information Agency and sets of indicators (predictors) integrated into forecasting models. The methodology consisted in adjusting predictors of the forecasting models into a Driving Force-Pressure-State-Impact-Response (DPSIR) framework and their sensitivity analysis enables their choice into forecasting models and their verification using appropriate data. DECWASTE supports decisions made by the Ministry of the Environment to improve the implementation of the national Waste Management Plan.

Keywords: Waste generation · Waste categories · Forecasting Modelling · DPSIR · Multi-linear regression models

1 Introduction

Making decisions in waste management is not only very capital-intensive, but also difficult from the environmental, economic and social points of view. There is a need to develop, master and implement simple but reliable models and application software that will help decision-makers in public administration (PA) to analyse waste management processes, follow national and European Union (EU) legislation, the implementation of the Waste Management Plan (WMP) for the respective PA level [1] and to consider also EU Circular Economy tasks [2].

J. Hřebíček et al. (Eds.): ISESS 2017, IFIP AICT 507, pp. 433–445, 2017.
https://doi.org/10.1007/978-3-319-89935-0_36

Therefore, we have developed an improved version of the information system, DECWASTE, forecasting the quantity of waste generated for each waste category listed in Section 2(1) of Annex I of Regulation (EC) No 849/2010 amending Regulation (EC) No 2150/2002 of the European Parliament and of the Council on waste (WSR). We have updated the previous information system, DECWASTE [3], forecasting the quantity of waste generated for each category of waste on the European list of waste (LoW) established by the Commission Decision 2000/532/EC.

The new DECWASTE can forecast these quantities for the prescribed years 2016–2025. It uses linked open data of the Czech eGovernment system, i.e. historical waste data (2009–2015) of the waste information system (ISOH) [4] of the Czech Environmental Information Agency (CENIA) at the national level of Czech Republic and transforms them into quantities of waste categories of the WSR. It downloads and parses linked open data to populate appropriate sets of indicators (predictors) for the forecasting models. The predictors are then used in the Driving Force-Pressure-State-Impact-Response (DPSIR) framework [5] which also integrates linked open data from the Czech eGovernment system [6] and from the Czech Statistical Office (CSO) [7].

DPSIR analysis was carried out by Delphi method [10] undertaken by the partnership on the basis of an assessment of the underlying data and searching for causal links of waste category production to the management of "driving force" (economic sectors of human activity), through the "pressures" (emissions, waste), on the "states" (physical, chemical and biological) and "impacts" on ecosystems, human health and function, that eventually lead to political "responses" (the setting of priorities of waste management, setting goals of the WMP and its indicators [1]), see [8, 9].

The Delphi method was carried out with the assistance of a chosen expert group of finding solutions to the survey group experts' opinions. The group of experts carried out, independently of each other, predictors designated mediator were summarized, also distributed for the next round. Use of standardized questionnaires and the procedure was repeated until the approximate match.

Each group was assessed from the perspective of the individual parts of the DPSIR cycles. From the perspective of the production of waste category and the environment impacts we understood the individual parts of the DPSIR cycle, the following [5]:

- Driving forces are human activities or activities caused by the lifestyle of society. They lead to pressures on natural resources and the environment, which disrupt the ecological stability and impair the quality of the environment (e.g., emissions and waste).
- State is what is usually measured in the environment: waste category generation, the quality of water, soil, air and the environment (nature), energy and material flows.
- Pressures and states effect impacts: health problems, change in ecosystems, e invasion of alien species etc.
- Responses are responses of society to the identified problems in the form of specific measures (e.g. legislation).

The result of the implementation of DPSIR analysis was the description of the predictors of the individual parts of the DPSIR cycle, including identification of driving forces of the 51 waste categories of the WSR, expressed as the time series input data for calculating the forecast model [11]. The most relevant predictors were chosen through a selection process that included experts' opinions and literature reviews based on the relevance and applicability to different waste categories of WSR settings [9].

A verified multilinear regression model is presented. The construction of the forecasting model consisted in the construction and definition of the predictors based on the DPSIR framework; a sensitivity analysis of the models; implementation of the forecasting models. The presented results follow the authors' results from the iEMSS 2014 [8] and iEMSS 2016 [3] conferences.

2   Material and Methods

The development of the new information system DECWASTE includes the following consequent steps:

1. Identification of each waste category listed in Section 2(1) (51 items) and waste generating activity listed in Section 8(1) (19 items) of Annex I of the WSR and development of computation formulae for their amounts of using the Table of equivalence of Annex III of the WSR between the European Waste Classification for Statistics, version 4 (EWC-Stat Rev 4) (substance oriented waste statistical nomenclature) and the European List of Waste (LoW) established by the Commission Decision 2000/532/EC.
2. Processing of the historical annual waste generation and treatment reports (2009–2015) based on the LoW provided by waste generators and facilities in the Czech Republic to the ISOH and creating their data sets of waste categories of the WSR.
3. Identification and development of socioeconomic and demographic predictors for waste categories and activities based on the DPSIR framework (which have influence on the generation of waste categories) using linked open government data (eGovernment systems) of the Czech Republic.
4. Development of the multi-linear regression model of waste category generation with predictors from the DPSIR framework analyses.
5. Forecasting of predictors from the DPSIR framework and the calculation of waste category forecasts.
6. Processing of sensitivity analyses of predictors of waste category generation models.
7. Visualization scenarios forecasting the quantity of waste categories for the prescribed period 2016–2025.

We briefly describe the above steps.

Firstly, we implemented simple meta-computation formulae in DECWASTE using the Table of Equivalence of Annex III of the WSR between the EWC-Stat Rev 4 and the LoW, which enabled us to calculate the amount of every item of waste category of the WSR from items in the LoW.

Data sets of the ISOH keep the quantity of waste generation and treatment by generators and data from facilities to treat, recover and dispose of waste [3, 8] from 2009–2015. Every year, the ISOH records more than 70,000 different generators' reports in all 6,500 municipalities of the Czech Republic and more than 3,000 facilities' reports. The annual ISOH database contains more than 50,000 records of municipal waste generation and 10,000 records concerning their treatment. The database is available to the public for the years 2009–2015 and we calculated all appropriate waste categories for these years.

The Czech eGovernment systems provide sources of linked open data of necessary input data for the DPSIR framework predictors for different waste categories and activities [5–8]. Parsing of the linked open data of eGovernment systems is divided in the DECWASTE information system into five phases [8]: definition of the appropriate data; data export; data processing; data import and optimization.

Identification and development of socioeconomic and demographic predictors based on the DPSIR framework [5] of the third step have been described [3, 9]. In the next section, we discuss the fourth step.

2.1 Development of a Multi-linear Regression Model of Waste Generation Based on DPSIR

We need to predict the amount of waste generated on the national level of the Czech Republic for the given year t and the chosen waste category $w^f(t)$ of the WSR $f = 1, \ldots, 51$. We have developed mathematical forecast models based on the DPSIR framework [5] predictors according to the work of [8, 9]. They use available linked open data on DPSIR predictors from eGovernment systems [4] and data of past waste generation from the ISOH (2009–2015).

Let us assume that for a given waste category f, the amount of waste $\hat{w}_t^f$ and predictors $\hat{A}_{i,t}^f$, $i = 1, \ldots, K^f$; in years $t = 2009, \ldots, 2015$ are known, where K^f is the number of predictors for the waste category f of the WSR. Let waste category generation $w^f(t)$ at the given year t fulfil the equation

$$\log\left(w^f(t)\right) = a_0^f + \sum_{i=1}^{K^f} a_i^f \cdot \log\left(A_i^f(t)\right) + \varepsilon_t^f, \tag{1}$$

where

- $A_i^f(t)$, $i = 1, \ldots, K^f$ are predictors in the given year t derived from the DPSIR analysis of the waste category f,
- $\varepsilon_t^f = \log\left(w^f(t)\right) - \log\left(\hat{w}_t^f\right)$, for $t = 2009, \ldots, 2015$ are approximation errors.
- Coefficients $a_0^f, \ldots, a_k^f$ in (1) for each waste category f are calculated using multiple regression on the basis of the values of waste generation $\hat{w}_t^f$ and predictors $\hat{A}_{i,t}^f$, $i = 1, \ldots, K^f$; $t = 2009, \ldots, 2015$. Approximation errors ε_t^f, $t = 2009, \ldots, 2015$, have the mean equal to 0 and the normal distribution.

If we want to establish the confidence interval of predictors $A_i^f(t)$, it is necessary to restrict their number to $K^f \leq 5$, since we only have a time series of six past known values. If we have the values of $\hat{w}_t^f$ and $\hat{A}_{i,t}^f$ for the next years $t = 2016, \ldots$, the model (1) will be more accurate and the approximation error $\varepsilon_t^{f,ps}$ will be smaller.

Furthermore, we assume that the predictors $A_i^f(t)$, $i = 1, \ldots, K^f$, for $t = 2016, \ldots, 2025$ have either known values (e.g. GDP, population, household consumption, etc.) from the eGovernment systems [6, 7] or are determined by an appropriate extrapolation method or are chosen by decision makers using DECWASTE.

These models are implemented in DECWASTE, written in language R and they use predefined predictors $\hat{A}_{i,t}^f$, which were parsed from linked open data [6, 7]. The outputs $w^f(t)$ are time series of the amount of waste generated for the years $t = 2016, \ldots, 2025$ of waste category f.

An estimate of the waste category generation $w^f(t)$ can be expressed after treatment (1) as

$$w^f(t) = A_0^f \cdot \prod_{i=1}^{K^f} A_i^f(t)^{a_i^f}, \tag{2}$$

where $A_0^f = \exp\left(a_0^f\right)$, while we have neglected the error ε_t^f.

2.2 The Sensitivity of Estimate of Waste Generation with Respect to the Statistical Significance of Predictors

The local sensitivity of the model (1), (2) for the ith predictor $A_i^f(t)$, in the year t and waste category f can be estimated using the partial derivatives of the waste category $w^f(t)$ in (2) according to the ith predictor $A_i^f(t)$:

$$a_i^f \cdot \frac{w^f(t)}{A_i^f(t)} \tag{3}$$

It follows from (3) that if the value of predictor $A_i^f(t)$ is increased by 1% then the amount of waste $w^f(t)$ in waste category f will increase or decrease by a_i^f percent, if $a_i^f > 0$ or $a_i^f < 0$, for $i = 1, \ldots, K^f$. This knowledge is important for users of the model. We continue in the further analysis of the developed model, i.e. assessment of the statistical significance of predictors.

The predictors $A_i^f(t)$, $i = 1, \ldots, K^f$ in (1), (2) were determined for each waste category f on the basis of the analysis of the DPSIR framework and experts' assessment. Therefore, we will conduct an assessment of their statistical significance in the multiple linear model (1) depending on the input values of the predictors in the years 2009 to 2015. Firstly, we consider in the model (1) all predictors $A_j^f(t), j = 1, \ldots, K^f$ in (1), in the waste category f where we calculate its sample variance, i.e.:

$$s^2 = \left(\sum_{t=2009}^{2015} (\varepsilon_t^f)^2\right) / (K^f - 1). \tag{4}$$

The statistical significance of each predictor $A_i^f(t)$ is calculated using the F-test of the difference of two sample variances, i.e. the sample variance s of the model (1) with all predictors and sample variance s_i of the model (1) where the ith predictor $A_i^f(t)$ is excluded and the rest of the predictors, i.e. $K^f - 1$, are recalculated and its sample variance is calculated

$$s_i^2 = \left(\sum_{t=2009}^{2015} (\varepsilon_{t,i}^f)^2 \right) / (K^f - 2), \tag{5}$$

Where $\varepsilon_{t,i}^f$ is the approximation error of multiple linear regression of the model (1), where the ith predictor was excluded.

Then we set the number of degrees of freedom for both samples: $n_1 = K^f - 1$ (for s^2) and $n_2 = K^f - 2$ (for s_i^2) and compute the value of the test criteria (statistics) F_i:

$$F_i = \text{the greater of } (s^2, s_i^2) \,/\, \text{the smaller of the } (s^2, s_i^2), \tag{6}$$

that has the Fischer probability density distribution

$$H(x) = \frac{\Gamma\left(\frac{n_1+n_2}{2}\right)}{\Gamma\left(\frac{n_1}{2}\right) \cdot \Gamma\left(\frac{n_2}{2}\right)} \cdot n_1^{\frac{n_1}{2}} \cdot n_2^{\frac{n_2}{2}} \cdot \frac{x^{\frac{n_1-2}{2}}}{(n_2 + n_1 \cdot x)^{-\frac{n_1+n_2}{2}}}, \tag{7}$$

for $x > 0$ and is equal to 0 for $x \leq 0$.

We use statistical software where it is more common to calculate the test p-value, which we denote as p_i. This is the smallest level of the F-test in which we would reject the hypothesis $H_0 : \{S^2 = S_i^2\}$. We set this value as $p_i = 1 - H\,(F_i)$.

This procedure is repeated gradually for other predictors $A_i^f(t)$, for which we calculate F_i statistics and the test p-values p_i, $i = 2, ..., K^f$.

Denote $V = \{F_i, p_i, s_i\}_{i=1}^{K^f}$ the set of predictor significance. We can now simplify the model (1) and exclude non-significant predictors.

Let us choose the level of significance α (values 0.05 or 0.1 are usually selected) of the predictors. We calculate p-values $p_i, i = 1, ..., K^f$ and compare them with this level of significance α:

- If $p_i > \alpha =>$ the null hypothesis $H_0 : S^2 = S_i^2$ is rejected. Conclusion: the variances of different models are statistically significant and the ith predictor $A_i^f(t)$ is significant.
- If $p_i < \alpha =>$ we cannot reject the hypothesis H_0. Conclusion: the variances of both models are not statistically significantly different (i.e., the selections originated from the same basic model with the common variance s^2) and the ith predictor is not significant.

In this way we can simplify the model (1), (2) if we exclude insignificant predictors $A_i^f(t)$, which we originally selected on the basis of the DPSIR analysis. In the developed model, only the statistically significant predictors $A_i^f(t)$ then remain. For some waste category f, however, it may happen that the original proposed predictors based on the DPSIR analysis do not remain in any model (1). The resulting forecast p of waste category generation is then constant and independent of the predicted values of the predictors of the future. In this case we can only reduce the statistical significance level α, i.e. reliability of the developed model and accept a greater risk of erroneous predictions.

2.3 Extrapolation of the Predictors

Let us suppose that for each waste category f the amount of waste category generation $\hat{w}_t^f$ and predictors $\hat{A}_{i,t}^f$, $i = 1, \ldots, K^f$; $t = 2009, \ldots, 2015$ are known and we have calculated for each waste category f the coefficients $a_0^f, \ldots, a_k^f$ in the model (1) by using multiple regression.

For the calculation of the forecast waste category generation $w^f(t)$ in the years $t = 2016,\ldots,2025$ it is necessary to know the values of predictors $A_i^f(t)$, $i = 1, \ldots, K^f$, $t = 2016, \ldots, 2025$. These values, however, may not always be listed in the sources (linked open data in the eGovernment systems) from which we draw the data predictors $\hat{A}_{i,t}^f$, $i = 1, \ldots, K^f$; $t = 2009,\ldots,2015$. In this case, the procedure is as follows:

- Enter the values of the predictors based on experts' estimates or other appropriate sources;

- On the basis of the values of the predictors $\hat{A}_{i,t}^f$, $i = 1, \ldots, K^f$; $t = 2009, \ldots, 2015$ the values of predictors $A_i^f(t)$, $i = 1, \ldots, K^f$, $t = 2016, \ldots, 2025$ are calculated using either linear or exponential extrapolation.

2.4 Modelling Measures in Waste Management and Scenarios

The developed models (1), (2) of forecast waste generation $w^f(t)$ for the waste category f should also reflect the trends in changes in this waste category as a result of the anticipated N measures o_j, $j = 1, \ldots, N$ (WMP, EU and national legislative changes etc.), which will have an impact on the given waste category f in the year t.

Therefore, we introduce the function $P^f(t,o_1,o_2,\ldots,o_N)$ in the form:

$$P^f(t, o_1, o_2, \ldots, o_N) = \prod_{j=1}^{N} \left(1 - \frac{P_j^f(t)}{100} \right), \tag{8}$$

where functions $P_j^f(t)$ are time-dependent functions of the impact of given measures (e.g. prevention, kind of collection, permitted treatment, delivery distance to waste facilities, etc.) on the waste category f in the given year t (generally in the whole waste management of the Czech Republic) and for simplicity, we assume that

$$0 \leq P_j^f(t) < 100, j = 1, \ldots, N; t = 2016, \ldots, 2025. \tag{9}$$

The functions $P_j^f(t)$ for the year t are set as a percentage which should be achieved in years $t = 2015, \ldots, 2025$, as a result of the measures o_j (on the basis of the WMP, WPP or other strategic documents). For the period $t = 2009, \ldots, 2015$, zero values of these functions are considered. In most of the waste categories f simple function values

$P_j^f(t)$ for the given year $t = 2016, \ldots, 2025$ will not be provided, therefore, they will be estimated on the basis of expert assessment. If it is not possible to set them realistically, we consider them to be equal to 0.

The forecast of the waste generation $w_{prognosis}^f(t)$ for the given waste category f-let us consider now as the product of the function $P^f(t, o_1, o_2, \ldots, o_N)$ and estimated waste category generation $w^f(t)$ of (2):

$$w_{prognosis}^f(t) = \prod_{j=1}^{N} \left(1 - \frac{P_j^f(t)}{100}\right) \cdot A_0^f \cdot \prod_{i=1}^{K^f} A_i^f(t)^{a_i^f} \qquad (10)$$

To compute logarithms (10) we obtain the resulting equation of our developed model for the forecast of the waste category generation f in the year $t = 2016, \ldots, 2025$:

$$\log(w_{prognosis}^f(t)) = a_0^f + \sum_{i=1}^{K^f} a_i^f \log\left(A_i^f(t)\right) + \sum_{j=1}^{N} \log\left(1 - \frac{P_j^f(t)}{100}\right). \qquad (11)$$

The values of the waste category generation $\hat{w}_t^f$ and the values of predictors $\hat{A}_{i,t}^f$ are known for each waste category f and $P^f(t, o_1, o_2, \ldots, o_N) = 0$ in the years $t = 2009, \ldots, 2015$ and the coefficients $a_0^f, \ldots, a_k^f$ from (1), (2) are calculated using the method of multiple regression. The forecast of the amount of waste category generation $w_{prognosis}^f(t)$ in the years $t = 2016, \ldots, 2025$ depends on the values of the predictors $A_i^f(t)$ and functions $P_j^f(t)$, $i = 1, \ldots, K^f; j = 1, \ldots, N$ for each waste category f.

Using the functions $P_j^f(t)$, the decision makers at the PA could simulate different scenarios for the anticipated impact of the individual measures o_j, $j = 1, \ldots, N$ on the total waste generation in the given waste category f and year t.

They could choose, for example, the value of $P_j^f(t)$, which was achieved for the year 2025 and the values of the function $P_j^f(t)$ in the previous years from 2016 to 2024, until the year 2015, where they choose this equal to zero and examine what the impact of the forecast value on the waste category generation $w_{prognosis}^f(t)$ is.

3 Results and Discussion

The DECWASTE information system enables the outputs of the above forecasting models for 51 waste categories listed in Section 2(1) of Annex I of Regulation (EC) No 849/2010. We present this for forecasting the household waste category.

3.1 Household Waste Forecast Generation Analysis Outputs

Firstly, we describe the process of development of DPSIR analysis and the choice of predictors for the household waste category [11].

The basic *driving force* behind the production of household waste is the size of the population, which is also significantly affected by urbanization of the population, when residents with higher incomes and stronger consumer behaviour live in cities and their surroundings. High population density together with higher purchasing power also limits their own waste management options (e.g. composting) and creates requirements for faster replacement of goods, which affects household consumption and composition of the consumer basket. The driving force for the production of municipal waste is also the age structure of the population and the amount of the unemployment benefit, when families with small children, students, pensioners and partially unemployed remain throughout the day near the residence where their activities produce waste.

The main *pressure* influencing the amount of household waste generation is environmental education and enlightenment in the prevention of and management of household waste.

The *state* of household waste generation is annually evaluated by indicators of the WMP [1], data from information systems of the MoE relating to the amount of emissions/imissions from energy recovery waste, the landfilling of waste, the status of surface water and groundwater etc.

The *impacts* of the generation and treatment of household waste on the environment have not yet manifested themselves to distort the landscape; mainly landfills, incinerators and industrial areas with waste treatment plants, the potential threat to groundwater and surface water and air pollution, etc. Furthermore, collection and transport of household waste and pollution in the case of collection containers, etc.

The *response* to generated household waste is increasing the number of collection places for sorting waste and streamlining the system of collection and treatment of household waste. There is, along with improving municipal waste management systems, the education of the population in the context of environmental education. Together with education legislative measures are used, which are operated both by the municipality as the originator of household waste, so the whole system for the collection and processing of waste, i.e. throughout the life cycle of the household waste. Legislative instruments are accompanied by economic instruments, in the form of charges (waste disposal in a landfill), and the amount of the tax rates and subsidies directed towards the development of systems for the municipal waste management.

The expert group choose the most significant four predictors for household waste for which past time series are available or can be estimated [11]:

- Driving forces: population; number of retired; unemployed rate; household expenditure on food, footwear and clothing.
- Press: prevention percentage according to environmental awareness (sorting rate, influence of ecological education etc.) which decreases the amount of household waste.
- State: household waste generation.

The outputs of every forecasting model consist of four basic output steps, which are presented for the household waste category forecasting, in the following figures.

1. In the first step, Fig. 1, basic data inputs over the time $t = 2009, ..., 2015$ for modelling are provided: previous household waste generation and time series of the

known values of the above DPSIR predictors (implicit values are parsed from linked open data) and forecasting model outputs.

Step 1: Input data for household waste generation model

Initial year of the model: (first year with modelled generation).	2016
Statistical significance: (percentage of probability that error not occurs when evaluate predictors).	95
Previous HW generation: (metric tons in years, separated by comma; for unknown value insert NA).	3646367.209,3732837.508,3598752.269,3424688.198,3348157.697,3398917.2,3
Previous households expenditures in food, footwear and clothing: (billions of CZK, values separated by comma; for unknown value insert NA).	495.01,502.25,527.19,545.84,561.8,589.77,620.82
Previous population: (thousands of persons, values separated by comma; for unknown value insert NA).	10491,10517,10497,10509,10510,10525,10543
Previous number of retired: (thousands of persons, values separated by comma; for unknown value insert NA).	2790,2881,2873,2866,2858,2863,2874
Previous unemployment rate: (percentagess, values separated by comma; for unknown value insert NA).	7.12,7.4,6.77,7.37,8.17,7.46,6.24
Previous waste genration prevention: (percentagess, values separated by comma; for unknown value insert NA)	0,0,0,0,0,0,0

Input values into model

Fig. 1. Step 1. Input data for MSW generation. Source: authors.

2. In the second step, Fig. 2, users can specify the values of the predictors (pre-filled values are available with hyperlinks to the linked open data sources) expected in the model (1), (2) or choose their possible linear/exponential extrapolation. Users can also input expected prevention measures (three possible scenarios of household waste prevention are available).

Step 2: Expected development up to 2025

Households expenditures in food, footwear and clothing: [bil. CZK]	2016	2017	2018	2019	2020	2021	2022	2023	2024	2025	Source: https://vdb.czso.cz/vdbvo2/faces
	632.62	653.79	674.76	695.73	716.69	737.66	758.63	779.59	800.56	821.53	/index.jsf?page=statistiky#katalog=30847

Population [thsds. persons]	2016	2017	2018	2019	2020	2021	2022	2023	2024	2025	Source: https://www.czso.cz/csu/czso
	10491	10439	10388	10336	10284	10271	10257	10244	10231	10217	/inhabitanIssIvo_hu

Retired [thsds. persons]	2016	2017	2018	2019	2020	2021	2022	2023	2024	2025	Source: http://www.cssz.cz/cz/o-cssz/informace
	2944	3011	3078	3146	3219	3291	3365	3441	3518	3597	/informacni-materialy/statisticke-rocenky.htm

Unemployment [%]	2016	2017	2018	2019	2020	2021	2022	2023	2024	2025	Source: https://vdb.czso.cz/vdbvo2/faces/cs/index.jsf?page=vyslup-objekt&pvo=ZAM06&zo=N&z=T&f=TABULKA&verze=-1&nahled=N&sp=N&filtr=G-F_M-F_Z-F_R-F_P-_S-_null_null_&katalog=30853&str=v95&c=v3__RP2014
	5.19	6.08	5.89	5.69	5.5	5.3	5.11	4.91	4.71	4.52	

Prevention [%]	2016	2017	2018	2019	2020	2021	2022	2023	2024	2025	
	2	4	5	7	8	10	11	12	14	15	

Input values into model

Fig. 2. Step 2. Scenario of forecasting future development in household waste generation in 2016–2025 with expected prevention measures. Source: authors.

3. In the third step, we conducted the assessment of predictor' statistical significance $\alpha = 0.05$ in the model (1) depending on the input values of the predictors in the years 2009 to 2015 and we excluded insignificant predictors: number of retired;

unemployed rate; household expenditure on food, footwear and clothing. We obtained a linear model with the predictor amount of population. In Fig. 3, results are shown in the form of a table, mathematical expression of (1) and a time-plot, showing the development of future household waste generation and the effects of

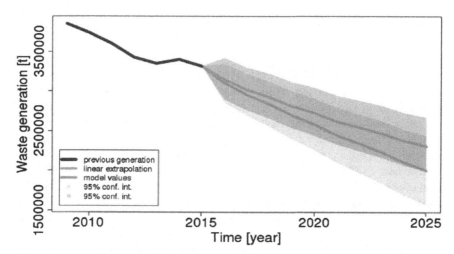

Fig. 3. Step 3. Final prediction of household waste generation. Source: authors.

	2016	2017	2018	2019	2020	2021	2022	2023	2024	2025
Model generation	3142702	3015105	2924115	2807124	2724773	2616872	2541862	2469916	2373191	2307163
Lower border	2892087	2757503	2656426	2532306	2440366	2326659	2243432	2164017	2064174	1992307
Upper border	3415033	3296770	3218778	3111766	3042326	2943285	2879990	2819056	2728469	2671778
Linear extrapolation	3100954	2951460	2835405	2692198	2580633	2443711	2336636	2231357	2103416	2002627
Lower border	2855472	2689412	2552168	2389578	2254724	2097809	1966937	1837807	1690913	1566925
Upper border	3346435	3213508	3118642	2994818	2906541	2789614	2706336	2624907	2515918	2438328

the prevention measures taken (the curves represent the prediction interval and shaded areas show the confidence intervals).
4. In the fourth step, Fig. 4, a sensitivity analysis is presented, showing decision makers the estimated effect of the individual predictors from the model (1) and the quality of forecasting.

Table of model results (in log form):

Predictor	Degrees of freedom	Sum of squared residuals	F statistics	p value
Variable: households	1	0.017	40.3	0.024
Variable: inhabitants	1	0	0.9	0.437
Variable: retired	1	0.001	2.6	0.25
Variable: unemployment	1	0.001	2.1	0.286
Residuals	2	0.001	NA	NA

Fig. 4. Step 4. Sensitivity analysis of forecasting household waste generation. Source: authors.

4 Conclusion

The construction of the DECWASTE waste information system is presented. It uses historical waste data of the ISOH [4] and linked open data [6, 7] of the chosen predictors [8, 9] based on the DPSIR framework [5, 9]. Integration of the appropriate predictors into the forecasting model is discussed. The forecasting model was implemented as open source software DECWASTE and was verified using appropriate household waste data, whose outputs are presented.

The new DECWASTE information system allows decision makers at the national level of the Czech Republic to make sustainable environmental decisions, focusing on waste management data requirements, national strategies for waste data acquisition, management and processing in a similar way as was done previously. They assisted in identifying alternative waste management strategies of the Czech Republic and support the national WMP that meet the objectives of EU legislation and Circular Economy principles [2].

References

1. Preparing a Waste Management Plan. A methodological guidance note. http://ec.europa.eu/environment/waste/plans/pdf/2012_guidance_note.pdf
2. Closing the loop - An EU action plan for the Circular Economy. COM/2015/0614 final. http://eur-lex.europa.eu/legal-content/EN/TXT/?qid=1453384154337&uri=CELEX:52015D C0614
3. Hřebíček, J., Kalina, J., Soukopová, J., Valta, J., Prášek, J.: Decision support system for waste management. In: Sauvage, S., Sánchez-Pérez, J.M., Rizzoli, A.E. (eds.) Proceedings of the 8th International Congress on Environmental Modelling and Software, Toulouse, France, 10–14 July (2016)
4. Waste Management Information System. http://www1.cenia.cz/www/odpady/isoh

5. Liao, M., Chen, P., Ma, H., Nakamura, S.: Identification of the driving force of waste generation using a high-resolution waste input-output table. J. Clean. Prod. **94**, 294–303 (2015)
6. Soukopová, J., Hřebíček, J., Valta, J.: National environmental data facilities and services of the Czech Republic and their use in environmental economics. In: Denzer, R., Argent, R.M., Schimak, G., Hřebíček, J. (eds.) Environmental Software Systems: Infrastructures, Services and Applications, ISESS 2015. IFIPAICT, vol. 448, pp. 361–370. Springer, Heidelberg (2015). https://doi.org/10.1007/978-3-319-15994-2_36
7. Czech Statistical Office. https://www.czso.cz/csu/czso/home
8. Kalina, J., Hřebíček, J., Bulková, G.: Case study: prognostic model of Czech municipal waste production and treatment. In: Ames, D.P., Quinn, N.W.T., Rizzoli, A.E. (eds.) Proceedings of the 7th International Congress on Environmental Modelling and Software, pp. 227–332, San Diego, 15–19 June (2014)
9. Hřebíček, J., Kalina, J., Soukopová, J., Prášek, J., Valta, J.: The forecasting waste generation model based on linked open data and the DPSIR framework. Case study concerning municipal waste in the Czech Republic. In: Proceedings of the Cyprus 2016 4th International Conference on Sustainable Solid Waste Management, Limassol, 23–25 June (2016)
10. Seker, S.E.: Computerized argument Delphi technique. IEEE Access **3**, 368–380 (2015). https://doi.org/10.1109/ACCESS.2015.2424703
11. Horáková, E., Kalina, J., Hřebíček, J., Prášek, J., Soukopová, J., Buda Šepeľová, G., Valta, J.: Vyhodnocení DPSIR rámce pro vybrané skupiny odpadů stanovené výzvou TB940MZP003. (Evaluation of the DPSIR framework for selected groups of waste laid down a challenge TB940MZP003). Internal report. CENIA, Praha (2015)

Planning and Scheduling for Optimizing Communication in Smart Grids

Miroslav Kadlec[✉], Barbora Buhnova, and Tomas Pitner

Faculty of Informatics, Masaryk University, Brno, Czech Republic
{miroslav.kadlec,buhnova,tomp}@mail.muni.cz

Abstract. Smart grid is a concept defining future electricity distribution network with the purpose of improving its reliability, efficiency and reducing its ecological impact. To achieve that, massive volumes of data need to be sensed and transmitted between the elements of the grid. A robust and efficient communication infrastructure is thus as essential part of smart grid. Some of the data transmissions are not time-critical, providing an opportunity to improve the communication network performance. In this paper, we present a new approach to optimize smart grid communications through time-based scheduling. Additionally, we provide a review of communication technologies in smart grids and published approaches to avoid congestions and transmission failures.

Keywords: Smart grids · Communication · Scheduling · Optimization

1 Introduction

The traditional electricity distribution infrastructures were developed during the first half of the 20th century and nowadays, they are undergoing complex transformation to fully satisfy the needs of modern society. The electricity consumption has doubled in the past 20 years and it is supposed to keep rising at least the same speed. Since the majority of electricity generation relies on coal, oil and gas resources, the growth in power usage brings more and more significant environmental problem. Additionally, more aspects of modern life are dependent on the electricity supply. Though, incorporating renewable resources based generators (e.g. photovoltaic power plants and wind turbines) as well as making the whole infrastructure more monitorable and controllable become an important strategic act to preserve power grid sustainability.

The need to employ more power generators based on renewable sources brings several challenges to be solved. First, both wind and solar power plants provide rather unstable electricity production varying with current weather that is difficult to be predicted, but may be estimated from short term weather forecast. Nowadays, end electricity users are also encouraged to install their own small power sources in order to save money lowering the electricity consumption and potentially send electricity back to the network in cases of overproduction. Since storing energy or transmitting it over long distances causes significant losses, the task of keeping the power grid capable of maintaining these changes is nontrivial.

© IFIP International Federation for Information Processing 2017
Published by Springer International Publishing AG 2017. All Rights Reserved
J. Hřebíček et al. (Eds.): ISESS 2017, IFIP AICT 507, pp. 446–456, 2017.
https://doi.org/10.1007/978-3-319-89935-0_37

The concept of smart grid represents a complex approach to improve current power distribution infrastructure in order to provide application such as demand response, use of distributed energy resources (DER) or real-time state monitoring [1]. The overall goals are to lower energy losses and to make the electricity network more reliable, efficient and environmental-friendly. In order to achieve the previously mentioned applications, smart metering and remotely controllable devices, communication infrastructure and computational systems for data collection and decision making are supposed to be added to the existing power distribution network.

To make the grid state analysis and decision making as relevant as possible, a large amount of up-to date complete data will be needed. Typically, the data will be generated in metering/monitoring points all over the network and then collected in central offices and, conversely, control commands will be sent from central offices to elements of the grid. Hence, a bidirectional, robust and reliable communication network is a critical part of smart grid. Due to its complexity, expenses associated with deploying a communication infrastructure of this scale are supposed to be high and strongly dependent on concrete technology used.

The communication requests are expected to have variable data sizes and requirements on latency and reliability of delivery. Since some of the data transfers are not time critical, the communication may be planned using proper scheduling techniques, request importance evaluation, real time adaptation and predictions of network traffic load and message sizes in order to balance traffic load and to prevent and manage communication network overloads. Thus, a given communication infrastructure will be capable to maintain bigger number of communication requests and to provide most relevant data possible at the time, so a better trade-off between quality and price of the communication infrastructure may be earned. To schedule the messages efficiently is a new optimization problem with many aspects specific to smart grid environment.

In this paper, we propose new approach to optimize smart grid communications through time-based scheduling. As the first step, an analysis of smart grid communication was conducted, based on existing literature as well as our practical experience from the smart grid design and implementation projects that we actively contribute to within the context of the Czech Republic. Then, the optimization problem is identified along with its inputs as well as techniques to find the solution are outlined.

The rest of the paper is organized as follows. In the Sect. 2, messages exchanged between smart grid elements are summarized with emphasis to their communication requirements. In the Sect. 3, communication technologies usable for smart grids with their specifics and challenges are listed. In the Sect. 4, the opportunity to use a scheduling algorithm in order to optimize traffic load is described and design of a potential solution is outlined and the specifics of given optimization problems are described.

2   Communication in Smart Grids

As long as smart grids are being developed as enhancement of current electricity distribution networks rather than brand-new infrastructures, the concrete implementations vary through different countries according to the existing power grids specifics. On the other hand, the overall structure, high-level applications and other general characteristics remain the same. In order to provide a standardized model of smart grid basic structure, SGAM (Smart Grid Architecture Model) framework has been presented in [2]. Although the model omits technical and implementation details, it provides a good insight into the organizational structure and defines several levels of abstraction the smart grids may be looked on, Fig. 1. Along the "interoperability" axis, several layers are listed, where each one is supported by layers located below. For example, the function layer describes functions and services provided by the smart grid in order to fulfill business requirements and policies. Similarly, the information layer summarizes all the data needed by the functions.

According to the SGAM framework, communication infrastructure serves as the support element for all the upper layers. Indeed, having up to date data transmitted by communication infrastructure is necessary for the data-analysis and decision-making systems incorporated in smart grids [1, 3]. Thus, deploying a robust communication infrastructure capable of satisfying smart grid requirements is one of major tasks in smart grid development [4, 5].

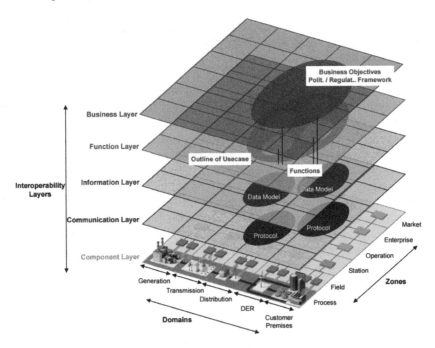

Fig. 1. Smart grid architecture model [2].

According to [6, 7], the communication network itself may be divided into three domains according to the coverage range and involved devices:

- **Home area network (HAN)**, that realizes communication between the smart meter and other household appliances, for example local power generators, controllable consuming devices, electric cars and other devices equipped by communication interface.

- **Neighborhood area network (NAN)** interconnects smart meters and data conce-trators, that collect metering data and send them to central systems. Complementarily, control commands coming from central systems are passed to smart meters.
- **Wide area network (WAN)** cover data exchange between data concentrators and the central systems, where the collected data is analyzed and potentially reacted to.

A graphical representation of described architecture is in Fig. 2, showing HAN, NAN and WAN with typical communicating elements. Such a multi-layered model is expected to be used since the smart grid communication network is needed to cover entire region with the intention to connect a large set of nodes [8].

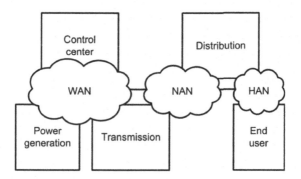

Fig. 2. Multilayer structure of the smart grid communication network [8].

2.1 Communication Requirements

Several papers have been published aiming to describe communication requirements of smart grids. The general objective of making the power distribution network more efficient, reliable and intelligent is expected to be achieved through implementing certain smart grid applications. The following requirements on the smart grid are the most commonly presented in existing studies [3, 9–11]:

- **Automatic metering reading (AMR)** refers to a technique that uses a communica-tion infrastructure to automatically collect metering data, events and alarms from the smart meters. Typical AMR communication scenarios are meter readings (both on-demand and previously scheduled readings), meter events and alarms (e.g. health events, unauthorized meter access), grid events detected by meters (temporary power outages) and others. AMI itself may be viewed as the most basic and simple appli-cation that serves as a platform supporting other applications [3, 9].
- **Wide area situational awareness** will monitor and manage all the components of the electric power system. Through predicting and modifying behavior of smart grid elements potential problems in the infrastructure may be detected or avoided [3].
- **Demand response and consumer efficiency** aims at balancing the overall electricity consumption by encouraging customers to cut their usage during peak times. In order to achieve this behavior, dynamic electricity pricing will enable the consumers to

lower their expenses by postponing some consumption, that is not time critical (e.g. electric water heater or air conditioning) to off-peak times [3, 9].

- **Distributed energy resources** uses load prediction and balance techniques in order to optimize integration of big number of small electricity generators based on renewable sources [11].
- **Grid-to-vehicle, vehicle-to-grid (G2V, V2G)** tends to use integrated accumulators of electric and hybrid vehicles as temporary electricity sources in order to overcome short-term consumption peak times [12].

Although, the overall smart grid system is lacking widely accepted standards, for particular smart grid applications, standards and protocols have been published. In [13], major smart grid standards are listed and described, e.g. ANSI C12.1, ANSI C12.19 (Advanced metering infrastructure), OpenADR (Dynamic pricing) and SAE J2836 (Electric vehicles communication).

With the purpose of defining technical requirements on smart grid communication network, research has been conducted to analyze general business communication requirements. According to [14, 15], reliability, latency, security and interoperability are the key characteristics of communication network in the context of smart grids requirements.

Concrete messages exchanged within smart grids are supposed to have various requirements depending on related smart grid application. In [16], utility operation practices, planned implementations and experience from other research groups have been analyzed in order to enumerate particular communication events with its estimated packet sizes, frequency, and delay objective. In the presented results, there are considerable differences between separate events requirements – while interval data reading is stated to have 480 Bytes data size, it is not considered to be delay time critical; on the other hand, meter remote disconnect requests size is only 20 Bytes, but the delay objective is 2 s.

Even more exhaustive summary has been published in [17], presenting typical data size, sampling frequency, maximum latency and desired reliability for various NAN and WAN applications. Twelve groups of smart grid operations have been investigated, for example:

- Advanced metering infrastructure applications including on-demand, scheduled and bulk metering data reads
- Pricing applications, e.g. TOU (time-of-use) commands, real-time pricing and critical peak pricing
- Electric service prepayment
- Demand response communication

According to the results presented, there is a big variability of both data size and latency requirements of separate operations.

2.2   Communication Technologies

Various communication technologies have been considered for smart grids including both wire-line and wireless solutions with respect to their abilities to maintain the requirements listed in the previous section and additionally to other aspects like coverage range and deployment costs, comparing their suitability for smart grids needs.

Wireline technologies represent one option to build up communication network separate from the power distribution infrastructure itself. Construction of such a network would require extra investments; on the other hand, it is capable of providing higher data transmission rates and not shared with other application [18]. Some national-scale wireline networks have already been deployed for other purposes, e.g. cable television or telecommunications. Various transmission media may be possibly used.

Fiber-optic networks provide both the highest data rate (for SONET/SDH architecture, the maximum theoretical rate is 10 Gbps, for VDM technology up to 40 Gbps) and large coverage range (up to 100 km) [17].

DSL (Digital Subscriber Line) technology relies ordinary telephone lines. ADSL (Asynchronous DSL) is capable of max theoretical data rate 1–8 Mbps downstream with coverage up to 5 km. High-speed versions of DSL (HDSL, VDSL) provide higher data rates, but smaller coverage range [19]. Although, DSL architecture is already deployed for many premises that would lower the initial installation expenses, it may not be suitable for smart grid applications due to possible down time problems and low reliability especially for more distant customers [17].

Coaxial cable transmission network uses cable television infrastructure. For high-speed data transfer over existing hybrid fiber-coaxial network, DOCSIS (Data Over Cable Service Interface Specification) may be used. This technology provides 172 Mbps maximum data rate and up to 28 km coverage range [17].

Ethernet is a technology often used to build local networks in houses and workplaces providing data rates between 10 Mbps and 10 Gbps [14]. Unlike DSL and Coaxial solutions, there is no Ethernet based large-scale network currently deployed.

Powerline Communication (PLC) may be viewed as a special case of wireline technology, but has several unique characteristics. PLC is realized through power distribution network. To transmit both the power and data, electric signal modulation is used. As long as the theoretical data rate is about hundreds of kbps and the transmission channel is rather noisy, PLC is not as effective as e.g. DSL [17]. However, it is not shared with other applications, that generate external traffic and though, cause inpredictable and unbalanced load.

Wireless communication technologies are also often inspected for the use in smart grids, mainly due to the fact, no wires need to be installed. Concrete wireless technologies may represent appropriate solutions for NANs or WANs.

Wireless Local Area Network (WLAN) is high speed communication technology often used for wireless Internet access commonly known as WiFi. It provides reliable secure communication with data rate up to 2–600 Mbps (depending on standard), but its maximum range is lower than 100 m and the cost and power consumption are higher making WLAN less suitable for massive smart grid use [17].

ZigBee operates on unlicensed bands (shared with WLAN) and its maximum theoretical data rate is 250 kbps. Due to its low speed, short range coverage (up to 100 m), ZigBee may be suitable for in-home applications [14, 17].

Cellular networks, e.g. GSM, GPRS, LTE, have the potential to enable wide area wireless smart metering deployment. The technology is based on a large number of transceivers dividing the covered area into communication cells. Communication devices connect to them do send and receive messages. In [20], GSM is considered a possible solution for smart grid communication since it is already deployed in most of inhabited areas. On the other hand, performance reduction during peak traffic and the problems connected to maintaining QoS over noisy channel.

Along with comparing technical parameters, Cost Benefit Analysis is an important procedure to assess the suitability of a particular technology for smart grid solutions. In [21], a comprehensive assessment framework of smart grid projects is proposed with purpose to provide guidance and advice for conducting cost-benefit analysis. According to the presented research, for monetizing possible benefits related to the smart metering roll-out, following aspects are critical (not exhaustive):

- Hardware cost including investments in communication infrastructure installation
- Data transfer costs (in GPRS, Radio Communications,…)
- Communication success rate
- Number of smart metering installed

Hence, achieving a good trade-off between communication network costs and its robustness and capability is an important step in order to make the smart grid deployment effective and beneficial. Both PLC and GPRS are mentioned as technologies potentially usable for smart grid. Additionally, a comparison is presented, regarding PLC as more suitable for "concentrated" deployments (bigger number of clients concentrated in a limited area e.g. an entire city) and more initial-costs intensive, while GPRS is stated to work well in "scattered" deployments (e.g. only clients with higher consumption in each network).

3   Optimizing Smart Grid Communication

In recent years, several papers have been published with the purpose to identify opportunities to optimize smart grid communication, describing possible approaches and solutions to the presented optimization problem.

3.1   Communication Infrastructure Design

Proper technology choice and topology design is the first step to build a sustainable communication infrastructure. In [16], an approach is presented to estimate communication profiles for selected smart grid application. Then, the capacity utilization ratio is applied with respect to the traffic described while considering two scenarios (Blue Sky Day and Storm Day Scenario). As an output of this analysis, both the regional and WAN capacity requirements are derived. In [22], the scalability of three communication architectures for advanced metering infrastructure (including i.e. AMR) is inspected. Accumulated bandwidth-distance product (ABDP) is defined as a performance metric. For each architecture, an optimization problem is defined in order to obtain the solution for minimizing the total costs considering both the ABDP and the cost of meter data management system. Additionally, the scalability of the total expenses for the centralized and distributed infrastructure is analyzed and compared, while the distributed architecture is said to have significantly lower total cost [22].

3.2 Congestion Avoidance

The problem of potential congestion caused by huge number of data samples has already been addressed in literature. TCP based networks may possibly be overloaded due to excessive packet retransmission in case of communication peak times. To overcome this problem, so-called transport aggregator operating on communication transport level is presented in [23]. The aggregator node is added between the data sources and the data collection server in order to split the TCP connections between the mentioned elements. Its task is to collect data from sources (e.g. smart meters) and to forward to the central server while adjusting the transmission rate and achieving congestion control.

Another investigated method is to identify the most salient data to be communicated [18]. Through Singular Value Decomposition (SVD) analysis, the authors have determined, that typical grid admittance matrices have only small number of strong components. SVD sparsity proved to be able to find out, what parts of the system are strongly coupled [18].

In [24], an intelligent traffic volume reduction of the communication flows is presented. The authors note that beside of "essential" data that must reach the target, there is a "non-essential" part. An assumption is made, that due to limited bandwidth, the communication infrastructure is not capable to transmit all the data successfully. Quality-aware reduction of the non-essential data component is used to utilize the overall revenue of communication flows processed.

In [25], a systematic priority-based approach is described to model and optimize communication in sensor networks over cognitive radio (CR) infrastructure. The proposed algorithm performed well in simulations, however is tightly connected to the concrete technology used.

To the best of authors knowledge, time-based scheduling of data transmissions in order to optimize communications in smart grids has not been investigated exhaustively. We have addressed this problem in cooperation with the major electricity distribution company in the Czech Republic. An AMR (Automated Meter Reading) pilot project is being executed within particular regions providing an opportunity to explore ways to optimize communications. In the current setting, all the data collection are executed at fixed times that were assigned considering neither the network specifics nor the current state if the infrastructure. As long as particular communication requests have various requirements in scope of delivery time and message size, proper time-based scheduling may be used to prevent the network from congestion and potential message interferences. In the first part of the research described in this paper, we focus on WAN communication scheduling, thus the messages in following text are the ones transmitted between a central management system and Distribution Transformer Stations (DTS).

3.3 Time-Based Communication Scheduling Problem

We have analyzed the current AMR environment identifying the following groups of characteristics important for implementing an appropriate communication scheduler.

First, we have inspected the specifics of cellular network that is going to be used in the scope of the Czech Republic (and likely also in other European countries) for WAN communication. The cellular network consists of base transceiver station (BTS) distributed within the covered area. The following aspects have been considered crucial for the scheduling process:

- Sending big amount of data through a single BTS may lead to undesired interferences and potential overload of given transceiver.
- It is uncertain, which BTS a concrete element communicates through.
  - Nevertheless, the probability that two DTS will communicate through the same BTS might be partially estimated according to their geographic location.
- The BTS capacity varies (due to external traffic, weather conditions). Estimation and detection of critical periods would help to avoid scheduling requests in such intervals. Single DTS is typically unable to serve more simultaneous communication requests.

Additionally, we have determined, which attributes each communication request should be assigned with in order to describe its characteristics and requirements:

- target device,
- desired interval, when the given request needs to be processed, determined by start time and deadline.
- priority preference describing, when the request should be preferably processed (e.g. control commands should be scheduled as soon as possible; on the other hand, in some cases of metering data reading, it may be beneficial to schedule them later, providing data concentrator with extra time to collect more data),
- estimated data load and duration of the request.

Since neither the data describing communication network nor the requests characteristics (data load, processing time) are often available, collecting message sizes, failure rate and processing times will be an important part of the scheduling algorithm in order to build a sufficient knowledge base. Gathered information will be then used to enhance the accuracy of predicted values essential for proper scheduling.

We assume that not all the communication requests will be known during schedule creation. Though, the scheduling needs to be done on both a strategic and operational level. While the strategic-level scheduling algorithm of previously known requests (e.g. periodic meter readings) is not necessarily time critical (and may be able to analyze all the inputs mentioned), light-weight techniques need to be implemented to dynamically readjust scheduled messages in case of sudden latency-critical messages generation (e.g. ad-hoc meter readings, smart meter commands).

Finally, since the meter data readings represents a significant part of all data transmitted, the overall traffic may be reduced through identifying less critical data (e.g. periodic metering data of low-consumption places) and potentially omitting them in case of overload.

3.4 Future Work

Proposed analysis was conducted as part of a pilot project defined by Czech energy distribution company aiming to deploy AMI in particular areas. In the scope of the Czech Republic, the PLC is most probably to be used for NAN communication, while the WAN will mostly use cellular network (GPRS and LTE).

Future effort will aim at implementing systems for data collection, analysis and prediction in order to obtain the essential inputs described in the previous section and then, to design and implement a prototype of the proposed communication scheduler itself.

4 Conclusion

Smart grid is a complex approach to make currently existing power grids more robust, efficient and sustainable. Beside other applications, smart grids aim at balancing electricity consumption, incorporate renewable energy resources, monitor the whole system and avoid or recover from faults. To achieve that, a communication infrastructure is used to interconnect smart metering devices deployed in the area with central systems for data analysis, prediction and decision making.

To maintain huge amounts of data, a sufficient communication network needs to be deployed. Along with optimization techniques listed in Sects. 3.1 and 3.2, time based messages scheduling is believed to be able to decrease the risks of network overloading and congestion. Hence, a better trade-off between capability and price of the communication infrastructure can be earned. In this paper, an approach to optimize smart grid communication through communication requests scheduling is presented along with identification of essential input data of the proposed scheduler. As a part of the work presented in this paper, an extensive review of the state of the art of technologies and existing literature resources have been performed, which became part of Sects. 2 and 3, to underline the reasoning that follows these sections.

References

1. Saputro, N., Akaya, K.: A survey of routing protocols for smart grid communications. Natl. Inst. Standards Technol. **11**(1), 2742–2771 (2012)
2. Smart Grid Coordination Group: Smart Grid Reference Architecture (2012). CEN-CENELEC-ETSI
3. Gao, J., Xiao, Y., Liu, J., Liang, W., Chen, C.P.: A survey of communication/networking in smart grids. Future Gen. Comput. Syst. **2**, 391–404 (2012)

4. Madueno, G.C., Stefanovic, C., Popovski, P.: How many smart meters can be deployed in a GSM cell? pp. 1263–1268 (2013)
5. Kouhdaragh, V., Tarchi, D.,Vanelli-Coralli, A., Corazza, G.E.: Smart meters density effects on the number of collectors in a smart grid, pp. 476–481 (2015)
6. Yu, R., Zhang, Y., Gjessing, S., Yuen, C., Xie, S., Guizani, M.: Cognitive radio based hierarchical communications infrastructure for smart grid. IEEE Netw. **5**, 6–14 (2011)
7. Gungor, V.C., Bucella, C., Hancke, G.P.: Advance metering infrastructure and DLMS/ COSEM standards for smart grid. Int. J. of Eng. Res. Technol. **1**(2) (2012)
8. Bojkovic, Z., Bakmaz, B.: Smart grid communications architecture: a survey and challenges. In: Proceedings of the 11th International Conference on Applied Computer and Applied Computational Science, vol. 1, pp. 83–89 (2012)
9. Khan, R.H., Khan, J.Y.: A comprehensive review of the application characteristics and traffic requirements of a smart grid communications network. Comput. Netw. **57**, 825–845 (2013)
10. Locke, G., Gallagher, P.D.: NIST framework and roadmap for smart grid interoperability standards, release 1.0, p. 33 (2010)
11. Brown, R.E.: Impact of smart grid on distribution system design. In: Power and Energy Society General Meeting-Conversion and Delivery of Electrical Energy in the 21st Century, vol. 1, pp. 1–4 (2008)
12. Khan, R.H., Khan, J.Y.: A comprehensive review of the application characteristics and traffic requirements of a smart grid communications network. Comput. Netw. **3**, 825–845 (2013)
13. Gungor, V.C., Sahin, D., Kocak, T., Ergut, S., Buccella, C., Cecati, C., Hancke, G.P.: Smart grid technologies: communication technologies and standards. IEEE Trans. Ind. Inform. **7**(4), 529–539 (2011)
14. Wang, W., Xu, Y., Khanna, M.: A survey on the communication architectures in smart grid. Comput. Netw. **15**, 3604–3629 (2011)
15. Gungor, V.C., Sahin, D., Kocak, T., Ergut, S., Buccella, C., Cecati, C., Hancke, G.P.: A survey on smart grid potential applications and communication requirements. IEEE Trans. Ind. Inform. **1**, 28–42 (2013)
16. Luan, W., Sharp, D., Lancashire, S.: Smart grid communication network capacity planning for power utilities. In: IEEE PES T&D, vol. 1, pp. 1–4 (2010)
17. Kuzlu, M., Pipattanasomporn, M., Rahman, S.: Communication network requirements for major smart grid applications in HAN, NAN and WAN. Comput. Netw. **67**, 78–88 (2014)
18. Wang, Z., Scaglione, A., Thomas, R.J.: Compressing electrical power grids, pp. 13–18 (2010)
19. Habib, A., Saiedian, H.: Channelized voice over digital subscriber line. IEEE Commun. Mag. **40**(10), 94–100 (2012)
20. Usman, A., Shami, S.H.: Evolution of communication technologies for smart grid application. Renew. Sustain. Energy Rev. **19**, 191–199 (2013)
21. Giordano, V., Onyeji, I., Fulli, G., Jimnez, M.S., Filiou, C.: Guidelines for cost benefit analysis of smart metering deployment. JRC Sci. Tech. Res. (2012)
22. Zhou, J., Hu, R.Q., Qian, Y.: Scalable distributed communication architectures to support advanced metering infrastructure in smart grid. IEEE Trans. Parallel Distrib. Syst. **23**(9), 1632–1642 (2012)
23. Khalifa, T., Naik, K., Alsabaan, M., Nayak, A., Goel, N.: Transport protocol for smart grid infrastructure, pp. 320–325 (2010)
24. Allalouf, M., Gershinsky, G., Lewin-Eytan, L., Naor, J.: Data-quality-aware volume reduction in smart grid network, pp. 120–125 (2011)
25. Huang, J., Wang, H., Qian, Y., Wang, C.: Priority-based traffic scheduling and utility optimization for cognitive radio communication infrastructure-based smart grid. IEEE Trans. Smart Grid **1**, 78–86 (2013)

3D Volume Visualization of Environmental Data in the Web

Eric Braun[1(✉)], Clemens Düpmeier[1], Stefan Mirbach[2], and Ulrich Lang[2]

[1] Karlsruhe Institute of Technology, Karlsruhe, Germany
{eric.braun2,clemens.duepmeier}@kit.edu
[2] Ingenieurgesellschaft Kobus and Partner GmbH, Stuttgart, Germany
{mirbach,lang}@kobus-partner.com

Abstract. The environmental community has an increasing need for visualizations because of the rapidly growing amount of data gathered from various sources e.g. sensors, users and apps. This paper presents a complex visualization for the Web that can be used to get insight into 3D volume data. Volumes like air, lakes and seas are often visualized using 2D slices or one dimensional diagrams that display measured values in a specific point of the volume. To get new insight the 3D volume has to be visualized in 3D. A technique called ray marching, which is known in the computer graphics field in combination with modern web technologies, can be used to create such visualizations for the Web. In addition to the new visualization, this paper also presents the usage of such complex software in a visualization framework created in the same research team. This framework hides the complexity behind user friendly web interfaces that allows one to configure the 3D volume visualization without any programming skills.

Keywords: Environmental information systems · 3D volume visualization
WebGL · Lake Constance

1 Introduction

The demand for dynamic visualizations of data in the Web grows with the popularity of mobile platforms and many solutions, especially for the visualization of charts and maps, already exist. The WebIS group at the KIT (Karlsruhe Institute of Technology) works on a modern microservice based visualization framework (FlexVis) that is modular, highly configurable and allows the utilization of state-of-the-art technology for implementing reusable and easy to use interactive visualization components which are embeddable into web pages. A new research focus refers to implementing reusable 3D volume visualization components for FlexVis to display complex multidimensional environmental data in the Web. In cooperation with kup (Ingenieurgesellschaft Kobus and Partner GmbH) the development of such 3D data visualizations for displaying the propagation of chemical substances (e.g. sodium chloride, phosphate…) in Lake Constance ("Bodensee") is explored. Within the existing Web based information system BodenseeOnline one and two dimensional data visualizations of the substance flow in Lake

© IFIP International Federation for Information Processing 2017
Published by Springer International Publishing AG 2017. All Rights Reserved
J. Hřebíček et al. (Eds.): ISESS 2017, IFIP AICT 507, pp. 457–469, 2017.
https://doi.org/10.1007/978-3-319-89935-0_38

Constance are already implemented by kup for the LUBW (State Office for the Environment, Measurements and Nature Conservation of the Federal State of Baden-Württemberg). However, since substance flows in a lake essentially depend on three dimensions the new 3D visualization already proves that 3D volume visualizations can provide more information to users of Web based applications like BodenseeOnline.

In this paper, the concept of the 3D volume visualization component will be described in the context of the BodenseeOnline application as one use case. Also, basic concepts of the overall FlexVis framework for data visualization [1] and the integration of the 3D visualization component into this framework will be described. The paper will show that users of web based information systems can benefit from more complex multidimensional visualizations which can be implemented with modern web technologies. Additionally, the paper will show that the usage of the FlexVis framework provides many advantages for the implementation of complex web based information systems.

2 BodenseeOnline

Lake Constance is a transboundary lake situated partly in Germany, Switzerland and Austria and it is an important drinking water reservoir. More than 4 million people get their water at home from the lake without considerable treatment. Beside this, the lake is also used for a fishery, recreational purposes and tourism. For improved monitoring of potential risks which can be caused by emissions into the lake (e.g. from industrialized areas or the intensive use of agriculture around the lake), the environmental decision support and information system BodenseeOnline was developed in an interdisciplinary research project from 2005 to 2008 by five project partners including kup. Using three-dimensional numerical models, the distribution of hydrophysical and biochemical parameters in the lake is simulated on a daily basis using up to date data from measurement stations around the lake. Additionally, results from weather forecasts are used to provide a forecast for the next 78 h. Measurement data from a wide variety of meteorological and hydrological data are gathered and stored in a database. The results from the simulations as well as the measurement data are visualized on a website and represent an important basis for decision making in case of accidents, disturbances or extreme events in or around the lake for local water authorities, disaster management and drinking water supply companies. The system is currently monitored, maintained and developed further by kup.

Currently, the visualization of the three-dimensional model data is based on an interactive map application which allows the display of time series, profiles and longitudinal as well as transverse sections of data at arbitrary, user-defined positions in the lake. Additionally, the simulated movement of the flow field of substances can be visualized using animated vectors. The propagation of substances in the flow field can be calculated using a particle tracking algorithm. These 1D and 2D visualizations offer extensive possibilities for data analysis and are sufficient for most use cases, like the evolution of water quality parameters at water extraction sites, the vertical distribution of critical parameters such as dissolved oxygen and the movement of substances or objects at the water surface. However, in case of the 3D propagation of local plumes of substances the current methods of 1D and 2D visualization are of limited suitability to capture the dispersion in all three directions. Typical examples are the dispersal of wastewater plumes or the inflow of sediments during flood events, which can form complex patterns of propagation in different depths of water in the lake. Figure 1 shows an example of the latter by visualizing the suspended sediment concentrations at 140 m water depth in the lake during a flood event in the river Rhine. Not unlike an avalanche, the denser riverine water forms a turbidity current, flowing along the lake bottom into deeper regions. The limitations of a 2D visualization in capturing the propagation and extent of the current in the lake are clearly visible. In these cases, a 3D visualization could offer a much more convenient and intuitive analysis of the plume propagation on a qualitative and, maybe with certain limitations, on a quantitative basis.

The users to be reached by this application are mainly:

- sailors who are interested in the wind speed at the surface of the lake
- fishermen who use information of wind speed and the height of waves for their advantage
- divers who are looking for water flow and water temperature information in several depths
- bathers who are also interested in the water temperature (mainly at the surface)
- experts who want to track more complex information about the lake (e.g. suspended sediment concentration)

With the current application, these users are provided with a limited view on the data because of the missing 3D visualizations. However, especially divers and expert users are interested in more detailed data since they want to see a full 3D picture of the lake. The next chapters describe enhanced types of visualization for those users.

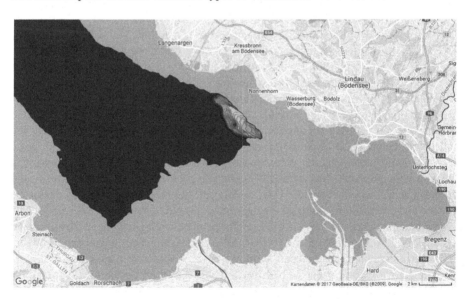

Fig. 1. 2D slice at 140 m water depth visualizing suspended sediment concentration

3   3D Volume Visualization

One technique to visualize 3D volumes (e.g. the propagation of substances in a lake) is known from the medical area and is called volume visualization. It is used to visualize MRI scans, for example. However, there are many more use cases since a volume visualization only requires a 3D volume containing spatial information, e.g. density information. This could be the anatomy of a human body (for MRI scans) or the density of different substances that are present in a lake. The rendering of such visualizations is commonly accelerated using a graphics adapter.

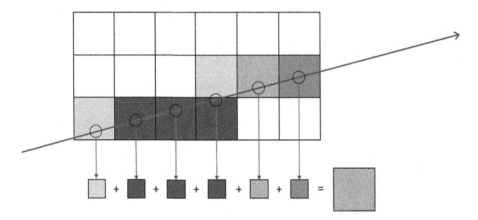

Fig. 2. Ray marching and alpha blending

To visualize 3D information on a 2D screen, a ray marching algorithm can be used. The idea of ray marching is that for each pixel a ray is cast through the volume, starting at the camera. The values hit by this ray are captured as a specific step size along the ray. These different values can be translated into a color and the different colors can be accumulated by the graphics card using alpha blending, which is the combination of multiple colors with a specific transparency. Figure 2 shows this technique. The step size in Fig. 2 is approximately equal to the length of one square. Therefore, the ray collects the colors of six squares and adds them up to receive a resulting color.

This can be implemented by drawing a cube in the scene which has the same size as the data volume itself. Afterwards, this cube can be shaded with custom vertex and fragment shaders to visualize the volume. The performance depends on the size of the volume and the resolution with which the ray samples the volume (i.e. step size).

Volume visualizations on desktop computers are typically implemented by using the OpenGL API. As for the Web, the WebGL API, which is supported by modern browsers on a decent computer, can be used. It allows the browser to directly render scenes on the graphics card. The current WebGL version is 1.0 and it implements the OpenGL ES 2.0 [2] features. This OpenGL version was released in March 2007 and it lacks various features of modern graphics adapters. One very important feature for volume visualization is 3D texture support which is unfortunately not included in WebGL 1.0.

Therefore, the implementation of such visualizations for the Web has to simulate 3D textures with 2D textures which costs a lot of performance. Figure 3 displays how a 3D texture can be unpacked into a 2D texture. The 3D texture with the size of X * Y * Z is converted into Z different slices of 2D textures with the size of X * Y. This workaround adds a lot of complexity to the fragment shader but it is necessary until WebGL 2.0 is released. More details about the implementation of volume visualization in WebGL 2.0 can be found in the bachelor thesis by Becher [3].

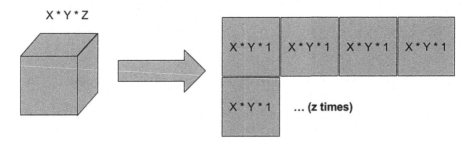

Fig. 3. Transformation of a 3D texture into a 2D texture

4   Lake Constance Volume Visualization

Volume visualization as described in the previous chapter can now be applied to a volume that represents a specific substance present in Lake Constance, e.g. the density of sodium chloride (salt) in the water. The challenge is to determine a good mapping from values to specific colors. If the visualization only uses a grayscale color mode, the values for each step will be normalized between 0 and 1 and the resulting color c in the RGB color scheme would be rgb(c, c, c). The color scheme can be improved by the creation of a non-linear scaling which matches the human perception more closely. A screenshot of this color mapping for salt in Lake Constance is depicted in Fig. 4.

Fig. 4. Densities of sodium chloride in Lake Constance using the grayscale mode

A second approach is to use different color ranges for different density ranges. As shown in Fig. 5, the lake is divided into 3 colors. The area with the highest salinity is shown in green, medium salinity is colored in blue, and low salinity is colored in red.

The comparison between both screenshots shows that different colors provide much more options to show the distribution in the volume.

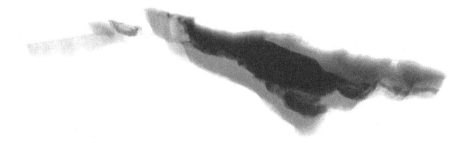

Fig. 5. Different densities of salt in Lake Constance (Color figure online)

This second approach allows the user to perceive more details from the visualization, especially if the values are not evenly distributed between the extremes or if there exist clusters of values. Figure 6 shows the color settings of the previous screenshot. The gray lines show the distribution of the different values between the minimal value (left border of the rectangle) and the maximal value (right border). The distribution has one cluster which was broken down into three different colors to visualize the different parts of the distribution in a clear way. The height of the color line indicates the brightness of the color.

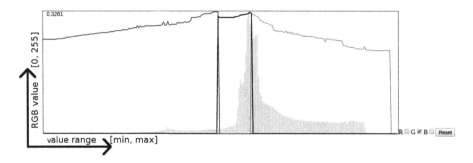

Fig. 6. Color mapping and distribution of values

Figure 7 depicts how the volume visualization can be combined with an interactive user interface to build a complex interactive 3D volume visualization component. The color mapping can be dynamically changed and the user sees the changes immediately in the visualization. Furthermore, the user can rotate, zoom and pan the camera of the visualization to look at the volume from different perspectives. The black box in the right upper corner can be used to change parameters that the graphics adapter uses to create the visualization. Such settings might not be included in the interactive user interface of final versions of the volume visualization component because they add too much complexity for the user. However, they can be exposed as configuration parameters to web page creators.

A feature of the 3D visualization component currently missing is some kind of orientation help. The data in our example have geographical meaning and users that know the structure of the Lake Constance should be able to see this structure at first glance. A possible enhancement is an option for the user to enable marks that show the nearby cities or villages. With additional markers, for example Constance and Lindau which are two cities near the lake, the user can immediately recognize familiar points of orientation. A second method which could help with spatial orientation is to add a compass of some sort which shows markers for north, south, east and west. These changes can easily be added to the current prototype and this will be the next step to improve the software. Additionally, in order to help the user select appropriate mappings, future user studies can be conducted to create a more intuitive and user friendly interface.

The prototype presented in this chapter can be integrated in the FlexVis framework for data visualization as an additional visualization type. The procedure for achieving this integration will be discussed in the next section.

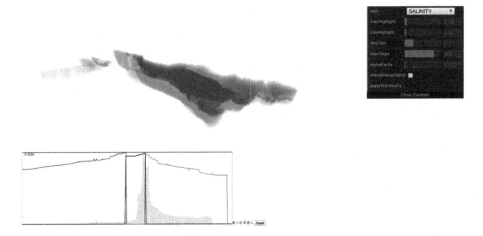

Fig. 7. Complete user interface

5   Integration of the Visualization in FlexVis

The FlexVis framework for data visualization in the Web can be used to provide web page creators the opportunity to add highly complex visualization components (such as the volume visualization) to web pages without the need to write any code. Instead, the web page creator can add the volume visualization component to the web page by configuration only. Such a configuration allows the user to change the features that the visualization provides, the behavior of the different features, the style of the visualization, as well as the selection of data sources which determine the data behind the volume visualization.

The data model of the FlexVis framework stores configuration information needed for a visualization in three separate services: a template, a data source and a visualization instance service. The most important configuration information for integrating the new 3D component into FlexVis is the definition of a new visualization type template for the new 3D visualization type. It contains a URL to an HTML5 web component that contains the implementation of the new component. This link allows the FlexVis framework to load the implementation of the 3D component into the web browser. The template also contains formal descriptions of configuration parameters which are used in the source code and will be customizable by a web page creator while embedding the component. Once defined, a template can be instantiated indefinitely on arbitrary web pages with different parameters each time. Finally, the visualization template also describes what parameters have to be defined by a web page creator when instantiating a visualization so that the framework can load data into the component e.g. from external data sources. In its simplest form, the location of data can be defined as simple REST URL that returns a JSON file when the components get instantiated.

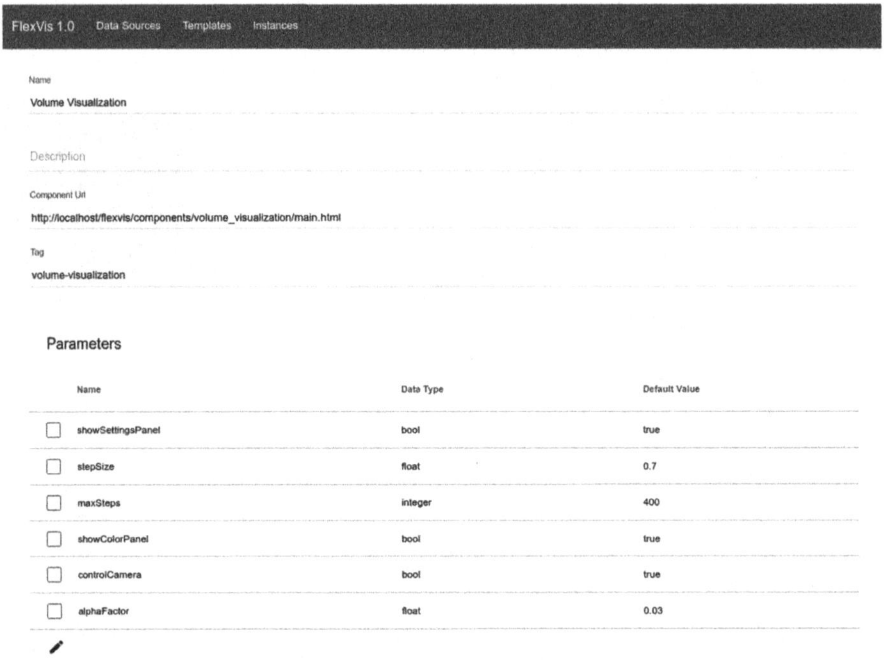

Fig. 8. Web user interface to configure a template

After a visualization template is defined for the 3D component, one or more instances of the template can be created which contain, beside a link to the template, concrete parameter configurations including the parametrization for data loading for this particular instance. It is important to note that the instance configuration should connect the right data source to the template, e.g. the data model of the data returned by the data source should match the data model used in the web component implementation. If this requirement is fulfilled, the web component should be able to load the data based on the given configuration. The instance can be further customized according to the other configuration parameters that the template features. For displaying a visualization instance on a web page, only the tag of the FlexVis wrapper component with a data parameter specifying the instance id of the visualization instance has to be specified. The wrapper component itself will then load the code of the component and configure it accordingly to the instance parameter configuration.

To illustrate these steps the next figures will show how a new visualization template and visualization instance can be configured. Figure 8 shows the configuration of the template for the new 3D visualization component. The component URL points to the main file that defines the web component for the volume visualization. This file has to be accessible by the frontend browser. The tag defines the name of the web component which is important to embed the visualization into a web page. Finally, the parameters section contains different configuration parameters that are used in the source code. In our example, the configuration allows the settings panel and the color panel to be shown or hidden, the camera control can be enabled and three further parameters control the rendering behavior of the visualization (*stepSize, maxSteps, alphaFactor*).

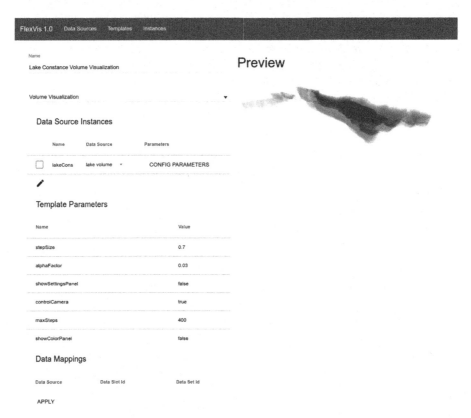

Fig. 9. Web user interface to configure a visualization instance

The data source for the volume visualization is a URL that points to a volumetric data set to be loaded. The next section discusses the format of this data set. The resulting visualization instance (Fig. 9) can be customized according to the template parameters.

The instance can be embedded in any web page by adding the FlexVis web component and specifying the ID of the created visualization instance.

The main advantage of the FlexVis framework is that only the creation of the template requires some programming knowledge but the rest of the parts, e.g. the data source and the visualization instance, can be created and edited by configuration only. This section illustrates that even quite complex visualizations can be integrated in the framework and do not require any programming knowledge once the appropriate template is registered in the framework.

6   Data Management for 3D Volumes

The 3D volumes of Lake Constance used in the prototype for this paper are provided by a backend service that stores data in NetCDF files [4]. The exchange format between the service and the visualization is a JSON object that includes a few parameters and the data itself as a three dimensional array. The client visualization converts the array into a JavaScript Typed Array. Figure 10 shows an overview of the used JSON format. The data are serialized as a flattened three dimensional array. The dimensions and interval properties are metadata that describe the size of the data and the range that the values describing the measured substance lie in.

```
{
  "dimensions": {
    "width": 673,
    "height": 230,
    "depth": 57
  },
  "interval": [0, 0.02]
  "data": ...
}
```

Fig. 10. JSON object for the phosphate data set

Data management can still be improved in different areas:

- The data sent to the frontend can be reduced in size by varying the resolution of the data if the user zooms out of the scene and vice versa. This can be achieved by precomputing the volume in different resolutions and selecting the appropriate resolution depending on the zoom level in the frontend. The disadvantage of this change is the higher storage need which scales with the amount of different precomputed resolutions.
- A second way to reduce the size of the data sent to the frontend is to transmit only parts of the whole volume depending on the region the user wants to see. In this case the server has to precompute at least a second resolution that has more detail. This resolution will only be send partially depending on the selection the user makes.
- The backend and both previous improvements can be further improved by storing data in an appropriate database or data structure. This decreases the access time to retrieve

the desired data and speeds up queries that only need a part of a volume (as described in the previous improvement). Additionally, the data will be preprocessed before inserting it into the database or data structure to eliminate any processing at runtime. This preprocessing can include handling of missing data and normalizing data.

These features are not yet included in the prototype but can be extended in the future without changing core concepts of the architecture.

7 Evaluation

After a detailed description of the different aspects of the volume visualization concept, this section evaluates the web application. The main advantage of the new form of visualization is that BodenseeOnline users who are interested in 3D data sets can profit from new insights on the data. Especially divers and expert users, as mentioned in the second section of this article, can use the full advantage of 3D information. Divers can have a look at the water temperature for all depths at the desired diving location. They can immediately see the differences in temperature in a specific volume they are considering to dive in. This is an improvement in contrast to the 1D/2D visualization of the existing web application. Furthermore, expert users benefit from new 3D visualizations of different substances in the water. Figure 11 shows that a simple 3D visualization of the temperature reveals not only information about the temperature itself but also information about the flow of the water which is correlated with its temperature.

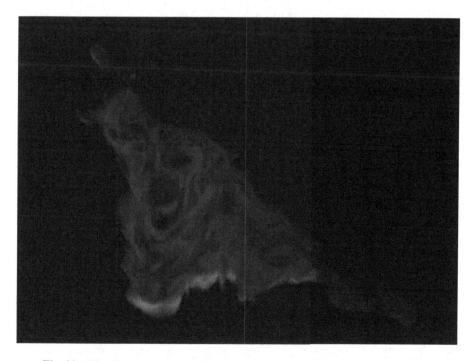

Fig. 11. Visualization of a small interval of temperature values in Lake Constance

A second advantage of the visualization component is the customizability of colors. Users can define their own color mapping to customize the visualization to their needs. A user with color blindness for example can select different colors in order to get better contrast. Average users however do obviously not want to customize the colors in such a complex manner that the current implementation allows them to. Therefore, such users can be provided with some predefined color settings that are easy to understand. An expert on the other hand might want to operate on the full color mapping interface.

The evaluation shows that the requirements for the 3D visualization are met and that new insights on the volume data can be acquired. In order to further enhance the visualization, user studies can be conducted that lead to more specific requirements especially for the color mapping interface.

8   Conclusion and Outlook

A volume visualization constitutes a complex example of a visualization in the Web. However, its implementation for BodenseeOnline shows that even complex visualizations can be included as easy to use interactive web components into the FlexVis framework to provide a simple configurable interface for web page creators who want to add such visualizations to their web page but do not have the skills to develop a visualization on their own. The different configuration options mentioned in the previous section show that the volume visualization component can help the web page creator to visualize any kind of 3D volumes (not only substance flows in Lake Constance). This can be helpful in many environmental fields. For example, the tracking of substances in water and in air can be visualized in a new way providing 3D insight into the data that cannot be achieved with one or two dimensional visualizations. The flexibility that the visualization framework provides allows the creation of easy to use visualizations for the general public but also rich visualizations with many features for expert users. The only downside of volume visualization is that the client device, which renders the visualization, requires access to an appropriate GPU chip and that the backend has to manage the volumetric data accordingly. However, the number of devices that have no GPU chips has decreased substantially over the past few years. Even most mobile devices have a graphics card that can render visualizations presented in this paper. Furthermore, most of the browsers nowadays support WebGL [5].

In the future, volume visualization can be used in many different areas for the visualization of environmental data. As a short term goal, other water bodies can be visualized. As a long term goal, the visualization can be used to show the propagation and the density of pollutants in the air. The scenario is similar to the previous one but the amount of data can be much bigger since lakes or rivers can have much smaller volumes than a volume in the air. Thus, visualizations that cover the air of a whole city can raise new data management challenges and demand big data solutions and smart services for data management.

A further future enhancement could lie in the animation of a volume visualization. Such an animation can display the change of the volume over time. Again, this feature raises new data management challenges because the amount of data increases tremendously. Such an animation also raises new visualization challenges because the animation has to be visualized which means that the graphics card has to compute an image for every frame, including those frames that lie between two volumes that were captured consecutively.

Finally, the user interface consisting of the settings panel, color panel and main visualization can be enhanced in many ways. A more space-saving design can help the user to have more space on the screen for the actual visualization and a common theme for both panels gives the application an enhanced appearance.

References

1. Braun, E., Düpmeier, C., Kimmig, D., Schillinger, W., Weissenbach, K.: Generic web framework for environmental data visualization. In: Wohlgemuth, V., Fuchs-Kittowski, F., Wittmann, J. (eds.) Advances and New Trends in Environmental Informatics. PROIS, pp. 289–299. Springer, Cham (2017). https://doi.org/10.1007/978-3-319-44711-7_23
2. Khronos Group: OpenGL ES 2.X. https://www.khronos.org/opengles/2_X/. Accessed 26 Sept 2016
3. Becher, M.: Interactive volume visualization with WebGl. Bachelor thesis (2012). https://elib.uni-stuttgart.de/handle/11682/2973
4. Unidata: NetCDF. http://www.unidata.ucar.edu/software/netcdf/. Accessed 26 Sept 2016
5. "Can I use": WebGL - 3D Canvas graphics. http://caniuse.com/#feat=webgl. Accessed 26 Sept 2016

Mobile Location-Based Augmented Reality Framework

Simon Burkard[1], Frank Fuchs-Kittowski[1,2($\boxtimes$)] (iD), Sebastian Himberger[1],
Fabian Fischer[1], and Stefan Pfennigschmidt[2]

[1] HTW Berlin, Wilhelminenhofstr. 75a, 12459 Berlin, Germany
{S.Burkard,Frank.Fuchs-Kittowski,s.himberger,
fabian.fischer}@htw-berlin.de
[2] Fraunhofer FOKUS, CC ESPRI, Kaiserin-Augusta-Allee 31, 10589 Berlin, Germany
Stefan.Pfennigschmidt@fokus.fraunhofer.de

Abstract. GeoAR, or location-based augmented reality, can be used as an innovative representation of location-specific information in diverse applications. However, there are hardly any software development kits (SDKs) that can be effectively used by developers, as important functionality and customisation options are generally missing. This article presents the concept, implementation and example applications of a framework, or GeoAR SDK, that integrates the core functionality of location-based AR and enables developers to implement customised and highly adaptable mobile application with GeoAR.

Keywords: Augmented reality · Location-based AR · Geo-based AR
AR-SDK

1 Introduction

The mass distribution of powerful and easy-to-use mobile devices (smartphones, tablets, etc.) has led to the increased availability and use of location-based services. While location-specific information on mobile devices is often displayed on maps or in lists, an innovative user interface consists of information displayed as an augmented reality (AR) layer over the camera image of the mobile device.

The term "augmented reality" refers to the supplementation of the human visual perception of reality with digital, context-dependent information [1]. In mobile augmented reality (mAR), the image from the camera of mobile devices is used to extend the real, local environment of the user by displaying additional digital information in real time [2]. The tracking method employed to acquire the position and viewing direction of the user (pose) can be used to differentiate between two forms of mAR: in the geo-based approach (also known as location-based AR, or GeoAR), the pose is determined using the built-in GPS sensors and inertial measurement unit (IMU) of the smartphone. In the image-based approach (vision-based AR), the pose as well as objects in the vicinity of the user are identified using optical tracking methods [3].

© IFIP International Federation for Information Processing 2017
Published by Springer International Publishing AG 2017. All Rights Reserved
J. Hřebíček et al. (Eds.): ISESS 2017, IFIP AICT 507, pp. 470–483, 2017.
https://doi.org/10.1007/978-3-319-89935-0_39

Mobile augmented reality has great economic potential. In spite of this, there has been little research and development in the area of location-based AR in recent years. The first available GeoAR software development kits (SDKs) such as Wikitude, Layar, and Metaio, have only a rudimentary range of functionality with few customisation options, or have disappeared completely from the market [4]. Instead, commercial companies as well as researchers have focussed on the development and improvement of vision-based AR (SLAM/3D tracking) in order to achieve the most exact positioning [5], but mobile vision-based AR is still not ready for the mass market. However, precise positioning is not necessary for many users and areas of application. The disadvantages of location-based AR compared to vision-based AR are therefore acceptable in many cases. The current example of Pokémon Go demonstrates that AR technology that is not based on complex image-based recognition methods can be very successful. However, there are currently no established GeoAR SDKs on the market for the implementation of custom applications without the need for expert knowledge in the areas of AR and computer vision.

In this article, a GeoAR SDK will be presented that supports the custom development of a wide range of GeoAR applications and simplifies and accelerates the development process. The framework is aimed primarily at experienced app developers who wish to create location-based AR applications with their own concrete ideas of functionality and design, but who do not wish to have to acquire expert knowledge in computer vision and AR in order to do so.

The article is structured as follows: starting with a brief introduction to mAR, the functionality of location-based AR is discussed in more detail (Sect. 2). A distinction is made between location-based and image-based AR, and both technologies are evaluated with regard to robustness and accuracy. Following this, common applications of mobile GeoAR are presented and on their basis, general functional requirements necessary for a wide range of GeoAR applications are derived (Sect. 3). Comparing these requirements with existing mobile GeoAR SDKs (Sect. 4), it is found that current SDKs lack certain functionality, and there is a market potential for a novel framework. The concept of such a novel GeoAR framework is detailed in Sect. 5. Finally, two mAR applications that have been implemented with the framework are presented in Sect. 6.

2 Mobile Location-Based Augmented Reality

In this section, a brief introduction to mobile augmented reality is given, followed by a discussion of the functionality of location-based AR.

2.1 Augmented Reality

The term "augmented reality" refers to the enrichment of the human perception of reality with additional, context-dependent, digital information in real-time [1]. The user of an AR application is presented with supplementary, virtual information within his/her field of view. This data has a fixed spatial relationship with objects in the real world. For example, computer-generated content can be superimposed on an image of the real world from the camera. This idea is already well established in many areas of everyday life, e.g., in TV broadcasts of soccer matches in which virtual off-side lines or virtual distance measurements are displayed over the real-life field (Fig. 1).

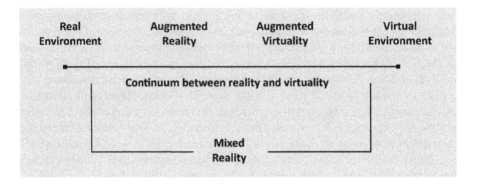

Fig. 1. Reality-virtuality continuum [6]

Augmented reality defines a reality-virtuality continuum. At either end stands complete reality or complete virtuality. In between the extremes lies the realm of mixed reality, which is characterised by different degrees of virtuality. In pure virtual environments, virtual reality (VR), the real surroundings are completely replaced by virtual ones and the user is totally immersed in the virtual world. On the other hand, the representation of additional information is at the forefront of AR; it is merely a supplement to the real world. Although the user must enter ("dive into") the virtual world and therefore interrupt contact with the real world, he/she continues to perceive the real surroundings. The real and virtual world, perceived simultaneously by the user, are unified.

2.2   Mobile Augmented Reality

In recent years, AR technology has become increasingly relevant in the context of mobile devices. In mobile augmented reality, mobile devices are used to merge the real and digital worlds in order to facilitate the perception of real and digital information on the local surroundings [2].

The real world is viewed through the camera of a mobile device (e.g., a smartphone) and is supplemented in real time with location-specific computer-generated content. The digital, geocoded information is put in spatial context and the view of the world is enriched by its presence. This enables a new way of perceiving places by presenting information from the past, present, or future, e.g., the representation of a building that is no longer/not yet visible. It also allows a better understanding and analysis of digital data on-site, allowing for better decision-making.

For a long time, mAR was a form of fundamental research with only a few expensive specialised applications for the few experts in the field. Today, modern mobile devices are a suitable hardware platform for mAR due to their high performance abilities. In particular, the most important sensors for implementing mAR are already integrated into smartphones. In addition to the camera for recording images, these include the IMU for determining the orientation (rotation) of the device as well as a GPS receiver for roughly determining the position. Moreover, these powerful mobile devices are widespread, user-friendly, and affordable so that mass usage of mAR applications is possible for everyone (workers, citizens, etc.).

In the past several years, mAR applications have been developed for various purposes [7, 8], e.g., in Tourism [9] (e.g., for displaying nearby hotels or tourist attractions), medicine [10], education [11], culture/museums [12], advertising/marketing [13, 14] (e.g., for visualising furniture in one's own home in 3D), and entertainment [15] (e.g., Pokémon Go). An example of some of these applications is shown in Fig. 2.

Fig. 2. Typical applications of mobile augmented reality: display of nearby points of interest (location-based AR) and visualisation of virtual furniture (image-based AR).

Due to the simple nature and widespread availability of mobile devices, the technical basis of mAR, and the numerous potential applications in many different fields, mAR has great economic potential [16]. Market research companies predict strong growth in this area in the coming years. For example, Juniper Research estimates the market will be worth over US$6 billion in 2021 [17].

2.3   Geo-Based (Location-Based) and Image-Based AR

In the implementation of mAR applications, it is fundamentally possible to differentiate between two different technologies based on the method employed by the device to determine its own position in 3D space. Establishing the position of the mobile device is an essential requirement for the implementation of AR, as information corresponding to objects in the field of view can only be positioned correctly on the screen given a knowledge of the camera position and projection. The position and pointing of the camera in 3D space is described by six degrees of freedom: three degrees of freedom for the orientation (rotation) and three for the position (translation).

With location-based AR (GeoAR), the rotation is determined solely by the IMU of the device, i.e., by a combination of readings from the gyroscope, accelerometer, and magnetometer. The GPS signal is used to roughly fix the location. This AR technology is based on established, robust, simple technology that is not very CPU-intensive, but it is primarily suitable for outdoor applications and is problematic inside buildings where no GPS signal is available. Additionally, the IMU sensors tend to "drift" during the rotation determination and often the viewing direction cannot be calculated exactly due to local disturbances in the global magnetic field [18].

In contrast, image-based AR calculates the position of the camera based solely on an analysis of the camera image using image processing techniques. By recognising prominent points in the video feed from the camera (markers or natural feature tracking), both the rotation and translation of the camera relative to its environment can be determined [19]. Very complex and CPU-intensive algorithms are necessary to interpret and analyse the images. However, in ideal conditions, this method can facilitate very accurate and realistic AR overlays. A major challenge is to cope with external influences and produce acceptable results even with poor lighting conditions (e.g., in darkness), moving objects in the images, or featureless surroundings. Another disadvantage is that this technology does not scale in large environments, such as streets, and does not scale well to various distances to objects. This AR technology is more suited to applications relating to the direct environment of the device, e.g., displaying virtual information about objects in the immediate vicinity (see Fig. 2).

The robustness of image-based technology can be further improved by creating 3D models of the environment (model-based AR). The user can then pinpoint him/herself within the virtual model at runtime and further extend the model (SLAM) [20]. However, other sensors that are not yet built into commercially available smartphones (e.g., infrared sensors for depth measurement or a second camera for stereo vision) are typically required to do this.

Table 1 summarises the above-mentioned key characteristics that determine the reliability and utility of mobile augmented reality approaches (and provides quantitative information from [29]). These key characteristics are: (1) *localisation*, which determines the users' viewpoint in order to derives real world objects in the current scene and to display the relevant digital information in the correct position, (2) *speed* of determining the users' position, the relevant information and the visualisation of the information in the correct position, (3) *robustness*, like dependence on external infrastructure or battery consumption, and the ability to work with dynamically changing environments, (4) *scalability*, like scaling to larger areas, number of objects, and size of objects.

Table 1. Comparison of mobile augmented reality approaches

Metrics	Location-based	Image-based	Model-based
Localization accuracy	1.5–35 m	0.5–2 mm	0.5–20 mm
Localisation area	Large (GPS area)	3 m (markers)	10 m (objects)
Localisation speed	100–200 ms	20–140 ms	5–240 s
External infrastructure	GPS satellite	Optical markers	External sensors, model
Resistant to drifts	No	Yes	Yes
CPU/battery consumption	Low	High	Very high
Scale to large scenes	Yes (outdoor)	No (room)	No (building)

Overall, however, it seems that image-based AR is not ready for the mass market due to its high error rate and lack of robustness. Image-based AR can - under ideal conditions - allow very accurate and realistic AR visualisations, but it is very error-prone.

On the other hand, the disadvantages of location-based AR technologies (inaccurate positioning/orientation) are acceptable for many (outdoor) applications. These general advantages and disadvantages of the AR technologies are roughly sketched in Fig. 3.

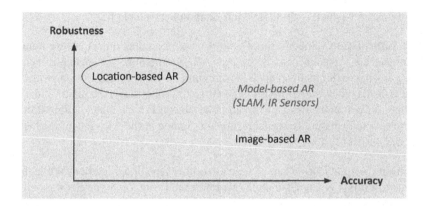

Fig. 3. Comparison of robustness and accuracy of mAR technologies

3 Applications of Geo-Based AR

Based on the typical usage of location-based AR applications, general functional requirements of an SDK for developing custom AR applications are derived in the following.

In the classical mAR applications, nearby points of interest (POIs) are displayed as markers in the camera overlay. However, location-specific information may not always be just simple markers. Complex 3D models referenced with a geographic coordinate or objects defined by several connected coordinates can be displayed as polylines or polygons. Considering even more complex uses for mAR, four different types of applications can be defined (cf., [21], see Fig. 4).

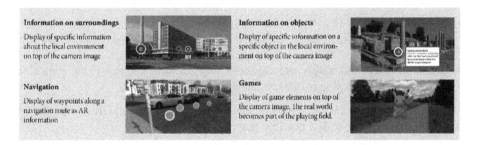

Fig. 4. Types of applications of location-based AR

Area Information. Specific information about the user's environment is displayed as additional AR information in the camera image. The information is displayed when relevant objects are within the field of view of the camera, e.g., tourist attractions, petrol stations, or rivers. Georeferenced data can be presented in very different formats on the image, for example, individual POIs can be displayed as icons (e.g., hotels or tourist attractions), polylines (e.g., rivers), polygons (e.g., flood risk maps), or georeferenced 3D objects (e.g., wind turbines). As an example, the GewässerBB app shows rivers as blue polylines for which hydrological information is available [22].

Object Information. Specific information on a particular object in the immediate environment can visualised as additional AR information, for example, details of building facades, exhibits in an open-air museum, an excavation site, or a product. The content is displayed by superimposing the virtual information on the image of the object when the user points the device at a particular object. For example, certain details, on which further information is available, are highlighted in the AR view of the historical House of Olbrich [23].

Navigation. AR navigation can be seen as another type of application. While the user proceeds towards a given destination, georeferenced waypoints (or arrows) as well as simple navigational information are shown in the camera image along a route. This provides an alternative form of displaying the information to the classic map-based navigation. An example of such navigation, which also provides the user with ecological information in order to promote sustainable living, is given in [24].

Games. maR games present a game as an overlay on the camera view of the real world. Location-specific game elements are represented as AR objects. The playing field is thereby an extension of the real world. Known examples of mAR games are Pokémon Go or Ghost Hunter. In Ghost Hunter, the player hunts ghosts which come through the walls of the room. A ghost-hunter gun, with which the player can target and shoot the ghosts, is displayed in the camera image [25].

A large number of different functionalities are required from a developer's perspective in order to individually create such applications. Based on an analysis of the typical (aforementioned) geoAR application types (object information, environmental context information, navigation, and gaming) as well our own existing geoAR applications in the context of

- **flood management** (e.g. flood risk maps, current water levels and flood warnings, historical flood markers, and an educational flood trail) developed in several projects like MAGUN [22] and
- **urban disaster and safety management** (e.g. incident reporting, navigation in disaster situation) developed in several projects like City.Risks,

the following general functional requirements were derived for an SDK envisioned for the development of the widest possible range of applications:

- **Presentation of spatial objects with one geographic reference (POI, 3D model) or several geographic references (polyline, polygon).** Location-specific objects with a single coordinate (3D model, POI) or several coordinates (polyline, polygon) must be displayed in the correct position on the screen.
- **Dynamic creation of adaptable content.** It must be possible to dynamically generate and flexibly scale the AR content. This means that it must be possible to

create and delete objects at runtime. The objects themselves must be as customisable as possible so that the design and appearance of the AR content (size, colour, icon style, etc.) is determined by the user context.

- **User interaction with AR objects.** The developer should have control over certain user events. These events include, for example, instances when an object is clicked or when objects appear in or disappear from the camera focus.
- **Access to camera controls and picture.** Access to the camera is desirable in order to control the camera or gain access to the camera image, for example, to process or store the current camera image.

4   SDKs for Location-Based AR

There are a number of AR SDKs available that are designed to facilitate and accelerate the implementation of AR applications [26]. In a market analysis, existing SDKs were systematically studied with regard to their functionality and possible applications in order to determine the extent to which the functional requirements identified above are fulfilled (Fig. 5).

#	name / provider	licence	last update	comments
1	3DAR	Unkown	2010	not up-to-date / no longer available
2	52 North: GeoAR	Apache 2.0	2013	not up-to-date / no longer available
3	Argon3	Open Source	2015	only iOS / browser-based
4	ARlab	Commercial	2013	not up-to-date / no longer available
5	Inglobe Technologies: ARmedia	Commercial	2016	barely documented; focus on image-based 3D tracking
6	ARPA	Unkown	2014	not up-to-date / no longer available
7	ARToolKit	GPLv3	2016	focus on image-based AR; GPS/IMU integration only on iOS
8	AugView	Commercial	2016	GIS system with AR functionality; no actual SDK
9	aumentia	Custom	2014	focus on image-based AR; geo-location only in iOS
10	Awila (Esri)	Commercial	2014	not up-to-date / no longer available
11	beyondAR	Apache v2	2014	some customization possible (low level); slighty outdated
12	Droidar	GPLv3	2013	some customization possible (low level); outdated; V2 is closed source
13	Hoppala	Unkown	2011	not up-to-date / no longer available
14	Instantreality (Fraunhofer IGD)	Unkown	2016	AR framework not available for mobile AR
15	Kudan	Commercial	2016	GPS integration apparently only on iOS ; focus on SLAM
16	Layar	Commercial	2016	customization possible according to docs; SDK currently not available
17	LibreGeoSocial	Unkown	2010	not up-to-date / no longer available
18	Metaio	Commercial	2015	not up-to-date / no longer available (bought by Apple in 2015)
19	Minvera	GPLv3	2011	not up-to-date / no longer available
20	Mixare	GPLv3	2012	not up-to-date / no longer available
21	PanicAR (Vuframe)	Commercial	2014	some customization possible (low level); free for non-profit projects
22	WearScript	Apache 2.0	2014	supports GPS-based AR; apparently only for Google Glass
23	Wikitude	Commercial	2016	some customization possible with certain limitations (high level)

Not up-to-date / not available
Limited GeoAR support
Solid GeoAR support

Fig. 5. Overview of available SDKs with GeoAR support

In a comprehensive literature analysis, relevant AR SDKs were identified and selected using search engines, link collections (e.g., [27, 28]), and established scientific literature databases (e.g., ACM Digital Library, IEEE Xplore Digital Library, Science-Direct, SpringerLink). The SDKs found in this search were subsequently examined and evaluated with respect to the functionality listed in the previous section as well as non-functional requirements (such as supported programming languages and platforms, available licences and licence cost, documentation, and current status).

Approximately 50 mAR SDKs were identified in this way. Of these, about 20 explicitly support location-based AR technology, facilitating mAR using GPS-based positioning and georeferenced content (GeoAR SDK). However, it is clear that most of the GeoAR SDKs are highly outdated or even officially discontinued or bought out (e.g. Metaio, Vuforia). This confirms the trend that many development studios and research companies are currently focusing purely on image-based tracking methods for AR solutions.

The few available, up-to-date GeoAR SDKs (Wikitude, DriodAR, PanicAR, and beyondAR) only support some of the aforementioned functionality. The depiction of objects with a single geographic coordinate (POIs, 3D models) is supported as a classic use case by all SDKs. However, the visualisation of geographic objects that are defined by a collection of coordinates (e.g., a river as a polyline) cannot be directly implemented with the available SDKs.

Customisation of the appearance of AR objects is also not generally possible to the desired extent. Thus, the developer is often bound to the design specifications of the SDK. Furthermore, access to the two-dimensional screen coordinates of the rendered objects is usually restricted, meaning that objects cannot be dynamically expanded or superimposed with their own additional content. Similarly, access to the underlying camera image in high resolution is generally restricted, making it impossible to further process or save the image.

Overall, there are very few usable SDKs available for location-based AR applications. Existing SDKs are either out-of-date or only offer limited functionality with few options for customisation such that they do not support the development of a broad range of custom mAR applications.

5   Concept of a Mobile Location-Based AR Framework

The weaknesses of the existing GeoAR SDKs reveal the need for a new framework that offers more extensive functionality and possibilities for customisation. The concept of such a framework is presented in the following.

The framework is intended to facilitate and speed up the development of as many of the aforementioned applications as possible while still allowing the developers as much freedom as possible to implement their individual ideas with regard to appearance and functionality. The framework is therefore designed as a low-level framework with the intention of internally performing the mathematical and core technological functions of location-based AR that would otherwise require expertise in the field of computer vision. It is suitable for app developers who have experience in writing mobile applications but who do not wish to have to acquire expertise in the fundamental mechanics of AR technology. Figure 6 shows the basic concept of the framework.

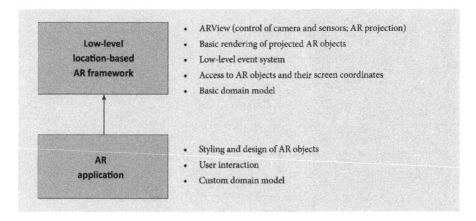

Fig. 6. Concept of a low-level location-based AR framework

A central part of the framework is an AR view (GeoARView) with its own lifecycle that displays the camera image as well as the overlayed, rendered AR objects. This core component consists of several layers which take care of internal functionalities like initialising and displaying the camera video stream (CameraLayer) or displaying AR objects (ARLayer) as well as user interface elements (e.g. radar and debug views). AR specific calculations and processes are encapsulated in separate classes, i.e. the conversion of three-dimensional geographic coordinates into corresponding two-dimensional screen coordinates on the basis of the current position and rotation of the device using the intrinsic camera projection matrix (e.g. ProjectionTranslation) or the rendering of an AR object (e.g. ARObjectRenderer). These classes are parts of the ARLayer.

Furthermore, an underlying model is created for the GeoAR objects to be displayed on the screen. This can either be represented by a single geographic reference point (POI) or by a list of connected reference points (polyline, polygon). Individual geographic points are initialised with their geographic coordinates, i.e., longitude, latitude, and height above sea level (optional). The appearance and design of these points on the screen (icon style, colour, size, transparency, etc.) can be changed at any time. Their appearance can also be adjusted according to context, for example, changing the transparency of a point depending on its distance from the user. Access to the distance between the user and the respective objects, as well as the 2D screen coordinates of the rendered objects, is always possible. The user of the framework has full control to the styling by implementing their own custom renderer.

A simple event model can be used to react to user interaction. Listeners exist to react when, for example, the device is rotated and new objects become visible or objects disappear out of the field of view. Additionally, all objects can be found within a definable region of the screen. This allows a reaction to click events from the user, for example. The listeners can also access the current feed from the camera in full resolution. Figure 7 shows the class diagram of the framework.

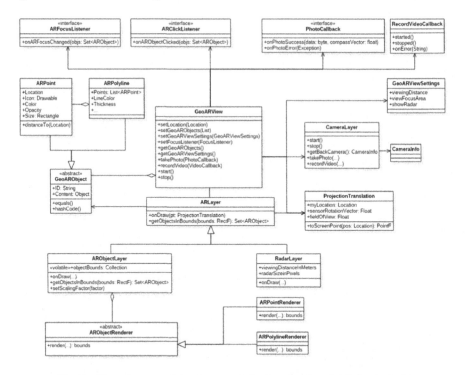

Fig. 7. Class diagram of the framework for location-based AR for Android

6   Implementation and Usage

A prototype of the framework was implemented for the Android platform and was used in two applications of the EU project, City.Risks. The overall idea of this project is to develop IT solutions to prevent and mitigate security risks in urban areas. With the aid of smartphones in smart cities, citizens actively contribute to combatting crime and increasing the sense of security.

Two applications for different use cases with integrated AR were developed using the location-based AR framework described in this article (see Fig. 8). One application uses mAR to show information about ongoing crime incidents in the city, explore crime-related data in this area, and to actively report issues. Another application allows the user to navigate out of a dangerous area to a safe destination using AR methods.

Fig. 8. City.Risks mAR applications: nearby incidents (left), Safety-aware navigation (right)

7 Summary

With the new generation of ubiquitous, powerful mobile devices (smartphones, etc.), a technical infrastructure is available that allows the development of a wide variety of mobile AR applications – especially in the field of location-based AR – as well as widespread use of these mAR applications by anyone.

In this article, the concept of a low-level development framework that facilitates the creation of a broad range of custom location-based AR applications has been presented. Geo-based AR technology has disappeared from sight in the last years as many companies have focused more on the optimisation of image-based AR technologies. Despite inaccuracies in the position determination, location-based AR is useful for many applications. However, developing one's own GeoAR application is often not possible without special expertise. The few existing SDKs can only be used under certain conditions as important functionality is missing or there are very few customisation options.

In contrast, the framework presented here allows the implementation of custom ideas with regard to appearance and functionality, thus enabling the creation of a wide range of different types of AR applications. It has been designed as a low-level framework for experienced app developers with no expertise in the field of computer vision. For this reason, it performs the mathematical and core technological functions of location-based AR.

Two applications from the EU project City.Risks were prototyped on Android using the framework. Later in the project, the viability of the framework will be more closely investigated. In particular, the degree of inaccuracy in the determination of the position and orientation of the device that can be tolerated will be explored. The extent to which this inaccuracy can be compensated by the use of additional methods (e.g., use of GPS bearing or feature tracking to improve the estimate of the rotation) will also be studied.

References

1. Azuma, R.T.A.: A survey of augmented reality. Presence - Teleoperators Virtual Environ. **6**(4), 355–385 (1997)
2. Höllerer, T., Feiner, S., Terauchi, T., Rashid, G., Hallaway, D.: Exploring MARS: developing in-door and outdoor user interfaces to a mobile augmented reality system. Comput. Graph. **23**(6), 779–785 (1999)
3. Fuchs-Kittowski, F.: Mobile Erweiterte Realität. WISU **41**(2), 216–224 (2012)
4. Rautenbach, V., Coetzee, S., Jooste, D.: Results of an evaluation of augmented reality mobile development frameworks for addresses in augmented reality. Spatial Inf. Res. **24**(3), 221–223 (2016)
5. Amin, D., Govilkar, S.: Comparative study of augmented reality SDK's. Int. J. Comput. Sci. Appl. **5**(1), 11–26 (2015)
6. Milgram, P., Takemura, H., Utsum, A., Kishino, F.: Augmented reality - a class of displays on the reality-virtuality continuum. In: SPIE Conference on Telemanipulator and Telepresence Technologies, vol. 2351, pp. 282–292 (1994)
7. Adhani, N.I., Awang Rambli, D.R.: A survey of mobile augmented reality applications. In: International Conference on Future Trends in Computing and Communication Technologies, pp. 89–95 (2012)
8. Mehler-Bicher, A., Reiß, M., Steiger, L.: Augmented Reality - Theorie und Praxis. De Gruyter Oldenbourg, München (2011)
9. Linaza, M.T., Marimon, D.: Evaluation of mobile augmented reality applications for tourism. In: Fuchs, M., et al. (eds.) Information and Communication Technologies in Tourism, pp. 260–271. Springer, Vienna (2012). https://doi.org/10.1007/978-3-7091-1142-0_23
10. Maier-Hein, L., et al.: Towards mobile augmented reality for on-patient visualization of medical images. In: Handels, H., Ehrhardt, J., Deserno, T., Meinzer, H.P., Tolxdorff, T. (eds.) Bildverarbeitung für die Medizin - Algorithmen - Systeme - Anwendungen, pp. 389–393. Springer, Berlin (2011). https://doi.org/10.1007/978-3-642-19335-4_80
11. Bischoff, A.: Dienste für Smartphones an Universitäten - ein plattformunabhängiges Augmented Reality Campus-Informationssystem für iPhone und Android-Smartphones. In: Roth, J., Werner, M. (Hrsg.) Ortsbezogene Anwendungen und Dienste. 8. GI/KuVS-Fachgespräch, pp. 127–135. Logos, Berlin (2011)
12. Haugstvedt, A.C., Krogstie, J.: Mobile augmented reality for cultural heritage. In: IEEE International Symposium on Mixed and Augmented Reality (ISMAR 2012), pp. 247–255 (2012)
13. Stampler, L.: Augmented reality makes shopping more personal - new mobile application from IBM Research helps both consumers and retailers. IBM Research (2012). http://www.research.ibm.com/articles/augmented-reality.shtml
14. Scott, G.D.: Enabling smart retail settings via mobile augmented reality shopping apps. Technol. Forecast. Soc. Change **124**, 243–256 (2016). https://doi.org/10.1016/j.techfore.2016.09.032
15. Joseph, B., Armstrong, D.G.: Potential perils of peri-Pokémon perambulation: the dark reality of augmented reality? Oxf. Med. Case Rep. **10**, 265–266 (2016). https://doi.org/10.1093/omcr/omw080

16. Inoue, K., Sato, R.: Mobile augmented reality business models. In: Mobile Augmented Reality Summit, pp. 1–2 (2010). www.perey.com/MobileARSummit/Tonchidot-MobileAR Business-Models.pdf

17. Barker, S.: Augmented Reality - Developer & Vendor Strategies 2016–2021. Juniper Research (2016)

18. Blum, J.R., Greencorn, D.G., Cooperstock, J.R.: Smartphone sensor reliability for augmented reality applications. In: Zheng, K., Li, M., Jiang, H. (eds.) MobiQuitous 2012. LNICSSITE, vol. 120, pp. 127–138. Springer, Heidelberg (2013). https://doi.org/10.1007/978-3-642-40238-8_11

19. Marchand, E., Uchiyama, H., Spindler, F.: Pose estimation for augmented reality: a hands-on survey. IEEE Trans. Vis. Comput. Graph. **22**(12), 2633–2651 (2016). https://doi.org/10.1109/TVCG.2015.2513408

20. Lahdenoja, O., Suominen, R., Säntti, T., Lehtonen, T.: Recent advances in monocular model-based tracking: a systematic literature review. Technical report, no. 8 (August 2015), University of Turku (2015)

21. Jeon, J., Kim, S., Lee, S.: Considerations of generic framework for AR on the web. In: AR on the Web, vol. 6 (2010) http://www.w3.org/2010/06/w3car/generic_framework.pdf

22. Fuchs-Kittowski, F., Simroth, S., Himberger, S., Fischer, F.: A content platform for smartphone-based mobile augmented reality. In: International Conference on Informatics for Environmental Protection (EnviroInfo 2012), Shaker, Aachen, pp. 403–412 (2012)

23. Keil, J., Zollner, M., Becker, M., Wientapper, F., Engelke, T., Wuest, H.: The House of Olbrich — an augmented reality tour through architectural history. In: IEEE International Symposium on Mixed and Augmented Reality - Arts, Media, and Humanities (ISMAR 2011), Basel, pp. 15–18 (2011)

24. Yu, K.M., Chiu, J.C., Lee, M.G., Chi, S.S.: A mobile application for an ecological campus navigation system using augmented reality. In: 8th International Conference on Ubi-Media Computing (UMEDIA 2015), pp. 17–22 (2015). https://doi.org/10.1109/umedia.2015.7297421

25. Armstrong, S., Morrand, K.: Ghost hunter – an augmented reality ghost busting game. In: Lackey, S., Shumaker, R. (eds.) VAMR 2016. LNCS, vol. 9740, pp. 671–678. Springer, Cham (2016). https://doi.org/10.1007/978-3-319-39907-2_64

26. Amin, D., Govilkar, S.: Comapartive study of augmented reality SDK's. Int. J. Comput. Sci. Appl. (IJCSA) **5**(1), 11–26 (2015)

27. SocialCompare: Augmented Reality SDK Comparison. http://socialcompare.com/en/comparison/augmented-reality-sdks

28. Wikipedia: List of Augmented Reality Software. https://en.wikipedia.org/w/index.php?title=List_of_augmented_reality_software&oldid=743628426

29. Bae, H., Walker, M., White, J., Pan, Y., Sun, Y., Golpavar-Fard, M.: Fast and scalable structure-from-motion based localization for high-precision mobile augmented reality systems. mUX J. Mob. User Exp. **5**(1), 4 (2016)

Author Index

Printed in the United States
By Bookmasters